D.E. BRISTOW

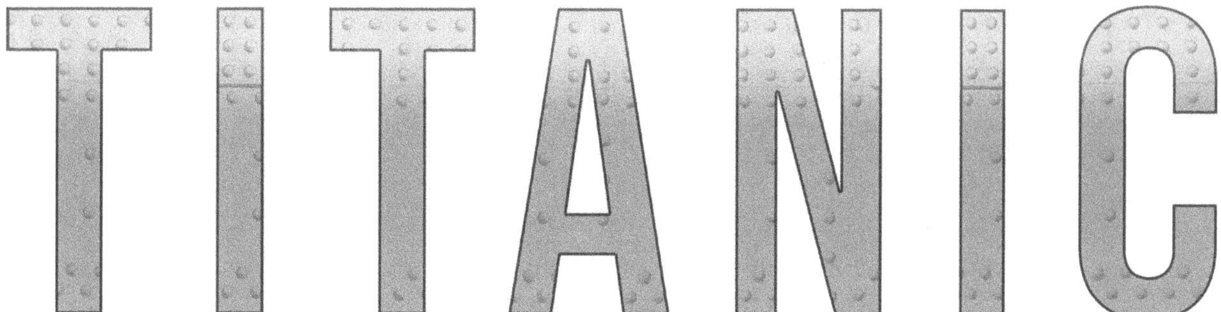

TITANIC

SINKING THE MYTHS

With a New Preface by Ryan Katzenbach

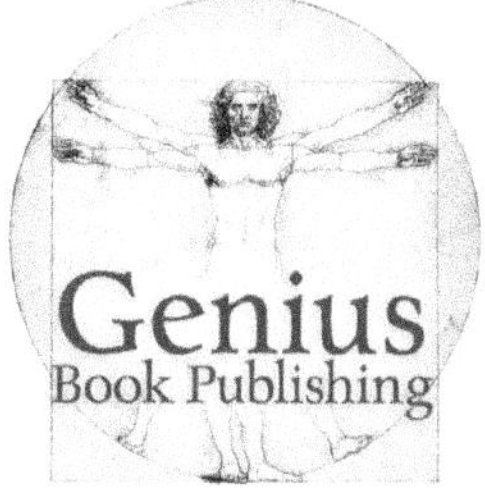

Milwuakee Wisconsin USA

By The Same Author...
TITANIC: *R.I.P., Can Dead Men Tell Tales?*
TITANIC *Calling* (a novel)

"The love of the ocean, that took me to sea as a boy, has never left me. In a way, a certain amount of wonder never leaves me, especially as I observe from the bridge a vessel plunging up and down in the trough of the seas, fighting her way through and over the great waves. A man never outgrows that."

Captain Edward John Smith,
Commander of White Star's ***ADRIATIC,***
Maiden Voyage, 1907.

TITANIC: Sinking the Myths

Originally published in 1995 by Katco Literary Group, Fresno California

Cover artwork by James Allen Flood

Preface by Ryan H. Katzenbach

Published by:
Genius Book Publishing
PO Box 250380
Milwaukee Wisconsin 53225
GeniusBookPublishing.com

Paperback ISBN: 978-1-958727-26-3
Hardcover ISBN: 978-1-958727-27-0

240404 Letter

Table of Contents

In memory of

Diana E. Bristow

1929 – 2011

You were loved.
You are missed.

Preface: God's Fist

BY RYAN KATZENBACH

Ryan Katzenbach on James Cameron's soundstage, Manhattan Beach, California

It was just minutes before 7 a.m. when I heard the phone's text alert. I glanced at the clock, saw the time, and thought "come on, Lauren... isn't it a bit early for texting?"

Lauren Parker is one of my friends who shares a lot of similar interests in all things history related. We've been friends for a long time, and she's also, in a lot of ways, my polar opposite. She's the consummate hard-charging go-getter drill-sergeant who is up bright and early every morning whereas I'm the go-getter who stays up until three in the morning. Lauren has two kids, Cass and Rylan, who have to be at school by 7 AM, so that's part of why Lauren is always up with the sun. I think she figures that if she has to be up, then I should be, too. So, hence, I did what I always did: I ignored the phone and rolled back over.

A few minutes later, however, the phone chimed again.

Then it alerted again.

I turned over and opened my eyes. Bear, my lab, and Hitchcock, my chihuahua stirred, too, unhappy that they were being disturbed by my movements in bed.

I grabbed the phone with a firm tug which disconnected it from its charge-cable.

But none of these messages were from Lauren.

"Hey, I am sure you've already heard about this, but what is your take on the sub at the ***TITANIC*** situation?" read the message from a friend in Central California.

Another friend said: "I hope none of your friends were on that sub that is missing."

One from a Midwest friend, who was a bit less kind about the situation, read: "Hey, is seeing your favorite wreck still on your bucket list? If so, you might want to make it the last thing on the list? :)".

In an instant I knew what had happened.

In the weeks leading up to this, I had heard several reports that OceanGate, a Seattle based undersea tourism company, was returning to the ***TITANIC*** wreck for another mission. Since 2018 this company had been on my radar when I was told of their experimental design for a craft that would take tourists to the ***TITANIC*** wreck. The ***TITAN*** submersible, as it would come to be named, was shaped like a Tylenol capsule. It consisted of two titanium pressure caps that sealed off an elongated carbon-fiber passenger compartment "tube." The design, even from my lay perspective, seemed flawed. I had asked, to no one in particular, in 2018, "How are they going to connect two titanium caps to a carbon fiber tube? I mean… don't those materials expand and contract under pressure at different rates?"

The appalling answer to my question: OceanGate was going to glue the components together.

This, in my humble opinion, was a recipe for disaster that was going to get people killed. You didn't have to be an engineer to know what glueing multiple pieces of differing materials together for an application in the deep ocean where the pressure is 6,000 pounds-per-square-inch is an all-around terrible idea.

Explorers had been diving the ***TITANIC*** wreck since July 1986 when Dr. Robert Ballard had taken the Woods Hole Oceanographic Institute vehicle, Alvin, to the site with Jason Jr., their newly-developed ROV. Ballard, on a joint French-American expedition, had discovered the wreck only a year earlier in September 1985 and photographed the bow, and some of the debris field, with the unmanned Argo/Angus camera-sled system. It was Ballard's discovery that had caught my attention as a 10-year-old living in Ohio, and I became obsessed with the ***TITANIC*** story. I was glued, every day, to the television soaking up the latest images and discoveries that were broadcast via satellite almost nightly on the news. The most exciting moment came when Ballard and Jason Jr's pilot, Martin Bowen, descended into the wreck through what was once the great glass and iron dome that crowned ***TITANIC***'s first class grand staircase. There, suspended in time and legend were rows of chandeliers.

Soon, it would not be enough to just photograph the wreck.

In 1987, the French Research Institute for Exploitation of the Sea (IFREMER) conducted an expedition and recovered items. Subsequent dives over the next few decades would continue to do the same, while also mapping and exploring the wreck in much greater detail. And, of course, we're all familiar with James Cameron's epic 1997 film ***TITANIC*** which brought us more stunning views of the wreck through his dives in the MIR1 and MIR2 Soviet submersibles.

There had been no accidents, no loss of life in nearly four decades of ***TITANIC*** exploration. Every submersible that had been to the wreck shared common tried-and-true technology: a foot-thick spherical titanium pressure hull. Imagine, if you will, a baseball in the palm of your hand. If you take the baseball and squeeze it, you make that baseball stronger by applying pressure. The deep ocean, and the nearly 6,000 pounds of pressure-per-square-inch of the ***TITANIC*** wreck site did the same to the titanium hull of the submersible craft. The design was like taking three human lives, putting them in a pressure sphere, and then putting that sphere in God's fist. Could he crush it? He certainly could. But the odds were unlikely that he would do so because this human design acted in accordance with His physics.

The OceanGate design challenged traditional wisdom. It put a tube-like center-capsule between two titanium end caps that was not made of titanium and glued together. Care to put this in God's fist and see what happens? As much as I personally wanted to visit the ***TITANIC*** wreck, I would not have taken OceanGate's ***TITAN*** to the ocean floor on a dare. However, they had conducted a few expedition dives to the wreck and returned safely. Everyone seemed to think that the design was in the clear; tested, true, and without reproach. It seemed as if everyone who was considering purchasing a $250,000 ticket to the wreck seemed to suddenly accept that just because you made a dive once, or twice—or even a dozen times—nothing could possibly go wrong. Did they not understand that these submersibles are no different than the commercial aircrafts that we travel on a daily basis? The Airbus or Boeing jets that fly you from one coast to another… or one continent to another… are regularly torn down and reassembled for the sake of maintaining structural integrity and safety. Joints are scrutinized for work hardening (colloquially referred to as "metal fatigue"). Wiring is removed and replaced… flight systems are updated. Engines are overhauled or replaced entirely. The subs that carry their explorers to the ***TITANIC*** are no different. They are certified. They dive. They are examined, tested, scrutinized, overhauled, and then re-certified. They dive again. Use, wash, dry, examine, certify, repeat.

Knowing this, I knew from the second I read those text messages that those five on the ***TITAN*** submersible were not missing—they were dead.

It was Monday, June 19, 2023.

I showered quickly and ventured to the kitchen where I found coffee that had been made earlier that morning. My friend and roommate, and another constant creative collaborator, Liza Asner, the daughter of my late and dear friend and legendary actor Ed Asner, left daily for work from our Woodland Hills home around 6:30 a.m. She always made coffee before she left, and I could always count on a few cups that just needed to be microwaved. As I did so, I turned on the TV in my office which was right off our kitchen. With a cup of coffee in hand, I plopped down at Ed's desk, which was now mine, complete with one of his Emmys as a paperweight on a pile of papers pertaining to the various things I was working on. The morning news coverage centered on the U.S. Coast Guard mobilizing for search and rescue operations in the North Atlantic.

"Why bother?" I commented to myself, sipping on the coffee. "They're dead."

It wouldn't take long for my assessment to be confirmed.

Over the next few hours I would receive several phone calls.

The first was from a friend and colleague, a lifelong student of the ***TITANIC*** disaster who had visited the wreck a number of times on various research and mapping expeditions. The call confirmed what I suspected—the ***TITAN*** had been lost. They explained that the U.S. Navy had heard the implosion on Sunday, right around the time the submersible had lost contact with the support ship, the ***POLAR PRINCE,*** at the surface.

Starting around the time of the Cold War between the United States and the Soviet Union, the U.S. military had developed and deployed state-of-the-art listening technology in the world's deep oceans. The intent, at that time, as it remains today, is to listen for submarine traffic. However, it's also been useful in other instances—such as when the nuclear Navy sub, the ***USS SCORPION*** went missing off the Azores in May 1968. The U.S. Navy heard the implosion of the submersible long before the ***SCORPION*** was officially declared missing. The U.S. Navy knew, almost immediately, where the sub had been lost and was able to photograph the remains in 9,000 feet of ocean within months. In the decades since the ***SCORPION***, the technology has only improved as the U.S. government has been forced to stay ahead of new technologies that make submarines quieter and harder to track. It was this same system that had heard the pressure-cabin of the ***TITAN*** implode the day before, I was told.

The next call, which came a little while later, was from a friend who is not as connected to the ***TITANIC*** side of things as he is to the U.S. Military. He had more specific information. Yes, he confirmed, the Navy had heard the implosion and he added that the failure occurred "beyond 7,000 feet." Specifically, however, he noted that the implosion hadn't been heard as much as it had been felt. According to him, it was seismic sensors in the deep ocean that had picked up the anomaly.

Another friend called to report that he, too, had been informed by colleagues in the commercial and research diving community, as well as the Navy, that ***TITAN*** had been lost as the result of a catastrophic pressure-cabin failure. This particular friend also confirmed that ***TITAN*** had been quite deep when tragedy struck. However, he had new details that I had not heard at this point.

Apparently, OceanGate CEO Stockton Rush, and his four passengers, had become aware that ***TITAN*** was in trouble. The sub had jettisoned weight and had blown ballast in an attempt to return to the surface. What was most disturbing was that, according to him, there had been an internal alarm system that had indicated that there was distortion taking place in ***TITAN's*** pressure cabin. If this were, indeed, the case, then those on the sub knew they were in trouble. While an implosion would kill these crew members in a nano-second—something they would have no time to even register—if there was an alarm sounding, one cannot imagine the sheer terror they must have been feeling in the moments leading to the end. This truly horrified me more than anything I had heard at this point.

Later, transcripts would emerge that were claimed to be the actual text dialogue between the surface aboard the ***POLAR PRINCE*** and the ***TITAN.*** These would document how the ***TITAN*** was descending, according to some sources, too fast and how the crew aboard came to realize that they were in trouble. However, as of the time of this writing, the transcript's legitimacy is not confirmed. Though if those transcripts were faked, as one source noted to me, they had a definite degree of authenticity to them. As of this writing, the official cause of ***TITAN***'s loss, and the specific details surrounding it, are the subject of an investigation. The findings, when released, will likely be scrutinized, studied, and examined in the years to follow.

I had no way of knowing it at the time I received these calls, but within days, filmmaker and deep ocean explorer James Cameron would go on various news outlets to state, and thus confirm, ALL that I was told on this Monday morning and afternoon. I thought, in watching his interviews, that Cameron came off as the most credible, authoritative voice on the subject. He had, as many in the deep-diving community expressed, been a vocal opponent of the OceanGate carbon-fiber design. He was but one of many voices that had told Stockton Rush that his design was likely flirting with disaster.

Listening to the news in the days that followed can best be described as mind-numbing. The stupidity, disconnect, and utter lack of understanding of the deep ocean displayed by the endlessly-say-nothing-talking heads of CNN and other networks infuriated me. None of them had a clue what they were talking about, and given the 24-hour news cycle, the media just seemed to spew supposition and utter fabrication purely as a means of retaining viewers. They interviewed people on the "fringe" of the ***TITANIC*** community who had no real insider knowledge of the situation and seemed to only be interested in their "fifteen minutes" of fame. This is why, eventually, when we heard from James Cameron, it was a breath of fresh air. He provided real content, real context as to what had happened.

In the effort to create a dramatic narrative to keep news consumers glued to their televisions while boosting ratings, there began the "countdown" of the 96 hours of oxygen that ***TITAN*** allegedly carried for her crew in the event of an accident. The news programs painted the picture of a submersible that had lost connection to the surface, and possibly power, and had sunk to the ocean floor. There, mired in the muddy sea floor, in the murky depths, the five "mission specialists," as OceanGate called them, awaited a heroic rescue by the U.S. Coast Guard. What the newscasters failed to understand was that even if there were 96 hours of oxygen on board, what about the electrical system that maintained and powered these life-saving emergency systems? The battery banks on the submersible were not capable of providing power for that long. This is why ***TITAN,*** and all submersibles capable of reaching ***TITANIC,*** free fall for the two-and-a-half-hour descent—to conserve electrical power. These subs have battery power for a four- to six-hour day of exploration on the bottom, followed by a powered-thruster ascent to the surface that takes another two hours.

Thus, for argument, let's say that a maximum diving day is 8 hours. Pray tell, CNN, how were they going to have the juice to sustain life for 96 hours?

The issue of electrical power was outweighed by one other very critical factor: temperature. Not once on any of the networks did I ever hear any discussion of this.

At ***TITANIC***'s depth of 3800 meters (roughly 12,500 feet, or if you prefer fathoms, 2,100) the temperature is a year-around-frigid 28 degrees. Without battery, without heat, the occupants of the ***TITAN***, on the sea floor, were likely to face the same fate of those at the surface on April 15, 1912—hypothermia. And this fate would not take 96 hours.

The U.S. Coast Guard followed normal protocols and rushed to round up the assets needed to conduct a search and rescue mission—one that was unprecedented in maritime history. Even if the United States government knew that tragedy had befell ***TITAN***, without confirmation, a search and rescue mission was an appropriate priority. Until there was confirmation of a catastrophic loss and confirmed death of the vessel, rescue was the focus. The effort would be suspended, of course, when a remote operated vehicle eventually discovered the shattered remains of the ***TITAN*** just off ***TITANIC***'s bow.

In all of this, I couldn't help but think of my late friend, the author of this book, Diana E. Bristow. The lessons of ***TITANIC*** were not lost on her when she wrote ***TITANIC:*** *Sinking the Myths* between 1992 and 1995. Unfortunately, the lessons of ***TITANIC*** had, quite apparently, been forgotten by many in the 112 years between the original disaster and the loss of ***TITAN***. Once again, the arrogance of man and his belief that he had triumphed over nature and the elements led to catastrophe. At least, this was my initial analysis. Regardless, I couldn't help but imagine what Diana would have said if she were alive.

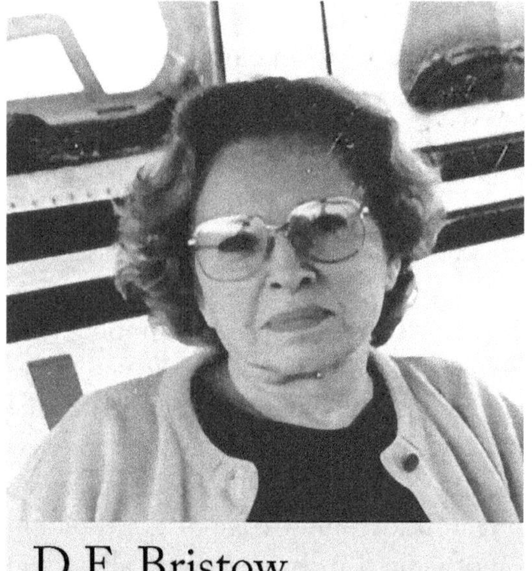
D.E. Bristow

•••---•••

"So, who is this DaBristrol woman again?" my mother asked.

With a sigh of teenage frustration at how square my mother could be, I replied "It's not DaBristol. Her name is Dee. Eee. Bristow."

On this Saturday morning, the 23rd of September 1989, my mother was driving me to meet Lonni Roberts at her house at the top of the "corkscrew" near the Valley High Ski Resort outside of Bellefontaine, Ohio. I was 14 years old.

Four years earlier, Dr. Ballard had found the wreck after being lost to man in the depths of the North Atlantic for 73 years. The discovery was all over the news, and upon hearing about the lost shipwreck, now two and a half miles deep in the North Atlantic, I was beyond mesmerized. I acquired every book that I could and saw every movie and documentary available. I, and the entire world, had become transfixed on the disaster.

Just as Dr. Robert Ballard was planning to return to the ***TITANIC*** wreck in the summer of 1986 for a follow-up manned exploration, an article appeared in the local Columbus Dispatch about a Sidney, Ohio man named John Whitman who was preparing to open a ***TITANIC*** museum.

TITANIC Museum, Sidney Ohio

John Whitman

Sidney, an hour or so west of where I grew up in rural Ohio, was hardly the place where you would expect to find a maritime museum. As word of this spread, a lot of reporters and newspapers found folly with Whitman and his ***TITANIC*** museum in the "middle of a Shelby County cornfield."

I wrote to Whitman, who was also the owner of the Artist Cove Institute of Fine Arts, and told him of my interest and fledgling collection of ***TITANIC*** memorabilia. To my surprise, a week or so later, Whitman called to say that he had received the letter and invited me and my parents to see his collection.

With my 5th grade school year having just ended, on June 7th, 1986, my parents took me to visit with Whitman. Upon entering his art studio, I was immediately mesmerized with his artwork. On one wall was an 8' x 24' mural depicting the starboard side of ***TITANIC*** as she brushed against the iceberg. On the opposite wall was "First Rockets Fired," which was a 6' x 16' mural which Whitman bragged had been sold to the Southampton Maritime Museum and would be delivered to them upon its completion. The visit, which lasted all day, further ignited my passion for the subject as well as for art.

John Whitman opened the ***TITANIC*** Memorial Museum in Sidney, Ohio on March 15, 1987. From 1987, until I moved to California in 1992, I would be a regular fixture at the museum and the art school.

Now, on this September day in 1989, the Museum was holding a "fellowship weekend," and the key attraction was a book signing with author Diana Bristow. Bristow had written a book entitled ***TITANIC*** *RIP: Can Dead Men Tell Tales*. The book was self-published through Harlo Press in Michigan, and Bristow had been selling the book by running small ads in some of the maritime and shipping publications.

One of the Museum's board members, and an Artist Cove art instructor, Lonni Roberts, had seen the ad in one of the magazines and decided to order a copy. She sent a personal check drawn on her bank in Bellefontaine, Ohio to Diana Bristow in Miami Springs, Florida. Diana, upon receiving the check dispatched the book and a note to Lonni stating that she was a native of Bellefontaine and had grown up there. This ignited a conversation that led to her being invited to come to the museum, and ultimately led to all of us becoming close friends.

Diana Bristow (left) and Ryan Katzenbach (second from right)

Lonni Roberts lived within about 15 miles of my home, so, as would commonly happen on Saturday mornings, one of my parents would drive me to her house where I would ride with her to Sidney. As I grew older, into my teenage years, I became a tour guide for the museum and worked on the weekends giving tours through the museum and talking with guests about all things ***TITANIC.*** This particular September weekend would forever change my life.

I won't go into the reasons that Diana wrote *RIP* or this, her more-thorough follow-up volume as she does a very thorough job of explaining this later in the book. What I will, however, write about is our relationship and how I became so extensively involved in the publication of *Myths*.

Diana and I hit it off that weekend. She was 59, and I was 14. It would seem that we should have nothing remotely in common. However, we were both artists and shared a mutual interest in ***TITANIC***, and that was enough.

After the weekend in Ohio, and upon returning to Florida, Diana and I became pen-pals, of sorts, and we would write back and forth. Initially, we wrote about all things ***TITANIC,*** but as the relationship progressed, it became far more personal. She wrote about the challenges she had in life and her relationships; I wrote about this girl, or that girl, I had a crush on or what was going on through junior high and high school. She would tell stories, in her writing, of her days as a student at the Dayton Art Institute with fellow classmate Jonathan Winters. She would regale me with adventures from her days in flight… as a pilot and as an Eastern Airlines flight attendant, from which she had just retired in 1986 as the airline was facing financial struggles.

Diana Bristow in her Eastern Airlines uniform

To say that Diana and I learned a lot from each other would be an understatement. Our relationship transcended the generational divide. She made me a better student, artist, writer, and researcher because of the wisdom and experience she imparted. She taught me that, in order to be a student of history, you had to look at history from the perspective of those participating in it. You had to see the world as they saw it. This is a lesson that has stuck with me through my entire adult life and career.

Diana also learned a lot from me, I do believe. When she began corresponding with her multi-page letters, she was writing on a typewriter. Around this time, I had just acquired my very first Macintosh SE computer. So I would key my lengthy letters on the Mac and print them. She became intrigued with my Mac, and this led to her throwing out her typewriter and buying a new Mac for herself.

In 1992, at 17, I moved to California. My friendship with Diana continued. As the years progressed, she became a bit more bitter and disenfranchised with the way her 1989 book had been received by what she called the "***TITANIC*** establishment." At some point, after being dismissed by the "experts," she had started talking about a new book—a book that couldn't be argued or refuted by the "establishment." Sometime between 1990 and 1993, the effort congealed and our discussions, which were now almost entirely by telephone, turned to the new manuscript.

After years of furthering her research, by 1994 she was approaching completion of the book. However, she wasn't getting any traction with the mainstream publishers and would often complain to me about her literary agent, Gus, not putting enough time, energy, or fight into the effort to get the book published.

"No woman is supposed to be an expert on this subject," she would complain to me, citing that the ***TITANIC*** "establishment" was made up entirely of men. She theorized that her manuscript, which had been rejected numerous times, would be put on ice and then would, eventually, be rewritten by another well-known MALE author, and thus her extensive research would be stolen. I initially, naive to the way the world sometimes works, thought her to be paranoid. Now I know that this sort of thing does happen, more often than anyone would like.

When I graduated from high school, I started my own boutique advertising agency. Given my media experience, Diana asked, "What would it take to start a publishing company?" Her intent was clear: She wanted to start an independent press that would publish her book and thus assure that her title would make it marketable just as she had written it.

After a lot of discussion and research, I eventually agreed that, while it would be difficult, it would not be impossible to start a small niche publishing company. With that, in 1994, we began production on her book which was eventually released in September 1995. While this book was in print, it sold amazingly well both in the domestic United States and overseas.

The book remained in print for several years, but my life and career was steadily changing. In 1998 the publishing company optioned one of its titles to a movie studio and, with this unanticipated event, I suddenly found myself heading into the entertainment business and leaving the book publishing world behind. When we sold off the last of the initial first run of Diana's book, it simply went out of print. Little did we realize that the demand for the book would only grow as the years progressed.

Diana and I remained friends through the years, until her death in July 2011. The day I received the call from our mutual friend, Kevin Reck, that Diana had passed was one of the saddest days of my life. I knew that I had lost a friend who was irreplaceable. As the dedication page of this book says: "She was loved; she is missed."

A few years after Diana's passing, I found myself engaged in a unique opportunity to adapt her book into a docudrama for the cable channel REELZ here in the United States. I was excited, as a producer, writer, and director, to tell the ***TITANIC*** story through Diana's lens. But, more importantly, I wanted to tell HER story about how and why she wrote the book to begin with. I

Bill Müller (Edward Asner) and Diana Bristow (Frances Fisher) in the 2017 REELZ Original docudrama "TITANIC: Sinking the Myths," directed by Ryan Katzenbach.

wanted the film to be a tribute to her life and research and I was thrilled to work with my longtime friends Ed Asner and Frances Fisher on the film. Frances took on the role of Diana with gusto, reading *Myths* and interviewing me extensively about her mannerisms and demeanor. When I directed Frances in the film, I sometimes felt like I was watching Diana.

The two-hour show debuted to terrific ratings in January 2017, and a year later, we released a "Director's Cut" of the show which was four hours in runtime. This version of the show was also very popular.

In doing the film, and adapting the book for screen, I, of course, had to re-read a book I hadn't looked at in years. When I began to read and study it in preparation of the screenplay I was even more impressed with the volume than I had been when I originally published it in 1995. The book was thorough and dense, and I could hear Diana's voice whispering in my ear: "Remember, I deal in FACTS, not theories."

In writing the screenplay, I also read a lot of other books about the ***TITANIC*** disaster just to get a feel for what new works had been authored and what new revelations had been revealed about the disaster in the years since *Myths'* publication. I came to realize that so much of Diana's work had been "borrowed" by other authors and experts in the years since *Myths* had been published. For instance, Diana Bristow had been the first author to study the coal fire that had been burning in ***TITANIC***'s stokehold since before she left Belfast. Diana was the first author to weigh in on this fire and extensively contemplate how it affected ***TITANIC***'s sinking on a structural level. Now, in the years to follow, it seemed a lot of authors were suddenly talking about this fire, and in some cases, trying to minimize or discredit Diana. At the same time that I was finishing my film, another documentary aired that attempted to capitalize on Diana's research into the coal fire, blaming that fire for the sinking.

I often wonder what Diana would have thought about being immortalized on film. In fact, I often wonder what Diana would think about a lot of things if she was still here to talk about these varied subjects. This is why, when the ***TITAN*** submersible went missing, the first person I thought of was her.

I could hear her voice in my head. "In 100 years, we haven't learned anything. Man is still arrogant and has to be reminded of his inferiorities."

Then I could hear her draw the parallels between White Star's ***TITANIC*** and OceanGate's ***TITAN.***

Like ***TITANIC, TITAN*** was a new design, larger than any other submersible before it in terms of passenger capacity.

From 1907 to 1912—a span of just five years—ocean liners had nearly tripled in size, starting with Cunard's ***LUSITANIA*** and ***MAURETANIA***. Immigrant trade was the key to survival and dominance of the shipping lines. The ***OLYMPIC***-class liners, of which ***TITANIC*** was the second, were even bigger than these two Cunard greyhounds, coming in just short of 900 feet in length. And Albert Ballin's Hamburg-Amerika was in the process of building liners even larger than the ***OLYMPIC***-class. In fact, ***TITANIC,*** had she not met her fate on April 15th, 1912, would have held the title of largest ocean liner for a only a few months before Ballin's ***IMPERATOR,*** which was nearing completion would steal the title.

Given the sudden increase in the length, breadth, tonnage, and power of these new ocean liners, it became apparent that not all was immediately understood about their handling dynamics, such as, for instance, hydraulic interaction between them and nearby ships.

OLYMPIC had had a collision with the ***HMS HAWKE***; ***TITANIC*** had had a near-collision leaving Southampton with the moored ***S.S. NEW YORK.*** Both the smaller ***HAWKE*** and the ***NEW YORK*** were being pulled into the wake of each ship by the larger vessel's screws. The "pull" was so strong, in fact, that it literally snapped the mooring lines of the ***NEW YORK*** and only quick interaction of nearby tugs prevented an impact between ***TITANIC*** and the smaller liner. Given these incidents, it seems clear that there had been no consideration of this hydraulic interaction between the vessels and the fact that smaller liners needed to maintain a considerable distance from the ***OLYMPIC***-class liners to avoid potential collision.

One must wonder how many design and performance "considerations" were not taken into account by Stockton Rush and OceanGate when they dreamt up ***TITAN***'s design; shortcomings in the engineering that would only be exposed through the application of an expedition into the deep. Considering that the sub was carrying a payload of human beings, this hardly seemed to be the appropriate proving grounds, when any engineer will likely agree that there is a difference between what a slide rule or engineering software will say is acceptable, and what actually happens to that design under 6,000 pounds-of-pressure-per-square-inch will reveal.

Then, there's the financial considerations of both White Star Line and OceanGate.

As you will read in this book, White Star Line was under tremendous pressure, given the changing circumstances of world politics and the market. Britain had to maintain dominance of the world's shipping lanes, which necessitated the very need for bigger liners that could move more cargo and immigrants between the continents. Furthermore, given the booming demands, these new, larger ships within the British fleet had to maintain a breakneck schedule at all costs.

With OceanGate, as a private company, similar financial considerations held true. It was not enough to build a submersible that could carry three people to the ***TITANIC*** wreck; it needed to carry *five, or more*, to be financially viable, even at $250,000 per seat. OceanGate, like White Star and the International Mercantile Marine that owned it, were *businesses*. Businesses must turn profits to remain in business and to satisfy owners, investors, and stockholders. OceanGate's Stockton Rush faced the very issue that Joseph Bruce Ismay had dealt with over a hundred years earlier—how to move more cargo, in his case human, from point "A" to point "B," while having only one submersible to do it. Every dive had to count to maintain financial viability.

As I noted earlier, one of my friends sarcastically asked me if I still had a visit to the ***TITANIC*** wreck on my "bucket list," given what happened to the ***TITAN***. My answer, without hesitation, is "yes." *If* I were ever lucky enough to be invited to tag along on a scientific expedition, I would absolutely seize the opportunity to join the club of the under 300 people on the planet who have visited the ***TITANIC***'s grave. I specifically noted "scientific" expedition here, for a reason. Scientific expeditions are not-for-profit. They generally follow stringent safety protocols, as noted by my friends who have been to the wreck. While there is always a chance that something can go wrong, it is my opinion that when you create a for-profit business model, like that of OceanGate, the risk factor increases tremendously. Scientific expeditions are generally well funded, whereas a commercial endeavor relies on customer revenue. If you have 10 "customers" willing to pay the admission, but you ideally need 12, will the expedition still happen? Most likely. The difference between those two customers could be the difference between a profit or a loss. And, what happens when there isn't an abundance of cash? Corners get cut. I speak hypothetically here as I have no idea what the break-even of OceanGate's expeditions was, but the average reader will understand what I am saying. Too many times I've seen colleagues—fellow business owners—say "well, we'll make it work." And this means that risks are taken, often unnecessary ones. I, myself, have had to make compromises in film production when we're not working with a budget as large as we need. I've cut crew, or trimmed the length of a shoot to work around budget constraints. The bottom line is that business owners are often forced to "make it work." When you're making a film, and you cut a Production Assistant from the shoot, or you scale down your craft services, no one is going to die. The same cannot be true when you're dealing with submersibles and the deep ocean where even under perfect circumstances there is still tremendous risk.

Are the ***TITANIC*** and ***TITAN*** not similar in the course they both took to the wreck site? They absolutely are. ***TITANIC***, as you will read in this book, took a shorter, more perilous northern shipping lane which she was not supposed to follow in April weather. ***TITAN*** skirted U.S. regulations and certifications by chartering the research vessel ***POLAR PRINCE*** with a port of departure from St. Johns, Newfoundland. Both vessels, succinctly stated, bent the rules which resulted in catastrophe and loss of human life.

I could go on, as I am sure Diana would if she was alive today to pen this updated preface herself, about the parallels between these two accidents. But the point, regardless, is still reached: Human arrogance and our belief that we are masters of the universe led to the deaths of 1,500 and 5 people, respectively. I envision both Ismay and Rush saying "it'll be all right" as they executed their decisions, both believing that they had anticipated all the unknowns.

Joseph Bruce Ismay drove his ship on a shorter, northern course for New York, only deviating with a turn south to take a rival German tanker under tow for the sheer spectacle of doing so. Stockton Rush ignored the concerns expressed by the deep submergence community who worried that his design was flawed. Some would argue that greed was the motivating factor; I assert that business survival was the reason for such perilous decisions. Both men helmed companies that needed—had to—cut corners to make a profit as means of staying in business. And we cannot forget vanity which, in my view, exceeds arrogance.

When I set out to make the film adaptation of this book in 2015—twenty years after the books initial publication—I questioned whether Diana Bristow's research had held up sufficiently in the passage of the decades to support the film. I realized, quickly, that it had. My position, today, as this book goes to reprint, is unchanged.

Diana did not get mired in the romantic haze (as she called it) of the disaster. The acts of heroism, the men who nobly stood by and watched their women and children depart in the lifeboats while they accepted death, didn't move her as much as her desire to find out HOW this disaster was allowed to occur in the first place. She stripped the haze away as she delved into the original source materials. Diana Bristow, as she told me so many times, "dealt in facts, not theories."

The ***TITAN*** disaster, sadly, has made her work even more relevant today than it was on its publication date in September 1995.

The lessons that we learned from the ***TITANIC*** disaster have faded with time. The ***TITAN*** disaster serves as a reminder that nothing has changed between 1912 and the present. As ***TITANIC*** survivor Eva Hart said, speaking of her mother's unease with crossing the Atlantic on ***TITANIC,*** "To say a ship is unsinkable is to fly into the face of God and that is why I am frightened."

Stockton Rush didn't just "fly into the face of God." He taunted God by putting his fate, and that of the four other "mission specialists" who descended with him on that fated Sunday morning in June 2023, in God's fist. Can we be surprised that God felt we needed a reminder—a refresher—on what happens when we as humans decide to challenge the Almighty?

Ryan Katzenbach
March 8, 2024
Los Angeles, California

Foreword

Readers will surely wonder why there should be yet another ***TITANIC*** book. Everything has been said, written and filmed in the more than eighty years since the great White Star liner went to her grave in the icy North Atlantic, has it not? Surely all of those so-called "mysteries" have been solved by now, have they not?

Unfortunately, no.

TITANIC has become almost a cult, with organizations all over the world devoted to preserving her memory. She has also become a business. For very few she has brought fame and fortune. For many she brings a life and a limited bit of prestige they would not have without her. For others, devoted to her memory and dedicated to uncovering the truth about her, there is only a great deal of frustrating hard work, with no monetary rewards, no recognition.

Official ***TITANIC*** documents are often obscure and many of the most important ones have rarely been perused even by those who claim the title of "researcher." ***TITANIC*** authorship is often fraught with intense rivalry and "moles" are everywhere. Blatant censorship exists when big publishing houses send ingenuously submitted manuscripts and queries on nonfiction subjects to "experts" for approval. Because *"**TITANIC** authorities"* are almost always rival authors who recommend rejection if their own theories are jeopardized, it is assured that the public will never read any serious new research on the subject.

There is far more to accident research, however, than merely collecting official data and memorabilia, and endlessly debating non-debatable facts.

The primary reason that ***TITANIC*** remains engulfed in mysteries and theories is simply that there has been, and still is, a stifling tendency throughout the ***TITANIC*** Establishment to disregard any evidence that does not fit perfectly into the official version of the accident, in spite of the fact that most ***TITANIC*** researchers admit that the official story makes little sense. The tendency to compartmentalize, or as the Dutch say, *hokjes geest,* "spirit of little boxes," is especially alarming because it has done much to hamper serious research. The cliché *"All sailors always lie,"* has often been used as a smug explanation for any statements made by mariners about the disaster which do not agree with official records, despite the fact that they are the one professional group who should know the answers. Obviously when witnesses give conflicting evidence it may be difficult to decide who is telling the truth, who is lying, and who is merely mistaken. I have preferred to rely heavily upon statements and testimony given to newspapers and inquiries as soon as possible after the event. Police detectives and intelligence officers know that when a certain amount of time has passed, especially after a disaster of such magnitude, witnesses tend to rationalize rather than remember what happened. In particular, those whose behavior was less than heroic will block painful memories from their conscious minds. As for those who were not involved but merely read about it, the majority will usually prefer to believe whatever is most dramatic, rather than whatever is most accurate and logical. Statements made by survivors long after the ***TITANIC*** disaster have obviously been influenced by what they have read about it.

To separate accuracy from drama it is necessary to study far more than the ship herself. First it is necessary to study seamanship and navigation from the same manuals that ***TITANIC***'s officers used. Then the serious researcher must study the social customs, morals and problems of the day, everything to get the "feel" of the era right down to the economics, the clothing, the food, the education available, state-of-the-art technology in all fields, and in particular the political climate prevailing in the countries affected by ***TITANIC***'s loss. I have been criticized for including details about other shipwrecks in my books about ***TITANIC***. I maintain that most of the so-called mysteries surrounding the sinking of ***TITANIC*** will be dispelled only by studying other shipwrecks, and therefore learning that they are not mysteries at all. It is the perpetuation of those mysteries and legends that makes ***TITANIC*** big business. In fact, there was nothing unique about her at all.

In its own time the ***TITANIC*** disaster was soon eclipsed by the even more horrible shipping catastrophes which followed close upon its heels. In those halcyon days when the great liners raced endlessly back and forth across the Western Ocean, maritime accidents were as common as airplane crashes are today. Many accidents at sea were hushed up if there were no fatalities among passengers. Certainly nobody ever reported the near-collisions, or "near misses" as they are called in aviation parlance, any more than they are reported today. It is true that ***TITANIC***'s death toll exceeded any previous maritime disaster simply because passenger ships were getting bigger with each new one built, but that would have created only transient interest if all of those who died had been "nobodies." Who, outside of Germany for example, remembers the ***WILHELM GUSTLOFF***, the refugee-crowded German ex-cruise ship torpedoed by a Russian submarine in 1945 with her death toll at least 7,500?

And yet, who forgets Astor, Guggenheim, Stead, Thayer, Widener, and dashing presidential aide-de-camp Major Archie Butt? Were these men more important simply because they were wealthy or famous? In our money-worshiping society, of course they were.

TITANIC was relegated to her proper place in maritime history after the gruesome mid Atlantic burning of the 3,600-ton Uranium Steamship Company liner ***VOLTURNO*** in October, 1913. Some twenty miles from her *SOS* position, ***VOLTURNO*** suffered no shortage of rescue ships, which raced to her aid guided by flames that often exploded hundreds of feet into the air, but these vessels lay helpless around the fire-gutted liner, unable to launch boats in the raging seas. ***VOLTURNO***'s passengers were mostly poor, European Jewish emigrants, therefore "of no consequence," and so ***VOLTURNO***, with but 146 lives lost although her overall drama and prolonged agony were far greater than ***TITANIC***'s, is forgotten.

The following year at the end of May Canadian Pacific's 14,500 ton ***EMPRESS OF IRELAND*** was rammed by the Norwegian collier ***STORSTADT*** near Father Point in the St Lawrence River. The ***EMPRESS*** sank in less than half an hour, with the loss of 964 lives. There are no books and films, no organizations endlessly devoted to the memory of the ***EMPRESS OF IRELAND***, but she lies in relatively shallow water, a mecca today for amateur divers.

A year later Cunard's hapless ***LUSITANIA*** gained her measure of fame when she was torpedoed by a German submarine off the South Irish coast. Like the ***EMPRESS***, ***LUSITANIA*** went down in less than half an hour, with the loss of 1,198 lives. Controversy still rages today over the exact cause of her sinking, but there is little doubt that she carried ammunition in her cargo holds. In spite of her passenger manifest ***LUSITANIA*** was built as an armed merchant cruiser, and Germany and Britain were at war.

On 25 July, 1915, Americans had their own peacetime shipping disaster to think about. The Great Lakes excursion steamer ***EASTLAND***, owned by the St. Joseph-Chicago Steamship Company, was loading at her pier in the Chicago River, carrying 2,500 Western Electric employees on a company outing. When her load limits were exceeded ***EASTLAND*** began listing to starboard, slowly at first, then suddenly she turned turtle, spewing her passengers into the water where the majority of them drowned. The death toll was 1,810, most of them women and children, the weaker ones who either did not know how to swim, an accomplishment usually denied women in those days, or they had no chance to swim in the crowded water. The ***EASTLAND*** disaster was the more horrible because it all happened within a few feet from shore, in sight of helpless bystanders.

Many liners were sunk in World War I, and in the second great War which came just one generation later, yet only ***LUSITANIA*** is remembered by the general public, and she has never been declared a memorial as ***TITANIC*** has. Her wreckage has been repeatedly violated, no doubt destroying valuable evidence necessary to learning the true cause of her sinking. All shipwrecks are fair game if they have gold or other valuable commodities aboard whether bodies remain trapped inside or not, yet only ***TITANIC*** enthusiasts cry "foul" when her artifacts are salvaged and displayed.

TITANIC remained the subject of obscure novels, occasional published memoirs, and one German propaganda film made in the late thirties, until suddenly, as the fiftieth anniversary of ***TITANIC***'s death approached there began an endless stream of books, articles, films, and television specials devoted ad infinitum to solving her "mysteries" and keeping her memory alive.

Why did she sink so quickly? Why did her master and her watch officer, with ice known to be in the vicinity, take her headlong into disaster? Was her watch officer warned of an ice field ahead less than an hour before impact? Did a nearby vessel's master lie in his cabin in a drunken stupor, within sight of the sinking liner, and do nothing to save her people? Did another ship steam past within two miles of ***TITANIC*** and ignore her "distress" rockets? And why did Fate send one stray iceberg into the path of this speeding, magnificent vessel with her splendid passenger manifest? Did those debonair and chivalrous American millionaires really line ***TITANIC***'s rails, clad in evening clothes, calmly smoking cigarettes, waiting, doing nothing to save their own lives, so that all the women and children might be saved? Did perfect calm really prevail on those ominously slanting decks, with the band courageously playing *"Nearer My God to Thee"* (or did they actually play the Episcopal hymn *Autumn?)* as the mighty ship slipped quietly beneath the waves... *intact?*

These are some of the questions allegedly still unanswered, yet there were answers in 1912, and in order to sink ***TITANIC's*** myths it is necessary to return to 1912, to view the incident through the eyes of a 1912 sailor.

I began my ***TITANIC*** research for a novel I wanted to write using her as a background. When you write historical fiction you must literally put yourself into the era about which you write. I quickly discovered that every previous author had a different version of the few moments which decided ***TITANIC's*** Fate, those moments when the iceberg was sighted and evasive action was taken. Only one man knew exactly what happened, and he had died. He was ***TITANIC's*** watch officer at the time of impact. First Officer William McMaster Murdoch. I was driven to wonder what kind of man he had been, what kind of seaman he was, and how he felt during those last two hours of his life. Murdoch became my ***TITANIC*** specialty, and for a time my obsession.

To understand Will Murdoch and his shipmates I studied seamanship and navigation from the manuals they would have used. I had some sailing experience in my youth, and I knew navigation from flying. I learned to fly when dead reckoning was the usual way to navigate a light plane, and when we had to learn Morse Code to pass the private pilot's written examination.

I was a flight attendant for many years with one of this country's leading pioneer airlines... Eastern. I've seen first-hand how people react in emergencies. Passengers are passengers, crews are crews, whether in a ship or an airliner. Sailors said it for centuries, and I said it after I had been on the line for a month... passengers are the most dangerous cargo that can be carried.

I've studied enough airline accident reports to understand how investigations work and how the public comes to believe what the cause of a crash was, often erroneously. Shipping accidents are no different, although even more obscure to the general public. Many things go on at sea which only sailors know about. Coverups are easy, for ships are out of sight, in 1912 and today.

In the summer of 1989 I collected some of my research notes into a book titled ***TITANIC:*** *R.I.P., Can Dead Men Tell Tales?,* hoping to pique the interest of other researchers and encourage them to look in new directions. I planned to finish my novel and let others who had priority in ***TITANIC*** investigation forge ahead toward the truth about that fatal night. Although it soon became apparent that most of them would continue to cling to the official legends, I did make many new friends through the book. I finally obtained the complete transcript of the British inquiry, and I interviewed Wilhelm Müller in person for the first time. Müller, a German deck officer-turned farmer whose 1962 ***TITANIC*** article intrigued me was the real reason I kept going in my own research. Bill was ninety-six years young when I interviewed him in Canada just before Christmas in 1989. His mind was clear, his memory excellent. He had carried a passionate desire to show the truth about ***TITANIC*** to the world since 1914, and with very good reason. Bill talked to me because he had read my book, and he told me his terrible secret because he knew that the end of his life was near. Bill passed away m 1991. To me he entrusted his crusade to let the world know what really happened to ***TITANIC.*** Still, his words meant nothing without testimony at both the American and British ***TITANIC*** inquiries which backs up his incredible story completely. Yet not one member of the "official" ***TITANIC*** *community* even bothered to talk with Bill, their opinion being that I "made him up."

For fifteen years, awake and asleep, I have lived with ***TITANIC***... walked her decks, paced her bridge, roamed her engine rooms and stokeholds. I know her all too well. It is time for her to come alive again, time to strip her of the myths and legends which have enveloped her in a rosy haze of romantic fantasy for over eight decades. Come follow me into an era of stark contrasts, a time of great luxury and even greater naiveté, when the gilded opulence of the upper classes sharply contradicted the barest poverty of those who toiled their lives away to merely survive, a time when the world teetered on the brink of a conflagration like humankind had never seen, a time of headlong industrial expansion, of dizzying social and technological changes, a not-so-gentle golden age gone forever.

D. E. Bristow
Miami Springs, Florida, 1994

TITANIC

SINKING THE MYTHS

Chapter One

A Ship Is A She

Excepting the transition from sail to steam, the language of the sea has changed little in the past few centuries. Many sea-words used today originated in sail, and many have found their way into common usage in every language. The nomenclature of aviation, a relatively infant discipline, has derived from nautical language. The *cockpit* of an aircraft, for example, derived from the nautical *cockpit,* the space from which a small boat is steered. The very word *pilot* came to aviation from the sea, where it meant one who *pilots,* or guides, ships through coastal channels, bays and harbors. *Piloting* is a type of navigation by which one guides an aircraft or ship by determining course using reference to a visible object on the earth's surface, or by *soundings,* which refer to ascertaining the depth of water by using a weighted line thrown over the side of a ship. Aircraft running lights derived from ships, the port wingtip light being red, the starboard wingtip light being green, and the tail light being white, as ships' stern lights are white. Aviation law has derived from maritime law. Because my vocational background is in aviation, and I believe that most of my readers will be more familiar with airplanes than with ships, I often use aviation analogies. Airplanes are easily seen, flying overhead every day, but ships still remain mysteriously at sea where vast numbers of the American population never see them, and thus never think about them.

On the sea as well as in the air distances are measured in *nautical miles.* One nautical mile is equal to about one minute of arc along a great circle, the Equator for example, and the standard figure accepted for that measurement for use in navigation and chart construction, is 6080 feet. In 1912 in the United States the figure 6080.27 ft., was accepted for the nautical mile, while in France, Germany and Austria the figure 6076.23 ft. was used, and in England the *Admiralty mile* was 6080 ft. The statute, or land mile measurement in the United States was, and is, 5,280 ft. One *nautical mile per hour* is one *knot,* abbreviated *kn.* It is therefore redundant and absolutely incorrect to say *knots per hour,* although this phrase was used even by some seamen as late as 1912, and it is found several times in both the American and British ***TITANIC*** inquiry transcripts. The term knot is still sometimes erroneously used to mean the measurement of one nautical mile. The word knot, then, is the nautical and aeronautical measure of speed, not distance.

TITANIC was a steamship of 1912. There are very few steamships operating today, their identity disclosed by the letters "*SS*" before the vessel's written name. When turbine-driven steamships were new and few, they were often designated by the prefix *"TSS,"* meaning *"Turbine Steam Ship,"* to distinguish them from steamships driven by reciprocating engines. It had quickly become apparent to regular ocean travelers that turbine-driven vessels had less uncomfortable vibration and more speed, therefore shipping companies capitalized upon their vessels which were equipped with the new turbine propulsion. ***OLYMPIC*** and ***TITANIC*** were frequently advertised under the designation "**TSS**" because their center engine was a turbine. The designation *"MV"* for *"Motor Vessel,"* (sometimes *"MS"* for *"Motor Ship")* is the usual prefix today and means that the vessel is driven by internal combustion engines. A ship's name is always painted on her bows, and across her stern above her port of registry.

It will be helpful to recognize and understand 1912 sea jargon before learning about ***TITANIC,*** for despite legend, she was basically no different from other vessels of her day.

Although, sadly, it may be politically incorrect to use the feminine pronoun when referring to a ship today, in ***TITANIC***'s era a ship was always a *she,* never an *it.* There have been many theories put forth to explain that, but perhaps it was something as simple as lonely sailors substituting their love of a ship for the feminine love they left ashore. Additionally, sailors expected their ships to nurture, sustain and support them, and isn't that what men have expected of women since Eve? Using the feminine pronoun when referring to ships is certainly not derogatory to women. I have no quarrel with this, and neither should any other woman; in fact, I like it. To me ships are all lovely creatures and each has her own personality. Beauty is not just an exterior quality. A plodding, ancient cargo vessel may have as much beauty in her character as a sleek passenger liner has in her perfect lines. Ships are always individuals, even among their own class. Ships have souls; ask any professional mariner, ships talk to you. And you must listen when your ship talks, for she will tell you at once if she's in trouble. Throughout this book I will therefore use the feminine pronoun when referring to ships, just as ***TITANIC***'s crewmen did. However, because in 1912 there were no female deck or engineering officers in the transatlantic liners I will for the sake of expediency use the masculine pronoun when referring to ships' officers and other crew members, excepting stewardesses.

A ship is called a *liner* when she follows a regular schedule between two or more ports, whether she carries passengers, cargo, or a combination of both. She is a *tramp* if she follows no schedule, but calls where her owners, represented by her master, can find cargoes, and sometimes passengers.

A ship is commanded by a *master mariner,* that is, one who has passed the requisite time at sea along with sequential written and oral examinations to gain the *master's certificate.* In ***TITANIC***'s era, in the British mercantile marine, there was also an *"extra master's certificate,"* one step above the usual master's. Many of ***TITANIC***'s officers, including First Officer William Murdoch, had the extra master's, although for purposes defined in later chapters it was expedient to downplay this information at both ***TITANIC*** inquiries. The term "master" mariner is still used today, even though an increasing number of women hold the certificate.

The British have generally favored the use of the rank description *officer,* while in sail and in the American merchant marine the term *mate* was, and is, frequently used, but the words are synonymous.

The captain, or *master,* holds a master mariner's certificate and is the commander of a merchant vessel, in complete charge, and completely responsible for everything that happens in the ship. The master's word is law aboard ship, as it must be, for when in danger the life of the ship and everyone aboard her depends upon discipline and absolute obeyance of orders. When dangerous circumstances demand it a good master is on the bridge, even though that might mean being on duty for many hours without rest. In the transatlantic liners it was not uncommon in bad weather, in fog or ice, for the master to be on the bridge for days without sleep. The master legally is always responsible for everything that happens to the ship, whether the master is on the bridge, or elsewhere in the ship, or even ashore. It is also the master's responsibility to ascertain that the vessel is seaworthy before going to sea. A ship's commander is always addressed as *"Captain,"* but referred to as *"the master,"* regardless of gender. When sailors turn in *all standing,* they retire fully clothed, ready to leap into action at a moment's notice. Both Captain Smith of the ***TITANIC*** and Captain Lord of the ***CALIFORNIAN*** ha*d* turned in all standing on the night of 14 April, 1912, as had, no doubt, many other masters in the area. The best master kept away from the bridge excepting in unusual circumstances, leaving the *conn,* or control, of the ship, to the watch officers. The master had full confidence in those senior officers, or they did not remain in the line.

Senior officers are the *watchkeepers,* or *watch officers,* meaning that they are in full charge of the ship when they are on duty and the master is not on the bridge, and they make the emergency decisions. They have their standing orders, they obey them completely, and call the master only when circumstances warrant it according to the master's instructions. In ***TITANIC***'s case. Captain Smith had left *night orders* for his watch officers as the ship approached the Grand Banks area where fog prevailed, where ice was known to accumulate at that time of year, where sailing craft abounded. Every well-regulated vessel has a *Night Order Book* on the bridge. The watch officer coming on duty checks the Night Order Book for the master's instructions, which have been written out each evening. The officer about to relieve the watch reads the Night Order Book, and initials it to signify that the orders are understood. *Standing orders* are the usual admonitions concerning weather changes, fog, ice, heavy rain, all of which are reasons for the watch officer to call the master immediately. Captain Smith's standing order was to call him if it "came on the slightest bit hazy," meaning if visibility decreased the slightest bit. Smith's instructions then no doubt would have been to reduce speed, and increase the lookout. Responsible watch officers did not, and do not, do these things on their own when the master has left such standing orders. *Special orders* relate to change of course and/or speed, lights expected to be sighted, and so forth. The watch officer *never* has the authority to change the cruising speed without permission of the master. If the master wants to give the conning officer that authority for a short time, he, or she, will so state, but then only for that particular time. If the watch officer initiates an emergency turn or slackens speed the master feels the ship heel or slow down, no matter how slightly she does, and the master comes to the bridge immediately.

In ***TITANIC***'s era the watch officer on duty was never relieved until the course had been passed to the relieving officer. At night the relieving officer entered the bridge about five minutes prior to the actual duty period, allowing time to check the Night Order Book, to get his night vision, to hear from the officer being relieved such pertinent information as ships in sight, and any passed during the course of the previous watch, weather changes, any special orders from the master pertaining to speed, course, lookouts, steering, and so on. Upon the course being passed, in the era of open bridges, the relieving officer stepped to windward of the officer being relieved, and the new watch had taken over. The reason for this ritual, performed swiftly and as a matter of fact, was simple, but extremely important. If an emergency arose while the two officers were on the bridge together it had to be absolutely clear which one was in charge. If the vessel was in the middle of a maneuver, for example in crowded waters, the relieving officer did not take over until the maneuver was completed.

Every watch officer must have a thorough knowledge of the *International and Inland Rules of the Road,* being able to make instantaneous decisions based upon them in emergency situations.

The *International Rules of the Road* are international laws, not merely "gentlemen's agreements," and they apply to *all vessels* navigating the international high seas. They were adopted by *all* maritime nations in 1889. In 1897 the United States adopted its own system of *Inland Rules of the Road,* which applied *"in all harbors, rivers, and inland waters of the United States, except the Great Lakes and their connecting tributary waters as far east as Montreal, and the Red River of the North and rivers emptying into the Gulf of Mexico."* In addition the United States adopted *Pilot Rules,* which supplemented the *Inland Rules,* and were drawn up by the U.S. Board of Steamboat Inspectors. Many other countries have their own set of rules for their local waters, but in countries where there are no prescribed local rules for navigation the *International Rules of the Road* always apply. In studying the ***TITANIC*** disaster it is absolutely necessary to have at least a rudimentary knowledge of certain *Rules of the Road,* and to understand that they are *laws* under which *every vessel* plying the high seas must operate. That certainly included ***TITANIC***. While *The International Rules of the Road* were originally intended to be "watertight," leaving no ambiguity in their interpretation, there were and are certain cases when a Court of Admiralty has been forced to interpret a rule, establishing precedent for later, similar cases. Because knowledge of certain *Rules* is so necessary to the understanding of what happened to ***TITANIC,*** those *Rules* are featured in their entirety in the appropriate portion of the chapters which follow. They are given verbatim from seamanship manuals of ***TITANIC***'s era, for that is the time period in which we are interested. I will say it often, it is *absolutely essential* to view the ***TITANIC*** disaster only from her own time frame, not ours. The *Rules of the Road* have changed little, however, differing only in reflecting technological advances made in the years since ***TITANIC*** sank, and lessons learned from her disaster.

Duty periods aboard ship are *watches,* and off duty time is called the *watch below.* In sailing vessels watches were usually four hours on duty, with only four hours off. By ***TITANIC***'s era senior officers. Chief, First and Second, kept somewhat more civilized hours, being four hours on duty and eight hours off. Junior officers in ***TITANIC*** kept the old four-on-four-off "*toe and heel*" watches. They therefore had to sleep fast when on their watch below, and as ***TITANIC***'s Fifth Officer Lowe commented, *"When we sleep, we die."* However, even when senior officers are not on watch on the bridge, they may have many shipboard duties to perform, related to their rank and assignments, particularly when the ship is in port.

Ship's time was marked by bells, struck by a quartermaster, with each watch always beginning with one bell, and each watch named for the purpose of eliminating confusion. The *Middle Watch* began with one bell at 12:30AM, or 0030 in 24-hour time. Two bells were struck at 1AM, or 0100. Three bells announced the next half hour, 0130, and so on with bells increasing in number on the half hour until four hours had passed, with eight bells being 0400. The bells began again with the *Morning Watch,* one bell signifying 0430, and so on until the end of the Morning Watch at 0800 with eight bells. The *Forenoon Watch* proceeded in the same manner, followed by the *Afternoon Watch* which ended with eight bells at 4PM, or 1600. At this point the watch was broken into two two-hour periods called *dog watches.* The *First Dog Watch* began with one bell at 1630, ended with four bells at 1800. *The Second Dog Watch* then repeated with one bell at 1830, two bells at 1900, three at 1930, and eight bells struck at 2000. The *First Watch* began at 2030, with one bell struck, continued in the regular manner until midnight when eight bells were struck. In many British ships a single bell was struck shortly before eight bells to give the watch coming on duty the chance of getting a meal. The reason for the divided Dog Watches was to give a crewman who had only four hours rest one night eight hours rest the following night. In ***TITANIC's*** time and later, there was a sailors' superstition that in the Middle Watch, in the middle bunker of a coal-burning ship at sea, the ghosts of all the souls who had drowned in shipping disasters would congregate to mourn their lost ships and lives. (See Appendix, *Bell Table)*

The master, and his engine room counterpart the chief engineer, never keep a watch. Titles may differ somewhat in various shipping lines, but in the White Star the watchkeeping deck officers were the Chief Officer, First Officer and Second Officer. Junior officers, that is Third, Fourth, Fifth and Sixth in ***TITANIC,*** shared the bridge, with two juniors to one senior officer. Today in the British *Merchant Navy* the same ranks are usually used, although fewer junior officers are carried, being for the most part replaced by modern electronics. "Merchant Navy" was the name given to Britain's mercantile marine after World War I by King George V to show appreciation for the valor and indispensable service of British merchant sailors during the Great War. The term is thus incorrectly used if applied to any other country's merchant marine service, although it has become common practice to do so.

Deck officers below the rank of Chief were addressed simply as *"Mister,"* while engineering officers below the rank of Chief were referred to by their rank, for example *"First, Second, Third,"* and so on.

There are two major departments responsible for operating a ship, the *Deck Department,* comprised of all navigating officers, deck seamen and their support crew members, and the *Engine Department,* where the *Chief Engineer* is in charge. The watchkeeping engineers were the First, Second and Third. Each in his watch would be responsible for the propelling and auxiliary machinery in the entire vessel, while junior engineers. First Assistant Engineer and so on, would be in charge in their own sections, always responsible to the watchkeeper, who in turn was responsible to the Chief Engineer. Like the master, the chief was always technically on duty. In Britain in ***TITANIC***'s time engineers usually had experience ashore with one of the marine engine manufacturers before going to sea as an apprentice. Having worked his way up from apprentice engineer the chief was experienced, and was able to feel every variation in his beloved machinery, knowing instantly when something had gone wrong. Like the navigating officers, engineering officers had their standing orders, from which they did not deviate. In ***TITANIC,*** or any other express liner on the high seas, that usually meant full speed-ahead at all times.

In a coal-burning ship there were the *greasers,* who attended to the ship's machinery, the *trimmers,* who brought coal from the bunkers into the stokeholds, for the *stokers* and *firemen* to feed into the ravenous furnaces. The trimmers did just what their name implied, they kept the vessel "trimmed" by moving coal in even amounts from each bunker, thereby keeping weight evenly distributed. Each man knew his duties and if he shirked them in any way he did not remain in the line's employ, for the crew was like the ship's machinery a… breakdown in any component meant lost time, and therefore lost revenue. The men who fed the yawning furnaces of the transatlantic liners were a tough lot, usually Liverpool Irish in British ships, often Hungarian or Roumanian in German ships. Their job was a hard one, requiring great stamina, although not necessarily brute strength as legend has it. Merchant Navy engineer and author William McFee, in his review of Eugene O'Neill's play *"The Hairy Ape"* (from *Sailors" Wisdom,* Jonathan Cape, Ltd., London and Toronto, 1938) wrote that contrary to legend, firemen were not chosen for their brawn. "No *vast agglomeration of muscles could ever take the place of skill,"* wrote McFee. Engineers who had the duty of picking firemen for the Western Ocean liners had learned the hard way to pass up the Neanderthal types in favor of men of normal stature, or even smaller, who knew their work. A high tolerance for heat was mandatory, the temperatures in stokeholds sometimes reaching 120° Fahrenheit, and higher if the vessel was in equatorial waters. It was common for firemen and stokers to be hauled unconscious from heat stroke to the upper decks where a reviving bucket of water was thrown on them.

And always in a coal-burning ship there were the ashes. Working a hand winch in the ventilator, each watch would raise ten or twenty buckets of ash and dump them through a canvas chute into the sea. The ventilator being some ten feet above the fireroom floor plates made this procedure especially difficult and hazardous in heavy weather. As the ship rolled in a seaway the men staggering to the side with the ash buckets had to be agile, no matter how tired they were, for if they missed the ashes would fall back on those below. Even in 1912 most port authorities permitted no ash-dumping in their waters. Consequently, while the ship was in port the refuse from the boilers accumulated on deck until the vessel was like a big slag-heap. In passenger liners this had to be hidden below, where it filled firerooms and empty bunkers. At sea a speeding liner or warship ejected a steady torrent of ashes. The men who toiled their lives away in this hellish atmosphere were always black with coal dust, and dripping with sweat. They inhaled the fine dust and ash, shortening their lives by years. They needed the intelligence to pace themselves, the ability to work as a team. ***TITANIC***'s firemen who testified at the British inquiry were often articulate and obviously intelligent, yet they were treated as if they were a subhuman species, an attitude born of the tremendous class distinction of the period.

There has always been a traditional rivalry and antipathy between Deck and Engine Departments, particularly in British ships. There is a saying even today in the Merchant Navy: *"Oil and water don't mix,"* meaning that the two departments are antagonistic. An old nautical joke along these lines considers the constant bickering between master and chief engineer, each of whom believed the other's job was not as important as his own. Finally they decided to settle the dispute by trading places for one voyage. They were not yet under way when the master in the engine room phoned the chief engineer on the bridge. *"I can't get these bloody engines started,"* groaned the master. *"It doesn't matter,"* answered the chief. *"We're fast aground."*

The third segment in the ship's operation was, in the White Star, called the *Victualing Department.* This was comprised of all persons who provided service to passengers... the stewards, stewardesses, waiters, bellboys, lift operators, chefs, and so on. They were all under the supervision of the Chief Steward, or of the Chief Purser, whose department handled all ship's paperwork, of which there was an enormous amount. The Chief Purser was responsible for all of the customs and immigration documents, and the manifest for passengers, crew and cargo had to be absolutely correct when the vessel arrived at her destination. This holds true today, and governments impose heavy fines on shipping companies and airlines when these regulations are not complied with to the letter. A complete and correct manifest is absolutely necessary at the port of entry for immigrations and customs officials. In a passenger ship the size of ***OLYMPIC*** and ***TITANIC*** it was impossible to have a perfect, accurate manifest until after she had sailed because there were always passengers who booked from the pier, and crew members who signed on at the last minute to replace those who did not show up by sailing time, to say nothing of the always possible stowaway. Therefore the only complete passenger manifest for ***TITANIC*** was that taken after she departed Queenstown, and it went down with her.

In the Deck Department *able seamen,* abbreviated *A.B.*'s, are those who have completed a prescribed length of time, usually three years, of seagoing deck service and passed a qualifying examination. At the bottom of the Deck Department hierarchy are the *ordinary seamen,* serving their apprenticeships to become able seamen. *Quartermasters* and *boatswains* (pronounced and often spelled *bo'suns)* were picked, experienced A.B.'s with a slight increase in pay. In the mail steamers they ranked as petty officers. The quartermaster's duties consisted of attending to the steering, the binnacle, telegraphs, flags, taking temperatures of air and water, heaving the log and reading the *patent log* (a device for registering a vessel's speed through the water). The bo'sun's duties were concerned with the ship's rigging, anchors, cables and boats. The usual way of referring to or addressing the boatswain was simply *"Boats."* Lesser ships of the White Star and other major lines, that is, the intermediate passenger liners and cargo ships, carried apprentices, or *cadets,* those in training to become officers. The transatlantic express liners did not carry cadets.

Calling a *ship* a *boat* is a serious breach of seagoing etiquette. A *boat* is generally defined as a "small craft which can be hoisted aboard a large vessel," hence *"lifeboat."* However, we speak of riverboats, *tugboats, houseboats,* and the goliaths of the Great Lakes are often called *"boats."* Submariners, as well, call their underwater ships *"boats."* ***TITANIC***'s officers spoke of the Atlantic express liners as *"mailboats,"* because they operated under government subsidies to carry the mails. A mariner, therefore, may call a ship a boat, just as an aviator may "drive" an airplane and put it in a "garage," instead of a hangar. But these are the privileges of those inside their intimate professions, professions which have their own languages and which close ranks to outsiders because the very nature of them is so complex that outsiders are not just capriciously unwelcome, they are often a nuisance .

One can be *in* a ship, never *on* a ship, although one may be *on* the bridge, or *on a* particular deck. The Royal Navy was always fussier about this than the merchant service was, and cruise lines today, who utilize so many shorebound employees who never learn the lingo of the sea, would never correct passengers who go on a cruise *on* a particular ship. A professional mariner, however, will be *in* a ship. The landlubber's analogy is simply that you can be in your house, never on it, unless you happen to be on the roof.

A ship lies in her *dock,* or *berth,* which is a water area, thus you never, ever, walk on the dock. As with so many words erroneously used over a long period of time, the true definition of dock being rarely known, the word is now commonly understood to be synonymous with *pier,* a structure built out into the water to be used as a landing area for boats or ships, or with *quay,* and *wharf,* formerly areas built along a shore where ships could come alongside for loading and unloading.

A graving dock, or *dry dock,* is where a ship goes when it is necessary to inspect or repair her bottom. It is an excavation that fills at high water. The vessel is floated into the dock, a gate is closed and the water is pumped out of the dock, leaving the ship resting on *keel* and *bilge blocks,* held by *wale shores* which support her sides.

A sailor makes a *pier-head jump* when he, or she, ships from the pier, without going through the usual rotation system. This is done only when necessary to prevent the vessel from sailing shorthanded.

Ships, like us, have skeletal structures. The backbone of a ship is her *keel,* her ribs are her *frames.* In ***TITANIC***'s era when a ship was laid down for building, her keel was put down first. Framing was built up from the keel, and that framing was *plated,* which made the watertight box, or *hull. A* sleek racing yacht has a keel which extends below the hull, and that keel may even be moveable, so it can be raised in shallow water. But the *keel* on a big steel vessel, such as ***TITANIC,*** lies entirely within the ship. It is made up of heavy steel plates and angles to form an I-beam shape, which runs the length of the ship. Between the lower flange of this structure, which is called the *flat plate keel,* and the upper flange, called the *rider plate,* is the ship's *inner bottom.*

The space between the inner bottom and the *outer bottom* is called the *double bottom.* When this double bottom is divided into subdivisions, as ***TITANIC***'s was, it is called a *cellular double bottom.* All liners of ***TITANIC***'s era had cellular double bottoms. The advantages to having this type structure if a ship runs aground are obvious. Some warships even had cellular *triple bottoms.* An inner keel which extends above the keel inside of the ship is called a *keelson,* pronounced *"kel-son." Cells,* or subdivisions, in the double bottom can be used as tanks to store water or oil, which may be utilized as ballast. If, through damage, a vessel takes in water on one side, thereby developing a *list,* (a prolonged *heel,* or roll out of the perpendicular) tanks on the opposite side can be flooded to bring her upright.

Imagine an invisible vertical plane which runs through the ship along the line of her keel. This is called the *center line,* and it divides the ship exactly in half. When you're standing on the center line facing forward, everything to your *left* is on the *port* side, while everything to your *right* is on the *starboard* side. Everything in the ship is designated by its position with reference to the center line, for example the *starboard gangway,* (the opening in a ship's side which gives access to *the gangplank,* which is the moveable bridge between ship and pier) the *starboard* running light, (which is always green) or the *port* propeller, the *port* emergency boat, or the *port* running light (which is always red). Objects which are permanently located on the starboard side, such as lifeboats or cabins, are usually given *odd* numbers, while those on the port side have *even* numbers. Numbering of compartments, cabins, lifeboats, frames, etc., usually starts at the stem with number 1 and continues aft, although in ***TITANIC*** and her sisters boiler rooms and coal bunkers were numbered from engine rooms forward, while all other objects and compartments were numbered in the ordinary way. As an object moves away from the center line it is said to be moving *outboard.* Conversely, if it moves toward the center line it moves *inboard.*

The word *port* may also refer to openings cut into the hull or deckhouses, on either side of the ship, to admit light, air, coal or cargo. A *blind port* is one fitted with a steel door, which closes flush with the side. *A port light* (not to be confused with the port running light) is the heavy, circular glass framed with metal, which screws against the port openings in cabins and "tween decks. *Dead lights* are the steel discs that screw down over the port lights to secure them in heavy weather.

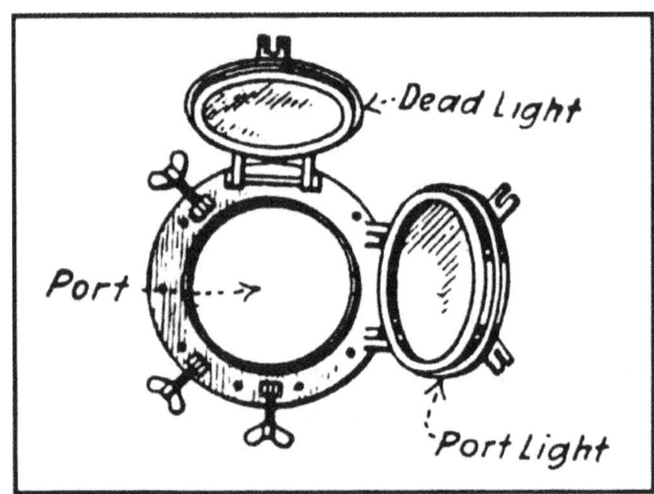

THE PORTLIGHT

In 1891 the Anchor Line's ***ANGLIA*** stranded in the Jellingham Channel of the River Hooghly, and rolled over so fast that five men were trapped in the forecastle by a shifting deck cargo of coal. The ports were too small for a man to get through, so the luckless five, despite heroic efforts of their shipmates to free them, drowned when the tide came in. Legend has it that one seaman "became insane" when he had to watch helplessly while his trapped brother died.

It took the disastrous fire at Norddeutscher Lloyd's Hoboken docks on 30 June, 1900, however, when men were again trapped below decks by small ports in the 440 ft. ***SAALE,*** to instigate a regulation that all ports leading to housing and working spaces must be large enough to permit the passage of an adult person.

An imaginary plane which crosses the ship at right angles to her keel, or center line, is said to be *athwartships.* This is not to be confused with a similar term, *amidships,* which defines the part of the ship which is equidistant between the forward end of the ship, her *bow,* and the after end, her *stern.*

Moving toward the ship's bow you always *go forward,* never, ever "toward the front." Moving toward the stern you always go *aft,* never, never "toward the back." If you are farther forward than an object in the ship, you *are forward* of that object, never "in front of it." If you are farther aft of the object, you are *aft of it,* or *abaft* it, never, never "in back of it." The area forward of amidships is generally referred to *as forward,* while the area abaft amidships is *aft. A* ship's keel runs *fore and aft.*

The moveable blade-like device attached to the stern for the purpose of directional control, is the *rudder.* Merchant ships of ***TITANIC***'s era usually had the entire area of rudder abaft its axis of rotation. When the rudder is parallel to the ship's keel it is *amidships,* and she is said to have *no rudder on her.* The rudder was moved in ***TITANIC***'s era by means of *steam steering gear,* controlled by a system of wires, pulleys and drums which transmitted the movements of the steering *wheel* made by the *helmsman.*

The word *helm* is derived from the old Norse word *hjalm,* the name for the lever which turned the rudder on a Viking longboat. Helm is therefore synonymous with *tiller,* the solid metal or wooden lever which moved the rudder on all early sailing vessels, and is still used in small craft today Helm is *not* synonymous with rudder, although long erroneous common usage has made it such. In ***TITANIC***'s time turning orders were given in terms of the position of the ship's helm/tiller rather than the rudder position.

When the steering wheel of a car is turned, the car instantly tums in the same direction the wheel has been turned, pivoting about its back wheels. Turning is not so simple in a ship. When the helm/tiller is moved away from the ship's center line it moves the rudder in the opposite direction to which the helm itself is put. Thus if the helm is put to starboard, the rudder goes to port. When the ship is making *headway* (going ahead) water piles up against the forward side of the rudder, forcing the stern off to starboard, which in turn forces the ship's head in the direction to which the rudder has been put, but in the opposite direction to which the helm has been put, and in this case the head goes to port. It may be difficult for landlubbers to grasp, but it is extremely important to understand that the ship's stern goes off first when the helm has been moved to initiate a turn or change in course. In this example the stern is "kicked" to starboard, forcing the head to port. The ship pivots about a point near the middle of her length called her *pivoting point.* The more headway, or speed, the ship has the faster water piles up against the forward side of the rudder and the quicker the stern goes off, thus the quicker she tums, or *answers her helm. A* ship always answers her helm faster at higher speeds. Thus it takes a greater angle on the rudder to turn a slowly moving ship than it takes to turn the same ship at higher speeds, and this is the reason why speed was not reduced when running in ice zones, until ice was actually sighted. It is not prudent, however, to put full rudder on a ship moving at high speeds, for the ship will heel sharply, putting high stresses on her hull. Therefore the helm is not put hard over at top speeds excepting in emergency situations when danger is close aboard. The rudder develops its greatest efficiency at an angle of about 40 degrees with the ship's fore and aft center line. In ***TITANIC***'s time stops or buffers were fitted on the deck of a vessel in the way of the quadrant to prevent the rudder from going over too far. When a ship's headway has been reduced to the point where she will no longer answer her rudder because not enough water is piling up against its forward side, then she has *lost steerageway.* It must be understood, for it is important to realizing how ***TITANIC*** was maneuvered prior to her collision with ice, that a ship has steerageway *as long as she is moving forward fast enough to let water pile up against the forward edge of her rudder.* Thus even if her engines have been put full speed astern, and her screws are backing, she will still have headway and answer her rudder for some time, usually the distance of at least three or four ship lengths, possibly more, depending upon her individual handling characteristics, for the backing screws must first bring her to a stop before the ship can actually begin making sternway. The interval between the order given to run the engines "full speed astern" and the time when the shaft has been stopped and reversed, was about ninety seconds in ***TITANIC***'s era of reciprocating engines. There is a period of time, then, when the ship is going ahead although her screws are backing, and she will answer her helm.

After the helm has been put hard over, as ***TITANIC***'s was first put to starboard and then to port, she ranges ahead along her original track, perhaps to leeward of it, for some distance, again depending on her individual handling characteristics, before she takes up her new direction.

It should be understood that even vessels which are identical "sister ships" will not handle exactly the same, nor will airplanes which are "identical models." ***OLYMPIC*** and ***TITANIC*** were slightly different although their hulls were of the same dimensions. Only her watch officers would have known ***TITANIC***'s handling characteristics, for they were the only ones who actually had the opportunity to get the feel of her. It was generally agreed among naval architects after ***TITANIC*** sank that her rudder area was too small for her size, and some experts argued that such large ships were impractical unless steering engines were redesigned for them.

A ship's *bridge* might be called her brain. All commands and instructions are issued from the watch officers, or the master, on the bridge. Bridges run athwartships the breadth of the vessel and were pretty well standardized in ***TITANIC***'s time. Outboard, open ends of the bridges of this era were called *bridge wings.* Small shelters on the outboard ends of the bridge wings were *bridge cabs. A* wood or canvas windbreaker on the forward bridge rail was called a *dodger.* Inboard, in the central, enclosed part of the bridge structure, were the *wheelhouse,* the *charthouse* or *chartroom.* Aft of and in many ships one deck below the navigating bridge, were the master's quarters, the officer's quarters and the wireless cabin. Located in the wheelhouses of ***TITANIC***'s era were the various navigating instruments, the timepiece or *chronometer,* the *wheel* by which the ship was steered, and directly in front of the wheel was the *binnacle,* the stand which houses the *steering compass.*

Felix Reisenberg, Master Mariner in Sail and Steam, Lieutenant Commander USNR, and Commander of the Schoolship *NEWPORT* from 1917 through 1919, and again from 1923 through 1924, first published his *Standard Seamanship for the Merchant* Service in 1922. (D. van Nostrand Co., Inc., New York) The ideal bridge, according to Reisenberg, had an open walkway which ran athwartships the breadth of the ship forward of the wheelhouse so that a watch officer had equal access to both wings without impairing his night vision by passing through the wheelhouse. When this open walkway was broken by a wheelhouse cutting across the center of the bridge, a favorite design with the Germans, said Reisenberg, if you closed the weather door to the wheelhouse it made the weather wing of the bridge useless. The bridge must have unobstructed vision and be high enough that the watch officer could see all around the horizon, Reisenberg recommended. The helmsman must be in the wheelhouse, but the watch officer did not belong inside. The officer, declared Reisenberg, should be actively on his feet, outside, walking back and forth in the fresh air, his eyes sweeping the horizon all around, noting the direction of wind and sea, and the surface of the water as well as everything about his ship. If a passenger or crew member should fall overboard it was much better to have the watch officer out in the open to immediately toss over a lifebuoy and call away the emergency boat while stopping the vessel as quickly as possible and yet maneuvering the screws away from the victim, rather than have someone run into the wheelhouse to call the officer first. The officer outside on the bridge *"is liable to be more active and able than the chap inside,"* wrote Reisenberg. ***TITANIC***'s bridge conformed to Reisenberg's criteria. Forward of ***TITANIC***'s wheelhouse the open bridge ran the full breadth of the ship, with engine telegraphs just forward of the wheelhouse. Passenger ships today usually have bridges well forward, while tankers and cargo vessels may have their bridges amidships or well aft. Modern bridges on large, ocean-going vessels are fully enclosed, a fact which probably created the legend of ***TITANIC***'s First Officer lounging in the wheelhouse waiting for the lookouts to tell him what lay ahead of the ship. (See Appendix; *Bridge photograph)*

The *engine order telegraphs,* or *annunciators,* (See page 63) were the means by which watch officers communicated with the engine room. Ideally the engine telegraphs were always within jumping distance of the watch officer, and Reisenberg advocated duplicate telegraphs on both quarter points of the bridge. This was an added building and maintenance expense, however, and most bridges had only the single set of telegraphs forward of the wheelhouse, as in ***OLYMPIC*** and ***TITANIC,*** where an agile watch officer could reach them quickly in an emergency. The engine telegraph transmitted engine and propeller orders to the engine room, where there were duplicate telegraphs. Experienced engineers could tell who was working the telegraph on the bridge by the officer's technique. Some watch officers and masters would bang the telegraph handle from one extreme to the other one or more times before settling on the order they wanted to convey, while the engineer on the starting platform below waited, usually not too patiently, for the pointer on his duplicate telegraph to settle down so he knew what to do with the engines. *Docking telegraphs* were also on the bridge, and their purpose was to transmit unmistakable orders to the docking bridge aft.

TITANIC and her sisters were among the first ships to have telephones with which officers could communicate from the bridge to major parts of the vessel. In 1912 the technology for automatic switching was not yet available, which meant that direct lines were hooked to individual telephones. In ***TITANIC***'s wheelhouse there were four telephones, one a direct line from the *crow's nest,* or observation post, on *the foremast,* one from the engine room, one from the *docking bridge,* (a small bridge structure on the poop, used during docking because visibility aft from the main, or navigating bridge, was obscured by deckhouses) and one from the forecastle. In addition there were direct lines between the various pantries and galleys, between the engine room and the chief engineer's cabin. Telephones in passenger cabins and suites were part of a separate system which utilized a switchboard, with an operator on duty at all times. Because telephones on ships were relatively new, and expensive, in 1912 older vessels and most cargo ships used *speaking tubes* for communicating. To initiate a call the officer would whistle into the tube, then speak into it after he received an answer from the person on the other end of the tube. Legend has it that several passengers and crewmen later "recalled" hearing ***TITANIC***'s lookouts shout the ice warning to the bridge from the crow's nest. The lookouts, however, used the telephone in ***TITANIC***'s crow's nest to communicate with the bridge. *Never* did officers or crew "shout" anything, for on an open bridge, an open crow's nest, voices would carry to passenger quarters and promenades, and it was never wise to allow passengers to know of anything they might construe as danger. Passenger ship crews, just like airline crews, were and are cautioned to always maintain an appearance of calmness, no matter what. Panic can be a much greater problem than the situation that already demands their urgent attention.

Lookouts always reported objects in terms of *relative bearings,* measured in *points* in ***TITANIC***'s time. Today relative bearings are given in terms of *degrees,* with the starting point of 000° always being the ship's head, or *dead ahead,* continuing clockwise with 180° being *dead astern.* One point is equal to 11 1/4 degrees. The *reciprocal* of a bearing is its opposite, and is figured by adding 180° to the bearing. If the sum is over 360° then you subtract 360 from it. For example if the bearing is 060° its reciprocal is 240°. If the bearing is 200° its reciprocal is 380°-360, or 020°. The bearing from the object to the observer is the reciprocal of the bearing from the observer to the object. Bearings now are always expressed in three digits, adding the prefix zero where necessary. (See illustrations in Chapter 4; The Tracks, beginning on page 88; *Relative Bearings, Points and Equivalent Degrees,* and *Compass Rose.)*

In the chartroom there was always a bunk or settee upon which the master could rest all standing, and here were all of the ship's navigating charts, in rows of long, flat drawers, along with a large table upon which the current working chart would be laid out. *Sextants,* which are instruments used to observe the angle between two objects and used in navigation to obtain the angle (called *altitude)* between a heavenly body and the visible horizon, were also kept in the chartroom. Even the most junior officer had a personal sextant, its value being a source of great pride. While the word *sight* might mean that something was seen for the first time, as in to *"sight* a ship on the horizon," when used as a noun it meant the observation of a celestial body, as in to "take a *sight* of the star Rigel," for example. In this way a ship's latitude and longitude coordinates would be determined within reasonable accuracy. From this position until further sights could be taken the ship's position would be figured by *dead reckoning,* the word "dead" being a corruption of "ded." an abbreviation for the word "deductive." In the Western Ocean mailboats it was the usual practice to take a noon sun sight each day when weather permitted. This ritual was made into quite a production for the benefit of the passengers, with the master as well as officers not on watch participating. The subject of ***TITANIC***'s navigation is dealt with more extensively in the chapter covering North Atlantic Tracks. To British sailors the North Atlantic was the *Western Ocean,* naturally because it lay west of the British Isles, to them the center of the universe.

You never go downstairs, or upstairs in a ship. In fact, there are no stairs in the working parts of a ship, where sailors call them *ladders.* Only in passenger quarters are there "stairs" because passengers are not expected to know any better. An *accommodation ladder* is a ladder rigged out and lowered from the gangway, on either side, to facilitate boarding of the ship from boats.

If you go to a lower level, you go *below,* while the area below the main deck is generally called simply *below decks.* When sailors are on their watch below they may be in the *forecastle,* sometimes spelled as it's pronounced, *fo'c'sle,* which in the merchant service is the term applied to crew living quarters, separate from officers' quarters. As a specific part of a ship the forecastle is the elevated structure extending from the stem to the forward end of the forward well deck. The *forecastle head* is the deck of the forecastle. The part of the forecastle head nearest the stem is known as the *eyes of the ship.* In American merchant vessels before the use of navigating radar a lookout was usually stationed here at night and during daylight when visibility was low. This is why Senator Smith at the American ***TITANIC*** inquiry persisted in asking the White Star officers if ***TITANIC*** had a lookout in the *eyes of the ship,* although the British officers either did not know what Smith was talking about, or more likely, pretended to not know, for ***TITANIC*** had no extra lookout posted there.

Mess is the term applied to a group of crew members who dine together, for example the *officers" mess,* which may be in the *officers" saloon* in a merchant vessel, while passengers dine in the *saloon,* never the "salon."

The area above the main deck is generally referred to as *topside.* Any area above a ship's solid structure, such as her masts, rigging, or stacks, is *aloft.*

An object which is in the water, for example on the port side of the ship, is *off* the port side. If it is *abeam* of her, it is on a relative bearing of 90° (abeam to starboard) or 270" (abeam to port). If it is in the water against the ship's side it is *alongside.* If the object is ahead of the ship it is *forward* of her, or simply *ahead* of her. If the object is to the ship's rear it is *astern* of her, never, never "in back of her." If the object is suspended against the ship's side, it is *over the side,* or *over* the bow or stern, as the case may be. An object thrown overboard may also be *over the side,* while a person leaving the ship is said to be *going over the side,* and one coming aboard is *coming over the side.* An object that is *close aboard* is in very close proximity to the ship. If a ship rolls over on to her side she is *on her beam ends.* The word *beam* may also mean the vessel's overall width, or it may refer to a transverse frame supporting a deck. *Panting beams,* and *panting stringers,* reinforce forward frames to take up *panting stresses,* which are caused by wave action.

The *weather,* or *windward* side of a ship is, obviously, that side from which the wind is blowing, while the opposite, sheltered side is the *lee* side. In the era of open bridges such as ***TITANIC*** and her sisters had, a watch officer took up his station on the *weather wing* of the bridge, from which side sailing ships would approach. In 1912 there were still millions of tons of large sailing craft afloat. Most watch officers of this era had apprenticed in sail. They knew instinctively from seeing a sailing ship's lights and always being aware of wind direction, exactly what the sailor was doing, and could do, in relation to their own vessel. Sailers, being less maneuverable than steamers, always had, and still have, the right of way.

A *weather helm* means "tiller to windward." *Helm alee* means the helm/tiller goes toward the side *to* which the wind is blowing, or downwind. Conversely, *aweather* means toward the direction *from* which the wind is blowing. *Weather,* when used as a verb, means to survive the onslaught of the elements, as in to *"weather* a gale."

An *anchor* is any device used to make a ship fast to the bottom. All large vessels have at least two anchors. These are tested and certificated, and the size of the anchor and its chain is matched to the size and tonnage of the ship which uses it. A vessel's safety may depend upon the good design and sturdy construction of this important gear.

Anchors stowed in a ship's bows are, not surprisingly, called *bowers.* They are the heaviest anchors a ship has. In addition to her bowers she may carry one or more medium-weight *stream anchors* as spares, usually located about the decks in convenient locations. About half as heavy as the bowers, stream anchors are used for stern mooring in congested waters. She may have a spare bower, usually carried on deck, or on the forecastle head, where it can be put over the side by a boom and tackle from the foremast head. ***OLYMPIC*** and ***TITANIC*** each carried a stern anchor worked through an extra hawsepipe in the stern, as did most of the larger liners of that era. Many large ships carried a stern anchor as well. When sailors retire from the sea they *"swallow the anchor"*

Ground tackle is the term applied to all equipment used in anchoring. Sailors pronounce it ground *taykel,* with the *"ay"* pronounced as in the month of May. This includes the anchors themselves, their *cables* (usually *chain* cables), connecting fittings, anchor hoisting machinery, all the devices used in the process of anchoring, mooring or securing. Because anchor cable was once called *hawse,* the pipes in the bow through which the anchor cables pass from the deck out through the side, and into which the stockless anchors stow, are called *hawsepipes,* while the openings in the deck and in the side which accommodate the hawsepipe are called *hawseholes.* The *hawse* is that part of the bow in which we find the hawsehole. An officer who has risen from the ranks is said to have *"come up through the hawsehole."* A *hawser* is any heavy wire or line used for mooring or towing. The expression *athwart the hawse* means "across the stem."

The *windlass,* or *anchor engine* as it is sometimes called, is used for *heaving up,* or *weighing anchor.* When hoisted and secured the anchor's *shank* is stowed in the hawse pipe, while its *flukes* rest snugly against the vessel's side. The chain passes over a sprocket wheel (called a *wildcat)* on the windlass, which engages the chain, link by link, and thereby applies the power of the engine to the chain when heaving in. When letting go, the wildcat is thrown out of connection and revolves freely, excepting that it has a brake lever or wheel to stop it if necessary. Coming up through the hawse pipe the anchor chain usually passes through *riding chocks* used for taking stress off the windlass when riding at anchor in heavy weather.

The chain, after passing over the wildcat, drops into the *chain locker* located immediately below. The chain locker is usually built either just forward or just abaft the collision bulkhead. Chain lockers are deep compartments divided by a stout bulkhead which separates the starboard and port anchor chains. The chain is not *tiered,* or stowed, when heaving in the anchor. The chain is confined by the sides of the locker, falling and resting in irregular short fakes, one on top of the other. In ***OLYMPIC*** and ***TITANIC*** the chain locker was forward of the collision bulkhead, extending to the forepeak tank top. Several surviving crewmen described hearing a sound like anchor chain running out when ***TITANIC*** struck ice. She apparently struck in such a manner that the impact damage caused a rift in her collision bulkhead, allowing her starboard chain to fall into either the cofferdam or the forepeak.

The deck chain pipes, abaft the windlass, are provided with efficient watertight stoppers, called *hawse plugs* or *hawse stoppers.* They are effective when the bows plunge into heavy seas in the normal course of a voyage in severe weather. A *manger* is a dam built abaft the hawse pipes, to collect water washing into the hawse.

Anchor may also be a verb, meaning to make fast to the bottom. A ship *weighs* anchor, meaning the anchor is hoisted clear of the bottom, and then she is *under way,* meaning that she is not anchored or made fast to the shore or aground, although she may not necessarily be making headway.

If a vessel is backing through the water, she is making *sternway.* She *heaves to* when she reduces headway to nil, or to just enough to maintain *steerageway* or manageability. Lying in this condition she is *hove to.* If she is made fast to a pier she is *moored alongside,* and secured with *mooring lines.*

As mentioned earlier, a ship's ribs are her *frames, or framing,* upon which rests her *shell plating,* or skin, which is further divided into *side plating* and *bottom plating.* The side plating is generally referred to simply as the *side,* and where side and bottom meet is the *turn of the bilge.* At the forward end of a ship the upward extension of the keel is called the *stern.* At the aft end of the keel a similar upward extension is called the *stern post.* The sharply curved shell plate which connects to the stern post is the *oxter plate.* The whole structure, plating fastened to frames, makes a watertight box, the top of which is the *main deck,* that being the uppermost deck which runs continuously from stem to stern. Where main deck meets the side is *the gunwale,* pronounced "gunnel." Roughly, from gunwale to waterline is the ship's *freeboard.* More accurately, freeboard is the distance, measured at the side of the vessel amidships, from the upper edge of the *deck line* to the upper edge of the *load line.* Load line *marks* are painted on the sides of merchant vessels to indicate the legal limits to which they may be loaded. These are also called *Plimsoll marks,* for Samuel Plimsoll, a member of Parliament who first introduced the system of marking as a means to protect British sailors from the dangers of overloaded vessels. With the passing of the Merchant Shipping Act of 1876 it became mandatory for every British vessel, excepting those under 80 tons engaged in the coasting trades, to have a circular disk with a line drawn horizontally through the center painted amidships on each side. This line indicated the greatest draft to which the vessel could be legally loaded. The enforcing of this act was ambiguous, however, and led to many disputes. Therefore in 1890 a load lines act was passed, decreeing that regulation and enforcement fell to the Board of Trade. This was reinforced by the Merchant Shipping Act of 1894, sections 437 to 443. When a ship is *down to her marks,* she is loaded to her legal limit, which will vary with the waters in which she sails, and the time of year. The deck from which this measurement is taken is *the freeboard deck,* and it is the uppermost complete deck where all openings can be permanently closed.

The complete structure of shell plating on frames, from keel to main deck, is the *hull.* Anything above the main deck, with the exception of mast(s), stack(s) and rigging, is the *superstructure. A* ship is said to be *hull down* when she is far enough over the horizon that only her superstructure, mast(s) and stack(s) are visible. She may also be *hull down* when she has sunk to the level of her main deck.

Individual *shell plates* were usually rectangular in shape. The joints between the short ends of the plates were *butts,* while the long edge joints were *seams.* Joined together at the butts, the plates formed long horizontal strips known as *strakes.* The uppermost strake in the side was the *sheer strake.* The strake on either side of the keel was the *A-strake,* sometimes called the *garboard strake.* ***OLYMPIC/ TITANIC***'s shell plates were generally 30 feet long and about 6 feet wide, weighing in at 2 1/2 to 3 tons each. The largest of their plates were 36 feet long and weighed 4 1/4 tons each.

Ships of ***TITANIC***'s era had their shell plates joined by riveting, and the seams thus formed were *caulked.* Caulking was accomplished in a steel vessel by bending down one part, or edge of a plate, in close contact with its neighbor, rather than ramming caulking material such as oakum into the seams, as was the practice in wooden ships. If rivet heads showed leakage they were also caulked, although this was not considered good practice. If it was discovered during construction, any such faulty rivets were backed out and new ones driven in.

Every major maritime country had, and has, its shipbuilding regulatory agency. The Admiralty and the Board of Trade in Britain, and the American Bureau of Shipping in the United States, were government agencies which regulated shipbuilding in 1912. They had rigid specifications for size and placement of rivets. The distance between the centers of rivets was called the *pitch.* The strength desired in a particular joint, the thickness of the plating and the shearing strength of the rivets were factors in determining the pitch. The largest rivets in ***OLYMPIC*** and ***TITANIC*** were 1 1/4 inches in diameter. Each vessel was said to have about three million rivets in her, half a million being in each ship's double bottom. In all it was estimated that the total number of rivets in each ship weighed about 270 tons. Hydraulic riveting was used wherever practical, the seams of the double bottom being double riveted, the topside plating triple and quadruple riveted. The butts of the bottom plating were overlapped and quadruple riveted.

While electric arc welding of shell plating had been tried in ships in the 1920s, it was the necessity of wartime that brought welded hull construction into general use with the American-built Liberty ships of World War II. Like many new processes the first electric arc welding used in ships had its flaws, and a few Liberty ships developed cracks in their hulls after working in a seaway. One of the early all-welded tankers, the ***SCHENECTADY***, even broke up while lying alongside her outfitting quay. Of the 4,694 ships built by the electric arc welding method in the United States between 1942 and 1946, eight broke in two at sea and foundered. Four others broke, but were salved. Naval architects debated the relative strengths of welded versus riveted hulls for years. It had been estimated that the electric welded ship contained about 15% less steel, required 40% less labor, took 25% less time for construction, required 2% less power for propulsion, had 5% greater carrying capacity, and was cheaper to maintain. As welding and steel processing techniques progressed the advantages of a smooth, welded seam plus the economics of being able to prefabricate large sections of the hull changed ship construction forever, although perhaps not for the better as far as looks were concerned. To this author the slab-sided, "prefabricated" cruise ships with their "stern castle" saloons which are in vogue today, are strangely reminiscent of ancient, clumsy galleons rather than the sleek Western Ocean greyhounds from the heyday of transatlantic travel. The first all-welded passenger liner, the Orient Line's *ORSOVA,* was not built until 1954. There are still many ships in service today with sturdy riveted shell plating, their hulls as sound now as when they came from their builders forty, fifty, even sixty years ago.

On some ships, including ***TITANIC*** and her sisters, a keel-like protuberance ran along the bottom on each side near the turn of the bilge, its purpose being to reduce rolling. This protuberance was called a *bilge keel.* ***OLYMPIC*** and ***TITANIC*** had bilge keels 25 inches deep which extended along 300 feet of their length amidships. Their double bottoms extended to the bilge keel, but unfortunately ***TITANIC*** struck ice just above her starboard bilge keel.

The word *bilge* may be used as a verb, meaning to rupture the shell of a vessel at any point below the waterline. When *bilge* is a noun, it is a somewhat ambiguous term meaning the rounded portion of the hull between the bottom and the sides of a ship and the space enclosed therein. Because this is the lowest part of a vessel water may collect in her bilge, thus one hears of *bilge pumps,* which do just that... pump water out of the bilge space. *Bilge* is also used as an adjective, to describe any appliance, plating, frame or stringer which is a part of this area of a ship.

The part of the stem which is above water is called the *prow,* while the part of the stem below water is called, appropriately enough, the *cutwater.* ***TITANIC*** and her sisters, like most ships of their day, had *straight stems,* that is the stem line dropped almost perpendicularly from its top to the keel in a plumb line, thus giving straight stems another name... *plumb stems.* A forward *rake,* or inclination from the vertical, of the stem piece gives the *flaring* bows that we see in ships today. The exact point where the keel rounds up to meet the stem piece is *the forefoot,* sometimes split into two *words, fore foot.* A broad fore foot was called a *clubfoot.* When a speeding ship cuts through the water she creates a *bow wave.* Traveling at top speed, throwing a spectacular bow wave, a ship is said to *have a bone in her teeth.* The *wake* is the trail of disturbed water left by a vessel under headway. The spreading series of undulations in the water caused by the wake is the *backwash,* or simply *wash.* The backwash of a large vessel can easily capsize a small boat, always a danger when sightseers came in too close to the big liners.

Captain Reisenberg warned against the dangers of ships with straight stems, which in collision with other ships would cut them straight down the side to the waterline. When the Italian Lloyd's ***SS FLORIDA*** struck the White Star liner ***REPUBLIC*** in February, 1909, this danger was well illustrated. On 25 April, 1908, a lesser known collision occurred in the Solent. The American Line's ***ST. PAUL*** and His Majesty's Ship, the cruiser ***GLADIATOR,*** were making their way through this narrow channel much as White Star's ***OLYMPIC*** and ***HMS HAWKE*** would be doing three years later. The big difference lay in the fact that for the officers of ***ST. PAUL*** and ***HMS GLADIATOR*** visibility was cut to a few hundred feet by gust-driven snow squalls. Finally, flurries blinded the men on the bridges of both vessels at a crucial moment, precluding evasive action by either ship. ***ST. PAUL***'s straight stem struck the cruiser obliquely on the warship's starboard side, ripping ***GLADIATOR***'s shell plating all the way to the turn of her bilge. A hole fifty feet long allowed water to enter with such force that it carried the warship to the bottom in a few minutes. Reisenberg advocated the adoption of a forward rake to the stem piece, doing away with the dangerously sharp, plumb stem. It seems a moot point when two ships collide, for the ramming vessel is not apt to stop until her cutwater is well into her victim's shell plating, and as ***STOCKHOLM*** *proved* when she struck ***ANDREA DORIA*** in July of 1956, a flaring prow may enter far into the stricken ship. ***STOCKHOLM*** pushed into the Italian liner's side for about thirty feet, one third ***DORIA***'s beam, with the breach being about forty feet across at the top, tapering to a point below the waterline. The ***DORIA*** was holed all the way to her double bottom. The unwritten rule of the sea, in what Reisenberg called "the hard old days," was simply *"hit the other fellow first"* when collision was inevitable. The ship that took the full brunt of impact on her bow could usually depend upon her especially strengthened collision bulkhead to remain afloat. When such a collision did occur deck officers were cautioned that the ramming vessel should endeavor to remain in place to plug the hole and keep the usually mortally wounded victim upright as long as possible, rather than backing out as instinct dictated. This was easier said than done, of course, and too often metal rubbing against metal generated dangerous sparks which ignited fuel and other combustible materials in both vessels. At any rate, the quest for efficient speed was the ultimate reason for doing away with the lovely, old straight stems.

There are many different ways to measure ships. Length, for example, if given unqualified, generally means *length over all,* which is the distance between the forward and after extremities of the hull. *Length between perpendiculars* is the distance between the forward side of the stem and the after part of the rudder post. When the stem or rudder post are raked, the measurement is taken through their intersection of the upper deck. When the stem is bent the straight middle part is extended up to meet the line of the deck from which measurements are taken. *Length registered* is the distance from the fore part of the stern to the after side of the head of the sternpost. *Length for tonnage* is measured in a straight line along the *tonnage deck,* (the second deck from below in ships having three or more decks and the upper deck in vessels having no more than two decks) from the inside of the inner plate at the bow to the inside of the inner plate at the stern. *Floodable length* is the extreme length of compartment which can be flooded and the ship will remain afloat, though with decks *awash* (level with or just below the water's surface). This measurement differs with the location of compartments in the fore-and-aft line. Under the rules for bulkhead safety, a margin of safety which is called *the permissible factor* must be allowed. This factor varies with the length of the ship. If a vessel has a permissible factor of 0.5, for example, it means that the permitted length of each compartment is half the floodable length, or, there are two compartments watertight in the floodable length. The *permissible length* is the maximum distance between two watertight bulkheads for that area in the ship. White Star's ***OLYMPIC**-class* ships were built to the usual bulkhead standards of their day.

Breadth moulded is the greatest breadth, or width, of hull measured between the outer surfaces of the frames. *Breadth registered* is the greatest width measured outside of the shell plating.

Depth moulded is the distance from top of keel to the level of the top of the upper deck beam at the gunwale. *Depth registered* is the distance from the top of the double bottom amidships to the top of the upper deck beams.

Much confusion arises over tonnage figures. The word itself is confusing, for it derives from *tun,* a name given to the great casks in which wine was carried in the earliest days of commerce between England and France. The carrying capacity of vessels engaged in this trade was expressed in this unit. A tun of wine weighed about 2,000 pounds, thus a standard *ton* today is 2,000 pounds.

Three measures of tonnage are commonly given for a ship. *Gross tonnage,* sometimes called *gross registered tonnage,* or *GRT,* is the internal capacity of the vessel expressed in units of 100 cubic feet. *Net registered tonnage,* sometimes referred to simply as *registered tonnage,* is a figure expressing the amount of space available for carriage of passengers and/or cargo, and it is figured by deducting from the gross tonnage all of the space taken up by necessities, for example, machinery, boilers, engines, shaft alleys, steering apparatus, chain lockers, chart room, wheelhouse, officers' quarters, crew forecastle, etc. *Deadweight capacity* is the actual carrying capacity of the vessel. *Displacement* is the actual weight of the entire ship and everything in her. This varies with the draft, and is figured in long tons, which are 2,240 pounds each. Displacement varies in fresh and salt water, thus a vessel loaded to her marks in fresh water will lift clear when coming into salt water. ***TITANIC's*** registered tonnage was 21,831; her GRT was 46,328, while she displaced about 52,250 tons. Displacement figures are often used simply to make a ship seem larger to the general public.

A ship's skeleton, or framing, may be *transverse* or *longitudinal. Transverse frames* run athwartships and support the decks as well as strengthen the sides. *Longitudinals* run fore and aft, and strengthen against *hogging,* or buckling amidships. A tremendous amount of stress can be placed on the longitudinals when a vessel is working in a seaway. Stress on ***TITANIC***'s longitudinals when her still-buoyant stern naturally tried to refloat her waterlogged bow was bound to break her in two as she sank, something that might not have happened in a much shorter vessel.

Where longitudinals intersect frames, one must be cut to make way for the other. Those which are not cut are *continuous,* while those which are cut, and therefore weakened, are *intercostal.* Either longitudinals or frames can be continuous, with the other being intercostal. The continuous members must be increased in number to compensate for the weakening of their opposite numbers.

There are frames and longitudinals extending from the inner to the outer bottom, dividing the double bottom into cells which not only contribute to the ship's strength but also provide a series of tanks for fresh water and ballast, and for fuel oil. Portions of the inner bottom above these tanks are *tank tops.*

The vertical partitions which divide the interior of a ship are *bulkheads,* never, ever "walls." A bulkhead may be a watertight *structural bulkhead,* or it may be nonwatertight, a partition only, in which case it is a *joiner bulkhead.* Either watertight or nonwatertight bulkheads may be transverse or longitudinal. Structural bulkheads are an integral part of a ship's framing, adding to her strength and rigidity, tying shell plating, framing and decks together into one stout structure. A *collision bulkhead* is a specially strengthened watertight bulkhead with no openings, protected by a *cofferdam,* which is a small space left open between the collision bulkhead and a second bulkhead which shields it from fire hazard or collision. Joiner bulkheads are usually strong enough to hold back water for some time. When ***TITANIC*** struck ice on her starboard bow she immediately listed to starboard, pulled down on that side by the weight of incoming water. Apparently a nonwatertight longitudinal joiner bulkhead in the forward part of the ship contained the water for a time. Ships are designed to float upright and level, just as airplanes are designed to fly straight and level. Their ability to maintain these positions and return to them when their equilibrium is disturbed by outside forces is called *stability.* As ***TITANIC***'s inherent stability righted her, water eventually leaked through to her port side forward, and she began listing to port. Harland & Wolff naval architect Edward Wilding, testifying at the British Board of Trade inquiry into the cause of ***TITANIC***'s foundering, believed that had she remained afloat her natural stability would have righted her again. There was much discussion at the B.O.T. inquiry about the merits of transverse watertight bulkheads only, such as the ***OLYMPIC**-class* ships had, versus transverse *plus* longitudinal bulkhead systems, such as Cunard's ***LUSITANIA*** and ***MAURETANIA*** had. The latter vessels were built to Admiralty specifications, their bulkhead systems being designed like those in warships as both liners were intended for conversion to armed cruisers in wartime. History proved, however, that the extra longitudinal bulkhead system was not infallible. When ***LUSITANIA*** was torpedoed off the Old Head of Kinsale on 7 May, 1915, there was no time to flood ballast tanks and internal damage was too great to right her. She sank less than twenty minutes after the torpedo struck her. ***ANDREA DORIA*** took longer to roll on to her beam ends, but a longitudinal bulkhead system did not save her because impact damage was extensive amidships on the starboard side. It would appear, however, that had ***TITANIC*** had a longitudinal bulkhead system she would have survived, simply because her impact damage was not as extensive as legend has it, and had water been confined to her starboard side tanks on her port side could have been flooded to right her.

Just abaft the stem in all ships is a relatively small compartment called the *fore peak*, or *forepeak*. At the stern there is a similar compartment called the *after peak*, or *afterpeak*. The *peak tanks* are deep tanks, and they are the principle *trimming tanks* of the vessel. Being small neither of these compartments contributes much to a vessel's buoyancy, thus flooding of them alone, provided their bulkheads remain secure, is not serious. The forepeak lies between the stem and the collision bulkhead, and it is usually divided into two parts vertically The lower part is the forepeak tank, the upper part is used for stowing forward cargo gear, boatswain's gear, spare parts, etc. The afterpeak lies between the stern frame and afterpeak bulkhead, and is usually filled by the afterpeak tank. Just below the afterpeak tank is the *stern tube*, which houses the propeller shaft. ***TITANIC***'s forepeak tank was flooded upon impact, indicating that her bottom was holed there. The forepeak itself was dry, however, and therefore it can be concluded that there was no impact damage above the tank top in that area of the ship. Judging from statements given by engine room survivors, it appears that impact damage may have extended in a continuous line from the forepeak tank through the cofferdam just abaft the forepeak, then, as ***TITANIC*** answered her opposite helm order, *"hard aport,"* her stern began to swing outward away from the berg but she struck one more sharp blow near the after end of Number 6 boiler room, bounced off again and very lightly rubbed against the ice just aft of the watertight bulkhead between Number 6 and Number 5 compartments.

While bulkheads divide a ship vertically, she is divided horizontally by a series of *decks*. The underside of each deck forms the *overhead* for the compartments below it. The deck of a compartment is never a "floor" nor is the overhead ever a "ceiling." The only *floor* in a ship is that portion of framing located in the double bottoms, while the only *ceiling* is a layer of planks put over the tank tops to protect cargo from contact with the metal.

Any deck which is exposed to the elements is called a *weather deck*. Those decks which are above the waterline are usually arched from center line to gunwale so that water will drain off of them. This arch is called *camber*. *Scuppers* are drains, openings in a ship's sides or solid rails, which allow water to run overboard. A similar word, *scuttle*, when used as a verb means to deliberately sink a ship. When a vessel sinks by filling or flooding, she is said to *founder*. As a noun *scuttle* is a small opening, usually circular in shape, to provide access for stowing fuel, water and stores. A cover, either hinged and dogged, or sliding, is provided to close the scuttle securely when it is not in use. *Scuttlebutt* was the name given to the casks which held drinking water in sailing ships, and sailors often gathered around these casks for conversation which was not allowed while they were on watch. Thus the word scuttlebutt today means any rumor, or non-authenticated piece of information.

A *hatch*, sometimes called *hatchway*, is any square or rectangular opening in a deck. The fore and aft pieces which frame a hatch are called *coamings,* while those pieces which run athwartships are called *head ledges. A batten* is a long strip of steel which is wedged against the edges of *tarpaulins* (sheets of heavy canvas) used to waterproof the hatchway, and this process is called *battening down.* Hatchways in ***TITANIC***'s era were secured against pressure from above only, for example when water spilled over the vessel's weather deck in a seaway. Modern hatches are secured also against pressure from below.

A deck which extends from stem to stern, from one side to the other, is a *complete deck.* On passenger vessels decks are designated by letter, and it is the custom on cruise ships to give them fancy names as well, to appeal to passengers. *Partial decks* are those which do not extend all the way to either side, or all the way fore and aft.

Some of the names given to partial decks are *the forecastle, or fo'c'sle deck,* which is a partial deck above the main deck at the bow. The *poop deck* is a partial deck above the main deck, located all the way aft. Ships with raised fo'c'sle and poop decks, such as ***TITANIC*** and her sisters, had *well decks,* the *forward well deck* lying between the forward end of the upper deck and the after end of the fo'c'sle deck. The *after well deck* is that area of the main deck which lies between the forward end of the poop deck and the after end of the upper deck. *Well decked ships* were sometimes called *three islanders,* for in profile they looked as if they were composed of three sections.

From the top down ***TITANIC***'s decks amidships were the *boat deck; promenade deck, (A); bridge deck, (B); shelter deck, (C); saloon deck, (D); upper deck, (E); middle deck, (F);* and *lower deck, (G).* Beneath G Deck, deep in the bowels of the ship, were the *orlop* and *lower orlop* decks, the decks which housed machinery, engines, boilers, bunkers, stores, etc. These are the general names of decks in cargo and passenger ships. In passenger liners the decks were lettered beginning with *A* as the highest deck on which passengers were housed, and so on through *B*, C, D, E, and in ***TITANIC***, *F* and *G*. This was obviously done for the benefit of passengers who could not be expected to remember the names sailors gave to a ship's many decks. Throughout the ***TITANIC*** inquiries crew testimony indicated that the men often did not know the letter of the deck being talked about, but they knew the sailor's name for that deck. Bulkheads, plating and decks divide a ship into *compartments.* Interior compartments between decks are, appropriately, the *"tween decks.*

The part of the hull which is under water is called the *underwater body* of the ship. The line of water level along the hull is, naturally, the *water line* or *waterline.* From keel to waterline is the ship's *draft.* If the draft forward equals the draft aft, the ship is *in even trim.* If draft is deeper forward she is *by the head,* as ***TITANIC*** was after impact when her forward compartments were flooded. If her draft is deeper aft, a ship is said to be *by the stern.* It is extremely important that a ship's officers are familiar with her draft under all conditions. When the ***QUEEN ELIZABETH 2*** ran aground off Cape Cod in August of 1992, it was assumed that her draft of 32 feet would allow her to negotiate an area marked on charts where water was 39 feet deep. However, uncharted boulders projected upward to 35 feet below the surface. Running at 25 knots, the ***QE2*** was expected to *plane,* or settle her stern about two feet while raising her bow, when actually she *squatted,* that is her stern settled, nine feet.

Ballast is weight added, usually in the form of concrete or pig iron, to increase a ship's stability. *Ballast trim* is her draft when she is carrying ballast only, in which case she is said to be *in ballast.*

The lines of the gunwales curve outward from the stem, until they reach the ship's extreme breadth, and then run more or less parallel amidships where they are known as the *port* and *starboard beams.* Where the gunwales curve inward again toward the stern are the port and starboard *quarters.* Where the lines of the gunwales curve into the sharp line of the cutwater the ship's bows *flare* upward and outward from the waterline, causing an *overhang,* extremely pronounced in modern passenger ships. A similar overhang at the stern is called a *counter.* As did most merchant ships of her day, ***TITANIC*** and her sisters had *counter sterns,* which were part of their overall exceptionally graceful lines. Warships of the era were already acquiring sterns which dropped from gunwale to below the waterline with only slight curvature, and this type became known as a *cruiser stern.* Where the sides of a vessel curve slightly inward from gunwale to keel, the amount they flare from the perpendicular is known as the *tumble home.*

Where the underwater body of a ship tapers from cutwater to more or less straight lines at her beams is called the *entrance,* while a similar taper toward the stern is the *run.* A ship with a long, tapering entrance and run, and a comparatively short area where the lines are parallel at her beams is said to have *fine lines.* The fastest and most graceful of the transatlantic liners had fine lines.

Early steamships were built with wooden hulls and were propelled through the water by paddlewheels. From the end of the eighteenth century onward experiments were made simultaneously in Europe and America to perfect such propulsion, to lengthen the range and conquer the Atlantic. Paddlewheels had a great many disadvantages, chief of which was the simple fact that when a ship was equipped with one paddle on each side, as most were, every time she rolled one wheel would come out of the water, putting tremendous strain on the engine and hull. Because they were outside of the hull, paddlewheels were subject to being easily damaged. In a warship they were virtually useless, because a direct hit in a wheel put the vessel out of commission immediately.

Between 1833 and 1836 four engineers took out patents on their marine propellers, all devices modeled after *Archimedes' screw.* Believed to have been invented in the third century BC by the famed Greek mathematician and physicist, this was a large, continuous screw inside a cylindrical chamber, used to lift water from a river. Englishman Francis Pettit Smith's propeller was at first the choice of shipbuilders, but an improved design by Swedish engineer John Ericsson soon won out when it was demonstrated in 1838 in a small steamer appropriately named ***ARCHIMEDES.***

Famed English engineer Isambard Kingdom Brunel had laid down his innovative iron-hulled ***GREAT BRITAIN*** in 1839, intending to equip her with paddlewheels. Ericsson's demonstration convinced Brunel to re-design ***GREAT BRITAIN***'s propulsion machinery. After a series of experiments Brunel outfitted her with four engines, developing a total of 1,500 horsepower, driving a six-bladed Ericsson propeller 15 feet 6 inches in diameter, at 53 revolutions per minute. Although ***GREAT BRITAIN*** could spread 15,000 square feet of canvas in an emergency, only once did she need sails to complete a voyage, when her propeller fell off in midocean. She ended her working career in 1886 by being towed to the Falkland Islands for use as a coal hulk. Fortunately for historians, in 1970 ***GREAT BRITAIN*** was raised and brought home to Bristol to serve as a memorial to Brunel and as a perfect example of an early propeller-driven, iron-hulled ship.

Brunel had proven the superiority of iron over wood and propellers over paddlewheels, yet the subject was still being argued until in March, 1845, two nearly identical 880 ton, 220 HP Royal Navy frigates, the propeller driven ***HMS RATTLER*** and the paddlewheel-equipped ***HMS ALECTO,*** raced over a 100 mile course. ***RATTLER*** won by several miles. Not convinced, the Admiralty set up another test, a tug of war between the two ships, which were bound together with a towing hawser, and then driven full power in opposite directions. ***RATTLER*** towed ***ALECTO*** stern first at a speed of 2.7 knots, proving for all time the superiority of propeller over paddlewheel.

William Inman, born in Leicester in 1825, started what became generally known as the premier line of the North Atlantic when he bought Tod and McGregor's ***CITY OF GLASGOW*** *in* 1850. Although always known as the Inman Line, the company's proper name was the Liverpool and Philadelphia Steamship Company. ***CITY OF GLASGOW*** *never* won the *Blue Riband*, that legendary symbol of speed on the North Atlantic, but she was the first iron-hulled screw steamer to be financially successful on the Atlantic. The Cunard-Collins feud was over when the last of the big wooden paddle boats, the 380 ft. Collins liner ***ADRIATIC***, which had introduced searchlights to the Western Ocean, was not enough to offset the loss of ***ARCTIC*** after her collision with the ***VESTA*** in 1854, and the disappearance of the ***PACIFIC*** in 1856. Cunard had already introduced the wrought iron-hulled ***PERSIA*** in 1855. In 1862 Cunard brought out the last, largest and fastest paddle boat of them all, the 400 ft. wrought iron-hulled ***SCOTIA***, which won the Blue Riband in December, 1863, with an eastward passage of 8 days, 3 hours. But in the same year Cunard had put into service the iron-hulled screw steamer ***CHINA***. The figures were impressive enough to convince Cunard that paddlers were finished. The ***CHINA*** was not quite, although very nearly as fast as ***SCOTIA***, but she made her speed with 2,250 indicated horsepower against 4,000 for ***SCOTIA***'s paddle engines, while ***CHINA*** consumed a modest 82 tons of coal per day, half of ***SCOTIA***'s daily 164ton consumption. Propellers were on the Western Ocean to stay.

During the transition period from propeller to paddlewheel, when both were afloat but paddlers still predominated, those vessels equipped with propellers were called simply that... *propellers.*

A ship's underwater body must necessarily be pierced to accommodate her propeller *shaft* or shafts. In ***TITANIC***'s era, the age of the big, fast transatlantic flyers vying for the Blue Riband, speed was more important in passenger liners than the economics which ruled lesser merchant vessels. A passenger liner then would have up to four *propellers,* also called *screws,* or *wheels. A* ship with a single screw would have her underwater body pierced well aft on the center line, but for twin, triple or quadruple screws, the underwater body had to be pierced farther forward on either side, necessitating the support of *propeller struts.* ***TITANIC*** and her sisters had triple screws, one being mounted on the center line while the other two were mounted outboard on struts.

If a ship has but one propeller the blades might turn in either direction, and could have an effect upon her turning characteristics. The blades of the screw in the lower half of their circle of rotation are going through denser water, thus each blade meets with greater resistance as it passes through this portion of its revolution. This resistance is transferred to the end of the shaft, and thus to the hull itself. For this reason, a right-handed screw, turning backward, throws the ship's stern to port, and head to starboard. Equipped with a right-handed single screw, that is when viewed from astern the screw turns clockwise, when the vessel is going slowly ahead with rudder amidships and other influences such as wind and tide are eliminated, the screw tends to cause the ship's stern to travel to starboard, forcing her bow to port. As the speed is increased this tendency is diminished. In backing this effect is reversed, because the screw is then turning counter-clockwise. Therefore when backing her stern will travel to port, her bow to starboard, and as the backing speed increases the turning effect of the screw increases. The single screw in going astern will have its greatest turning effect when full backing speed has been reached. When a single screw ship is brought to an emergency stop by going full speed astern her head will swing to starboard. A left-handed screw will bring the opposite result. Going ahead at top speeds, however, none of this is relevant. The piling up of water against the rudder's forward surface is the chief cause for the ship's turning at high speeds, and she turns to port or starboard with equal facility.

Twin screws came into general use in the 1870's. Twin screws always turn in opposite directions, usually with the tops of the blades turning outward, thus the effect of the screws on turning is neutralized. While some vessels were equipped with inward turning screws, it was found that this arrangement generally gave less effectiveness to the rudder when turning. A vessel may be turned from very slow speeds by reversing one screw, going full ahead on the opposite one. But at high speeds this maneuver, known as *warping ship,* has little effect. The greatest turning effect on a ship going full speed ahead, is produced by the rudder. Twin screws, or more, provided reliability, and they also provided maneuverability at lower speeds. A vessel could reach port safely if she lost one screw, and if she lost her rudder or her steering apparatus broke, she could be steered with her screws, the preferred method being to run one engine at a constant speed, while maneuvering by decreasing or increasing the speed of the opposite engine.

Twin screws or more provide much greater efficiency in stopping a ship than a single screw. A twin-screw vessel running at a top speed of approximately 23 knots would come to a stop in about six or seven ship lengths from the time her screws begin backing at full speed astern, unless she had a good head wind to knock down her speed more quickly. When ***TTTANIC***'s watch officer reversed her engines it was not part of any turning maneuver to avoid striking the iceberg, as legend has it. Backing the screws was the last, desperate way to slow her if and when she did strike, thus lessening the force of impact.

Masts are the main upright spars of a vessel, once used to carry sails. During the transition from sail to steam, all steamships carried a complete set of sails for emergency use, because breakdowns in machinery were frequent and they could be fatal if a ship had no other means of propulsion and control. By ***TITANIC***'s time machinery had become so reliable and twin screws, or more, so common that sails were no longer needed, but masts still supported the ship's wireless antenna, the required lights, the crow's nest, signal stays, yards and trucks, cargo booms and gear. ***TITANIC*** had two masts, the forward one being, naturally, the *foremast,* the after one the *mainmast.* A third mast, from the stem, would have been the *mizzenmast,* and a fourth would have been *the jiggermast.* If there were five masts they were the *fore, main, middle, mizzen* and *spanker,* or sometimes *fore, main, mizzen, jigger and spanker.* Six masts were named *fore, main, mizzen, jigger, driver* and *spanker.*

Masts on cargo ships were often built in two sections, a heavy, strong *lower mast*, and a lighter *topmast.* In passenger liners the mast was usually in one piece, as ***TITANIC***'s was, and named a *pole mast.* The top of a mast is called the *truck.* A small pulley, called a *sheave,* admitted the *truck halyards,* which were light lines used for hoisting and lowering *signal flags.* The *gaff* was a small, light spar set at an angle abaft the upper part of a mast. *Halyards* (hoisting lines) running to the *peak,* or upper end of the gaff, were called *peak halyards.* Some ships had a light spar mounted horizontally athwartships on the upper foremast or fore topmast to carry a number of sheaves for signal halyards. In older vessels this spar also carried Morse signal lamps keyed from the bridge. By the time of ***OLYMPIC*** and ***TITANIC*** Morse lamps were usually mounted on top of the bridge cabs.

A ship's flags should always be properly flown. They might be old, even slightly soiled, but never torn, never frayed. On entering a foreign country, and while there, a vessel flies that country's flag at the foremast. Some countries imposed fines if that courtesy was omitted. The *jack* fa small national ensign) is flown from the *jack staff* at the stern, but is never flown when under way. One signal flag always flown in port by merchant vessels is the *blue peter,* the code flag for the letter *"P,"* an unmistakable white square on a blue field. The blue peter is hoisted at the foremast head, in ***TITANIC***'s era 24 hours prior to sailing, and signifies that the ship's departure is imminent. It was traditionally used to call her crew on board, and to notify all merchants to conclude their business with the ship. On modern vessels, especially cruise ships, the blue peter is sometimes hoisted as soon as the ship arrives in port because turnaround time for the new seagoing resorts is now so short that they are due to depart within a very few hours from arrival. The blue peter, and the jack, are always hauled down as the lines are cast off and a ship begins to move away from her pier.

A ship is said to be *dressed* when she is flying signal flags or lights from stem to stern. *Dress ship* is done by naval and passenger vessels when entering and while in certain ports, on holidays and ceremonial occasions of the vessel's country of registry, and when in a foreign port, on national holidays and ceremonial occasions of that country as well. During daylight hours this includes stringing signal flags, bunting, oversized ensigns and jacks, fore and aft. At night lights are strung in place of flags. ***TITANIC*** was dressed overall just once, on Good Friday at Southampton.

Dipping is a salute which involves lowering a flag or ensign partway down the staff. The flag or ensign is then said to be *at the dip.* Merchantmen dip to men-o-war.

Masts were supported fore and aft by wires called *forestays* and *backstays.* Similar supporting wires running athwartships were called *shrouds.* The stays and shrouds, together with similar wires supporting the *stacks* were known as the ship's *standing rigging.*

All rope aboard ship that is not made of wire is fiber rope. It is always called *line,* never rope, unless it is designated for a special purpose, such as *footropes* on the yards of sailing ships, or *manropes* on gangways. Fiber rope is made from various plants, for example *manila,* from the fibers of the abaca plant native to the Philippine Islands, or *sisal,* from plants grown in Indonesia, East Africa, Mexico and the Bahamas. The plant fibers are twisted together in the same direction to form *yarns.* The yarns are then twisted together in the opposite direction to form *strands,* and the strands are twisted together, again in the opposite direction to form the line. Most line is *right-laid,* meaning that the strands in the finished line spiral in a right-handed direction as one looks along the line. It is a serious breach of seamanship to coil a right-laid line left-handed. Right-laid line must always be coiled down right-handed, or clockwise.

A wire rope is called simply a *wire.* It is composed of single wires twisted together in the same direction to form strands. As in fiber ropes, the wire strands are then twisted together in the opposite directions to form the wire rope. The foremost manufacturer of wire ropes in 1912 was John A. Roebling's Sons Company, founded by the Prussian ancestor of Washington A. Roebling 2nd, a passenger who died in ***TITANIC.*** Roebling's wire ropes were used not only for ships, but in the construction of many famous bridges, including the Brooklyn Bridge over the East River, which links the boroughs of Manhattan and Brooklyn in New York City. This was the first steel-wire suspension bridge in the world. At the time of its construction between 1869 and 1883 it was also the longest suspension bridge in the world. It was designed by John Roebling, who died from tetanus incurred after an accident during its construction. John's son, Washington Augustus Roebling, took over the Trenton, New Jersey, company after his father's death and completed the bridge, although he was in poor health after he, too, suffered a construction accident.

Any line smaller than 1 3/4 inches in circumference is referred to as *small stuff*. The art of caring for, handling and working all kinds and sizes of fiber and wire rope is called *marlinespike seamanship*. The term is usually thought of as meaning knotting, splicing, and intricately fancy work done with rope.

A ship's *funnels,* sometimes called *stacks,* or simply *pipes,* were the large pipes which carried off smoke and gases from the furnaces. Stacks of ***TITANIC***'s era were usually *raked,* leaning slightly aft in proportion to the rake of the masts, as were those of ***TITANIC*** and her sisters. This rake seemed especially pronounced and well-balanced in Harland & Wolff ships, and was an important part of their overall beauty. ***TITANIC*** and her sisters had four stacks, the fourth, counting from the stern, being a dummy used for engine room ventilation. She has often been erroneously painted by overly enthusiastic artists with smoke belching from all four stacks. The first liner with four stacks was Norddeutscher Lloyd's ***KAISER WILHELM DER GROSSE,*** built by the Vulcan yard of Stettin, Germany, in 1897. Because she quickly won the Blue Riband passengers erroneously equated the number of stacks with the safety and speed of the vessel, thus other shipyards of necessity designed and built ships with four stacks, whether they were needed or not.

The wider, lower section of a stack, which is below the main deck, is the *uptake. The funnel casing* is the part we actually see, built around the inside stack for strength and insulation. A *fiddley* is an open grating in the deck around the funnels, or it may refer to the enclosure around the heads of the engine room ladders.

Early marine steam engines were *reciprocating* engines. Water boiled into steam increases about 1,600 times in volume. The pressure thus created by confirming the steam can be used to produce a force that will move a piston up and down in a cylinder. The piston is attached to a crankshaft which creates rotary motion which in turn is geared to drive a ship's propeller. Marine reciprocating steam engines were classified as *compound, triple* or *quadruple expansion,* meaning that the steam passed successively through two, three or four cylinders, which gradually increased in size before exhausting into the condenser, where it became water again for re-use. Scottish inventor James Watt had patented the first practical steam engine in 1769 and coined the word *horsepower,* thus effectively beginning the Industrial Revolution.

One horsepower is 33,000 foot-pounds of work performed per minute, or 33,000 pounds lifted one foot in one minute. Or, 550 pounds lifted one foot in one second. *Indicated horsepower* is developed in the cylinders of an engine. This calculation does not take into account any losses arising from friction in the machinery. *Shaft horsepower* is the brake horsepower measured on the shaft, thus it is the amount of twist given the shaft in units of foot-pounds and time. *Effective horsepower* is the actual power expended in moving the hull through the water. It is the final measurement of power after all losses in engine and shaft and slip of the propeller are deducted.

The most powerful set of reciprocating engines ever built for a ship were those installed in Norddeutscher Lloyd's ***KAISER WILHELM II*** of 1903 and in the same company's ***KRONPRINZESSIN CECILIE*** in 1907. Each ship had four four-cylinder, three crank, quadruple expansion engines, a set of two driving each of the twin screws. ***KAISER WILHELM II*** won the Blue Riband in June, 1904, with an eastward run from Sandy Hook to Eddystone Light at an average speed of 23.58 knots. On one day her run averaged 24.35 knots. It was thought that

KRONPRINZESSIN CECILIE would be at least a quarter of a knot faster, but before she could establish herself the two turbine-driven Cunarders, ***LUSITANIA*** and ***MAURETANIA***, had proven to be the fastest vessels in the North Atlantic trade. They were driven by the smoother, quieter and more powerful Parsons turbines.

Charles A. Parsons was born in London in 1854, the fourth son of William Parsons, third Earl of Rosse, and famed astronomer. Charles received his early education from private tutors at the family seat, Birr Castle in Ireland, and later attended Cambridge University. Shortly after graduation he began his career as a premium apprentice at the Armstrong Works, Elswick. From there he went to Messrs. Kitson of Leeds for a year. From 1884 to 1889 Parsons was a partner in Messrs. Clarke, Chapman and Company of Gateshead. He had become interested in the turbine, a type of steam engine much older than the reciprocating engine, which derives its power from the velocity of steam compressed and forced through nozzles to impinge against guides and blades, which in turn causes rotation of the shaft upon which the blades are mounted. Parsons was convinced that turbines had much more potential than the reciprocating engines then in use to drive ships.

In the year 150 BC Hero had exhibited a crude form of steam turbine at Alexandria. During the middle part of the nineteenth century several inventors had tried to give Hero's toy a practical use. One of the major problems had been that the velocity of the steam jet was always too high, for it created blade and rotative speeds which were then too great to harness by any known methods. Parsons set out to build a steam turbine which could run at reasonable speeds and could be built large enough to drive a ship.

His solution was to expand the steam gradually through a series of turbine wheels which increased in size, thus the pressure drop and resulting steam velocity in each stage was relatively small. The first turbines developed by Parsons were used to drive electric generators. In 1889 Parsons founded his own company devoted to the further development and manufacture of steam turbines, and he turned his attention to marine power plants.

In 1894 Parsons built a small, experimental vessel which he named ***TURBINIA***. She was 100 ft. long, with a beam of only 9 ft. Lightly built of steel, ***TURBINIA*** weighed only about 44 tons, complete with machinery, fuel and water. Her first engine, which drove a single shaft, developed about 1,800 horsepower and gave a disappointing speed of only 18 knots. But Parsons was sure that the fault lay not in the turbine engine, but in the little ship's propeller. He made tank tests with model propellers running at various speeds, and photographed them in such a unique way that they appeared to be stopped, so that he could study the phenomenon of *cavitation*, which is caused by a propeller revolving so fast that the head of water pressure cannot supply solid water for it to work in, so that the blades cut across the suction column of the screw instead of working in it. This creates uncomfortably heavy and damaging vibrations, and consumes additional power without effective thrust.

From these experiments Parsons determined that ***TURBINIA*** would perform better with a triple shaft installation, each shaft driven by a separate turbine. Upon each shaft Parsons mounted three screws, giving the little craft an unheard of total of nine propellers. Steam turbines are not reversible, so it was necessary to fit ***TURBINIA*** with an astern turbine on her center shaft. This remarkable machinery produced 2,100 horsepower, which drove the tiny ship at an unprecedented speed of 32.75 knots. Subsequent improvements increased ***TURBINIA***'s speed to 34 knots.

Secretly taken to Spithead for the naval review in honor of Queen Victoria's diamond jubilee in 1897, ***TURBINIA*** upstaged the fleet when Parsons arranged for her to make a sudden and dramatic appearance. The little steamer seemed to fly down the long line of warships, startling their officers with speeds they thought impossible. Parsons' showmanship was superb, and it accomplished what he intended. Not only were senior Royal Navy officers impressed, but the German Kaiser, Wilhelm II, was attending the naval review in honor of his grandmother's sixty years as England's Queen. Always intensely interested in maritime developments, Wilhelm was determined to learn more about this man Charles Parsons and his new engines.

But Parsons never sought speed only. He proved in ***TURBINIA*** that speed could be obtained with his turbines utilizing a lower fuel consumption than reciprocating engines.

It was not surprising that the first operational warships to receive the new power plants would be the innovative "torpedo boat destroyers," small vessels which depended upon speed for their effectiveness. The first turbine-equipped ships other than the sleek ***TURBINIA*** and an even smaller experimental vessel, ***CHARMIAN***, were ***HMS VIPER***, and ***HMS COBRA***, built on the Tyne in 1899.

Bad luck dogged both of these little ships from the start. ***COBRA*** should have been completed first, but she was run into by a collier as she lay at her berth at the Turbinia Works. She was badly damaged, and extensive repairs delayed her completion so that ***VIPER*** went into commission first.

HMS VIPER was 210 ft. long, with a beam of 21 ft. and a depth of hull of 12 ft. 9 in. She displaced a mere 370 tons, a fraction of the displacement of later destroyers. ***VIPER*** was equipped with two power units, each of which drove two shafts. Each power unit was a combination of a high pressure turbine mounted on one of the outboard shafts, and a low pressure turbine mounted on the adjacent inboard shaft. The inboard shafts carried reversing turbines which idled when the ship was going ahead. Each shaft had two propellers, the after screw having greater pitch than the forward screw. Coal-burning water tube boilers of the Yarrow type worked under forced draft at maximum pressure of 200 pounds per square inch, giving the little ship a total of 11,000 maximum horsepower.

On 21 November, 1899, ***VIPER*** began her first informal trials, during which she reached a speed of over 32 knots, using about three quarters of her power. Parsons was elated, and predicted that with some modifications ***VIPER*** would easily work up to 35 knots. Government inspectors were equally enthusiastic.

Modifications took longer than expected, and spring weather turned sour for the anxious Parsons. After several postponements the final trials were undertaken on 4 May, 1900. ***VIPER*** made ten test runs, achieving her highest speed of 34.75 knots. On Friday, 13 July, ***VIPER*** did even better. On six consecutive rims over the measured mile she averaged 36.58 knots. By August she was deemed ready for maneuvers with the fleet.

Attached to Admiral Noel's squadron for scouting duty, ***HMS VIPER*** departed Portsmouth commanded by Lieutenant Speke, under orders to reconnoiter near the islands of Alderney and Guernsey and report back to Portsmouth the same day. By 4PM she was approaching her scouting area, loafing along at 22 knots. Near the Casquets half an hour later visibility was restricted by a light haze. Shortly afterward heavy fog closed in and ***VIPER***'s speed was reduced to about 16 knots. At 5:23 her helm was put hard astarboard when land was sighted off the starboard bow, but it was too late. Two minutes later ***VIPER*** struck a rocky ledge which tore a gaping hole in her bottom plating forward and smashed her shafts. In less than an hour it was obvious that ***VIPER*** was doomed, but her stern was fast on Renonquet Rock, north of Burhow Island near Alderney, which kept her from sinking. Lieutenant Speke gave the order to abandon ship. There was no panic and evacuation was accomplished in orderly fashion, the crew being careful to place the ship's mascots, two kittens, in a lifeboat along with the signal book and log book. Minute guns were fired from the ***VIPER*** until the last of the officers pulled away.

VIPER's loss was naturally a great blow to Parsons, but no lives had been lost and there was still ***HMS COBRA***. Built by Armstrong Whitworth and Company at their Elswick works, ***COBRA*** was similar to ***VIPER***, but not a sister ship. ***COBRA*** was slightly the larger, with her length of 223 ft., and beam of 19.5 ft. Her machinery was similar to ***VIPER***'s.

COBRA seemed ill-fated from the start. She finally passed her acceptance tests, but never quite came up to ***VIPER***'s speed, perhaps because she was larger and heavier, while her power plants remained the same. On Tuesday, 17 September, ***COBRA*** steamed out of the Tyne with Lieutenant Bosworth Smith commanding. On board were her crew of 54, as well as 25 builder's men, including Robert Barnard, manager of the Parsons Marine Steam Turbine Company.

The little vessel ran into heavy weather as soon as she cleared the Tyne. In the short seas off the east coast of England ***COBRA*** was soon rolling heavily and Smith reduced her speed to 10 knots to ease her, while fires were put out in the forward stokehold. During the night speed was reduced still further, but by early morning ***COBRA*** was still plunging and rolling heavily. At 7:15 there was a sudden heavy shock and most everyone on board thought ***COBRA*** had struck a rock as ***VIPER*** had. Immediately she buckled and began to settle amidships. Water rushed into the fire rooms, hit the boilers and furnaces, and sent great clouds of steam swirling throughout the ship, driving the engine room force on deck. With bow and stern rising high in the air, ***COBRA*** sank so quickly that only one small boat got away.

Fortunately, the mate of the Outer Dowsing Light Vessel witnessed the whole disaster. His report noted that ***COBRA*** had settled down amidships, "as though she had burst."

At first ***COBRA***'s loss was attributed to her striking the Outer Dowsing Shoal off the coast of Lincolnshire. Further investigation, however, proved that she could not have struck bottom where she sank. The depth was at least 6 fathoms (36 ft.), and ***COBRA***'s draft was only 6 feet. It was obvious that she had broken her back, tearing open her bottom plating for most of her length. There was some supposition that she had struck underwater wreckage, or a whale. According to *Engineering* magazine, a large whale with a big gash in its side had been found in the vicinity of the wreck. The small boat with 12 survivors was picked up that evening six miles southeast of Dudgeon Lightship by the PO steamer ***HARLINGTON***, Captain W. H. Young.

The area where ***COBRA*** sank was carefully dragged, but no wreck other than hers was found. The whale theory, too, was dropped. Chief Engineer Percey had survived to give good evidence at the inquiry. The conclusion was that ***COBRA***'s loss was due to structural failure. Experiments were made in which the destroyer ***HMS WOLF*** was driven at speeds up to 15 knots in seas as heavy as ***COBRA*** had encountered. The wreck committee concluded that something more than the action of the sea had caused ***COBRA*** to break up.

There then began a theory which gained wide acceptance, that ***COBRA*** had broken her back because gyroscopic action of her turbines prevented the hull from working in the normal way as the ship steamed through heavy seas. There was considerable debate over this in the technical press, so that finally Sir Hiram Maxim, engineer, inventor and munitions maker, defended Parsons' turbines, explaining that the action of two turbines on one side rotating in one direction and two on the other side rotating in the opposite direction would neutralize any gyroscopic effect. The behavior and the laws of the gyroscope are difficult to explain to the layman, however, and the ***COBRA*** incident undoubtedly delayed acceptance of the turbine as a marine power plant. Parsons was forced to postpone his practical work while he convinced a skeptical maritime world that his turbine was superior to and just as safe as reciprocating engines.

Built by Mssrs. Denny of Dumbarton, the first commercial vessel to be driven by Parsons' turbines was the 250 ft. Clyde excursion steamer ***KING EDWARD***. Her turbines produced 3,500 horsepower, driving no less than five propellers, two on each of the wing shafts, and one on the center shaft. Even at her top speed of 20.48 knots there was a noticeable lack of vibration. So successful was ***KING EDWARD*** that she was soon followed by a slightly larger but similar ***QUEEN ALEXANDRA.***

In rapid succession there followed two more Clyde steamers, and the Admiralty built two turbine-driven destroyers, ***HMS VELOX*** and ***HMS EDEN***. The cruiser ***HMS AMETHYST*** was equipped with turbines while a sister ship received reciprocating engines. This experiment, which proved ***AMETHYST*** to be the superior vessel, convinced the Royal Navy that the reciprocating engine's days were over.

Cunard then conducted its own experiment, installing turbines in the triple screw ***CARMANIA***, and reciprocating quadruple expansion engines in the twin screw ***CARONIA*** in 1905. ***CARMANIA*** proved more economical and about one knot faster. This sealed the fate of the reciprocating engine for use in the fast passenger liners. Cunard's next pair, ***LUSITANIA*** and ***MAURETANIA*** in 1907, were equipped with turbines driving quadruple screws. But these ships were equipped with astern turbines for maneuvering.

Why then, did White Star, with all this evidence of the turbine's superiority, equip their new giants ***OLYMPIC*** and ***TITANIC*** with reciprocating engines? The answer was elementary. It was a matter of economics.

The first Atlantic liners to use the Parsons turbines and triple screws were the Allan Line's ***VICTORIAN*** and ***VIRGINIAN***, introduced in 1905. In each of these vessels all three screws were driven by turbines, which can only revolve in one direction, driving the ship ahead, and therefore require an extra turbine on each shaft for going astern, an added expense which White Star could avoid by its combination of power plants.

The advantage in reciprocating engines lay in their ruggedness and simplicity of operation. It was easier, therefore cheaper, to train engineers to operate and repair reciprocating engines. This meant that there were more experienced engineers to work on reciprocating engines, thus they could be hired at less pay. There were few turbine-qualified engineers available in 1912. As late as 1947 the majority of vessels under United States registry were driven by reciprocating steam engines. During World War II Liberty ships were equipped with reciprocating steam engines, which could be built much faster than more complicated turbines.

The first ship to use a combination of reciprocating engines and a turbine was ***OTAKI***, of the New Zealand Shipping Company, fitted in 1908 with the same combination ***OLYMPIC*** and ***TITANIC*** would have in 1911 and 1912. In that same year Harland and Wolff tested this combination for the White Star in ***MEGANTIC*** and ***LAURENTIC***. Launched at the end of 1908, the former was powered by conventional quadruple-expansion reciprocating engines driving twin screws, while ***LAURENTIC*** had three screws, the outboard ones driven by triple expansion reciprocating engines which exhausted their steam into the center low-pressure turbine connected to the center screw, a test for the propulsion system proposed for the ***OLYMPIC*** class superliners. ***LAURENTIC***'s maiden voyage, in White Star's new Canadian service, came first, in April, 1909. Her running mate ***MEGANTIC*** followed with her maiden voyage in June of that year. ***LAURENTIC***'s performance was so much superior to that of ***MEGANTIC*** that the triple screw combination of outboard reciprocating engines and center turbine was immediately adopted for the then-building ***OLYMPIC***. With the two outboard screws, which are most needed in maneuvering, driven by reciprocating engines no extra expense for astern turbines was required. The maneuverability was there, where it was needed on the outboard shafts, and the center turbine was for speed where it was needed, going ahead. If the ships were being turned the center shaft was simply stopped and made little difference. The fallacy in this reasoning lay in the fact that the center shaft of the three White Star giants had no means for reversing in an emergency. Because astern power is always less than ahead power, less than two thirds of their total horsepower was available for going astern and stopping the ship if danger lay dead ahead and close aboard. But how often might such a thing happen?

Legend has it that the propulsion systems of the three White Star goliaths were unique, innovative, or "high-tech" as we might say today. But the truth was they were an economic compromise, already well-tested in other ships.

Whether reciprocating or turbine, a ship's engines were driven by steam pressure, and steam was generated by fires which heated water in huge boilers. There were two general classifications, *fire tube boilers,* wherein water and steam surrounded tubes through which the fire was led (the principal type of fire tube boiler was the Scotch boiler). In *water tube boilers,* which gradually supplanted fire tube boilers, the fire and hot gasses surrounded tubes of circulating water, while steam was collected in suitable drums. Both types of steam engines were fueled by coal at first, and later by oil or a combination of coal dust and oil known as *colloidal fuel.*

British ships of this period were still using the Scotch boilers. The three leading German ships built just prior to WWI, Hapag's ***IMPERATOR***, ***VATERLAND***, and ***BISMARCK***, had their quadruple screws driven by direct-connected turbines similar to the Cunarders, but the Germans used water tube boilers which were a decided improvement over the British Scotch boilers.

Parsons had been experimenting with reduction geared turbines as early as 1897, in the 22 ft. twin screw ***CHARMIAN***. Turbines, running at speeds much too fast for the propellers they drive, must be geared down to an efficient propeller speed. Up to ***TITANIC***'s time turbines were still running with the compromise of turbines turning too slowly, propellers rotating too fast for maximum efficiency.

By 1909 Parsons was ready to try his reduction gear in the freighter ***VESPASIAN***, which was fitted with a single screw driven by means of a helical gearing of the type developed by the Swedish inventor DeLaval for use in small, extremely high speed turbines. ***VESPASIAN*** was such a success that the Anchor Line adopted the same reduction gearing in their ***TRANSYLVANIA***, but not until 1915. The first successful installation of geared turbines was in the U.S. Navy collier ***USS NEPTUNE*** in 1912. But warship building soon took precedence over modifying or building new passenger liners, and it was not until 1929 that geared turbines became common on the North Atlantic.

Readers now have a very rudimentary knowledge of shipping development, with a very basic nautical vocabulary. Terms pertinent to specific subjects, such as navigation, lifeboats, oil firing and ship stability, for example, as they pertain to ***TITANIC*** will be explained in their appropriate, succeeding chapters.

It is important to realize that seamanship and its accompanying vocabulary cannot be learned from reading books, however. These subjects can only be learned through years of experience at sea.

Chapter Two

The Pretty Triplets

In spite of the heroic efforts of seamen's union strike leaders, the White Star Line's new superliner departed Southampton on her maiden voyage on time, without incident. Tom Maim at Liverpool, Ben Tillett at London, and Havelock Wilson at Southampton did their best to whip up enthusiasm among the rank-and-file of the International Seaman's Union for a strike which would keep even the elite Atlantic liners tied up. But to men who, at best, made barely enough money to feed and clothe their families sparsely, a strike meant more than extreme hardship. It very probably meant death from starvation. Arresting al participants was the usual way to end a strike, and every man knew perfectly well that he would be blackballed by shipping lines, forever, after he finally got out of jail. The union men also knew there were hordes of foreigners eagerly waiting to take their jobs at half the pay, or less.

In the eleventh hour White Star, Canadian Pacific, and the Holt Line conceded an advance in pay equal to $2.50 per month, half of what the union leaders had asked for, yet more than they had hoped to get. Although the departure of White Star's ***MAJESTIC*** was cancelled, that line's ***TEUTONIC*** and ***BALTIC***, and Canadian Pacific's ***EMPRESS OF IRELAND*** sailed on time, as did White Star's new pride and joy, with full crews of experienced men.

The new vessel was the largest ever built. She exceeded the length of her nearest rival, Cunard's ***MAURETANIA***, by more than one hundred feet, while her gross registered tonnage surpassed the Cunarder's by over 14,000 tons. Some experienced voyagers thought, however, that ***MAURETANIA*** and her elder sister ***LUSITANIA*** still held the edge on luxury as well as speed. Others were so fascinated by the new ship's immense size that they saw little else. Her overall length was 882 feet, 9

S.S. TITANIC leaving Southampton on her Maiden Voyage April 10. 1912

ABOVE: *J. Bruce Ismay*

inches, with her breadth extreme being 92 feet. She was driven by three giant screws, the center one weighing 22 tons, while those outboard weighed 38 tons each. Her bower anchors weighed 15 1/2 tons each, and her gargantuan electrically-operated rudder weighed in at 100 tons. She had four funnels, although the fourth was merely a dummy.

The graceful White Star giant boasted three electric elevators, or lifts as the British call them, in the First Class area, and one lift in Second Class. Experienced travelers sagely remarked that the new liner's bows were more bluff than those of her Cunard rivals. She resembled another lovely White Star favorite, ***ADRIATIC***, and no wonder. All of the line's ships had been built by Harland & Wolff at Belfast, a yard renowned for trim, fine-lined vessels.

Her builders and owners were so proud of her that they invited thousands of people to inspect her at Belfast, at Liverpool, and again at Southampton. On a fine Wednesday forenoon thousands more gathered on the White Star quay at Southampton to cheer her off on her maiden voyage.

Her manifest listed many wealthy, prominent Americans. James Bruce Ismay, Chairman and Managing Director of the White Star Line, was aboard to observe the new ship's performance. Although White Star did not officially use the title "Commodore" at this time, reporters used it freely to describe the line's senior commander. Captain Edward John Smith, master of the new liner, as he had been the maiden voyage master of White Star ships for many years.

"She's like a city," enthused one satisfied passenger. *"She's a bridge, not a ship,"* another sang her praises. She had nine decks, the uppermost, or boat deck, being 550 feet long. The forward end of this deck contained the navigating bridge, and the deckhouse which held the officers' accommodations. And on this deck the superliner carried twenty lifeboats, four more than the British Board of Trade required.

Great crowds lined the banks of the River Test and Southampton Water, watching proudly as the new symbol of Britain's sea supremacy steamed *majestic*ally down the channel, dwarfing every vessel she passed. She swept serenely past the Isle of Wight, where more onlookers cheered her. Flying the Royal Navy Reserve blue ensign of her commander, she graciously received a salute from the British fleet anchored at Spithead. Quickly she steamed the short distance across the English Channel to her first port of call, Cherbourg. After discharging, and embarking passengers and mails, she steamed north to Queenstown. From there she swept out across the North Atlantic, her mighty engines throbbing confidently, her First Class passengers congratulating themselves on their choice of ship.

Her maiden voyage was blessed with good weather, and she exceeded the hopes of both her builder and owner, by averaging 21 knots for this first westward crossing. Congratulatory messages flew through the ether as she sped across the unusually calm North Atlantic.

She passed Daunt's Rock on Thursday afternoon at 4:22. By noon on Friday she had steamed 428 miles. Her next day's run was 534. By noon on Sunday she had made another 542 miles. To noon Monday she made only 525 miles, having run through fog at reduced speed for four hours.

At 6:58 on Tuesday morning she was 433 miles east of Ambrose Channel Lightship, making 22 knots. Captain Smith wirelessed that he expected to reach Quarantine about 8 o'clock on Wednesday morning. Accordingly, a revenue cutter was dispatched at 6:30AM to meet her.

Actually, she did better than that. At 12:17AM on Wednesday she was a splendid sight, coming in at full steam, lights blazing, just east of Fire Island. With her clean bill of health she was not detained at Quarantine, and she docked at White Star Pier 59, at the foot of West Nineteenth Street, at 8:30AM. On board were 489 First Class passengers, 263 Second Class, and 563 Third Class. Her crew numbered 850.

No, this is not a fictionalized account of ***TITANIC***'s maiden voyage, and how she would have landed at New York had an iceberg not changed her destiny.

To a died-in-the-wool ***TITANIC*** enthusiast it is heresy to suggest that she was not unique.

Unfortunately, the legend of ***TITANIC***'s singularity has been perpetuated for so long that it is believed as truth by casual ***TITANIC*** readers.

TITANIC was not the first of her class. ***OLYMPIC,*** whose maiden voyage has just been recounted, and her younger sister ***TITANIC,*** were built side by side in Harland & Wolff's Belfast shipyard. Each vessel had the same dimensions. Overall length for each was 882 ft. 9 in., with length between perpendiculars being 850 ft. Breadth extreme for each vessel was 92 ft. 6 in., while the total height from keel to bridge was 104 ft. Each vessel was designed to have a gross registered tonnage of 45,000.

The Belfast yard site was first leased to the firm of Robert Hickson & Company, which began to build iron-hulled sailing ships in 1853. In 1854 twenty-three year old Edward James Harland came from the Tyne to manage the new firm. Hickson retired in 1859 and Harland took over the yard. One of Harland's financial backers was Gustav Schwabe, a partner in the Bibby Line of Liverpool. Schwabe was from Hamburg, and was one of many Germans who had found a more favorable business climate in England.

ABOVE: *Captain Edward John Smith*

***ABOVE: TITANIC** off Roches Point, Queenstown. (Artwork by James A. Flood.)*

Schwabe's affiliation insured that Harland & Wolff would build all of the Bibby liners, and the first contract was for three Bibby steamers, a large order for that time. In 1857 Harland had taken Schwabe's nephew, Gustav Wolff, as manager of the drawing office. On 1 January, 1862, Wolff was taken into full partnership.

In 1874 W. J. Pirrie (he was raised to the peerage in 1906) was taken as a partner. In 1885 the firm was turned into a private limited liability company, with capital of £600,000, divided into six hundred shares of £1,000 each. In 1895 Sir Edward Harland died, and in 1906 Wolff retired, leaving Lord Pirrie in complete control of the firm. By this time Harland & Wolff, Ltd., had earned an excellent reputation in the shipbuilding industry, a reputation which has endured to the present day.

When construction began on ***OLYMPIC*** and ***TITANIC***, Harland & Wolff had eight building slips and employed 14,000 men. Three regular-sized slips were converted into two, numbered 2 and 3, especially for the construction of three White Star superships, the number considered necessary to maintain the line's planned express service between Southampton, Cherbourg, Queenstown and New York. Huge gantries were built, of a size necessary to handle the extra-long hulls. There were ten walking cranes, each of which could lift five tons. A central cantilever revolving crane had a lifting capacity of three tons at 135 feet, or five tons at 65 feet. Over each berth were three traveling frames, each of which supported two traveling cranes with lifting capacities of ten tons each. This entire structure weighed over 6,000 tons.

Harland & Wolff boasted its own electric power station, with a capacity of 4,000 kilowatts. Another unique feature was the firm's complete engine shop, for Harland & Wolff built its own propelling machinery and did its own fitting out.

***ABOVE: TITANIC** at Queenstown.*

OLYMPIC's keel was laid on 16 December, 1908. Her last frame was raised on 20 November, 1909, while **TITANIC**'s keel had been laid on 31 March, 1909. **OLYMPIC**'s shell plating was complete by 1 April, 1910, while **TITANIC** was fully framed in the first week of April, the same year.

OLYMPIC was launched on 20 October, 1910. **TITANIC** was by then fully plated. **OLYMPIC**'s construction was completed by 31 May, 1911, the day **TITANIC** was launched. During this period Harland & Wolff was also fitting out the two White Star tenders **NOMADIC** and **TRAFFIC**, which would be based at Cherbourg, as well as the Aberdeen liner **DEMOSTHENES**, the Union Castle Line's **GALWAY CASTLE**, and the Peninsular and Orient liner **MALOJA**.

Before her sea trials **OLYMPIC** was thrown open for public viewing. Thousands of visitors paid 5s each during the first two hours and 2s each for the remaining three hours. Proceeds were donated to Belfast hospitals.

Contrary to legend, it was **OLYMPIC**, not **TITANIC**, which startled the shipping world with her size and splendour. Visitors gaped at her magnificent grand entrance and stairway, lighted from the top deck by an immense, yet delicate wrought iron and glass dome. On the top landing the sightseers paused to admire a carved panel containing a clock, with intricately carved female figures symbolizing Honour and Glory crowning Time. They marveled at the convenience of the smoothly operated First and Second Class lifts. They stood awestricken amid the elegance of the First Class saloon, 92 feet wide and 114 feet long, the largest afloat, with its virginal linen-clad tables intimately arranged for private dining and set with the finest crystal, china and silver. Visitors shook their heads, positive that there could be no finer restaurant ashore, and moved on to ogle the reception room, 92 feet by 54 feet, with its Axminster carpeting, French tapestries, deeply upholstered chairs and sofas, and its gleaming grand piano.

Thousands of people duly admired the soft patina of fine marble, the polished sheen of rare wood paneling, the genteel rustle of silk curtains, the sparkling glitter of electric light fixtures, and the ornate splendor of molded plaster ceilings. **OLYMPIC**'s Turkish bath, swimming bath, squash court and gymnasium, her elegantly appointed staterooms with telephones and electric heaters, were luxuries rarely seen by any except the very rich. Improvements to Second and Third Class that

ABOVE: RMS OLYMPIC

placed them well above those classes in any other ship afloat, were something the visitors could more readily comprehend, and fit into their own travel plans. It was, after all, the emigrant trade which kept the liners running, whether the swells in First Class could comprehend it or not.

On the morning of May 28th ***OLYMPIC*** proceeded down Belfast Lough to adjust her compasses and carry out her steaming trials. She was attended by Harland & Wolff's tug ***HERCULES***, as well as the Mersey tugs ***ALEXANDRA***, ***HERCULANEUM***, ***HORNBY*** and ***WALLASEY***, and the new White Star tenders ***NOMADIC*** and ***TRAFFIC***. Several important guests, including J. Bruce Ismay and J. Pierpont Morgan, had been brought to Belfast in the specially chartered steamer ***DUKE OF ARGYLL*** to attend ***TITANIC***'s launch. As they approached Belfast on the morning of May 31st, they had a magnificent view of the newly completed ***OLYMPIC*** as she lay in the Lough. ***OLYMPIC*** had exceeded the expectations of both her builders and owners by making speeds up to 21.75 knots during her trials.

After ***TITANIC***'s launch the guests were taken in ***NOMADIC*** from the Belfast quay to ***OLYMPIC***, which departed at 4:30PM, passing her newly-launched twin sister ***TITANIC***, a memorable sight for those who beheld them together on what no one could have guessed would be a rare occasion. ***OLYMPIC*** then proceeded to Liverpool, arriving off the Mersey on June 1st, where she again was open to the public. That same evening she departed for Southampton, where thousands more inspected her. She sailed from Southampton on her maiden voyage on Wednesday, 14 June, 1911, Captain Edward J. Smith commanding.

OLYMPIC's arrival was anxiously awaited in New York. Mr. and Mrs. Ismay were accompanied by Colonel Thomas Denny, of the famous Dumbarton firm of shipbuilders, who made the voyage to observe the functioning of the combination of turbine and reciprocating engines. Both men planned to return to England on the following Wednesday in ***OLYMPIC***. Seven hundred First Class passengers had already booked the first eastbound passage, the largest number ever taken from New York in First Class in one voyage.

Reporters, some of whom had been on the maiden voyage, displayed their Edwardian flair for dramatic writing when they described the new liner's appointments. On Sunday, 25 June, 1911, the *New York Times* carried several pages of prose and photographs, praising ***OLYMPIC***'s splendor and size. Again thousands of visitors crowded aboard, paying 50 cents each for a complete view of the new ship, which required at least an hour of fast walking. Proceeds went to the Seamen's Charities.

One reporter who made the first voyage wrote that when he had booked his passage at Oceanic House in London he had been informed that arrival time in New York would be the following Wednesday at 3 o'clock in the afternoon. He had been greatly impressed when ***OLYMPIC*** arrived on Wednesday morning instead. Ismay was quoted as saying that ***OLYMPIC*** had more than realized the company's expectations, in every way. She had not been driven at her full speed, yet she had averaged over 21 knots for the westward passage. On the return eastbound voyage she would be run the first day at about 21 knots, Ismay declared, and then she would gradually have her speed increased until they had a good idea of what she could do. It was common gossip that fires under five of her boilers had not been lighted at all, the explanation being a shortage of coal caused by the strike of Southampton dockworkers.

Twelve tugs aided ***OLYMPIC***'s departure from New York on Wednesday, 28 June, at 3PM. She carried 1,205 cabin passengers, the record number ever carried by a single ship from any port in the world. Of that number 730 were First Class, including 60 maids and valets. Among these passengers was ***OLYMPIC***'s designer Thomas Andrews, who would perish less than a year later in the sister ship ***TITANIC***. ***OLYMPIC***'s estimated earnings were between $325,000 and $350,000 for the round trip, while her expenses would be no more than $175,000, including wages, coal and food for crew and passengers, thus giving White Star a profit of at least $150,000 for the three weeks' round trip.

On this first homeward run ***OLYMPIC*** starred in another maiden drama. An American passenger from Philadelphia had broken his eyeglasses the day before sailing. He had left instructions that they were to be repaired and sent on to England on the next available vessel. But the firm who did the repairs happened to have its own wireless station. They made contact with ***OLYMPIC***, which had just departed New York, and sent the glasses with British aviation pioneer T. O. M. Sopwith, who dropped them from his airplane via a tiny parachute on to ***OLYMPIC***'s deck.

Experience gained from ***OLYMPIC***'s early voyages indicated that ***TITANIC*** could be improved. Salt spray stained the elegant clothing of First Class promenaders, for instance, therefore ***TITANIC***'s forward promenade was given vertically sliding windows that could be closed to inclement weather, or left open on those rare occasions when the North Atlantic provided gentle swells and soft breezes.

As ***OLYMPIC***'s popularity was assured, and cabin passengers actually had to be turned away, it was deemed advisable to increase the number of ***TITANIC***'s First Class staterooms. Other alterations included addition of the intimate Cafe Parisien, and a reception room was added to the popular *a la carte* restaurant. This new construction increased ***TITANIC***'s registered tonnage to 46,328, thus allowing her billing as the "largest ship in the world." Physically, however, the ships were identical in appearance, and impossible to tell apart unless viewers were close enough to discern names on stern and bows, or ***TITANIC***'s forward promenade windows. All too often photographs of ***OLYMPIC*** have been represented as ***TITANIC*** because the latter's photos are naturally in short supply.

The third sister, ***BRITANNIC***, still on the stocks at Harland & Wolff when ***TITANIC*** sank, was slightly longer than the first two ships, but still her lines were indistinguishable at a distance from ***OLYMPIC*** and ***TITANIC***. Unfortunately she did not live to see regular passenger service. Her construction was delayed after ***TITANIC***'s unfavorable publicity and she was eventually completed as a hospital ship for service in WWI. What probably would have been an illustrious career was cut short when ***BRITANNIC*** struck a mine laid by the German submarine U-73 in the Aegean Sea, four miles west of Port St. Nikolo, on 21 November, 1916. It was one of Fate's odd twists that placed nurse-stewardess Violet Jessup aboard both ***TITANIC*** and ***BRITANNIC***. Fate was kind, however, and Jessup survived the second sinking as well. Another coincidence, ***BRITANNIC*** struck her mine in a manner startlingly similar to ***TITANIC***'s collision with ice on the starboard bow.

Cunard's famed running mates, ***LUSITANIA***, built by John Brown and Co., Ltd., at Glasgow, and ***MAURETANIA***, built on the Tyne by Swan, Hunter and Wigham Richardson, were faster and more maneuverable than White Star's ***OLYMPIC*** class ships, but more expensive to build and operate. When Cunard threatened to join American financier J. Pierpont Morgan's shipping conglomerate, the International Mercantile Marine Company, which already controlled the greater part of Atlantic shipping. His Majesty's Government advanced the money to build two large, fast steamers, at 2 3/4 per cent per annum interest with twenty years to pay, provided that Cunard remained entirely British. Both Cunarders were launched in 1906, with maiden voyages in 1907. The first ship in service, ***LUSITANIA***, promptly returned the Blue Riband to England, and for more than a year the two Cunarders passed it back and forth between them. ***MAURETANIA*** eventually proved to be slightly the faster.

The three White Star giants were designed to make almost the speed of the Cunarders, but money saved in construction and operating costs was used to provide the seagoing luxuries demanded by affluent First Class passengers, mostly nouveau riche Americans who skipped back and forth across the Western Ocean with the nonchalance of today's jetsetters.

It is certainly possible, indeed probable, that ***TITANIC*** would have bettered ***OLYMPIC***'s speed, just as ***MAURETANIA*** had bettered ***LUSITANIA***. Certainly builders would utilize knowledge gained from prototypes to incorporate improvements in succeeding vessels. Even something so small as improved draft in ***TITANIC***'s huge furnaces could have increased her sea speed. However, since speed was a factor in disproving liability of the White Star it was an item better left uninvestigated after ***TITANIC*** sank. It is known, however, that ***TITANIC***'s owners were more than satisfied with her speed trials. Because ***OLYMPIC*** had exceeded her expected speeds in her trials, it is fair to assume that ***TITANIC*** would have been faster than ***OLYMPIC*** had she lived to have her engines properly run in.

In September, 1911, ***OLYMPIC*** was involved in a collision with the Royal Navy cruiser ***HMS HAWKE***. Damage to the liner was slight but it was necessary for her to return to Harland & Wolff for repairs. She remained out of service for about six weeks. When she departed Belfast more historic photographs were taken of the pretty sisters together, as ***OLYMPIC*** steamed past ***TITANIC*** in the fitting out basin.

In February, 1912, ***OLYMPIC*** dropped a propeller blade in mid-Atlantic and once again returned to her birthplace for repairs, where ***TITANIC*** was almost completed. Thus the sisters were seen afloat together only three times. Two months later ***OLYMPIC*** was homeward bound. Captain Haddock commanding, when her stricken sister called for help. Five hundred and sixty miles away, ***OLYMPIC***'s officers could only listen helplessly to ***TITANIC***'s final wireless messages. ***OLYMPIC*** completed her summer season, then once more returned to Belfast, this time for extensive refitting, a tacit admission that the sisters had design flaws. For six months during the winter of 1912-1913 ***OLYMPIC*** went through a major reconstruction program which cost about one quarter of a million pounds. Her double bottom was extended above her bilge keel, some of her watertight bulkheads were extended upward, and she was fitted with side bunkers to give her additional protection from collision as well as added buoyancy. When she returned to service she was one of the strongest, safest ships afloat. Her identical consort now gone, ***OLYMPIC*** was reduced to running with the aging 10,147 ton ***MAJESTIC***, built in 1889, and the 17,272 ton ***OCEANIC***, built in 1899.

In 1914 Cunard brought out ***AQUITANIA***, one last fourstacker which looked surprisingly like ***OLYMPIC***. Built by Messrs. John Brown & Co. of Clydebank, who had built the ill-fated ***LUSITANIA***, ***AQUITANIA*** was often referred to as "the ship beautiful." Although a popular ship, ***AQUITANIA*** was neither innovative nor particularly speedy. Her quadruple screws, powered by four Parsons turbines, drove her at 23 1/2 knots, about the same as ***OLYMPIC***, but she was only 19 ft. longer between perpendiculars than her White Star competitor, her gross tonnage of 45,647 being about the same. She did have, however, a complete double hull, with from 5 ft. 4 in. to 6 ft. 3 in. between the inner and outer hulls. She was also equipped with anti-rolling tanks for a more comfortable ride in a seaway, a factor which probably accounted for much of her popularity.

Almost two years to the day after her maiden voyage ***OLYMPIC*** and British sea supremacy were challenged by the 51,969 ton Hapag liner ***IMPERATOR***. Built by Vulcan of Stettin, the German supership was laid down as ***EUROPA***, her name being changed to ***IMPERATOR*** at the request of the Kaiser. ***IMPERATOR*** averaged about 22 knots on her voyages, again about the same as ***OLYMPIC***, and was not a threat to Cunard's Blue Riband. But ***OLYMPIC*** was no longer the largest ship afloat. On 14 May, 1914, Hapag brought out the 54,282 ton ***VATERLAND***, laid down by Blohm & Voss as ***EUROPA***, with the Kaiser again requesting a name change. (When a ***EUROPA*** was finally launched in 1928, without the Kaiser's name-changing, she was seriously damaged by fire while fitting out.)

OLYMPIC continued to be a popular ship despite her new competition. As comfortable and spacious as any of them, she rode easily in a seaway and remained almost free of the vibrations which plagued the German liners. On her westbound passage when war started in August, 1914, ***OLYMPIC*** continued on to New York, then returned to Southampton. In October, 1914, she rescued most of the crew of the British battleship ***HMS AUDACIOUS***, which had struck a mine near Lough Swilly. She remained in commercial service until September, 1915, when she was commissioned His Majesty's Transport.

OLYMPIC safely carried troops to the Dardanelles and Gallipoli, evading submarine attacks on three occasions. Early in 1916 she was overhauled and fitted with six 6-inch guns for defense against submarines and raiders. In April of that year she carried a British diplomatic mission to Nova Scotia and the United States. From then until the end of the war she brought American and Canadian troops to Europe. On one of these voyages ***OLYMPIC*** evaded a torpedo fired by the German submarine U-103, then rammed the sub and sank it.

By the end of the war ***OLYMPIC*** had safely carried 41,000 civilian passengers as well as 24,000 Canadian and 42,000 American troops. She had also carried 12,000 Chinese laborers to work behind the lines on the Western Front. Her affectionate nickname, "Old Reliable," had been well earned.

When the war was over ***OLYMPIC*** reversed her trooping voyages, bringing American and Canadian soldiers home. Then it was back to Belfast again for complete reconditioning to bring her up to peacetime luxury standards. At this time she was converted to oil firing, which reduced her engine room staff from 350 to about 60 men and increased her speed.

Her first post war commercial voyage began on 21 July, 1920. In the same year she crossed from the Ambrose Lightship to Cherbourg at an average speed of 22.53 knots. She was soon joined by new running mates, former rivals, yet more worthy of her than the old ***MAJESTIC*** and ***OCEANIC*** had been. The former Hapag liner ***BISMARCK*** became White Star's new ***MAJESTIC***, and Norddeutscher Lloyd's ***COLUMBUS*** became White Star's ***HOMERIC*** when Germany's surrender terms demanded that she give up her best liners as compensation for those sunk by German submarines. Hapag's ***IMPERATOR*** became Cunard's famed ***BERENGARIA***, while ***VATERLAND*** became the United States Line's flagship ***LEVIATHAN***. ***LUSITANIA*** was gone, but ***MAURETANIA*** was faster than ever.

Now and then rumors circulated throughout the shipping world that a new consort for ***OLYMPIC*** would be built by Harland & Wolff, but nothing came of them. In 1928 ***OLYMPIC*** was again modernized to compete with Compagnie Générale Transatlantique's popular new ***ILE DE FRANCE***, and a new class was added... "Tourist." Austerity became a trend on the North Atlantic as severe restrictions on U.S. immigration quotas virtually eliminated the lucrative emigrant trade and shipping lines wooed thrifty vacationers to keep the express passenger liners running.

In July of 1929, just months before the October Stock Market crash and the start of the Great Depression, Germany's Norddeutscher Lloyd brought out the innovative ***BREMEN***, 899 ft. long, 51,656 GRT. Long and sleek, with only two squat funnels and a slightly raked bow, ***BREMEN*** had a bulbous forefoot which increased her speed and kept her screws well submerged even when running through heavy seas. With her single reduction geared turbines, twenty water-tube boilers fired by oil fuel, a steam pressure of 350 pounds per square inch driving quadruple screws at 180 revolutions per minute, ***BREMEN***'s 130,000 shaft horsepower was over twice that of Cunard's ***MAURETANIA***. On her maiden voyage ***BREMEN*** made the passage between Cherbourg and New York in 4 days, 17 hours and 42 minutes, averaging 27.83 knots, and bringing the Blue Riband back to Germany.

In 1933 ***OLYMPIC***'s engines were overhauled, while White Star's new motor ship, ***GEORGIC***, a sign of things to come, took her place on the Western Ocean.

In February, 1934, the old rivals White Star and Cunard merged into Cunard-White Star, Ltd., to ride out the economic depression that forced the laying up of many fine ships. The British Government encouraged the marriage with a much-needed financial subsidy.

On 16 May of that same year ***OLYMPIC*** acquired the only blotch on her career. She rammed the Nantucket Lightship in thick fog, killing seven of the lightship's crew. The liner was held solely to blame. The U.S. Government was reimbursed by half a million dollars for the loss of seven of the crew and the vessel itself.

The following year CGT brought out its spectacular 79,280 ton, 29-knot ***NORMANDIE***. She was France's first and only Blue Riband winner. ***NORMANDIE***, too, had a bulbous forefoot. Built for speed, she also brought new luxury to the North Atlantic. In contrast ***OLYMPIC*** was showing her age. Four stacks were obsolete and so were straight stems, counter sterns, reciprocating engines and triple screws. ***NORMANDIE***'s quadruple screws and turbo-electric drive had driven her at 31 knots during her trials.

Cunard-White Star retaliated by completing the delayed, almost 82,000 ton ***QUEEN MARY***, which had been launched on 26 September, 1934, *while* ***MAURETANIA*** had been laid up that summer. On 27 March, 1935, ***OLYMPIC*** departed Southampton for the last time. Upon her return home she was sold to industrialist Sir John Jervis for a mere £100,000. He then sold her for the same amount to the shipbreaking firm of Thomas Ward, with the condition that she should be broken up at their Jarrow yard to provide work for those suffering from the economic slump. The famous old *"**MAURY**,"* said to be Franklin D. Roosevelt's favorite ship, was scrapped in July of the same year, the end of an era. ***QUEEN MARY*** departed on her maiden voyage from Southampton and Cherbourg to New York on 27 May, 1936, the largest liner yet built, and the Blue Riband came home to England once more.

OLYMPIC's hull was as sound as the day she was launched. It was stripped, then towed to Ward's Inverkeithing yard and finally broken up in 1937. ***OLYMPIC*** had steamed over one and a half million miles, and made 257 round trips across the Atlantic. But time had marched on, and how quickly she was forgotten as the race for speed and luxury at sea continued until it was brought to a crashing halt by the second Great War.

But for that quirk of Fate which sent ***TITANIC*** to the bottom of the North Atlantic on her maiden voyage, none except liner enthusiasts would remember ***TITANIC*** today. A superb vessel for her time, ***OLYMPIC*** was the first of her class, and deserves that place in maritime history, unshadowed by her ill-fated younger sister.

The Middle Sister

TITANIC departed the busy double-tide port of Southampton at midday on Wednesday, 10 April, 1912. Exactly like her sister before her, she followed the River Test to Southampton Water. Down the Water she steamed, to the Solent, past Spithead, and across the Channel to Cherbourg. From that French port she steamed overnight to Queenstown from whence she sailed on the afternoon of 11 April. Her voyage was uneventful, the weather was fine, cold but clear, excepting for a few patches of fog. She passed at least one rain squall that we know of, but remained clear of it.

Her departure from Southampton had been slightly marred, and much has been made of this, by an incident in which the American Line's ***NEW YORK*** broke her moorings when the smaller liner (also owned by the International Mercantile Marine Company) was pulled away from her berth by suction created by the much larger ***TITANIC*** as she passed. Contrary to legend, this "suction"' was understood in 1912, and ***TITANIC***'s master acted quickly to avoid collision by slowing his engines while an alert tug master got a line aboard ***NEW YORK*** and towed her to safety. It was the sort of incident which is all in a day's work to a mariner, but the public quickly seized upon it as unusual, and it has been often used to suggest that ***TITANIC*** was doomed from the beginning of her maiden voyage.

On Sunday evening, 14 April, ***TITANIC*** was just south of the Grand Banks, an area notorious for fog, ice, and sailing ship traffic. At 6PM ship's time Second Officer Lightoller took over the watch from Chief Officer Wilde. At 10PM First Officer Murdoch took over the watch from Lightoller, and both officers allegedly discussed the fact that they would come up to the ice area during Murdoch's watch.

At about 11:40PM Murdoch spotted a low-lying berg, or growler, ahead. He immediately ordered ***TITANIC***'s helm *"hard astarboard,"* and rang her engines through *"Stop"* to *"Full speed astern."* He would later be criticized for doing this. At any rate, it was too late. ***TITANIC*** *was* too close to the ice when it was sighted on the moonless night.

TITANIC slipped beneath the waves at about 2:20AM on Monday, 15 April, about two hours and forty minutes after impact. Survivors were rescued from all of ***TITANIC***'s lifeboats a few hours later by Cunard's ***CARPATHIA***, Captain Arthur Rostron.

Legend has it that the only vessel within sight of ***TITANIC*** was the Leyland liner ***CALIFORNIAN***, Captain Stanley Lord commanding. ***TITANIC*** survivors, even those few left today, will say, "We *saw the* ***CALIFORNIAN*** th*at night,*" adding fuel to the myths. The truth is, of course, that ***TITANIC***'s people saw the lights of at least one ship, which were described by every reliable witness immediately after the disaster as moving, while ***CALIFORNIAN*** was known to be stopped. Captain Lord was a convenient scapegoat because his employer, the Leyland Line, was owned by the same conglomerate that owned ***TITANIC***, Morgan's I.M.M..

While ***CARPATHIA***, originally bound for the Mediterranean, turned around and headed for New York, a United States Senate investigative committee, chaired by Michigan Senator William Alden Smith, was hastily convened to search for the cause of the accident. A second investigation was conducted by the British Board of Trade in England, as soon as surviving crewmen could return home. Although ***TITANIC*** is remembered as a British ship, registered in Liverpool and flying the Union Jack, she was owned by an American shipping trust, which was financed heavily by British and Dutch money.

TITANIC is memorialized in every corner of the world, because her manifest listed passengers and crew members from almost every country. The bulk of her passenger list, as well as a disproportionately greater part of her casualty list, was comprised of Third Class, commonly called steerage, which along with government mail subsidies provided the financial impetus to keep the big liners running.

Chapter Three

The Harter Act

Born in acquiescence to the *Harter Act of 1893,* the legend of ***TITANIC's*** incompetent officers and their "bad seamanship" can be refuted by a few facts and, as always, a little common sense.

The Harter Act stated *"That if the owner of any vessel transporting merchandise or property to or from any port in the United States of America shall exercise due diligence to make the said vessel in all respects seaworthy and properly manned, equipped, and supplied, neither the vessel,* ***nor owners****, agents or charterers* ***shall become or be held responsible for damage or loss resulting from faults or errors in navigation or in the management of said vessel****, nor shall the vessel, her owner or owners, charterers, agent or master be held* ***liable for losses arising from dangers of the sea*** *or other navigable waters, acts of God, or public enemies, or the inherent defect, quality, or vice of the thing carried, or from insufficiency of package, or seizure under legal process, or for loss resultant from any act or omission of the shipper or owner of the goods, his agent or representative,* ***from saving or attempting to save life or property at sea, or from any deviation in rendering such service."***

"Dangers of the sea" were defined as *"all accidents and marine casualties caused by seawater, heavy weather, collision, stranding or* ***any peril which may be encountered at sea and against which the carriers could not take precautionary measures."***

"Seaworthy" meant that the vessel was in every way fit for the contemplated voyage, that she was in a condition to meet the risks which might reasonably be expected, and that she was also in a position to ensure safe carriage of the cargo, and/or passengers.

If, however, the shipowner was privy to or participated in any alleged errors or mismanagement of the vessel, then said shipowner *was* liable. This is why it was so important to prove that J. Bruce Ismay, who qualified as "shipowner" due to his position as White Star's Managing Director, was aboard solely as a passenger who had absolutely nothing to say about, and no knowledge of, how ***TITANIC*** was being navigated. At the American inquiry Ismay went so far as to deny any knowledge of navigation at all, a strange admission for a shipowner.

Throughout the inquiries into the cause of the ***TITANIC*** disaster there is continual confirmation of the vessel's seaworthiness and compliance with equipment regulations. The myth of a shortage of lifeboats being the sole cause of ***TITANIC's*** high loss of life made the British Board of Trade an early scapegoat, for it had granted ***TITANIC*** and her elder sister ***OLYMPIC*** their sailing certificates under the Board's antiquated requirement of a minimum of sixteen boats under davits for a passenger ship of 10,000 tons and upwards, regardless of the number of persons aboard, or how far "upwards" the tonnage went.

The legendary "stray," recently-calved growler which turned its "impossible-to-see" dark side toward the onrushing ***TITANIC,*** on a calm, moonless night with no wind to stir up a telltale white froth at the foot of the berg, obviously complied with the Harter Act's definition of *"dangers of the sea."* It was a one in a million chance that all these conditions had come together at once, declared White Star and ***TITANIC's*** obedient officers. There was no way that any action by ***TITANIC's*** officers could have prevented the accident under such *unforeseeable* conditions. *"Any peril which may be encountered at sea and* ***against which the carriers could not take precautionary measures."*** said the Harter Act. As the senior surviving officer. Herb Lightoller dutifully insisted that the circumstances were so extraordinary they would never happen again in many years. The Second Officer even recounted his alleged conversation with Captain Smith about the peculiar conditions which prevailed that night, saying that they had discussed the fact that ice would be unusually difficult to see. Lord Mersey, Wreck Commissioner at the British Board of Trade Inquiry, found it hard to believe that Lightoller was not making this up as it was just too contrived to sound like a routine conversation.

In fact, there was nothing unusual about the circumstances at all, as every Western Ocean watch officer knew. The truth was simply that ships had been crashing into, and having near misses with ice from the beginning of commercial North Atlantic traffic. Ships had limped into port with ice damage for years, and some had simply gone missing, the consensus of nautical opinion being that they had struck ice and sunk without trace. In February, 1892, White Star's freighter ***NARONIC*** had joined the missing, having departed from Liverpool for New York never to be heard from again. The fact that none of the express liners of ***TITANIC***'s era had yet sunk from collision with ice was testimony to the topnotch brand of seamanship demanded in their officers by all the lines which habitually pushed their ships and crews to extremes to make smart passages and keep their imperative schedules, whether they tried for the coveted Blue Riband or not.

The Harter Act *declared that "neither the vessel, nor owners, agents or charterers" could be held responsible for damage or loss resulting from* ***faults or errors in navigation or in the management of said vessel,*** *"* thus it had to follow that ***TITANIC***'s officers were guilty of *"bad seamanship,"* a legend loudly and irrationally perpetuated to this day, in spite of 1912 testimony and knowledge to the contrary. Indeed, her officers would not have remained long in the White Star, or any other passenger line, if they had not only been completely competent, but superior.

TITANIC was brought from Belfast to Southampton under the command of Captain Edward John Smith. Her senior, watchkeeping, officers were Chief Officer William McMaster Murdoch, First Officer Charles Herbert Lightoller, and Second Officer David Blair. Her junior officers were Third Officer Herbert John Pitman, Fourth Officer Joseph Groves Boxhall, Fifth Officer Harold Godfrey Lowe, and Sixth Officer James Pell Moody.

On 9 April, the day before ***TITANIC***'s departure from Southampton, Henry Tingle Wilde replaced Murdoch as Chief Officer, allegedly at the request of Captain Smith, who, according to Lightoller, wanted a Chief Officer with experience in the sister ship, ***OLYMPIC***. It would be Murdoch's watch when ***TITANIC*** struck ice.

Murdoch dropped to First Officer, the same position he had held for almost a year in ***OLYMPIC***. Lightoller dropped to Second Officer, a position he had held often enough in other White Star ships. A very lucky Davy Blair was left ashore. The junior officers remained the same. Of the above. Smith, Wilde, Murdoch and surprisingly, the most junior man, Sixth Officer Moody, would perish with the ship.

Lightoller testified at the inquiries that this change, made so abruptly at the last minute, threw all of the senior officers *"off stride."* It may have thrown Lightoller off stride, for he had come from the smaller ***OCEANIC***, and the step up to First Officer in the line's newest ship was a tremendous boost in prestige. Wilde and Murdoch, however, now held the same positions they had held in ***OLYMPIC***. The ships being almost identical in their passenger quarters, and literally identical in their working areas, Wilde and Murdoch would hardly have felt "off stride." Both men were seasoned professionals, who were accustomed to maiden voyages. Both were also used to abrupt changes, for a career at sea is like a career in the air, the only thing constant about either profession is change. Moreover, Wilde and Murdoch were old shipmates, at home in ***OLYMPIC***, thus at home in ***TITANIC***, and certainly accustomed to working with each other. Lightoller mentioned needing sometime to find his way around in ***TITANIC***, but Murdoch and Wilde came aboard knowing their way around. There is some evidence that Wilde did not want to go in ***TITANIC***, but the reason for that was probably more mundane than a premonition of disaster.

When a man chose the sea as his profession in Britain, and in ***TITANIC***'s era, he usually began his career at about fourteen years of age as an apprentice. Most senior, watchkeeping mailboat officers of this period had apprenticed in sailing ships. By 1912, however, many were apprenticing in steam, and most of the lines carried cadets on their crew rosters, in all but the prestigious Atlantic liners. After this period of on-the-job learning, which might take as long as four years, for voyages in sailing vessels were often counted in years rather than months, they took the Board of Trade's examination for a Third Mate's certificate. As they gained the required experience they studied whenever they found time aboard ship, usually under the auspices of a kindly officer, and they progressed to the examinations for Mate, Master and perhaps the special Extra Master certificates. While advancing in certificates they also were advancing in rank commensurate with the examinations they passed and the experience they acquired. Those who apprenticed in sail usually progressed quickly to Second Mates in sailing vessels. Perhaps they then made a voyage in the same or comparable vessel as First Mate, and then moved into steam, most knowing that the future of shipping lay there. The most ambitious men looked for berths as junior officers in one of the big passenger lines. The epitome of the profession was command in one of the elite Western Ocean liners. Not every officer had what it took to achieve this, of course, but few did not aspire to it, dream of it, and work toward it.

White Star paid top money for its officers, and in turn demanded the best men afloat. That Wilde and Murdoch had risen so high in the line indicated that they had served well, from apprenticeship through their first appointment in the White Star, and so on up through the line's ranks. In the White Star a man who came from sail began his career as a junior officer, usually in the Australian trade. He was closely watched by the master and senior officers with whom he sailed, and if he did well he became a senior, or watchkeeping, officer in one of the line's lesser ships as openings occurred. In the White Star this meant either the Australian run, or cargo. He would either move up one rank at a time in the same ship, or a ship of comparable size, or he would be posted to a larger vessel at a lower rank, again depending upon where there was an opening, and how well he was recommended by the senior officers and masters with whom he served. In the White Star he would go from the Australian run to the North Atlantic when he exhibited the unusual qualities necessary for crewing an express passenger liner, for the best men needed even more than superior seamanship. They would have to deal well with passengers, an attribute that does not necessarily go along with professional competence. Being good-looking certainly helped his chances, for the lines were very much aware that their female passengers often liked to flirt with the officers. In passenger ships officers were, and are, always encouraged to behave as gentlemen toward the ladies, which sometimes creates misunderstandings because most women are not used to being treated so gallantly. The officers' uniforms also seemed to enhance what was called in 1912 their "manly bearing." Women passengers often developed "crushes" on the officers and booked passage in their ships again and again, another plus for the line. At the Senate subcommittee investigation into ***TITANIC***'s loss a young woman hysterically pushed her way into the hearing room, demanding to know what had happened to First Officer Murdoch. When told that he had drowned, she fainted dramatically and was carried out of the room. No doubt this was one of White Star's passengers who had sailed with Murdoch and found him attractive, not an uncommon scenario in passenger ships then, or now.

Having thus worked his way up the ladder of rank from Second to First, to Chief Officer, he could go no further but to ships larger than the ones he had first been posted to as Chief, or to command. From Chief in the flagship there was no promotion except to command, and that depended entirely upon openings. Commands opened up only when a master retired, died, or was booted out of the line for negligence which resulted in an accident or near accident.

The new master's first command would take him again to the line's smaller ships, usually cargo carriers. If he did well, he worked his way up again through a progression of larger and newer ships, until, if he had no blemish on his career, and if he lived long enough to see an opening before he reached retirement age, he would be in the position of Captain Smith… he would command the "flagship," the newest and finest in the fleet. In ***TITANIC***'s time White Star did not use the title "commodore" for this coveted position, but other lines did. England rewarded the commodores of its elite passenger fleets with knighthood. A mariner could aspire to no more, and for many men, no less.

Harry Wilde had been Chief Officer in ***OLYMPIC***, with Murdoch being First Officer in that ship. According to ***TITANIC*** legend, while Murdoch was promoted to Chief in ***TITANIC*** Wilde remained in ***OLYMPIC*** as Chief Officer until he was called at the last moment to supersede Murdoch as Chief in ***TITANIC***.

But Wilde was available for ***TITANIC*** because he had *not* been at his post in ***OLYMPIC*** when she sailed from Southampton for New York on April 3rd. This suggests that Wilde had already been posted to a command, and probably was on leave until that command was available. It would have been perfectly normal for him to have a period ashore while he waited for his new ship to arrive from a voyage, or even to be finished by the builders. That Murdoch had been posted as senior officer in the newest ship confirms his wife's later assertion that he was to be the line's next commander. Because Wilde was senior to Murdoch, he would have a command before Murdoch. Had it been otherwise, Wilde would have been ***TITANIC***'s Chief Officer, while Murdoch would have moved up to Chief in the older ***OLYMPIC***, which would have been the normal progression. The one voyage as Chief Officer in ***TITANIC*** would have postponed Wilde's promotion, as well as its accompanying pay raise, which certainly would have been enough to make Wilde "out of sorts."

It is necessary to understand the mystique of command to comprehend Wilde's disappointment. To savor for many years that moment when he first paces his own bridge, when he is first addressed as "Captain," and when he first assumes that tremendous responsibility for his ship and all aboard her, and then to have it postponed even for one voyage is something that would be impossible for the average person, who never commands anything larger than an automobile, to understand. It is entirely possible that Wilde knew that what was to be his first command would sail without him while he was away on ***TITANIC***'s maiden

ABOVE: *William McMaster Murdoch, First Officer,* ***TITANIC***

voyage, postponing his promotion still further, while pulling another master from holiday leave. There has always been, unfortunately, a dearth of information about Henry Wilde. That Captain Smith was very close to retirement is further confirmation of Wilde's promotion and Murdoch's impending promotion to command. Had Wilde not been posted to ***TITANIC*** at the last minute, and had ***TITANIC*** not struck ice on her maiden voyage, Wilde would have had his command. Smith would have retired, and ***OLYMPIC***'s master, Captain Haddock, would have moved up to ***TITANIC*** as the line's senior commander, with all masters junior to him moving up in the natural progression, leaving a command open at the bottom of the hierarchy in a cargo ship, which Murdoch would have taken, leaving Lightoller as Chief in ***TITANIC***. As it turned out. Captain Haddock almost blundered aground in ***OLYMPIC*** just a few weeks after ***TITANIC*** foundered. Haddock was forced to quietly resign shortly thereafter, and another command opened up at the bottom of the line, which would have been filled by ***TITANIC***'s current Chief Officer, Lightoller. If ***TITANIC*** had not sunk, the third sister ship, ***BRITANNIC***, would have been completed and entered service on time and the whole process would have been repeated, with another new master at the bottom of the echelon of command. Murdoch would have understood Wilde's disappointment, but he had little reason to be disappointed himself. On the contrary, he had much to look forward to. When ***TITANIC*** was sinking, however, both Murdoch and Wilde knew that even if they survived, their careers were virtually finished. No passenger line wants a commander, or even a watch officer, whose name is associated with disaster. Murdoch would have found himself on the beach, scrambling for a berth no doubt in a tramp with no prestige and far less remuneration, even though the accident was not his fault. Wilde was not even on the bridge at the time of impact, yet Harry Wilde would never have achieved command in the White Star. In fact, the shortage of information about Wilde and the knowledge that he was soon to be a commander is enough to focus attention upon him as the officer who shot himself.

ABOVE: *Charles Herbert Lightoller, Second Officer,* ***TITANIC***

Several survivors told of seeing an officer on the bridge put a gun to his head and pull the trigger shortly before ***TITANIC*** took her fatal plunge. At least one crewman said it was the "Chief Officer" who committed suicide. Because Murdoch had originally been ***TITANIC***'s Chief Officer and thus many crewmen still thought of him as such, and because it seemed to everyone that Murdoch had the motive for suicide, legend has pointed the finger at Murdoch all these years. Wilde, however, had a motive in that he would have known at that moment beyond all doubt that he would never have a command, that his whole brilliant, coveted future had been destroyed in but an instant. It mattered not how competent he had been, how deserving he had been, or that it had not even been his watch. It mattered not that Wilde must have known that Murdoch himself was not responsible for the accident, for Murdoch had behaved exactly as Wilde would have done. Harry Wilde surely knew in his last two hours of life that but for the Grace of God it could have happened in his watch. If he survived, the name of Henry Wilde would ever after be associated with ***TITANIC***'s loss and his career would have gone down with the ship. That Lightoller remained in the White Star at all is testimony to the fact that he was part of the coverup initiated by the White Star (read IMM) to protect it from financial loss as well as to his heroism in remaining with the ship to the end. Another damning piece of evidence for Wilde is that he was the officer who first searched for the ship's weapons. It is also entirely possible that Wilde preferred a quick bullet in his head to a slow death by drowning. He came from the era of sailing ships when sailors usually chose *not* to know how to swim. When a man fell from the lofty spars of a squarerigger, as often happened in the cruel world of sail, there was rarely any hope of rescue in raging, or shark-infested seas. His death was mercifully quicker if he did not instinctively struggle to survive as a swimmer would. If a man had struck the rail on the way overboard his shipmates would run to look for blood and hope that he had been knocked unconscious, making his death that much easier. But some men yearned and worked so hard for command that to lose it for any reason made life no longer worth living. This was the reason that captains often chose to go down with their ships.

Occasionally a master who loses the ship but not any lives will be given obscure employment in the line, but never again a command. He may leave the sea altogether in such a case, as did Captain Inman Sealby, master of White Star's ***REPUBLIC***. Forsaking his native country after losing his ship, at the age of fifty-one Sealby enrolled in the University of Michigan's law school to take up the profession of admiralty law. But suicide either by gunshot or remaining on the bridge as his ship sank was the usual choice. It was considered the "manly" thing to do rather than the "coward's way out." In fact, a male passenger who told of seeing one of ***TITANIC***'s officers shoot himself commented *"There was a man!"*

Wilde probably did not take his own life until he had done all he could do for ***TITANIC***'s passengers. That Murdoch did not commit suicide was affirmed by witnesses who saw him still trying to free the last Engelhardt as the sea engulfed ***TITANIC***'s bridge. In fact, Lightoller testified at the Board of Trade inquiry that he had seen Murdoch and Moody at the starboard collapsible, still trying to attach the falls as ***TITANIC*** went under. But Lightoller had not seen Wilde for "quite a long time before the ship went down." Murdoch, like Lightoller, simply remained on board, doing what he had to do until the end. Fate alone decreed which man would go down with the ship, but come up again to survive, and which would not. Murdoch had no doubt rejected wearing a life vest because it hampered his movements. Surviving crewmen commented that Murdoch had been "everywhere," doing more than any of the other officers to aid the passengers.

"Mister Murdoch had overlooked nothing that could help save the passengers when the final moment came. He ordered doors, chairs, chests of drawers... everything on board that would float to be thrown into the sea," said A.B. George McGough.

In meeting the Harter Act's criteria for *"damage or loss resulting* **from faults or errors in navigation or in the management of said vessel**," it was not prudent to dwell on the fact that ***TITANIC***'s two most senior watchkeeping officers were considered by the White Star Line to be competent enough for command. For the same reason, the fact that Wilde and Murdoch both held Extra Master's certificates was downplayed at both inquiries, the Senate investigation even listing Murdoch as having only an ordinary master's certificate. White Star walked a tightrope, needing desperately to satisfy terms of the Harter Act, yet not wanting passengers to feel that the line might hire incompetent officers.

When Lightoller insisted that Murdoch had been replaced at Smith's request, because Smith wanted a Chief Officer with experience in the sister ship ***OLYMPIC***, his assertion perpetuated the slur against Murdoch's competence which still exists in ***TITANIC*** legend, although it made no sense at all, and therefore was undoubtedly what Lightoller was instructed to say. Murdoch had as much experience in ***OLYMPIC*** as Wilde had, from her acquisition by the line, until he was transferred to the newly-completed sister ship ***TITANIC***. The watchkeeping duties of Chief and First Officers were exactly the same. Lightoller knew all this perfectly well, but his assertion fits neatly into the provisions of the Harter Act. Lightoller and Murdoch were old shipmates, therefore Lightoller knew full well of Murdoch's competence.

When ***TITANIC*** called at Queenstown, White Star's Marine Superintendent at that Irish port was Captain James McGiffin, who had been Chief Officer in ***MEDIC*** ten years earlier when Lightoller and Murdoch were Second and First Officers respectively in that vessel. McGiffin came aboard at Queenstown not just in his official capacity but to have a chin-chin with two old shipmates and friends. In fact, McGiffin was Murdoch's closest friend. One of the oddities in the British Board of Trade ***TITANIC*** inquiry is the absence of Captain McGiffin's testimony as the last Marine Superintendent to have visited the ship. Captain Benjamin Steele, Marine Superintendent at Southampton was called, and so was Captain Charles A. Bartlett, Marine Superintendent at Liverpool. Although ***TITANIC***'s port of registry was Liverpool, as all White Star ships were registered there, she had never called at that port, thus asking Captain Bartlett to testify at the Board of Trade inquiry merely increases the questions about the absence of Captain McGiffin. After ***TITANIC*** sank, Lightoller saw McGiffin and naturally told him all about the disaster, including the fact that Murdoch had been forced to shoot a crewman who led a rush on one of the lifeboats, pushing aside women and children. The bullet struck the man's jaw.

Shortly after the ***TITANIC*** inquiry in England McGiffin left the White Star and the sea, suggesting that the disaster and what he learned about it later from Lightoller had a profoundly traumatic effect upon him. Among other things. Captain McGiffin must have known about the fire that was already smoldering in one of ***TITANIC***'s forward bunkers when she called at Queenstown. He knew that White Star's Managing Director, J. Bruce Ismay, was aboard to push Captain Smith into making a record passage for the Southern Track. While Blue Ribands were won on the shorter northern routes, ***TITANIC*** had not the speed to take a Blue Riband from the swift Cunarders ***MAURETANIA*** and ***LUSITANIA***. However, if she made up for that lack of speed by taking the usual shorter northern route, Ismay could tell reporters in New York that she had in fact been on the longer Southern Track, the track agreed upon by White Star and other lines, making ***TITANIC*** seem faster. On subsequent voyages, with engines properly run in, ***TITANIC*** should have made 24 knots easily, thus maintaining the speed which Ismay would attribute to her maiden voyage. In fact, perhaps McGiffin knew too much and was too devastated by Murdoch's loss to risk having him testify at an inquiry. The late Jim McGiffin, who was the Captain's son, remembered Will Murdoch, the kindly officer who used to visit his father. He also remembered that his father was "a broken man" after ***TITANIC***'s loss.

Lightoller himself may have been more than a little distressed at having to carry out the charade of Murdoch's incompetence, but he had little choice unless he wanted to find himself serving in a low-paying tramp for the rest of his life, and lucky to be there. Lightoller had recently purchased a large and expensive home in Netley Abbey, near Southampton, which was beyond the means of even a White Star First Officer. And Lightoller himself eventually wrote in his autobiography that there would be others still living if they had been able to put the catastrophic events of that night out of their minds. That Lightoller was a man of very strong character was evidenced by his subsequent life, including his heroism during the Dunkirk evacuation of World War II. This

***LEFT**: Captain James McGriffin, White Star & American Lines' Marine Superintendant, Queenstown, Northern Ireland, 1903-1912, and a close personal friend to **TITANIC**'s First Officer, William Murdoch. (Photo courtesy of the late J.O. McGriffin.)*

was an era when men gave absolute and unquestioning loyalty to employers, and Lightoller was no exception.

The truth was simply that Captain Smith knew what Ismay expected of ***TITANIC***, for it was the same thing the line's Managing Director had expected of ***OLYMPIC***'s maiden voyage... early arrival at New York with its accompanying favorable publicity to assure future bookings. Smith also knew perfectly well that April was not the time of year to make such a fast passage because of ice along the regularly-used shipping lanes (not necessarily the "official" Tracks) which would not be

***ABOVE**: The officers of White Star's **MEDIC** in Melbourne, Australia, 1902. Standing L-R: Apprentice and Junior Officer Names Unknown, Second Officer Charles Herbert Lightoller, First Officer William Murdoch, Junior Officer and Apprentice Names Unknown. Seated L-R: Chief Engineer, Name Unknown, Captant Trant, and Chief Officer James McGriffin. (Photo courtesy of the late J.O. McGriffin.)*

present in June, the month of ***OLYMPIC***'s maiden voyage. Smith wanted his best men on the bridge when ***TITANIC*** was most likely to encounter ice, and experience had taught Smith just when that would be. Wilde and Murdoch were White Star's two most experienced watch officers, and Smith had sailed with both of them many times, thus he had complete confidence in them. While Smith may have had confidence in Lightoller and Blair, he knew that they did not have experience in handling the big triple screw superliners which were less maneuverable than the smaller twin screw ships. Of all deck officers afloat, in any lines, only Wilde, Murdoch and one other officer had that experience. The third man who had the expertise, who had been Second Officer in ***OLYMPIC***, has never been considered in this scenario. Why did Smith not ask for all three watch officers from ***OLYMPIC***? Because the third man had already moved up in ***OLYMPIC***, had already sailed in her for New York, and at any rate Smith only needed his best officers during the period of time when ***TITANIC*** would be crossing the Grand Banks area, and that was during the First and Chief Officer's watches. Smith was also aware that on this particular voyage the most hazardous period of traversing the ice wne would have no moon to reflect its telltale "blink," which would have enabled a watch officer to see ice from a greater distance than he would on a moonless night. But the over-confident, desperate Ismay knew that all eyes would be upon ***TITANIC*** now, not later. If she did not arrive early on the maiden voyage while reporters waited anxiously to meet her in New York, nobody would notice if she arrived early on subsequent voyages. Ismay knew perfectly well that White Star was the prime jewel in I.M.M.'s crown, and he knew that I.M.M. was not doing well financially. Trying to live up to his father's shipping heritage, Ismay had desperately wanted these three superliners for an express service second to none on the Western Ocean. Now he needed to prove that only the three vessels could carry out what should have been the work of four ships at their speeds. With no great reserve of speed such as the Cunarders ***LUSITANIA*** and ***MAURETANIA*** possessed, Ismay's three ships had to be driven hard to maintain their schedules. Those who insist that White Star no longer sought the Blue Riband and point out that ***TITANIC*** and her sisters had not the speed to take that symbol from the rival Cunard miss the point entirely. It was not the Blue Riband that Ismay was after with ***TITANIC***. The pretty triplets would make up in size and luxury what they lacked in speed. Ismay simply wanted, and needed, to beat his own schedule to attract future bookings. Ismay knew perfectly well why Captain Smith wanted Wilde in ***TITANIC***, and Ismay knew perfectly well of Murdoch's competence, but when ***TITANIC*** was gone he had to sacrifice Murdoch's reputation for the good of the White Star Line. Captain McGiffin, and Murdoch's widow Ada Banks Murdoch, undoubtedly understood this, but they naturally remained bitter over the incident, for they knew that Murdoch had been the real hero of ***TITANIC*** and for the rest of their lives they saw Murdoch vilified in the press, in books and movies, by those who knew nothing of the events leading up to the disaster.

Armchair mariners, without the slightest knowledge of 1912 seamanship, seized upon Lightoller's statements, and added to it the speculation raised at both inquiries to satisfy the Harter Act, that if Murdoch had run ***TITANIC*** straight into the ice she would have survived, merely crumpling her bows to the collision bulkhead, probably killing a few minor human beings in the forward steerage and crew quarters, but theoretically saving the ship and the lives of those all-important millionaires in First Class.

It is true that when collision is inevitable between two vessels, the ship which takes the impact on her bows will usually be the survivor. Every watch officer knows this theory and should stand ready to maneuver the ship into this "enviable" position just prior to impact if at all possible. In actual practice it is a different story, of course, and psychologically it would be very difficult to deliberately

C.

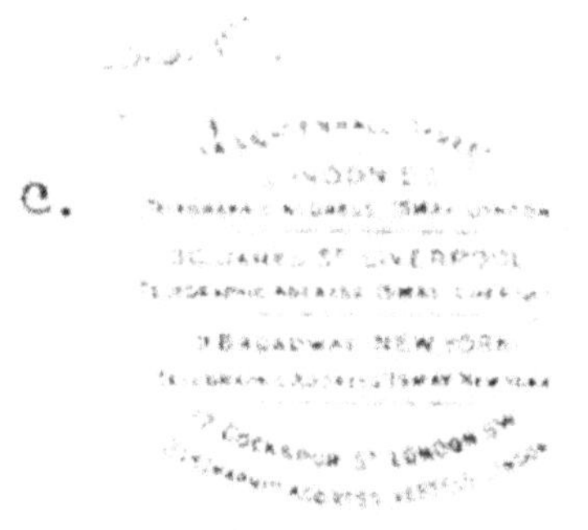

Steamship DEPARTMENT

LIVERPOOL March 17th. [illegible]3.

Captain James McGiffin.

73, Kingsley Road,

Liverpool.

Dear Sir,

We duly received your letter of the 14th instant applying for the appointment of Marine Superintendent at Queenstown, and we have pleasure in appointing you to the position named, subject to three months notice on either side, at a salary after the rate of £200 per annum, and a bonus of £50, conditional upon the duties being performed to our satisfaction.

It is understood that you will continue in the Insurance Scheme of the White Star Line.

The appointment is made on trial for the present, and in the event of it being decided, for any cause other than misconduct, to cancel same we will replace you in the Service in a similar position to that you now hold on the first opportunity.

Yours faithfully

ABOVE: Letter appointing Captain James McGriffin to the position of Marine Superintendant for the White Star and American Lines at Queenstown. (Courtesy of Captain McGriffin's great nephew, Alan McGriffin.)

Captain James McGriffin,
Marine Superintendent,
White Star & American Lines,
QUEENSTOWN.

Dear Sir,

Your many friends in Queenstown cannot permit your leaving this port where you have for so many years discharged the duties of Marine Superintendent of the White Star and American Lines without placing on record their estimate of your career and conduct whilst living amongst them.

You came here a stranger to many of them, but it soon became evident that you were an official whose worth and efficiency tact and courtesy stamped you as one possessing the qualities essential to the proper discharge of the onerous duties of the impotant Office you held. Your courteous manner to all with whom you came in contact - your thorough knowledge of your business - your great experience and intelligence combined, enabled you to secure the good will of your confreres in Office, to earn the gratitude of the thousands of passengers using the White Star and American fleets and we feel sure to increase the confidence and favour of the Directors of your Companies.

All this you accomplished without deflecting from the strict line of what you duties demanded.

We desire your acceptance of the accompanying small token of our esteem and regard for your many sterling qualities and also as a souvenir of the happy years you spent in Queenstown.

In your new position we wish you every prosperity, and we shall always to rejoice to hear of the future happiness of yourself, Mrs. McGiffin and family.

signed.

Charles O'Callaghan. Chairman J.P. C.U.D.C.

H.R. Greene. Hon. Treasurer. Agent, Bank of Ireland.

T.W. Scoggins. Hon. Secretary. Aroral Villa.

ABOVE: *The letter to Captain James McGriffin upon his retirement from the White Star Line. (Courtesy of Alan McGriffin.)*

ABOVE: *The plaque honoring Captain James McGriffin upon his retirement from the White Star and American Lines in 1912. (Plaque photograph courtesy of Alan McGriffin.)*

***ABOVE*: *TITANIC*'s *First Officer William Murdoch, pictured aboard* ***MEDIC*.** *(Photograph courtesy of the late J.O. McGriffin.)*

***ABOVE*:** *William Murdoch pictured in 1909. (Photograph courtesy of Ada Murdoch's nephew L.R. Webley.)*

***ABOVE*:** *Will Murdoch's wife and widow, Ada Banks Murdoch, pictured in 1909. (Courtsey of Ada Murdoch's nephew, L.R. Webley.)*

steer at another ship. But if any officer could coolly decide when to abandon all possibility of avoiding collision and deliberately steer his ship into another vessel or object, then Murdoch was that officer.

It is also true that a watch officer would endeavor to strike small ice with the bows. Murdoch, however, unlike the armchair strategists, had plenty of experience with ice in both the southern and northern oceans. He alone knew what he had to avoid, and he knew perfectly well that the most dangerous part of a berg was what he could *not* see. Had he run straight at what he could see, he knew that invisible, submerged spurs extending outward from the main part of the berg could have torn out ***TITANIC***'s bottom. He was completely obligated to avoid the ice that he could see, to the best of his and ***TITANIC***'s ability, and hope that in so doing he would also avoid the more dangerous spurs of ice that he could *not* see. A ship colliding with another vessel will yield somewhat on impact, although those aboard her will hardly believe it. Icebergs are a different story. With ***TITANIC***'s great mass behind her 22 1/2 knot speed, running stem-on into a berg, or even a growler, would undoubtedly have meant fatal damage, while the glancing blow that ***TITANIC*** suffered should not have. It is truly amazing how those who have studied ***TITANIC*** for years have been willing to ignore the capabilities of the officer who was on the spot that night. Only one man in ***TITANIC*** knew exactly what had happened, and that man was Will Murdoch. To ignore the fact that he was a thoroughly professional and competent officer is incredibly arrogant and naive. Even the conclusion of the Board of Trade inquiry supported Murdoch. He was, said Lord Mersey, the only man who knew what had happened, and he was dead and could not defend himself. If Murdoch had steered head on into the iceberg he would have had to defend himself for that action, declared most Board of Trade investigators. Therefore his maneuver to try to avoid the ice was entirely proper, concluded the Board, although Murdoch's second helm order was ignored.

Will Murdoch was born at Dalbeattie, in the Stewartry of Kirkcudbright, Scotland, near the beautiful but treacherous Solway Firth, on 28 February, 1873, into a long line of seafarers. In fact, John Paul Jones, credited with founding the United States Navy, came from this same area of Scotland and had his place on the Murdoch family tree. Will's father, Captain Samuel Murdoch, had a reputation as one of the best-liked masters in the British merchant service. Will graduated at the top of his class from Dalbeattie High School, where a memorial plaque and scholarship still commemorate his heroism in the ***TITANIC*** disaster.

Unfortunately, some sources give the J &J Rae iron barque ***ST. CUTHBERT*** as Will's first ship, and I used that information in my first book ***TITANIC**: R.I.P.* Information in family archives, however, indicates that Will was First Mate in ***ST. CUTHBERT*** from 17 May, 1895, to 29 July 1896. *(**ST. CUTHBERT*** foundered in a pampero off the coast of Uruguay in October 1897). From 3 April, 1897, to 2 May, 1899, he was First Mate in the steel four-masted barque ***LYDGATE***, owned by John Joyce and Company of Liverpool. Leslie Harrison, in his book *A **TITANIC** Myth: The **CALIFORNIAN** Incident* (Second Edition Revised, S.P.A. Ltd., Units 7 /10 Hanley Workshops, Hanley Swan, Worcs., 1992) wrote that Captain Lord said he met Will Murdoch in Rotterdam when Will was an apprentice in the Vaughan & Co. Liverpool barque ***IQUIQUE*** and Lord was an apprentice in J.B. Walmsley & Co.'s barque ***NAIAD***. Considering that Will's uncle, Captain John Murdoch, had been master of Walmsley's barque ***RAVENSWOOD***, out of Liverpool, it is possible that Will did indeed make a voyage or two in ***IQUIQUE*** at about this time, but probably not as an apprentice. Will may have apprenticed in either ***ESKDALE*** or ***NORTHBROOK***, both having been under his father's command at about the time that Will would have gone to sea. According to information obtained from the Maritime Archives of the University of Newfoundland, the ***ST. CUTHBERT*** *crew* agreement listed ***IQUIQUE*** as Will's previous vessel, but the archives lacked any corroborating 1894-1895 documents. Records do show that Captain Samuel Murdoch, Will's father, commanded ***IQUIQUE*** from her maiden voyage in 1892 until 1898. There is no doubt, however, that Will began his apprenticeship at the usual age of fourteen. Like all boys who survived their first Cape Horn voyage in a windjammer, young Will necessarily progressed into responsible manhood at a rate that would terrify most of today's teenagers. He had acquired his Extra Master's Certificate (no. 025780) in 1896, at the age of 23. It was not at all unusual for shipmasters in sail of that era to be under 25 years of age.

By 1912 Murdoch had been posted successively to ***MEDIC, RUNIC, ARABIC, ADRIATIC, OLYMPIC***, had done occasional relief stints in other White Star ships, and had been appointed Chief Officer in the line's newest ship, ***TITANIC***. (There has been and still is controversy over just which ships Murdoch had served in. Because Lloyd's does not list ***MEDIC*** as one of his ships, there are researchers who refuse to believe that Will did serve in ***MEDIC***. Officers, however, were and are routinely transferred among ships of the same class, and even outside the class, but there is no need to notify the underwriters unless a vessel's permanent master is transferred. Lloyd's is not infallible, simply because it publishes only the information furnished by the shipowner. Murdoch had been promised White Star's next command, which along with his appointments to maiden voyages was indicative of the company's confidence in his abilities.

Along the way Will Murdoch had earned a reputation among his colleagues as *"the best and smartest sailor afloat,"* and *"one of nature's gentlemen."* An incident related by White Star Captain Edwin Jones years after the ***TITANIC*** disaster has often been used to demonstrate Murdoch's extraordinary abilities as a watch officer, but it bears repeating because it is never fully explained for the benefit of readers who have no knowledge of shiphandling.

Jones, then a junior officer, had just come on to ***ARABIC***'s bridge with Murdoch, who was taking over the watch. That many years later Captain Jones would still remember the incident and want the world to know of it was indicative of the respect that other White Star officers had for Will Murdoch.

ARABIC was running smoothly through patches of fog late at night. In that awkward few moments before Murdoch had his night vision and was officially ready to take over the watch, the lookout struck one bell to indicate sighting something off the port bow. Murdoch dashed to the port bridge wing, while the watch officer still on duty instinctively gave the order *"Hard aport!"*

Murdoch, however, immediately saw a red light glimmering through the mist *off* ***ARABIC***'s port bow and he at once recognized it as the port running light of a sailing ship. Fearing confusion if he countermanded the watch officer's order. Will sprang to the wheel himself. Pushing the helmsman aside he held the wheel steady amidships while the watch officer, who had by this time seen the light himself, realized his error and countermanded his first order, calling for *"Midship's the helm. Steady as she goes!"*

This incident demonstrates Murdoch's superior eyesight, and his extraordinarily fast reflexes. Even though he had just come up to the darkened bridge he had seen that red lantern and it was close aboard. Had the helm been put hard aport, as the watch officer still on duty ordered, ***ARABIC***'s course would have been altered to starboard, her stern swung directly across the path of the great steel-hulled windjammer that came swinging down her port side.

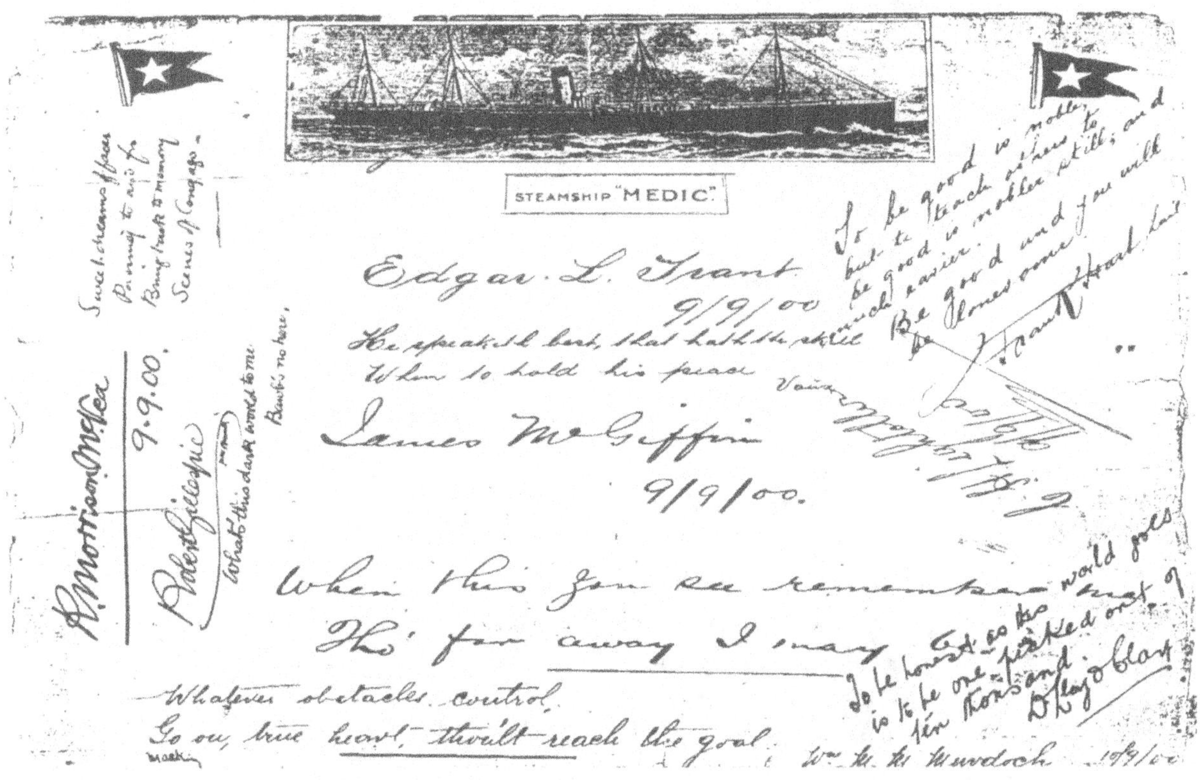

ABOVE: *A menu cover signed during an officers' party aboard* ***MEDIC****. Note the bottom right hand corner is signed by William Murdoch, and* ***TITANIC*** *historians will also note C.H. Lightoller's signature in the middle of the menu. (Menu cover courtesy of the late J.O. McGriffin.)*

***ABOVE: TITANIC's** First Officer, William McMaster Murdoch in his first White Star uniform. **INSET**: Will Murdoch as a mate in sail.*

"Green to green, or red to red,
All is well, go ahead;
Green to red, or red to green.
Take care until your way is seen.
But if you see both green and red,
Better stop before you're dead!"

Thus runs one version of the old sailors' teaching rhymes, and one of the first things taught to every apprentice deck officer.

Red and *green,* of course refer to a ship's running lights. In the ***ARABIC*** example Murdoch was dealing with the sidelight of a sailing vessel, which had no electricity. Lanterns were hung over the sides of sailers, properly shielded to conform to the *Rules of the Road,* and when correctly maintained these lanterns could be surprisingly bright, yet an officer of Murdoch's experience could immediately recognize the difference between a sailer's lanterns and a steamer's electric running lights. In addition, a steamer carried white mast lights, which were never carried by sailing vessels under way. Far less maneuverable than a steamer, sailers always had the right of way.

When two ships are meeting head on, each must by the *Rules of the Road* alter her course to starboard so that each will pass on the port side of the other, thus showing *red* light to *red* light. This *Rule* may be broken in extenuating circumstances, when proper signals are given indicating a deviation from the *Rules.* To understand all this, it is necessary to know something of helm orders, watchkeeping and shiphandling.

The so-called "reverse helm orders," explained in Chapter 1, were used in some merchant ships as late as the 1930s, although they had long been phased out in naval vessels, where orders are given in terms of the desired actual position of the rudder. Again, it is important to understand that it is the ship's stern that moves first when a change in course is initiated by moving the helm.

With the helm/tiller to port, the rudder goes to starboard and the stern is thrown to port. The ship's head is resultantly forced to starboard. As explained in Chapter 1, she will range ahead nearly along the line of her original course, for a distance that may be roughly two or three ship's lengths, depending on her size and individual handling characteristics, before she takes up her desired new heading. In the case of the ***ARABIC,*** in such close proximity to the sailing vessel that the officers on the liner's bridge involuntarily ducked as the windjammer swept past them, any alteration of her helm to port, as her watch officer had instinctively ordered, would have swung ***ARABIC***'s stern to port, putting her vulnerable side directly across the path of the sailing vessel. For this reason, when vessels meet nearly head on, but do not discover each other until they are in close proximity, it may be best for both to hold course rather than alter it as the *Rules of the Road* dictate. It is the watch officer's call in this case, and experience teaches him or her what the best action may be. It is conceivable that if both ships conform to the letter to the *Rules of the Rond,* with each altering course, for example to starboard when they are going to pass red to red and very near each other, they may well bring their sterns into collision.

It is interesting to note that ***ARABIC***'s master that night was Captain Bertram Hayes, later Sir Bertram Hayes, commodore of the White Star fleet when he retired and wrote his autobiography, *"Hull Down"* (The Macmillan Company, New York, 1925). Obviously Hayes knew Murdoch well, and he must have known that Will had literally saved ***ARABIC*** that night. Yet Hayes never once mentioned Murdoch in his book, although he made a great point of mentioning the fact that White Star Line officials *never* went near the bridge when they traveled in company ships. Thirteen years later Hayes was still supporting Ismay's contention that he never went near ***TITANIC***'s bridge or had anything to do with her navigation. But privately, to friends and to Murdoch's family, Hayes always maintained that ***TITANIC***'s officers had been scapegoats. One can hardly blame Hayes, however, for being a "company man" to the end, and for knowing who paid his pension.

On Sunday evening, 14 April, ***TITANIC*** was a few miles southeast of the Grand Banks when, at 6PM ship's time. Second Officer Lightoller took over the watch from Chief Officer Wilde. About two hours later Lightoller sent the standby Quartermaster, Robert Hitchins, to the carpenter with orders to check the fresh water supply because the air temperature had dropped to near freezing. Next Lightoller summoned the deck engineer and told him to turn on the electric heaters in the alleyway of the officers' quarters, the chartroom and the wheelhouse. At 8PM the junior officers changed their watch, with Sixth Officer Moody and Fourth Officer Boxhall coming on the bridge. Lightoller's next order was to Moody to tell the lookouts in the crow's nest to keep a sharp lookout for small ice and growlers, indicating that the Second Officer was aware that ***TITANIC*** was near ice fields. In fact, Lightoller had Moody repeat the order because the junior officer had left out the part about growlers. At 10PM First Officer Murdoch took over the watch from Lightoller, and both officers allegedly discussed the fact that during Murdoch's watch they would come up to the ice area which had been reported by wireless. It would have been a logical discussion, and at any rate Murdoch was well aware of the fact. Also at 10PM the two quartermasters on duty changed places, with Hitchins taking over the wheel from Alfred Olliver, who then took the standby duty. At the same time in the crow's nest Frederick Fleet and Reginald Lee took over the lookout duties from George Symons and Archie Jewell, who passed on Lightoller's orders about small ice and growlers.

At about 11:40PM, ship's time, Murdoch spotted a low-lying berg, or growler, in the ship's track. Murdoch immediately ordered ***TITANIC***'s helm *"hard astarboard,"* and rang her engine telegraphs through *"Stop"* to *"Full speed astern."* As Murdoch was acting, Frederick Fleet in the crow's nest rang three bells, the signal for something sighted dead ahead, and telephoned the

***ABOVE: TITANIC** at sunset. (Artwork by James A. Flood.)*

bridge as ***TITANIC***'s head swung to port on the starboard helm. Sixth Officer Moody answered one of the four telephones in the wheelhouse. Because it was a direct line from the crow's nest Moody knew when he answered it that he was speaking to the lookouts and he answered with the question, *"What did you see?"* It should be noted that contrary to legend the three bell signal from the lookout did *not mean "iceberg ahead."* It merely meant that there was *something* dead ahead, and it could have been simply a light.

To Fleet's reply *"Iceberg right ahead,"* Moody answered calmly, *"Thank you."* Moody's noncommittal reply has been used for over eight decades as evidence that Murdoch ignored Fleet's warning. The fact is that Murdoch had already seen the growler, had begun evasive action, and was doing all that he could do. The warning from the lookouts was redundant. Murdoch's critics apparently believe that the First Officer himself should have dropped whatever he was doing and dashed into the wheelhouse to answer the lookouts with something like this: "Really? Thank you so much. We'll do something about it straight away!"

The truth is that while no responsible watch officer would ignore his lookouts, neither would he depend upon lookouts to tell him what lay ahead of his ship. I cannot repeat often enough that in 1912 a watch officer, quite simply, *kept watch.* He took up his station on the weather wing of the bridge and he stayed outside during his entire four hour watch. This was the reason that bridges were designed with the open walkway running athwartships forward of the wheelhouse. If the watch officer on the starboard bridge wing happened to notice a light off the port bow, for example, he could dash across the bridge to the port wing to get a good view of the light without going through the wheelhouse and losing his night vision or losing sight of the light.

Being lower than the crow's nest by about twenty feet, with a clear view ahead, Murdoch was in a position to see the growler first. Legend has it that because of the moonless night, with no wind and an oily calm sea there was no telltale white froth at the lip of the berg to enable Murdoch or the lookouts to see the ice while far enough away to take successful evasive action, conditions that had never before been seen on the North Atlantic. Legend also has it that the berg was literally a "mountain of ice." The truth is that the oily calm sea was a dead giveaway that ***TITANIC*** was in the lee of an ice field where growlers, bergy bits and small pieces of ice abound. Murdoch knew it, Lightoller obviously knew it when he warned the lookouts about small ice and growlers. In his lower station on the open bridge wing Murdoch was in a better position to see the low-lying growler silhouetted against the night sky, to see the "blink" of starshine reflected off its glassy surface. He was also in a better position to see through any haze which might exist. Earlier in the evening when he relieved Lightoller so that the Second Officer could have his dinner, Murdoch had ordered ***TITANIC***'s forward hatch covers tightened to make sure that not one bit of light interfered with his view into the darkness ahead. He did this because he knew that ice would be hard to see, that every bit of his senses had to concentrate on what lay ahead of the ship. But it was nothing new to a Western Ocean mailboat's watch officer with Murdoch's experience and expertise.

Murdoch's order to ***TITANIC***'s helmsman was *"Hard astarboard!"*, meaning that ***TITANIC***'s helm was put to starboard by turning her wheel to port, thus moving the rudder to port. Her stern then was pushed to starboard by water piling up against the forward edge of her rudder, which in turn threw her head to port. Murdoch told Captain Smith that he intended to *"port around it,"* meaning that he intended to throw the stern first to starboard, and then to port as the berg was passed. It was the emergency method employed to avoid collision with an object dead ahead and close aboard. It was a reaction fast and by the book, and it had worked many times, not only for Murdoch, but for every watchkeeping deck officer in every steamer afloat. It still works today. The maneuver involves "kicking" the stern to push the bow away from the object ahead, turning in the direction where the most searoom lies. When the object is missed by the bow, but not yet one third of the ship's length along the side, the helm is reversed to literally push the stern away from the object. This would not be something done with the legendary "mountain of ice" dead ahead, but it would be done with a *growler*, a smaller chunk of drift ice which has little height above water, but a great mass below its waterline. Growlers are so named because of the sound they make as they rasp along the side of a vessel.

There has been much speculation within the ***TITANIC*** establishment as to why Murdoch turned to port rather than starboard. Many authors and researchers believe that a ship turns more easily to starboard, and after all, according to the lookouts the iceberg was "dead ahead," therefore Murdoch erred in a tum to port. The very fact that Murdoch turned to port indicates that he did indeed see the ice before it was seen and reported by the lookouts, and that Murdoch perceived the tum to port as being the most advantageous course of action.

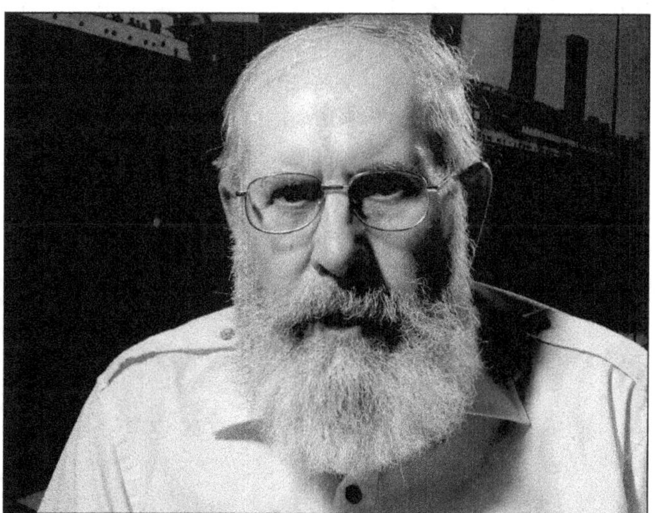

ABOVE*: Second Officer Larry Fosgate*

"The 'berg had the right of way," says Second Officer Larry Fosgate, an American Merchant Marine watch officer with twenty six years' experience at sea. *"Murdoch would*

have turned in the direction wherein lay the best advantage," Fosgate declares. Whether it was a lead, open water, or the shape of the berg as he saw it, with perhaps its flat side facing ***TITANIC***'s starboard bow, the fact that he did make the decision to turn to port indicates that he did see the object and make the decision on his own perception, not that of the lookouts. No responsible watch officer would initiate evasive action without seeing what he was evading, and we have the ***ARABIC*** incident to prove that Murdoch not only was responsible, but he had extraordinarily fast reflexes and keen eyesight.

A watch officer's *instinctive* reaction to a lookout's bell signal for something sighted dead ahead would be a turn to starboard, not port, as the ***ARABIC*** incident clearly showed. Less than a year prior to ***TITANIC***'s maiden voyage White Star's ***BALTIC*** had been involved in a mid-ocean collision with a Standard Oil tanker named simply ***STANDARD***. Because this incident must have been on every White Star watch officer's mind, if Murdoch had reacted solely on instinct after the lookout's bell warning he would have turned to starboard as the *Rules of the Road* dictated when two ships were meeting head-on. This alone leads to the conclusion that Murdoch did not react instinctively to the lookout's warning, but he saw the ice first himself.

Murdoch also knew that more ice lay to the north and therefore he turned to the south. The reason for the sudden drop in wind velocity and the "oily calm" on the sea's surface described by survivors was simply that ***TITANIC*** was in the lee of an ice field, and the wind happened to be out of the north-northwest, a fact proven by the ice fields' charted direction of movement during the two weeks preceding ***TITANIC***'s accident. Another proof of wind direction lay in Lightoller's statement that he had taken up his watch position on the starboard bridge wing, which therefore was the weather side. The fact that some ships do turn more readily in one direction than the other, especially if they are driven by single screws, has no bearing upon this case. This factor is never a consideration in an emergency turn, even with a single screw vessel, and ***TITANIC*** had triple screws.

It was always difficult to cover up the fact that one of the express liners had been involved in collision with ice, or another vessel. Reporters routinely met the liners upon their arrival at New York, to interview celebrities aboard. When ***BALTIC*** arrived at New York after her collision with the ***STANDARD***, the White Star liner betrayed the accident by displaying a hole in her bow six feet in diameter, yet her officers tried to make light of the incident and hush it up. But for nearly two hours after the collision ***BALTIC*** was dead in the water, rolling in the heavy swell, her passengers crowding on deck expecting to take to the boats, while Captain Ranson sent crewmen below to patch the hole with canvas. Finally repairs were made and ***BALTIC***, which had been the largest ship on the North Atlantic until Cunard's ***LUSITANIA*** went into service, was able to proceed, arriving at New York nearly on time. ***BALTIC***'s officers, surprisingly, were quoted as believing that the tanker had sunk after backing off into the fog, yet they had not initiated any search for her or her survivors. Obviously they had been able to read ***STANDARD***'s name on her bows, yet no report of the collision came from the Standard Oil Company, or from its German subsidiary, Deutsche Amerikanische Petroleum Gesellschaft GmbH, in whose name one tanker named ***STANDARD*** was registered. One ***BALTIC*** seaman had been lost, apparently being knocked overboard by the force of the collision. Captain Ranson had sent a coded message to White Star offices in New York, apprising company officials of the incident and the ensuing delay. Otherwise ***BALTIC***'s wireless remained silent, her Marconi operator refusing to answer queries. The collision had occurred about 1,000 miles east of Fire Island in heavy fog, a position not far from ***TITANIC***'s collision with ice. Obviously both ***BALTIC*** and ***STANDARD*** were on the shortest route, one westbound, one eastbound. It is interesting to note that Captain Ranson did not lose his command over this incident. He was still commanding ***BALTIC*** when ***TITANIC*** sank.

When Norddeutscher Lloyd's twin-screw flyer ***KRONPRINZ WILHELM*** struck ice at 12:30 AM on 8 July, 1907, off the Grand Banks on a night that was also moonless, dark and clear, just as Murdoch would do in the ***TITANIC***, the German watch officer ordered the helm hard astarboard, the engines full speed astern. ***KRONPRINZ WILHELM*** was running at 16 knots, a good speed considering that she had a green crew of strikebreaking scabs in her stokehold, but not near her rated sea speed of 22 knots. Captain Richter, on the bridge at the time, reported that the ship responded quickly to her helm, but did not appear to lose headway before striking. He estimated that the top of the berg was about fifty feet above the waterline.

The German ship struck, lurched, and her bows lifted a bit. As her forefoot cut through a submerged ice spur the ship suddenly returned to an even keel. Officers heard a grinding, crunching sound as the hull rubbed along the side of the iceberg, leaving paint on the ice. The watch officer used a control lever on the bridge to close all watertight doors throughout the ship. A few tons of ice reportedly fell on the forward deck, and came through forward ports in the crew quarters. But the German officers made light of the incident when they were interviewed by reporters in New York. It was all in a day's work when your workplace was the North Atlantic.

In 1890 NDL's ***SAALE*** had a similar experience. Her helm was put hard aport, her engines reversed, but she struck a submerged spur, then was shot off into deep water sideways which shifted her cargo and coal. ***SAALE*** limped into New York with her port rail barely out of the water. In 1900 Hapag's ***NORMANNIA*** also struck ice, but she had been turned just in time to avoid a head-on impact. She scraped alongside the berg, shearing off pieces of ice which fell onto her decks. She, too, limped into New York with her rail awash.

For over eight decades authors and ***TITANIC*** enthusiasts have argued that Murdoch was wrong in sending the *"Full Speed Astern"* command to the engine room. He should have run the starboard engine *full ahead,* while putting only the port *engine full astern,* thus turning the ship faster, assert those who have never conned a ship. ***TITANIC***'s shafts had first to be braked to a complete stop, then her outboard reciprocating engines had to be put into reverse. This whole procedure took at least ninety seconds from the time engineering officers received the command and went into action. ***TITANIC***'s center turbine had no astern turbine, so it was merely stopped. Murdoch knew all this, while the armchair strategists did not. Porting around an object required precise timing, born of instinct, experience and feel for his ship. Murdoch had that feel, that experience, and he knew what he was doing. ***TITANIC*** continued to have way on her, to answer her helm, for a short time after her screws had begun backing. Tests on her trials, and those made later with ***OLYMPIC*** showed that ***TITANIC*** maintained steerageway through a forward speed of 6 knots.

Second Officer Fosgate has this to say about Murdoch's order *"Full Speed Astern"*: *"If the ship were at full cruising speed, which would be excessive in an ice region even with good radar, she would not turn appreciably faster by reversing one engine (warping the ship). If she were at 'maneuvering combinations,' meaning that the engines were not at full speed and that the engineers could direct the power as necessary or even stop without damage, that would be the maneuver of choice to turn the ship most rapidly. If the engines are at full pressure, the only bell that the engineers can answer is a 'crash back,' directing the steam pressure on the backing nozzles but not damaging the boilers or condensers, in the case of turbines. With reciprocating engines the procedure is more complicated, taking from ninety seconds to two minutes to accomplish the reversing."* In the ninety seconds minimum time to reverse a reciprocating engine ***TITANIC*** could have turned twice by means of her rudder, and that is exactly what she did.

LEFT: *A typical engine telegraph for a reciprocating steam engine. Note the watertight door settings.*

The telegraph, or annunciator, on the bridge was connected by wiring, cables, and pulleys to a similar telegraph on the starting platform in the engine room. When the watch officer or master rang the telegraph to a setting, it appeared at the same setting on the engineer's telegraph, thus the watch engineer knew what to do with the engine. When the **TITANIC** *broke in two as she foundered, the connecting cables were severed. Therefore, it is impossible to say what her final telegraph setting was. A watch officer as professional as William Murdoch, however, would have rung it to "stop" or "finished with engines."*

We do know from engine department survivors that ***TITANIC***'s engines *were* at full pressure. The order was *"full speed ahead,"* and she was running at her top speed, or very near it, considering that all of her boilers were not yet lighted. Therefore ***TITANIC***'s engineers could only respond to a crash back, or *full speed astern.* One experienced Merchant Navy chief engineer, who wishes to remain anonymous, told this author that if a watch officer or the master rang *"full speed astern"* while the ship was in mid-ocean running at full speed ahead, he might be inclined to ring up the bridge and ask *"What in the bloody hell are you trying to do to my engines?"*

There has also been a great deal of controversy over whether ***TITANIC***'s engines were stopped or run full speed astern. The confusion apparently comes from the fact that the center turbine was simply stopped because it had no astern turbine. The turbine telegraph, then, had no astern speeds on its indicator, and thus was rung to *"Stop,"* where it would have remained, while the reciprocating engines had to be rung *through* the *"Stop"* position into the astern speed indications.

Running ***TITANIC***'s engines full speed astern had no effect on her turning, which had already been accomplished prior to her screws going into reverse, nor was it part of a maneuver to avoid the ice. Backing screws would slow her faster than simply stopping the engines, and this was done to lessen the force of the impact if she did hit the ice.

Did Murdoch actually give that second command, *"hard aport,"* and was it acted upon? All evidence says a definite *"yes."*

Late in the afternoon of 25 April, Ohio Senator Theodore Burton began taking testimony separately from thirty-two-year-old ***TITANIC*** Quartermaster George Thomas Rowe, whose experience at sea included two years in the merchant service and fourteen years in the Royal Navy. Unfortunately Burton concentrated on Rowe's observance of Ismay entering a lifeboat. But eventually Burton did get around to asking some surprisingly pertinent questions. On page 522 of the U.S. Senate Inquiry transcript. Burton asked Quartermaster Rowe, *"Just where were you when you saw the iceberg?"*

"On the poop, sir; underneath the after bridge," Rowe answered.

"And the iceberg, when the boat rubbed against it, was right near, was it?" Burton had not been told the difference between a ship and a boat.

"Yes, sir."

"How far, would you say?"

"It was so near that I thought it was going to strike the bridge," was Rowe's answer. Unfortunately it is not clear whether Rowe meant the navigating bridge, or the docking bridge where he was.

"Did it strike the bridge?"

"No, sir, never. "

"Only ten or twenty feet away?" Burton persisted.

"Not that far, sir," Rowe answered.

"Did you notice the iceberg when the boat got clear of it?" Burton asked.

"No, sir; I went on the bridge then, to stand by the telephone." Rowe is here clearly referring to ***TITANIC***'s after, docking bridge.

"Could you hear the ice scraping along on the boat where you were?" was Burton's next very pertinent question.

"No, sir."

"So you do not know whether it was rubbing against the hull there or not?"

"No, sir."

"What is your best judgement about that?" Fortunately for posterity Burton persisted in this line

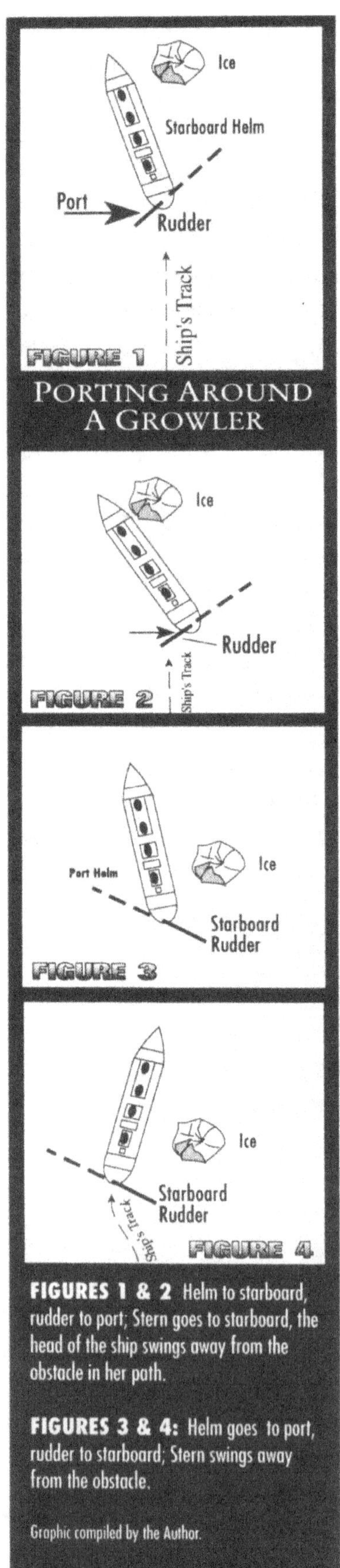

FIGURES 1 & 2 Helm to starboard, rudder to port; Stern goes to starboard, the head of the ship swings away from the obstacle in her path.

FIGURES 3 & 4: Helm goes to port, rudder to starboard; Stern swings away from the obstacle.

Graphic compiled by the Author.

of questioning.

"I do not think it was," Rowe answered.

"You are positive you heard no rubbing?" Burton remained surprisingly persistent.

"Yes, sir," Rowe was positive.

And Burton's next amazingly intelligent question, *"Do you not think that if the helm had been hard astarboard the stern would have been up against the berg?"*

"It stands to reason it would, sir, if the helm were hard astarboard," Rowe answered. He alone estimated the height of the berg as about 200 feet, and said it looked like "ordinary ice," with no "black side" that he could see.

Burton digressed to Rowe's experiences in the lifeboat, then returned to the subject of ***TITANIC***'s impact with ice to ask, *"How long did the rubbing or grinding against the ice last?"*

"I never heard anything except the first contact; the first jar was all I knew about it. I never heard any rubbing at all," Rowe confirmed his earlier statement.

"Do you think the propeller hit the ice? Did you feel any jolt like the propeller hitting the ice?" Burton asked.

"No, sir."

"Do you not think the propeller would have hit the ice if the helm had been turned hard astarboard?" Burton asked.

"Yes, sir," replied Rowe, further confirming the fact that Murdoch had reversed his original helm order.

If ***TITANIC***'s helm had remained in the hard astarboard position, her rudder would have remained to port. As we have seen, this position of the rudder would push the stern to starboard, holding the side of the ship against the ice as long as the helm was in the hard astarboard position. In retrospect it seems surprising that Senator Burton understood this, but no doubt he was coached by George Uhler, Supervising Inspector-General of the Steamboat Inspection Service, Department of Commerce and Labor, who was present at the inquiry. But as we will see, while legend has it that ***TITANIC***'s entire side was ripped by the ice, the truth is that there was no serious damage aft of the no. 6 boiler room, less than one third her length, and the point at which Murdoch would have had the helm hard aport to complete his maneuver of "porting "round" the growler.

Senator Burton continued in this line of questioning when he interrogated Quartermaster Alfred Olliver on the same day. Olliver had been trimming the lights in the standing compass when he heard the lookout strike three bells. He looked ahead but did not see anything, so he left the standing compass and ran to the bridge, which he was just entering when the shock came.

Olliver described hearing "a long grinding sound."

"How far aft did the grinding sound go?" Burton asked.

"The grinding sound was before I saw the iceberg. The grinding sound was not when I saw the iceberg," Olliver replied.

"Do *you know whether the wheel was hard aport then?"* Burton asked.

"What I know about the wheel... I was standby to run messages... but what I knew about the helm is, hard aport," was Olliver's interesting reply.

"Do you mean hard aport or hard astarboard?" Burton seemed to understand the importance of this testimony and fortunately for posterity he wanted to get it absolutely correct.

"I know the orders I heard when I was on the bridge was after we had struck the iceberg. I heard "hard aport," and there was the man at the wheel and the officer. The officer was seeing it was carried out right," Olliver was positive.

"What officer was it?"

"Mister Moody, the Sixth Officer, was stationed in the wheelhouse. "

Who was the man at the wheel?" Burton asked.

"Hitchins, Quartermaster," replied Olliver.

"You do not know whether the helm was put hard astarboard first, or not?"

"No, sir, I do not know that," Olliver answered.

"But you know it was put hard aport after you got there?" Burton persisted.

"The iceberg was away up stern... when the order hard apart was given," Olliver replied.

"Who gave the order?"

"The First Officer."

"And that order was immediately executed, was it?"

"Immediately executed. And the Sixth Officer saw that it was carried out," Olliver added.

Judging from these statements made by Quartermasters Rowe and Olliver it is obvious that Murdoch had indeed given his second helm order, which would have completed his maneuver to port around the ice if Fate had not decreed that one submerged tentacle would reach out and clutch at the speeding intruder into its frigid realm. *"I intended to port around it,"* Murdoch had told Captain Smith, *"but it was too close. She hit it."*

But the second helm order did keep the ice from tearing a lengthy gash in ***TITANIC***'s hull. When it was necessary to "prove" a 300 ft. or more gash in order to conceal the real cause of ***TITANIC***'s rapid demise, then it was necessary to also conceal Murdoch's second helm order.

Olliver said that to the best of his knowledge the ice did not rub against the hull aft of the bridge. He thought the ice was dark blue, it was about the height of the boat deck, and pointed on top. It was impossible to see its length from where he was standing. Olliver's description fit a growler... not the legendary "mountain of ice."

While Quartermaster Rowe testified at the British Board of Trade inquiry, it is interesting to note that Olliver did not, and he was the one man who had overheard Murdoch's second order to ***TITANIC***'s helmsman. Fourth Officer Boxhall might have overheard it although he had not entered the wheelhouse prior to impact, and Quartermaster Hitchins at the wheel certainly knew of it, but neither man volunteered the information at the inquiries as Olliver did.

In London on 24 May Rowe was interrogated by Mr. Butler Aspinall, Counsel on behalf of the Board of Trade. Aspinall elicited the interesting information that ***TITANIC***'s course had been altered at 5:45PM ship's time, when Rowe was at the wheel, from S 85°W by the steering compass to N 71°W, the course still being steered six hours later when she struck ice. Most of the questions directed to Rowe pertained to the starboard Engelhardt boat in which he escaped from the ship, but one important bit of information did come from him. While nobody else, including ***TITANIC***'s navigation specialist. Fourth Officer Boxhall, seems to have thought of looking at the brilliant stars which were numerous and highly visible that night to figure which direction ***TITANIC*** was heading when she finally stopped after impact, Rowe noted that her head was facing north, and the lights of the "mystery ship" were then two points off ***TITANIC***'s port bow. She would only have ended up facing north if that second helm order had been given and acted upon, thus turning her head back to starboard, or toward the north. Undoubtedly this is the reason why none of ***TITANIC***'s officers seemed to "remember" which way she was heading after she stopped. For over eight decades authors and ***TITANIC*** enthusiasts have assumed that ***TITANIC*** was on a southwesterly heading as she sank, an extremely important factor in identifying the mystery ship two points off her port bow.

On 3 May A.B. Joseph Scarrott testified that he had been on watch from 8PM to midnight on 14 April. At about half past eleven Scarrott was "just about the forecastle head" when he heard the lookout in the crow's nest strike three bells. He estimated that it was anywhere from five to eight minutes later that he felt the ship shake in the same manner "as if the engines had been suddenly reversed to full speed astern." His estimate of time from the lookouts' signal to impact seems much too long and disagrees with estimates by other witnesses, a fact that Scarrott himself attributed to his paying little attention to the lookouts' three bell signal.

Scarrott rushed below to tell his mate what had happened. Together they hurried back on deck in time to hear the boatswain order boats uncovered and turned out. Scarrott looked over the rail and saw an iceberg, which he took to be what the ship had struck, abaft the starboard beam. When asked if the berg was close, Scarrott replied that it seemed as if the ship had acted on her helm and had swung clear of the iceberg. The berg, said Scarrott, was then not a ship's length away. He was asked to be specific about ***TITANIC***'s helm, and Scarrott replied that she was under *port helm,* and her stern was *"slewing off the iceberg."* Her starboard quarter was going off the berg, and the starboard bow was going as if to make a circle around it. Lord Mersey wanted Scarrott to be more specific, and the seaman replied once more that ***TITANIC*** was under port helm with her head going to starboard.

There can be no better evidence that Murdoch had indeed given the second helm order. ***TITANIC*** had turned first to port, then to starboard, the second helm order saving her from being ripped open for any great length.

Scarrott's testimony is undoubtedly one of the reasons why many researchers believe the official story that watch officers depended upon lookouts, that Murdoch took no evasive action until several minutes after the lookouts rang three warning bells and telephoned the bridge.

Scarrott appears to have begun another legend when years later he and a few former passengers insisted that they had heard the lookouts *shout* a warning to the bridge. This is absurd for several reasons. On open bridges the sound of voices carried quickly to passenger quarters. For this reason officers always gave orders and spoke in low tones so passengers would not be alarmed. Crew members in passenger ships as well as airliners were and are always admonished to keep voices low in order to avoid panic. This author can attest to the fact that passengers are acutely sensitive to the slightest changes in facial expressions or voice intonations. The remotest suggestion that crew members might be alarmed about something can create panic far more dangerous than the existing situation.

When Frederick Fleet was recalled before the Senate subcommittee in Washington on 24

April he was asked by Senator Burton, *"Could they have heard you on the bridge if you had cried out?"* Fleet's response was, *"I dare say they could."* If he had indeed eschewed using the telephone and shouted to the bridge instead he would have said so at this time. The fact is that Fleet properly, routinely, used the bell signal and the telephone, a direct line from the crow's nest to the bridge.

On 23 April Lookout Frederick Fleet was interrogated for the first time by Senator Smith. Fleet was twenty-five years old, had served four years as lookout in White Star's ***OCEANIC***, had been going to sea for "five or six years." Fleet knew that Murdoch was the ship's First Officer, a fact that several other seamen did not know due to the last minute shake-up. He did not know any of the other officers on the bridge. Fleet and his mate, Reginald Lee, had gone up to the crow's nest on the foremast to take over the lookout at 10PM. The order to be on the watch for small ice and growlers had been passed to them by Lookouts Jewell and Symons as they were relieved. Like helmsmen, a lookout's duty period was two hours at a time. Surprisingly, even in 1912 these duties were recognized as so stressful that going beyond the two hours impaired a man's efficiency. On this particular watch the time was to be put back, at midnight, giving Fleet and Lee an extra twenty minutes on duty Just after seven bells Fleet saw the ice ahead and rang three bells to warn the bridge.

"Would you be willing to say that you reported the presence of this iceberg an hour before the collision?" Senator Smith asked.

"No, sir," Fleet answered.

"Forty five minutes?"

"No, sir."

"A half hour before?" Smith persisted.

"No, sir."

"Fifteen minutes before?"

"No, sir."

"Ten minutes before?"

"No, sir."

"How far away was this black mass when you first saw it?" Smith changed his tactics.

"I have no idea, sir," Fleet answered.

"Can you not give us some idea? Did it impress you as serious?" Smith asked.

"I reported it as soon as ever I seen it," Fleet answered defensively. *"I struck three bells first. Then I went straight to the telephone and rang them up on the bridge."*

Senator Smith repeated Fleet's statement as a question, to which Fleet replied, "*Yes.*"

"Did you get anyone on the bridge?" Smith asked.

"I got an answer straight away... what did I see, or 'what did you see?'"

Fleet naturally did not know to whom he spoke on the bridge, and he had already said that he did not know any officers except Murdoch.

Smith asked Fleet what the three bell signal meant, to which Fleet replied, *"That denotes an iceberg right ahead."* This statement by Fleet apparently was responsible for the erroneous assumption by researchers that the three bell signal actually meant that there was an iceberg in ***TITANIC***'s track. The three bell signal merely meant that **something** was dead ahead, not necessarily an iceberg, and this was explained in later testimony at the Board of Trade inquiry. It was up to the watch officer to ascertain **what** lay ahead and act upon that information. When Fleet was recalled on the following day he explained this himself. Three bells meant *"anything right ahead; any object."*

When Smith asked directly if Fleet had received a prompt response to his telephone call.

Fleet replied, *"I did."*

"Then what did you do?" asked Smith.

"After I rang them up?"

"Yes, sir," Smith replied

"I kept staring ahead again," Fleet answered.

Senator Smith persisted in wanting to know how close the ice was when Fleet first saw it, but unfortunately Fleet either was not good at estimating distances, or he had already been told that this was information better not given. Fleet managed to evade all of Smith s questions on the subject, saying finally that the berg had been the size of two tables in the committee room put together when first sighted. Fleet did note that when the berg was alongside it was only *"a little bit higher than the forecastle head"* which Fleet suddenly was able to estimate as about 50 or 60 feet above the waterline. Again, a description fitting a growler.

"Do you know whether the ship was stopped after you gave that telephone signal?" Smith asked.

"No, no; she did not stop at all. She did not stop until she passed the iceberg." Fleet's observation supports testimony that ***TITANIC*** still had headway and answered her port helm.

"She did not stop until she passed the iceberg?" Smith repeated.

"No, sir."

"Do you know whether her engines were reversed?" Smith asked.

"Well, she started to go to port while I was at the telephone," Fleet answered.

"She started to go to port?"

"Yes; the wheel was put to starboard." Fleet was wrong about this. The wheel had been put to port, it was the helm that had been put to starboard.

"How do you know that?"

"My mate saw it and told me. He told me he could see the bow coming around," Fleet answered.

"They swung the ship's bow away from the object?" Smith asked.

"Yes; because we were making straight for it."

"But you saw the course altered? And the iceberg struck the ship at what point?"

"On the starboard bow, just before the foremast."

"How far would that be from the bow's end?" asked Smith

"From the stem?" Fleet corrected.

"From the stem," Smith repeated.

"About 20 feet."

"About 20 feet back from the stem?"

"From the stem to where she hit."

Fleet had not thought the impact was serious. He felt no heavy shock, just a slight grinding noise, and thought they had a narrow shave. A little ice, not much. Fleet said, had fallen on the forecastle light and the weather deck.

Lee had not had much to say. Fleet remembered, he just kept looking ahead while Fleet was on the telephone, and reported that the ship's head was going to port. Both lookouts had seen the ice simultaneously, but Fleet had been the one to act. None of the other lookout teams had reported seeing ice earlier in the evening, said Fleet.

From that point much of Smith's questioning concerned the fact that there had been no binoculars in the crow's nest. There has been much speculation on this subject, and it has been maintained that the lack of glasses hampered the lookouts' view ahead. The truth, however, is that glasses were a help to identify an object after it had been sighted with the naked eye, and the identification was

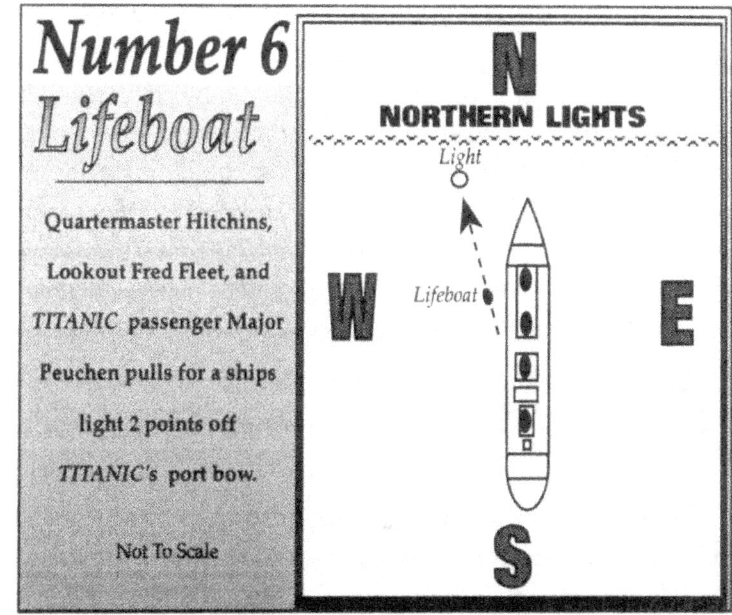

the duty of the watch officer, not the lookouts. Each watch officer had his own binoculars. Several shipmasters testified at the British Board of Trade inquiry that they never gave binoculars to the lookouts because it lessened their effectiveness if they were spending their time looking through the glasses, which had limited vision. One needs only to use binoculars to understand that. In any case, a lookout identifying a light or any object without being asked would have been accused of usurping the watch officer's duty.

Number 6
Lifeboat
Quartermaster Hitchins, Lookout Fred Fleet, and TITANIC passenger Major Peuchen pulls for a ships light 2 points off TITANIC's port bow.
Not To Scale
N
NORTHERN LIGHTS
Light
Lifeboat
W
E
S

Fleet had eventually been ordered into No. 6 lifeboat by Second Officer Lightoller. Fleet estimated that there were about 30 people in the lifeboat. They had pulled for the light of the "mystery ship," which Fleet described as "two points off the port bow," just as others had described it.

One passenger in this boat was Major Arthur Godfrey Peuchen, his commission being in the Canadian militia. Peuchen was a yachtsman from Toronto, Ontario, and he had been ordered into the boat by Lightoller to act as crew because the only seamen in the boat were Hitchins and Fleet. Peuchen believed that they had pulled to the north because he had seen the Northern Lights. They had departed ***TITANIC*** amidships on the port side. He was certain that the light they pulled for was imaginary. It looked more like a "glare," said Peuchen, and he believed it was the Northern Lights reflected from ice.

To digress for a moment, if ***TITANIC*** did lie facing about due north after she came to a stop, as Quartermaster Rowe had testified, and lifeboat no. 6 with Hitchins in command, departing from amidships on the port side, pulled toward a light two points off ***TITANIC***'s port bow, then they were pulling toward the north-northwest and they would have seen the Northern Lights.

Peuchen had spoken with Fleet about the telephone call to the bridge warning of an iceberg right ahead. This conversation and Peuchen's misunderstood testimony may have been the beginning of the legend that insists that Murdoch did not respond immediately to Fleet's call.

When Senator Smith asked Peuchen if he had spoken with Fleet the Major's reply was, *"I was interested when I found he was in the crow's nest, and I said, 'What occurred?' In the conversation he said he rang three bells, and then he signaled to the bridge."*

Smith wanted to know if Fleet had told Peuchen how far off the berg was when first sighted from the crow's nest. But Fleet had not said, nor had he said what the berg looked *like. "The only thing he said was that he did not get any reply from the bridge,"* Peuchen remarked.

"From the telephone?" Smith asked.

"I heard afterwards that really the officers were not required to reply."

"That is, the information is imparted from the crow's nest to the officer at the bridge, and that is the end of that information?" Smith asked.

Peuchen replied that he had later spoken to Lightoller about this, and the Second Officer had explained that the watch officer would decide whether he wished to reply to the lookouts, to tell them what was going on. In this case obviously Murdoch had no time for chitchat, and no watch officer was obligated to tell the lookouts anything. This, then, is all that Fleet meant when he said that he had received no reply from the bridge, yet legend has insisted for over eighty years that Murdoch was negligent in **acting upon** the lookout's warning. Second Officer Fosgate's comment on this subject, *"The normal response to a telephone report or any report from a lookout is 'Thank you' or a repeat of what was said to avoid confusion, e.g. "Ice right ahead, aye." There would be no reason for a watch officer to launch into an outburst of praise for a lookout doing his job."*

Frederick Fleet's answers, and his actions and statements after the accident indicate that he may have felt unusual and unnecessary guilt for not seeing the ice in time for ***TITANIC*** to avoid it. If Fleet did carry this guilt to his grave (and he did commit suicide by hanging many years later) he should not have.

When Second Officer Lightoller was interrogated on this subject by Senator Bourne, Fleet should have heard Lightoller's response to Bourne's question: *"The principal reliance is placed upon the man in the crow's nest, or the men in the crow's nest?"*

"We place no reliance on them," Lightoller answered emphatically.

"What are they there for?" asked a surprised Senator Bourne. *"They are there to keep a lookout; to assist us,"* Lightoller replied.

"Then, why is no reliance placed upon them?"

"Because, speaking personally, I never rely on any lookout. I keep a lookout myself, and so does every other officer," Lightoller was again emphatic.

It takes only a moment of thought to understand that relying upon lookouts literally puts the vessel into the hands of seamen, not officers, and that in itself should be enough to convince anybody that officers must keep their own watch. Time and time again, however, at both inquiries, lookouts made reference to the fact that if they reported too much to the watch officer he would say that the lookouts were interfering with his job, and this says it all.

Quartermaster Hitchins had been in command of the lifeboat with Fleet and Peuchen rowing. Peuchen had nothing good to say about Hitchins, nor did Fleet.

Two days earlier the *New York Times* had printed an article written by an enterprising reporter who had sneaked aboard White Star's ***CELTIC***, where the 25 ***TITANIC*** seamen who were to testify before the Senate Committee were held incommunicado. Private detectives had accompanied the sailors to their quarters and stayed to guard them. ***TITANIC***'s survivors had been told they would be dismissed from the White Star service *"for good and all"* if it were ascertained that any of them had disobeyed the instructions against talking about the accident. The reporter especially wanted to interview Fleet and Lee because they had been in the crow's nest at the time of impact.

Fleet explained to the reporter that Hitchins, who had been at the wheel when ***TITANIC*** struck ice, was *"not one of us."* Hitchins, said Fleet, was making his first trip and *"hadn't been drilled in the sailor's way of sittin' tight and waitin' for the boss's word."* Fleet added that when Mr. Ismay said not to talk it meant as far as he was concerned, that there was nothing to be said. Years later Fleet would tell acquaintances that he was promised a job and pension for life if he "forgot" his claim that he had rung up the bridge about three quarters of an hour prior to impact and told the officer that he had "smelled ice." He had been ignored, said Fleet.

The question here is simply "how logical is Fleet's assertion?" Would he have rung up the bridge with such a warning? Possibly, but it is not probable. If he had taken it upon himself to issue such a warning, it was overstepping the limits of his job which was simply to report what he saw. Fleet's suicide indicates that he may not have been emotionally stable enough to handle what he perceived as his guilt, and thus his subconscious mind conjured up the early ice warning that was somehow consoling to him. This is an absolutely normal psychological reaction among disaster survivors. Today, after such a catastrophe as ***TITANIC,*** teams of psychologists and counselors would work with surviving crewmembers to ease them over the guilt of survival, but in 1912 survivors were left to work out their own problems. Fleet, then, did not lie about this, he really believed it. No doubt Fleet had smelled ice, for it was all around, but if he could smell it so could Murdoch. Fleet had no idea of ***TITANIC***'s position. Murdoch did. Fleet had no notion of wireless ice warnings, excepting perhaps for fo'c'sle scuttlebutt. But Murdoch had seen every ice warning which reached the bridge. Murdoch knew perfectly well that ice was near. He had been that way many times before, in every month of the year. Moreover, Murdoch had apprenticed in sail, stood his first watches in sailing ships, where an officer was necessarily alert to his surrounding environment. He literally "read" the sky and the sea around him. He had to be aware of every instant of the wind direction and velocity, the sea's behavior, the proximity of land or other obstructions, which included ice. An officer then developed a sixth sense about hazardous conditions of any kind, or he did not survive long. Murdoch had that keen sixth sense. He knew about the proximity of ice. Like Captain Smith and ***TITANIC***'s other senior officers, Murdoch needed no wireless ice warnings.

On the 8th of May Fleet's mate Reginald Robinson Lee testified before the Board of Trade inquiry. Lee was forty-one years old, had first gone to sea in 1887. He had spent fourteen years in the Royal Navy, had been in the Atlantic Transport Line's ***MINNEHAHA,*** and had served in ***OLYMPIC.*** He was questioned by the Attorney General, Sir Rufus Isaacs, about the availability of binoculars, and Lee affirmed that although he had occasionally had them in other ships there were none in ***TITANIC*** for the lookouts, excepting for the trip from Belfast to Southampton. These glasses had belonged to ***TITANIC***'s original Second Officer, David Blair. When he left the ship he took the glasses with him.

Lee was the first, and only witness to voluntarily mention that there had been a slight haze, which he saw all around the horizon, just before ***TITANIC*** struck ice. Lee confirmed Fleet's statements in the U. S. to the effect that they had seen nothing at all until about ten minutes after seven bells, or about 11:40PM, when they spotted the iceberg ahead. Lee said that the helm must have been put hard astarboard, or very close to it, as soon as the reply *"Thank you,"* had come from the bridge, "because ***TITANIC*** *veered to port.*" Lee thought she was going to clear it, but he guessed that there must have been ice under water. ***TITANIC*** struck just forward of the foremast, Lee said.

When Fleet had been recalled on 24 April he had been asked by Senator Fletcher, *"To what extent did she change her course from the direct line?"* with reference to the fact that ***TITANIC***'s head had gone to port as Fleet was talking on the telephone to Moody.

"You mean how far did she go?" Fleet asked.

"Yes."

"A little over a point, or two points."

On the basis of this testimony tests were made later with ***OLYMPIC*** traveling at ***TITANIC***'s speed which indicated that it took 37 seconds from the time the helm was put hard over until the ship's head had turned two points. It is important to understand that this does *not* mean it took 37 seconds for ***OLYMPIC*** or ***TITANIC*** to *respond* to her helm. It means that it took 37 second for her head to *turn two points **after** the helm had been put hard over.* This indicates that Murdoch had indeed seen the ice before Fleet rang three bells, therefore prior to the telephone warning, and it puts a time factor into the proof of this. From the time Fleet finished ringing three bells and Moody answered the telephone should not have been more than 10 seconds, probably less. Therefore it was at least 27 seconds earlier that Murdoch had ordered *"Hard astarboard,"* because ***TITANIC***'s head was swinging to port *as Fleet spoke with Moody.* The order had first to have been given to the helmsman before he would turn the wheel to put the helm hard over. If Murdoch had merely reacted when he heard the *end* of the three bell signal (he needed to hear it all to know how many bells would be struck, to know what it signified) and then he acted instinctively without having the berg in sight himself, he would have been ordering the helm hard over, probably to port, even as Fleet telephoned the wheelhouse, and it would have been another 37 seconds before Lee could have seen ***TITANIC***'s head turned through two points. This is also impossible because at that moment Moody would have been relaying the helm order to Quartermaster Hitchins at the wheel, which he would have considered took precedence over answering the telephone, when he already knew the call was from the crow's nest. But Moody calmly answered the telephone with *"what did you see?"* while ***TITANIC***'s head *was already swinging to port on a starboard helm.* Had Murdoch already told Moody that there was ice dead ahead? Probably not. Murdoch was a man of action and quick thinking, as *the* ***ARABIC*** incident proves. Murdoch of all people knew there was no time to waste. He was busy giving the helm order to Moody to relay to Hitchins, and even as he gave the helm order Murdoch was springing to the engine telegraphs forward of the wheelhouse to push the handles into the *full speed astern* position for the outboard reciprocating engines, the *stop* position for the center turbine. The watch officer had no obligation to explain what he was doing to the junior officer, who should have been able to figure it out for himself. When Moody answered Fleet's telephone call, the Sixth Officer already knew that something lay ahead, although he was not in a position to have seen it. Because Murdoch's order was *"hard astarboard"* and because Moody surely knew of the proximity of ice from Lightoller's earlier order to the lookouts if from nothing else, the Sixth Officer must have guessed it was ice. If it had been a ship Murdoch's helm order would probably have been *"hard aport."* Not even the most junior officer in a transatlantic passenger liner was going to panic so easily, and Moody's reply *"Thank you"* therefore was perfectly calm, and perfectly correct.

On 21 May Second Officer Lightoller was questioned by Sir John Simon about who had first seen the ice, Murdoch or Fleet. Lightoller had discussed this with Fleet aboard ***CARPATHIA***. The helm had been put hard over "distinctly before" the report from the lookouts, said Lightoller. Fleet had told him that "practically at the same moment he struck the bell" he noticed that the ship's head commenced to swing, showing that the helm had been altered "probably a few moments before he struck the bell." When Sir John confronted Lightoller with Quartermaster Hitchins' statements to the contrary Lightoller capitulated. *"If Hitchins is right, then Fleet must be wrong,"* answered Lightoller obediently. But further testimony as well as Lightoller's statements on the subject eventually convinced Board of Trade attorneys, and even Lord Mersey, that Murdoch had indeed seen the ice first and reacted before Fleet rang three bells.

Tests made with ***OLYMPIC*** traveling at 11 knots, slightly less than half of ***TITANIC***'s final speed of 22 1/2 knots, indicated that with the helm put hard over at the slower speed it would take 74 seconds for her head to turn about two points. This demonstrates the reason why commanders did not slacken speed in areas of scattered icebergs. There was no appreciable safety advantage to the slower speeds, because the vessel responded more quickly to her helm at higher speeds. Mr. Roche, Attorney for the Marine Engineers' Association, pointed out that the safety factor in lower speeds lay in the fact that the ship could be stopped more quickly by reversing engines at lower speeds. This safety in lower speeds, however, would apply only if she was about to run up on field ice, as ***CALIFORNIAN*** stopped to avoid such ice. When dealing with the bergy bits and growlers, the type of ice obviously expected in ***TITANIC***'s track, the matter of reduction of speed became a matter of dollars and cents, or pounds and pence, as well as safety. Porting around small bits of ice did not involve losing any time enroute, and time lost was money lost. The real factor involved in this equation of time to port around the ice was ***TITANIC***'s lack of maneuverability with her triple screws and too-small rudder area. She needed the extra speed to enhance what maneuverability she had.

In order to put some of these time passages into proper perspective and understand what can be accomplished during an emergency situation, let me suggest to my readers that the next time they travel in an airliner, especially a jumbo-jet with 400 to 500 passengers aboard, imagine evacuating that aircraft full of passengers, using only half the exits, in just ninety seconds. That is precisely what has to be done to certificate any airliner in the United States, regardless of size, and ninety seconds evacuation time is the goal in any real emergency evacuation. I can assure readers that time appears to stand still in such a situation, just as it would have on ***TITANIC***'s bridge and in her crow's nest. A great deal more than one would think can be accomplished in but a few seconds when the adrenaline is flowing during an emergency.

When Lee was asked if he had communicated to the watch officer that it was hazy, he replied *"Certainly not. The watch officer would wonder whether you were interfering with his duty,"* giving further confirmation that watch officers did not depend upon lookouts and lookouts knew it.

When Sir Robert Finlay questioned Lightoller on the matter of who saw haze first, the lookouts or the watch officer, Lightoller replied that the watch officer would see it quicker, or just as quick, because "we always see the little blur on the green light." In other words, the haze, or moisture in the air, tended to show up as a halo, or what Lightoller called a "beard," around the sidelights, which the watch officer would notice immediately. He would then notify the commander at once.

When Lee was asked if he knew that ice was about, he affirmed Fleet's comment that *"you could smell it,"* which seemed to surprise Lord Mersey.

Lee, too, had seen the "mystery ship's" white light, but he was not convinced that it was a ship's light. He clung to his assertion that there had been a low-lying haze all around the horizon, until after ***TITANIC*** sank. Eventually with some prompting. Fleet remembered the haze, too.

But Lightoller blew hot and cold, seeming to say what he thought was expected of him.

While he had originally described a perfectly clear night with good visibility, he, too, eventually recalled haze and he also changed his mind about relying upon lookouts. *"You were relying at this time exclusively upon the lookout; you were not taking any measures to reduce the speed?"*

"None, my Lord," replied Lightoller.

"And therefore you were relying for safety entirely on the lookout?"

"Yes," replied Lightoller again. No wonder Fleet lived with guilt.

Several shipmasters from various IMM-controlled lines, as well as the Cunard, were called upon to give their opinions at the conclusion of the Board of Trade inquiry. All insisted that they did not rely upon lookouts, that the officers on the bridge almost always saw objects ahead before the lookouts in the crow's nest or stem saw them. Captain Rostron testified that while on their way to ***TITANIC*** they had seen icebergs from the bridge before the lookouts saw them. Explaining the reason for that, Rostron said that the watch officer was "more intelligent, more conscientious," than the sailor on the lookout.

Lord Mersey concluded that the evidence showed only that there could have been a low-lying haze enveloping the iceberg itself, a haze caused simply by the difference in temperature between the berg and the water. This type of haze would rise only about two feet off the water, said Lightoller. He had not seen any such haze in his watch, which ended at 10PM, nor had he seen haze when he came to the bridge after the collision. Lightoller reminded his interrogators that if there had been such a haze they would not have seen the distant lights of ships from the lifeboats.

In Fleet's lifeboat they had pulled for the light, but they had never been able to reach it. They pulled away from the ***TITANIC,*** far enough to avoid the expected suction as she went down. Fleet said. None of ***TITANIC***'s crewmen had the experience to know that a vessel sinking by bow or stern creates comparatively little suction. Of course nobody knew how much suction might be created by a sinking ship the size of ***TITANIC,*** there being only two vessels of that magnitude in existence at the time.

This single white light seen two points off ***TITANIC***'s port bow is generally considered to be *the* "mystery ship." There were undoubtedly other lights in sight, but ***CALIFORNIAN***'s running lights were not among them. Fleet insisted that while he was in the crow's nest he had seen no ship's lights at all. Nor had he seen any other icebergs besides the one he had reported. At sea, especially on a clear, moonless night when stars and planets sparkle brightly, unless one can give undivided attention to a particular light for sometime it is not difficult to lose sight of it. Deck officers in other ships the night ***TITANIC*** sank described mistaking ships' lights for stars and vice versa. With ***TITANIC***'s crewmen as distracted as they must have been it would have been easy to lose sight of a single white light, which was allegedly the mastlight, or stern light, of the mystery ship.

Five men had assigned duty on ***TITANIC***'s bridge at the moment of impact. First Officer Murdoch as the watch officer, the two junior officers Boxhall and Moody, and the two quartermasters, Hitchins and Olliver. Only two of these men died. Why then, has so little been known about what happened in those few seconds prior to impact?

Boxhall testified that he was just approaching the bridge as Murdoch rang the engine telegraphs to *"full speed astern,"* and Boxhall testified that he heard Murdoch give the helm order *"hard astarboard,"* actions that would have been simultaneous. Murdoch would have given the helm order to Moody as he sprang to the engine telegraphs. Boxhall's testimony at both inquiries was strangely ambiguous, about a lot of things. There is still speculation about why the Fourth Officer was not on the bridge, and what errand he was returning from just prior to impact. Was he returning from the loo, had he gone for a cup of tea, or as he himself declared, had he been making rounds?

There is no reason not to believe the latter. Part of his duty was to make rounds, to check around various parts of the ship at certain intervals. Deck officers had their own stewards to bring them tea, so it is highly unlikely that Boxhall had gone to make tea, or anything else. Some researchers speculate that Boxhall had been sent to fetch the master, which mission Murdoch might have sent him on if it had "come on the slightest bit hazy." Where Boxhall was is moot and has no bearing on anything pertinent to solving ***TITANIC***'s "mysteries." The fact that Boxhall did enter the bridge and hear Murdoch's first order *"hard astarboard,"* but not the second order *"hard aport"* when others did hear it or know about it is in itself suspicious. Added to other ambiguous testimony from Boxhall, it is all highly suspect.

And what of Quartermaster Robert Hitchins, the man at ***TITANIC***'s wheel, the man who had carried out *both* helm orders according to other witnesses?

Hitchins was not called upon to testify until the sixth day of the U.S. Senate investigation. After Senator Smith ascertained that Hitchins was thirty years old, married with two children, had been a quartermaster for seven or eight years. Smith asked on what ship Hitchins had been employed on *"April 14th last."* This question seemed too difficult for Hitchins, or perhaps he had not been programmed to answer it and after a long pause Senator Smith rephrased the question.

"Were you filling such a position on the ***TITANIC*** *at the time when she suffered this collision?"*

"Yes," Hitchins finally replied.

"Were you at your post of duty the night of the collision?" Smith asked.

"Yes."

"What was your post of duty; where was it?"

Now Hitchins was on familiar ground. *"At the time of the collision I was at the wheel, sir, steering the ship."*

After eliciting the information that Hitchins had come on duty one hour and forty minutes prior to impact, instead of asking pertinent questions as other senators had done. Smith simply told Hitchins to tell what had happened in his own words. Hitchins had obviously "sat tight" long enough to "get the boss's word," and now his lengthy speech tumbled out as if rehearsed.

Hitchins began with *"I went on watch at 8 o'clock."* He continued through Lightoller's sending him to the carpenter about the fresh water supply, with the carpenter's subsequent report that it had been taken care of. Hitchins repeated Lightoller's order to the lookouts about small ice, and he continued through the known sequence of events up until he heard three bells from the lookouts in the crow's nest.

"The Chief Officer [sic] rushed from the wing to the bridge, or I imagine so, sir. Certainly I am enclosed in the wheelhouse, and I cannot see, only my compass," explained Hitchins. *"He rushed to the engines. I heard the telegraph bell ring; also give the order 'Hard astarboard,' with the Sixth Officer standing by me to see the duty carried out and the quartermaster standing by my left side. Repeated the order, 'Hard astarboard.' The helm is hard over, sir."* Here Smith interrupted him.

"Who gave the first order?" Smith asked.

"Mr. Murdoch, the first officer, sir: the officer in charge. The sixth officer repeated the order, "The helm is hard astarboard, sir." But, during the time, we was crushing the ice, or we could hear the grinding noise along the ship's bottom. I heard the telegraph ring, sir. The skipper came rushing out of his room... Captain Smith... and asked, 'What is that?' Mr. Murdoch said, 'An iceberg.' He said, 'Close the emergency doors.'"

"Who said that, the captain?" Senator Smith interrupted.

"Captain Smith, sir, to Mr. Murdoch; 'Close the emergency doors.' Mr. Murdoch replied, 'The doors are already closed.' The captain sent then for the carpenter to sound the ship. He also came back to the wheelhouse and looked at the commutator in front of the compass, which is a little instrument like a clock to tell you how the ship is listing. The ship had a list of 5° to starboard."

"How long after the impact, or collision?" Smith asked.

"I could hardly tell you, sir. Judging roughly, about 5 minutes; about 5 to 10 minutes. I stayed to the wheel, then, sir, until 23 minutes past 12. I do not know whether they put the clock back or not. The clock was to go back that night 47 minutes, 23 minutes in one watch and 24 in the other."

During the summary of the Board of Trade inquiry there was much discussion about the fact that impact had been great enough to "wake the captain." But Captain Smith had done what Captain Lord did that night, he turned in all standing, in the chart room. A commander will feel every tiny nuance in the ship's movement and sound. Even in a deep sleep the subconscious will screen out normal vibrations or noises, but like a mother with her baby, the slightest deviation from the normal registers at once and the commander is wide awake.

Hitchins had remained at his post, at the wheel of the stopped ***TITANIC***, until Murdoch told him, *"That will do with the wheel. Get the boats out."* He had, he thought, been in command of No. 6

boat, and one of the officers, probably Murdoch, had told him to pull for the light seen two points off the port bow. Hitchins thought the light belonged to a fishing boat. Other boats around No. 6 had also been pulling for the light, said Hitchins.

Hitchins also put the time of impact at twenty minutes to midnight. He explained that Murdoch had told the standby quartermaster, Olliver, to take the time, and then the First Officer told one of the junior officers, Moody no doubt, to enter the time in the log book.

At the American inquiry, and again at the Board of Trade inquiry, Hitchins mentioned that "the quartermaster" had been standing at his left side as he carried out Murdoch's helm order, with Moody at his right side seeing that it was done. Nobody ever asked who that quartermaster was, but there were only two quartermasters on ***TITANIC***'s bridge in each watch. When ***TITANIC*** struck ice the two quartermasters assigned to the bridge were Hitchins and Olliver. Olliver had testified that he returned to the bridge when he heard the three bell signal from the lookouts. Hitchins' testimony supports that, and Olliver was positive about hearing the helm order *"hard aport."* Hitchins never mentioned any helm order except *"hard astarboard."* Hitchins was under oath, but he did not lie, he just never volunteered the whole truth. This is perfectly normal behavior at an inquiry of this type. Nobody at the American inquiry ever asked Hitchins to verify Olliver's statements, and nobody ever asked him to identify the quartermaster who had overheard the second helm order, both items that should have been covered in a thorough investigation… unless the second helm order was better left uninvestigated. Nor was Olliver asked to testify at the British inquiry, a strange oversight indeed.

As standby Quartermaster, about ten minutes before he went to the wheel, Hitchins had taken the temperature of the water and air. This was done routinely every two hours, for reports to the Hydrographic Office, not to ascertain the proximity of ice. Hitchins had also taken the temperatures in his watch twelve hours earlier. He could recall only the air temperature at night, but he was sure that it was colder than it had been in the morning, hardly a notable observation considering that it usually is colder at night than in the daytime. He recalled that the air temperature had been 31 1/2 degrees Fahrenheit at 8 o'clock on Sunday evening. Hitchins had overheard Lightoller's order to the lookouts to keep a sharp watch for small ice until daylight.

Hitchins did remember that he had still been steering North 71° West (by compass) when ***TITANIC*** struck ice. The remainder of his testimony was concerned with defending himself against the complaints made about his behavior in the lifeboat. One of the ladies in the boat had a flask of whisky and she had offered him a drink to warm him as he stood at the tiller. Others in the boat accused him of drinking it all. This was hardly as important as it would have been to ask Hitchins about Murdoch's second helm order but it did take up time and it did take everyone's mind off of Olliver's allegation that he had overheard the second helm order. After leaving the witness stand, at his request and while he was still under oath, Hitchins told Senator Smith that ***TITANIC*** had been making 22 1/2 knots at 10PM. Hitchins was allowed to return home to England without further questioning.

On 7 May, interrogated in England by Sir Rufus Isaacs, Hitchins could not recall the air temperature, only that it had been "intensely" cold. Isaacs took Hitchins through his American testimony almost word for word. The Quartermaster dutifully repeated everything about Lightoller's order to the lookouts, and he repeated the course he had been steering, N 71° W.

Hitchins' testimony about the helm order was ambiguous, but Lord Mersey finally got him to say that the helm had been hard over, and ***TITANIC*** had turned about two points before she struck the ice. He repeated that the reading on the Neptune taffrail log had been 45 nautical miles in two hours. At this point both Isaacs and Mersey also led Hitchins into saying that he had heard first the three gongs from the lookouts, then the telephone call which Moody had answered with *"Thank you,"* and *then* Murdoch had rushed to the engine telegraphs while giving the helm order *"hard astarboard."* This does not concur with the lookouts' testimony that ***TITANIC***'s head had already gone two points to port as Fleet was talking to Moody on the loud speaking telephone, but none of the interrogators seemed to catch this discrepancy, or perhaps they did not want to call attention to it.

When he testified in England Hitchins did change one statement he had made in the United States. In England he was positive that they had pulled for the light of a "steamboat," while in America giving his first statements Hitchins was sure that it was a fishing boat, a sailer. While sailing vessels under way never carried white lights, fishing vessels hove to with drift nets out were required by the *Rules of the Road* to show two white lights. Open boats, such as the dories sent out by larger fishing sailers, were required to carry one all-round white light when outlying tackle extended more than 150 feet into the seaway. But identifying the "mystery" light as that of a steamer helped to draw the net of contrived circumstantial evidence tighter around the ***CALIFORNIAN*** and her master, Captain Stanley Lord. Nobody seemed to notice that Hitchins had changed his story, although the British interrogators had the text of the American inquiry in front of them.

Finally, Hitchins was examined by Mr. L. S. Holmes, counsel for the Imperial Merchant Service Guild which represented officers of the mercantile marine. All of ***TITANIC***'s officers were members of this guild. Holmes asked Hitchins directly about the second helm order *"hard apart."* ***TITANIC***, declared Hitchins, had never "come under the port helm." He had but one helm order, Hitchins said, and that was "hard astarbord." It is a pity that Holmes never had the opportunity to cross examine Quartermaster Olliver, but perhaps there was good reason for that. Present at the B.O.T. inquiry to protect ***TITANIC***'s officers. Holmes might have been the one man to ferret out that second helm order from Murdoch.

Clearly someone was lying. What was the logical motive? Hitchins' statement in answer to Holmes' question did one important thing… it successfully concealed Murdoch's second helm order for all time, firmly entrenching the myth of the lengthy gash in ***TITANIC***'s hull, thus concealing the fire damage to the crucial watertight bulkhead as the real reason for ***TITANIC***'s rapid demise. But why was it only Hitchins who lied? Because it is easier to control just one man, if one will do the trick. Hitchins was the logical man to control because he was at the wheel. People differ greatly in integrity, some can be bribed or threatened easily, some not so easily, some not at all. It is impossible to know why Hitchins lied about the second helm order, yet he must have done so in light of so much testimony to the contrary. Probably his family, his two children, were incentive enough for Hitchins to say whatever was necessary to keep his job.

According to many witnesses there were three distinct shocks, or shudders, as ***TITANIC***'s starboard bow grazed the ice spur. One of these shudders, however, was probably caused by the outboard screws going into reverse. ***TITANIC***'s momentum carried her at least another mile, possibly farther, beyond the berg, indicating that she still could answer her helm.

Within seconds after impact Captain Smith was on the bridge. *"What have we struck?"* he asked Murdoch.

"We have struck an iceberg, sir I put her hard astarboard and ran the engines full astern, but it was too close. She hit it." He added, *"I intended to port around it,"* and, *"The watertight doors are closed, sir."*

There was nothing unique, then, about ***TITANIC***'s striking ice or about Murdoch's evasive action. What *was* unusual was the rapidity with which ***TITANIC*** sank, especially the ratio of her survival time to her immense size and the slight impact damage.

The myth of Murdoch lounging in the wheelhouse waiting for ***TITANIC***'s lookouts to tell him what lay ahead of his ship is just that and no more. It is legend without basis in fact, begun by poor research, perpetuated by lack of further research into seamanship of the era and into the 1912 inquiries of the accident.

The enclosed bridge areas of modern ships are far more comfortable than the bridges of ***TITANIC***'s time. Modern deck officers are no longer exposed to the discomforts of the elements and an old salt would say they have no real *"feel"* of the sea around the ship, just as modern aviators no longer fly *"by the seats of their pants."* Ships today have automatic pilots, radar, computerized engine controls and navigation equipment, all technology which theoretically replaces human intellect, reflexes, and eyesight. Again, this is a matter of economics. Computers and autopilots are not paid, fed or given vacations and health insurance. The automatic controls work fine, as long as they are backed up by human vigilance and expertise. The expertise, the vigilance and the sense of responsibility which accompany them unfortunately are eventually lost when too much reliance is placed upon automation.

Quite simply, a watch officer in 1912 *kept watch.* He accepted full responsibility for the safety of his ship during his watch. In the White Star Line at night when the relieving officer came on to the open bridge wing, he took a few minutes to allow his vision to fully adjust to the darkness. Once the course had been passed and he had officially taken over the watch he did not then jeopardize his night vision by entering even the dim light of the wheelhouse. Those used to the modern comforts of glass-enclosed, heated and air-conditioned bridges and homes obviously find this too rigorous to be believed. But to the man who had apprenticed in sail, who had often spent weeks on end exposed to the worst that Nature could offer, who had climbed to the loftiest spars while battling the wildest winds of a Cape Stiff snorter, who had often gone without sleep for several days and nights at a stretch, who had eaten, when he happened to have the chance to eat at all, soggy, moldy, insect-infested food, while his saltwater-soaked clothes rubbed open sores all over his body, who had his hands and face lacerated bloody by wind-driven rain, sleet or hail while he struggled to furl heavy canvas frozen stiff as iron, all the while balancing precariously on flimsy footropes a hundred feet above a deck which frequently disappeared in the surging seas beneath him, only four hours on the open bridge of a liner, even in a Western Ocean winter, was not such a tough billet.

Captain Jones said of his old shipmate Will Murdoch, *"There never was a better officer. Cool, capable, on his toes always… and smart toes they were. That man let nobody down on the* ***TITANIC****, I'm sure of that."*

Will Murdoch was handsome, intelligent, affable, yet tough when necessary. One of those rare men adored by women, yet respected and liked by other men, he would have been a superb mailboat commander. ***TITANIC*** First Class Steward Edward Wheelton was among those who would speak out with special tribute to Murdoch at the inquiries. When asked by Senator Newlands if there was anything else he would like to tell about, Wheelton replied, *"I would like to say something about the bravery exhibited by the first officer, Mr. Murdoch. He was perfectly cool and very calm."*

"And he was lost?" asked Newlands.

"Yes, sir," replied Wheelton. *"He was lost."*

Chief Second Class Steward John Hardy had this to add about ***TITANIC***'s First Officer: *"Of course I had great respect and great regard for Chief Officer Murdoch."* Hardy had been walking along the forward deck with Murdoch when he said, *"I believe she is gone, Hardy,"* and that was when the steward first realized that ***TITANIC*** was going to founder.

When Captain Smith requested that Wilde replace Murdoch as ***TITANIC***'s Chief Officer for the maiden voyage, it had nothing to do with Smith's lack of confidence in Murdoch. Smith knew that Lightoller would get the feel of ***TITANIC*** in the round trip maiden voyage, and then Blair could return to gain experience in the next one, as the weather progressively improved and ice moved farther south. The lovely superships were clumsy, with their center turbines and small rudder areas. Smith, Wilde and Murdoch knew it. Lightoller and Blair could learn it, but Smith wisely did not want to have to teach them under the conditions that prevailed on ***TITANIC***'s maiden voyage.

In a perfect example of not seeing ***TITANIC*** from her own era, ***TITANIC*** legend makes much fuss over the fact that three wireless ice warnings may never have reached ***TITANIC***'s bridge. Captain Smith and his watch officers did not need wireless warnings to tell them they were in the ice wne. They had been there before, many times, at every season of the year. They had survived without wireless for decades at sea, as had every other senior officer on the Western Ocean in that era. Ice reports had been wirelessed to ***TITANIC*** at Queenstown, and no doubt inbound shipmasters had warned Smith at Southampton, too.

Smith had first gone to sea as an apprentice in the clipper ***SENATOR WEBER***, in 1869. By 1876 he was an officer in the square rigger ***LIZZIE FENNEL***. Four years later he was Fourth Officer in White Star's old ***CELTIC***. In 1884 Smith was Third Officer in the ***COPTIC***, calling at San Francisco, his foot now firmly on the ladder to command. In 1887 Smith went into the old ***REPUBLIC***, and from there to the old ***BALTIC***. His first command was White Star's freighter ***CUFIC***. He then went to ***RUNIC***, on the Australian run. His progress was rapid and he successively commanded the old ***ADRIATIC***, ***CELTIC***, ***BRITANNIC***, and ***COPTIC*** in the Pacific trade. From there he went to the Atlantic, and the liners ***GERMANIC***, ***MAJESTIC***, the new ***BALTIC***, the new ***ADRIATIC***, then ***OLYMPIC*** and ***TITANIC***. He sailed many times with Murdoch, Lightoller and Wilde. His rise in rank was commensurate with the quiet professionalism and safety of his commands. When Smith brought the ***ADRIATIC*** into New York on her maiden voyage in 1907 he told reporters, *"When anyone asks me how I can best describe my experiences of nearly forty years at sea I merely say 'uneventful' of course, there have been winter gales and storms, and fog and the like, but in all my experience I have never been in an accident of any sort worth speaking about. I have seen but one vessel in distress in all my years at sea, a brig, the crew of which was taken off in a small boat in charge of my Third Officer I never saw a wreck and have never been wrecked nor was I ever in any predicament that threatened to end in disaster of any sort."*

Smith added, *"The love of the ocean, that took me to sea as a boy, has never left me. In a way, a certain amount of wonder never leaves me, especially as I observe from the bridge a vessel plunging up and down in the trough of the seas, fighting her way through and over great waves. A man never outgrows that."* One must wonder how Smith would have fared had he lived to retire, with his strong emotional attachment to the sea.

It was during this interview that Smith made the oft-quoted statement that he was sure of shipbuilding being *"such a perfect art nowadays that absolute disaster involving the passengers on a great modern liner is quite unthinkable."* No matter what happened, he concluded, there would be time before the ship sank for every person on board to be saved. Whether this was an example of company public relations or really Smith's belief, he tempted Fate even further. *"I will say that I cannot imagine any condition which could cause a ship to founder. I cannot conceive of any vital disaster happening to this vessel. Modern shipbuilding has gone beyond that."*

It is impossible to know whether Smith believed everything he said in a public interview. The masters of Atlantic liners were necessarily company men, diplomats, public relations experts, who knew what they were supposed to say to reporters. The safety image was paramount in booking ships to capacity.

The first accident in which Captain Smith was involved is the one now used as an example of his poor seamanship. It is understandable that the White Star Line based its official version of the ***TITANIC*** accident on the requirements of the Harter Act, but it is incredible that writers are still dragging the ***OLYMPIC-HMS HAWKE*** collision of 1911 into the limelight to condemn Smith's abilities more than eighty years after the fact. In 1911 the shipping world knew perfectly well what had happened in the Solent, and many mariners were openly incredulous when ***OLYMPIC*** was declared to be at fault, yet her officers were exonerated because she was *"under compulsory pilotage"* at the time, an ambiguous verdict at best.

On 20 September, 1911, ***OLYMPIC*** departed Southampton on her fifth voyage, with Captain Smith commanding, Henry Wilde as Chief Officer and William Murdoch as First Officer. Trinity House Pilot George Bowyer shared the bridge with Captain Smith as ***OLYMPIC*** proceeded down Southampton Water. She had just rounded Calshot Spit at the harbor speed of 19 knots, and was slowing to negotiate the tight turn "round Bramble Bank," when her officers spotted a warship coming up the Solent, about three and a half to four miles away. The warship turned out to be ***HMS HAWKE,*** a cruiser of 7,350 tons, built in 1891.

When first sighted by the liner's officers, ***HAWKE*** was off ***OLYMPIC***'s starboard bow, which made ***HAWKE*** the privileged vessel, while ***OLYMPIC*** was the burdened ship, obligated to give way to the cruiser. *International and Inland Rules of the Road Article 19* stated, *"When two steam vessels are crossing, so as to involve risk of collision, the vessel which has the other on her own starboard side shall keep out of the way of the other."*

In this case, however, there were mitigating circumstances. Calshot is a shingle spit which

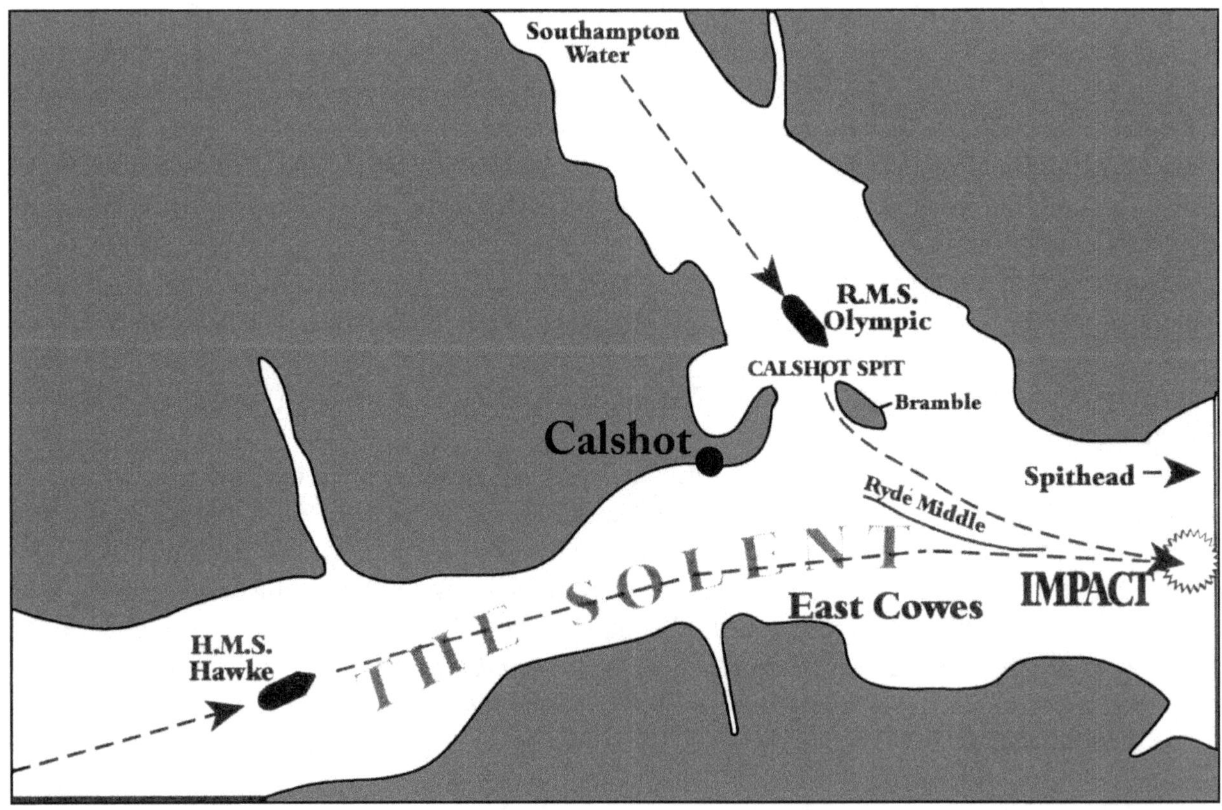

projects about half a mile into Southampton Water. Approaching Calshot ***OLYMPIC*** was headed directly for the East Knoll, which is the shallowest part of the Bramble Bank, where sand is exposed during very low tides. From here ***OLYMPIC*** had to make about a 75 degree turn to bring her into the Western Approach Channel. About a mile and a quarter farther she had to make another alteration in her course, to round the West Brambles Light Buoy. A vessel of ***OLYMPIC***'s size cannot turn tightly around a buoy, like a racing boat might. ***OLYMPIC*** would be well south of the South Brambles Buoy before she could be steadied on her new course toward the West Ryde Middle Buoy. The men on ***OLYMPIC***'s bridge were well aware of the tricky maneuvering necessary to get her to the relatively wide open spaces of the English Channel, and their attention had to be devoted to safely conning the liner. ***HAWKE***'s commander ought to have known this. Had ***OLYMPIC*** been slowed to give way to the warship, she would have lost what little maneuverability she had at the time when she needed it most. She would then have been in great danger of running aground. In addition to this the liner had a schedule to keep and ***HAWKE***'s commander should have known this, too.

When ***HAWKE*** was sighted, ***OLYMPIC*** signaled properly to the cruiser, her mighty siren giving two piercing blasts, each of about one second's duration, which announced, *"I am directing my course to port."* ***OLYMPIC*** continued her turn, taking up her new track, ahead of ***HAWKE***, traveling in the same direction. Still ***HAWKE*** continued on at her speed of 19 knots, rapidly closing with the liner because ***OLYMPIC*** had lost ground while making her turn. Had ***OLYMPIC*** been in this position relative to the warship when ***HAWKE*** was first sighted, ***OLYMPIC*** would have been the overtaken, or privileged vessel, while ***HAWKE*** would have been the burdened ship.

Article 24 of the *International and Inland Rules of the Road* stated: *"Notwithstanding anything contained in these rules every vessel, overtaking any other, shall keep out of the way of the overtaken vessel." Article 25* spelled out the rules in a narrow channel: *"In narrow channels every steam vessel shall,* ***when it is safe and practicable****, keep to that side of the fairway or mid-channel which lies on the starboard side of such vessel."*

But there was another *Rule, Article 27*, the *General Prudential Rule*, which should have come into play at this point, even for a Royal Navy commander. *"In obeying and construing these rules due regard shall be had to all dangers of navigation and collision,* ***and to any special circumstances which may render a departure from the above rules necessary in order to avoid immediate danger.****"*

By every *Rule* in the book, as well as every moral code and common sense, ***HAWKE***'s commander was obligated to avoid coming near ***OLYMPIC***, and that should have been easy. All he had to do was slacken speed, briefly, while ***OLYMPIC*** regained hers. Yet ***HAWKE*** continued her onward rush. Both ships were now headed toward Spithead, a Royal Navy anchorage. It is difficult to believe that ***HAWKE***'s commander knew this channel less well than Smith or Bowyer. Incredibly, ***HAWKE*** came up close on ***OLYMPIC***'s starboard quarter.

On 17 November (note that date) Murdoch's testimony at the Admiralty Inquiry was terse. With question #1070, page 99, Mr. F. Laing, Counsel for the White Star Line, affirmed that Murdoch was the First Officer of the ***OLYMPIC***.

Laing then asked Murdoch if he held an Extra Master's Certificate, to which Will replied simply, *"Yes."* Next Laing asked Murdoch if he was a Lieutenant in the Royal Naval Reserve. Again Murdoch replied, *"Yes."*

When Laing asked if Murdoch's station was on the poop. Will corrected him with *"On the after end of the ship."* In reply to Laing's next question, Murdoch affirmed that he had some men under his control at that station.

Then Laing asked what, if anything, had drawn Murdoch's attention to the ***HAWKE.*** Murdoch replied that he had heard the two short blasts on ***OLYMPIC***'s steam whistle, and naturally looked to see who the signal was for. It was then that he saw the cruiser coming along off ***OLYMPIC***'s starboard bow.

Next Laing asked Murdoch to give ***HAWKE***'s bearing at that time, and Will replied that ***OLYMPIC*** was swinging, head to port on the starboard helm when he first saw the cruiser, so it was difficult to give a bearing from his ship.

In answer to Laing's next question, Murdoch replied that ***HAWKE*** was then about three miles away from ***OLYMPIC***, but he had taken no particular notice of the warship at that time.

He had no reason to. First, he was not on the bridge. But more important, Murdoch and the other White Star officers were quite used to seeing warships in the channel. Whether they expected ***HAWKE***'s commander to do the gentlemanly thing and stay clear of ***OLYMPIC*** or not, there was nothing that ***OLYMPIC***'s officers or Pilot Bowyer could do. The situation was entirely under the control of ***HAWKE***'s commander at this point.

OLYMPIC rounded the Bramble Buoy under starboard helm, and took up her proper course, down the middle channel, south of the Ryde Middle. ***HAWKE*** closed rapidly, and Murdoch next noticed her about three points on the liner's starboard quarter, and only a quarter of a mile away. Murdoch proceeded to the aft end of the boat deck, in performance of his regular duties.

Laing next asked Murdoch if anything attracted his attention while he was on the boat deck. Murdoch replied that he now saw the cruiser coming up almost parallel to ***OLYMPIC***'s course, on the starboard side. ***HAWKE*** had never slackened speed. Murdoch judged the warship's distance from ***OLYMPIC*** now as only about 1000 feet, dangerously close to the liner. Still it remained for ***HAWKE***'s commander to avoid collision, for ***OLYMPIC*** was in no position to do so.

Laing asked what was now done on the part of the liner.

"Our ensign was dipped," was Murdoch's surprising reply.

The inference here is that the maneuver was all jolly good fun, a "boys will be boys" game with the smaller cruiser dashing smartly past the big liner. It was later rumored that cameras were seen in the hands of several officers on the bridge of His Majesty's Ship, but it was never an issue at the Inquiry. Dipping the ensign is the usual salute at sea, which merchant ships give to men-of-war. The ensign is hauled down in plenty of time so that the intention to dip can be observed by the vessel being saluted, and reply made while the ships are nearly abreast. Murdoch, by the time of impact, had gone to the port side of the boat deck, and did not see the collision.

Murdoch acquired a new interrogator, Mr. Bateson, who suggested in his first question that Will apparently knew very little about the collision.

Murdoch responded tersely, saying that he had already told all he knew about it.

Bateson continued to question the liner's First Officer, making the same mistake as Laing by asking what Murdoch had been doing *"aft on the poop."*

"The after end of the ship," Murdoch corrected again. One can imagine that by this time it must have been said through clenched teeth. Bateson asked Murdoch about his duties, and Will named them. Murdoch was then obliged to go through the whole interrogation again, answering the same as he had answered Laing.

But Bateson asked one more important question. He asked if Murdoch had seen ***HAWKE*** three points off the starboard quarter and only 1000 feet away *shortly* before the collision. Murdoch's reply was astonishing. He estimated that it was about *five to six minutes* from the time when he had first seen ***HAWKE*** only 1000 feet from ***OLYMPIC***'s starboard quarter, to the time of impact.

Five or six minutes is an adequate length of time for any vessel, particularly one as small and maneuverable as the cruiser, to alter her course, or slacken her speed. Still ***HAWKE*** ran on, very close to the liner. Murdoch continued his testimony. ***HAWKE***'s midships had been almost opposite his station right aft, or just abaft ***OLYMPIC***'s fourth funnel. When ***OLYMPIC*** dipped her ensign, Murdoch's view of ***HAWKE*** was shut out by the deckhouse. When he saw the cruiser again, it was after the impact. ***HAWKE*** struck ***OLYMPIC*** on the starboard side, at a point about 80 feet forward of the liner's stern.

This testimony makes it obvious that the relatively tiny ***HAWKE*** was deliberately running in much too close to the huge liner. It was no doubt a common sight to the men on ***OLYMPIC***'s bridge, to see smaller vessels coming close enough for good photographs; she was, after all, unique, the largest ship in the world. In any case, it was entirely up to ***HAWKE***'s commander to keep far enough away to avoid collision.

Finally Bateson asked for Murdoch's opinion... if ***HAWKE***, just about 1000 feet from ***OLYMPIC***, had starboarded her helm, would she have struck the liner?

Murdoch's enigmatic reply was that it was "questionable."

The verdict was questionable, too. All evidence indicated that the cruiser was at fault, yet ***OLYMPIC*** was named the culprit, with the buck passed to Pilot Bowyer. When a ship is under pilotage, whether compulsory or not, her master does not abdicate command. (Excepting in the Panama Canal, and as of 1990 when entering all ports of the State of Florida, U.S.A.) The master remains fully in control of the vessel, with the obligation to intercede if it appears that the pilot might be putting the ship in danger. Yet the Admiralty Inquiry found ***OLYMPIC*** at fault, then absolved the liner of blame because she was under compulsory pilotage at the time! Neither Pilot Bowyer nor Captain Smith had their certificates suspended, and less than a year later confidence in the two men was such that they took the new liner ***TITANIC***, a replica of ***OLYMPIC***, down the same channel, hardly a suggestion that either had been at fault in the collision.

"Suction" then was named as the real culprit, the cause of the accident. The liner's greater displacement, it was said, had created a tremendous suction which had drawn the smaller vessel into her.

"Suction" was a loosely used term which in this case meant that the turn of ***OLYMPIC***'s screws had created a force which was at its most powerful and dangerous abreast the quarter, exactly where ***HAWKE*** struck, where the water has the least apparent motion, and appears to be the least harmful. Yet such a thing could not have happened if ***HAWKE***'s commander had stayed at a prudent distance from ***OLYMPIC***. The effects of "suction" were known in 1911, as evidenced by seamanship manuals of the day.

Naval architects declared that interaction between the two vessels would have commenced when ***HAWKE*** was about two cables distant from ***OLYMPIC***, a cable being a measurement of 600 feet. ***OLYMPIC***'s officers contended that the ships were about one and a half cables apart, while ***HAWKE***'s officers estimated the distance as only three-quarters of a cable. At any rate, ***HAWKE*** should have been carrying a large amount of starboard rudder to maintain a course parallel to ***OLYMPIC***. She was carrying only 5 degrees, much too little, until a frantic last moment helm order gave her 15 degrees, at which point it was said that the rudder jammed.

The inquiry was obviously a whitewash. But why? The answer lies in at least three important factors, one of which was the last name of ***HAWKE***'s commander. *Blunt.*

From the end of the Plantagenet dynasty with the death of Richard III at Bosworth Field in 1485, Britain had been ruled by about 200 great families, who intermarried, and therefore were all pretty much related to each other. By the turn-of-the-19th into the 20th century, this ruling class was being challenged by a new "working class," created by the industrial revolution and led by men like union leader Keir Hardie. The laws had been changed to allow such poor men to enter Parliament with pay and for the first time the lower classes had a voice in government. Hitherto Britain had been entirely governed by its aristocracy and landed gentry, who were rich enough to serve in Government offices without pay. To their credit many did have some sense of responsibility toward the lower classes, although it never occurred to most of them that all human beings had the same needs, and ought to have equal opportunities. Toward the end of Queen Victoria's long reign, a group of avant-garde, intellectual aristocrats who called themselves the *"Souls"* had a firm grip on England's Government. They tended to have large families. Titles, along with responsibilities, fell from eldest son to eldest son. Younger sons gravitated toward the elite regiments of the British Army, and to the Royal Navy, in itself Britain's aristocratic "senior service." Officers' commissions were automatic. The Souls' children naturally grew up trying to outdo their parents, and they became known as the *"Coterie."* By 1911 the Souls had presented England with such notable statesmen as Herbert Henry Asquith, Arthur Balfour, George Curzon, William Grenfell and George Wyndham, to name only a few. The Coterie contributed Raymond Asquith, son of H. H. by his first wife Helen Melland. Raymond would play a great part in the ***TITANIC*** inquiry, and would be killed in 1916 at the Battle of the Somme. The Souls were aging, but their influence on British Government would not wane until after the First World War, which killed so many of Britain's young male aristocrats, including most of those belonging to the Coterie.

One highly influential Soul was Wilfred Scawen Blunt. Married to Lady Anne King-Noel, the granddaughter of poet Lord George Byron, Blunt was equally known for his passionate *affaires de coeur* and his fiery liberalism. He was anti-imperialist at a time when the British Empire was at its zenith. He had been imprisoned for demonstrating in support of Home Rule for Ireland, and he had been defeated in his only attempt to run for Parliament. Having spent much time in Egypt, where he maintained a home. Blunt had become a champion of Islam, and used his influence as best he could to ease British restrictions in Egypt, while he urged English withdrawal and independence for that country on the Nile. Blunt lived comfortably on his estates' income, and was part of the vast network of luncheon and dinner parties, hunts and weekend socializing, where many of Britain's policies were decided. Frequent guests at the Blunt homes were Winston Churchill and his wife, "Clemmie." Churchill became First Lord of the Admiralty on 25 October, 1911, *before* the ***OLYMPIC-HAWKE*** verdict was handed down.

No way would any kinsman of Wilfred Blunt, no matter how distant, be charged with anything that might be detrimental to his career. A word to Winston at dinner, another to Prime Minister Asquith (married now to Soul Margot Tennant, an old friend of Blunt's), and the matter would have been discreetly taken care of. After all, no real harm had been done, no casualties, only some inconvenience to the liner's passengers, many of whom were rich Americans, and Blunt made clear his attitude toward them in his diary's entry for 16 April, 1912, when he commented on the ***TITANIC*** disaster: *"One thing is consoling in these great disasters, the proof given that Nature is not quite yet the slave of Man, but is able to rise even now in her wrath and destroy him. Also if any large number of human beings could be better spared than another it would be just these American millionaires with their wealth and insolence."*

OLYMPIC was officially charged with the accident. Her officers were all Royal Navy Reservists who dared not protest.

The second aspect was simply that Britain liked her dashing, aristocratic naval officers, who had a certain audacious style reminiscent of those old seadogs Drake, Hawkins, Frobisher, Nelson and others who had helped to fashion, and keep, the Empire. Young male aristocrats vied with each other to prove their bravery, their derring-do. ***HAWKE***'s commander no doubt was emulating the style of Lord Charles Beresford, who had harassed the Russian Second Pacific Squadron on its way to destruction at Tsushima by chasing the ponderous, outdated warships all the way to Gibraltar after the unfortunate Dogger Bank Incident when the paranoid Russian gunners had fired on British fishing vessels, believing them to be Japanese torpedo boats. In a splendid example of naval maneuvering Beresford had his ships dart around the overloaded and slow-moving Russian vessels, cutting so close across their bows that collisions were avoided only by such superb seamanship that the Russian Admiral Rozhestvensky remarked with tears of envy in his eyes, *"Those are real seamen."* Apparently the Admiral was too modest to realize what superb seamanship was taking his pathetic, rag-tag fleet 18,000 miles from the Baltic Sea to attempt the relief of Vladivostok on Russia's Pacific coast.

Still a third, and very important consideration, was the attitude of Royal Navy officers toward men in the mercantile marine. Wardroom toasts were often drunk to the derision of merchant officers, who were, after all, only commoners. It was the usual practice to expect merchant vessels to give way to RN ships, regardless of the *Rules of the Road.* Even today naval vessels from almost every nation are known to run in too close for the comfort of merchant ships' watch officers. In fact, merchant ships give warships a wide berth whenever possible.

It was a difficult decision to make. Britain's premier liner, or a vessel of her prestigious senior service, either at fault lost face for the country that ruled the seas. Neither dared be a loser, but unfortunately legend without regard to facts made Captain Smith the scapegoat, a blotch which in all fairness deserves to be removed from his reputation. The fact that Smith commanded ***OLYMPIC***'s new sister ship less than a year after the ***HAWKE*** collision is tacit admission that he was not at fault, and White Star Line officials knew it.

In spite of anything said publicly to the contrary, there were some matters in which Captain Smith did have to defer to Ismay when the Managing Director was aboard. Smith knew what was expected of him in every maiden voyage, when the public eye was necessarily upon him and his ship. But to suggest, as legend does, that Captain Smith *took it upon himself* to make a record passage is absurd. Two fine seamen have thus fallen victim to the terms of the Harter Act of 1893. It is time to erase that stigma from their records.

Chapter Four

The Tracks

The first witness called before the United States Senate subcommittee investigating the wreck of the ***TITANIC*** was White Star's Managing Director, Joseph Bruce Ismay.

Suave, sophisticated, handsome in the studied, urbane style of the era, Ismay was tall enough to intimidate, commanding enough to hold the U. S. senators at bay. Forty nine years old, he had inherited the White Star Line from his father, Thomas Henry Ismay, who had in 1867 bought the White Star Line of sailing packets which ran out of Liverpool to the west coast of South America, and to Australia. In 1864 the elder Ismay had become a director of the National Steam Navigation Company Limited, which traded between Liverpool and New York. Soon after this Ismay met Gustavus C. Schwabe, uncle of that Gustav Wilhelm Wolff who had become a junior partner in the shipbuilding firm of Harland & Wolff. Schwabe helped Ismay raise the capital to start a new line of steamers, with the provision that all of the ships would be built and repaired by Harland & Wolff. The new company was officially named the Oceanic Steam Navigation Company Limited, but popularly known as the White Star Line, after its house flag which consisted of a five-pointed white star centered on a red burgee. The line quickly gave the established Cunard plenty of competition by running the fastest and most luxurious steamers on the North Atlantic. Bruce Ismay thus grew up in the shipping business, and was ready to take over the line when his father died on 23 November, 1899.

When J. Bruce Ismay had arrived in New York aboard ***CARPATHIA*** he had been vilified by the press, and spat upon by strangers in the streets because he had survived ***TITANIC***'s foundering when women and children had died. Ismay insisted, and his officers dutifully supported him, that he had entered the last boat to leave the ship when no women were present on the boat deck and there was space available in the boat. Had Ismay not survived, the direction of the inquiries might have taken a different turn. It is therefore entirely possible and in fact quite probable that Ismay did not enter that lifeboat because he was a coward, as everyone in his time supposed, but because he knew that he was the one man who could save the White Star Line from the financial devastation that was sure to follow the loss of its newest superliner. Rumors had been flying about Ismay's arrogant behavior aboard ***CARPATHIA*** and about the coded messages wirelessed to and from White Star's New York office under Ismay's cable address, "Yamsi." In fact coded messages were the normal procedure under such circumstances, and every shipping line had its own code. While to this day ***CARPATHIA***'s messages pertaining to Ismay have never been decoded, they apparently used a method quite common for the time. Foreign words were substituted for the English words, and were used in a pre-arranged sequence from special dictionaries carried on board.

Ismay had not been "officially designated" to make ***TITANIC***'s maiden voyage, he declared in response to one of Senator Smith's first questions, thus at once establishing his position as "merely a passenger" to satisfy terms of the Harter Act. He was not privy to the ship's navigation at all, and in fact knew nothing about navigation in general, Ismay insisted repeatedly. Ismay did admit to consulting with Captain Smith and Chief Engineer Bell after ***TITANIC***'s impact with ice, but not before. According to Ismay, Chief Bell had told him that he hoped the pumps would keep her afloat, although both Bell and Captain Smith knew the ship was seriously damaged. Later, at the Board of Trade inquiry, there was much discussion over Ismay's choice of words to describe his conversation with Chief Bell. ***TITANIC***'s Chief Engineer had said either that he "hoped' or he "thought" the pumps would keep her afloat. Ismay could not recall exactly which word was used, but the distinction was obviously important.

A rumor had started in Queenstown among the First Class passengers, spreading naturally to Second and Third Classes, that Ismay had already arranged with Chief Bell to drive ***TITANIC*** at her top speed to reach New York early, arriving on Tuesday, 16 April, rather than at the scheduled Wednesday arrival time. Part of Ismay's speech concerned the fact that he made a point of telling the subcommittee that there was no *"attempt to arrive in New York at the lightship before five o'clock Wednesday morning."* Ismay apparently assumed that none of the senators had read the shipping pages in any of the New York newspapers, where inbound liners routinely wirelessed their estimated times of arrival. ***TITANIC***'s message to Marconi's Sandy Hook wireless station dated 14 April had read *"**TITANIC**, Southampton to New York, 1,284 miles E. at 2:15 AM .; due 16th 4PM. White Star Line."*

In reply to Senator Smith's question, *"Had you ever been on this so-called northern route before?"* Ismay replied, *"We were on the southern route, sir."*

"On this Newfoundland route?" Smith asked.

"We were on the long southern route, not the northern route," Ismay repeated.

"You were not on the extreme northern route?" Smith persisted.

"We were on the extreme southern route for the westbound ships." Once more Ismay said it, and in so doing he set the course for White Star's defense, and the legend of ***TITANIC***'s having been "right on" the Southern Track.

Legend also insists that because ***TITANIC*** struck ice *"right on the Southern Track,"* then she had to have been on the *Track* all of the way across the ocean. Right?

Wrong.

At least part of the reluctance to believe otherwise seems to come from a misconception about what the *"steamer tracks"* were, and are. Merely naming them *"tracks"* appears to generate as much confusion today as it did in 1912. These are not something like railroad tracks across the North Atlantic, something a ship locked on to at her port of origin and could not leave until she arrived at her destination, an idea apparently fostered by Senator Smith's unfortunate reference to them as being *"like a double-track railroad."* To understand the tracks it is necessary to learn how they originated, plus some basic principles of navigation.

The *ARCTIC-VESTA* Collision

In 1836 American Edward Knight Collins had founded the Dramatic Line of sailing packets which operated between New York and Liverpool. When the United States Postmaster-General advertised in 1845 to offer a mail contract between Europe and America, Collins proposed a fortnightly steamer service between the same two ports during eight months of the year, with a monthly service for the remaining four months. Although Congress rejected the Collins tender in June, 1846, less than a year later it was approved and Collins formed the New York and Liverpool United States' Mail Steamship Company, always known by its popular name, the "Collins Line."

By the middle of the nineteenth century the Collins Line's four wooden-hulled paddlewheel steamers, ***ATLANTIC, PACIFIC, ARCTIC*** and ***BALTIC***, were the fastest, most luxurious vessels in the North Atlantic service. They had introduced such innovative seagoing amenities as steam heat, electric call bells, barber shops and special smoking rooms for male passengers. The ships were immensely popular with the traveling public, who immediately dubbed them *"floating palaces."*

All of the line's vessels were built in the United States, and thus flew the Stars and Stripes of U.S. registry and were manned by American officers. The four ships were designed by George Steers, who would later become famous as the designer of the yacht ***AMERICA***.

The British, who were used to absolute supremacy at sea, found that the popularity of the new American liners encroached sharply upon *their* Western Ocean, and they immediately cried "foul," contending that a subsidy from Congress gave Collins an unfair competitive advantage. The subsidy had been won after lengthy debates, on the grounds that the Collins steamers would be built primarily to be used as warships should the need arise, with their use as passenger and mail carriers strictly secondary. This was especially galling to the British, for up until this time Britain had been the only country with which the Americans had waged war on the high seas.

Nevertheless, many Englishmen gave credit where credit was due. One Royal Navy "Captain McKinnon" voyaged from Liverpool to New York in a Cunarder, then returned in the Collins steamer ***BALTIC***. McKinnon felt compelled to write that the American ship had been far superior not only in speed and luxury, but also in comfort. *"No sea ever came aboard, there was no violent plunging; the steaming of the **BALTIC** was the absolute poetry of motion,"* proclaimed Captain McKinnon. Daringly, the Royal Navy officer went even further, *"The reason why we allow brother Jonathan to beat us on our own element is patent to the world, the British model is far inferior to the American."* The British publication *"Punch"* commented drily on the superior speed of the American ships in a limerick which suggested that British agents would do well to buy the ***BALTIC***, this *"Yankee Doodle Nation,"* just to *"tow the Cunard packets over!"*

At a time when the United States Navy had only recently converted to steam, naval inexperience left doubts as to the actual role a liner might be expected to play in wartime, with ensuing confusion over the proper building specifications. Charles H. Haswell, who had been chief engineer on the ***FULTON***, criticized the Collins vessels, citing the inferior timbers used in hull construction and combined with iron boilers, plus their lack of spars, rigging and armament. Any attempt to utilize them as warships would be "disastrous," Haswell told Congressmen. But the Collins Line alone stood in the way of Cunard's North Atlantic monopoly, and that plus the postal revenue gained from having the fastest steamers afloat swayed Congress in the end to grant the needed subsidies to Collins.

Launched by William H. Brown of New York in January, 1850, ***ARCTIC*** was 285 feet long, with a beam of 46 feet inside her paddle boxes, an overall beam of 75 feet and a gross registered tonnage of 2,856. ***ARCTIC*** and her running mates had straight stems and no bowsprits, an innovative design that was many years ahead of its time. Their hulls, which had extra internal bracing, were said to be the strongest ever made of wood. Built by the Novelty Iron Works of New York City, ***ARCTIC***'s two-cylinder engine had a bore of 96 inches and a stroke of 10 feet. With steam at maximum pressure of 17 pounds, the engine indicated 2,000 horsepower and drove ***ARCTIC*** at better than 13 knots. The Collins quartet challenged for the first time the speed supremacy of the British Cunarders. In September, 1850, ***PACIFIC*** broke the westbound record with a time of 10 days, 4 hours and 45 minutes from Liverpool to New York.

ARCTIC had her trials on 18 October of the same year and departed on her maiden voyage nine days later. Bad weather slowed her homeward passage to over 14 days. ***ATLANTIC*** made the worst trip of all, departing Liverpool on 28 December, 1850, going overdue and causing great anxiety in New York until it was learned that she had arrived at Queenstown under sail on 22 January, after breaking her main shaft 900 miles from Halifax. In 1851 ***BALTIC*** beat the westbound record with a passage of 9 days, 19 hours and 51 minutes. In February, 1852, ***ARCTIC*** made the fastest eastbound passage of 9 days, 17 hours and 4 minutes, at a time of year when adverse weather conditions usually precluded record breaking. Collins skippers were known for driving their ships hard, which placed enormous strain on the wooden hulls and heavy wear on the engines. It was the usual thing for squads of mechanics to meet the ships and repair their engines after each passage. In 1851 Collins carried almost 50% more passengers than Cunard, yet operated at a loss which mandated more financial aid from Congress to keep the line in business.

A great debate raged in the Senate over the subsidy, which amounted to more than $3 million, a huge sum of money for 1852. Collins and his associates secured the support of Senator Seward from New York and Senator Miller from New Jersey, who swayed enough votes to pass the amendment on 28 May while the House passed it on 12 July. A major argument in favor of the subsidy was the need for American ships which could challenge Cunard's North Atlantic monopoly. In 1852 there were many men still living who recalled the War of 1812 and even the Revolution of 1776. Ohio's Senator Wade, however, called the subsidy amendment an act *"to gratify national vanity, by beating John Bull in a boat race across the Atlantic,"* a race which Senator Wade suggested might be better won by the natural skill and enterprise of the American people.

In the fall of 1853 ***ARCTIC*** ran aground on the Burbo Bank in dense fog, but sustained no damage, and continued her voyage to Liverpool. Six months later, on her westbound passage, she struck a submerged object near the Irish coast and had to return to Liverpool for repairs.

At 11 o'clock on the morning of Wednesday, 20 September, 1854, ***ARCTIC*** departed Liverpool, bound for New York. Mrs. Edward Knight Collins, wife of the line's General Manager, was aboard with their daughter and younger son. Accompanying them were Mrs. Collins' brother, James E. Woodruff, and his wife. Also on board were the two daughters of James Brown, the line's President. Traveling with them were Brown's son William and his French-born wife, and their two children. ***ARCTIC***'s manifest listed many other well-known and wealthy men and women, among them the Duc de Grammont, a young French nobleman who had been dispatched to the United States as an attaché to the French embassy at Washington. The ancestors of the twenty-one-year-old Duc had occupied a prominent place in both the political and literary history of France.

Captain James Luce, the forty-eight-year-old master of the ***ARCTIC***, had brought his physically handicapped younger son, eleven-year-old Willie, on the voyage, hoping to raise the boy's spirits. Luce had married a second time after being widowed, and he had an older son by his first wife. ***ARCTIC*** carried a total of 233 passengers, most of whom were Americans, with a crew of 175, including officers.

At noon on Wednesday, one week later, ***ARCTIC*** was in latitude 46 degrees, 45 minutes North, longitude 52 degrees West, steering West by compass. The weather had been unusually good for the entire passage, and all hands were relaxed and looking forward to only three more days at sea, after which they would be safely home with families and friends. The usual fog in this area near Cape Race would later be described as everything from *"occasional patches of mist,"* to *"so thick that one could not see the length of the ship."* At any rate. Captain Luce did not consider it necessary to sound the ***ARCTIC***'s bell or whistle. Luce got a good noon sight and retired to his chartroom to work out the ship's position, while passengers went below for lunch. The sea would later be described as very calm, by everyone except Fourth Officer Mark Graham, who insisted that it was quite rough.

Running at her rated top speed of 13 knots, ***ARCTIC*** entered a patch of fog. Suddenly Luce was startled to hear his watch officer on the bridge cry, *"Hard astarboard!"*

Through the engine room skylight those on deck could hear the jangle of signal bells. Chief Engineer Rogers muttered, *"What is it now?"* then boomed the order, *"Unhook her!"* Like most paddle steamers of her time, ***ARCTIC*** was maneuvered by disconnecting her eccentric rods and then operating her valves with hand levers. A moment later there was a shock so light it was not taken seriously. Straggling out of the saloon to see what the commotion was about, passengers saw a small, iron-hulled, barque-rigged screw steamer with all sails set, sweeping along ***ARCTIC***'s starboard side. Striking the guards at the forward end of the paddle box, the stranger sheered off into the mist, where she lay for a few moments, just barely visible to those aboard the Collins ship. ***ARCTIC*** circled the smaller vessel, then came to a stop.

The stranger's bow was torn off, to about ten feet abaft her stern, and the cargo in her forward hold was clearly visible to those aboard the ***ARCTIC***. *A* babble of voices rose from the stranger's decks, where passengers screamed for boats, yet hindered crewmen from swinging them out. Several men jumped overboard and swam for the ***ARCTIC***, which appeared sturdy and safe.

Captain Luce immediately ordered First Officer Robert Gourley and Second Officer William Baalham to lower the guard boats and pick up the swimmers. Sure that the little propeller would sink quickly. Luce ordered Gourley and Baalham to stand by and rescue her people.

Gourley took six sailors and quickly launched one boat, but Baalham was somewhat slower. Just as the Second Officer was ready to lower away. Captain Luce received ominous news from the engine room. The bilge injectors had been started immediately after the collision, and the big jet condensers of the main engines were now drawing water from the bilges instead of through the usual sea water intakes. The Worthington bilge pumps were working, too, but water was gaining fast. Through openings in the engine room floor plates, a flood of black, oily water could be seen swirling around the engine bearers.

Luce now ordered his Second Officer over the side to assess the extent of damage to ***ARCTIC***'s hull. What Baalham found were three huge holes in the ship's side, two of them below the waterline. Parts of the stem and cutwater of the other ship were wedged into one of the openings, which was

ABOVE: *Stricken in the fog, Captain Luce has realized the fate of his command, the Collins liner* ***ARCTIC***, *and had ordered women and children to the boats after discovering three large holes in the side of the vessel—two below the waterline. The* ***ARCTIC***'s *stem severed the bow of the French liner,* ***VESTA***. *(Artwork by Ryan Katzenbach)*

at least 5 1/2 feet long by 1 1/2 feet wide.

Luce ordered sails put over the side and hauled in close to cover the openings, in what proved a vain attempt to stop the leaks. Next, Carpenter George Bailey was sent over the side to stuff mattresses and pillows into the holes. ***ARCTIC*** was now down by the head, and passengers were mustered on the port quarter deck to raise her bows and cant her to port, with the hope that more of the damage could be brought above the waterline. Passengers and crew worked together, throwing every moveable object overboard to lighten the forward part of the ship. Anchors and anchor chains were jettisoned. These heroic efforts proved futile, as did attempts to plug the leaks through the forward hold.

This exertion had actually occupied only a short space of time, but Gourley's boat and the other steamer had now disappeared in the fog. Luce assumed that the propeller had already sunk, and realizing that ***ARCTIC*** had not long to live, he decided to make a desperate run for Cape Race. The engine room signal clanged again, to *"Full speed ahead."* There was no time to waste looking for Gourley. The First Officer had a seaworthy boat, a capable crew, and he knew the course and distance to Cape Race.

ARCTIC's boilers had two tiers of furnaces, the lower ones being only a few inches above the floor plates. The upper row was four feet above the plates, and was fired from a moveable platform. Chief Engineer Rogers reported that water would reach the lower fires in a few minutes.

Slowly ***ARCTIC*** gathered way in the now dense fog. Without warning a small boat that had escaped from the other ship appeared under ***ARCTIC***'s bow, too close for Luce to avoid it. One man in the boat grabbed a line hanging over ***ARCTIC***'s side and pulled himself to dubious safety as the tiny boat and its occupants were smashed under the liner's 35 ft. paddlewheel. Luce knew it was useless to stop. None of the men could have survived, and ***ARCTIC***'s time was quickly running out. The rescued man proved to be French-Canadian. With ***ARCTIC***'s French Second Cook acting as translator, a few people aboard the Collins liner learned that they had been struck by a three-masted French propeller named ***VESTA*** taking fishermen from the island of St. Pierre to Granville, France. She had about 200 persons aboard.

Chief Rogers reported that the lower fires had been extinguished. ***ARCTIC*** was now so deep in the water that her paddlewheels had lost their efficiency. At the hand pumps passengers worked alongside the crew. About an hour after the collision firemen came up from below, reporting that all fires were out. The mighty paddlewheels slowed, hesitated, stopped.

At this point Captain Luce lost control of his crew. He had ordered all boats ready when the engines stopped, and one boat had been lowered. Passengers and crew alike began jumping into it without any semblance of order. Luce then ordered the boat towed astern, to be brought alongside when order was restored so women and children could get into it safely.

But someone cut the painter, and the boat was free with a mere fraction of the complement it should have carried.

Second Officer Baalham, in command of the starboard guard boat, begged Luce to let Willie come with him. Vowing that the ship's fate would be his. Luce replied, *"I will not allow it until other people are provided for. The boy will have to take his chances with me."* Baalham shoved off. Luce shouted to him to drop astern as firemen began leaping into his boat.

A third boat, lowered with women and children and a few sailors to man it, dropped stern first when a fall was allowed to run free, spewing all of its passengers into the sea, except for one woman who clung to a thwart. Many witnesses would later claim that Mrs. Collins and her children were in this boat. Luce would deny that, saying that he had seen them on deck just before the ship foundered.

Engine room personnel took places in boats which Luce had ordered held for women and children. Passengers crowded around boats, making it impossible for crewmen to work the falls. Chief Engineer Rogers, with several of his assistants, got away in one of the smaller boats. Although ***ARCTIC*** carried a weapons chest, it never seemed to occur to Luce or his officers to use the force that might have maintained discipline.

The spilled boat, still hanging from its forward davit, was finally freed and about fifteen passengers managed to get it away. Only the sixth and last boat was left on board. All seamen were gone. An apprentice engineer, Stewart Holland, continued to fire the ship's signal gun.

Luce checked below and found African-American stewardess Anna Downer alone, working at the pumps with all her strength. Luce wrote later, "I *told her she was to come up, that she was only exhausting herself, that it was as useless for her to attempt to pump out the ship as it would be to attempt to pump out the ocean."* Anna replied, *"Captain, I'm willing to pump as long as I can work my arms."* Again Luce told her that she had better come up with the others. Anna asked him if he would take her into the boat with him, and Luce answered that he was not going to get into a boat, that he would go down with the ship. Arma replied that she would then *"wait a while."*

Only Third Officer Francis Dorian remained with Luce and the ***ARCTIC***. Assisted by passengers, Dorian began to build a makeshift raft, using the fore and main yards, stateroom doors, anything that would float and could be cut free. In order to facilitate this work the last boat was lowered. Intending to use this boat for women and children when the raft was completed. Luce removed its oars and tholepins to keep men from stealing away with it.

Luce and some of the male passengers were holding back the crowd while Dorian and his passenger-crew worked on the raft. Suddenly panic seized all on board. Passengers and some remaining firemen threw themselves into the raft.

To stop the rush, Dorian ordered the boat's painter cut. Using their hands and axes, the men in the boat paddled free of the almost swamped raft. Dorian cried out to Luce, *"For God's sake. Captain, clear the raft so we can work! I won't desert the ship while there's a timber above water!"*

The sea was now even with ***ARCTIC***'s deadlights. Luce could do no more than pass out life preservers to women and children. A few moments after Dorian's impassioned plea, about four and a half hours after the collision, ***ARCTIC*** rolled over until her upper deck rail was level with the water. The sea foamed over a tumbling heap of human beings who still clung to her stern. Many people fell against her pipe as she plunged stem first into her watery grave. Dorian and the men in the boat could do nothing. They managed to pick up two more men, but with the boat overloaded, without oars, they had difficulty avoiding pieces of the wreck, while all around them were the bodies of women floating in life preservers, Anna Downer among them. Dorian secured a floating pumpkin and a cabbage to ward off immediate starvation, and lashed a spar taken from the wreckage to the boat's painter to keep its head into wind and sea. Cramped, drenched in the 45 degree water, half naked, the men drifted around the wreck area through the long night and into the following morning.

At 5 o'clock the next afternoon Dorian sighted a sail, which proved to be the barque ***HURON*** of St. Andrews, New Brunswick, Captain A. Wall, bound for Quebec. With his men safe on board the ***HURON***, Dorian took some of the barque's crew and rescued a man he had spied on what was left of ***ARCTIC***'s makeshift raft. This turned out to be Peter McCabe, a waiter, who had counted 72 men and 4 women, including William Brown and his family, on the raft with him when ***ARCTIC*** sank. By 8 o'clock in the evening of the same day McCabe was the only one alive. By morning there were only two bodies, *"much eaten by fishes,"* beside him.

During the night of the 28th Captain Wall hung out extra lights, fired rockets and kept a horn blowing, with hope of attracting the remainder of the boats. His endeavors were in vain. At 4:20PM on the 29th Wall spoke the ship ***LEBANON***, Captain Story, bound for New York. ***LEBANON*** took eighteen of ***ARCTIC***'s survivors, including the four passengers and Dorian. Once again the Third Officer was lucky, for nine years and seven days earlier, a shipwrecked Dorian had been picked up just 150 miles east of where he was rescued this time.

Soon after ***ARCTIC*** disappeared Second Officer Baalham's boat fell in with an overloaded boat commanded by Purser John Geib. Baalham transferred several men from Geib's boat into his own, leaving 26 in his, 19 in Geib's. Unanimously elected to command the two boats, Baalham brought them safely to Broad Cove, about twelve miles north of Cape Race, after pulling for forty hours with only the run of the sea and an occasional glimpse of the North Star to guide him in the fog. They landed at daybreak, then walked six miles to Renews where Baalham and Geib chartered a small schooner. Getting under way at eleven the same morning, they cruised to the wreck area, searching for survivors until 3 o'clock the following morning, when a strong northeast gale forced them to put into Trepane. Captain Leitch, commander of the Inman Line steamer ***CITY OF PHILADELPHIA***, which had run aground at Cape Race on 9 September without loss of life, also sent two local vessels that he had employed about his own ship. Several other vessels, including the New York, Newfoundland and London Telegraph Company's 200 ton steamer ***VICTORIA***, the brig ***ANN ELIZA***, dispatched by the American Consul, and the Reverend Doctor Fields' yacht ***HAWK***, joined the search, but found nothing. Of ***ARCTIC***'s 86 survivors, all were men and 50 were crew. Three of the six boats were never found, including the first boat sent away commanded by First Officer Gourley, and the boat stolen by Chief Engineer Rogers and his men.

Baalham's schooner stopped again at Renews, then proceeded to St. John's, arriving there on Tuesday morning. Here these ***ARCTIC*** survivors learned for the first time that they had collided with the French steamer ***VESTA***, which now lay at St. John's being repaired. The liner's survivors then went to Halifax, where they boarded the Cunarder ***EUROPA*** for New York. ***EUROPA*** had herself been in collision with the American steamer ***CHARLES BARTLETT*** in 1849. ***EUROPA*** would again be involved in a collision, off Cape Race in 1858, with another Cunarder, ***ARABIA***, but without fatalities in either incident.

VESTA had made St. John's safely on 30 September. When Captain Duchesne had realized that ***VESTA***'s collision bulkhead was holding, he had cut down and jettisoned the foremast, pitched freight from the forward hold overboard, and shored up the bulkhead while he made for St. John's at reduced speed. Two of ***VESTA***'s boats had been launched before Duchesne had been able to restore order. The first boat was the one smashed under ***ARCTIC***'s paddlewheel, and the second boat, taken forcibly by two crewmen and several passengers, was never seen again. One ***VESTA*** crewman had been killed in the collision. Captain Duchesne had assumed that ***ARCTIC*** was sound when he saw her circling his ship after the collision. He was sure of it when he saw the liner steam away in a westerly direction, which put ***VESTA*** upwind of ***ARCTIC***, so that those aboard the French ship were out of hearing range of the Collins liner's signal cannon. Duchesne had estimated that ***VESTA*** could live at least four days, possibly longer, enough to reach Halifax, or even Boston. Had he realized ***ARCTIC***'s true condition, Duchesne said later, he could have saved everyone aboard her.

On 13 October the barque ***CAMBRIA***, Captain John Russell, out of Glasgow for Montreal, brought nine of ***ARCTIC***'s survivors into Quebec, Captain Luce among them. Captain Russell was no stranger to shipwreck, having been rescued from a former command, the barque ***JESSIE STEVENS***, by Captain Nye, master of the Collins liner ***PACIFIC***.

Luce had remained true to his word and gone down with his ship. In his own words, *"As I went down after the sinking of the vessel, I was carried a great distance, with my son Willie in* my *arms. I opened my eyes, to see if I could discover light through the water. It was sometime before I could do so, and then it seemed a very long time before I reached the surface. When I did so, I could only have held out a few moments. I saw Willie near me, with a life preserver on him, and was just struggling to reach him when a piece of the paddlebox came up with great force and fell upon him, striking him on the head.*

"I struggled to get away, and on looking around, I saw that the box was sliding upon the water. A short distance back, poor little Willie was lying dead. During my struggle I had cut my head badly, which caused it to bleed very profusely, and I was compelled for sometime afterwards to wash it frequently, to keep the blood from blinding my eyes. Mr. Allen and I got upon the paddlebox at about the same time. By some it is supposed, from the newspaper accounts, that the piece we were on was the entire paddlebox. This is not so; it was only a part of it, about twelve feet square and we stood in the concave."

Luce contradicted statements made by passengers and crewmen who claimed to have seen Mrs. Collins and her children in the boat that dumped its passengers into the sea to drown. Third Officer Dorian confirmed Luce's statement, claiming that he had seen the Collins family still aboard the ***ARCTIC*** just three minutes before she sank. Later, however, Dorian told E. K. Collins that he had seen Captain Luce personally place the Collins family into the first boat to leave the ship. It was well provisioned, said Dorian, and commanded by First Officer Gourley. It would have been the logical thing for Luce to do, to put his employer's family into the first boat, to see to their safety first. However, other accounts mention that Luce had actually sent Gourley to rescue ***VESTA***'s passengers, before he knew that ***ARCTIC***'s wound was mortal. Luce would hardly have placed the Collins family in a lifeboat so quickly, before damage had been assessed. This is something that is frequently seen in disaster psychology. Survivors, who may not be able to remember much of this period under dire stress, but who want to comfort families of those lost are quick to make it seem that victims met their deaths calmly, and that everything humanly possible had been done for them.

In this case there was something else to cover up, the faulty lowering of the first boat, when Luce had lost control of passengers and crew alike. Reporters were already speculating that Collins' intense grief had turned him into a "maniac." Obviously it would be better to leave him with a mental picture of his family waiting calmly, patiently resigned to their final moments. Luce did reveal that he had seen the Duc de Grammont make a desperate last minute leap for the bow of Dorian's boat, but the young Frenchman was driven away from it and drowned.

Nineteen days after the wreck, on the morning of 16 October, Captain Luce left Montreal for New York City. When his train reached Troy, New York, 5,000 people were waiting to greet the hero of the ***ARCTIC***. The Hudson River Railroad set apart a private car for Luce and his friends. At each station Luce was greeted with cheers, and hundreds of people insisted upon shaking his hand.

The wreck of the ***ARCTIC*** was, in her day, just as important as ***TITANIC***'s wreck in her time. Each ship was the epitome of transatlantic luxury. Each carried an impressive manifest of elite passengers. When each sank American cities were paralyzed with mourning, and eulogies rang from every pulpit. The number of persons lost in each was great in comparison to the population of the time. And each made a unique contribution to the future safety of seagoing passengers and crew.

In the ***ARCTIC-VESTA*** collision, as in every shipwreck including ***TITANIC***, we see exactly the same clichés of human behavior, not only among those who were actually in the wreck, but among those at home who confidently proclaimed what they would have done in the same situation, while they remained safe and comfortable by their own firesides. As always, there were the heroes and heroines, the villains and the cowards, those who fought valiantly to live, and those who resigned themselves to death without a struggle. There are always those whose stories contradict each other, leaving mysteries forever. There are always miraculous survivals. And always the greatest hero is the senior surviving officer who has not deserted his post, who has gone down with his ship in the exultant tradition of the sea. In the ***ARCTIC*** it was the Master himself who cheated death. In ***TITANIC*** it would be her Second Officer. The adulation would be the same.

With the ***ARCTIC*** disaster came tales of premonitions, just as these precognitive fears would be dredged up as evidence that something about ***TITANIC***'s demise was supernatural, that some people had psychic warning, and thus escaped.

George C. Smith, of the firm of Leupp & Company, perished in the ***ARCTIC***. His son died on 3 October, six days after the wreck, but several days before it became generally known. Before young Smith died he told relatives that he had seen his father, and he was dead. When it was suggested to him that it was merely a dream, young Smith replied emphatically that it was not, and that they would know the truth of it soon.

Publisher Mahlan Day had reluctantly consented to the sea voyage to take his English wife home to visit her family. *"He had voiced many apprehensions and fears lest he should never return,"* said the *Daily Times.* Perhaps this was not a true premonition; Mr. Day might simply have been apprehensive because of the frequency of shipwrecks he saw reported in the newspapers.

It was rumored that three or four days before news of the wreck reached New York, a man came into Mr. Collins' office in a state of great excitement, saying that the ***ARCTIC*** was wrecked and there were only thirty passengers saved. His brother, said the unnamed man, was on board, and was lost.

Another unnamed gentleman in America had written to his wife and daughter in England, begging them not to travel in the ***ARCTIC*** because he was sure that harm would befall that ship. The ladies, however, had several friends who were sailing in the Collins ship, and so embarked in ***ARCTIC*** despite the warning. The gentleman's wife, it was said, was so distraught about disobeying her husband that she was apprehensive for the whole voyage. Of course all of the women were lost. Reports of psychic warnings come after every disaster, not only shipwrecks.

And always there are suggestions from armchair, and sometimes from real, mariners who would have handled it better, who knew how to prevent similar catastrophes in the future. Occasionally good ideas come from these shoreside mariners, and sometimes these ideas will be acted upon to the benefit of those who come after.

ARCTIC, said one writer to the *New York Daily Times,* should have backed to Cape Race, thus forcing sea water out of, instead of into, her hull. The Collins Line was culpably negligent in not providing boats enough for all on board, wrote another. Most pointed out the crew's dereliction of duty. They should have stuck to their posts, filling each boat, building rafts, saving all on board. Certainly more passengers would have been saved, probably even some of the frailer sex and the helpless children, had the crew been better disciplined.

"Future ships must utilize the tops of paddleboxes and the wheelhouse as lifeboats which would simply float free when the ship sank," was a suggestion made after ***ARCTIC***'s loss. Similar suggestions were made after ***TITANIC***'s loss, yet never has a ship with such capabilities been designed.

Ships must carry lifeboats capable of saving every soul on board, was the suggestion which had much support, yet as ***TITANIC*** would prove over half a century later, it was never acted upon.

But paddlewheels and wooden hulls were already obsolete when ***ARCTIC*** sank. The British were building iron hulls, with watertight compartments that were impossible to install in wooden ships, and the new screw-propellers were rapidly replacing paddlewheels.

"Baalham," said Luce, *"could have maintained order."* Fireman Patrick Tobin told the *Daily Times* that First Officer Gourley could have controlled the crewmen. Why did Captain Luce lack that power?

The answer to that question undoubtedly lies in the origin of the United States itself, and the system of command at sea which exemplified in the American merchant marine that rebellious beginning. The United States of America had been conceived in a defiant demand for individual freedom. In 1854 the "frontier ethic" still prevailed, for there were still frontiers, in the former British colonies as nowhere else in the world. Men were used to taking care of themselves, while their women fought alongside them, their survival almost always entirely dependent upon their own actions. In the American merchant marine, with few exceptions, a ship's captain remained aloof from his men, leaving hard discipline to his "bucko" mate, who ruled with fists and belaying pins cruelly applied to the nearest available flesh. No doubt Baalham and Gourley had come from sail, perhaps they were known to have been among those notoriously brutal mates of the infamous American "hell ships."

Fireman Tobin related, *"When I first attempted to leave the Captain caught me and tore the shirt off my back to prevent my going, exclaiming 'Let the passengers go in the boat.' He also seized a kind of axe and attempted to prevent the firemen reaching the boat; but it was everyone for himself, and no more attention was paid to the Captain than to any other man on board. Life was as sweet to me as life to the others."* Tobin said of Luce, *"He paced the deck as if there was no resort but to sink with his ship. He could easily have saved himself had he sought his own safety."*

Only two years and seven months earlier, on 26 February, 1852, the British troopship ***BIRKENHEAD***, Captain Robert Salmond, had struck submerged rocks off the southern coast of Africa at two o'clock in the morning. ***BIRKENHEAD*** was bound for Algoa Bay, from Cork, with members of the 91st, 74th and 12th Infantry regiments and their families. She had called at Madeira, Sierra Leone, St. Helena and Cape Province. There were 648 souls aboard the 1,400 ton iron-hulled paddlewheel steamer.

At first impact the rocks tore a huge hole in ***BIRKENHEAD***'s bows. She filled rapidly and many soldiers sleeping below were quickly drowned. Pumps were started immediately, while anchors were set out with the hope of stabilizing the vessel so lifeboats could be safely launched. The senior Army officer took command of his men, and established perfect discipline. While the boats were carefully loaded with women and children, regimental horses were brought up from below and pushed overboard, giving them the chance to swim two miles to land. Many of the animals, as disciplined as the men who rode them into battle, did reach safety, but several of the poor beasts were caught by the packs of sharks that always roamed the area. All on board the doomed ship could clearly hear the screams of dying horses, yet soldiers remained at perfect attention while their wives and children were calmly placed in the ship's few boats, all of which were launched successfully and cleared the wreck safely. The sea was soon enough littered with shrieking, drowning men, many of whom were torn apart by the sharks. Force was used to keep those struggling in the water from swamping the boats. ***BIRKENHEAD***'s mainmast remained partially exposed above water and afforded refuge to about fifty men. Almost half of these died of exposure and exhaustion, while the rest were eventually rescued by the schooner ***LIONESS***. Of the 648 on board, 193 survived, including for the first time ever in a shipwreck all of the women and children. The procedure of placing women and children first in lifeboats became known as *"The **BIRKENHEAD** Drill."*

*"Had **ARCTIC**'s crew stood to their posts all on board could have been saved. Those who did not do their proper duty should be fired, never to find work on any passenger vessel again,"* declared one writer to the *Times.* It was said that a seaman who survived ***ARCTIC*** had signed on the ***ATLANTIC*** on Saturday, but just as the steamer was about to depart. Captain West discovered the coward, grabbed him by the collar and marched him ashore, saying he wished no *such* men to go to sea with him!

One editorial insisted that speed meant safety, even in fog. *"High speed on a steamer, while increasing her own safety, does add to the danger of smaller craft with which she comes in contact. But those smaller craft surely could be handled more rapidly, and thus it was their business to keep out of the way."* Obviously, it was this type of thinking that spawned the "ram-you-damn-you" school of seamanship in transatlantic liners. Eventually, the *International Rules of the Road* would give precedence to those smaller, sailing craft which could not be maneuvered so easily as the writer believed.

Firing a cannon at sea, as ***ARCTIC*** had done, was understood to be a distress signal. But there was no fixed signal for a ship in fog to let other vessels know her whereabouts when she could not be seen. One writer suggested coded blasts on the steam whistle, which could give the direction a ship was steering, one of the few really practical suggestions to come out of ***ARCTIC***'s demise.

Watertight bulkheads defining multi-compartmentation must be mandated by law, suggested one writer. On only one ship had this writer ever seen printed emergency instructions for passengers posted in conspicuous places. On a few ships he had seen the posting of crew stations, but all this needed to be law. And there must be definite rules and signals for two ships approaching one another, so they could signal intent and thus avoid each other.

The writer went on, *"The British steamer commanders, who do not succeed as well as the Americans in gaining the admiration and friendship of their passengers, and who, I believe, are themselves no better seamen or navigators, do maintain a better, more exact and orderly discipline in their ships. Their crewmen might work with less spirit and rapidity, but they work more by rule and routine and they are consequently more to be depended upon. Discipline does not mean forced or frightened obedience, as too many young officers suppose. Discipline means **system**.*

In American steamers the commander had little authority, while in all other mercantile marine services he had absolute authority, over everyone on board. But in American ships each department had its own commander, owing allegiance to none above him. The system adopted in American river boats had gone to sea. The Chief Engineer was absolute in his department, for example, and did not obey any commands of the Captain, nor could he be required to perform any other duty. No wonder Luce lost control.

The American merchant marine had long been infamous the world over, from its inception during the Revolution until the First World War when seamen's unions finally gained enough clout to stop the horrors of life afloat in American hell ships. Sailors quickly realized that the hard-fisted, belaying-pin-soup type of discipline they had long suffered under bully captains and bucko mates would never do in front of passengers in the new transatlantic floating palaces. When a man found a berth in one of the elite liners he was suddenly, gloriously free, and he could hardly be blamed for taking advantage of it. Sadly, not one man aboard the ***ARCTIC,*** except for Captain Luce and Third Officer Dorian, had shown any concern for the women and children. Discipline would have to prevail if the Stars and Stripes intended to compete with the Union Jack on its Western Ocean.

For Collins it was too late. On 16 February, 1856, ***PACIFIC*** departed Liverpool, never to be seen again. It was generally believed that she had struck an iceberg and sunk with all hands.

Although Collins chartered the steamer ***ALABAMA*** to search for ***PACIFIC*** as soon as she went overdue, it was in vain. No trace of her was ever found, although it was probable that many of her people did get away in boats, only to die slowly of exhaustion and exposure to the harsh North Atlantic winter.

The loss of ***ARCTIC*** and ***PACIFIC*** so close together destroyed public confidence in the line. Although the remaining ships were fitted with compartments, the company was criticized because the bulkheads defining those compartments were made of wood and not iron, and therefore could not be watertight. While Cunard continued to advance with iron-hulled, screw-propelled ships, Collins built one last wooden-hulled paddlewheel steamer, ***ADRIATIC***, the biggest of all the wooden paddlers. But she was too little, too late, and Collins suspended operations in February, 1858. He lived another twenty years, but never again took part in the shipping business.

The nineteenth century ocean traveler expected shipwreck. Hardly a day passed that the major newspapers missed a wreck notice in their shipping columns. Sailing ships were often lost with all hands, simply sailing away from port never to be seen again. Life at sea was extremely harsh at best. Transatlantic vessels continued to collide with each other, and with icebergs. At the time of the ***ARCTIC-VESTA*** collision it was estimated that each ship on the Western Ocean had to herself 75 square miles of water to ensure her safety. Why, then, did these ships so often find another sharing the same few feet of ocean?

The answer was obvious. Every shipmaster was admonished by his company, or owner, to follow the shortest route, which was naturally also the most economical. With both east and westbound ships on the same shortest route, or "track," collisions were inevitable. That there were not more of them was no doubt due to luck, and the fact that navigation was not precise.

One man had a practical solution to this problem.

Lieutenant Matthew Fontaine Maury has often been called the Father of Oceanography. Born in Virginia on 14 January, 1806, Maury began his career in the infant United States Navy nineteen years later. The developing United States of America had no naval academy yet, and Maury's sea training began aboard a man-o-war.

There was no classroom training, no books had yet been written on the ways of the sea, so Maury taught himself. Always an astute observer of nature, Maury set out to write the textbooks SO that others would have the benefit of his studies. During his naval career Maury charted the prevailing winds and currents of all the oceans by distributing questionnaires to shipmasters all over the world. It is interesting to note that the most cooperative masters in this extensive project were German. For each voyage these sailing ship commanders filled out one of Maury's special logs and expedited its mailing to him. Painstakingly he put all this information together over a period of many years and in 1847 he published the first *Wind and Current Chart of the North Atlantic.* From these charts Maury plotted sailing directions for the fastest, most economical routes between major ports. With wind-driven vessels it was obvious that the shortest routes might not be the fastest, for it was better to sail a longer distance with the wind than to try to beat into a strong wind over a shorter route. With steamships this is not so obvious but wind and current are still important considerations.

Because Maury was not university-educated he unfortunately encountered much professional jealousy which generated many political enemies in the Navy and ashore. When the Civil War broke out he returned to his native Virginia and worked for the Confederacy, thus ending his career with the United States Navy. But he had virtually founded the U.S. Navy's Hydrographic Office, and he had pioneered the first serious studies of meteorology with his meticulous research, for which he had been lauded by scientists, governments and mariners the world over. Wind did not stop when it reached land, Maury pointed out, and wind charts for land areas were just as valuable to farmers as sea wind and current charts were for sailors.

Lieutenant Maury believed that there were paths across the seas, just as there were passes through the mountains ashore. It followed that Maury produced the idea of the North Atlantic sealanes, to prevent collisions at sea, and to keep ships from the areas where ice drifted down from Greenland and Newfoundland during the Spring months. It took the horrors of *the* ***ARCTIC-VESTA*** collision to convince the public and many politicians that Maury's sealanes could prevent further catastrophes. With this impetus Maury worked out his *"North Atlantic Tracks."* They would keep ships separated, free from collisions, because they would provide an eastbound and a westbound lane. They would keep ships away from the dangerous ice and fog areas by providing a northern set of sealanes, and a southern set of sealanes to be used during the months when ice came farther south. Maury's Southern Track, westbound, which ***TITANIC*** was supposed to be following, was to be used from 14 January to 14 August. His Northern Tracks were considered safe for the remainder of the year. The Northern Tracks were shorter than the Southern Tracks, yet not as short as the usual routes which came very near Cape Race, and which ships had been following since the beginning of commerce between Europe and America.

But Maury's "tracks" were doomed to failure, for he based them upon safety, not economics. Ships made money when they delivered their cargoes, either freight or passengers, or both at once. Enroute they did not *make* money; they *used up* money for fuel, food, wages. The longer the passage the fewer voyages per year, the higher the shipowner's expenses, the less money the vessel made for her owner. It was that simple. So nobody used Maury's tracks and ships continued to collide with each other and with ice.

In 1889 at the International Marine Conference in Washington, D.C., representatives of twenty six maritime nations ruled against mandating use of these North Atlantic tracks by international law. However, the Conference representatives did recommend that individual steamship companies should agree among themselves for safety's sake to establish routes for their own vessels. Reluctantly, in 1891, long after Maury's death in 1873, the Guion, Cunard, Inman, National and White Star Lines agreed in writing to use Maury's tracks.

But these lines were then at a competitive disadvantage with the lines which had not signed the "gentlemen's agreement," and still followed the shortest route. In 1898 all of the North Atlantic steamship companies finally joined in an agreement to use Maury's longer tracks, but in reality not one of them did, for there was a clause which gave the master of every vessel leeway to choose his own path over the sea commensurate with his best judgement. Today, these sealanes are often called "company stripes," and are not used any more than they were in ***TITANIC***'s time. Their use was not, and is not mandatory by law. Many shipmasters rationalized their use of the shorter northern routes during the Spring months because experience had taught that by going farther north they could be in water left clear by the southward drifting ice.

Ships continued to collide with each other, and with ice, and they still do. Many collisions were not fatal to either vessel, and thus were never heard of ashore. Near misses are never reported publicly unless somebody blows the whistle and forces the issue. It would be rare for a merchant seaman of any nation to destroy his livelihood by "squealing" on his employer. By the same token shipmasters are protected whenever possible and the master's word is always taken about shipboard incidents, above that of a lesser crew member. Far out at sea it is very easy to conceal what happens.

After the ***TITANIC*** disaster Captain William S. Sims, USN, was quoted on the subject of

Atlantic navigation. *"The shortest course between New York and the English Channel lies across Nova Scotia and Newfoundland. Consequently the shortest water route is over seas where navigation is dangerous by reason of fog and ice. It is a notorious fact that the transatlantic steamships are not navigated with due regard to safety; that they steam at practically full speed in the densest fogs. But the companies cannot properly be blamed for this practice, because if the 'blue liners'* slow *down in a fog or take a safe route, clear of ice, the public will take passage in the 'green liners,' which take the shortest route and keep up their schedule time, regardless of the risks indicated."*

An editorial comment on 18 April, 1912, described *Great Circle Perils and Profits. "A good many landsmen find it difficult to understand why there is such a strong preference among the managers of steamship lines, and consequently among the masters of their vessels, for a route across the Atlantic that seemingly bends northward between the points of departure and destination. This route takes them through the stormiest part of what used to be called the 'Western Ocean,' while one with a like deflection southward would cross waters appreciably calmer, comparatively free from fog and wholly free from any chance of meeting ice.*

"The explanation is that by the northern route there is a fairly close approximation of the navigator's ideal, which is 'great circle sailing.' His love of the 'great circle,'... of a line which, if sufficiently prolonged, would divide the earth into two equal parts... is due to the fact that such a line is the shortest that can be drawn or followed on a sphere between two points.

"Now, that shortest line means shortening of the time of passage, something of which the public, except just after a great disaster, is extremely fond, and it means for the owners a saving of coal, smaller demands upon the kitchen, the possibility of making more frequent voyages, and half a hundred other economies, in the aggregate always considerable and sometimes constituting the difference between profit and loss in operating the line."

After ***TITANIC*** sank there were many letters to editors of East Coast newspapers, just as there had been after ***ARCTIC***'s loss. One writer told of a conversation he had with one of the French Line's commanders who complained that the position of the master in most transatlantic lines was "precarious and uncomfortable." If he did not make the best time in crossing of which his ship was capable, he would soon find employment elsewhere. There would be many willing to fill his shoes, willing to take the necessary risks, for the prestige and financial remuneration were worth it.

"On the other hand," continued the letter writer, *"if they met with accidents in obeying their companies' orders, they were sure to be superseded as their names would hurt business."* Since accidents were not all that frequent in spite of the risks, most masters preferred to take the chances, and most also preferred the challenge, for that was why they chose the profession in the first place.

Navigation

If a plane could be passed through the center of the earth, like cutting an orange in half, its intersection with the earth's surface would be a *great circle.* If a string is stretched between any two points on a globe it will represent the *great circle track,* which is the shortest distance between the points. On long east-west voyages, particularly in the higher northern or southern latitudes, the distance saved by great circle sailing is of great importance economically.

Meridians can best be described as halves of great circles which extend from pole to pole always at right angles to the equator. Thus meridians always run true north and south. In 1912 British and American navigators used the meridian of the Greenwich Observatory in England as the *prime,* or zero degree, meridian, just as we use it today. Most charts aboard ships flying the flags of Argentina,

Austria, Belgium, Brazil, Chile, Denmark, Germany, Italy, Japan, Norway, Russia and Sweden also used Greenwich as the prime meridian. For all charts published in Batavia and for some published in The Hague, The Netherlands used Greenwich as the prime meridian. A few charts published in The Hague, however, used the meridian of the west tower of Wester Kirk at Amsterdam, in longitude 4 degrees 53 minutes 01.5 seconds east of Greenwich as the prime. Portuguese charts constructed on a scale of 1:100,000 used the meridian of the observatory of Lisbon Castle, 9° 07' 54.86" west of Greenwich, while Portuguese charts constructed on a scale of 1:50,000 carried two graduations, one based upon the meridian of Greenwich, the other based upon the meridian of Lisbon Castle. Spanish charts used as their prime meridian that of the San Fernando Observatory at Cadiz, in longitude 6° 12' 18" west of Greenwich. Russian charts sometimes used the meridian of the Pulkowa Observatory at St. Petersburg, in longitude 30° 19' 40" east of Greenwich as their prime. Older Italian charts still in use in 1912 were based upon the meridian of the Royal Observatory at Naples, in longitude 14° 15' 26" east of Greenwich. The meridian of the observatory at Christiania, in longitude 10° 43' 23" east of Greenwich was still used as the prime on some Norwegian charts. French vessels used the meridian of the Paris Observatory, which was *2*° 20' 15" east of Greenwich, as their prime. One can readily see the confusion that could result in ships from different countries exchanging position reports prior to standardization of Greenwich as the prime meridian. Vessels passing each other prior to the general use of wireless would report their longitude by chronometer for comparison, using flag signals, and indicating which meridian they used as their prime. In the matter of a distress position sent out by a vessel seeking assistance it was especially important to identify her country of registry, and/or her prime meridian. This is important also in the matter of positions given for ships which might have been near ***TITANIC***. Owners of vessels registered in any of the above countries which did not always use Greenwich as the prime meridian could have given a position report for one of their ships which placed her an honorable distance from the sinking ***TITANIC***, when working out her position using the proper prime meridian would have shown that she was indeed very near, even in sight of the White Star liner.

Longitude defines position on the earth's surface in degrees east or west of the *prime meridian.* Longitude of a place on the earth's surface is the arc of the equator between the prime meridian and that of the place. Longitude cannot exceed 180 degrees, which is halfway around the earth, where east meets west. At sea longitude was found by taking the difference between the hour angle of a celestial body from the prime meridian and its hour angle, at the same instant, from the local meridian. The local hour angle was found by *sextant,* a device used to measure the angle, or *altitude,* between a celestial body and the visible horizon. When no celestial bodies were visible due to inclement weather, longitude was measured from the prime meridian by means of a *chronometer,* a mechanical timepiece which had, in ***TITANIC***'s era, a surprisingly high degree of accuracy. The chronometer was a clock of unusually fine construction, built to withstand shock, vibrations and great variations in temperature. Chronometers were handled with the utmost care and were mounted in gimbals to protect them from the pitching and rolling motions of the ship. Chronometers in British and American ships were always set to Greenwich Mean Time (GMT) by the manufacturer and were never reset aboard ship. They were always wound at precisely the same time every day. If there was more than one chronometer aboard they had to be wound in the same sequence every day to ensure accuracy. Most larger ships carried three chronometers so that one could always be cross-checked with the other two. Usually one chronometer was considered the most accurate after careful observation of longitude by celestial observations, and this primary chronometer was used to check the others. The chronometer was the only means of determining longitude in 1912 if a celestial

The Marine Sextant

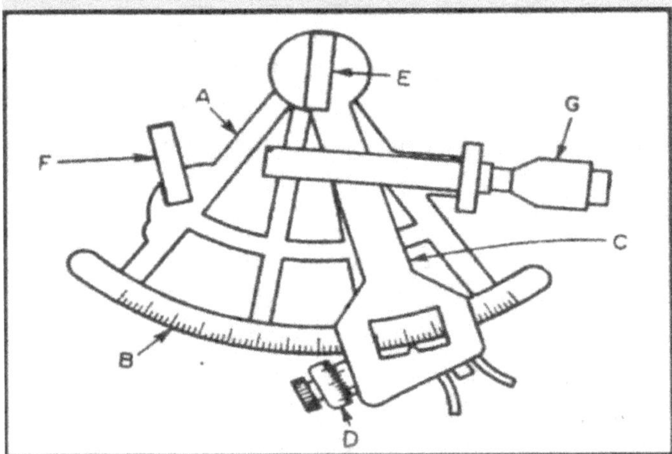

ABOVE: The parts of a a marine sextant: **A**: *Frame;* **B**: *Limb,* which is graduated in degrees. Originally, the limb was 1/6 the arc of a circle. *Sex* being the Latin word for *six*, accounts for the name *'sextant.'* **C**: *Index arm;* **D**: *Vernier;* **E**: *Index mirror;* **F**: *Horizon Glass;* **G**: *Telescope.*

observation could not be made. On the equator one minute of longitude equals one nautical mile. A 1-minute error in time produces a 15-minute error in longitude, regardless of latitude. Fifteen degrees of longitude equals 1 hour of time. All the fury of the master would thus descend upon the hapless officer who forgot to wind the chronometers in proper sequence and time.

The *error* of a chronometer was the difference between the time indicated and the correct time to which it had been set, in this case to Greenwich Mean Time. The *daily rate* was the amount that the chronometer gained or lost each day. It was not necessary that the rate or the error be zero, as long as both were known, and that the rate remained uniform since its last determination. The error could be determined by time signals given in port, usually the dropping of a time ball at the correct instant given telegraphically from an observatory, such as Greenwich. In some ports a gunfire or other sound was used in place of the time ball, but in such instances allowance was made for the length of time necessary for the sound to travel from the point of origin to the observer. For example, if a time ball dropped precisely at 5 hours 0 minutes 0 seconds GMT, and the chronometer reading at that instant of observation was 4 hours 57 minutes 52.5 seconds, the chronometer error was 2 minutes 07.5 seconds. This error correction would then be considered in every longitude observation made until the next opportunity to check the chronometer for error and reset it.

Celestial observations were timed according to the time at the prime meridian at the instant of observation. As the earth rotates on its axis, we have the apparent motion of the sun around the earth. When time is measured by the apparent motion of the sun it is called *apparent time.* When it is noon, or the sun is directly overhead the meridian we are on, it is noon *local apparent time.* At that same instant it is midnight local apparent time on the meridian which is 180^0 from the one we are on. Because the earth is not stationary in space… it travels in an elliptical orbit around the sun, and its speed relative to the sun varies with its position in this orbit... the time required for a complete revolution of the earth about its axis varies too much for accurate navigation. To do away with this problem in navigation an *imaginary mean sun* is used. *Mean, or civil* time is calculated from the motion around the earth of this imaginary *mean* sun, which always makes its 360° trip around the earth in precisely 24 hours. Therefore, when it is noon by local civil time, this is taken as the mean rather than the true sun being precisely over the local meridian. Four times a year the mean and true suns coincide. Otherwise there is always a difference, which is called the *equation of time,* and this is listed in the *Nautical Almanac* for Greenwich Civil Time. The equation of time

The Marine Chronometer

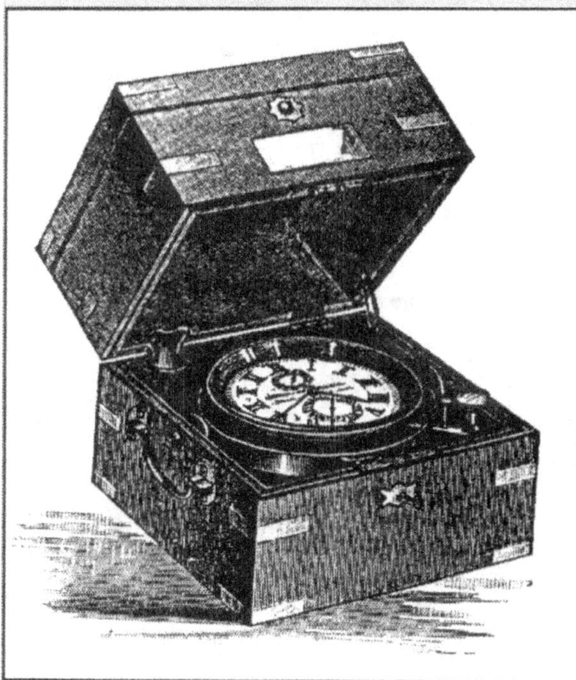

ABOVE: A Marine Chronometer, circa 1912

reaches a maximum of about 16 minutes 30 seconds. *Zone,* or *standard time* was established to eliminate the confusion that might occur because in actuality every time you move a few feet from east to west you change longitude and thus change time. Within a time zone, which encompasses 15 degrees of longitude, or one hour, all clocks may be set to the same time. *Sidereal* time, also used in certain navigation procedures, is calculated from the motion of the stars around the earth. It is measured by the motion around the earth of the *First Point of Aries,* and a *sidereal day* is about 4 minutes shorter than a solar day Many researchers have gone extensively into the differences in ship's time aboard the several vessels in ***TITANIC***'s vicinity, and aboard ***TITANIC*** herself. Remembering that one hour is fifteen degrees of longitude is all we need to know. The times between ***TITANIC*** and ***CALIFORNIAN***, for example, were so near each other because there was a difference of only seven minutes longitude between the two ships. Therefore the difference in ship's times was important in only one instance, as we shall see. The ship's activities were timed by her various clocks, which were set ahead or back, depending upon her direction of travel, usually at noon each day, although some ship's clocks were reset at midnight. This is what causes much confusion when reconstructing events aboard ***TITANIC*** as related to ***CALIFORNIAN***. ***TITANIC***'s clocks were due to be set back at midnight, but events prevented that. ***CALIFORNIAN***'s clocks were set back at noon.

Latitude defines position on the earth north or south from the equator. Thus *parallels* of latitude are smaller circles around the earth, parallel to the equator. Latitude on the equator, which is a great circle, is zero degrees, and latitude never can exceed 90 degrees. If you are on latitude 90 degrees North you are at the North Pole, and everywhere you look is south. Conversely, if you are at latitude 90 degrees South you are on the South Pole, and everywhere you look is north. Parallels always run true east and west and obviously become shorter in length as they get closer to the Poles.

In ***TITANIC***'s time latitude in the northern hemisphere, when visibility was good, was usually figured by using a sextant to measure the altitude of Polaris, often called the North Star, or the Pole Star, which is always about one degree from the celestial north pole. With a slight correction, the altitude of Polaris is the latitude of the observer, because the altitude of the celestial pole equals the latitude of the observer. The proper correction is taken from *Nautical Almanac* tables.

While meridians and parallels are imaginary lines, and there are, for the use of navigation instruments, one meridian or parallel for every one of the 21,600 minutes around the circle of the earth's circumference, and one for each of the 1,296,000 seconds around it, there is no limit to the number of meridians and parallels one can imagine. Every place on the surface of the earth is located at the intersection of a parallel and a meridian, and thus every location is described in terms of latitude and longitude, which are called that position's *coordinates.*

In ***TITANIC***'s era navigation instruments were the sextant, chronometer, magnetic compass, charts, dividers, protractors, paper and pencil and various publications and tables, a cumbersome, only reasonably accurate system at best. Master Mariner Perry Vosseller, in his *Navigation,* (Rudder Publishing Company, New York, 1935) wrote that there was *"an inclination to exaggerate the precision of navigation and to claim undue skill for navigators."* The accuracy of the average fix from celestial observations was a subject for debate even among mariners. It was said that the third mate would carefully mark a dot on the chart and say, *"This is our position."* The second mate would just as carefully draw a circle around this dot and say, *"We are somewhere in here."* The mate would surround this circle with a larger, freehand sweep, with the same comment. Then the master would place his huge, beefy hand over dot and circles, and say, *"somewhere under here."*

As noted earlier, most navigation was *dead reckoning,* the "dead" being a corruption of "ded.," the abbreviation for "deductive." It was true that ships had been known to run for days on dead reckoning alone in bad weather when no celestial observations could be made, to end up as little as a mile off course. That was highly unusual, however, and was due probably to phenomenal luck as much as navigational skill. Today a handheld computer called GPS, for Global Positioning System, utilizing a multiple-satellite network can give your position anywhere on the earth within a few decimeters, by simply pushing a few buttons. By pushing a few more buttons GPS will give you your heading, time and mileage to your destination. This assumes that the batteries do not go dead and the ship does not lose all power due to an accident of some nature. In that case the wise sailor has a chart, sextant, dividers, pencil and paper handy, and remembers how to use them.

Dead reckoning, or *D.R.,* represents the navigator's *best judgement* of the ship's position, therefore it is an *estimated position. A* D.R. position is figured from the *point of departure,* using the distance run computed from time and speed, and the direction steered, taken from the compass, but assuming that the ship has not been influenced by any unknown factors such as current, wind, bad steering or irregular speed. When these latter factors were estimated and applied to the dead reckoning it was called *Current Reckoning,* or *C.R.* The influence of wind speed and direction, as well as surface current and its direction were mostly guess work in ***TITANIC***'s time. Compass *variation* and *deviation,* two more components used in figuring a ship's course and position, were measurable.

A D.R. position thus may be erroneous because of any one of several factors, including an error in the point of departure (which in ***TITANIC***'s case was the 7:30PM celestial observations); compass deviation errors (common in a new ship in ***TITANIC***'s era); bad steering (also common in a new ship of that period); errors in distance run from the earlier fix, which in ***TITANIC*** came from Fourth Officer Boxhall's faulty estimation of her speed, and errors in correcting for the wind and current effects. While the D.R. position should have been carried forward from hour to hour in a well-run vessel because it would always be ready for a distress position if needed, there is no direct evidence of this practice in ***TITANIC***. After ***TITANIC***'s collision with ice Boxhall said he worked up her position by dead reckoning from the 7:30PM star sights. His coordinates, meaning ***TITANIC***'s distress position, were subject to an error of several miles based on any one or more of the above factors. In ***TITANIC***'s era navigation consisted of finding the ship's position by taking celestial sights, then running on D.R. until time for the next celestial fix. When weather permitted the sun sight was always taken precisely at noon.

The noon sight, usually called LAN for *local apparent noon,* had for several centuries been a convenient and simple practice in navigation. At local apparent noon the true sun is on the meridian. An observation taken at that instant gives an altitude which can, using a simple formula, give a fairly accurate latitude, provided the *meridian altitude* is properly determined. The method used in ***TITANIC***'s time was one commonly called *following to maximum altitude.* Starting about ten minutes before watch time of local apparent noon, the observer began taking repeated altitudes. The altitude increases as the sun rises toward the meridian, but that increase lessens as the sun approaches the *instant of transit.* The observer would continue to take altitudes until the sun would *hang* for an instant, when there was no observable change in altitude. When the sun began to dip its maximum altitude was shown on the sextant, a reasonably accurate meridian altitude was obtained, thus giving the ship's position at noon. In passenger ships this was an occasion for a ceremony wherein the distance covered in the past 24 hours was computed by the ship's officers who had lined up with the master on the boat deck. The passenger who had come closest to guessing this distance correctly won a sum of money from a pool of wagers.

To make a map or navigation chart the earth's spherical surface must be projected onto a flat surface. The most commonly used charts for navigation at sea are *Mercator's projections,* adopted by the sixteenth century Flemish cartographer Mercator, upon which meridians are represented as vertical straight lines, while parallels are represented by horizontal straight lines. A great circle course on a Mercator chart is represented by a curved line. Any straight line on a Mercator chart is a rhumb line, which crosses each meridian at the same angle. For relatively short distances the rhumb line will be almost coincident with the great circle. Just because parallels and meridians are neatly marked into squares, usually of five degrees, on the charts does not mean those are the only tracks a ship can follow. As we have already learned, there are an infinite number of parallels and meridians on the Earth's surface, and they are measured in degrees, minutes and seconds of arc.

Great circle charts differ from Mercator charts in that they use a *gnomonic projection* and are so constructed that a great circle appears as a straight line between two points on the chart, while a rhumb line is curved. Meridians are shown converging at the poles, while parallels are curved.

A nautical mile is about the length of one minute of arc of any great circle of the earth. For navigational purposes the nautical mile is now a standard figure, 6080 feet, about one seventh longer than the statute mile, 5,280 feet. In 1912, in the United States, the nautical mile was measured at 6,080.27 feet, while in Germany, Austria and France the length of a nautical mile was considered to be 6,076.23 feet. The Admiralty nautical mile was then 6,080 feet. It can readily be seen that while these differences seem infinitesimal they would have an effect on reporting mileage between ships from different countries. Identifying the country of registry of any ship making a position report was always a necessity. All experienced navigators were well aware of the differences. This merely emphasizes the fact that navigation was hardly as precise as early ***TITANIC*** investigators took it to be, nor would ***TITANIC*** investigators today be able to compute positions of ships suspected of being near her if they were not aware of these differences in measuring the nautical mile and in the use of various prime meridians. While one minute of latitude always measures one nautical mile, one minute of longitude varies with latitude, because meridians converge at the poles.

When following a great circle a ship must have her steering course changed frequently. Therefore, before autopilots and electronic navigation on ships, there were several methods of navigating which were employed because they were simpler than great circle sailing. One of these methods, called *parallel sailing* was often employed. The simplest way to describe this is to say that the vessel would steer due east or west along a parallel, changing course to the north or south on to the next chosen parallel. The distance was not appreciably longer by this method, which was much simpler than plotting a great circle by hand methods, and it was much easier for a helmsman to steer due east or west. This could have been the navigation technique used by ***TITANIC***'s master,

Captain Smith, for at least part of the voyage. Captain Smith, and other masters who knew their way across the North Atlantic like a commuter today knows the way to work, simply navigated from memory. Leaving the Fastnet astern Smith knew perfectly well what heading to steer for about how long. He had merely to work his ship in a direction slightly south of west, changing headings at known time intervals, until he picked up the latitude of the port of New York, which was 40°42'N. He then had to steer due west until a familiar check point was sighted, the Nantucket Light Vessel, for example. If there were obstructions along any given parallel, such as land or ice, the ship was steered north or south around the obstructions until another due west course could be steered.

Composite sailing is just what it sounds like... a combination of great circle and parallel sailing, and it is used when the great circle reaches latitudes that might not be desirable. When figuring a composite track the shortest track between points which takes into consideration the latitude which must not be exceeded will be based upon three things: 1: A great circle through the point of departure tangent to the limiting parallel; 2: A course along that parallel; 3: A great circle through the point of destination tangent to the limiting parallel.

The great circle between the Fastnet and New York cuts directly through Newfoundland, which works fine for airliners but not for ships. Therefore, the latitude which must not be exceeded is a latitude which gives a safe distance from Newfoundland's most southern point, Cape Race. The closer a ship can come to Cape Race, therefore, the shorter will be the distance she must traverse, plus she will have a westerly set to help her along. Using the word *"track"* in navigation has nothing at all to do with Maury's *Tracks.* A ship's *track* is the *line of her true course.*

Prior to ***TITANIC***'s accident a ship leaving Queenstown, bound for New York, and intending to follow Maury's Southern Track, steered a great circle but nothing south from the Fastnet to latitude ***42*** *degrees North, longitude* ***47*** *degrees West,* thence a rhumb line to a position just south of the Nantucket Light Vessel, and thence directly into New York. After ***TITANIC***'s disaster all tracks were moved southward thirty minutes of latitude, or thirty miles. The coordinates vary today, with an Extra Southern Track added. The position chosen for the change from great circle to rhumb line, or vice versa, is known as *"the corner."*

Nicholls's Seamanship (and Viva Voce) Guide, the "bible" of British seamen of ***TITANIC***'s era, contained *"All the prescribed subjects for each grade of the Board of Trade Examinations from Second Mate to Master."* In the *Questions and Answers* section, used to study for the Master's Certificate examination, the question *"How would you take a steamer from England to the United States?"* was answered thus:

"From mid-January to mid-July I should go on the great circle from the (English) *Channel to a point in* ***about 42*** *degrees North and* ***49*** *degrees West, and thence direct for my port. From mid-July to mid-January I should go on the great circle to* ***about 46*** *degrees North and* ***49*** *degrees West, and then direct for my port. Mind the fogs and keep a good lookout for ice."* (Emphasis by the author.)

So much for Maury's tracks.

Nicholls's considered the 42nd parallel a safe distance south of expected ice limits in April, but intersecting the 49th meridian at the 46th parallel was the shorter distance. The point to these explanations is simply that there were an infinite number of ways ***TITANIC*** could arrive at her distress position without being anywhere near the Southern Track prior to this or without any intention on the part of the White Star or Captain Smith to use the Tracks. The fact that she was close enough to Maury's Track that her position could be given as on it was pure luck. Had she struck ice farther north, then White Star's defense would necessarily have been that Captain Smith had erred in choosing to deviate to avoid ice farther south. As events happened, Ismay could choose to use the Southern Track defense.

That at least one other British shipmaster was concerned with the 42nd parallel is supported by an ice warning wirelessed from Cunard's ***CARONIA*** to ***TITANIC*** on Sunday morning, 14 April. The warning read *"Westbound steamers report bergs, growlers, and field ice in 42 N. from 49 to 51 W."* This indicates that ***CARONIA***'s master probably had made his "corner" at 42"N, 49"W, as *Nicholls*'s prescribed, and he undoubtedly expected other British ships to be steaming on or near the 42nd parallel, as he was.

As noted above, the latitude for the port of New York is 40°42'N. A true course from 42°N, 49°W, to New York would have taken ***TITANIC*** right over the position in which she sank, given the 1912 state-of-the-art navigational errors. She would have been steering about S 86° W true. It must be noted that a ship's *heading* (the direction in which her stern is pointing) or her course or track will have nothing at all to do with her *position.* She may steer the same course in an infinite number of positions on the earth's surface. It is interesting to note that another British ship, the Leyland liner ***CALIFORNIAN***, out of London for Boston, was being navigated in accordance with *Nicholls*'s recommendation for taking a steamer from England to America. ***CALIFORNIAN*** had followed the parallel of 42°05'N for some time, as far as 50°07'W longitude. Her course had been S 89° W true. Her master testified at the British inquiry that the *variation* in that area was 24°W. ***CALIFORNIAN***'s *deviation* at that compass point was 2°E, making a total compass error of 22°W.

The *variation* would have been the same for ***TITANIC.***

Can Dead Men Vote Twice? Every student of navigation begins with this perplexing question. Some dead men have been known to vote at least once, of course, but this is an easy way to remember the formula for figuring *compass course* and *true course.*

CDMVT also will stand for *Compass Deviation Magnetic Variation True.* The *true course* is the track you want your ship, or airplane, to make over the earth's surface. The *compass course* is what you have to steer by the compass to make good that true course.

The *magnetic compass* was used by the Arabs as early as 1100 AD, and it was the only type of compass used in 1912. It was not until shortly before World War II that the more accurate gyroscopic compass came into general use, although it had been used in most naval vessels and a few transatlantic liners as early as the latter days of World War I. A magnetic compass is subject to errors caused by *variation* and *deviation,* while a gyro compass is not.

The magnetic compass itself consists of a circular compass card which, in ***TITANIC***'s day, was graduated in the cardinal (North, South, East and West) and intercardinal (Northeast, Southeast, Northwest and Southwest) compass points. It is mounted on magnets in such a way that when its needle points to North (000°) it is pointing to the magnetic north pole, which is different from the true north pole. This difference is called *variation.* The compass card and magnets floated in a cast bronze bowl filled with a mixture of 55% distilled water and 45% pure alcohol, a brew that has been the downfall of many a thirsty sailor. The bowl was mounted in double rings called *gimbals,* which allowed the card to ride steady no matter how the ship might roll. The gimbals were mounted in an upright stand called the *binnacle. A* light was provided to illuminate the compass card at night.

On the inside rim of the compass card chamber was a mark known as the *"lubber's point."* In steering the lubber s point was held steady on the point of the card indicating the course to be steered. The binnacle was always set directly in front of the wheel, and the helmsman always concentrated on the compass card and lubber's point. This is why ***TITANIC***'s helmsman. Quartermaster Robert

Merchant Service Compass Card

ABOVE: *A Merchant Service Compass Card of 1912 with corresponding degrees.*

Hitchins, testified that he could see nothing but his compass.

The compass card in use in the merchant service of ***TITANIC***'s time was graduated in degrees which began at North and at South, and ran 90 degrees toward East or West. Thus a course might be given in the North-east quadrant as North 01 degree East, N 02° E, and so on up to N 90° E, which was due East, or 090° on a modern compass card. In the Southeast quadrant the course might be S 01° E, S 02° E, and so on until it became S 90° E, again due East or 090°. In the North-west quadrant it would be N 01° W, N 02° W, and so on until N 90° W, which was due West, or 270° in modern compass language. Similarly, in the Southwest quadrant it was S 01° W, S 02° W, etc., until S 90° W was reached, again due West.

TITANIC's helmsman said he was steering N 71°W by the compass at the time of collision, which according to her officers was S 86° W true.

While voyaging west to find the East, Christopher Columbus noticed on 13 September, 1492, that his compass needle, which had been pointing slightly east of the North Star since leaving Europe, was now pointing slightly west of the North Star, and it continued to do so as the little fleet traveled farther west. Columbus had just discovered what others would also note in various parts of the world. Columbus had also passed through a point just west of Fayal in the Azores, where the needle pointed to True North. A few years later English explorer Sebastion CaB.O.T. observed the same phenomenon somewhat farther north. These two observations thus roughly located for the first time an *agonic line,* an imaginary line on the earth's surface upon which magnetic and true north converge and variation is zero degrees. It was assumed for some time, however, that this was merely a mechanical error in the construction of the compass itself. In about 1570 George Hartmann, a maker of compass sundials, discovered that near Rome a compass needle pointed 6 degrees east of true north. It was another 125 years, with more such observations coming in as sailors reached out to explore trade the world over, when it was found that at London between 1580 and 1634 the needle had changed its direction of pointing from 11 1/2 degrees east to 4 degrees east, or a change to westward of 7 degrees. This phenomenon is the *secular variation* of the earth's magnetism. Changes in the distributions of the earth's magnetism occur continually. These changes are constantly observed and marked on aeronautical and nautical charts, by lines of equal variation called *isogonic lines,* and by the compass rose.

While *variation* varies in different parts of the earth, it usually increases or decreases in the same locality at known rates which are indicated on charts and can therefore be computed on different dates with reasonable accuracy. Variation is the same for any ship on any heading in that vicinity at that particular time. Variation may be east or west, and will be so indicated on the charts. If it is east it is subtracted, if it is west it is added in order to convert true heading to compass heading. *East is least and west is best* is the way navigators remember this.

Deviation is the amount a magnetic compass needle is deflected by the metal used in the construction of the ship. The amount of deviation for a particular ship is computed and the compass is adjusted by placing magnets in such positions that they act in a direction opposite to and of equal force to the deflecting metals in the vessel. But no magnetic compass was perfectly adjusted, thus its deviation was, in ***TITANIC***'s era, checked in a newly built vessel by a process known as *swinging ship*. The ship was turned slowly through 360 degrees near an object on land the bearing of which from the ship was known. She was steadied on each point of the compass card as indicated by the lubber's line, and the bearing of the object was observed from the compass. The difference between the compass and the known magnetic bearing of the object is the deviation for that point of the compass only. Deviation varied from point to point on the compass, and a deviation chart was made up and posted near the compass. Before swinging ship it was ascertained that the ship was upright, that the lubber's line was in the exact fore and aft line of the ship and that everything in the vessel that was made of iron or steel was in the same place it would be when she was at sea. It was also necessary that no other ships were closer than two cables from the ship which was having a compass check. There were other methods of swinging ship, but this was the simplest and undoubtedly was the method used to check ***TITANIC***'s compass. Changes in cargo carried, such as iron ore and metallic objects, could also affect a ship's compass and great care thus had to be used in cargo vessels. Adjusting the compass to compensate for the presence of new magnetic substances was considered too complicated by some officers, but Reisenberg recommended that any officer in training for command should master it.

The Compass Rose

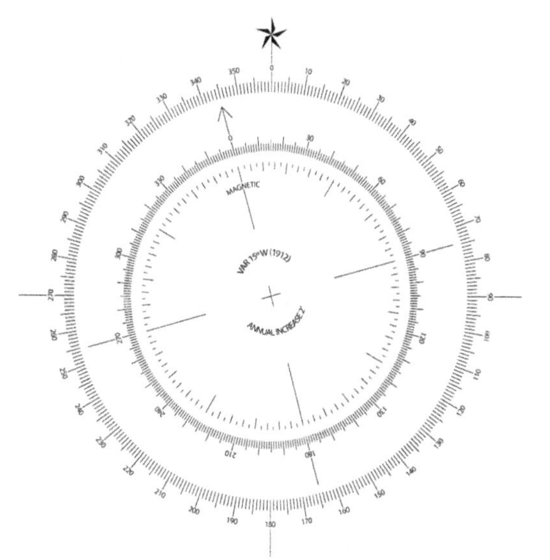

ABOVE: *A Compass Rose from a nautical chart showing 15° westerly error, increasing 2 minutes annually.*

Due to the earth's lines of magnetic force which pass through a ship while she is on the stocks, and to the continual hammering on her metal parts during building, by the time she is launched she has become a giant magnet, but with an amount of magnetism in excess of what she will permanently carry. Therefore, during her trials and for the first few months of service her navigators must continually watch for compass error, which may be constantly changing. A navigator in a new ship of ***TITANIC***'s era had to be constantly double-checking the compasses by taking frequent celestial observations. This possible compass error in a ship on her maiden voyage could have been one reason for Boxhall's dead reckoning position being off by a few miles. The magnetic *steering* compass was located in the wheelhouse, where it was considerably affected by deviation. The *standard* compass was located somewhere above the bridge, where magnetic forces were not so strong. Courses and bearings given from these two compasses were carefully differentiated, those taken from the standard compass designated *p.s.c.* (per standard compass) and those taken from the steering compass designated *p.stg.c.* (per steering compass).

To go from true course to compass course you first add or subtract the variation, and then apply the deviation. Westerly deviation is added, easterly is subtracted.

The Compass Deviation Table

DEVIATION TABLE					
BEARING P.S.C.	DEVIATION	BEARING P.S.C.	DEVIATION	BEARING P.S.C.	DEVIATION
0°	14° W	120°	15° E	240°	4°E
15°	10° W	135°	16° E	255°	1°W
30°	5° W	150°	12° E	270°	7°W
45°	1° W	165°	13° E	285°	12°W
60°	2° W	180°	14° E	300°	15°W
75°	5° W	195°	14° E	315°	19°W
90°	7° W	210°	12° E	330°	19°W
105°	9° W	225°	9° E	345°	17°W
				360°	14°W

***ABOVE:** The typical compass deviation table chart that was posted near the compass.*

We can therefore figure ***TITANIC***'s deviation. Her true course according to Fourth Officer Boxhall was S86°W, which is 266°. Adding 24° westerly variation we get 290° Quartermaster Hitchins testified that he was steering N71°W, which is 289°. This meant that ***TITANIC***'s deviation was computed as 1° E for that particular compass heading. Mariners had known for over a century that variation in the vicinity of the Grand Banks was particularly large due to iron ore deposits in the area.

The *true bearing* of a place or object is the angle that a line from the object to the observer makes with a line from the observer to the true North Pole, measured clockwise from the Pole through 360°. *Relative bearing* is the angle between the ship's head and the object, and this may be expressed in either degrees or points. In degrees a bearing is measured clockwise through 360° from the ship's head. By points it is measured from dead ahead through 16 points on either side to dead astern. One point is 11 1/4 degrees. Bearing was measured by an instrument called a *pelorus,* or *"dumb compass,"* located on either bridge wing. The pelorus consisted of a *dumb compass card,* which could be manually rotated to bring any heading in line with the lubber's line. A pair of sighting vanes were mounted on the card, and they could be aimed at the object whose bearing was desired. The whole thing was mounted inside a nonmagnetic metal ring mounted in gimbals on an upright called a *pelorus stand.* The inside of the ring was graduated either in degrees from 000°, which corresponded to the ship's head or a lubber's line, through 360° or it was graduated in points, the usual method in merchant vessels of ***TITANIC***'s era. Provided that the ship was exactly on course at the instant the bearing was taken, and that the dumb compass card was set to the ship's true course, the bearing by pelorus would be a true bearing. This, however, was seldom the case. It was the custom for the person taking the bearing to call out *"Mark!"* at the instant he took it, while he clamped down on the sighting vanes. At the instant the helmsman heard *"Mark!"* he noted the compass course as shown on the lubber's line. If the ship was right on course, the bearing thus obtained was a true bearing. But if she was off course a correction had to be applied to the bearing. Relative bearings were taken by setting the dumb card's 000° heading to the lubber's line. *Azimuth* and true bearing had pretty much the same meaning, except that azimuth was applied only to bearings of celestial bodies. When ***CALIFORNIAN***'s watch officers referred to the relative bearings of ships seen from her bridge or when ***TITANIC***'s crewmen referred to the relative bearings of lights seen from her boat deck and bridge, these bearings were undoubtedly guessed at rather than measured accurately by pelorus because ***CALIFORNIAN*** was swinging with the wind and surface current, and ***TITANIC*** had a list as well as being by the head. It is unlikely that ***TITANIC***'s officers, busy with more important tasks, took time to use the pelorus to check the bearing of ships' lights.

Boxing the compass referred to naming all the points and quarter points of the compass card in proper order, one of the first tasks an apprentice had to learn.

The speed of vessels in ***TITANIC***'s era was computed by means of a *patent* (mechanical) *log*, a device which consisted of a "rotator," in principle very much like a ship's propeller, which was towed through the water and thus made to rotate with a velocity that varied with the speed of the ship. A series of gears transmitted this motion to dials which registered the distance traveled in a certain time span corresponding to the revolutions of the rotator. All patent logs had their errors. In a ship which had been in service for sometime the revolutions of the engines gave at least as reliable an indication of the speed as any patent log. Speed, track and time were the factors used in determining position by dead reckoning. Boxhall used 22 knots as ***TITANIC***'s speed, while Quartermaster Hitchins, who had read the patent log at 2200, said it showed 45 nautical miles covered in two hours, which indicated a speed of 22.5 knots. From 1930, the time of the last celestial observations that Boxhall had used as the starting point for his dead reckoning distress position, to 2340 when ***TITANIC*** stopped, was four hours and ten minutes. If the speed that Boxhall used was in error by half a knot that meant that his position was off by about two miles. Boxhall had "guesstimated" speed by engine

Relative Bearings

Dead Ahead	000°
1 Point On Starboard Bow	11.25°
2 Points On Starboard Bow	22.50°
3 Points On Starboard Bow	33.75°
4 Points (Broad) On Starboard Bow	45°
3 Points Forward of Starboard Beam	56.25°
2 Points Forward of Starboard Beam	67.50°
1 Point Forward of Starboard Beam	78.75°
On The Starboard Beam	90°
1 Point Abaft the Starboard Beam	101.25°
2 Points Abaft Starboard Beam	112.50°
3 Points Abaft Starboard Beam	123.75°
4 Points (Broad) On Starboard Quarter	135°
3 Points On Starboard Quarter	146.25°
2 Points On Starboard Quarter	157.50°
1 Point On Starboard Quarter	168.75°
Dead Astern	180°
1 Point On Port Quarter	191.25°
2 Points On Port Quarter	202.50°
3 Points On Port Quarter	213.75°
4 Points (Broad) On Port Quarter	225°
3 Points Abaft Port Beam	236.25°
2 Points Abaft Port Beam	247.50°
1 Point Abaft Port Beam	258.75°
On The Port Beam	270°
1 Point Forward of Port Beam	281.25°
2 Points Forward of Port Beam	292.50
3 Points Forward of Port Beam	303.75°
4 Points (Broad) On Port Bow	315°
3 Points On Port Bow	326.25°
2 Points On Port Bow	337.50°
1 Point On Port Bow	348.75°

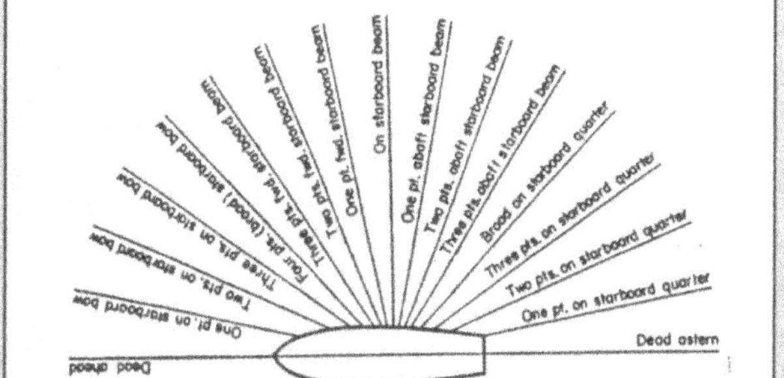

Above & Inset; relative bearings in points and their degree equivalents

revolutions, although he admitted that he was not sure of the number of revolutions that ***TITANIC*** was making. But that was speed through the water, not over the ground, which is different because wind and current must be factored in to get a proper position on the earth's surface.

In the 1920s tests which recorded the helm movements made by different helmsmen found that they made from 85 to 565 movements of the wheel in one hour. A helmsman who "cut snakes" in the wake not only could get a vessel off course, but he would slow her down as well, and increase her fuel consumption.

There was one more, very important reason for ***TITANIC***, and other ships, *not* to be on the Southern Track in April, or on any of Maury's idealistic Tracks at any time of year.

Maury described the Gulf Stream as a *"river in the ocean." "The Gulf of Mexico is its fountain,"* he wrote, *"and its mouth is in the Arctic Seas."*

While it was once thought that the Gulf Stream was one continuous current originating in the Gulf of Mexico, flowing through the Florida Straits, moving swiftly up the east coast of the United States and finally branching out eastward across the Atlantic, oceanographers now believe that there is a system of separate currents involved in this journey, like river systems ashore. The Florida Current originates in the vicinity of the Dry Tortugas, curves through the Straits of Florida, between the Keys and Cuba, to join the Gulf Stream proper, which gives northbound vessels swift passage along the east coast of the United States, while southbound vessels must hug the coastline so closely to avoid the fast moving northerly current that they sometimes run aground on fragile coral reefs. Northbound ships utilize the rapid set of the Stream, which varies from 1 to as much as 5 knots, to save fuel and increase speed over the ground, thus making the most economical passage. It may appear from glancing at a chart that vessels coming from the Gulf of Mexico to northern European ports and the Channel would save distance by striking out from the Florida Keys directly across the Atlantic. In reality they usually ride the Gulf Stream to a point near Cape Hatteras, then strike out with the combination of great circle and easterly setting North Atlantic Drift, the most economical route, which is commensurate with the great circle from northeast U.S. ports to northern Europe and the English Channel

A glance at a current chart will explain how the North Atlantic Drift affects shipping. The current flows steadily at average speeds from 1/2 to 2 1/2 knots *against* westbound vessels. Add to this the fact that prevailing winds are also westerly (winds are named for the direction from which they originate) and it can readily be seen that the westbound passage would be much slower than the eastbound, unless a ship is navigated to follow the path of least resistance. *(See North Atlantic Current Chart for April in Appendix)*

One of the earliest explorers of the Gulf Stream was American patriot and statesman Benjamin Franklin. American sailors had long noted the effects of this great river within the ocean which carried them to European ports, but colonial mariners had not shared this valuable information with their British rivals.

Franklin, who had made many voyages to England and the Continent on behalf of his young country, enlisted the aid of his cousin, Timothy Folger, to chart the limits of the easterly setting current in order to utilize it for speedier passages eastbound, and to avoid it westbound. It was quickly noted that westbound ships must slip between the easterly set and the coasts of Newfoundland and Nova Scotia where they would find a helpful westerly set. This coincided with the route of least mileage, the great circle, but it meant that ships had to be navigated perilously close to shore to take advantage of wind and current as well as the shortest distances.

Although much has been made of ***TITANIC***'s distress position being "right on the Southern

Track" it would have been extravagant navigation for her to buck the current, and take the longer route, ice or no ice. The longer, slower passage, would have cost the White Star too much in extra fuel, wages and supplies, something no good shipmaster did except in extreme conditions, if he wanted to keep his job. In fact, if he met "extreme conditions" and took the longer route too often he did not remain long in the line. Mailboat commanders were not only topnotch navigators and seamen, they were willing to take necessary risks. To be south of that eastward flowing "river in the ocean" would have meant much longer mileage and no helpful westerly set. Every mile, every minute saved was important to a liner's tight schedule. But to satisfy insurance and liability clauses, after the collision and subsequent loss of the ship, ***TITANIC*** *had* to appear to have been on that "proper" Southern Track. Additionally, because the British lines had signed the 1898 Tracks agreement, if they were known to not use the Tracks it impugned British integrity.

It is often erroneously assumed that if ***TITANIC*** was not on the *Southern* Track, then she must have been on the *Northern* Track. It cannot be emphasized enough that *nobody* conscientiously followed Maury's tracks. Every master navigated his vessel in the most economical manner commensurate with a *reasonable* degree of safety. As we have seen, there were an infinite number of ways ***TITANIC*** could have arrived at her distress position, even if that position was "right on the Southern Track."

Firmly entrenched in ***TITANIC*** legend is the alleged meeting of the Furness-Withy steamer ***RAPPAHANNOCK*** with the White Star liner just one hour and ten minutes prior to ***TITANIC***'s impact with ice. ***RAPPAHANNOCK***'s Chief Officer Alfred Smith, who claimed years later that his ship, out of Halifax bound for Liverpool, had passed ***TITANIC*** on *Sunday* night, 14 April, at 10:30PM, also claimed that as ***RAPPAHANNOCK***'s acting master he had Morsed a warning to ***TITANIC***'s watch officer about the ice field dead ahead, through which ***RAPPAHANNOCK*** had just steamed. According to Smith, ***RAPPAHANNOCK***'s rudder had been damaged by the ice.

But Chief Officer Smith told a different story less than a fortnight after ***TITANIC***'s loss. In a special dispatch from London dated 26 April, 1912, ***RAPPAHANNOCK***'s Chief Officer told how his ship ran out of a heavy rain squall on *Saturday night, 13 April,* and found herself abeam of ***TITANIC***. "With all of her lights glowing," said Smith, "***TITANIC*** was a splendid sight." It should be noted that Smith had no difficulty in identifying ***TITANIC*** as a large passenger liner. *She was traveling at about 21 knots,"* said Smith, *"and soon disappeared into the darkness. We had come through the icefield, which* **TITANIC** *struck later on. It stretched some hundred miles northward. It had come thus far south a month before the usual time, and we could not escape it, but ran into it, suffering considerable damage. Our rudder was twisted and our bows dented and other injuries were inflicted on us by the ice. I saw some packs of a thousand square feet in area, and the ice was bunched together and heaped up in some cases. This is, in all probability, the pack which* **TITANIC** *struck. The ice was three or four feet above the surface of the sea and twenty-odd feet thick. It is astonishing to me that Captain Smith should have struck the pack if he sighted it in time. Of course, he may have taken it to be slob ice, which is soft, and through which it would be safe to run even at 21 knots; but the ice we encountered was not slob ice, and when we sighted it we went dead slow. The* **TITANIC**, *if she scraped one of those ice packs, would have had the bottom practically ripped out of her going at the speed she was. What I cannot understand, and what most seafaring men wonder at, is why it should have been necessary for the* **TITANIC** *on a clear night to strike an ice pack at all. I may say that we did not see any icebergs during the voyage."*

Chief Officer Smith did not mention any Morsed warning to ***TITANIC*** in his 1912 statement to the press. In actual practice Morse lights for night signaling were used sparingly because they temporarily blinded not only the officer receiving the message, but the sending officer as well. Smith did not see icebergs, which indicates that ***RAPPAHANNOCK*** was not in the same ice field that ***TITANIC*** skirted on Sunday night. In fact ***RAPPAHANNOCK*** was probably in ***BRINKBURN***'s ice, which will be discussed in the next chapter. If Murdoch did receive a Morsed warning from ***RAPPAHANNOCK*** on Saturday night, then he, and Captain Smith, had 24 hours warning of the ice fields. It is more likely, however, that Chief Officer Smith simply embellished his story when he told it years later to an author. This is the reason why it is always better to use statements taken soon after any incident, when it is remembered rather than enhanced. The fact remains, however, that ***TITANIC*** passed ***RAPPAHANNOCK*** on *Saturday* night, not Sunday night as legend has it.

If, as legend has it, she was out of Halifax, bound for *Liverpool*, ***RAPPAHANNOCK*** was certainly not on the Southern Track for vessels bound for New York. Furness-Withy, however, used London as its eastern terminal, not Liverpool, and Chief Officer Smith's 1912 statement was issued from London. While it is possible that for certain voyages ***RAPPAHANNOCK*** might have called at Liverpool, her normal route was Halifax-London. Whether London or Liverpool makes only a slight difference in where she would have passed ***TITANIC***. We will, however, study both tracks for ***RAPPAHANNOCK***, because taking C/O Smith's information along with two wirelessed positions given from ***TITANIC*** prior to her collision with ice, we can figure very closely what ***TITANIC***'s track actually was.

The latitude of Queenstown (now Cobh) is 51°50' 50"N. The latitude of the Fastnet, the junction point for ships departing or bound for Cobh, or Liverpool on the Irish Sea, is 51°20' 00"N. The Channel entrance junction point. Bishop Rock is 49°45' 00"N. Departing Halifax at 44°39' 00"N, ***RAPPAHANNOCK*** had to clear Cape Race not much farther north than the 46th parallel before heading direct for her port. Bound for either Liverpool or London ***RAPPAHANNOCK*** was not going to be south of the 49th parallel excepting for the beginning of her voyage when she passed Cape Race. From there she would have curved northward to pick up one of three courses… a great circle to either Fastnet or Bishop Rock, the parallel of Fastnet or the parallel of Bishop Rock.

Studying the great circle chart we can see that ***RAPPAHANNOCK*** would have cut close to Cape Race, across the Virgin Banks, near the Flemish Cap, on a direct track to the Fastnet, and on into the Mersey if she was bound for Liverpool. From the time she departed Halifax ***RAPPAHANNOCK*** was steering either due east or slightly north of east true, whether bound for the Mersey or the Thames, while ***TITANIC*** departing Queenstown for New York, which is in latitude 40°42' 00"N, was steering slightly south of west true for much of her voyage. It is clear from Chief Officer Smith's account of his adventures in the ice field that he did not waste fuel trying to go around it.

At 7PM (1900) GMT on 12 April ***TITANIC*** reported her position to ***LA TOURAINE*** as 49"45'N, 23"38'W. The reason that Greenwich Mean Time was qualified in this position report was simply because ***LA TOURAINE*** was owned by Compagnie Générale Transatlantique, the French Line, and therefore she used the meridian through the Paris Observatory as the prime meridian for navigation. Thus Captain Smith had to make it clear that he used Greenwich as the prime meridian when he gave the position and time. This position for ***TITANIC*** was about 27 hours prior to her passing ***RAPPAHANNOCK***, assuming the 10:30PM (2230) time given by Chief Officer Smith to be accurate for Saturday night also. If ***TITANIC*** steered due west for some time, remaining on the same parallel where she had given her 12 April position report, 49°45'N, this was the parallel of Bishop Rock, for which ***RAPPAHANNOCK*** was heading if she was bound for London. ***RAPPAHANNOCK***'s track should never have been south of this parallel. If she was bound for Liverpool ***RAPPAHANNOCK*** would never have been south of the Fastnet, or 51°20'N, excepting at the beginning of her voyage when she cleared Cape Race. ***TITANIC,*** intersecting the parallel of 49°45'N on her second day out of Queenstown, would have at that moment been just about on the Southern Track great circle, but it would have been the only time she was on the Southern Track until she reached her distress position two nights later. This would be commensurate with *composite sailing* explained earlier. ***TITANIC*** thus should have passed ***RAPPAHANNOCK*** somewhere between the 35th and 38th meridian, along the parallel of 49°45'N, *or* the two ships passed close to the 38th meridian as ***RAPPAHANNOCK*** steered slightly north of east toward the parallel of either Fastnet or Bishop Rock and ***TITANIC*** was steering just south of due west, heading for perhaps the 45th parallel. This would have put ***TITANIC*** north of the ice reported by NDL's ***GEORGE WASHINGTON*** to ***HANNOVER*** on the evening of 11 April, in 44°34'N, 40°22'W, and north of ***RIO PIRAHY***'s ice at the 45th parallel, but ***TITANIC,*** once more steering south of due west true, would have been well south of the ice through which ***RAPPAHANNOCK had*** passed, the ***BRINKBURN*** ice which was near the Flemish Cap. Now needing to go south of Cape Race, ***TITANIC*** could then have intersected the 45th parallel, then continued safely along a course of due west true for some time, staying north of ice reported by ***CARONIA, CARMANIA, EXCELSIOR, NIAGARA, ETONIAN, COLUMBIA, etc.***, until Captain Smith received the legendary message from ***BALTIC.*** At this point Captain Smith decided that it was safe to steer a course to intersect the 41st parallel anywhere west of the 50th meridian, as explained in the next chapter.

ABOVE: *The chart represents* ***TITANIC****'s track on her maiden voyage.*
A. TITANIC *position 1900 GMT on 12 April.*
B. TITANIC *position, 2340 ship time, 0250 GMT on 14-15 April, Distress Position.*
C. *Probable parameter for* ***RAPPAHANNOCK*** *meeting.*
D. DEUTSCHLAND*'s position and direction of drift.*

But why did ***RAPPAHANNOCK***'s Smith change his story years later and say that he had passed ***TITANIC*** on *Sunday* night, just a little over an hour before she struck ice? It could very well have had something to do with the fact that Furness-Withy and the Leyland Line were affiliated, and thus both came under the aegis of Morgan's International Mercantile Marine Company which owned ***TITANIC***.

The Furness Line was founded by Christopher Furness in 1877 when he persuaded his brother and partner in the family business, Thomas Furness & Company, merchants and ship chandlers of West Hartlepool, to establish a line of steamers between West Hartlepool and North America. In 1882 Thomas, who had no real interest in shipping, dissolved the partnership amicably and returned to the merchant business while Christopher took over the management of the shipping firm. Furness steamers began service from London to Boston, Halifax, St. John and New York. In 1883 the West Hartlepool shipbuilding yard of E. Withy & Company joined Furness and in September, 1891, the firm of Furness, Withy & Company Limited was founded. In 1895 Furness joined Leyland in the Wilson's & Fumess-Leyland Line Limited, which operated between London and New York and London and Boston. In 1898 Fumess-Withy acquired the Canada & Newfoundland Line of Steamers, and in 1901 began a joint service with the Allan Line, which became known as the Furness-Allan Line. In 1902 Wilson's & Furness-Leyland Line became part of Morgan's shipping trust, which owned the White Star Line as well. It is also possible that years after the fact an old man grabbed his one chance at immortality by enhancing his story to make it more interesting to an author.

The truth, of course, is that we will never know exactly how ***TITANIC*** was being navigated, because her logbook went down with her.

A ship's log is a legal document which can be used in any inquiry concerning her navigation or management if she has a mishap. It can exonerate her crew, provided they have done nothing wrong in managing the vessel.

Two hours and forty minutes, the time span between impact and foundering, was time enough to place ***TITANIC***'s logbook in a lifeboat with an officer in charge of it. This should have been done. Probably it was *not* done at Ismay's order, rather than Captain Smith's. Ismay was astute enough to know that positions written into the log would have given away the fact that ***TITANIC*** was *never* on the Southern Track. If a logbook carries incriminating evidence which could be used in the investigation of an accident, the usual method of destroying that evidence is simply to "deep six" it, or weight it and pitch it over the side. The disappearance of ***TITANIC***'s log is tacit admission that something in it was incriminating.

It is also entirely possible that ***TITANIC***'s logbook, as well as her position report to ***LA TOURAINE*** on 12 April were not "honest." Readers may be surprised to learn that as late as the 1950s, in fact until our air traffic control system was equipped with radar, airline pilots routinely made position reports giving the positions where they were *supposed* to be rather than where they actually were. That would be much easier to do at sea, especially in ***TITANIC***'s era.

While we cannot now know how ***TITANIC***, or any of the other ships which reported contact with her, were being navigated, we can certainly assume on the basis of knowing standard navigation practices of the era, that ***TITANIC*** was on the shortest route commensurate not with safety, but with the earliest arrival time in New York.

We do, however, have one other position report from ***TITANIC***, given at 0215 on 14 April. This and the aforementioned 1900 GMT position on 12 April were probably reliable because they were given before the accident and the subsequent coverup. The 14 April report gives no qualification of the time used, and no coordinates. Marconi operators used New York time west of the 40th meridian and Greenwich Mean Time east of that meridian, therefore this report was probably given in New York time. GMT would be five hours faster than New York time. Unfortunately three times were used by ships in wireless reports, GMT, New York and ship's time. Unless qualified as GMT any wirelessed time was probably given at the Marconi operator's discretion. Taking these two position reports along with ***RAPPAHANNOCK***'s passing her, we can very closely approximate ***TITANIC***'s actual track, and it was not on the Southern Track.

Chapter Five

Ice!

On 1 April, 1912, the British steamer ***SAMARA*** rescued six seamen from the sinking schooner ***BLUE JACKET*** about 600 miles southeast of Newfoundland.

The 86-ton ***BLUE JACKET*** had departed St. John's, Newfoundland, on 12 March, bound for Oporto, Portugal, with a cargo of codfish. On the following day the little schooner was buffeted by gale force winds amid large fields of ice. ***BLUE JACKET***'s master, Captain Richard Jones, put into Bay Bulls, eighteen miles south of St. John's. Two days later when the weather looked more favorable. Captain Jones elected to continue the voyage. Although the weather was no better, Jones set his course for Portugal. The wind increased and water poured over ***BLUE JACKET***'s decks. Gales tore her rigging to shreds and ice crushed against her sides.

For a week the sturdy little schooner withstood the ferocious attacks of wind and ice. On 26 March she finally cleared the ice field. Jones and his five sailors breathed more easily. But the following day they encountered ice and wind greater than they had seen during the previous week. By 30 March ***BLUE JACKET*** had been holed in two places and her pumps could no longer control the water pouring into her hull. Ice had smashed the schooner's only lifeboat. Captain Jones ordered his men into the rigging, where they clung with frozen fingers, waiting for death, and praying. Their prayers were answered when ***SAMARA*** hove into view.

The master of the British steamer ***BRINKBURN***, arriving at Philadelphia from Narvik on 3 April, reported that on 26 March in lat. 47°N, long. 47°W, he had encountered field ice stretching for 100 miles and containing numerous bergs.

Captain Black, master of the British steamer ***COLUMBIA***, reported that on 4 April in lat. 43°20'N, long 49°W, he saw field ice trending to the north-northeast as far as could be seen. In lat. 43°40'N, long. 48°17'W, two small growlers were sighted.

On 7 April Captain Jacobson, master of the Leyland Line's ***ARMENIAN***, sent the following ice warning by wireless: *"Lat. 43°20'N, long 48"20'W, saw several large and small icebergs, and lat. 42°36'N, long. 49°36'W, heavy field ice. Indications are that there is an unusual quantity of heavy field and pack ice and numerous small and large icebergs on the Banks and well east of it. The southern limit of the ice appears on April 7th to extend from lat. 42°36'N, long. 49°36'W, in an east-northeast direction for seventy miles."*

On 8 April Captain Roberts, master of the British steamer ***ROYAL EDWARD***, flashed this ice warning: *"Lat. 42°50'N, long. 49°50'W, to lat. 43°30'N, long. 50°10'W, passed thick and heavy loose field ice, and in lat. 42°8'N, long. 49°40'W, a large iceberg."*

Captain Dunbar, master of the British steamer ***RIO PIRAHY***, at Philadelphia from Narvik via Halifax, reported that on 8 April in lat. 43°44'N, long. 49°34'W, he passed a large quantity of field ice, and numerous icebergs were seen for about seven hours altogether.

Arriving at New York from Stockton-on-Tees, Captain J. P. Barker, master of the British steamer ***LORD CROMER***, said it would take $30,000 to repair his ship's broken plates and rivets.

"On the 49th degree (latitude) *I encountered the ice field and backed out and took a course due south to the 43rd degree. I then tried to head due west for St. John's, but I had to cut through part of the field at that. I was in the ice from March 27th to March 30th, and before the first day was ended I had all the pumps working. I thought we were going to founder, but I made St. John's, and after temporary repairs came here,"* Captain Barker said. This statement apparently contained a misprint as to ***LORD***

CROMER's destination. If she steered due west on the 43rd parallel she was bound for Saint John, New Brunswick, not St. John's, Newfoundland.

The DAPG tank steamer ***DEUTSCHLAND***, out of Stettin on 23 March for Philadelphia, reported that from April 6th to April 10th, and from lat. 48°N to lat. 41°40'N, she passed continuous fields of pack ice and numerous large and small icebergs, during which she "started" some rivets in both bows. ***DEUTSCHLAND*** ran out of coal due to navigating around this ice, and at midday of April 14th she was taken in tow by the ***ASIAN***, out of New Orleans for Liverpool via Newport News. Both ships arrived safely at Halifax.

On 14 March the Norwegian steamer ***ROMSDAL*** left Norway with a crew of nineteen men. Captain S. A. Hole commanding. On 26 March, in lat. 45°50'N, long. 57°10'W, ***ROMSDAL*** ran into a field of ice. Her engines were slowed, but the fog was so dense that the ship ran up on the concealed ledge of an iceberg. Reversing the engines did no good, and the vessel was stuck.

ROMSDAL's officers saw another steamer of about 8,000 tons displacement, also trapped in the ice, about five miles away. That night the unknown steamer sent up distress rockets, but ***ROMSDAL*** was unable to move to render aid. About midnight all signaling ceased and all lights disappeared. At daybreak there was no sign of the unidentified steamer. She had apparently gone down with all hands.

ROMSDAL remained trapped in the ice until her lookout spied an opening in the field on 30 March. With full steam ***ROMSDAL*** managed to break loose from her icy prison, but her stern plates were damaged and one of her propeller blades was broken, which caused her to be delayed two more days. Although ***ROMSDAL*** moved cautiously, slowly through the field, jagged spurs of ice breached her plates in several more places. Water poured into her hull in such quantities that the pumps worked continuously. ***ROMSDAL*** put into Halifax for temporary repairs, and then proceeded to New York. It was thought in maritime circles that the missing steamer might have been the ***MOUNT OSWALD***, out of Newcastle-On-Tyne. A lifebuoy from this vessel had been found in lat. 48°55'N, long. 16°10'W, just about where the currents would have carried it from the position of the steamer seen from ***ROMSDAL***. Other maritime experts, however, believed that ***ROMSDAL***'s officers might have overestimated the tonnage of the stricken ship, for vessels of that size rarely go missing without being noticed after several weeks. Two other, smaller ships had disappeared within this time frame, one British, one Norwegian.

At 8AM on 10 April the German steamer ***EXCELSIOR***, Captain A. Courtin, for New York from Hamburg, in lat. 41°50'N, long. 50°25'W, encountered an ice field a few hundred feet wide and at least fifteen miles long in a north-northeast direction. ***EXCELSIOR***'s officers saw a barque pass through the ice.

On 11 April the Allan liner ***CORSICAN*** encountered an extensive ice field. Her master immediately ordered *"slow ahead,"* and for three days, steaming at less than five knots, the ship picked her way through the ice. Early on the following day ***CORSICAN*** crashed into a large berg, but she managed to reach St. John's safely on 14 April. No position for the ice was given in newspaper accounts of the accident. It is difficult to believe that this incident was not relayed via Marconi shore and ship stations to ***TITANIC***, as a matter of interest.

Officers of the Greek steamer ***ATHENAI***, at New York from Piraeus, reported passing a large quantity of icebergs and field ice in lat. 41°30'N, from long. 40° to 51°W.

Arriving at Boston from Liverpool, officers of the Cunarder ***LACONIA*** indicated that she had passed four large icebergs on 11 April at 7:22AM in lat. 47°07'N, long. 40°41'W. The bergs were six miles north of ***LACONIA***'s track.

The Atlantic Transport Line's ***MINNESOTA***, for Philadelphia from London, Captain Wylie commanding, reported that on 12 April at 7PM in lat. 42°N, long. 49°35'W, she passed through broken field ice, two miles wide and extending as far as the eye could reach, from the northeast to the southwest. ***MINNESOTA***'s position was 2 degrees and 35 minutes due west of the Southern Track corner. Morgan's International Mercantile Marine Company owned the Atlantic Transport Line.

Another British steamer, ***SS KINTAIL***, from Leith for Philadelphia, reported that on 12 and 13 April she encountered field ice in lat. 46°N, long. 46°18'W, to lat. 44°30'N, long. 49°20'W. ***KINTAIL*** steamed forty miles around the field, which was shaped like the letter "S" and contained numerous small and large icebergs. ***KINTAIL*** was not on any "official" track. She was crossing the Grand Banks.

Captain Hume, master of the British steamer ***AVALA***, at Philadelphia from Fowey, reported that on 12 April in lat. 41°46'N, long. 50°14'W, his ship passed through *pan*, or *slush*, ice for about one hour and a half, and sighted seven icebergs. This ice warning was flashed to the U.S. Navy Hydrographic Office and published in routine shipping news *two days prior* to ***TITANIC***'s collision with ice. The coordinates at which ***AVALA*** encountered slush ice were exactly the same coordinates which ***TITANIC*** gave as her final distress position. Slush ice, just as it sounds, is a mushy surface mixture of ice and sea water, not quite frozen into ice, but not quite liquid either. Floating on the sea's surface, slush ice dampens wave action, but it is safe to steam through.

Captain George Black, master of the British steamer ***BORDERER***, upon arriving at New York from Calais, reported that on 13 April in lat. 41°50'N, long. 50°01'W, for thirty miles along the direct course of steamers bound to New York, his ship passed through heavy field ice and in that distance he counted sixteen icebergs. The ice extended *"as far north and south as the eye could reach,"* said Captain Black, whose wife was a first cousin of ***TITANIC***'s First Officer, Will Murdoch. Black, like Murdoch, was from Kirkcudbrightshire, the birthplace of many seafaring Scots. Thus Captain Black had a special interest in retracing ***BORDERER***'s route through the ice. From the ship's logbook Black made up a chart showing the *two* ice fields, separated only by a narrow lane of clear water, the lead through which he had taken ***BORDERER***. At noon on 13 April Captain Black had prudently stopped his 8,000 ton cargo vessel after passing a small piece of ice in thick fog. Like Captain Stanley Lord of the

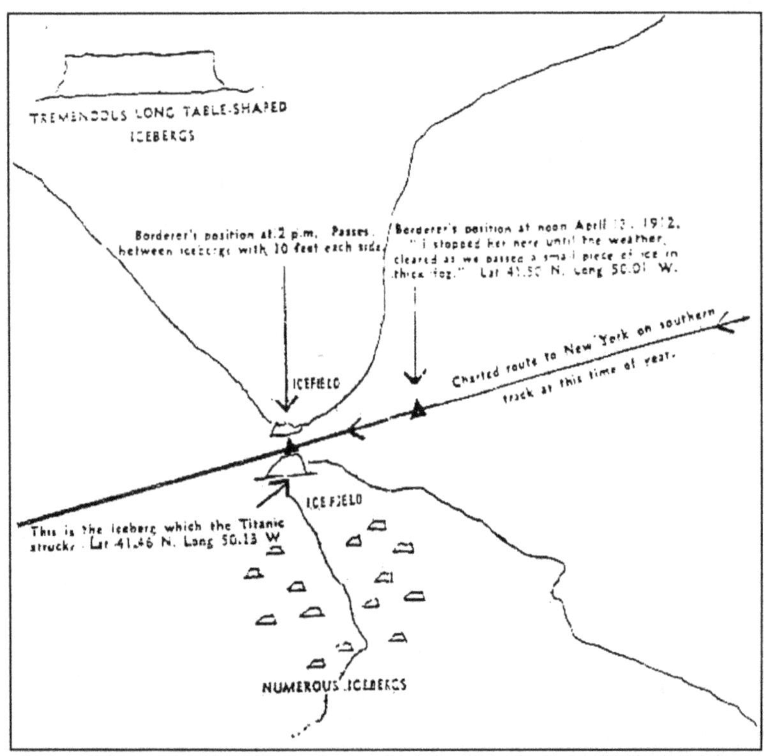

ABOVE: An ice diagram drawn by Captain George Black, Master of the ***S.S. BORDERER***.

CALIFORNIAN, Black had no impatient passengers to push for a fast passage. When the fog lifted, ***BORDERER*** proceeded at five knots through the narrow lead, with less than ten feet to spare on either side. Black later commented that ***TITANIC*** had to have struck the same iceberg he had seen, otherwise she would have been *"embedded infield ice before she could have hit any others in the position given."* By the time ***TITANIC*** struck ice ***BORDERER*** was at least 150 miles west of her, with a wireless range of only fifty miles. Captain Black commented further, *"The trouble with the* ***TITANIC*** *was that she was on her maiden voyage and was out to break records."*

From ***BLOOMFIELD***, a British steamer at Norfolk, en route from Emden to Galveston, came a report that in lat. 43°44'N, long. 49°20'W, ice was encountered and skirted for 160 miles. ***BLOOMFIELD***'s master reported sighting eight bergs, the largest being about 350 feet long and 150 feet high. He said that ice was seventy miles farther south than he had ever seen it before.

Captain Wood, master of the steamer ***ETONIAN***, at New York from Antwerp, reported that on 12 April, in lat. 42°N, long. 50°W, his ship passed about twenty icebergs and an ice field 108 miles in length. That night ***ETONIAN***'s officers saw the schooner ***DOROTHY BAIRD*** of St. John's drifting with the pack, with all sails lowered. They surmised that the schooner's master had decided to wait for daybreak to look for a way out of the ice.

At about 10AM on 10 April the watch officer on the bridge of the CGT liner ***NIAGARA*** sighted ice. Captain Juhan immediately ordered speed reduced and, with fog settling rapidly around them, ***NIAGARA*** began to pick her way cautiously through the floes.

At dinner time ***NIAGARA*** was still in the ice field and fog. Officers on her bridge could hear ice grinding alongside, and the ship brushed against several small floes. Tension ran high as the fog thickened and bergs of formidable size loomed up in the mist ahead, then slid dangerously close along the ship's side, disappearing in the grey veil astern.

Suddenly ***NIAGARA*** crashed into a big berg. The impact sent diners, china and glassware sprawling. For a time Captain Juhan and his officers had their hands full preventing panic among the passengers.

Wireless operator Herve Magny, who was at his key when the shock came, ran on deck and looked over the side to find that the ship was listing heavily while ice was still grinding against her hull.

Captain Juhan made an immediate inspection and found that some plates had buckled below the waterline and the ship was making water. He ordered his crew to start repairs and told Magny to flash out the international signal of distress, "SOS."

The ***CARMANIA*** was the first to answer ***NIAGARA***'s call for help, but the Cunarder was having her own problems with the ice. Fortunately, ***NIAGARA***'s repairs were effective and Captain Juhan was soon able to report that she was proceeding.

CARMANIA's master, Captain Dow, told reporters when his ship docked at New York, *"I entered the icefield on a southwest course, and when I saw the extent of the field I tried to find a northwest passage out of it. Failing to find one, I was compelled to follow a northeast course in order to get clear of the ice. In other words, it was necessary for me to swing back to a certain extent over my course."*

Captain Dow's brief report to the U.S. Navy Hydrographic Office read: *On voyage from Liverpool to New York, on April 11th, from noon to 8PM, passed about thirty large icebergs and extensive field ice, some bergs being 400 feet high and from one quarter to one-half mile in length. The ice was encountered from lat. 41°56'N, long. 50°20'W, to lat. 41°54'N, long. 51°30'W.*

In New York Dow gave reporters a fuller account of the ice he had encountered. *"At first it was foggy, and there were times when we stopped and drifted. I was feeling the way, every inch of it. When the fog lifted I was able to get my bearings by a star, and found that I was a little to the north of my course. I never saw so much ice and* so *little whisky and lime juice in all my life before. Had the ingredients been handy, there would have been a highball for every man in the world,"* Captain Dow quipped.

The log of the Red Star liner ***LAPLAND***, from Antwerp for New York, Captain H. D. Doxrud, showed that on Friday, 12 April, in lat. 42°N, long. 49°50'W, the vessel ran through ice, large and small, and that for several hours navigation was difficult because of the loosely packed ice. The Red Star Line was part of Morgan's International Mercantile Marine conglomerate.

Captain Doxrud was no stranger to the North Atlantic, or to shipwreck, and his harrowing experiences at sea are so indicative of the times that we will digress for a moment to note some events in his career. As an officer in Red Star's ***PENNLAND*** in December, 1890, he had been in charge of a boat that rescued the crew of the British brigantine ***DON JUAN***, drifting dismasted and rolling in the trough of high seas with the wind being Force 7 on the Beaufort Scale, or about 35 knots, a moderate gale. In October, 1892, as Chief Officer in Red Star's ***NOORDLAND*** he had been in charge of the boat crew that rescued the crew of the Norwegian barque ***KING OSCAR II***, off the Flemish Cap, with the wind being Force 6, or about 30 knots. On 7 May, 1898, Captain Doxrud had been in command of the American Line's aging ***PENNSYLVANIA*** when she encountered a hurricane so severe that he had to stop the ship and pour oil into the sea to somewhat abate the wave action. The ***PENNSYLVANIA*** herself was no stranger to severe weather. While bound from Liverpool to Philadelphia in February of 1874 she had survived a hurricane so violent that her master, two officers and two seamen had been swept overboard and drowned. In high drama reminiscent of modern airliner movies, a passenger, one C. L. Brady who had at one time been third officer in White Star's ill-fated ***ATLANTIC***, took command and brought the ***PENNSYLVANIA*** safely into port. In October, 1899, in command of Red Star's ***RHYNLAND***, Captain Doxrud had sent a volunteer crew of 8 men commanded by his Chief Officer to rescue the crew of the waterlogged British brigantine ***IDA MAUD***, off George's Bank, with the wind again at Force 6. These incidents were all in a day's work to a North Atlantic shipmaster and one must wonder why ***TITANIC***'s Captain Smith escaped such adventures... if he did. Probably he simply did not mention them to reporters for the simple reason that passengers would not travel if they realized the dangers of the sea. Doxrud's adventures also illustrate just how far north ships voyaging between Antwerp and New York were navigated, a route south of ***TITANIC***'s Queenstown-New York track. It would be difficult to believe that Captain Doxrud, for example, had changed his navigating habits after so many years on the North Atlantic, Track agreement or not. The Flemish Cap is about 47°N, 45°W, well north of any "official Tracks."

To return to Captain Doxrud on 12 April, 1912, near the ***LAPLAND*** and creeping through the fog, was the Hapag liner ***PRESIDENT LINCOLN***. Several times her engines had to be reversed to avoid dangerous-looking ice, said her commander, Captain Magin. The center of the field was in lat. 41°55'N, long. 50°14'W, a few miles north of ***TITANIC***'s eventual distress position, but two days prior to ***TITANIC***'s collision with ice.

Captain Polack, master of NDL's ***GEORGE WASHINGTON***, Bremen to New York, told reporters that ice conditions off the Banks were unusually bad. His vessel entered the ice fields on Friday, 12 April, in the afternoon. Two towering bergs were sighted, along with two others somewhat smaller. ***GEORGE WASHINGTON***'s log recorded ice in lat. 42°13'N, long. 49°49'W north of the Southern Track. The liner ran at reduced speed and did not come too close to any of the bergs.

Captain Stener, master of Holland-America's ***ROTTERDAM***, at New York from Rotterdam, told reporters that he had not actually seen ice, but he had encountered "a black fog" that shut in everything. "*I smelled ice and started south to keep clear,*" was Stener's terse comment.

Captain Stanley Lord, master of the Leyland Line's ***CALIFORNIAN***, reported to the U.S. Navy Hydrographic Office on 14 April at 6:30PM that his ship had passed two large icebergs five miles to the southward of his position, which was lat. 42°04'N, long. 49°10'W.

At 7:15PM Captain Lord reported again, when ***CALIFORNIAN*** passed two more bergs in lat. 42°05'N, long. 49°20'W. Fifteen minutes later Lord reported two more bergs, and at 10:20PM he reported again to the Hydrographic Office with an ice warning when he stopped his ship for the night after encountering heavy pack ice in lat. 42°05'N, long. 50°07'W. The pack extended north and south as far as he could see, and was about five miles wide, reported Lord. These routine ice warnings flashed to the Hydrographic Office and published on the shipping pages of East Coast newspapers on the morning of 15 April should prove to even the most skeptical that Captain Lord never lied about ***CALIFORNIAN***'s position to make it appear that she was farther from ***TITANIC*** than witnesses claimed the mystery ship was. The ice warnings were sent as a matter of routine several hours before ***TITANIC***'s collision with ice, and many hours before Captain Lord had heard of ***TITANIC***'s loss.

On 15 April in lat. 48°36'N, long. 43°43'W officers on the bridge of White Star's ***CYMRIC*** saw "a large piece of ice." In lat. 48°26'N, long. 44°28'W, to lat. 47°34'N, long. 46°20'W, one large and three small bergs were seen surrounded by pack ice. Bound for Portland, Maine, ***CYMRIC*** had the option of using Canadian Tracks, yet she was north of any of Maury's tracks for that time of year.

The British steamer ***CARTHAGINIAN***, at Philadelphia from Glasgow, reported that on 15 April from lat. 44°46'N , long. 47°31'W, to lat. 44°37'N, long. 48°18'W, she passed large and small icebergs. ***CARTHAGINIAN***, too, was north of the Tracks.

How could it have happened, when ice reports had been flashed through the ether for weeks, that on the night of 14 April the grand, new Royal Mail Ship ***TITANIC*** slammed full speed through one of these reported ice fields to strike an outlying berg on the western edge of the pack?

The answer is simple. She didn't.

The first clue came hidden in Captain Dow's jovial report of *backtracking* ***CARMANIA*** to the *northeast* to get out of the ice. Far more important clues came from ships that docked at Philadelphia on 17 April. They reported passing through fields of ice and seeing enormous bergs near where ***TITANIC*** had foundered.

When the Anglo-American Oil Company tanker ***LACKAWANNA*** arrived at Point Breeze from Manchester, her master, Captain Gray, reported that he and his officers had sighted more than a score of icebergs in the vicinity of where ***TITANIC*** had gone down. Captain Gray said that he was unable to explain how ***TITANIC*** failed to locate the bergs and so avoid them. The weather in that area was clear, and ***TITANIC***'s officers should have had no difficulty in sighting the mountains of ice, declared Captain Gray.

On Monday, 22 April, Captain Gray turned over a chart made by one of his officers, F. E. Townsend, to the U.S. Navy Hydrographic Office. Captain Gray had withheld this information until after the ***LACKAWANNA*** sailed. The chart was turned over to the pilot who took the steamer out, with instructions to place it in the hands of the officer in charge of the Hydrographic Office in the Bourse. The need for so much secrecy was questioned, but it came to be the general belief that if the chart was accurate, "*the statements that the* ***TITANIC*** *was not on the regular northern lane when the disaster occurred are likely to be found incorrect.*" To put this in simpler language the chart showed that ***TITANIC*** could not have been on the Southern Track.

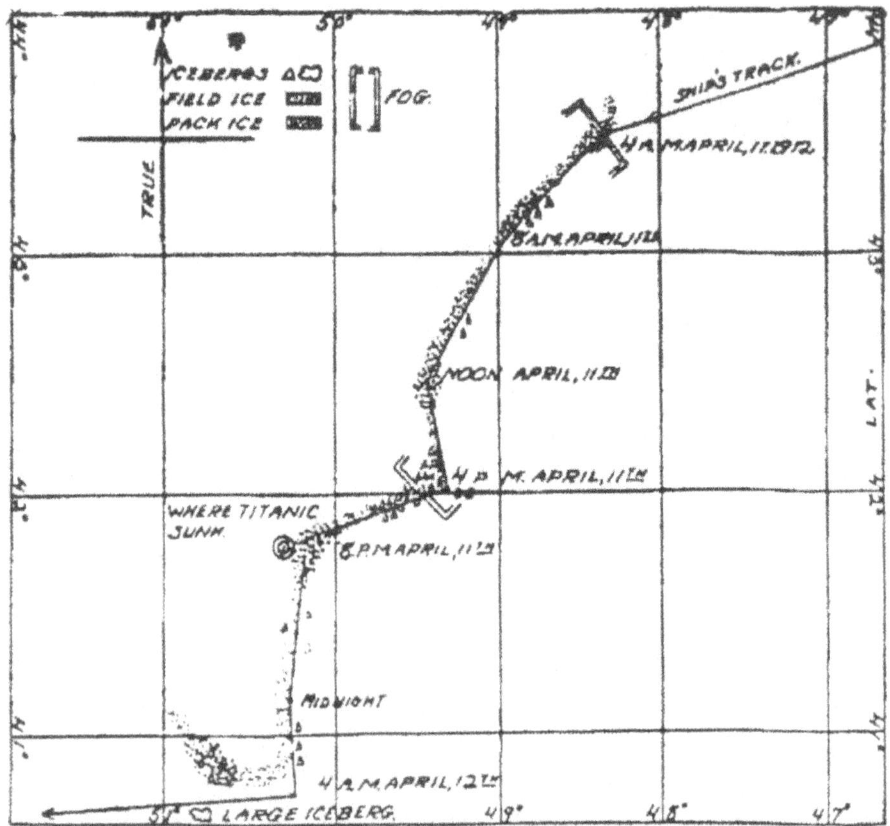

ABOVE**: A chart prepared by F.E. Townsend, Officer of the British tanker* **LACKAWANA**. *(Captain William Gray commanding, April 12th, 1912.) The position where* **TITANIC** *struck ice two days later is about two thirds of the way through the field, westbound. With the ice drifting east-northeast, it puts the field east of* **TITANIC's distress position, and was the basis for believing in 1912 that* **TITANIC** *was not on the Southern Track.*

Townsend had prepared a chart of the ice limits which was said to be one of the most complete ever submitted to the branch office of the Hydrographic Department. It showed 34 huge bergs, as many growlers, and a dense field of ice covering an area of more than 200 miles in length and more than 30 miles in width. Lieutenant Martin of the Hydrographic Office marked the place where ***TITANIC*** struck ice, on the *western* edge of the field.

It is clear that Captain Gray wanted to avoid being subpoenaed as a witness for the Senate Inquiry, thus his secrecy can be understood. It should be noted, however, that ***LACKAWANNA***'s owner, the Anglo-American Oil Company, was the English subsidiary of John D. Rockefeller's great Standard Oil Trust, and other Standard Oil tankers would be implicated as being near the sinking ***TITANIC***.

It is clear that ***LACKAWANNA***'s ice was the same ice sighted from ***BORDERER, LAPLAND, CARMANIA, MINNESOTA, GEORGE WASHINGTON, EXCELSIOR, SERVIAN*** *and* ***PRESIDENT LINCOLN*** It was also ***BLUE JACKET***'s ice.

When the NDL liner ***HANNOVER*** arrived at Philadelphia on 17 April, from Bremen, her master, Captain Proitzsch, reported that on the evening of 11 April his wireless operator, George Klee, received a message from NDL's ***GEORGE WASHINGTON***. The text of the message was: *"Lat. 44°34'N, long. 40°22'W, much ice. Steer* northward. *Run slowly."*

Captain Proitzsch declared that under ordinary circumstances he would have followed the path taken by the ***TITANIC***, and it was the message from ***GEORGE WASHINGTON*** that caused him to change his route. According to his calculations ***HANNOVER*** was 120 miles west and 180 miles north of ***TITANIC*** when the latter struck ice. ***TITANIC*** carried a copy of ***HANNOVER***'s manifest as well as other important NDL papers. It should be noted here that Norddeutscher Lloyd as well as its other German rival, Hapag, had a profit sharing agreement with J. P. Morgan's International Mercantile Marine Company which owned ***TITANIC*** and ***CALIFORNIAN***.

Captain Starck, master of the tank steamer ***SERVIAN***, which docked at Marcus Hook on 17 April, had a stranger story to tell. Captain Starck said that, as near as he could calculate, ***SERVIAN*** had passed over ***TITANIC***'s course about two hours after she had sunk. He saw no icebergs, lifeboats or bodies floating in the water.

When the Allan liner ***TUNISIAN*** arrived at Liverpool from Canada, her master reported that she had run into a large ice field 887 miles east of St. John's. For thirty six hours Captain Fairfull, one of the oldest commanders in the North Atlantic service, never left the bridge.

"The ship was practically surrounded by huge ice mountains," said one passenger. *"Pinnacles of jagged crags glistened in the rays of the sun with dazzling brilliancy. A sea of floating ice stretched for miles on every side of the vessel, and we counted no fewer than 200 huge bergs. It was a magnificent sight."* Passengers tended to dramatize accounts of their voyages.

About midnight on Saturday, 13 April, the Marconi operator in the ***TUNISIAN*** had signaled, *"Good luck,"* to the ***TITANIC***. The acknowledgement came back, *"Many thanks. Goodbye."*

From Boston came word that Captain James Jacobson, master of the ***ARMENIAN***, had just brought that Ley land liner over the *northern* route from England.

The *Daily Memorandum* of 15 April contained a message from the Hapag liner ***AMERIKA*** via steamship ***TITANIC*** and Cape Race, to the Hydrographic Office in Washington, DC, dated 14 April:

*"**AMERIKA** has passed two large icebergs in lat. 41°27'N, long. 50°08'W, on the 14th of April"— Knuth.*

Said Captain John J. Knapp, Chief of the Hydrographic Office of the Bureau of Navigation, USN, *"A trained seaman can and does estimate the probable speed and direction of drift of any dangerous obstruction, so that if he had knowledge of the existence of an iceberg or a derelict in a certain location at a given date, he reckons its future position for an interval of a few days."*

AMERIKA's ice warning, allegedly relayed through ***TITANIC*** to the Hydrographic Office via Cape Race, has been a matter of debate for over eight decades. Did the warning reach ***TITANIC***'s bridge, or did it not? Would ***TITANIC***'s Marconi operators have taken it upon themselves to intercept the message which they were bidden only to relay, a message not rated by them as "official" and not addressed to ***TITANIC***'s master, and deliver that message to the bridge?

Probably not. Marconi operators normally refused to communicate with German operators using Telefunken equipment. It is a moot point, however. Long. 50°08'W is east of ***TITANIC***'s final distress position by more than five miles. It is almost fifteen miles east of ***TITANIC***'s first CQD position of long. 50°24'W. The prevailing winds and current in this area as known to ***TITANIC***'s navigators were east-northeast. More important, ***AMERIKA***'s icebergs were south of ***TITANIC***'s track by nineteen miles, if the navigation of either ship had been precise. And even more important, ***AMERIKA*** reported "two large icebergs," and ***TITANIC*** did not strike a large iceberg. ***TITANIC***'s officers expected field ice to drift with the surface current, to the east-northeast. If they had ***AMERIKA***'s ice warning they would have believed that they were safe in their longitude and latitude on the night of 14 April.

At New York on 17 April Captain Caussin, master of the CGT liner ***LA TOURAINE***, stated that on 10 April in lat. 44°15'N, long. 50°40'W, (Paris) at five seconds past midnight his ship entered an ice field. Captain Caussin immediately slowed her to 12 knots, from her service speed of 19 knots.

LA TOURAINE emerged from the ice field at 1:15AM. The bergs and floes showed only a little above the water, said Caussin. But the same morning ***LA TOURAINE*** coasted along the southern edge of *another* ice field for three quarters of an hour, and her officers sighted two icebergs.

On Friday, 12 April, ***LA TOURAINE*** was in constant communication with ***TITANIC*** up to 9PM. Captain Caussin sent word by wireless of the position of the ice fields which he had encountered to the commander of ***TITANIC***. Captain Smith replied, sincerely thanking the French commander for the information. But ***LA TOURAINE***'s warning described two ice fields, and Captain Smith had acknowledged receiving these warnings. ***LA TOURAINE***'s longitude was taken from the meridian of the Paris Observatory, which was precisely 2°20'14.6" east of Greenwich.

From Washington on 17 April came news that Secretary of the Navy Meyer had attempted to keep from the newspapers the contents of ***AMERIKA***'s ice warning of 14 April. Meyer sent for Captain Knapp when he learned of the dispatch, and said that it must not be given out. Knapp said it had gone into the *Daily Bulletin* of the Hydrographic Office, which had already gone out to shipping interests, and would make its way into the newspapers. Nevertheless, Secretary Meyer said that it must not be given out by the Navy Department; if it leaked out from the branch Hydrographic Office that could not be helped. It was understood that the Secretary said that his reason for trying to keep the dispatch quiet was that the Hydrographic Office attachés and Navy officers would be called upon as witnesses in the impending investigation.

In fact, all routine wireless warnings transmitted to the Hydrographic Office on 14 April did indeed find their way into the shipping pages of East Coast newspapers, leaving mute testimony to the fact that ***TITANIC*** had ample warning of the ice fields.

TITANIC legend makes much of one ice warning which Captain Smith was known to have received from White Star's ***BALTIC*** on Sunday, while ignoring the most important part of the wirelessed message. Sent at 11:52AM New York time, the first part of the Marconigram repeated ***ATHENAI***'s report of passing icebergs and large quantities of field ice in 41°51'N, 49°52'W. Smith handed the written message to Ismay to read somewhere around lunch time, either shortly before or shortly after one o'clock, ship's time. Ismay could not remember, or did not want to remember, the exact time that Captain Smith had given him the message, which Ismay put into his pocket. According to Ismay neither man had commented on the message, but sometime between 7 and 7:30 PM Smith had asked Ismay for the message so he could post it in the chart room. The reason he was questioned about the ice warning contained in the Marconigram was simply because Ismay had violated the first rule that a junior officer in a passenger ship learns… do not talk to passengers about ship's business. Ismay had told Mrs. Thayer and Mrs. Ryerson about the message, and they told the press about it after ***TITANIC***'s loss. The logical question is *why did Captain Smith show only this one particular ice warning to Ismay?* The logical answer is *that only this one message contained something more than an ice warning.*

The second part of the message read: *"Last night we spoke German oil-tank steamer* ***"DEUTSCHLAND,"*** *Stettin to Philadelphia, not under control, short of coal, lat. 40°42"N, long. 55°11'W. Wishes to be reported to New York and other steamers."*

The wirelessed ice warning originated from the Greek *steamer* ***ATHENAI***, which had passed icebergs and a large quantity of field ice in 41°51'N, 49°52'W. As we have seen ***ATHENAI*** had transmitted a similar message to the USN Hydrographic Office. With ice drifting to the east as expected, the ***ATHENAI*** message indicated that ***TITANIC***'s track was safe if she stayed north of the 42nd parallel until she reached at least the 50th meridian, which is exactly what she did.

ABOVE: Built in 1908 by Flensberger Schiffsbau Gesellschaft, and intended for service to the Far East, transporting oil there, and bringing back general cargo, ***NIAGARA*** *and her sister* ***PHOEBUS*** *belonged to a rare class of liners—those tankers with their engines and bridge amidships. Owned by the DAPG (The Deutsche Amerikanische Petroleum Gesellschaft) of Hamburg, it is possible that she was in* ***TITANIC****'s vacinity on the fateful night of April 14-15, 1912. (Photo courtesy Arnold Kludas)*

This message has been blown out of proportion because it has been assumed that Smith showed it to Ismay because of the ice warning and because Ismay kept it for so many hours ***TITANIC***'s watch officers did not see it. However, the second part of the message, the information about the ***DEUTSCHLAND***, was the only logical reason why Smith wanted Ismay to read this message when he had not shown him the other Marconigrams regarding ice.

The latitude of the port of New York happens to be 40°42'N, thus ***DEUTSCHLAND*** happened to be very near ***TITANIC***'s projected track. It may be assumed that the master of a liner as prestigious as ***TITANIC***, with her imperative schedule on a maiden voyage would not deign to attempt something so menial as towing a tanker. But what a *coup de théâtre* it would have been for ***TITANIC*** to arrive in New York towing another vessel, and especially a German ship! Imagine the fantastic publicity for a maiden voyage, the exciting "entertainment" for the jaded American millionaires in First Class! ***TITANIC*** was already running ahead of her scheduled arrival time on Wednesday morning, and even ahead of her estimated arrival time of Tuesday at 4PM. In reasonably good weather it should not have been much of a feat to get a line on the ***DEUTSCHLAND***. The tanker was bound for Philadelphia, a port less than 100 miles south of New York. Captain Smith would have wirelessed for a tug to meet ***TITANIC***, a message which would have been immediately intercepted by every professional and amateur wireless operator on the East Coast and blabbed to the newspapers. ***DEUTSCHLAND*** would have been transferred to the tug, which, along with every available chartered craft would have been crawling with reporters and photographers. The transfer would have taken place somewhere highly visible, probably off Sandy Hook. Headlines would have blazed something like *"Giant New Liner* ***TITANIC*** *Rescues German Tank Steamer at Sea,"* with subtitle *"New White Star Liner So Powerful She Tows Tank Steamer Halfway Across Ocean and Still Arrives Early."* Stock prices for both I.M.M. and Marconi would have skyrocketed. There was also a definite propaganda opportunity with Germans in America already touting anti-British sympathy. Smith no doubt realized the publicity advantage, as did Ismay, and the salvage fee, which turned out to be £3,250 for the ***ASIAN***, was nothing to overlook, either. Each ***TITANIC*** crew member would have realized a share, the largest portion going to the master of course, while ***DEUTSCHLAND***'s hapless master undoubtedly found other employment. But while Captain Smith would not have consulted Ismay about routine navigation, he needed Ismay's approval for this stunt because the rescue would have required that ***TITANIC*** lose perhaps a couple of hours while negotiating with the tanker's master, then getting a line on the ***DEUTSCHLAND***. In addition the tow would have slowed ***TITANIC***, although at that time Chief Bell had not yet put on all her boilers. Thus Ismay no doubt had to discuss the matter with Bell, for it also would have caused ***TITANIC*** to consume more coal than originally planned, and that was why Smith gave the printed message to Ismay, to show to Bell.

Undoubtedly Ismay, when questioned by the two First Class passengers, simply mentioned the ice rather than risk ship's gossip discussing and looking forward to the tanker tow, which ***TITANIC*** could have missed. If the passengers had anticipated the incident they would have been lining the rails looking for the tanker, and have been greatly disappointed if she was not sighted. If she came as a surprise, however, the rescue would have been much more dramatic. The question that should have been investigated was whether or not Captain Smith learned that ***DEUTSCHLAND*** was taken in tow by the ***ASIAN*** earlier on Sunday, but with emphasis on the ice warning the second, and most important part of the message, has always been ignored. Probably Captain Smith did not know that ***DEUTSCHLAND*** had already been rescued because ***ASIAN***'s standard 1 1/2 KW wireless set did not have enough range to reach ***TITANIC***, nor would either Phillips or Bride consider such a message, if overheard, important enough to copy and take to the bridge. The ***DEUTSCHLAND***, then, is undoubtedly the reason why Smith chose to angle south as soon as he felt they were far enough west for safety.

But there was no time given in the message other than "last night" for the tanker's position. ***DEUTSCHLAND*** was drifting with the surface current, easterly with a slight northerly component, at a speed which could have been up to 3 knots. Thus ***DEUTSCHLAND***'s position at least 24 hours earlier had been about 225 miles west of ***TITANIC***'s longitude at the time she struck ice. During those 24 hours ***DEUTSCHLAND*** had drifted as much as 75 miles toward ***TITANIC***. The two ships were then closing at a combined speed of about 24 to 25 knots. Smith knew that sometime during the night, or around daybreak on Monday at the latest, they should meet up with the drifting tanker. But if he waited too long to head south he could miss her. All he had to do was ease ***TITANIC*** a bit south of due west (S 86°W true, for example) to the parallel of about 40°45'N and head due west along that parallel. If ***DEUTSCHLAND*** had already been taken in tow Smith had nothing to lose because he was going that way anyway. Because Smith believed that field ice was drifting east-northeast with the surface current he thought he was safe in coming south when he did. When Smith posted the wireless message in the chart room his watch officers were automatically alerted to be on the lookout for the helpless tanker. ***BALTIC***'s commander, Captain Ranson, had known the advantage of the publicity in this when he sent the message. Smith immediately realized it and hastened to show the message to Ismay, who naturally approved the scheme. It was not a matter that would have been discussed with the press after ***TITANIC***'s collision with ice, or admitted at either inquiry, however. In fact, it was a matter to conceal because Smith had cut it too close and come south too far east because of it. The fact that the Marconigram also contained the ice warning was naturally seized upon by investigators at both inquiries, and has remained therefore in the legends while the ***DEUTSCHLAND*** message has been ignored, probably because nobody noticed that ***DEUTSCHLAND***'s latitude and New York's latitude are the same, and nobody who has written about ***TITANIC*** has studied navigation practices of her era. But the fact is that ***DEUTSCHLAND*** thus became one more link in the chain to disaster, and it should be noted that she belonged to the German subsidiary of Standard Oil, Deutsche-Amerikanische Petroleum Gesellschaft.

About one hundred tidewater glaciers normally inhabit the west coast of Greenland and spawn the icebergs which generally spend their first winter in Baffin Bay. During the following summer these ice masses are carried southward with the Labrador Current, to end up spending another winter in Davis Strait. With the warming of spring the pack ice begins to break up, and the icebergs embedded in the packs are freed to drift still farther south, into the shipping lanes. Although icebergs have been sighted during all parts of the year, and as far south as the Azores, they are particularly numerous in the Grand Banks area in the Spring. ***TITANIC***'s master and watch officers were veterans of the North Atlantic service, and knew perfectly well in which areas to be wary of ice. All four of these men had navigated the Grand Banks area in every month of the year, prior to the use of wireless at sea. Whether or not they received specific ice warnings from other vessels was not particularly important. They would have, as a matter of habit, been on the lookout for ice in this vicinity. ***BALTIC***'s master, Captain Joseph Harlow Ranson, in fact was asked by Sir Robert Finlay if he was familiar with the route that took ships just south of the Virgins in the Cape Race direction. Ranson answered that he was indeed familiar with this route.

While legend has it that in 1912 ice had moved farther south than usual for April, the U. S. Navy Hydrographic Office's *American Practical Navigator* for 1914 says otherwise. In 1905, 1906,1907, and 1908, all years in which ***TITANIC***'s master and watch officers had been on the North Atlantic, the ice limits had indeed been as far south as the 40th parallel. In fact, from 1904 through 1913 in the months of April, May and June, icebergs were sighted as far south as 37°50'N, and as far east as the 38th meridian. This publication (formerly by Nathaniel Bowditch) states also that exceptional drifts had been seen as far south as the 30th parallel, between the 10th and 75th meridians. Ice of all kinds, warned Bowditch, was most apt to be found during the months of April, May and June, between the 42nd and 45th parallel, from the 47th to the 52nd meridians west of Greenwich. While this was an American publication, it is unlikely that British sailors were less aware of this.

Most of the bergs which appeared in the North Atlantic originated on the western coast of Greenland. From a small glacier in southern Greenland came the bluish bergs which were hard to see at night.

The *mass* (not the height) of ice that is invisible, underwater, varies with the ice density, and will be from five to nine times more than its visible mass above water. All mariners are, and were, well aware of this. Icebergs, having considerable underwater mass, are propelled more by surface currents than by wind. In fact, large bergs may act as icebreakers when they plow through an obstructing ice field, breaking it up as they go along, their movement often to windward. Vessels have moored to bergs with ice anchors, being towed through field ice in which they could otherwise make no headway. Field ice which has been penetrated by bergs will have leads, or open paths, in the lee of the bergs. The wise old commanders knew this and used it to their advantage in navigating through field ice.

Field ice, however, is propelled generally by surface winds, a fact unknown to ***TITANIC's*** navigators. It may become rafted when a field to windward drifts down on one to leeward. The field which is rougher on its surface gives the wind a better hold and thus it drifts faster. Fields may even

Ice Diagram Using Prevailing Wind & Current

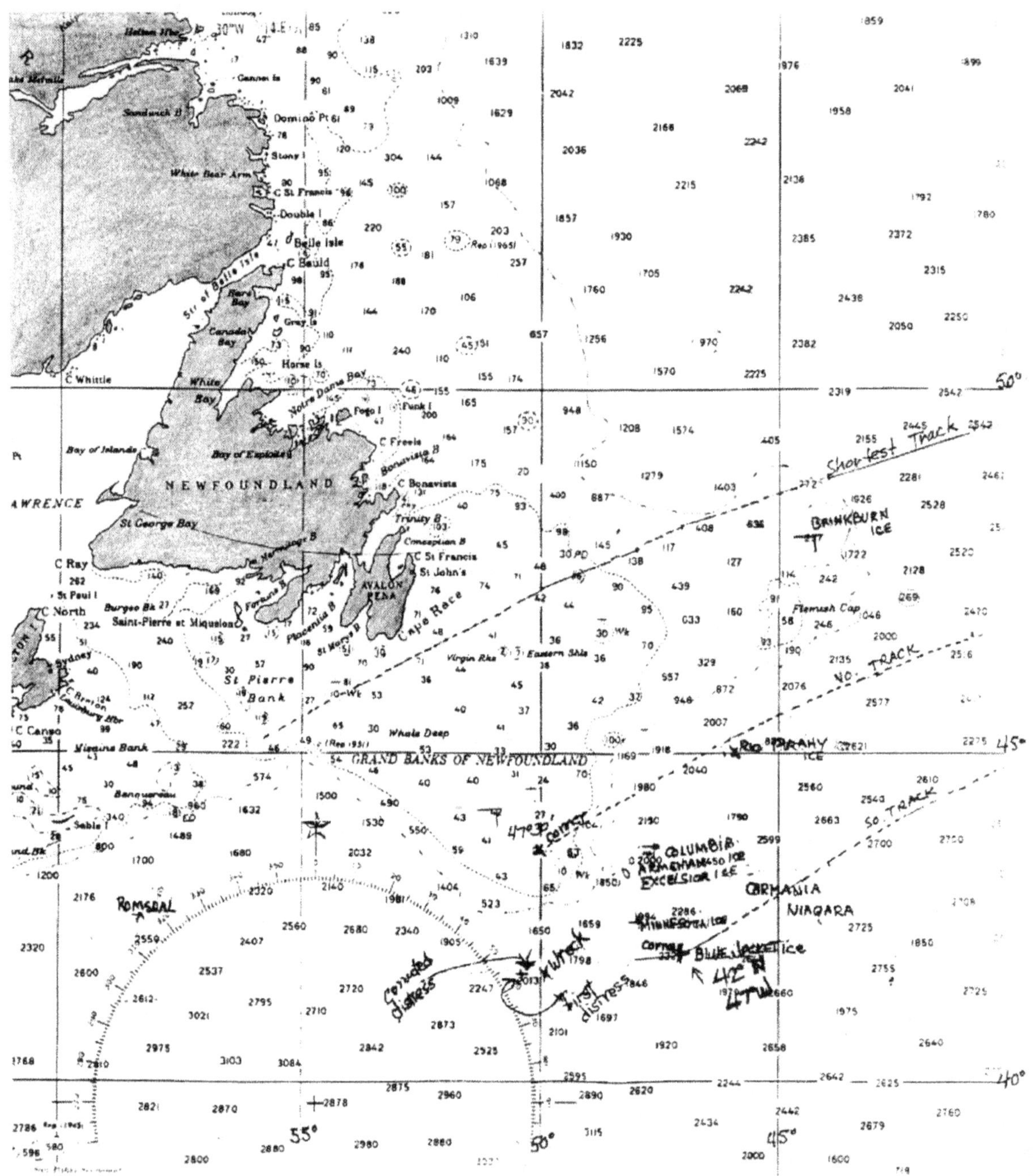

*ABOVE: In 1912, Mariners had not yet learned that field ice moves with the wind rather than surface current, nor had thay accepted that the direction of the surface current could be deflected by a strong wind. On Sunday, 14 April, 1912, the wind had been so strong out of the North that there had been no boat drill aboard **TITANIC**. If the field ice reported to **TITANIC** by wireless had moved only with the prevailing current as her navigating officers had expected, then the field ice would have been centered near the 'corner,' 42°N, 47°W, and **TITANIC** would have been safe in coming south at the 50th meridian. It was, therefore, state-of-the-art oceanography that brought **TITANIC** into collision with ice, and no fault of her navigation in any way.*

be pushed towards each other by winds from different directions. Small fragments of bergs that are mingled with ice fields may become frozen fast. When liberated as the fields drift into warmer water these small bergs become the dangerous growlers, low, dark, indigo colored masses just awash and rounded on top like a whale's back. Growlers are especially dangerous when in ice fields that are loose enough to permit the passage of vessels through them. Experienced shipmasters could tell by the field's appearance if it was safe to attempt passage through it. If doubt existed Bowditch suggested that a commander would be safe in entering the field at dead slow, and if he found the ice too heavy he could haul out. An ice field formed a good lee for riding out a gale, but it was wise not to come in too close to the field as pieces could break off from the main field with such force that they would stove in the bows of the sturdiest ship.

While one major flaw in ***TITANIC*** research has been the refusal to see the accident through the eyes of a 1912 sailor prior to the knowledge of ***TITANIC's*** foundering, a second fallacy, just as important, has been the lack of studying subsequent discoveries in seamanship, navigation practices and oceanography to learn of the lack of information in these areas in 1912. This is especially important in one major study… the drift of field ice.

The Coriolis effect, named for Gaspard Coriolis, the French civil engineer who discovered it, is the tendency of any moving body on or above the earth's surface to drift sideways from its course due to the earth's rotation, west to east. This effect is naturally greater for a surface point near the equator, and it is especially important in plotting the track of a ship although the frequent course changes necessary on a great circle mask the effect. Gunnery experts had long known of the Coriolis effect upon the trajectories of long-range shells, but mariners had not yet accepted it as a force that influenced wind direction and ocean currents although this had been hypothesized by Coriolis himself, who lived from 1792 to 1842. The effect would also be important in long-range air flight, but in 1912 this form of transport was still far in the future.

In 1912 mariners believed that field ice, with its relatively low freeboard, drifted with the surface current. Subsequent observations begun decades later proved that field ice drifted with the wind rather than surface current, and thus its drift was directly related to wind direction which in turn was influenced by the Coriolis effect.

A strong wind blowing over a period of several hours will cause a surface current or deflect the natural course of an existing current far out at sea. The velocity of the current is naturally dependent upon the velocity of the wind. There were two factors which 1912 mariners thus failed to consider... the Coriolis effect and field ice drift with wind rather than surface current.

In the northern hemisphere in open ocean areas where the Coriolis effect causes a marked deviation of the set, theoretically a wind-driven current should be deflected on the surface 45 degrees to the right of the wind direction. In the southern hemisphere the deflection is 45 degrees to the left. Continuous current observations made long after ***TITANIC***'s loss have verified the theories. In the open ocean with plenty of sea room the drift of wind-driven currents is approximately in knots 2% of the wind velocity in miles per hour. The earth's rotation deflects these wind-driven currents in the northern hemisphere about 40 degrees to the right of the wind direction. None of this was taken into account in plotting ***TITANIC***'s course or position by dead reckoning. And none of this was taken into account when ***TITANIC***'s officers figured the drift of field ice reported by wireless. Lightoller said at both inquiries that they expected the ice to drift east-northeast, with the prevailing current and wind as shown on current charts of the day. But the field ice was drifting south rather than east, a fact that Captain Smith did not know when he brought ***TITANIC*** so close to the western edge of the ice fields reported by wireless. When Smith came south to avoid missing the ***DEUTSCHLAND*** he assumed that the field ice had moved well east of ***TITANIC***'s track. It was made clear at the Board of Trade inquiry summary that field ice was expected to drift with the Gulf Stream, which was ENE. The ice could not have come south, said Mersey, on the basis of the information known to them.

But wind and current affect the track of ships, too, although Boxhall did not factor them into ***TITANIC***'s D. R. distress position. But if he had he would have figured them to be as shown on the current charts. In reality there had been strong winds out of the north and northwest for the two weeks prior to ***TITANIC***'s collision with ice, as we may conclude from studying ice reports during that period. On Sunday, 14 April, there had been such a strong wind blowing all day that there had been no boat drill, said Lookout A.B. Archie Jewell, the first witness interrogated at the British inquiry on 3 May. This wind, which did not abate until sunset, had thus created a surface current which would have set south, but for the Coriolis effect which deflected it to somewhat west of south. When Captain Lord said that the set was south, not east, nobody believed him. Lord had been so discredited in the media for so long that anything he said was construed as a lie to indicate that ***CALIFORNIAN*** had actually drifted closer to ***TITANIC*** than Lord said she was. Yet ***CALIFORNIAN*** was pushed along with the field ice, with the wind, deflected by the Coriolis effect. ***TITANIC***, not in the field ice, drifted with the surface current, east-northeast, after she stopped. For almost every surface current there is an opposite sub-surface current, however. As ***TITANIC*** sank she would have been subjected to the subsurface current. ***CALIFORNIAN*** continued to drift for several hours after ***TITANIC*** had hit the bottom. The two ships therefore did drift closer together, but not enough to alter the fact that at their closest they were from 20 to 40 miles apart and ***CALIFORNIAN***'s lights were not visible from ***TITANIC***'s boat deck, nor were ***TITANIC***'s sidelights or even her mastlights visible from ***CALIFORNIAN***'s bridge.

With the strong wind about 45 degrees on ***TITANIC***'s starboard bow, or on her starboard beam, as it must have been during most of Sunday, her track would have been deflected to port, or south, because the resulting current drift would have been setting about athwartship, or 40 degrees to the right of the wind direction. If the wind velocity had been as great as 35 knots, during a 24 hour period she would have been about 17 miles to port of the course laid down by her navigator. This would have been caught with the 7:30PM star sights and her compass course should have been adjusted accordingly. But the surface current would have continued for some hours even after the wind's velocity had decreased, a fact which ***TITANIC***'s navigators could not have known. Thus ***TITANIC***, and any other ships in that vicinity, were somewhat south of where their navigators thought they were. How much south, and how much that error affected ***TITANIC***'s collision with ice cannot be known because none of this was considered in 1912, nor has it been figured in any ***TITANIC*** investigation since then. The effects of wind and current were naturally greater upon a larger vessel than a smaller one because of the greater area upon which the wind and current could exert their pressure. In the case of ***TITANIC***'s unprecedented size this made quite a difference which the two watch officers with experience in ***OLYMPIC*** could have realized, yet they had not the knowledge of later observations to know about the drift of field ice with wind as well as the effect of the earth's rotation. That Captain Smith miscalculated in bringing ***TITANIC*** south as early as he did was greatly due to the as yet unknown effects of the Coriolis force on wind direction and the drift of field ice, something for which he cannot be blamed. If Smith had relied more on instinct and past experience rather than wireless ice reports he might not have come south until he was a few miles farther west and the collision would have been avoided. That the wind was still out of the north or northwest on Sunday night was also proven by Lightoller's statements that he had taken up his watch position on the starboard bridge wing, the weather side of the ship.

Bowditch did teach, however, that field ice is affected by wind more than current, and that fields often had a rotary motion when drifting, although Bowditch taught that this rotary motion was caused by contrary surface currents, an effect which could not be calculated. Perhaps Captain Smith and other shipmasters and watch officers of his era had noted this, yet Smith had only the known *prevailing* set and wind direction to guide him in assessing the movements of known field ice and bergs. If all of the ice reported during the two weeks prior to ***TITANIC***'s accident had drifted with the prevailing wind and surface currents, the ice mass would have been located very near the Southern Track corner, 42°N, 47°W. But as ***TITANIC*** unfortunately proved, the ice concentration was much farther west than that.

When the Department of Transport's Marine Accident Investigation Branch convened primarily at the instigation of Leslie Harrison, former General Secretary of the Mercantile Marine Service Association and Captain Lord's chief defender for many years, to reappraise the evidence relating to the ***CALIFORNIAN*** with reference to ***TITANIC***, the MAIB's Chief Inspector of Marine Accidents, Captain P. B. Marriott, released his conclusions in March, 1992.

Accepting the position of ***TITANIC***'s wreck at the bottom of the North Atlantic to be 41°43'06"N, 49°56'09"W, Captain Marriott thus accepted the southerly set as reported by Captain Lord.

Due to these uncharted, unknown forces, any attempt to make a definite diagram of the ice field encountered by ***CALIFORNIAN***, ***TITANIC***, or any other ship, can be only an approximation, and only for a few moments in time. The ice was drifting, moving, shifting, constantly. Its general drift can only be estimated. There were two distinct ice fields, not one as legend has it, which shifted positions during their southward drift, sometimes allowing a passage between them as ***BORDERER***'s master described, sometimes closing that passage. Many witnesses recalled large bergs within the field ice, and as we have seen, bergs drifting with the surface current were often seen pushing their way through and breaking up field ice which drifted with the wind. The truth is that we will never know the exact position of ice fields or bergs at the time of ***TITANIC***'s impact, but the best clues were given by ***CALIFORNIAN***'s much-maligned master, Captain Stanley Lord, by First Officer Murdoch's cousin-by-marriage. Captain George Black, master of ***BORDERER***, and by ***LACKAWANNA***'s master, Captain Gray, and his watch officer F. E. Townsend. Other limits of the field were given by ***MOUNT TEMPLE***'s master, Captain Moore, at the U. S. Senate Inquiry. Moore's ice coordinates, as well as the coordinates he gave for NDL's ***FRANKFURT***, were taken as absolutely accurate, and have never been questioned. But as we shall see, Moore had good reason to cooperate with those who needed to cover up the truth about ***TITANIC***. Recognizing that readers need some tangible idea of the ice limits on the night ***TITANIC*** foundered, the diagrams of ***LACKAWANNA*** and ***BORDERER*** ice are offered. Bear in mind, that they are only approximations. There is no way that we can know accurately and exactly where the ice fields were at 2340 on 14 April, 1912. The Board of Trade's conclusion, however, was that ***TITANIC*** evaded all ice mentioned in wireless warnings, except two. Those warnings which never reached her bridge were sent from the Atlantic Transport liner ***MESABA*** and from ***CALIFORNIAN***. ***MESABA***'s warning was transmitted to ***TITANIC*** around 11PM ***TITANIC*** time, but Phillips was too busy with paid messages to deliver it to ***TITANIC***'s bridge. Allegedly Phillips told Lightoller about the message just before the senior Marconi operator died and slipped off the overturned Engelhardt. The ***MESABA*** message warned of large icebergs and field ice from 42°N to 41°25'N latitude, from 49°W to 50°30'W longitude. This was precisely the area in which ***TITANIC*** struck ice. While the ***MESABA*** ice warning was sent to all eastbound ships as well as ***TITANIC***, no time for encountering the ice was ever mentioned in the message.

If field ice is approached from windward its edge is usually well-defined. If the pack is approached from leeward, however, the ice is apt to be loose and scattered, which fits in with Lightoller's warning to ***TITANIC***'s lookouts to watch for "small ice and growlers." It is therefore always wise to skirt pack ice and icebergs to windward, and that is precisely what ***TITANIC*** did. Approaching pack ice on its lee side the watch officer may notice that the sea has suddenly become calm, with no visible swell, but here the danger lies in small ice, bergy bits and growlers, exactly what Lightoller warned ***TITANIC***'s lookouts about. On a clear, dark night such as ***TITANIC*** encountered on 14 April, field ice may be visually picked up by its *blink,* a visual phenomenon which displays a markedly pale horizon over the ice area. In fact, an experienced watch officer could read a "sky map" created by this blink when ice fields were numerous and scattered, thus picking the safest way through the ice. When bergs were numerous within the ice field the noise made by their breaking up and capsizing was likened to the sound of breakers or distant discharge of guns. Often the appearance of herds of seals was an indication of nearby icebergs or fields. Studies made by the ice patrol in 1914 proved that no definite air temperature changes could be used as an indication of nearby ice, and that if there are temperature effects of sea water due to the presence of ice these temperature changes were indistinguishable from the normal variations in temperature. It was recommended, however, that when water temperature dropped below 40° Fahrenheit in spring, and below 50° in summer, it was well to be on guard for the presence of ice. At night an iceberg might be sighted by a glimmer of white froth at its base, caused by waves breaking against the hard surface of the ice. An iceberg can rarely be seen at a distance greater than one quarter of a mile under these conditions, although with binoculars an observer might spot the breaking waves at its base from as far as a mile. Much ado has been made over whether ***TITANIC***'s ice could have been seen by the lookouts if they had used binoculars, but it should be remembered that the watch officer *always* had binoculars. It was accepted by commanders that watch officers would see ice before the lookouts did.

Icebergs come in many sizes. They may be several miles in length and several hundred feet in height, as in ***TITANIC*** legend, but always they come in irregular shapes, and dangerous spurs of ice may extend from their bases for hundreds of feet into the sea, underwater and unseen. Contrary to Fifth Officer Lowe's impertinent reply to Senator Smith's question about the composition of icebergs, they are composed of more than ice. They carry rocks, silt, organic and other foreign matter, and they are subjected to differences in temperature of both the air above them and the sea below them, as well as the usual forms of precipitation. All of these factors determine a berg's shape, as well as its odor, and they influence changes in its equilibrium, which may cause the berg to capsize. It may then *calve,* that is, a piece will break off of the parent berg, forming a smaller berg. The side of this new piece of ice which had been underwater will remain dark until it is exposed to the elements long enough to *weather* it, giving it the characteristic crystal-white appearance seen in the classic photographs of icebergs. If the newly spawned piece of ice is about the size of a small, one-story house it is known as a *bergy bit.* If it is still smaller, yet large enough to inflict damage on a ship, it is called a *growler.* Legend has it that ***TITANIC*** struck an "ice mountain," but in reality she struck a bergy bit, or a growler, no higher than her bridge deck. While legend has it that "tons of ice" were deposited on the forward well deck as a result of the impact, there were reliable witnesses who said there was actually only "a little" ice there. It should be remembered that the forward well deck was *three* decks *lower* than the bridge deck.

The legend of one stray mountain of ice looming unexpectedly in ***TITANIC***'s path is just that...

legend… born to satisfy the Harter Act's criteria of *perils of the sea.*

Legend has ignored the fact that every ice warning excepting the final warnings from ***MESABA*** and ***CALIFORNIAN*** indicated to ***TITANIC***'s master, with the knowledge of his era, that the ice fields were east of the 50th meridian by the night of 14 April. We cannot hold Captain Smith responsible for information learned long after his time which would have told him different.

Chapter Six

In the Rockets' White Glare

The Leyland liner ***CALIFORNIAN***, Captain Stanley Lord commanding, arrived at Boston on 19 April at four o'clock in the morning. A combination cargo and passenger vessel of 6,223 GRT, ***CALIFORNIAN*** had departed London on 5 April, bound for Boston. On this voyage she carried no passengers, although she had accommodations for 47, with a crew of 55. With her four lifeboats, a gig and a pinnace, ***CALIFORNIAN*** could save 218 persons with her own boats alone, more than *double* the number of persons she would ever carry. Reporters, knowing from intercepted wireless messages that ***CALIFORNIAN*** ha*d* been near ***TITANIC***, naturally converged upon the ship, badgering crewmen for information. On 24 April ***CALIFORNIAN***'s Second Donkeyman Ernest Gill gave them the following notarized statement:

"I, the undersigned, Ernest Gill, being employed as second donkeyman on the steamer ***CALIFORNIAN***, C*aptain Lord, give the following statement of the incidents of the night of Sunday, April 14:*

"I am 29 years of age; native of Yorkshire; single. I was making my first voyage on the ***CALIFORNIAN***.

"On the night of April 14 I was on duty from 8pm until 12 in the engine room. At 11:56 I came on deck. The stars were shining brightly. It was very clear and I could see for a long distance. The ship's *engines had been stopped since 10:30, and she was drifting amid floe ice. I looked over the rail on the starboard side and saw the lights of a very large steamer about 10 miles away. I could see her broadside lights. I watched her for fully a minute. They could not have helped but see her from the bridge and lookout.*

"It was now 12 o'clock and I went to my cabin. I woke my mate, William Thomas. He heard the ice crunching alongside the ship and asked, 'Are we in the ice?' I replied, 'Yes; but it must be clear off to the starboard, for I saw a big vessel going along full speed. She looked as if she might be a big German.'

"I turned in, but could not sleep. In half an hour I turned out, thinking to smoke a cigarette. Because of the cargo I could not smoke "tween decks, so I went on deck again.

"I had been on deck about 10 minutes when I saw a white rocket about 10 miles away on the starboard side. I thought it must be a shooting star. In seven or eight minutes I saw distinctly a second rocket in the same place, and I said to myself, 'That must be a vessel in distress.'

"It was not my business to notify the bridge or the lookouts; but they could not have helped but see them.

"I turned in immediately after, supposing that the ship would pay attention to the rockets.

"I knew no more until I was awakened at 6:40 by the chief engineer, who said, 'Turn out to render assistance. The ***TITANIC*** *has gone down.'*

"I exclaimed and leaped from my bunk. I went on deck and found the vessel under way and proceeding full speed. She was clear of the field ice, but there were plenty of bergs about.

"I went down on watch and heard the second and fourth engineers in conversation. Mr. J. C. Evans is the second and Mr. Wooten is the fourth. The second was telling the fourth that the third officer had reported rockets had gone up in his watch. I knew then that it must have been the ***TITANIC*** *I had seen.*

"The second engineer added that the captain had been notified by the apprentice officer, whose name I think, is Gibson, of the rockets. The skipper had told him to Morse to the vessel in distress. Mr. Stone, the second navigating officer, was on the bridge at the time, said Mr. Evans.

"I overheard Mr. Evans say that more lights had been shown and more rockets went up. Then, according to Mr. Evans, Mr. Gibson went to the captain again and reported more rockets. The skipper told him to continue to Morse until he got a reply. No reply was received.

"The next remark I heard the second pass was, 'Why in the devil they didn't wake the wireless man up?' The entire crew of the steamer have been talking among themselves about the disregard of the rockets. I personally urged several to join me in protesting against the conduct of the captain, but they refused, because they feared to lose their jobs.

"A day or two before the ship reached port the skipper called the quartermaster, who was on duty at the time the rockets were discharged, into his cabin. They were in conversation about three-quarters of an hour. The quartermaster declared that he did not see the rockets.

*"I am quite sure that the **CALIFORNIAN*** was *less than 20 miles from the **TITANIC**, which the officers report to have been our position. I could not have seen her if she had been more than 10 miles distant, and I saw her very plainly.*

"I have no ill will toward the captain or any officer of the ship, and I am losing a profitable berth by making this statement. I am actuated by the desire that no captain who refuses or neglects to give aid to a vessel in distress should be able to hush up the men.

(signed) Ernest Gill

"Sworn and subscribed to before me this 24th day of April, 1912.

(signed) Samuel Putnam, Notary Public"

*ABOVE: A NOAA expedition discovered the case of **TITANIC**'s rocketrs on the ocean floor. The nose-cone of each rocket indicates the color; as can be clearly seen, **TITANIC** was carrying white rockets.*

Why, in over eight decades since ***TITANIC***'s loss, has no one ever investigated the rockets fired from the White Star liner's bridge on that fatal night?

The answer is simple. Because the rockets have been continually referred to and labeled as *"distress rockets,"* nobody has thought to find out if they were in fact *"distress rockets"* as defined by the *International Rules of the Road* which were in effect in *1912,* and by a ***1912 sailor's understanding*** *of the Rules of the Road definition* of a distress rocket. The *International Rules of the Road* are explicit in defining distress rockets, although it has been argued otherwise by the men involved in the 1912 ***TITANIC*** inquiries and subsequent ***TITANIC*** investigation.

*Article 31, Distress Signals, At Night: **First**... (called Class 1 by the British) A gun or other explosive signal fired at intervals of about a minute.* (This is usually called a "minute gun.") ***Second**... (Class 2) Flames on the vessel as from a burning tar barrel, oil barrel, and so forth. **Third**... (Class 3) Rockets or shells throwing stars of any color or description, fired one at a time, at short intervals. **Fourth**... (Class 4) A continuous sounding with any fog-signal apparatus.* (Explanatory information in parentheses by the author.)

Legend has it that ***TITANIC***'s rockets were all-white, as were *"all distress rockets,"* that they were *"detonators used in lieu of signal cannon shells."* The facts are quite different.

The first flaw in this explanation of ***TITANIC***'s rockets is that as a distress signal satisfying the *Class 1* criteria the detonations should have been made at about one minute intervals on the assumption that officers on the bridge of a vessel over the horizon could hear the minute gun, yet not be within sight of the ship from which it was fired. Fourth Officer Boxhall admitted that he fired the rockets as long as five minutes apart. The reason for being at least fairly specific about the timing of the detonations lies in *Article 12, International and Inland Rules of the Road, Special Signals,* which stated: *"Every vessel may, if necessary in order to attract attention, in addition to the lights which she is by these rules required to carry, show a flare-up light or use any* ***detonating signal that can not be mistaken for a distress signal.*** *Note 12… This may be very useful to attract the attention of* ***a ship whose duty it is to keep clear****, if she does not show a disposition to act. A detonating signal would be especially valuable, and such signals should be kept on the bridge."* (Emphasis by the author.)

Therefore, if ***TITANIC***'s alleged "detonators" were fired alone, at anything other than nearly one minute apart, they could have been mistaken for a signal other than distress. A vessel not under way, but not in need of assistance, might have used a flare-up light or detonating device as a means of attracting attention to the fact that she could not maneuver out of the way of another vessel, for example, if she was trapped in field ice perhaps in a lead which had closed around her. In other words, ***TITANIC***'s detonating signals coming several minutes apart literally meant *"keep clear of me."*

Further, an explosive device used in lieu of a signal cannon would be much like the salutes, or *maroons* as the British call them, used in fireworks displays, usually as part of the finale. As such, the explosion should have been felt as well as heard by anyone nearby. Such an explosive concussion at close range can be felt in the chest, in the gut, as well as in the ears. Not one survivor mentioned such a force although the detonation occurred at altitudes no more than 400 to 800 feet above them and should have been the most noticeable thing about the rockets. While it is true that during the firing of the rockets ***TITANIC*** was blowing off steam from her boilers because of her sudden stopping, and this noise could have drowned out sounds of the rockets' explosions, still the concussion should have been *felt,* and anyone who has dealt with pyrotechnics or ordnance can testify to that.

As we have seen with ***ARCTIC***, it is possible to not hear a signal gun, or detonator, if the listener is upwind of the sound source. Herein lay a fatal flaw in using only the detonator or signal cannon for a distress signal. Before the use of wireless, when ships relied only upon sound and visual distress signals, such as the cannon and rockets, the two were used simultaneously, or alternated, one for sound, one for sight, the rockets being strictly a night signal while during daylight hours other visual signals were used with the minute gun as prescribed by the *Rules of the Road.* However, the eye could sight a rocket's apogee many miles farther than an explosive device could be heard, or signal flags could be seen, so obviously the master of a vessel in distress during daylight hours might also use rockets. The visual pyrotechnic Signal could be seen in all directions, the sound signal could be lost to those upwind of its source. In other words, when you are in dire need of aid you use every means at your disposal to attract attention. If the weather was inclement, with a very low ceiling it was possible to lose sight of the rocket's apogee, of course, and the detonation would then be the only discernible signal unless the rockets could be aimed at launch to lower the apogee, keeping it below the ceiling. Such was the case of the fogbound ***BALTIC*** and ***REPUBLIC*** trying to locate each other after the latter's collision in 1909. (See Chapter 13, Other Shipwrecks) As we shall see, however, any lowering of the launch angle from 90 degrees would give a false impression of the position of a vessel in distress, and it could be enough of a difference to make a search for her difficult in foul weather.

The velocity of sound in quiet, open air the temperature of which is at the freezing point (32 degrees Fahrenheit, 0 degrees Celsius) is approximately 1,090 feet per second. Sound velocity decreases with temperature drop, increases with rise in air temperature. Sound travels more readily through moist air so that distant sounds are easily heard when the humidity is high. Sailors for centuries forecast weather by such signs, giving rise to rhymes which were surprisingly accurate. One such couplet ran:

Sound traveling far and wide,
A stormy day will betide.

Conversely, lower humidity would mean that sound did not travel as far. Sound signals can be erratic anyway. The watchword of a sentinel may be heard 10 1/2 miles across the water, while a cannon may be heard 20 miles. Wind naturally affects the traveling distance of sound. It has been noted that when sound has to travel against the wind it may seem to be thrown upwards, therefore a person aloft, in the crow's nest for example, may hear it when those on the bridge do not. In the case of ***TITANIC*** and ***CALIFORNIAN***, with wind out of the north, sound from ***TITANIC***'s rockets could have been impeded by wind which was not noticeable on the surface while at 670 to 870 feet, the altitude at which the rockets exploded and from which the sound emanated, the wind was strong enough to throw the sound upwards, well out of the range of ***CALIFORNIAN***'s bridge or crow's nest. This was one problem which could arise in using a rocket detonation at altitudes of up to 800 feet above bridge level instead of a signal cannon mounted on the fore deck of a vessel.

The argument has been put forth that ***TITANIC***'s rockets were both the visual distress signal prescribed by the *Rules of the Road,* ***Class 3***, *"rockets or shells throwing stars of any* ***color*** *or description,"* and the ***Class 1*** criteria for a sound signal, *"a gun or other explosive device,"* that there was no distinction between them.

The fact is that there *was* a distinction between night visual and sound signals, but ***TITANIC***'s rockets should have contained both components, visual and aural, *if* she was showing distress rockets which were recognized and accepted as such by seamen of the era.

Pyrotechnic displays approved in ***TITANIC***'s time by the Board of Trade for use as distress signals on board British passenger ships included *Holmes' danger signals* and *McKirdy*'s *danger signals,* both of which produced a simulation of *"flames on the vessel"* and were regarded as equivalent to the *Class 2* night distress signal of *Article 31, International Rules of the Road.* Had either of these two pyrotechnic signals been used at least most of ***TITANIC***'s people could have been saved, and the ship herself might have been saved because the simulated flames would have been unmistakable. Also approved were *socket distress signals,* their name meaning only that they were fired from a socket mounted on a bridge rail, from whence they ascended to a height of 600 to 800 feet, where they burst with the report of a gun and the stars of a rocket. *Socket light signals* as described by B.O.T. regulations rose to a height of about 500 feet where they burst with the stars of a rocket, but had no sound. In addition there was listed *Crundall*'s *distress signal,* which was a Roman candle throwing twelve brilliant red balls at short intervals. Crundall's distress signal and the socket light signal were regarded as equivalent to the *Class 3* night distress signal *"rockets or shells throwing stars of any color or description."* Because there was no sound with either of these signals they should have been used in conjunction with a signal cannon or other detonating device. The "socket distress signals" were regarded as equivalent to the *Class 1* distress signal or *explosive device fired at intervals of about a minute,"* as well as the *Class 3, "rockets or shells throwing stars of any color or description."*

VISIBILITY AT VARIOUS LEVELS OVER THE SEA

THE RELATIONSHIP OF DISTANCE AND HEIGHT ON THE OCEAN

Height In Feet	Distance In Nautical Miles	Height In Feet	Distance In Nautical Miles	Height In Feet	Distance In Nautical Miles
5	2.55	70	9.56	250	18.07
10	3.61	75	9.90	300	19.80
15	4.43	80	10.22	350	21.38
20	5.11	85	10.54	400	22.86
25	5.71	90	10.84	450	24.24
30	6.26	95	11.14	500	25.56
35	6.76	100	11.43	550	26.80
40	7.23	110	11.99	600	27.99
45	7.67	120	12.52	650	29.14
50	8.08	130	13.03	700	30.24
55	8.48	140	13.52	800	32.32
60	8.85	150	14.00	900	34.29
65	9.21	200	16.16	1,000	36.14

ABOVE; The Visibility Table gives the approximate geographic range of visibility for an object which may be seen by an observer whose eye is at sea level. It is necessary therefore, to add to these a distance of visibility corresponding to the height of the observer's eye above sea level. These distances may be increased by abnormal atmospheric refraction, or may be decreased by unfavorable weather conditions (i.e., fog, rain, haze or smoke). Colored lights are more easily obscured by such conditions. Distances corresponding to heights not included in the table may be found approximately by the formula $D= 8/7 \sqrt{H}$, in which H= the height in feet of the object above sea level, and D= the corresponding distance of visibility, in nautical miles. The formula is based on the mean curvature of the earth and is corrected for ordinary atmospheric refraction.

Clearly the Board of Trade did differentiate between *Class 1,* or aural signals, and *Class 3,* or visual signals, and properly so because the *Rules of the Road* were international law. In addition to the *Rules of the* Road-approved distress signals, the Board of Trade had approved a rocket throwing one white star to be used by British fishing vessels when they urgently needed aid from one of His Majesty's cruisers which were assigned to protect the fishing fleets. The point to this dissertation is simply that both *sound* and *visual* signals were needed concurrently to constitute a distress signal at night which would be unmistakable at maximum distances under all atmospheric conditions. If the vessel responding to the visual pyrotechnic signal was out of sound range of the vessel firing it, then there had to be some way to discern the difference between a pyrotechnic distress signal, and a pyrotechnic signal which was not a distress signal. The only way to do that was by the color of the rocket star burst. It must be clearly understood that in 1912 very few ships carried wireless equipment, therefore pyrotechnic signaling was the only means of communicating at night between those ships which had no wireless. While most latter-day ***TITANIC*** historians cannot comprehend an era before television, let alone radio, the common sight of rockets and flares at sea in ***TITANIC's*** time precluded having every vessel within sight of the pyrotechnic signals dashing madly over the waves with salvage in the mind of every crewman.

Because there were no prescribed colors for distress rockets in 1912 distress rockets could be any color, including white, so say those who believe the official version of ***TITANIC***'s all white pyrotechnic displays described as *"distress rockets."* ***TITANIC***'s rockets thus met both the *Class 1* and *Class 3* sound and sight criteria in that they exploded at their apogee with the sound of a signal gun while throwing stars. So say legend and officialdom.

The crux of the matter is the definition of *"color."*

We may study any artist's color wheel. Primary colors are red, blue and yellow. Secondary colors are mixtures of primary colors. If you mix red and blue, you get purple, a secondary color. If you mix blue and yellow you get green, a secondary color. If you mix red and yellow you get orange, a secondary color. A tint is any *color* to which *white* is added. Some dictionaries define white as *"the absence of color,"* which is what this author was taught in art school as the definition of white. Some dictionaries elaborate about wavelengths of light, a physicist's definition of color. Some define color as a *"hue, contrasted with white, gray or black."* Reading the directions on a box of any laundry detergent one finds that white and colored laundry items are treated differently, therefore it is obvious that white and colored items must be separated. If by chance they are not separated, today that might not be disastrous because most colors are *"colorfast,"* meaning that their dyes will not "run" or fade on to other items in the wash. But in ***TITANIC***'s era, when laundry was soaked in washtubs in strong lye soap and very hot water, colors did run, and thus they were washed separately from whites, which were bleached as well. Every housewife therefore knew the difference between white and colors, and so did every sailor who ever had to wash his own clothes.

If you ask me what color my car is, and I answer "white," it does not necessarily mean that I consider white a color, nor do I see any necessity to elaborate and answer "my car has no color, it is white." When available colors for garments sold through a catalog are listed with white among them, it does not mean that white is a color, only that the garment is also available in white, and this is understood by prospective customers. When the manufacturers of colored pencils, crayons, pens, pastels, inks, oils, acrylics and watercolors pack white pencils, crayons, pastels, inks and paints along with their colors it does not mean that they consider white a color. In fact, an English manufacturer of exceptionally fine artist's oils and acrylics does provide separate charts for its colors and whites. We distinguish in common usage between *color* film and *black and white* film. Some of us remember when movies came only in black and white. Many of us deplore the modern practice of *"colorizing"* those wonderfully dramatic black and white films. And in my medicine cabinet is a bottle of *"decolorized* iodine," which is also known as *"white* iodine." It is, among other things, an old folk remedy for brittle fingernails, and it is a clear liquid without the characteristic reddish-brown iodine *color.*

The major question, then, is simply, what did a 1912 sailor understand by the *Rules of the Road* criteria for distress rockets or shells *"throwing stars of any* color *or description?"* It is necessary to return to *pre-**TITANIC*** 1912 to see ***TITANIC's*** rockets through the eyes of a seaman of that era. What was his definition of color as opposed to white?

Theoretically one would expect that any pyrotechnic color could be used and recognized as a distress signal. After all. *Article 31* does say *"any color,"* does it not? In reality this was not the case simply because pyrotechnics manufacturers were, and are, limited by the chemical combinations used in the making of fireworks to produce certain colors. Pyrotechnic formulas existed in 1912 for yellow, blue, red, green and orange as well as white. In 1912 there was no pyrotechnic formula for making a clear, bright blue. Blues were either too pale and apt to be mistaken for white, or too dark to show up against a night sky. Even today a formula for a bright clear blue in fireworks is highly prized, a closely guarded secret among professional and amateur pyrotechnists alike. But even a clear, perfect blue, had it been available, would not have made enough contrast against a night sky, which can be an infinite number of shades of blue and gray, while at sunset turning into night the sky may take on any number of shades of yellow, orange, deep fuchsias, mauves and purples, which quickly become indigo shading rapidly into midnight blue, all of which were of interest to a sailor because the colors of the evening sky forecast the next day's weather. Remember that rockets of *any color or description* were a *night visual* signal as mandated by the *Rules of the Road.* Yellows were apt to be too pale, too easily mistaken for white. Orange had the same problems as yellow. What did that leave? Red and green, as the only clear, unmistakably bright, easily identified colors for distress rockets. The chemicals used for red and green pyrotechnics happened to be tried and true, and relatively stable, a necessity for storage at sea. Red and green were easily recognized at sea, for they were the colors of sidelights. And bright red or green could be easily seen during daylight hours for the master desperate enough to use rockets then. Therefore, whether colors were specified or not, rockets throwing *red* or *green* stars came into common usage and thus were exactly what a 1912 seaman expected to see as distress signals, because that was what was available to fireworks manufacturers. And distress rockets were nothing more, nothing less, than the rockets and shells we Americans see in every Fourth of July fireworks display. Whether the stars in distress rockets were red or green was entirely up to the manufacturer, but British manufacturers seemed to prefer bright green, which was also the one clear color that was not apt to be found in a night sky still lit by the lingering rays of a setting sun.

In his autobiography *Clipper Ships to Ocean Greyhounds* (Harold Starke Ltd., London, 1971) former Nourse Line and Cunard deck officer Hans de Mierre described a stormy night off the Goodwins and his first experience in steam.

The Nelson Line's ***HIGHLAND SCOT*** was an aging, rusting tramp bound for the knacker when de Mierre boarded her in London as Second Officer at the end of November, 1909. Among other supplies for which the Second Mate was responsible, were distress rockets. De Mierre saw to it that the requisite numbers and types of pyrotechnic signals were aboard.

Empty, bound for the Mersey, ***HIGHLAND SCOT*** rode dangerously light, her screw and rudder only half submerged. She passed Southend in freezing rain squalls raging out of the northeast, with the barometer plunging rapidly Dropping her pilot at Deal, ***HIGHLAND SCOT***, 3,060 tons, 320 feet long, continued on past the Downs, with her new Second Officer alone on the bridge. De Mierre was surprised to find that the master was not lurking in the wheelhouse to keep an eye on him. The wind grew stronger, accompanied by sleet and hail. Smaller vessels were running for cover.

Approaching Dungeness, ***HIGHLAND SCOT*** ventured out of the lee of the land, and felt the full force of the 60 knot gale. Pitching heavily, underpowered, with her stern now so far out of the water that her screw and rudder were useless, she refused to answer her helm. Helplessly she fell off into the trough and only de Mierre's recent experience in sail could save her. Two red globe-lamps were hoisted up the signal halyard, the lights to be shown by a vessel not under command, but not yet in need of assistance. Captain Brown told de Mierre to break out the distress rockets, to have them ready to use if necessary. De Mierre described the rocket-bombs, as he called them, and the process of firing them.

They were small canisters about six inches long and two inches in diameter. He put one rocket/bomb in one pocket of his jacket, placing the lanyard and detonator in another pocket. Bolted to the deck was the firing socket, a bronze tube something like a miniature howitzer. It pointed upward, outward from the ship's rail. De Mierre removed the protective wooden cap from the tube, and saw to it that there was no water in the socket. He put the detonator into the hole in the center of the rocket's bottom, hooked one end of the firing lanyard to the small wire loop in the detonator, and attached the other end to the rail, and then he inserted the rocket into the bronze firing tube. All it needed to fire and release its shower of bright *green* stars was a smart pull on the lanyard. De Mierre set up another rocket on the opposite side of the ship. Then de Mierre, with the aid of several seamen, rigged a foresail to bring ***HIGHLAND SCOT's*** head into the wind and sea where her engines and rudder could again control her. This story had a happy ending. ***HIGHLAND SCOT*** clawed her way off the Goodwins, made it safely back to the Downs and shelter, while not far away, off Beachy Head just west of Dover, two steamers were driven ashore. But de Mierre's description of distress rockets of the era remains one of the most comprehensive in maritime literature. And although the young Second Mate never had to fire them, he *knew* the distress rockets would throw *green* stars, a fact which he seemed compelled to mention. It should also be noted that the sockets mounted on the bridges of ships needed to be of standard diameter to accommodate rockets made by the hundreds and dispensed for emergency use in many different types of ships. Fortunately for ***HIGHLAND SCOT*** de Mierre never saw the rockets fired and therefore could not record the height of their apogee. Obviously the higher the apogee the more propellant needed, thus the larger the canister. A shipowner would spend as little as possible on a tramp bound for the knacker, her equipment being barely adequate no doubt to satisfy her underwriters if she were lost at sea, in which case her insurance would probably have paid better than breaking her up. The small size of her rocket canisters therefore did not match those fired from ***TITANIC*** but their method of construction and firing were necessarily exactly the same.

Did ***TITANIC***'s rockets even meet the distress rocket criterion *"throwing **stars**?"*

Maybe. Maybe not. Not one ***TITANIC*** survivor seems to have had the knowledge of pyrotechnics necessary to discriminate between stars, or debris falling from the explosion of a rocket carrying only flash powder to simulate the *Class 1* distress signal *(a gun or other explosive device).* Any rocket will explode at apogee to release its payload, but if the payload is only stars or other visual pyrotechnic material the explosion, although it might sound like the firing of a small-caliber gun, will not be anything like a maroon, or signal cannon.

From descriptions given later by witnesses we could never tell for sure just what ***TITANIC***'s rockets really were. Unfortunately nobody ever made any effort to clear up this subject while ***TITANIC***'s surviving officers were still living. But one thing we can be sure of... ***TITANIC***'s rockets were *not* distress rockets as prescribed by the *International Rules of the Road Class 3 criteria,* and as recognized *by a pre-**TITANIC** 1912 mariner.* It is exceedingly odd that the man who fired them. Fourth Officer Boxhall, an officer in one of the most prestigious passenger lines afloat, handpicked for the crew of that line's newest ship, did not seem to know what a distress rocket would look like, yet only three years earlier the young second mate of a British tramp knew exactly what to expect from a distress rocket.

A rocket used for signaling in ***TITANIC***'s era was essentially the same as one used in fireworks displays today. It was simply a hollow projectile, or tube, made of special heavy paper, filled with pyrotechnic material consisting of a propellant which burned through and ignited the payload of flash powder and/or stars at the height of the rocket's climb. A mixture of potassium chlorate or potassium perchlorate, sulfur and aluminum powder, flash powder was developed in the last century and gained extensive usage as a means of providing illumination for photographs. Flash powder explodes rapidly, with a bright, white flash, and a bang which can be perfect for salutes or "maroons." Black powder, a ground-up mixture of potassium nitrate, sulfur and charcoal, has been used from the 13th century until the present time. It burns slowly when ignited, is relatively noiseless, makes a good propellant if confined, and is relatively stable. Cotton treated with nitric acid came into use as a propellant in 1838, but its manufacture and storage resulted in many disastrous explosions, until about 1865 when a relatively safe method of manufacture and storage was discovered.

The rocket's propellant was ignited in ***TITANIC*** as in ***HIGHLAND SCOT***, by a lanyard which, when pulled sharply, created a friction-activated spark which set off the propellant powder. The slow-burning powder created gases which exerted tremendous pressure on the inside of the rocket casing, except where the gases escaped through a vent in the bottom of the rocket called the *"choke."* This pressure therefore manifested most strongly on the inner forward portion of the container, thus driving the rocket upward until the propellant burned through to ignite the bursting charge and release the payload. The rocket's manufacturer, having great experience, knew just how to pack the propellant and how much of it to use, timing it to burn through and ignite the payload at the desired altitude. In the case of a distress rocket the payload should have been flash powder for a loud report, and colored stars to spread out in the night sky and drift slowly to the water's surface.

The stars were pellets of varying sizes and number, often seeds from different plants, rolled and shaped, then dipped in the desired chemicals and coloring agents, shaped again until they were round, then inserted into the canister and ignited at the apogee of its climb by the bursting charge. Because much of the pyrotechnic material contained in a rocket is needed for propulsion, as opposed to a shell which acquires its propulsion from an external source, rockets can carry fewer stars than shells of the same size, and shells are most often used in fireworks displays today. Thus ***TITANIC***'s rockets may very well have been limited to a payload of flash powder for sound, without the stars for a visual show. Rockets have been around for many centuries, and originally were steadied and aimed on their upward course by long sticks, often made of bamboo, attached to the rocket casing at one end, the other end being pushed into the ground to provide a solid launch platform which gave the rocket direction. Ships' rockets were steadied and aimed not by bamboo sticks, but by firing them from a strong, metal tube, as we have seen in the account of ***HIGHLAND SCOT***.

The only record we have of ***TITANIC***'s rockets is what artists have painted of them using myth alone to guide them, and the ambiguous descriptions left to us by survivors, who have described those pyrotechnic signals with puzzling variety.

The first mention of ***TITANIC***'s rockets came in Washington on 22 April, from the man who had fired them ,Fourth Officer Joseph Groves Boxhall. *"They go right up into the air and they throw stars,"* said Boxhall, referring to distress rockets in general. The Fourth Officer had just described the ship's lights he had seen about two points off ***TITANIC***'s port bow. Boxhall explained to Senator Smith that he had fired rockets and used the Morse light to attract the attention of the mystery ship's watch officer.

"The failure to arouse the attention of this ship was not due to any impaired or partial success of these signals?" asked Senator Smith, referring to the rockets.

"Not at all, sir," replied Boxhall. What else would he say?

When Third Officer Herbert John Pitman was recalled in Washington on 23 April Senator Smith asked *"Did you see any rockets?"*

"I should say about a dozen rockets were fired."

"What did you see? What did they do?" asked Smith.

"They were fired from the rail. They make a report while leaving the rail, and also an explosion in the

air, and they throw stars, of course, in the air."

"Red in color?" asked Smith.

"Various colors," answered Pitman.

Later Senator Smith asked, *"Did the firing of the rockets make any noise like the report of a pistol?"*

Pitman's reply, *"Like the report of a gun."* Note that he did not say like the report of a *cannon.* Any rocket will make a report because it has to contain explosives of some kind for its propelling and bursting charges. To simulate a signal cannon, however, it needed much more. It needed flash powder or its equivalent to make the very loud boom which could be heard as far as 20 miles across the water.

The next description of the rockets came on the afternoon of 23 April, from Canadian passenger Major Arthur Godfrey Peuchen. Senator Smith asked Peuchen if he saw any rockets fired from ***TITANIC.*** When Peuchen answered in the affirmative. Smith asked, *"What colored rockets... red and all colors?"*

Peuchen's vague reply, *"A good deal like an ordinary skyrocket, going up and breaking, and the different colors flying down."*

On 24 April Fifth Officer Harold Godfrey Lowe described the rockets as "deafening." Lowe is the only one to suggest that the rockets may have satisfied *Class 1,* although as noted above, any rocket will explode at apogee and some people will find the noise more noticeable than others.

Quartermaster Rowe on 25 April told how he had been at his station aft, and had seen a lifeboat in the water. He had telephoned the navigating bridge to find out if the officers there knew that a boat had been lowered. The officer who answered had asked Rowe if he was the Third Officer. When Rowe replied that he was the Quartermaster, he was ordered to bring a box of detonators to the main bridge. Rowe explained that the detonators *"are used in firing distress signals."*

This is apparently the origin of the legend, and the excuse, that ***TITANIC***'s rockets were "detonators in lieu of signal cannon." But a detonator is a device used to fire, or detonate, an explosive. It may also be defined as an explosive, but Rowe's statement about the box of detonators being ***"used in firing*** *distress signals"* indicates that they were not distress signals in themselves, rather they were the device used to fire, or ignite the propellant in the rockets fired from ***TITANIC***'s bridge rail. De Mierre's description of the detonators inserted into the center of the distress rockets and connected to the firing lanyard supports this. Why would the detonators have been stored apart from the rockets themselves? Obviously, for safety. An accidental explosion of a distress or other pyrotechnic signal at sea could be deadly, especially in a passenger ship. Thus the rockets were kept separate from their firing device until they were to be used. Boxhall had told Senator Smith that "*... these distress rockets are dangerous things if they explode, and I had to keep people away clear while I fired the rockets."*

Legend also has it that because they were very new, the detonators in lieu of signal cannon were not recognized as distress rockets. But by 1912 signal cannon had been replaced in all but the oldest tramps for many years. Signal cannon had been long gone in transatlantic passenger liners by the turn of the century. The elite floating palaces in the North Atlantic trade no longer carried signal cannon for two simple reasons. Rockets were cheaper, and smaller, thus easily stored out of sight. The presence on the fore deck of the signal cannon always reminded passengers of the dangers of the sea. By 1912 distress rockets had replaced signal cannon for enough years that "rocket-bombs" like those aboard ***HIGHLAND SCOT*** were recognized by deck officers everywhere. Those officers who had not actually seen a distress rocket fired, however, had the description given in the *International Rules of the Road* to guide them. If, however, ***TITANIC***'s rockets were indeed merely *"detonators used in lieu of signal cannon"* then they should never have been used alone, especially at night, to signify distress.

On 26 April ***CALIFORNIAN***'s Second Donkeyman Ernest Gill gave Senator Fletcher different descriptions of the rockets all in one sentence. The rockets were *pale blue,* or *white,* said Gill. When Fletcher asked for clarification Gill answered that they were *"apt to be a clear blue,"* then changed that to *"I reckon it was white."* When asked if the stars spangled out. Gill was even more confused. *"Yes, sir; the stars spangled out. I could not say about the stars."*

In fact, every bit of Gill's testimony was confused and confusing. It almost seemed as if Gill had not seen ***TITANIC***'s rockets at all. Or, Gill had seen them at a great distance, did not see anything about them that indicated distress, and thus paid no attention to them at the time. After obtaining Gill's affirmation under oath that his signed statement taken two days earlier was true. Senator Fletcher asked, *"What direction was the **CALIFORNIAN** going?"*

"We were headed for Boston, sir."

*"In what direction were the rockets from the **CALIFORNIAN** when you first saw them?"* asked Fletcher.

"On the starboard side, forward," was Gill's frustratingly ambiguous answer. Few of the crewmen involved in the ***TITANIC*** inquiries seemed to have any real sense of direction, in spite of the fact that on such a brilliantly clear night any seaman worth his salt should have been able to tell direction by the stars. Even Gill should have recognized at least the Pole Star.

*"Was the **CALIFORNIAN** passed by the **TITANIC**, her course being the same as **TITANIC**'s course was originally?"* Fletcher asked.

*"I think she must have passed the **TITANIC**. The **TITANIC** must have passed us first, because we were floating, and that would take a lot out of her way. We were a slower boat."*

Again Gill's answer was so enigmatic that it made no sense at all. Belonging to the engine department he did not use nautical terms, and he would not have known anything about ***CALIFORNIAN***'s navigation. Obviously ***CALIFORNIAN*** was "floating," or Gill would not have been there to tell his tale. And ***CALIFORNIAN*** was hove to, drifting with wind and current, from 10:21PM ship's time throughout the remainder of the night. She could hardly have passed ***TITANIC***, under any circumstances. Being hove to would certainly "take a lot out of her way," for ***CALIFORNIAN*** was *stopped,* meaning she had no way on her at all.

Senator Fletcher apparently tried to connect the facts. ***CALIFORNIAN*** was supposed to be stopped. The "mystery ship" was moving. How could the two fit together?

*"After the **TITANIC** struck the iceberg did the **CALIFORNIAN** pass by the **TITANIC**?"* Fletcher asked.

"The only way I can account for this, we were stopped in the ocean, and it is not natural for a ship to keep her head one way all the time. She must have been drifting," was Gill's guess.

As we have seen, most single-screw steamships had right-handed propellers, that is, the screw turned in a clockwise direction when viewed from the stern, with the engines going ahead. A right-handed screw, turning over slowly ahead, with rudder amidships, has a tendency to cause the ship's stern to travel to starboard, resultantly forcing the bow to port. When the speed is increased, this tendency to force the stern to starboard diminishes. When the screw is backing, with rudder amidships, it turns counter-clockwise, forcing the stern to port and bow to starboard. As the speed in reverse is increased the stern goes to port, bow to starboard that much faster. When ***CALIFORNIAN*** was stopped for the night by backing her single screw, her head thus swung to starboard before she came to a complete stop.

A ship hove to, lying with engines stopped in a smooth sea, with the wind abeam, will gradually fall off from the wind. If her draft is even fore and aft, she will bring the wind abeam. If she is trimmed down by the stern, she will bring the wind abaft the beam. If her engine is reversed while she makes little headway, with head to wind, she will in a short time tum her stern to the wind by falling off to starboard. If she lies hove to, drifting in a current, she will sooner or later drift broadside to the set of the current.

Thus, when ***CALIFORNIAN*** was stopped by reversing her screw, her head first fell off to starboard. She then slowly turned to starboard until she finally drifted broadside to the set, which was southerly, and her heading thus became westerly.

Cross-examined in London by Leyland Line Attorney Dunlop, Gill admitted that at the time he had not thought they were distress rockets. Unfortunately Dunlop did not ask Gill why they did not look like distress rockets, but he did suggest that if Gill had believed they were distress rockets he would have immediately thought about salvage and told somebody about seeing them. Gill also admitted to Sir Robert Finlay that he had no idea which direction the "big passenger ship" he had seen was heading. *"My compass is the steam gauge,"* said Gill. In Gill's original statement there had been other flaws. He said he saw the "broadside" lights of a large steamer. Because nobody clarified that vague statement we have no way of knowing whether he meant her side running light, red for port, green for starboard, or white deck and porthole lights.

The Attorney General made a point of letting Dunlop know that he disagreed with the conclusion that nobody paid any attention to the rockets. In fact, Isaacs insinuated that Dunlop had privately seen Gill and persuaded the donkeyman to change his story.

It is worth noting that Gill's shipmates in ***CALIFORNIAN*** did not agree with him. Unfortunately nobody asked them officially about this, probably with good reason, although it was common talk in the forecastle that Gill had received a good sum of money for his affidavit. Gill's mate, William Thomas, told reporters that he was highly indignant that his name had been brought into Gill's notarized statement.

"I think that Gill would have told me if he'd seen rockets. I can't believe that he could see a ship ten miles off if there was one, because the change from the engine room to the deck partly blinds a man, and besides that night it would have been easy to take fixed stars for vessels' lights and shooting stars for rockets. Yesterday afternoon, the barman from a Marginal Street saloon came to me and said I was wanted at the 'pub.'" Thomas continued. *"I went over and when I got there, the bartender said to me, You're not the fellow. Where's the chap that was with you yesterday with a brown suit on?' I knew that was Gill,* so *went back and told him. He went away then without telling me where he was going. He came back sometime later, didn't say a word to me, but soon went ashore again. He must have taken all his dunnage with him, for there isn't any here now. Gill was engaged to a girl in England and I can see where the offer of a sum as large as reported in the forecastle would greatly tempt him. He could very easily set up a small shop in England, or get work in America with a comfortable nest egg in addition."*

When Senator Fletcher asked him how he could know exactly the time at which he had seen the big passenger ship. Gill replied, *"Because at five minutes to 12 I was working with the fourth engineer at a pump that kicked, that would not work, and while we were interested in our work we forgot the time; and I looked up, and I said, 'It is five minutes to 12. I haven't called my mate, Mr. Wooten. I will go call him.' And I got to the ladder to climb out of the engine room and get on deck. That taken me one minute, to get up there."*

Senator Fletcher asked next, *"Was this ship (**CALIFORNIAN**)* m*oving at that time?"*

"I did not take particular notice of it, sir, with the rushing to call my mate. I went along the deck. It

taken me about a minute, going along the deck, to get to the hatch I had to go down, and I could see her as I walked along the deck. Suppose I am going forward, now; I could see her over there (indicating), a big ship, and a couple of rows of lights; so that I knew it was not any small craft. It was no tramp. I did not suppose it would be a 'Star' *boat. I reckoned she must be a German boat. So I dived down the hatch, and as I turned around in the hatch I could not see her, so you can guess the latitude she was in.* As *I stood on the hatch, with my back turned, I could not see the ship. Then I went and called my mate, and that is the last I saw of it."*

"How long after that was it before you saw the rockets go up?"

"About 35 minutes, sir; a little over half an hour."

"Did you observe the rockets go up in the direction this ship was as you first saw her, from where the ***CALIFORNIAN*** was?" Fletcher asked.

"It was more abeam, sir; more broadside of the ship." Again Gill confused the issue with his reference to direction from the ship, and Fletcher failed to clarify Gill's description.

"In the meantime the ***CALIFORNIAN***, as *I understand, was drifting?"*

"Yes, sir."

"She was not under way at all?"

"No, sir."

"Was the ship too far away, when you saw the rockets going up, for you to see the lights on her?" Fletcher persisted.

"Yes, sir; no sign of the ship." Gill repeated.

This statement makes it obvious that Gill saw only the apogee of each rocket, that he never saw the running lights, not even the mastlights, of the vessel firing rockets.

"What time was it when you heard these officers discussing this matter that was mentioned in this statement?"

"Twenty minutes past 8 on Monday morning," Gill answered.

Fletcher asked Gill if he had been discharged from the ***CALIFORNIAN***, and Gill replied that he still belonged to the ship.

Senator Smith joined in the interrogation, bringing up the subject of the ***FRANKFURT.***

"Mr. Gill, did you ever see the North German-Lloyd ***FRANKFURT?"*** Smith asked.

"No, sir."

"What made you think that this ship you saw, or thought you saw, was a 'German ship'?"

"Because the German ship would be heading to New York at about that time."

"Heading for New York?" Smith asked.

"Or from New York. It is in that vicinity we meet those boats." Gill was vague again, did not seem to know which direction the liner he saw was heading. And Gill was making his first voyage in ***CALIFORNIAN***. How would he know where she met German ships? Like Fletcher, Smith did not pursue his line of questioning in order to clarify any of this. It was clear, however, that Senator Smith intended to delve further into the ***FRANKFURT*** matter.

In retrospect it is absolutely amazing that Captain Lord should have been judged guilty solely on the strength of Gill's vague statements. Gill's answers to the senators' questions were all so ambiguous that they made little sense other than to say that he may have seen the apogee of one or more of ***TITANIC***'s white rockets from a very great distance, and at the time he saw them he had no idea what they were.

Like all ***TITANIC*** researchers, in the beginning I was reluctant to suggest, or believe, that any of the witnesses lied under oath, yet the pieces to the puzzle fit together only when we accept the fact that someone did lie. Only by studying every word of both the American and British inquiries can we logically decide who the prevaricators were and what motivated them. The important point to make from Gill's testimony is that if he did see rockets at all he really did not know they were distress signals until he heard of ***TITANIC***'s loss the following morning. The most peculiar thing about Gill's statement is that so much attention was paid to it, while statements made against the master of the Canadian Pacific liner ***MOUNT TEMPLE*** were ignored.

TITANIC Quartermaster Arthur John Bright was not any more help in describing the rockets to Senator Smith, although Bright had helped fire them. When Smith asked what color the rockets showed. Bright replied, *"I did not notice the color; but they burst after they got up in the air."*

"And then what colors were displayed?" asked Senator Smith.

"I did not look to see," Bright answered.

When Fourth Officer Boxhall was recalled on 29 April in Washington, Senator Fletcher asked, *"What was the character of the rockets fired off on the **TITANIC**, as to colors?"*

"Just white stars, bright. I do not know whether they were stars or bright balls. I think they were balls. They were the regulation distress signals."

"Not red?" asked Fletcher.

"Oh, no; not red," replied Boxhall.

Eventually red would be the mandated color for pyrotechnic distress signals, to avoid such confusion as came out of the ***TITANIC*** inquiries. But Boxhall's answer to Senator Fletcher indicated that *never* would he expect to see a distress rocket throwing red stars, when that was exactly what he should have expected to see.

"Can you say whether any rockets fired at night by a ship under those conditions form a distress signal, or whether rockets may be sent up that are not distress signals?" Fletcher continued his line of questioning.

"Some companies have private night signals," Boxhall answered.

"What are they?"

"They are colored as a rule; stars, which you can easily see. These rockets were not throwing stars, they were throwing balls, I remember, and then they burst."

Boxhall's answer was incredible. Did he really not know what a distress rocket was supposed to look like? Could he really have believed that a rocket throwing colored stars was a company signal? Or had he just boxed himself into a corner in his explanation of ***TITANIC***'s rockets when he said that company's signals were *rockets throwing colored stars,* which was exactly the description of distress rockets given in the *International Rules of the Road?*

Fletcher continued. *"It seems that an officer on the **CALIFORNIAN** reported to the commander of the **CALIFORNIAN** that he had seen signals; but he said they were not distress signals. Do you know whether or not under the regulations in vogue, and according to the custom at sea, rockets fired, such as the **TITANIC** sent up, would be regarded as anything but distress signals?"*

"I am hardly in a position to state that, because it is the first time I have seen distress rockets sent off, and I could not very well judge what they would be like, standing as I was, underneath them, firing them myself. I do not know what they would look like in the distance." Another incredible answer from Boxhall.

"Have you ever seen any rockets sent off such as you say are private signals?" Fletcher asked.

Boxhall replied, *"Yes, sir."* When Fletcher asked under what circumstances he had seen such signals, Boxhall replied, *"Ships passing in the night, signaling to one another."*

Before all ships carried wireless telegraphy apparatus, and then radio-telephones, pyrotechnics were the only means of signaling at night. Every ship carried several different types of pyrotechnic signals. Reisenberg listed *Blue, Green, Red, White, Fog, Distress* and *Pilot,* under *"Lights in Use."* Vessels in need of a pilot burned a blue light, for example. *Coston rockets,* carried in American ships, rose to a height of 400 feet and burst into a shower of "red balls," wrote Reisenberg, which was undoubtedly why Senator Fletcher persisted in asking if ***TITANIC***'s rockets had been red. Pyrotechnic signals not classified as rockets, but as "lights," were flare-up lights, much like the emergency flares carried in the life rafts of airliners today. These modern flares have two ends, one which burns with the intensity of the fusées one sees in the streets after an accident or when a car has broken down, and one which spews out brightly colored smoke for use as a day signal. Ships today still carry pyrotechnic signals, for use when the power source is lost, as may well happen quickly in shipwrecks. When there is no radio excepting the battery-powered emergency locator beacon, which may have gone down with the ship, it can still be, and very quickly, too, back to the basic pyrotechnics for signaling. Only rockets carry their signals aloft to a height of several hundred feet.

Finally, Senator Fletcher asked, *"Were those rockets carried on the* ***TITANIC*** *for the purpose of being used as distress signals?"*

"Yes, sir; exclusively." What else could Boxhall answer?

"They were not carried or supposed to be used for any other than distress signals?"

No, no, sir. We did not have any time to use any of those things." Another ambiguous answer from Boxhall, which Fletcher did not pursue.

When asked if he had seen any rockets fired from any other ship that night, Boxhall described rockets sent up by the ***CARPATHIA***. *"An ordinary rocket. I think it was, so far as I could see, a distress rocket in answer to ours."* Here we have one of many examples of confusing semantics, a difference in British English and American English, or was it more than that? The difference between an *"ordinary rocket"* and a *"distress rocket"* was a matter that Senator Fletcher should have pursued.

In his memoirs *"Home From the Sea"* (Castle & Company, Ltd., London, 1931), Captain Sir Arthur Rostron gave no description of the rockets he ordered fired from ***CARPATHIA***'s rail that night. Nor did James Bisset, who was then Second Officer in ***CARPATHIA***, describe the rockets in his memoirs, *"Tramps and Ladies"* (Criterion Books, New York, 1959). Both men, however, mentioned seeing a green light on the horizon as they approached ***TITANIC***'s CQD position. According to Bisset this was at first identified as ***TITANIC***'s green starboard sidelight and they believed that she was still afloat. But as the light winked out they realized that it was the apogee of a rocket seen from 25 miles away. Rostron, however, said that it was a green flare from one of the lifeboats, but in his testimony at the Board of Trade inquiry on 21 June, 1912, Rostron told Attorney General Sir Rufus Isaacs that the green flare was White Star's company night signal. Seeing this green light did indicate to Rostron that ***TITANIC*** was still afloat, but he did not mistake it for her starboard running light. Boxhall had taken into his lifeboat from ***TITANIC*** a box of "green lights." Hardly a rocket, then, unless the Fourth Officer had figured some way to fire one from a crowded lifeboat without a socket, a rather dangerous proposition. Boxhall's "green lights' were undoubtedly just what Rostron said they were, company signal flares, much like those used today in life rafts, but why ***CARPATHIA***'s officers saw them from such a distance, if they did, must remain a mystery. Probably it was simply another example of "remembering" an event with too much imagination added many years later. From ***CARPATHIA***'s bridge a light on the water's surface should not have been seen more than 8 miles away.

In view of the many varied and ambiguous descriptions it appears that from the beginning someone knew that ***TITANIC***'s rockets were not all they should have been. The logical assumption is that *"someone"* was J. Bruce Ismay.

Descriptions of the rockets given at the Board of Trade inquiry were just as vague and confusing as those given in America. Quartermaster Hitchins on 3 May in London said that he had taken no particular notice of the colors in the rockets, but he then began to describe them as green, red, blue, all kinds of colors, and some were white. Then, Hitchins changed his mind again and said the rockets were blue, if he remembered them correctly. Attorney General Sir Rufus Isaacs continued to question Hitchins about the rockets, telling Lord Mersey that it was important to know about them. Isaacs quoted *Article 31, International Rules of the Road.*

Not every interrogator at the Board of Trade inquiry believed that white is a color. On 8 May the Attorney General asked Lookout Reginald Lee if the rockets he saw were *colored, or only white.* Lee replied that they were colored.

There was naturally a very detailed discussion of rockets when Captain Stanley Lord, master of the ***CALIFORNIAN***, was interrogated on 14 May in London. During this discussion it was stated that the rockets seen by ***CALIFORNIAN***'s watch officer were white. Because each rocket's apogee was seen apparently above a vessel which lay between ***CALIFORNIAN*** and ***TITANIC***, legend has it that ***CALIFORNIAN*** was only five miles from the sinking ***TITANIC***, the Leyland liner's officers ignored ***TITANIC***'s *"distress"* rockets and were criminally responsible for the deaths of some 1,500 people.

A vessel which Captain Lord and Third Officer Groves had seen coming from the east at about 11:30 PM Sunday, one hour and ten minutes after ***CALIFORNIAN*** had stopped, was similar in size to ***CALIFORNIAN***, and she showed them her green sidelight, said Lord. In the United States Lord had said of this unidentified vessel, *"She came and lay, at half past eleven, alongside of us until, I suppose, a quarter past 1, within 4 miles of us. We could see everything on her quite distinctly; see her lights."* Lord's American testimony was condensed. Senator Smith's questions being chiefly concerned with the matter of ***CALIFORNIAN***'s wireless operator not being on duty to catch ***TITANIC***'s *CQD.* But unfortunately Lord's first testimony, given in response to Senator Smith's questions, gave the impression that there was only one ship, that she had been within five miles of ***CALIFORNIAN***, and that *she* was the ship firing white rockets. Note, however, that Captain Lord did say that he and Groves could clearly see *everything* on this ship lying so close to ***CALIFORNIAN***.

In England Lord elaborated when asked about this steamer which approached ***CALIFORNIAN*** after the Leyland liner had stopped to keep from running into field ice. Lord had noticed the stranger only casually at first. She had approached from the east, showing her *single* mastlight. Lord had then gone to the wireless cabin and asked his wireless operator, Cyril Evans, what ships he was working. Evans told him *"only* ***TITANIC***."Lord remarked that the stranger approaching them was not ***TITANIC***. She was not large enough, not showing a blaze of light that would be normally displayed by an elite passenger liner of that size.

As the steamer came closer Lord and Third Officer Groves could see her green light, and a few deck lights. Lord estimated that at 11 o'clock the stranger was about six or seven miles away. At this point Lord Mersey proved that even he did not believe white is a color. Captain Lord had described seeing the white mastlight, and white deck lights, which might have been from portholes, doorways, anything. But Mersey asked if Lord had seen any *colored* light. Lord replied that he had not yet noticed the green light.

Lord said that he and Groves had continued to watch the stranger's approach until she stopped about half past eleven. She was about ***CALIFORNIAN***'s size, about 6,000 GRT. Lord later learned

ABOVE: A Photograph of Cunard's ***QUEEN ELIZABETH 2*** *at night. Because the* ***QE2*** *and the* ***TITANIC****, as well as any other ocean liner of this class would be ablaze with light in the evening, this picture serves as an excellent example of why the* ***TITANIC*** *could never have been mistaken for a tramp freighter. (Photograph by the Author, Copyright 1986.)*

that at midnight the stranger's bearing from ***CALIFORNIAN*** *was* SSE by compass, which is 157°30'. Asked if the compass was accurate. Lord said no, that ***CALIFORNIAN***'s compass deviation was about 2° East, the variation was about 24° West, making a total error of about 22° West. "East is least, and West is best," so adding 22° to 157°30' we get 179°30', meaning that the stranger was about due south of ***CALIFORNIAN***, due south being 180°. Lord estimated the distance between his ship and the stranger as about five miles. The rockets fired later appeared to come from beyond this unidentified vessel. There was an error in transcription of Lord's original statement concerning the mastlight of this unidentified ship, which he pointed out when the statement was later read back to him. While Lord had commented that it was a most "peculiar *night*," the stenographer transcribed it as "peculiar *light*," an entirely different matter. Captain Lord had gone on to explain originally, as he had to the Senate subcommittee, that he and his watch officers had been mistaking stars for ships' lights and vice versa all evening because of the very clear atmosphere with visibility at extreme limits. There was what is known as a "soft horizon," when it is difficult to tell where sea ends and sky begins.

This statement has given rise to a theory expounded by astronomers who suggest that ***CALIFORNIAN's*** watch officers as well as ***TITANIC***'s crewmen did not see ships' lights at all. They saw "stars and planets" and mistook them for ships. This is another example of not seeing the situation through the eyes of a professional mariner. Second Officer Fosgate's comments, *"When 'naviguessing' by the stars, the watch knows which planets are between 15° and 70° above the horizon. It's very rare for a sailor to mistake a star for a ship's light for more than a few seconds. The Gemini twins look like a pair of running lights crossing from port in the eastbound Med. when they can be seen 1° on the* *horizon. They are the most convincing mistake I've seen."*

Crewmen were interrogated at both inquiries by men who had for the most part never been to sea, and if they had it was merely as passengers. Years of keeping watch taught an officer to tell the difference between stars and planets, and ships' lights. An apprentice might make the mistake... once or twice... and someone from the engine room might make the mistake, more than once or twice, for engineering department officers and crewmen rarely came on deck at all. But as Mister Fosgate has stated, no watchkeeper would make the error for more than a few seconds. Captain Lord saw no need to explain his statement, nor indeed did anyone ask him to. Thus it has unfortunately been left that the mistakes made that night were permanent, when actually it was only a matter of a few seconds, as Mister Fosgate has explained.

There then ensued a confusing conversation between Lord Mersey and Sir Rufus Isaacs during which they tried to understand the bearing of the ship Lord had just described and the bearing of the rockets which ***CALIFORNIAN***'s Second Officer had seen later. This conversation makes it obvious why compass points were replaced by the method used today… a simple matter of 360 degrees. It is also obvious that neither Mersey nor Isaacs did understand, or they did not want to.

Assuming that the apogee of ***TITANIC***'s rockets was anywhere from 400 to 800 feet above her bridge rail, which was about 70 ft. above the sea's surface, her rockets theoretically could have been seen from ***CALIFORNIAN***'s bridge, which was 40 feet off the water, at a distance of from 32 to 41 miles. Because of the earth's curvature only the rockets' apogee would have been seen, breaking at an altitude of from 470 to 870 feet, making them appear very much like "shooting stars," which had also been present that night in unusual quantities. Had ***TITANIC***'s rockets showered red or green stars they would not have resembled "shooting stars." We have no accurate estimate of the height of the rockets' apogee as seen from ***TITANIC***'s boat deck or bridge. It is difficult enough for an aviator to estimate altitude at night, requiring some experience in night flying. In 1912 nobody had that experience. The 470 to 870 feet is merely a range of altitude from the American Coston rockets to the Board of Trade's various approved rocket signals, plus the approximate height of ***TITANIC***'s bridge above the waterline after impact flooding. Theoretical visibility from ***CALIFORNIAN***'s bridge to an object on the surface was 7.23 nautical miles. Assuming that the height of the bridge of the vessel stopped to the south of ***CALIFORNIAN*** was also about 40 feet, then theoretically her sidelight could have been seen as far as about 14 1/2 miles on such a clear night. Sidelights, however, needed by the *Rules of the Road* to be of sufficient candlepower to be seen only 2 miles. Mastlights needed candlepower to be seen by an observer 5 miles away on a clear night as prescribed by the *Rules of the Road.* In higher latitudes, on a cold, very clear night, visibility could be even greater. The highest number on the *Visibility Scale* is **9**, *Objects visible at more than 30 nautical miles.* Assuming that this mystery ship's mastlight was about 20 feet above her bridge, or 60 feet above the water's surface, theoretically her mastlight could have been seen as far as 16 miles from a height of 40 feet off the water.

I use the word "theoretical" because we do not know exactly how far anyone could see a light on the night of 14-15 April, 1912. We know that officers estimated that visibility was better than usual, that it was an almost moonless, clear night. Second Officer Fosgate comments, *"On a black night I can see a 60 watt bulb at five miles easily without binoculars. The lights on a raft, for instance, can be seen easily from the surface on a clear night because there are very few background lights. If the apogee of a rocket were 500 feet and it attained full altitude, it could be seen at 40 nautical miles in the ice without trouble. The only way to judge the distance to a star shell is by the size it appears. Not knowing how big it was to be, I could not determine distance at all. Sidelights can be hard to pick out on vessels with a lot of other lights, like a cruise ship or passenger liner, for example."*

To assume that in the 30 to 41 mile distance between ***CALIFORNIAN*** and ***TITANIC*** there could be no other vessel, considering the volume of transatlantic shipping traffic in the era before air travel, is absurd. There should be no doubt, then, that an unidentified vessel did stop between ***CALIFORNIAN*** and ***TITANIC***. She at first showed ***CALIFORNIAN*** he*r* green light, indicating that she was westbound because she was south of ***CALIFORNIAN***, possibly for an American port, but she could have been bound anywhere from Boston south to Miami, or to a Gulf port, such as Tampa, Galveston, New Orleans, Baton Rouge, Houston, or to Mexico, or any Central American port, or the northern coast of South America, or to Bermuda, the Bahamas or Cuba, or any of the Caribbean islands. She might have called quickly at one or more of those ports and then continued on around the world before reaching a home port, weeks, months later, after calling wherever cargoes took her. Had she been bound for any port north of Boston, which was also ***CALIFORNIAN***'s destination, she would not have been so far south, and it would have been likely that somebody in ***CALIFORNIAN***'s forecastle would have run into one of her crew in a local waterfront bar. She could very well have been flagged to any country in the world, not necessarily Britain or the United States. ***TITANIC*** enthusiasts have a tendency to lean too heavily upon information in Lloyd's publications of the day. Lloyd's was restricted to its communications system, and information given by shipowners. If a vessel was not insured by Lloyd's underwriters the owner was not bound to report to Lloyd's. And Lloyd's used Marconi wireless exclusively, therefore they could not communicate satisfactorily or routinely with ships using other systems. Because most ships did not carry wireless most ships did not communicate their whereabouts to anybody until they arrived in port. It is obvious that ***TITANIC***'s rockets came from beyond this mysterious vessel, and that meant that her watch officer must have also seen the rockets. While ***CALIFORNIAN***'s watch officer saw the apogee of the rockets bursting above the decks of this second mystery ship, from the unidentified ship's bridge an officer would have had an unobstructed view of the rockets, yet he should not have seen any of ***TITANIC***'s running lights either. The unidentified stranger had no electricity, therefore no wireless and no Morse lamp. Because watch officers purchased their own binoculars, and tramps did not pay well, it is possible that the stranger's deck officers had inferior glasses, probably not night glasses, if they had any at all. They would not have known of ***TITANIC***'s loss until they arrived in port, possibly several days, maybe weeks later. Then the master and his officers would have learned of ***TITANIC***'s loss, the accusations against ***CALIFORNIAN***, and the "mystery ship" seen from ***TITANIC***'s boat deck and lifeboats, as well as the mysterious vessel seen from the ***CALIFORNIAN***. Certainly they were not going to come forward after seeing what was happening to Captain Lord. Especially if they were from a country other than England, Canada or the United States it would have been easy for them to simply "disappear." It is even within the realm of possibility that her crew spoke little or no English, although her master and senior officers would have necessarily spoken some English in order to conduct business in America. Looking for a foreign tramp would have been like looking for the proverbial needle in a haystack in 1912, and it would be impossible now. But the point to implicating ***CALIFORNIAN***, thus allegedly "solving" the riddle of the mystery ship's identity, was simply that once Captain Lord had been accused nobody looked elsewhere. Even Captain Lord's defenders have chosen other, "official" routes to his defense, which is the reason why the controversy still rages. The official version has remained questionable for over eight decades because it makes no sense. ***TITANIC*** researchers have access to two primary sources to identify this, and other, mystery ships... newspaper shipping reports from 1912 (and because of two world wars the newspapers extant are generally American,

Canadian and British) Lloyd's various publications, including *Lloyd's Weekly Index of Shipping* as well as *Lloyd's Register of British and Foreign Ships,* and the latter's American counterpart, the *U.S. Maritime Register.* German newspapers from 1912 are few and far between, and printed in archaic German which even younger Germans today often cannot read. Cargo vessels and tankers were rarely listed in published newspaper shipping reports. Tramps especially arrived and departed unnoticed, unrecorded, with no regular ports of call. Few shipping companies survive today from ***TITANIC***'s era and 1912 ship's logs are rarely saved even by the big companies. Naming this vessel now is probably impossible. Sailors of ***TITANIC***'s era knew, of course, but nobody asked them, or listened to them. British marine engineer and prolific writer William McFee wrote in *Watch Below* (Random House, New York, 1940) that there were several British tramps without wireless near ***TITANIC***. No doubt McFee knew this as one in the profession, a profession which closes ranks to outsiders when it is necessary to protect its own. It is therefore not the purpose of this book to positively identify the two major "mystery ships," involved in the ***TITANIC*** disaster, the one which lay two points off the White Star liner's bow, and the one which lay between ***CALIFORNIAN*** and ***TITANIC***. It is, however, the purpose of this book to expose the reasons why Captain Lord took the blame for ***TITANIC***'s high casualty count. Lord was such a convenient scapegoat and his ignoring "distress signals" has been so firmly embedded in the public's mind by those who are neither historians nor merchant seamen that nobody looked for these mystery ships when their crews might still have been living, and the ***TITANIC*** establishment unfortunately has done little or no research outside of England and the United States. One contingent of the ***TITANIC*** establishment believes that the Norwegian sealing vessel ***SAMSON***, a small sailer with steam auxiliary, was the mystery ship seen from ***TITANIC***'s boat deck. There is no doubt but what ***SAMSON*** was in the vicinity, and no doubt her officers saw ***TITANIC***'s rockets. But ***SAMSON*** does not fit the description of the mysterious vessel seen from ***CALIFORNIAN***, nor does the little sailer engaged in illegal sealing fit the description of the "primary" mystery ship, the vessel with what Boxhall described as "good lights," meaning electricity, and range lights, seen two points off ***TITANIC***'s port bow. ***SAMSON***'s Chief Officer, Henrik Naess, on his deathbed in 1962, confessed that ***SAMSON***'s officers had seen ***TITANIC***'s rockets but mistook them for U.S. revenue cutters. ***SAMSON***, according to her Chief, was running without lights because she was operating illegally. This alone rules her out as either Boxhall's or ***CALIFORNIAN***'s mystery ship. Even so, if the Norwegian crew had seen red or green distress rockets they would have attempted a rescue, although their tiny vessel could never have taken aboard 1,500 people. But with ***CALIFORNIAN*** accused and found guilty nobody looked for another ship, which is precisely what the coverup intended. Bringing too many other crews into the investigation, especially those who were foreign or who had no allegiance to Morgan's IMM, would have been embarrassing, to say the least. ***TITANIC***'s officers were easily controlled, being British, with the Leyland Line being part of Morgan's shipping trust.

It is significant that ***CALIFORNIAN*** had turned after stopping, because of the action of her single screw, and she had swung to a heading of about ENE by the time the stranger ship appeared.

Fourth Officer Boxhall, who was the first to mention the primary mystery ship at the American inquiry, and one of the first aboard ***TITANIC*** to see her, had told Senator Smith on 22 April that he had seen the mystery ship's two mastlights and her *red* sidelight. He had first seen the mastlights, Boxhall said, then as she got closer he saw the red light. Had this stranger actually been ***CALIFORNIAN*** she would have shown her *green* light, or no sidelight at all, to those on ***TITANIC***'s bridge because the Leyland liner had by this time swung around to a heading of ENE, and ***TITANIC*** was south and a bit west of her. This is the first mention of the mystery ship and it is significant that Boxhall said she was moving, while ***CALIFORNIAN*** was known to have stopped at 10:21PM, the time given in her routine report to the USN Hydrographic Office, although Captain Lord himself later rounded that figure off to 10:20. It is extremely important to note the date... *two days after* Boxhall's first testimony and description of the mystery ship... that Gill made his notarized statement in which he claimed to have seen the large passenger liner and the white rockets. It is therefore significant that Boxhall, testifying again *after* Gill's statements, added that he had seen the mystery ship's *green* light, the light ***CALIFORNIAN*** would have shown to ***TITANIC*** at this time. This was the first salvo in the battle to make ***CALIFORNIAN*** into Boxhall's mystery ship, and it is possible that Gill had been instructed to say that he had seen the passenger ship and the rockets off ***CALIFORNIAN***'s starboard side so that his statement would match that of ***TITANIC***'s Fourth Officer.

A. B. William Lucas, in a lifeboat off ***TITANIC***'s starboard side, claimed to have seen a ship's *red* light off ***TITANIC***'s *starboard quarter.* The mystery tramp westbound between ***CALIFORNIAN*** and ***TITANIC*** would have initially shown ***TITANIC*** her red light, had she been no more than two miles from ***TITANIC***, while showing ***CALIFORNIAN*** he*r* green light, but she was about NNE of ***TITANIC***, not south of the White Star liner as a vessel off her starboard quarter would have been. If ***TITANIC*** was headed about due north after she stopped as some witnesses claimed, then a red light off her starboard quarter was a different vessel entirely, meaning that yet another "mystery ship" was involved, and this one was south of ***TITANIC*** heading east.

Fifty copies of the *Chronik der Waried Tankschiff Reederei GmbH* were privately printed by its author. Dr. Joseph Hunck, in Germany in 1938. The *Chronik,* and the veracity of Dr. Hunck, have been dismissed by certain ***TITANIC*** "researchers" on the grounds that Dr. Hunck was a Nazi and therefore he lied, although there is no evidence one way or the other about Hunck's alleged affiliation with the Nazi Party then ruling Germany. It is true, however, that in 1938 Europe was already alight with the first flames of World War II and that the Germans did make a propaganda film about ***TITANIC*** showing their version of how incompetent and cowardly British sailors had been. The *Chronik* contains statements made by the First Officer of the DAPG tanker ***NIAGARA***, identified only as Herr Hofmann, who claimed that this vessel was within sight of ***TITANIC***. But it also appears to be true that DAPG's ***NIAGARA*** in April of 1912 was in the Pacific Ocean, not the Atlantic. Usually when such a dilemma about a ship's position occurs it means that there are two vessels with the same name.

The Deutsche-Amerikanische Petroleum-Gesellschaft of Hamburg was the German subsidiary of the American Standard Oil Company In 1912 "trust-busting" was fashionable in American politics. Trusts were popularly considered "un-American," and Senate committees had been investigating two of the largest and best-known trusts in the United States, J. Pierpont Morgan's banking trust, of which the International Mercantile Marine Company was a part, and John D. Rockefeller's giant oil trust, the Standard. Both Morgan and Rockefeller had been under investigation for years, and they would continue to be hounded by Congressional committees long after ***TITANIC*** was lost, in Morgan's case until his death in 1913. In 1904 Ida Tarbell's lengthy and detailed exposé of the Standard Trust was published by McClure, Phillips & Co., New York. Tarbell was a reporter for *McClure*'s magazine, and her *History of the Standard Oil Company* had run in installments in that magazine for two years, adding fuel to the Senate trust investigations. Politicians were eager to please voters by defending small businesses against the crushing financial power of the big trusts. It is beyond the scope of this book to discuss the politics or business ramifications of the giant trusts begun in the early history of the United States. Whether right or wrong, Morgan had kept the greedy railroad robber barons from destroying themselves and the country's economy when he set them on the track away from chaotic, unlimited and destructive competition. Rockefeller's Standard Oil had acquired its name because it "standardized" quality in illuminating oil production, thus protecting consumers from the hazards of dangerously flammable products used for home lighting, products which often came from very small independent producers who raised enough money to buy a few barrels of crude and build a still.

The Standard Oil Company originated in the State of Ohio, and the first anti-trust suits were filed against the Standard by Ohio's idealistic Attorney Generals David K. Watson in 1890, and Frank S. Monnett in 1897. In 1900 the trust-busting, rough-riding Theodore Roosevelt was elected Vice President. In September the following year he became President of the United States after the assassination of William McKinley. In 1904 Roosevelt was elected President by a landslide. During his administrations over forty anti-trust suits were initiated under the Sherman Anti-Trust Law of 1890. In 1911 the U. S. Supreme Court forced the Standard to break up into several allegedly independent companies. In April, 1912, the one thing that the Standard did not need was the type of publicity which would have ensued if one or more of its tankers happened to be in the vicinity of the sinking ***TITANIC*** without rendering aid. Nor did Rockefeller need to have it known that there were so many tankers on the North Atlantic sailing under the Standard's aegis. The fact that the Standard tanker ***CITY OF EVERETT*** had gone to the aid of White Star's ***REPUBLIC*** in 1909, and been rebuffed by ***REPUBLIC***'s master, had been hushed up, as had the collision of the ***STANDARD*** with White Star's ***BALTIC*** in 1911. On the night of 14-15 April, 1912, the Standard had a fleet of tankers on the Western Ocean, flying at least three different flags. DAPG's ***DEUTSCHLAND*** had run out of coal and requested a tow, as related in a previous chapter. She had already attracted too much attention when wireless messages concerning this matter were used to cover up the truth about suppression of the news of ***TITANIC***'s loss until 16 April, a full 24 hours after the event, allowing time to reinsure ***TITANIC*** at 5:30PM London time on Monday, as well as protecting I.M.M. stock prices from a disastrously sudden collapse. It was known that DAPG's ***PAULA*** was in the vicinity of ***TITANIC***, allegedly too far away to be of any help. ***LACKAWANNA*** had become involved when her master gave a detailed diagram of the ice field encountered by ***TITANIC*** to the U.S. Navy Hydrographic Office, a diagram which showed ***TITANIC*** on the western side of the field ice. The *Chronik* listed the tanker and tank-barge combination ***IROQUOIS*** and ***NAVAHOE*** as also nearby, but the *Chronik* was the history of the Waried Shipping Company. Dr. Hunck wrote that these two vessels belonged to DAPG when actually they were listed by Lloyd's as belonging to the Anglo-American Oil Company, the English subsidiary of the Standard. As in all the big shipping trusts the vessels were transferred among subsidiaries of the Standard, wherever they were needed. They were owned, on paper at least, by a holding company, and there were sometimes more than one vessel within the Standard group with the same name. It is not at all unusual now, nor was it in 1912, for a ship to "disappear" for various reasons by steaming into port under one name, her paperwork being shuffled quickly so that she steamed out of that port under her new name and "new owner." It is therefore absurd to dismiss out of hand Dr. Hunck's statement from ***NIAGARA***'s First Officer. The ship's trail has been well covered, as one would expect, but Hofmann's story is so detailed that it makes sense. If it was made up, it was done with a reason, possibly to get another DAPG tanker off the hook as one of the mystery ships, possibly to conceal the ***FRANKFURT*** scandal. Possibly Hofmann simply forgot the name of the ship he was in that night, or ***NIAGARA*** had been her name but it was quickly changed to cover her trail. Second Officer Fosgate finds Hofmann's story plausible for the simple reason that a watch officer in an area of traffic or other obstruction, such as ice, pays little attention to ships which are no threat to his or her own vessel. Hofmann's veracity is enhanced by his statement that the German officers on ***NIAGARA***'s bridge saw lights of several ships, when legend and officialdom say that only two ships were in the vicinity... ***TITANIC*** and ***CALIFORNIAN***. There were at least two vessels besides ***TITANIC*** and Hofmann's ship that we know of... the mystery ship two points off ***TITANIC***'s port bow and the mysterious ship between ***CALIFORNIAN*** and ***TITANIC***. Whatever else can be said to discredit Dr. Hunck's *Chronik,* it is obvious that Hofmann's story was written by a seaman, and undoubtedly by one who saw ***TITANIC*** on that fatal night.

In a chapter titled *Keine Hilfe Für die **TITANIC**,* translated for my first book by Stephen G. Tucker, an Englishman who was then living in Germany and working as a translator for the West German government, ***NIAGARA***'s First Officer was quoted:

"We were crossing from New York to Hamburg and were steaming along the northern route. As *it was April we saw no risk in this. The air was crystal clear and fresh, and around 11 PM on a Sunday we noticed two bright masthead lights in the Northwest. Shortly afterwards we noticed two bright sidelights, but only for a short time as there were also a lot of other lights to be seen. We thought it must have been a passenger steamer which was disappearing at high speed over the horizon. We could, however, no longer occupy ourselves with the waters to our West, but had to keep a sharp lookout ahead as we were sailing through the iceberg zone. A quick glance aft, however, enabled us to spot the two brightly shining masthead lights again. The lights were now disappearing over the visual horizon, but unusually were still on the same bearing. At that moment the masthead light to the fore appeared remarkably to be sinking deeper and deeper into the visual horizon, whereas the aft light was climbing higher and higher. For one moment the thought crossed our minds that the ship might be sinking.*

"All this lasted only a short time. Then both lights disappeared suddenly and we only saw rockets being fired occasionally into the sky. A passenger ship which, during a celebration on board, fires rockets into the sky is nothing unusual. We estimated that we must have been at least fifteen nautical miles away and did not consider it necessary to investigate further because we had not seriously thought that an accident was happening.

"The horrid mistake first became clear to us on our arrival in Hamburg. Using the chart and the time we discovered that the lights and rockets we had observed could only have been those of the sinking ***TITANIC***. *The fearsome collision with the iceberg, which tore the ship open in her whole length, must just have happened. We did not see the iceberg ourselves, although it must also have moved on our route. But such low icebergs can hardly be seen from a distance. Had we been equipped with a wireless station it would have been no problem for us to turn around and save hundreds of lives.* Wie *were, after this experience, very depressed. It was not until the wireless station was installed shortly afterwards that we felt better again."*

Hofmann's story fits in perfectly with the red light seen off ***TITANIC***'s starboard quarter. If it was true, it had to be suppressed simply because Hofmann had said that ***NIAGARA*** was on the northern route, but saw ***TITANIC*** to the northwest.

At any rate, with so many Standard Oil tankers on the North Atlantic that night, and many of them going to the big refinery at Hamburg, there was more than the one reason to avoid publicity. In 1912 many politicians and top military and naval men in England and Germany, and in the United States as well, knew that war was inevitable and imminent in Europe. One major preparation for that war would be the stockpiling of enough oil to last through the hostilities. Churchill, trying to convert the Royal Navy to oil firing, knowing from intelligence reports that the Germans were not only equipping warships with oil-fired steam turbines, but also that German intermediate liners were already powered by oil-fired steam engines or Rudolf Diesel's new oil-fueled internal combustion engines, had estimated that a four year supply of oil would be needed for the coming hostilities. Oil had become a highly necessary commodity for warfare, with technology advancing so rapidly while internal combustion engines replaced horses and mules as the means of moving machines of war. There were the new aeroplanes, motorcycles, vehicles of all types, and of course the oil-powered ships, and in Germany the giant Zeppelins, all of which needed oil for propulsion and lubrication, while oil was still needed for illumination in many areas. If the ***NIAGARA*** story is true, and many historians in Germany believe that it is, the question comes full circle... why were ***TITANIC***'s rockets ignored by so many ships' officers and why was ***CALIFORNIAN*** singled out for censure?

CALIFORNIAN's Apprentice James Gibson and her Second Officer Herbert Stone were naturally interrogated at length during the Board of Trade inquiry because they had been on the bridge when the rockets were seen. The brunt of the investigation fell upon Stone's shoulders because he was the watch officer and therefore responsible for making the decision whether or not to call the master. Whatever Captain Lord said about the rockets, then, was hearsay. Apprentice Gibson, although he had also seen the rockets, was inexperienced, leaving Stone's testimony as the most important part of the rocket investigation.

At about 0200 on Monday Stone sent Gibson to the chart room where Captain Lord had turned in all standing on the settee. Gibson was supposed to tell the master that Stone had seen rockets going up beyond the steamer lying near them. Lord, in a deep sleep, allegedly answered the apprentice, but had no recollection of the conversation later. This is not at all unusual, but unfortunately it gave rise to the legend that ***CALIFORNIAN***'s master was drunk, when in fact he was a temperate man. Captain Lord, like every other shipmaster of his era, apprenticed in sail. The usual watches were four on-four off, and a boy quickly learned to sleep fast and deeply when he had the chance. It was a habit hard to break in later life. This ability to be completely rested from quick naps stood the master in good stead because he, like the sailing apprentice, would have to snatch sleep whenever and wherever he could, never knowing when he might have to remain on the bridge for days at a time in bad weather.

Later in the morning, when ***CALIFORNIAN***'s officers learned that ***TITANIC*** had sunk during the night, the matter of the rockets became extremely important. Allegedly Lord then learned that Gibson had indeed brought the information to him. The apprentice claimed that Lord had asked if there were any colors in the rockets, or if they were merely white. But again the testimony and the questions became convoluted and ambiguous. Why, asked Sir Rufus Isaacs and Lord Mersey, did Lord ask whether the rockets were white or colored? Lord's answers at this time made little sense and, in fact, appear to indicate that he was a party, albeit reluctantly, to the coverup. While Stone later in his testimony said that Lord asked if the rockets had any color... and Stone was specific in saying that Lord asked if they were *red or green*..... Captain Lord himself never explained this any way other than saying that he was thinking of company's signals, and yet because he specifically said *red or green* it was obvious that he was thinking of distress rockets, and so was Second Officer Stone, who properly told Lord that what he saw were *not* distress rockets. The emphasis here in the inquiry questioning began to be shifted to the matter of distress rockets always being all-white, when in fact they most certainly were not. Nobody ever asked why Lord specifically mentioned red or green, no doubt because they knew the answer perfectly well. Over and over, relentlessly, Isaacs and Mersey repeatedly inferred that distress rockets were *always white,* yet Isaacs had previously read *Article 31, Class 3 "rockets or shells throwing stars of any* ***color*** *or description."* And here began the repeated use of the brainwashing phrase *"the colour white"* with reference to ***TITANIC***'s rockets. Even Leyland Line attorney C. Robertson Dunlop stated during the Board of Trade inquiry summary, *"As to the colour, it is not of importance, because that is the colour of rocket you would expect if a rocket was sent up at all."* An absurd statement which indicates that Dunlop must have been a party to the coverup in spite of his alleged defense of Captain Lord and the Leyland Line. There again, however, how would you defend one line against another when they are both owned by the same conglomerate?

Dunlop's being privy to the coverup was an indication that a deal had been struck with Captain Lord because the question naturally arises: why did Captain Lord never invoke in his own defense the definition of *distress* rockets as understood by a mariner of his time? Why did he never fully explain why he had asked if the rockets had *"any red or green"* in them, a question answered, so Stone said later, with *"no, they are just white rockets"*? Why did Lord effectively squelch any further questioning along those lines by saying that he had been asleep and did not hear Gibson when in fact he apparently did? And why was Lord's question which named specifically red or green signals never pursued at the Board of Trade inquiry?

Two words explain it all... integrity, and patriotism. As we shall see in the many reasons for a ***TITANIC*** coverup, if Captain Lord had been approached on this subject of the rockets he *never* would have explicitly defended himself in the matter of distress rockets being red or green simply because he would have put his country first. He was a professional mariner and he was British. As such he would *never* have cast any aspersions on ***TITANIC***'s officers, not even to save himself. It is entirely possible also that Lord had by this time been so brainwashed by the constant reference to *"the colour white"* that he had come to believe that he was indeed wrong. But Lord and his officers, whether explicitly warned to back off on the subject of white as opposed to red or green rockets, or whether they realized on their own that this subject was *verboten,* would have understood that it was a matter which could reflect upon the integrity of the entire British mercantile marine, and therefore was not to be publicly aired. Britain's life blood was the sea. Without Britannia's sea supremacy she was lost economically, perhaps even physically, to foreign invaders. This was an era when a man's integrity was his most highly prized possession. Employers of all kinds, but especially shipowners required signed loyalty oaths from their employees, and it was integrity which made those employees abide by those oaths. McFee called it "principle," and lamented its decline in each succeeding generation that went to sea.

The fact that Captain Lord took the precaution of having Stone and Gibson write out statements about what they had seen and done on the night of 14/15 April before ***CALIFORNIAN*** reached Boston has unfortunately been turned against Lord and used as proof of his "guilt" by anti-Lordites. But Lord was obviously a prudent man who looked ahead, an admirable quality in a shipmaster, as we can see from his foresight in navigating ***CALIFORNIAN*** in the ice area. After he knew that ***TITANIC*** had sunk, that she had fired white rockets. Lord obviously knew what had happened, as did every shipmaster in the area. He knew there would be a big investigation, that was obvious. It was prudence, then, rather than guilt which motivated his request for the written statements from Stone and Gibson, and Lord knew that it must be written while it was fresh in their minds, before anyone had talked with them. We have no idea what similar measures were taken by masters of other vessels near ***TITANIC*** that night, for nobody ever asked them.

It was very easy to say that ***TITANIC***'s rockets were "regulation distress rockets," because after all they had been fired from her bridge while she was in distress. The reporters bought it, the general public bought it, but neither had the slightest notion of what a distress rocket might really be.

If ***TITANIC'***s rockets were merely detonators in lieu of signal cannon, that is aural rather than visual signals, they would have behaved exactly as ***TITANIC'***s rockets were described, excepting that they would not have thrown stars. Their payload would have been flash powder only, it would have exploded at apogee with a white flash, and there would have been some fallout from debris, bits of burning paper which might have been mistaken for stars. The only close observers to the rockets were obviously under great stress with better things to do than look upward and identify what was coming out of the rockets' explosions. But if ***TITANIC'***s rockets were merely detonators, then they should have been alternated, or fired simultaneously with the visual signal, rockets throwing *stars of any **color** or description.*

William Kerka, P.E., retired engineering professor and ***TITANIC*** enthusiast, has for many years been interested in this particular question, for Kerka has dealt with acoustics professionally. Kerka has prepared a detailed diagram showing that ***CALIFORNIAN*** had to have been at least 19 to 20 miles from ***TITANIC*** or Second Officer Stone could have heard the detonators. Nineteen or twenty miles is the distance given by Captain Lord between ***CALIFORNIAN*** and ***TITANIC***, but let us not forget the state-of-the-art navigational errors of the era. While the noise from ***TITANIC'***s blowing off steam due to her sudden stopping might have simulated the *Class 4 Rules of the Road* distress signal, *"continuous sounding with any fog-signal apparatus,"* and it may have seemed deafening to those aboard the White Star liner, it would not have been heard as far as a detonator or signal cannon, and certainly not as far as a rocket could be seen. It should, however, have been heard for a distance of five miles, the distance which legend and officialdom say that ***CALIFORNIAN*** was from ***TITANIC***.

Captain Lord did tell Sir Rufus Isaacs that if ***TITANIC'***s rockets had been distress rockets his watch officer would have heard them. While Lord was probably not fully privy to all of the reasons for the coverup, he may have guessed most of them, yet he wanted to defend his watch officer. Lord, of all people, knew that Stone had done nothing wrong. Either ***TITANIC'***s rockets were not detonators, or ***CALIFORNIAN*** was farther from her than even the 19 to 20 miles that Lord estimated. There is some confusion in this part of Captain Lord's testimony, in particular his answer to one of the Attorney General's questions. Sir Rufus wanted to know how far ***CALIFORNIAN*** had been from the ship which was in sight, not how far ***CALIFORNIAN*** was from ***TITANIC'***s distress position. When Captain Lord answered that ***CALIFORNIAN*** was about four to five miles away, he was referring to the ship which he and his watch officer had seen lying four or five miles south of ***CALIFORNIAN***. This was the ship *between* ***CALIFORNIAN*** and ***TITANIC***, but this answer of Lord's helped create the legend that ***CALIFORNIAN*** was only four or five miles from ***TITANIC***. The facts are quite different. Using Professor Kerka's sound diagram and the visibility table in the next image proves that ***CALIFORNIAN*** was anywhere from 20 to 41 miles distant from ***TITANIC*** because Stone obviously saw only the apogee of the rockets and heard no detonations.

As Stone's testimony progressed he said that the rockets which had at first appeared to emanate from some point beyond the deck of the ship which was only four or five miles south of ***CALIFORNIAN*** later changed their bearing and at least one rocket seemed to be fired from that closer steamer, that rocket being brighter than the rest. But remember that Stone saw only the apogee of the rockets, and at a very great distance. Only the very top of the star, or debris, burst was within Stone's range of vision because of the curvature of the earth. Stone therefore saw no more than a faint, split second white flash. The rockets were fired from the socket mounted on ***TITANIC'***s starboard rail, very close to the starboard emergency boat's bow. These bridge-rail sockets were aimed slightly outward from the rail to keep debris from falling back on to the deck.

Otherwise the socket formed a 90° angle with the keel, thus a 90° angle with the water's surface, *as long as the ship remained on an even keel.* The socket aimed the rockets and going straight up they would attain their maximum height before bursting which would give them their maximum range of visibility. Therefore the first rocket fired from ***TITANIC***'s bridge was going nearly straight up, its launch angle being 90° with the plane of the water's surface. Thus the apogee of this first rocket would appear to Stone at the highest point above the horizon of all the rockets fired. But as ***TITANIC***'s bow sank lower into the sea, the angle of her deck with the plane of the water's surface changed, causing the bridge-mounted socket, which had pointed almost straight up when ***TITANIC*** was on an even keel, to change its angle from the vertical, or 90° angle with the surface, to an ever decreasing angle with the surface. In addition ***TITANIC*** acquired a slight list to port which altered the rockets' trajectories still further, while the elevation of the bridge above the water's surface was decreasing steadily. The trajectories of the rockets varied with the decrease in their launch angle and height caused by the deck's changing elevation and angle with the surface. The time, and therefore the number of feet traveled by the rocket between ignition at the bridge rail to bursting charge at apogee remained the same because the size of the rockets and amount of propellant material was the same. The altitude of the bursting charge, or apogee, however, decreased as the elevation and angle of launch decreased, which caused the rocket to travel farther in a horizontal line to its bursting point. The gravity component thus became more influential as the

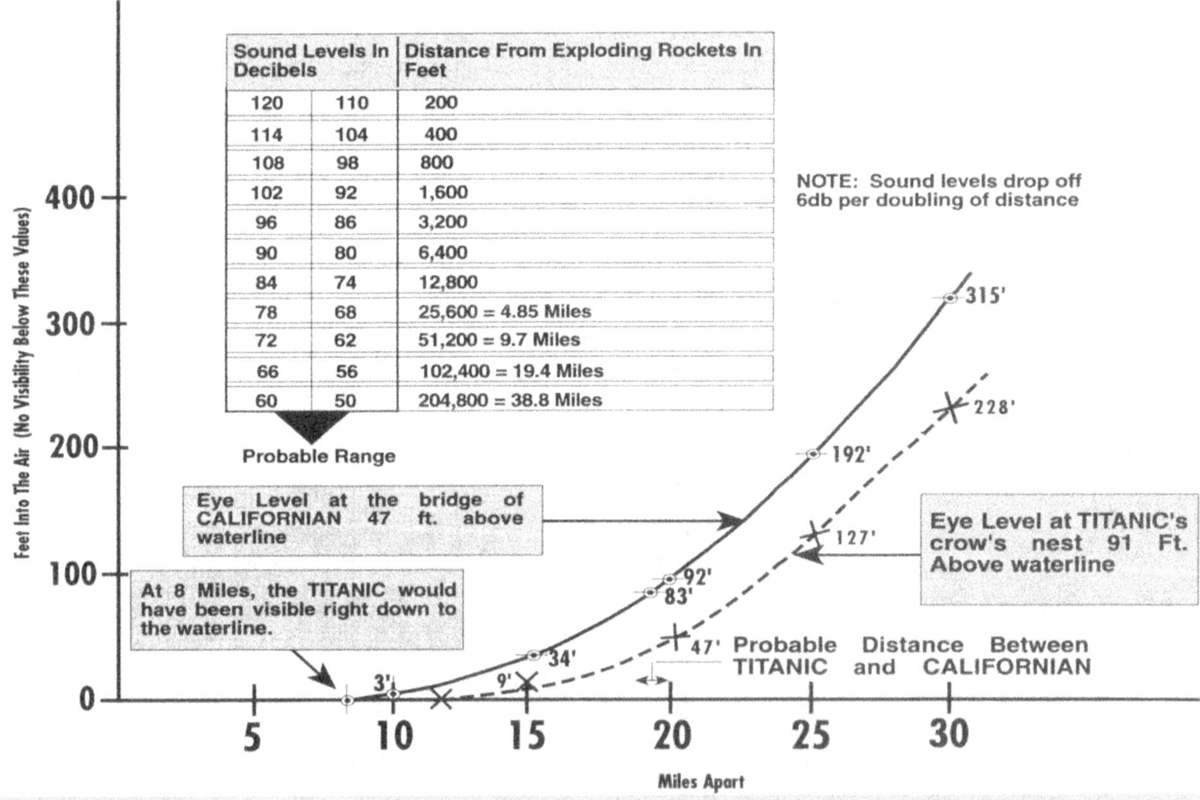

Sound Levels In Decibels		Distance From Exploding Rockets In Feet
120	110	200
114	104	400
108	98	800
102	92	1,600
96	86	3,200
90	80	6,400
84	74	12,800
78	68	25,600 = 4.85 Miles
72	62	51,200 = 9.7 Miles
66	56	102,400 = 19.4 Miles
60	50	204,800 = 38.8 Miles

***ABOVE:** A diagram by William Kerka, P.E., a retired engineering professor, showing the role that visibility and acoustics played in the **TITANIC** disaster on the fateful night of April 14-15, 1912. (Diagram courtesy of Mr. William Kerka, P.E.)*

WHAT STONE SAW

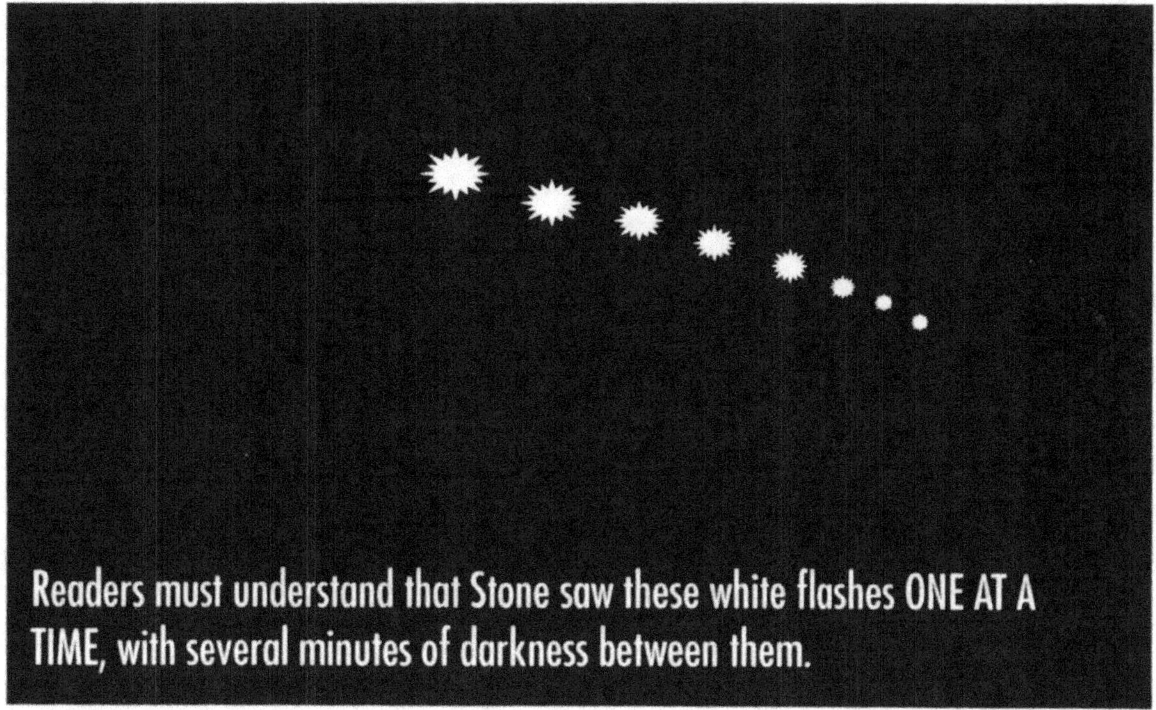
Readers must understand that Stone saw these white flashes ONE AT A TIME, with several minutes of darkness between them.

launch angle decreased, causing the trajectory to flatten toward the horizontal even more with each rocket launch as ***TITANIC*** sank further by the head; thus the apogee of each rocket decreased even more rapidly in altitude compared to the rocket preceding it. For example, with a difference of 25 degrees from the perpendicular 90 degrees, if the rocket's length of trajectory was 800 feet, there would be a visibility difference of about 8 nautical miles. If we had any accurate specifications as to the type of rockets fired, knowing the height achieved by the first one fired from the socket when ***TITANIC*** was still on a relatively even keel, we could figure the distance between ***CALIFORNIAN*** and ***TITANIC*** with a fair degree of accuracy. Whether these specifications were omitted deliberately as part of the coverup we will never now know. To an observer well over the horizon the path of the rockets' brief flashes, fired several minutes apart, descended lower and lower while the flash seemed dimmer with each burst because of refraction caused by the slight haze which would be above the field ice between the two ships, thus creating the illusion that the signals were being fired from a moving ship, a ship which steamed away over the horizon, her signals disappearing as she went hull down, then out of sight altogether. Actually the rockets did not stop because ***TITANIC*** sank but because the man firing them escaped in a lifeboat, about half an hour before she went under. This optical illusion was merely one more link forged in the chain of events leading to disaster. Because the rockets were white, it did not occur to Stone, or any other watch officer, that the ship firing the rockets was sinking. If she had been sinking she would have fired rockets throwing colored... red or green... stars. If the pyrotechnic display of brilliant red or green stars had marched in descending pattern across the night sky Stone would have known at once why they descended... because the ship firing them was descending, into the sea. Because the rockets were merely white and not distress rockets, because there were only eight rockets, and because the unseen ship

THE ROCKETS FROM A DISTANCE

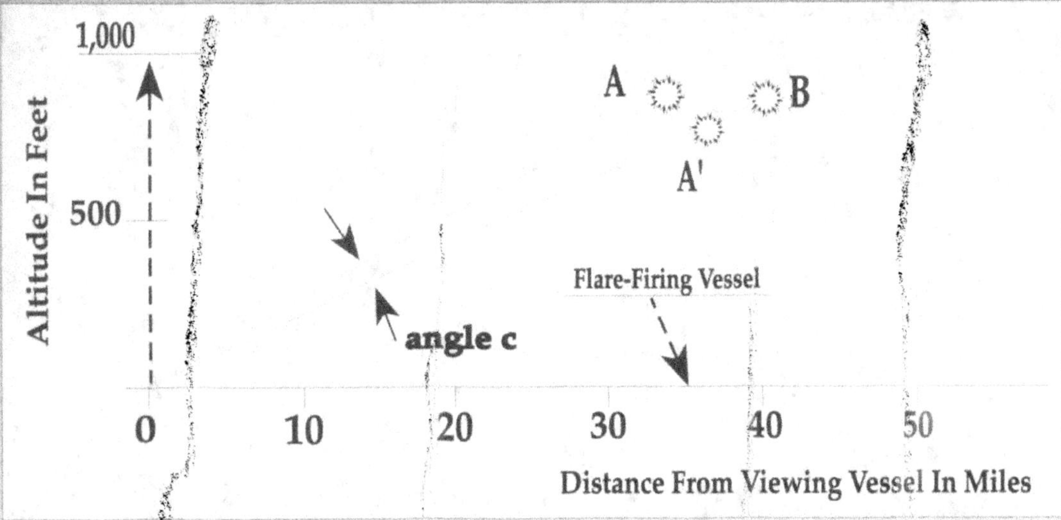

The Trajectories of a Moving Vessel Decreasing Angle of Launch

The above figure demonstrates, in graphic form, how the tilt of a vessel in pitch, and/or roll might influence the perception of its range as judged by an observer aboard another ship some miles away. The Vertical and Horizontal scales in this figure are different to accentuate the visual effect described.

The burst of a flare, marked A, corresponds to the location as seen from an observer's ship, located at the origin of abscissa of the graph, when the launch tube on the vessel which fired the rocket is vertical, due to the roll or pitch of the vessel--then the rocket would follow a curved trajectory and the flare would be ignited at a lower altitude, marked A' in the figure.

But, a point B exists where the burst would be observed if the vessel which launched the flare had merely moved farther away from the observing ship, with its hull and launch tube still in a vertical orientation. It can be seen that the elevation angle of burst B, as viewed from the observer's ship has turned down from an earlier sighting by an angle C, and for some distances this might match the angle to burst A'. If an alignment existed in the line of sight to A' and B, and in absence of contrary evidence, a crewman aboard the observing ship might mistakenly conclude that the vessel firing a succession of flares was continuing underway and the increasing depression of the sighting angle to subsequent flares was due solely to the increasing range, rather than anything catastrophic---as was the case for the **TITANIC**, where flooding below the waterline was responsible for a major list and downward slope of the hull.

Reprinted Courtesy of the Author, Mr. John Bryant Williams, P.E.

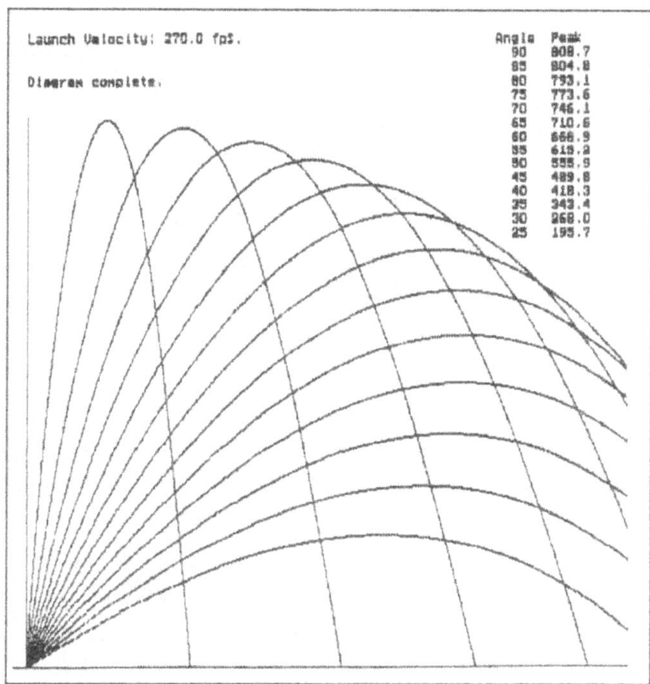

ABOVE: *This chart displays progressive decrease in apogee altitude as the launch angle decreases. (Chart courtesy of Mr. Jeff Anderson.)*

which fired them gave every appearance of moving in what seemed to be a perfectly normal manner, one could hardly expect Stone to comprehend that she was sinking. Remember that at no time did Stone see any lights on the ship firing the rockets. ***TITANIC***'s running lights were far out of Stone's range of vision. It cannot be said too often... *all Stone saw was the apogee burst of eight white rockets, which appeared to be fired from a moving ship because the apogee of each succeeding rocket was lower than the one preceding it.* It is impossible to show more than a rough approximation of this optical illusion in only two dimensions.

While Gibson allegedly discussed with Stone that "a ship would not fire rockets for nothing," a discussion that Stone denied, that would be true simply because rockets cost money and therefore were not dispensed lightly. But in this case, let us emphasize once more that these were not *distress* rockets, they could have meant anything other than distress, and they gave every indication of being what Stone judged them to be... a signal to other ships to stay away from the ice, or when the ship firing the rockets gave the appearance of moving it could have meant that she was signaling to show others a lead through the ice field. As for one rocket seeming brighter than the others, no doubt each handmade rocket, no matter how carefully constructed, was not of uniform quality to begin with, nor were their detonators. While the pyrotechnic material filling the rockets' canisters was carefully measured, variations in quantity and quality, in addition to deterioration caused by storage conditions prior to manufacture and at sea, were bound to occur and even minute variations would assure that the rockets' flashes would not all be exactly uniform. One or more might very well be brighter than the others.

It may be argued that the candlepower of the rockets' bursts might not be sufficient to allow them to be seen at the theoretical maximum range of visibility. Pyrotechnics and ordnance expert Jeff Anderson says otherwise. Jeff designed a software program to compute the external ballistics of a mortar firing a lightweight projectile. His comments on visibility:

"Candlepower was a VERY subjective parameter around the turn of the century. Pyrotechnic designers were just beginning to understand the affect of persistence-of-vision on the apparent brightness of an effect. Good pyrotechnics today can deliver over a million candlepower-seconds with high perceptibility. At the turn of the century I would not have expected more than 10% of this effect (100,000-CPS) and then only with poor perceptibility (a quick "wink" of light, too short to catch the attention or leave a strong afterimage). However, I would expect signaling "stars" to have a nice long burn (1/2 to 2 seconds) with a reasonable energy content (say 10,000 to 20,000 candlepower-seconds) spread out over this period. Visibility, even to the naked eye, would not be an issue at 40 miles as a mere 10,000 candlepower lighthouse lamp can be seen much farther. Whether it would be noticed is the real issue since the apparent size of the flare becomes

a tiny speck with distance. Once noticed, the signals could be observed closely with night glasses."

When Apprentice James Gibson first saw the mysterious ship stopped south of ***CALIFORNIAN*** it was about 0020, or fifty minutes after this vessel had stopped, and about twenty minutes after the time Gill had claimed he saw a large passenger ship passing ***CALIFORNIAN***. Gibson had the middle watch, from midnight to 0400, with Second Officer Stone. The Apprentice saw this unidentified vessel's red light, *one* mastlight and a glare of white lights on her after deck. When Gibson told the Solicitor General that he had seen one masthead light. Sir John admonished the young man, *"I don't think you quite answered the question I was putting to you. Did you or did you not see any second white steaming lights?"*

Gibson replied, *"Not distinctly, sir."*

"You are not sure whether you could see it or not?" asked Sir John.

"No," replied Gibson, not once, but twice to this same question. This was very important for two reasons... because ***TITANIC*** had *range lights,* and the white lights were referred to as *"steaming lights"* because sailing vessels never carried white lights when under way.

The above figure demonstrates, in graphic form , how the tilt of a vessel in pitch, and /or roll might influence the perception of its range as judged by an observer aboard another ship some miles away. The Vertical and Horizontal scales in this figure are different to accentuate the visual effect described.

The burst of a flare, marked A, corresponds to the location as seen from an observer's ship, located at the origin of abscissa of the graph, when the launch tube on the vessel which fired the rocket is vertical, due to the roll or pitch of the vessel-then the rocket would follow a curved trajectory and the flare would be ignited at a lower altitude, marked A' in the figure.

But, a point B exists where the burst would be observed if the vessel which launched the flare hod merely moved farther away from the observing ship, with its hull and launch tube still in a vertical orientation. It can be seen that the elevation angle of burst B, as viewed from the observer's ship has turned down from an earlier sighting by on angle C, and for some distances this might match the angle to burst A ". If an alignment existed in the line of sight to A' and B, and in absence of contrary evidence, a crewman aboard the observing ship might mistakenly conclude that the vessel firing a succession of flares was continuing underway and the increasing depression of the sighting angle to subsequent flares was due solely to the increasing range, rather than anything catastrophic—as was the case for the ***TITANIC***, where flooding below the waterline was responsible for major list and downward slope of the hull.

Reprinted Courtesy of the Author, Mr . John Bryant Williams , P.E.

The International Rules of the Road Section II – Lights and So Forth, Article 2, stated: *"A steam vessel when under way shall carry... (a) On or in front of the foremast, or if a vessel without a foremast, then in the fore part of the vessel, at a height above the hull of not less than twenty feet, and if the breadth of the vessel exceeds twenty feet, then at a height above the hull not less than such breadth, so, however, that the light need not be carried at a greater height above the hull than forty feet, a bright white light so constructed as to show an unbroken light over an arc of the horizon of twenty points of the compass, so fixed as to throw the light ten points on each side of the vessel, namely, from right ahead to two points abaft the beam on either side, and of such a character as to be visible at a distance of at least five miles.*

"Steam Vessels... Side Lights: (b) On the starboard side a green light so constructed as to show an unbroken light over an arc of the horizon of ten points of the compass, so fixed as to throw the light from right ahead to two points abaft the beam on the starboard side, and of such a character as to be visible at a

distance of at least two miles, (c) On the port side a red light so constructed as to show an unbroken light over an arc of the horizon of ten points of the compass, so fixed as to throw the light from right ahead to two points abaft the beam on the port side, and of such a character as to be visible at a distance of at least two miles, (d) The said green and red side lights shall be fitted with inboard screens projecting at least three feet forward from the light, so as to prevent these lights from being seen across the bow.

"Steam vessels... Range Lights: (e) A steam vessel when under way may carry an additional white light similar in construction to the light mentioned in subdivision (a). These two lights shall be so placed in line with the keel that one shall be at least fifteen feet higher than the other, and in such a position with reference to each other that the lower light shall be forward of the upper one. The vertical distance between these lights shall be less than the horizontal distance."

In addition *Article 5* stated: *"A sailing vessel under way and any vessel being towed shall carry the same lights as are prescribed by Article 2 for a steam vessel under way, with the exception of the white lights mentioned therein, which they shall never carry."*

Article 10... Lights for an Overtaken Vessel stated: *"A vessel which is being overtaken by another shall show from her stern to such last-mentioned vessel a white light or a flare-up light. The white light required to be shown by this article may be fixed and carried in a lantern, but in such case the lantern shall be so constructed, fitted, and screened that it shall throw an unbroken light over an arc of the horizon of twelve points of the compass, namely, for six points right aft on each side of the vessel, so as to be visible at a distance of at least one mile. Such light shall be carried as nearly as practicable on the same level as the side lights."*

Vessels built after about 1898 carried range lights because the two lights' relative positions along with the relative positions of visible sidelights indicated to watch officers in other ships how the ship was steering in relation to their own. This was obviously important in avoiding collisions at night. All such lights were to be shown between sunset and sunrise, during which time *"no other lights which may be mistaken for the prescribed lights shall be exhibited." "Visible"* meant on a dark night with a clear atmosphere.

Clearly, if this vessel stopped just about five miles south of ***CALIFORNIAN*** had range lights then she could have been ***TITANIC***. If she had but one mastlight, then she definitely could *not* have been ***TITANIC***. It was therefore extremely important to establish the number of mastlights carried by this mystery ship. Was it one, or two?

Gibson was sure the unidentified vessel was a tramp and not a passenger ship because the latter would have rows of lights from the waterline up.

A big passenger ship casts a glare of lights reflected from the water's surface which at night is unmistakable seen across the water or from the air. In fact, the loom of the lights of a large passenger ship will be seen from well over the horizon. In ***TITANIC***'s era, while lights were put out with the curfew in Third Class, usually about 11PM, it being assumed that all such lower class and "foreign" men and women were immoral and must be separated at night, there was no such curfew in First Class, where passengers often had cabin lights on quite late, where no moral restrictions applied. Public room lights, too, were bright until quite late while younger passengers danced and gentlemen smoked, drank and played cards. In addition lights were on in some crew quarters, there were minimum alleyway lights for safety, and there were lights in all areas where work was necessarily in progress. The bridge, of course, was dark, as was the entire area forward of the bridge to enhance night visibility. A passenger ship the size of ***TITANIC*** could not be mistaken for anything else. Nor would a ship with ***TITANIC***'s speed be mistaken for a slow tramp. *(See previous night photograph of Cunard's QE2.)*

If this mystery ship did the same thing that ***CALIFORNIAN*** had done earlier, that is, she had stopped by going full speed astern to prevent running up on the ice, she would then have done just what ***CALIFORNIAN*** had done, swung around to head ENE, thus then showing a red light to ***CALIFORNIAN***, after first showing her green light. This behavior would have manifested in a right-handed single screw ship, but if she was a tramp about the size of ***CALIFORNIAN*** then she no doubt did have but one screw, and most single screws were right-handed. Engines, shafts and propellers cost money to build and operate, and in a tramp money was the biggest consideration. Freight did not need speed when speed costs money. The fact that this ship had but one mastlight indicated that she was built at least fourteen years earlier, probably she was older, suggested by her oil lights. There were, however, ships built after the turn of the century for use as tramp freighters which were not equipped with electricity, because that, too, was expensive. Nobody was going to hoist two white lanterns aloft for range lights when one would satisfy the *International Rules of the Road.*

Additionally, it should be noted that a vessel's sidelights are shut out as soon as an observer is more than 2 points abaft her beam. Thus, if the bearing on which the light disappears is noted, the approximate direction of the ship's head at the time can be found. A red light being shut out indicates that the vessel carrying it was heading 6 points to the left of the bearing. A green light just being shut out indicates that she was heading 6 points to the right of its bearing. For example, when the mystery ship seen 2 points off ***TITANIC***'s port bow shut out her red light she had been heading about due west. (Two points on the port bow is 337°30'. Six points is 67°30'. Subtracting 67°30" from 337°30' we get 270°, which is due west.) This would hold true if Boxhall had seen only her red light, as he said in his first statement at the American inquiry, which was his first mention of this mystery ship.

Gibson's testimony supported Captain Lord's statements excepting that Gibson was sure the master had been awake when he reported the rockets to him at about 0205. It is interesting to note that Master Mariners Edward A. Turpin and William A. MacEwen, in their *Merchant Marine Officers' Handbook* (Cornell Maritime Press, Inc., Cambridge, MD, 1942), admonished young deck officers not to call the skipper in such a soft voice that it made him sleep all the sounder.

Gibson was also the first to mention that he and Second Officer Stone had remarked that the strange steamer's lights looked "queer," that she seemed to have a "big side out of the water" and to Gibson this meant that she had a list to starboard because he was seeing only her red, port sidelight. While one would assume that ***TITANIC***, bilged on her starboard side forward, would have a list to starboard, her most serious list was to *port.*

The testimony from Apprentice Gibson about seeing a list to starboard would be more credible if it had been made before ***CALIFORNIAN*** had been accused of being the mystery ship.

MOUNT TEMPLE's master would later report having seen a tramp while he was on his way to ***TITANIC***. It is also known that several German tramps without wireless searched ***TITANIC***'s wreckage for survivors on Monday after ***CARPATHIA*** and ***CALIFORNIAN*** had departed the area. These vessels were seen from the Hapag liner ***PRINZ ADALBERT.***

On Tuesday, 16 April, in latitude 41°40'N, longitude 50°15'W, officers on the bridge of ***PRINZ ADALBERT***, from Hamburg for Philadelphia, reported seeing ice. When the Hapag liner docked at Pier 34 her master, Captain Brambeer, told reporters that he had instructions from Hamburg-American to file his report with the local company agent, and not to discuss ***TITANIC*** in any way with reporters, or to discuss any part of his voyage from Hamburg to Philadelphia. A woman in Germany, learning of my search for any German tramps which had come across ***TITANIC***'s wreckage, wrote to me about her father, who had been a young seaman in ***PRINZ ADALBERT***, and who had often told his family about seeing several German tramps without wireless searching ***TITANIC***'s wreckage for survivors. (It must be noted that Hapag, as did the Lloyd, had a profit-sharing agreement with Morgan's I.M.M. shipping trust.) This young German sailor had not seen any survivors taken aboard any of the tramps, yet this story fits in with that of Seaman Arthur Edward "Pop" Blogg, who claimed to have been a "deckhand" in ***TITANIC***, who jumped overboard as the ship went down, clung to wreckage for many hours, and who was eventually rescued by *a German tramp without wireless.* Blogg turned up in New Zealand after jumping ship in Australia, sometime near the end of 1912 or beginning of 1913. Blogg's story, according to the ***TITANIC*** establishment without any research, is a hoax because he "had not been born yet" when ***TITANIC*** sank.

Arthur Edward Blogg was born on 4 February, 1888. His birth certificate is Number 406, Registration District, Deepwade; Sub District, Harleston, in the County of Norfolk, England. He was twenty four years old when ***TITANIC*** sank.

When Blogg was about eleven years old he had run away from home to get away from his father, a butcher, who was described by the family as a "very hard man." Young Arthur went to his uncle, who owned a small fleet of fishing boats on the Channel Coast. Arthur learned cooking and seamanship in his uncle's boats. When he was fifteen Arthur returned home. His father promptly sent him to Kew Gardens to be an apprentice gardener for five years. In about 1908, when Arthur was twenty, he went back to sea, signing on sometimes as a cook, sometimes as a seaman. He was still on the run from his abusive father and usually signed articles under the names Alf or Ned Daniels. Daniels was his mother's maiden name. Legend has it that a fireman named Thomas Hart was listed on ***TITANIC***'s manifest and was presumed lost. Hart appeared, however, in Southampton on 8 May, 1912, according to his mother, and said that his discharge book had been stolen and used by another to sign on ***TITANIC***. There is a discrepancy here in that Blogg's family recalled his saying that he had been a "deckhand," not a fireman. But Blogg's family were not seamen, and thus may have misunderstood. By the same token Hart and Blogg, or at least Blogg, may have signed on ships as either firemen or ordinary seamen, whatever they could get. Blogg's story fits too neatly with that of Hart's missing discharge book *and* the searching German tramps, neither of which Blogg could have known from reading newspapers or books about ***TITANIC***. Because no proper search of ***TITANIC***'s wreckage was ever conducted, if there had been survivors it would have been a very serious, in fact a *criminal* matter that they had been overlooked and in fact left to die. Captain Rostron had asked ***CALIFORNIAN*** to search the area, but had told Captain Lord that all survivors had been picked up, all others had drowned. The area searched, however, was the area where the lifeboats had been picked up, not the area where the ship's wreckage had surfaced after her plunge to the bottom. A proper search would have consisted of sending lifeboats into the wreckage area, examining every body and bit of wreckage and ice for signs of life. Assuming that everyone had either drowned or died of hypothermia was indeed criminal negligence. If even one person had survived, and there are almost always miraculous survivals in any disaster, that person should have been found by a thorough search. As it was, apparently two crewmen, a greaser named George Prangnell as well as Blogg, did survive after being left as dead. Legend has it that Prangnell, too, clung to wreckage and was picked up the following day by a British tramp without wireless and brought to New York, where he remained in hospital for about two weeks before returning to England. These two stories have never been thoroughly investigated, and are just the items that would have been officially covered up. As mentioned earlier, McFee wrote that several British tramps without wireless were in the area. Both accounts of survival are perfectly logical, and not unusual following shipwrecks. Prangnell was on ***TITANIC***'s manifest and did remain in White Star's employee after his return to England. Because of the lack of a thorough search we will never know how many victims actually survived the sinking but died hours later clinging precariously to wreckage. Imagine, however, the furor if the public had found out, or if the families of men like Astor, Guggenheim, Thayer, Roebling, Butt, Stead, for example, had learned that they might have survived if a thorough search had been conducted. Second Officer Fosgate's comments on the subject, *"I can surely believe that some captains were more conscientious about searching for survivors than others, and that the tramps would have been proceeding very slowly in the pack so they could have come across survivors a day later... if they were OUT of the WATER, which would kill a well dressed person in an hour or so. If the survivors were dry on ice or rafts (wreckage) they could survive for several days if warm enough."*

I would add that some people will always have more natural stamina and will to survive than others.

In Australia Blogg worked at various jobs, as a station cook, in the cane fields, as a grape harvester, and he traveled for a while with a circus. He used the name Ned Brown during this period. Sometime in 1914 he worked his way to New Zealand, took the first name of Alfred, but reverted to his real surname, Blogg. He was married in September, 1918, and for the next 27 years he worked as a baker or cook, and later as a gardener. In 1945 he moved to Geraldine, New Zealand, and became a respected member of the County Council. He died in November, 1974. Blogg's story would not have been known except for the fact that by remarkable coincidence he emigrated to an area in which lived Will Murdoch's widow, Ada Banks Murdoch, and Captain James McGiffin's son, J. O. McGiffin. It was the latter who sent a copy of Blogg's obituary from the *Christchurch Press* to me.

The tramp freighter ***LENA***, out of Fowey, England, for Portland, Maine, had no wireless set. Therefore it was not until ***LENA***'s arrival at Portland on 24 April that her officers learned of ***TITANIC***'s loss. Quickly they checked ***LENA***'s logbook and charts, and were sure that ***LENA*** was not one of the mystery ships seen from ***TITANIC***. However, Chief Officer Evan Elias figured that ***LENA*** had been 30 miles to the northeast of ***TITANIC***. We have no report on the height of ***LENA***'s bridge, thus no idea of her watch officer's extreme limit of visibility with reference to ***TITANIC***'s rockets, yet it seems that on such a clear dark night he should have seen at least some of the white flashes in the sky. Three westbound steamers had passed the heavily-loaded, slow-moving ***LENA*** earlier in the evening, reported Elias, and all of them were traveling at speeds which could have put them near ***TITANIC***. The tramp steamer ***KELVINDALE*** passed ***LENA*** at 4PM on Sunday, several miles to the south, moving about three knots faster. Four hours later a four-masted passenger steamer sped past ***LENA***, and later still another tramp passed her. Probably the latter was the mysterious vessel between ***CALIFORNIAN*** and ***TITANIC***, while the passenger ship was probably ***MOUNT TEMPLE.***

Also on 24 April the British tramp steamer ***DULWICH***, Captain John Dudley, having departed an unidentified Norwegian port on 29 March, arrived at Philadelphia. On 14 April Dudley ordered a course change to avoid field ice and scattered bergs. Captain Dudley could not understand how ***TITANIC*** had escaped the most dangerous part of the fields and struck ice as she was passing from the fields. Early on Monday morning one of the British sailors had sighted a drifting, empty lifeboat. On 13 April, in spite of Dudley's precautions, ***DULWICH*** had struck a submerged spur of ice, her bow running up over the ice, forcing her stern under water. Hull plating on the ship's port side had been damaged and it was necessary for her to remain in Philadelphia for repairs. With pumps working continuously, the little ***DULWICH*** had survived, yet the mighty ***TITANIC*** had not. Captain Dudley told reporters that ***DULWICH*** had been within 40 miles of ***TITANIC*** when the White Star liner was calling for help. In spite of her own wounds, if ***DULWICH*** had had a wireless installation Dudley said that she surely could have saved the lives of many passengers who had been left struggling in the water. Actually, of course, if ***DULWICH*** and ***LENA*** had been equipped with wireless they each would have had but one operator and he undoubtedly would have been asleep, as was Evans of the ***CALIFORNIAN***.

Unfortunately no officers from any other ships known to be in the vicinity were ever called upon for testimony, with the exception of ***MOUNT TEMPLE***'s master, Captain Moore, but his watch officers were never interrogated as ***CALIFORNIAN***'s watch officers were. A thorough and *impartial* investigation would have encompassed ship's logs and statements from officers and seamen, not just masters, in ***LENA, KELVINDALE, DULWICH, FRANKFURT, MOUNT TEMPLE, RAPPAHANNOCK,*** at the very least, along with a search for the unidentified tramp seen from ***LENA.*** The latter was surely not ***DULWICH***, as she had already struck ice and would have been moving very slowly. Sailors, however, live in a different world from landsmen, and sailors are very hard to pin down. The United States had no jurisdiction over foreign ships and their crews, thus any effort to detain them for the inquiry would have been a matter of courtesy on the part of shipowners, a courtesy which would have been tremendously expensive. Sailors, who would not have been paid while they remained ashore for the inquiry, were certainly not going to volunteer to go without pay. A Senate investigation of ***TITANIC*** was legal only because the White Star Line was part of the Morgan shipping trust, I.M.M., and because ***TITANIC*** was bound for an American port carrying American passengers.

Gibson went on to say that at 0340 he and Stone had seen three more white rockets. These, however, were the rockets fired from ***CARPATHIA*** as she approached ***TITANIC***'s distress position, signals to cheer ***TITANIC***'s people and let them know that help was at hand. Unfortunately we have no description of the rockets sent up by ***CARPATHIA***, excepting that Rostron said he had alternated distress rockets with Cunard's company pyrotechnic signal, which was a Roman candle, quite a different signal from a rocket, although one with no knowledge of pyrotechnics might well use the terms interchangeably. Gibson insisted that he and Stone had discussed the fact that a ship would not fire rockets for nothing, and of course she would not, but that reason did not have to mean distress. It is interesting to note that while an unknown vessel had fired rockets definitely identified as distress signals only three weeks prior to ***TITANIC***'s loss, the word of a nearby shipmaster was taken when ***ROMSDAL***'s master said that his ship could not move to the rescue, and he believed that the unknown steamer had sunk with all hands. In this case no search was instigated, even though it was not unknown for shipwrecked sailors to take refuge on the very ice that wrecked them, and the press gave very little coverage to just another tramp lost. The sea was, and is, a harsh way of life. Sailors and tramp steamers are expendable, American millionaires and large, new passenger vessels are not.

Gibson then reported how the mystery steamer which had stopped a few miles south of ***CALIFORNIAN*** had disappeared to the southwest, while ***CALIFORNIAN*** had by this time swung around to a WSW heading. At no time had Gibson seen the green light of this mysterious vessel, but her red light had disappeared as she steamed away. Gibson had not come on the bridge until midnight, nor had he according to his statement, even looked at the ship until twenty minutes later. He had not seen her arrive and stop. ***TITANIC***, with her waterlogged bow sinking ever deeper into the sea, would not have swung as a normally stable and buoyant vessel would. Nor would the triple screw ***TITANIC*** have swung to starboard when her outboard screws began to back, while the center screw was put out of action. Gibson was adamant, never did he see a green light, the mystery vessel had only *one* mastlight, and she was only five miles away from ***CALIFORNIAN***. This testimony has also been confused into legend which says that Gibson did see ***TITANIC***'s lights. He did not. ***TITANIC*** had *two* mastlights. Like Stone, the Apprentice saw only the apogee of ***TITANIC***'s rockets, which could have been seen from as far as 41 miles away, if the rockets had achieved an altitude of 800 feet from their firing point. The ship which showed first her green and then her red sidelight to ***CALIFORNIAN*** was between ***CALIFORNIAN*** and ***TITANIC***, and was merely another link in the chain of disaster. Had she not been there the issue would not have become so confused and difficult to assess. When this mystery ship did steam away, she was undoubtedly steaming in the general direction of ***TITANIC***, whether to investigate, or because coincidentally at that particular time her lookout had found a lead through the ice we will never now know, but probably it was the latter. This vessel's watch officer would also have seen the apogee of ***TITANIC***'s white rockets, and because they gave the illusion that the ship was moving away that would have given the impression that there was open water in that direction, and in fact there was. When Gibson said she showed a "big side" and her red light, she could have been turning tightly to starboard, showing her red light until she turned enough to close it out, preparing to follow a suddenly appearing lead through the ice. As she turned she would have eventually showed only her stern light to ***CALIFORNIAN***. The confusion arising over the persistent legend of Gibson and Stone actually seeing ***TITANIC***'s sidelights precluded identification of the mystery ship between ***CALIFORNIAN*** and ***TITANIC*** when an investigation should have been made, when those involved were still living. That is exactly what the coverup intended, and in fact the identity of this vessel may very well have been known in 1912… by someone involved in the coverup.

It must be noted that we can never know exactly how the ice lay that night. Captain Lord chose to stop rather than search for a lead during the night, a prudent choice. But the mystery tramp's master may have kept a constant vigil for a lead and chosen to follow it when he saw it, not an unusual choice for a master who probably had to study his coal supply very carefully. As we have seen, ***ROMSDAL***, ***DULWICH*** and ***RAPPAHANNOCK*** among other vessels plowed through field ice at night. Captain Lord was employed by a large, reasonably financially solvent company, the Leyland Line, affiliated with Morgan's IMM. This line's masters were allegedly told to stay out of field ice, and Lord said it was his first experience with this type of ice. The choice to continue or stop for the night was the master's decision to make, and one master will be more cautious than another. Questioned by Senator Smith, Lord stated that ***CALIFORNIAN*** had been surrounded by "a lot of loose ice," and that she had stopped about one quarter of a mile off the eastern edge of the ice field. Lord estimated that the field extended about 25 miles in a generally north-south direction, being about 1 to 2 miles wide. Therefore one could easily see across the ice in the east-west direction from the bridge of any vessel the size of ***CALIFORNIAN***. That the field area was long in the north-south direction, and that it had at times curved back on itself, much like the letter "S," we know from descriptions given by other shipmasters' wireless reports during the preceding two weeks. Lord also told Senator Smith that *"we had had a report of this ice three or four days before."* He read several ice reports from ***CALIFORNIAN***'s log, including one dated 9 April from the Holland-American liner ***NIEUW AMSTERDAM***, which warned of ice sighted on 4 April in 43°20'N, 49°W, *"extending as far to the north-northeast as horizon is visible."* There were undoubtedly leads, plowed by bergs moving through the field ice. As we have seen, ***BORDERER***, commanded by Will Murdoch's cousin-by-marriage, had gone through one of those leads less than 36 hours earlier. There had been enough sea room between ice fields that ***BLUE JACKET***'s master had believed his little vessel was clear of ice, when in fact she encountered another field within a few hours. ***LA TOURAINE***, too, had encountered two fields. In fact there may have been, and probably were, more than two fields as the entire mass of ice moved south, broken by bergs moving with the surface current, plowing through the wind-driven field ice, with all of the ice beginning to melt in the warmer water of the Gulf Stream. There was enough clear water for ***CARPATHIA*** and other ships to maneuver into ***TITANIC***'s distress position area early on Monday. Again, the only mental picture we can form of this area comes from artists who have exaggerated for artistic effect, authors who have used Captain Moore's coordinates as finite, and survivors who have dramatized even more with each passing year. The only reliable coordinates came from Captain Lord, because he had given them to the USN Hydrographic Office *before* ***TITANIC*** struck ice.

CALIFORNIAN's log also contained some interesting information about the wind direction and velocity. At 0400 on Sunday there had been a fresh, westerly wind, with an overcast sky and heavy showers. On the Beaufort Scale a "fresh breeze" is Force 5, or 24.3 knots. By 0800 the wind had been "moderate," Force 4, or 20 knots, the weather clear. The wind had gradually shifted from WNW, through NNW, remaining moderate, until by noon it was out of the north and remained so until 2200 when it died altogether, *or* ***CALIFORNIAN*** had moved into the lee of a larger ice field to the north.

While Gibson and Stone had tried to signal to the mystery ship with ***CALIFORNIAN***'s Morse light on top of her bridge, they had first believed that she was answering because they saw her mastlight flickering. In 1912 there were still many older vessels afloat which carried their Morse lights on their foremast spreaders. Later, however. Stone became sure that the flickering mastlight merely meant that the ship had oil lights, no electricity. William McFee wrote that many English watch officers in tramps did not know Morse at all, and in fact they had no reason to if they had served entirely in ships without electricity. Although it was a requirement for passing the examination for an officer's certificate, if the skill was not used it could quickly be forgotten. As far as communication was concerned, wrote McFee, they were no more advanced than Nelson. This statement would have held true for vessels of any registry.

It cannot be emphasized enough, to combat the tenacious myths, that when Gibson and ***CALIFORNIAN***'s watch officers talked about the ship firing rockets and the ship which lay only four or five miles south of them, they were talking about two different ships, which legend has fused into one vessel, deliberately. If blame was put on the ***CALIFORNIAN***, then no further investigation would be made. Further investigation might have brought to light several things that White Star wanted kept in the dark. If Stone and Gibson had indeed seen ***TITANIC*** at a distance of only five miles, as the Board of Trade interrogators insisted and legend perpetuates, both men would have known her at once. A passenger liner of that size on a clear night is absolutely unmistakable only five miles distant. In fact, the distance at which ***CALIFORNIAN***'s officers could have readily identified a large passenger ship with a bridge 70 feet above the waterline would have been nearly 17 miles on such a clear night. Her deck lights would have been seen farther than her sidelights. If ***TITANIC*** had indeed been only five miles from ***CALIFORNIAN***, Stone would have seen Boxhall's green flares as well as the lanterns that were in some of the lifeboats.

Leyland Line attorney Robertson Dunlop was the last to interrogate Gibson on 14 May. When Dunlop asked Gibson if he had seen passenger ships of all sizes, as well as many tramps during his three and a half years at sea, Gibson was positive. He had seen many, and he certainly could tell the difference between tramps and passenger ships, by the quantity of lights shown by the latter. It is a pity that Gibson did not testify in the United States before details of ***TITANIC***'s rockets had been given. Gibson remained adamant about the rockets, however. The rockets he and Stone saw from ***CALIFORNIAN***'s bridge were all white. They had heard no explosions. White Star's Attorney F. Laing obviously believed that white was not a color, because he asked Gibson if the rockets threw stars of any color, or were they merely white? Gibson knew that distress rockets threw stars. And by this time he replied that distress rockets were *"white... any colour at all."* Gibson also stated that he now knew that only distress rockets were used at sea, while private signals were used only near the shore! One of the more absurd statements to be given at either inquiry, yet it did indicate that somehow, someone, had been "educating" the officers of both ***CALIFORNIAN*** and ***TITANIC*** about white rockets as opposed to those throwing green or red stars. If Gibson really believed what he said one shudders to think what might have happened if he ever achieved command, or even watchkeeping status. Had he seen any pyrotechnic signals emanating red or green stars, accompanied by loud reports, near shore from a ship in distress he would have automatically ignored them as company's signals!

Second Officer Herbert Stone was interrogated next, by Mr. Butler Aspinall, Counsel on behalf of the Board of Trade. Stone held a First Mate's certificate and had been going to sea for eight years. Captain Lord had judged the twenty-four-year-old Stone to be honest, responsible, and somewhat stolid. He had been ***CALIFORNIAN***'s watch officer from midnight to 0400. On his way to the bridge to relieve Third Officer Groves, Stone had spoken with Captain Lord, who had pointed out the steamer which had approached from the east and stopped to the southward of ***CALIFORNIAN***. Stone described seeing one mastlight and a red sidelight, as well as two or three small, indistinct lights, and judged the stranger's distance from ***CALIFORNIAN*** as about five miles. Stone confirmed that the lights then were bearing SSE by the standard compass. Lord told the Second Officer that the Third Officer had already tried to contact the stranger by Morse light but there had been no response. The master then went into the chart room while Stone went on to the bridge, with orders to let Captain Lord know if the stranger altered her bearing or got any closer.

Stone relieved Groves. He then kept the unidentified ship in sight for the whole of his watch, simply because she was another vessel stopped in the ice, the same as ***CALIFORNIAN***, and she was fairly close. At about 0110 Stone called up the master on the speaking tube and told Lord that he had seen white lights, or flashes, in the sky immediately above the other steamer. Stone at first thought he'd seen a shooting star. When asked if this was a distress signal. Stone responded that it was just a white flash in the sky which might have been anything. He then used his binoculars and saw four more flashes which he now identified as white rockets, sent up at intervals of three or four minutes.

Stone was treated badly by Aspinall and by Lord Mersey, with questions and suggestions that today would be overruled in any court of law as "leading." When Stone said that he thought the white rockets might mean that the other ship was signaling that she had big icebergs around her, or she might have been signaling to a ship beyond her, out of sight of ***CALIFORNIAN***, Aspinall and Mersey bored in on Stone. He had not applied his mind, he had not been thinking for himself, he could not possibly have believed these white rockets were anything but distress signals. Mersey remarked that Stone did not make a good impression upon him. Stone remained adamant... he had not thought at all that the white signals were distress signals, until after he heard that ***TITANIC*** had foundered and had sent up white rockets.

Let us pause for a moment and study this exchange. Captain Edmund A. Gibson in his series of seamanship manuals (McGraw Hill, New York) advised that an unusual display of any kind is probably being shown by a vessel which is unable to keep clear of other ships. *"Give her a wide berth,"* advised Gibson. A white rocket fired in an area of the North Atlantic known to contain ice could very well have meant that a ship trapped in an ice field was warning others to keep clear and not fall into the same trap, which was exactly how Stone interpreted the white rockets. Watch officers still give a wide berth to any white light, which could mean a variety of things, from cargo clusters to fishing boats with nets out, to submarines operating on the surface. Boxhall, then, from ***TITANIC***'s bridge, instead of calling for help was warning other vessels to keep away, and they did, properly so. The fault lies entirely in ***TITANIC***'s signals, not in the response of watch officers in other ships. No prudent master would take his ship on a wild goose chase to investigate a signal which in itself indicated that the ship firing it wanted to warn other vessels away.

TITANIC, with over 2,200 lives in jeopardy, was emanating pyrotechnic signals which were not only *not* distress signals, but those signals literally said *"stay out of this area where I am."* Why, then, were the all-white rockets fired when ***TITANIC*** did carry regulation distress rockets, according to her manifest? The coverup was so complete, and historians have been so brainwashed by that coverup, that we may never know for sure. They were allegedly not company signals, which means only that they were not officially registered by the Board of Trade as White Star Line pyrotechnic company signals.

But if ***TITANIC*** carried regulation red or green distress rockets, why did Boxhall eschew them to fire white rockets? Did Boxhall choose the white rockets on his own initiative, did Captain Smith choose them, or did someone else choose them for him? Unfortunately nobody ever asked these questions when they might have been answered, although undoubtedly the answers were known in 1912. The meaning of ***TITANIC***'s white rockets will probably never be admitted, or proven at this late date. The logical conclusion, however, is that they were a private, unregistered White Star signal for aid, but not necessarily for distress in the context that they were sinking. Probably this was a pyrotechnic signal adopted after the loss of ***REPUBLIC*** in 1909. After ***REPUBLIC***'s collision with ***FLORIDA***, so many ships answered the CQD call, among them White Star's own ***BALTIC***, and Captain Sealby wanted no help from any vessel whose master asked a towing fee, nor did White Star's Marconi operators want to communicate with vessels equipped with other wireless services. In fact, the inference was that such vessels, notably the Standard Oil tanker ***CITY OF EVERETT***, were in the way. A shipmaster in trouble will first call on a company ship, then one of his own country's registry, and last a government ship of any country, because none of these will ask salvage fees. Captain Sealby waited for ***BALTIC***, waited for two little U.S. revenue cutters to tow ***REPUBLIC***. Sealby waited too long, lost his ship and his career, but Fate intervened and saved his life, as it did Lightoller's three years later. Even today there are cases of shipmasters waiting too long to ask for help from just anyone. But what do they have to lose? They gamble for very high stakes... their ships, their careers, and a few lives. If they win they win big, if they save their ships they might save their careers and they certainly save the lives. But if they lose, they lose big... their ships, careers, possibly their own lives among the rest of those lost. It is all very well for idealists and romanticists to assume that when they travel their safety is of paramount importance to the owners and stockholders of whatever transportation system they have chosen, but this is not the real world. The bottom line in any transportation company is profit, period, and corners will be cut whenever it means saving pennies, dollars, pounds, whatever. A good ship or a good airplane is an economic compromise. A compromise in safety, be it in maintenance, weather, crew training or otherwise, may be judged a calculated risk. When maritime law puts no value on human life it does not necessarily mean that human life is above monetary value. It is easy enough to take calculated risks with the lives of others when the stakes are high, the odds are in your favor. It takes but one misstep and the whole house of cards comes crashing down. Cut fares the day after the accident, however, and the traveling public quickly forgets in the rush to buy cheap tickets.

A private White Star pyrotechnic signal could avoid the confusion and ensuing publicity that accompanied the ***REPUBLIC-CITY OF EVERETT*** debacle. Wireless signals were heard by everybody within range, regardless of wireless service, thus were not private.

But what more logical private pyrotechnic aid signal for the White Star Line than a rocket which threw white stars? It told other White Star vessels within sight that one of their own needed help, while warning others away. Surely the signal was to be used by White Star ships not in acute danger, however, but it was to be used at the master's discretion. It was a private code, then, like the wireless codes adopted by shipping lines to conduct private business by wireless, with messages sent in codes to preclude eavesdropping by competitors. Clearly, if the white rocket signal was registered it would no longer be private. As we have seen, it could be argued that it was a regulation distress signal, as mandated by the *Rules of the Road,* if you believe that white is a color. But the average seaman in 1912 obviously did not believe that white is a color, nor did all of the attorneys and senators who questioned the seamen concerned believe that white is a color. And if this hypothesis is correct, then why did ***TITANIC***'s master allow only the white signals to be used when it should have been known that no other White Star ships were within sight? Probably for the same reason that ***TITANIC***'s wireless operator told ***OLYMPIC,*** over 500 miles away, to have her lifeboats ready. While ***TITANIC***'s officers, and apparently Bruce Ismay also, knew she was doomed, Ismay at least refused to accept the fact that she would die so soon. Ismay had conferred with Chief Bell, who allegedly had told Ismay that he thought the pumps would keep ***TITANIC*** afloat. Ismay, in shock no doubt, simply could not comprehend that his beautiful, big, new ship, upon which he had pinned so much hope for the future of the White Star Line, would sink any sooner than ***REPUBLIC*** had, for example. ***REPUBLIC,*** two thirds ***TITANIC***'s size, had lived for *39 hours, over a day and a half,* after her mortal wound, long enough for all of her people to be transferred to ***FLORIDA,*** and transferred again to ***BALTIC.*** Why should Ismay or anyone else, expect less of the mighty ***TITANIC?*** As far as the rockets were concerned, Ismay was no doubt calling the shots and Ismay above all people would have been aware of the enormous salvage fee which would have been asked and awarded by the courts later to whoever got a towing line on ***TITANIC.*** *Salvage* is a monetary reward granted by a court of admiralty for services rendered in saving a vessel or her cargo. The reward is generous to encourage others to do the same if the need arises, but no awards are made if human lives alone are saved. The saving of life is looked upon by all mariners as a duty owed to those whose lives are in peril. It is not customary for a government vessel of any type, or from any country, to press for salvor's fees. The possibility of making extra money from salvage is always before the merchant sailor, always somewhere in the adventure which lies ahead. And salvage is the one thing a shipowner, and his representative-on-board, the master, tries desperately to avoid. It may well be financially better for the shipowner to collect insurance. No doubt Ismay ordered the White Star signals to be used first, they could be followed by the regulation distress rocket-bomb when the situation became acute, but as it turned out, as Boxhall let slip at the American inquiry, they had no time to use *"any of those things."* Logically it might seem that the masters of other I.M.M. vessels would have known about the white rocket signal. But, when huge trusts control so many companies, the companies have their own executive officers, and they are operated as entirely separate entities as far as the general public is concerned. Even employees often do not know that their company is part of a trust. This gives the illusion of free competition, and indeed the separate companies do show their own profits and losses. But at the apex of this hierarchy sit the men who reap the profits from all of their "separate" companies, in this case Morgan and his stockholders. There was also, judging from the actions of officers in the ***REPUBLIC*** disaster as well as that of ***TITANIC***, a tendency to want to maintain elite service even in the face of catastrophe, incredible as it may seem. Relying far too much upon wireless, and exclusively Marconi wireless at that, actually indicated that they wanted another liner of nearly equal accommodations to make the rescue. Surely, however, Astor, Guggenheim and even Ismay would gladly have stepped on to a floating garbage scow had it been available. It undoubtedly was the first and last time the private signal was used. Never again would Ismay be aboard a sinking ship to use it, never again would any White Star master be in such a position to use it, and never again would the White Star allow such a choice after the ***TITANIC*** fiasco.

The only other answer is even more difficult to comprehend. If ***TITANIC***'s rockets were indeed merely detonators, then Boxhall erred in firing them alone as well as in firing them at such lengthy intervals. Captain Smith erred in allowing him to do so. As it turned out they were not heard, they were therefore not recognized as any sort of distress signal, and rightly so, as we have seen. Boxhall apparently was too eager to escape the sinking ship, and thus fired the rockets with one eye on the nearest lifeboat when he should have concentrated on the rockets. He should have fired a detonator from one side of the bridge, then raced to the other side to fire a socket light signal throwing green stars that would have been unmistakably a signal of distress, not a difficult task with one of the quartermasters to help him. For that matter, if Murdoch could dash from one boat to another to speed their launching, then Boxhall could have dashed from one side of the bridge to the other considering the urgency of the situation. Like ***ARCTIC***'s apprentice engineer firing her signal cannon to the end, Boxhall should have continued firing rockets until water closed over the bridge rail, just as Smith, Wilde, Murdoch, Lightoller and Moody continued launching lifeboats until the end.

Continuing with Second Officer Stone's interrogation, although Stone's answers were sensible and logical when he described the unidentified ship's departure in a manner which indicated that her lookout had merely spied a lead and she steamed away, a distinct possibility because she was several miles south of ***CALIFORNIAN***, and a scenario exactly like that which had surrounded ***ROMSDAL*** three weeks earlier, Aspinall and Mersey continued their harassment of ***CALIFORNIAN***'s Second Officer. The Commissioner appeared once again to have made up his mind that Stone had seen ***TITANIC***, that the White Star liner was only five miles from ***CALIFORNIAN***, and that Stone was lying, even though Mersey's arbitrary plot made no sense whatsoever.

At about 0330 Gibson reported to Stone that he saw a white flash in the sky to the southward of ***CALIFORNIAN***. Stone watched with his binoculars and saw another flash off the port beam, which would be due south as ***CALIFORNIAN*** was then heading about due west. When Lord Mersey asked how far away the flash had been, Stone replied that it was "a very great distance." These were undoubtedly ***CARPATHIA***'s rockets, the apogee of which could have been over 40 miles away if the rockets rose to an altitude of 800 feet. The bearing of these rockets from ***CALIFORNIAN*** was about due south. ***CARPATHIA*** had come up from the southeast to ***TITANIC***, which would have fit Stone's description of these later rockets' direction from ***CALIFORNIAN***.

At 0400 Stone was relieved by Chief Officer Stewart. It was shortly after four o'clock that Stone and Stewart saw another steamer. Stone had passed on all the information about the rockets to Stewart, who allegedly had said *"There she is; there is that steamer; she is all right."* Stone looked through his glasses and told Stewart that it was not the same ship. This one had two mastlights. Aspinall twisted Stone's testimony to suggest that Stone had told the Chief Officer that he was fearful that the other steamer "had gone down." "No," insisted Stone. *"I told him the steamer had steamed away from us in a south westerly direction."*

But Stone had just unwittingly done something else that had to be covered up. Stone's testimony had put ***TITANIC*** west of the one ice field. She could have been west of the field only by going around the northern edge of it, unless somehow she had managed to get through it unscathed at full speed. And if she had gone around the northern edge of the field, then she was not "precisely on the Southern Track" as Ismay and ***TITANIC***'s officers had already testified. Ernest Gill's revelation had shown that ***CALIFORNIAN***'s officers were in a position to disprove Ismay's Southern Track defense which was necessary to satisfy the Harter Act and evade liability. Stone had just proven that ***CALIFORNIAN***'s officers knew too much, whether or not they yet realized it. ***CALIFORNIAN***'s officers, particularly Captain Lord and Second Officer Stone, therefore had to be discredited. The quickest and best way to discredit them was to "prove" that ***CALIFORNIAN*** was the "mystery ship" that had "ignored ***TITANIC***'s distress rockets," allowing 1,500 people to die. When the public believed that, anything Lord and Stone said in their defense would be taken as lies to evade their guilt. And with ***CALIFORNIAN*** firmly locked in as the "mystery ship" with full blame falling on the shoulders of her master, Captain Lord, there was no need to call any other ships' officers for testimony, officers whose statements would bear out those of Stone and Lord, statements which would give the truth about ***TITANIC***'s rockets and track to the world, the last thing Ismay, and therefore Morgan, wanted. Further investigation might even have exposed the bunker fire and bulkhead damage, as well as the ***FRANKFURT*** blunder. The latter had already been emblazoned in headlines around the world and needed to be silenced at once. It was best to pin everything on ***CALIFORNIAN*** and get it all over with quickly, not to confuse the issue with more facts to which Lord Mersey would not listen.

Stone's ordeal was far from over. Next up was Mr. Thomas Scanlan, M.P., representing the National Sailors' and Firemen's Union of Great Britain and Ireland. It should be noted that this was not the officers' union, and apparently in 1912 one union owed no allegiance to another, which is rather strange considering the problems that all unions of that early era had in common. Scanlan bored in immediately and relentlessly. Had not Stone taken an examination for his First Mate's certificate which included the identification of distress and pilot signals? *"Yes,"* replied Stone. Did Stone mean to tell His Lordship that the throwing up of *"rockets or shells throwing stars of any colour or description, fired one at a time at short intervals"* was not immediately recognizable as a distress signal at night?

Stone replied that was the way it was always done as far as he knew.

Scanlan then asked if Stone had known that perfectly well on the night of April 14, and Stone simply replied *"Yes."*

Mersey interjected, *"And is not that exactly what was happening?"*

Impatiently Scanlan prompted, *"You have heard my Lord put that question. That was what was happening?"*

"Yes," replied Stone again.

"The very thing was happening that you knew indicated distress?" Mersey insisted.

"If that steamer had stayed on the same bearing after showing these rockets..." Stone began.

"No," said Mersey. *"Do not give a long answer of that kind. Is it not the fact that the very thing was happening which you had been taught indicated distress?"*

What could Stone reply but another simple *"Yes."*

Together Scanlan and Mersey hammered mercilessly at Stone. He *knew* he was seeing distress signals, did he not? He was not to try to explain anything, only to answer "yes" or "no."

"Think about what you are saying," seemed to be a favorite admonishment of Mersey's when he got an answer he either did not like or did not understand. The steamer lying between ***TITANIC*** and ***CALIFORNIAN*** became forever fused into the same steamer which fired white rockets that night; the tramp with one mastlight and no electricity became transformed into the giant ***TITANIC*** with two mastlights and a blaze of electric light. The legend has remained thus for over eight decades. The inference was, and is, that Stone, and subsequently Captain Lord, lied. They "made up" the second steamer, the unidentified stranger which happened to wander into the way to obscure ***TITANIC***'s rockets. Everyone did and they still do ignore the fact that ***TITANIC*** lying only five miles from ***CALIFORNIAN*** would have been visible right to the waterline, and she would have been unmistakable. At five miles the rockets would have been redundant... Stone could have seen her boats in the water. He could have seen her mastlights, seen the forward light sinking lower as the aft light rose higher. He could have heard the noise of escaping steam. Even more macabre... at five miles Stone could have heard the screams from those struggling in the water, the horrendous never-to-be-forgotten sound of their dying cries blended into one long, mournful wail. Can anyone really believe that Stone and Gibson could have ignored all this?

Together Scanlan and Mersey twisted Stone's words to prove his and Lord's guilt. They saw ***TITANIC*** firing distress rockets, they had done nothing. An absolute railroading of innocent men in order to cover up all of the links in ***TITANIC***'s chain to disaster and death.

Still they pounded away at ***CALIFORNIAN***'s hapless Second Officer. Although Captain Lord's name would become synonymous with ***CALIFORNIAN***'s guilt because the master is always responsible for everything that happens in, on, around and to his ship. Stone was the watch officer. A good master knows that a responsible watch officer can be trusted, and does just that. Yet the name of the man responsible for telling Captain Lord that the rockets he saw were definitely not distress rockets has never been bandied about in the media as Lord's name has been and still is, and only hard-core ***TITANIC*** enthusiasts are aware of Herbert Stone. But at the Board of Trade inquiry Stone was the man to break. And try to break him they did.

Testimony continued to be confusing because questions were confusing. The two ships, the tiny, mysterious tramp without electricity and the giant liner were being treated as one. When White Star attorney Laing asked Stone if he had ever seen "this vessel's" green light and Stone answered "no," Laing responded with the assumption that Stone should have seen her red light while she was crossing ***CALIFORNIAN***'s bow and heading southwest. But a vessel to the south of ***CALIFORNIAN*** would not "cross her bow" if heading southwest. As long as she was to the southward she would show a red light to ***CALIFORNIAN*** only if she headed in an easterly direction. Stone explained that by this time, when ***CALIFORNIAN*** had swung to a heading of WSW, the mystery tramp had closed out her red light and was showing only her stern light. (***CALIFORNIAN***'s heading had nothing to do with the relative bearing of the mystery tramp, or the lights that she would show to ***CALIFORNIAN***. This is exactly what she would have done had her officers seen ***TITANIC***'s white rockets and assumed that there was clear water to the south. She would have then turned to starboard, turning tightly to avoid loose ice around her, closing out the red port sidelight and then showing her stern light as she headed southwest toward open water. When a ship shows her stern light, her other running lights, sidelights and mastlights, are shielded so they do not also show in order to avoid confusion in estimating her track. But if the mystery tramp's watch officer, or probably her master was on the bridge then, had seen a lead and followed it they probably never got close enough to ***TITANIC*** to see what was happening, and by then of course there were no more rockets until some were fired from ***CARPATHIA*** shortly before 0400. By this time the tramp should have been at least 20 miles west of the scene but also at least 15 miles, probably more, north of it. While ***CALIFORNIAN*** was out of visual range of ***TITANIC***'s running lights from the beginning, the tramp, just five miles south of ***CALIFORNIAN*** at most, should have been, too, and after ***TITANIC*** sank at 0220 there were no more lights to be seen excepting Boxhall's few green flares and lanterns in the lifeboats, on the water's surface. A watch officer, or master, conning a ship through an area where there is known to be ice does not usually look aft, he looks where the ship is going, straining to see into the darkness ahead, looking for that faint glimmer of starshine reflected from an ice pinnacle that should give ample warning on a clear night. But, said Mersey, you *must* have seen her green light, you know. And that again was that.

Leyland Line attorney Dunlop asked Stone again about the tramp. Could she possibly have been ***TITANIC***, judging from the appearance of her lights? *"Not by any means,"* Stone replied.

Mersey asked if ***CALIFORNIAN***'s officers had been looking for this unidentified ship since the accident, if they had tried to find out her name, and Stone naturally replied that they had no way of doing this except by watching the newspapers. An impossible task considering how many "smallish" tramps plied the sea lanes between Europe and America. Dunlop asked about the second steamer that Stone and Stewart had seen later. Stone described her again; she had two mastlights, not one, but he had not been able to see funnels or sidelights. Stone had subsequently seen three steamers in the morning altogether.

Third Officer Charles Victor Groves was interrogated next. Groves had been on ***CALIFORNIAN***'s articles as Second Officer, but had taken the duties of Third. He was an ambitious twenty four year old officer eager to obtain his master's certificate. Captain Lord had considered it his duty to be on the bridge with Groves as ***CALIFORNIAN*** approached the ice area, a matter which might have antagonized Groves if he felt there was an insinuation that he lacked experience and competency. It should be noted that watch officers in ***CALIFORNIAN*** were not nearly as experienced as those in ***TITANIC***. It was the Third Officer's watch from 8PM until midnight on the 14th. Groves was the one other officer who had seen the mystery tramp, and Captain Lord had already testified that he and Groves together had watched the tramp approach and stop. Groves confirmed Lord's testimony about their conversation when she had come along from the east, and Groves put the time at about 11:10PM by his watch which he had set with the ship's clock at 6PM. (Note this, it is extremely important). Groves had seen one white light, which he at first thought was a star rising. But Groves claimed that as the vessel drew closer, he had seen *two* mastlights.

Groves claimed a lot of other things that were entirely different from statements made by

Captain Lord, Stone and Gibson. Groves had definitely seen a large passenger steamer, so he said. She had "come up obliquely" to them, ***CALIFORNIAN*** was then heading NE, the stranger was on a bearing of S 1/2 W from ***CALIFORNIAN***, but she was changing her bearing slightly to the south and west.

Because Lord, Stone and Gibson had already described the mystery steamer as having few deck lights, something had to be done to make this appear to be ***TITANIC*** with many lights. Groves' statement that the ship had already stopped and at the instant she stopped she put out her deck lights, before Lord first saw her, solved that problem, although Groves had already confirmed his conversation with Lord as the tramp approached. But the Third Officer's next statement was so absurd it is amazing that it has been taken as truth all these years. At precisely *11:40PM,* said Groves, he had seen the passenger ship stop and *put out her lights.* The legend thus was perpetuated that Groves saw ***TITANIC,*** that she was so close that all of her lights were within sight of ***CALIFORNIAN.*** Groves said he saw her put out her lights at 11:40, but actually that was *precisely* when ***TITANIC*** struck ice… *by* ***TITANIC****'s clock.* Groves, remember, had already testified that he had set his watch with ***CALIFORNIAN***'s clock. When ***TITANIC*** turned to avoid the iceberg, then struck it, her deck lights only appeared to go out because she turned abruptly So says legend which parrots the official story.

Examining this early statement from Groves it is obvious that someone was lying because it did not agree at all with the statements of Stone, Lord, or even Gibson. The natural conclusion reached by ***TITANIC*** enthusiasts has been that everyone lied except Groves, because Groves confirmed the "official" version of the disaster. Of course Lord and Stone had a "vested interest" in lying, say those who would continue to blame Captain Lord for ***TITANIC***'s deaths. But who *really* had the vested interest? The answer to that is perfectly simple… the vested interest lay with Ismay, White Star, and thus Morgan's IMM.

Groves said that he saw the stranger's lights go out precisely at *11:40.*

By this time everyone knew that ***TITANIC*** had struck ice at 11:40. Murdoch had ordered the time logged as 11:40, it had been thus reported in newspapers throughout the world. But ***TITANIC***'s time was not the same as ***CALIFORNIAN***'s time, yet Groves claimed that the ship he saw had stopped at 11:40 *by* ***CALIFORNIAN****'s* ***clock!*** The times were only minutes apart, because of the slight difference in longitude, and because ***CALIFORNIAN***'s clocks had been set back at noon while ***TITANIC***'s clocks were due to be set back at midnight, but never were. Leslie Harrison, master mariner, navigation instructor for the Royal Air Force in World War II, leading defender of Captain Lord, and author of *A* ***TITANIC*** *Myth, The* ***CALIFORNIAN*** *Incident,* (Second edition, revised, S.P.A. Ltd., Hanley Swan, Worcs., 1992) figured the time difference as 12 minutes, thus when it was 11:40 in ***CALIFORNIAN*** it was 11:52 in ***TITANIC.*** Or, ***TITANIC*** struck ice at 11:28 ***CALIFORNIAN*** time. Groves, however, was sure of the time because he had heard one bell to call the middle watch at the time he saw the stranger's lights go out. In many British ships of this era one bell was struck 20 minutes before eight bells to give the watch coming on duty a chance of getting a meal. The time given by Groves, 11:40PM in ***CALIFORNIAN***, is not only far too coincidental, it is blatantly ridiculous.

Nor would a passenger ship the size of ***TITANIC*** suddenly not look like a passenger ship simply because she turned two points, as Mersey insisted. Her porthole lights, lights from public rooms, would still shine across the water, reflecting from the surface, she still would look like a large passenger ship with a blaze of light easily distinguished by an observer as close as four to five miles. Clearly Groves was giving the answers his interrogators wanted to hear. And yet, if ***TITANIC*** was coming up obliquely, "foreshortened," as Groves said, then if she turned two points to port she should have presented a more broadside appearance.

Groves had seen the stranger's port side, her red light, another strange answer. ***TITANIC***, westbound and south of ***CALIFORNIAN*** when she struck ice, would never have shown her port, or red sidelight, to ***CALIFORNIAN***. But Boxhall and others had already said they saw the lights of a ship two points off ***TITANIC***'s *port* bow. Therefore Groves had to say he saw the stranger's port side, her red light, because that put ***CALIFORNIAN*** off ***TITANIC***'s port side, where Boxhall had seen the primary "mystery ship."

Ah, there was evidence, said Mersey, that ***TITANIC***'s lights had indeed gone out in one or more of the stokeholds. As if these lights in compartments below the waterline would have been visible at all. They had, however, not gone out at the time of impact, but minutes later, as we shall see in a later chapter. There then ensued a lengthy discussion on how stopping ***TITANIC***'s engines at 11:40PM would have shut off her lights. But ***TITANIC***'s engines did not stop at the moment of impact. Her engines stopped her by going full astern. After they had been run astern, then slow ahead briefly, her engines continued to provide power for the pumps and the electrical system until the end. ***TITANIC***'s engine rooms were in full running order when she foundered.

Supposing, Groves was asked, that the steamer he had seen had turned two points to port at 11:40. Would that account for the appearance of her lights going out? *"I quite think it would,"* replied Groves obediently.

Remember that there was evidence that ***TITANIC***'s last heading had been almost due west, that Murdoch had indeed given the second helm order, "hard aport," after his first "hard astarboard," which turned ***TITANIC*** first to port, then to starboard, and evidence that she had finally stopped on a heading of almost due north. At no time would she have shown her red light to ***CALIFORNIAN***, at no time would ***CALIFORNIAN*** have been off ***TITANIC***'s port side. But to make it appear that ***CALIFORNIAN*** was indeed the mystery ship, as well as put ***TITANIC*** east of the ice field. Groves had given all the right answers.

The discussion continued. *"A change of two points would conceal the lights in the ship?"* asked Mersey. *"In my own opinion it would,"* answered the obedient Groves again. Deck lights, lights from ports and windows, all would disappear when the ship turned two points! This is one of the most absurd statements to come out of either inquiry and yet it has been taken as truth, its absurdity deliberately ignored not only by the Board of Trade interrogators but by subsequent "researchers" as well.

Groves' job obviously was to do two things… make ***CALIFORNIAN*** into the mystery ship and put ***TITANIC*** directly on the Southern Track. If she had been on the Track, then she had to have been east of the ice fields. If she was east of the ice, then she would have shown ***CALIFORNIAN*** her red light after stopping because ***CALIFORNIAN*** would have been northwest of ***TITANIC***, not northeast of her. No way could ***TITANIC*** have gone through field ice full speed to strike one lone berg on the western side of the fields. And Groves effectively did this with some of the most blatant lies to come out of the inquiries.

But the conspirators forgot one small factor… if ***CALIFORNIAN*** was indeed northwest of ***TITANIC***, where the Leyland liner had to be to see ***TITANIC***'s port sidelight, and ***CALIFORNIAN***'s officers saw ***TITANIC***'s red light as they were allegedly two points off ***TITANIC***'s port bow, then ***TITANIC*** had indeed turned to starboard after her initial turn to port, and the conspirators knew it. If ***TITANIC*** had merely turned to port two points while heading just 4 degrees south of west, then stopped heading another 22 1/2 degrees south of west, *never* would ***TITANIC*** have shown

CALIFORNIAN her red light as long as ***CALIFORNIAN*** was north of the westbound ***TITANIC,*** whether northeast or northwest of her. This error in the conspiracy to prove ***CALIFORNIAN*** as the mystery ship two points off ***TITANIC***'s port bow confirmed either that the conspirators knew about the second helm order, that ***TITANIC*** had ended up on a heading of almost due north, or that they were desperate enough to try such a blatant lie believing that nobody of any importance would ever catch it. The conspirators knew, of course, what subsequent investigators insist upon ignoring, that Captain Lord had wirelessed his position to the USN Hydrographic Office when ***CALIFORNIAN*** stopped at 10:21PM. They knew what subsequent investigators have refused to see… that ***CALIFORNIAN***'s position was already a matter of record, therefore they could not move ***CALIFORNIAN*** as others have since tried to do. But they could "move" ***TITANIC,*** and it was to their advantage to move her east. And, as we shall see in a later chapter, they also had to "move" the ice field. While it can be argued that the position of the wreckage at the bottom of the sea would clear all of this, we must consider two factors… first, the state-of-the art errors in navigation, and second, the coverup was instigated by what was known, and/or suspected in 1912. And still we come to the relative positions of all the vessels involved that night, and the relative position of the field ice, which can never be fully known.

The first thing Groves had to do was discredit Captain Lord's, Second Officer Stone's and Apprentice Gibson's description of the tramp which had stopped four or five miles south of ***CALIFORNIAN,*** the position in which ***TITANIC*** had to be to make Lord and Stone guilty. This Groves did by saying that the stranger ship had put out her lights before Lord and Stone saw her. This statement effectively explained why Lord and Stone saw only a few white lights about the stranger's decks, not the glare of lights one would see in a giant passenger liner. Whoever put their heads together to engineer the coverup must have seen that as a marvelous chance to have Groves say that the lights went out at precisely 11:40, when it was known that ***TITANIC*** had struck ice at that exact time. But that someone either forgot that ***CALIFORNIAN***'s clock would not have said 11:40 at that precise moment as did ***TITANIC***'s clock, or they figured that nobody would catch that slight error. Sailors of that era knew, of course. But sailors in 1912 knew what had really happened anyway. Anyone who has seen a passenger liner at sea at night would know there was no mistaking one for a tramp freighter. Passengers rarely have that opportunity, but experienced merchant seamen do, and did. They do not mistake passenger ships, no matter which way they are heading. Nor do they mistake one mastlight for two because a seaman tells the direction another vessel is heading by her range lights. The first thing a watch officer notices about a vessel coming into his or her range of vision at night is the number, color and placement of lights she shows because this tells if the stranger is a threat in any way to the watch officer's ship. Today of course the watch officers might talk directly by radio, but in ***TITANIC***'s time they used their eyes, and radio or no, a good watch officer still does. It might surprise readers to know how many tramps still go to sea without working radios or running lights. Nor did a watch officer communicate by Morse without very good reason. The Morse lights momentarily blinded the officers for several minutes and seamanship manuals always warned against using Morse lights because the usual message was something unnecessary like *"What is that ship?"*

After Stone had relieved him Groves said he had gone to the wireless cabin and awakened Evans. Allegedly Groves asked the Marconi operator what ships he had been working and Evans replied *"Only the* ***TITANIC.****"* This statement, too, has remained in legend to make it seem as if only ***CALIFORNIAN*** and ***TITANIC*** shared that area of the Western Ocean that night. Evans had gone back to sleep and Groves had for a few seconds put the earphones on and listened, but Evans had shut down the power for the night so Groves heard nothing. Groves had gone to bed, and been awakened about 0640 by Chief Officer Stewart who told him that ***TITANIC*** had sunk. Groves allegedly then went straight to Stone's cabin to ask if Stewart had been right about ***TITANIC***. According to Groves, Stone had replied, *"Yes, old chap, I saw rockets in* my *watch."* Remembering that Stone had been the only watch officer to see the rockets, but that Groves, who had been relieved by Stone, did not yet know that, one must wonder why Groves would not take Stewart's word for such an important bit of intelligence, but he would take Stone's, especially considering that Stewart was the senior officer.

"This conversation was very important," said Mersey. Groves had gone immediately upon rising, not even bothering to dress first, to see Stone. Strangely, Groves was now vague about times. He had gone on the bridge to find that ***CALIFORNIAN*** was under way making a good speed through the ice. He saw three steamers, said Groves, ***CARPATHIA***, ***MOUNT TEMPLE*** and one small steamer with a black funnel. ***CALIFORNIAN*** had searched the area until 1040, and then resumed her course. Note that not even the obedient Groves mentioned seeing ***FRANKFURT***, for this is very important, as we shall see in a later chapter.

Groves was then asked about ***CALIFORNIAN***'s rockets, what type did she carry? *"Distress rockets,"* answered Groves. He had never seen one, did not know what they looked like either before or after firing, and would not know until he had to send one up for the first time. That effectively precluded any further questioning about the color of distress rockets.

Laing asked Groves only about ***CALIFORNIAN***'s mastlights. She had range lights, located on the foremast and the mainmast. ***CALIFORNIAN*** was a four-masted vessel, and Boxhall had already said the mystery ship seen off ***TITANIC***'s port bow had four masts... he could tell by the placement of her lights. Boxhall had said this *after* ***CALIFORNIAN***, known to have four masts, had been implicated by Ernest Gill. But this, too, is absurd. There was no way that Boxhall, looking merely at two white lights at such a distance, without seeing anything of the ship underneath them, could tell if they were on the fore and main masts of a longer four masted vessel, or on the fore and main masts of a shorter two masted ship.

Attorney Dunlop then asked Groves about the position entered in ***CALIFORNIAN***'s log, 42°05'N, 50°07'W, the position in which Lord had stopped the ship at 10:21PM. Was the position accurate, Dunlop wanted to know. It was bound to be if the master had entered it, answered Groves. An effective, yet subtle way of suggesting that Captain Lord may have lied about ***CALIFORNIAN***'s position, and subsequent investigators have seized upon this as proof of Lord's guilt. But remember that Lord had wirelessed that position to the USN Hydrographic Office well over an hour before ***TITANIC*** struck ice and several hours before anyone in ***CALIFORNIAN*** knew about the loss of the White Star liner. If Lord lied in his entry of ***CALIFORNIAN***'s 10:21PM position then he must have been psychic, because otherwise he had no reason to lie.

Dunlop questioned Groves closely about the position of ***TITANIC***'s wreckage found by ***CALIFORNIAN***. Dunlop made an error in giving ***TITANIC***'s latitude at this point, insinuating that her distress position latitude had been 41°33'N, when actually that had been the position of the wreckage seen from ***CALIFORNIAN***. This "wreckage," however, seems to have been merely the lifeboats and the items which Murdoch had caused to be jettisoned for use as makeshift rafts... deck chairs, chests, doors and so forth. This is not the same as the real wreckage which comes to the surface as a ship breaks up on her way to the bottom, and we have seen an example of that in pieces of ***ARCTIC***'s paddlebox popping up near Captain Luce. In World War II there was a legendary Merchant Navy engineer who, it was said, had been shipwrecked so many times that he could swim to precisely the area where the ship's wreckage would surface and take refuge upon it. The position of the jettisoned material and the lifeboats, which had been rowed toward ***CARPATHIA*** as soon as the Cunarder hove into view, was not necessarily the same as the position of ***TITANIC***'s actual wreckage and bodies of those who were still aboard as she went down. The actual wreckage and bodies were not seen from either ***CARPATHIA*** or ***CALIFORNIAN*** on Monday morning, and neither ship conducted a real search of the proper area.

Mersey suggested that when Stone allegedly told Groves that they must hurry and dress as they would be wanted in the boats, and then said, *"I saw rockets in my watch,"* that Stone was inferring he was sure the rockets he had seen were from ***TITANIC***. The insinuation in this is that Stone knew all along the ship firing rockets was in distress, but for some unfathomable reason chose to lie to Captain Lord about it, another absurdity.

Groves had gone to the bridge, and seen ***CARPATHIA*** about five miles away off ***CALIFORNIAN***'s port beam. The Cunarder's house flag was at half mast. Groves had then noticed ***MOUNT TEMPLE*** about a mile and a half off ***CALIFORNIAN***'s starboard bow. ***CARPATHIA*** and ***CALIFORNIAN*** ha*d* exchanged messages by semaphore. Captain Rostron telling Captain Lord that the Cunarder had ***TITANIC***'s survivors on board, including Ismay. Captain Lord then suggested that they search to leeward, which ***CALIFORNIAN*** did until 1040, then she resumed her course.

Scanlan then asked Groves if in the position ***CALIFORNIAN*** had swung to, could any person from the ship he described seeing have been able to see ***CALIFORNIAN***'s green sidelight? *"Yes,"* replied Groves. This effectively covered Boxhall's early statement about the mystery ship two points off ***TITANIC***'s port bow, when ***TITANIC***'s Fourth Officer said he had seen a green light as well as a red one for a short time. Yet it was another absurd statement from Groves, and Boxhall had made the statement *after* ***CALIFORNIAN*** was named the mystery ship and it was known that the Leyland liner would have shown her green light after swinging to an easterly heading. In Boxhall's first mention of the mystery ship to Senator Smith he had positively described seeing only two "white steaming lights" and a *red* sidelight. If ***CALIFORNIAN*** had been in the position Groves had already described, stopped on a heading about due west, and he had seen ***TITANIC***'s red sidelight, then no way could anybody aboard ***TITANIC*** have seen ***CALIFORNIAN***'s green light unless ***TITANIC*** was northwest of ***CALIFORNIAN***.

W.D. Harbinson, appearing on behalf of Third Class passengers was next to question Groves, asking if he had seen two mastlights, to which Groves replied, *"Yes."* Mersey interrupted with *"Do not take him through the whole thing again."* Perhaps the Wreck Commissioner was afraid that Groves would not be able to get the story straight twice. Harbinson then revealed his purpose in repeating the questions. Did Groves remember what Captain Lord had said when Groves told him that the steamer lying only a few miles south of ***CALIFORNIAN*** was a passenger ship? *"Yes, I do,"* replied Groves. *"He said 'the only passenger ship near us is the **TITANIC**.'"* A blatant manipulation of words that forever erased the small, unidentified tramp, and put in her place the giant ***TITANIC***. Harbinson reinforced this message when he asked Groves about going to see Evans in the wireless cabin. Evans, too, had said the only steamer he had been working was ***TITANIC***. Ergo, only ***TITANIC*** was near ***CALIFORNIAN***. There were only two ships in that area of the North Atlantic at that time, another absurdity perpetuated in legend.

Laing questioned Groves about ***CALIFORNIAN***'s mastlights, thus confirming that she fit Boxhall's description of the mystery ship two points off ***TITANIC***'s port bow.

And in response to Leyland Line Attorney Dunlop's questions. Groves affirmed that in his opinion the passenger ship he had allegedly seen, the ship which had been sending up rockets, the ship within sight of ***CALIFORNIAN***, was ***TITANIC***. But Dunlop questioned Groves again about his seeing a red light on a ship heading west and south of him. He had not said she was "heading" west, said Groves, she was "proceeding" west. Presumably this meant she was backing in a westerly direction! If she was going anywhere from north to west, and she was due south of ***CALIFORNIAN***, Groves claimed he would have seen her red light. In fact, if she was heading due north and was directly due south of ***CALIFORNIAN*** Groves might have seen both sidelights, but any alteration toward the west would have closed out her red light. Only if she was heading in an easterly direction could Groves have seen her red light alone for any length of time. Either he did not see ***TITANIC***, or he did not see her red light. And if Groves did not see her red light, then ***CALIFORNIAN*** *could* not have been the mystery ship two points off ***TITANIC***'s port bow.

It can be argued that because we know that ***TITANIC***'s engines were run briefly "dead slow ahead," and briefly "dead slow astern," that her position after stopping because of the impact with ice had changed. However, if she was run ahead for a few minutes she would have been run in a northerly direction because that was the way to shallow water and Cape Race. If she was run astern it was only briefly to ascertain whether she could be moved astern and avoid greater pressure on the crucial watertight bulkhead and therefore she would have been run astern with rudder amidships, thus she would have backed almost due south. Obviously neither had worked, but both were normal procedures after any damage which caused flooding, particularly when that flooding was forward. Many ships had been backed into port after collisions. At any rate, the information about ***TITANIC***'s northerly heading had been given after she had finally stopped altogether, and the questions were being put to Groves about the color of the sidelight after ***TITANIC*** had been completely stopped for at least forty minutes.

In answer to questions put by Mr. Cotter, appearing on behalf of the National Union of Stewards, Groves emphatically called Captain Lord

HOW MANY MASTS DOES EACH SHIP HAVE?

1

2

3

4

5

6

7

8

9

10

11

ANSWER KEY PAGE 463

ABOVE: By 1:25a.m., April 15th, the situation was growing serious aboard the ***TITANIC****. Water now lapped the 18" high gold letters on the bow, as* ***TITANIC*** *continued vainly to send up her white distress rockets. In fact, the rockets were not "distress" rockets at all. (Artwork by James A. Flood)*

a liar. Cotter said, *"The captain states that he was on the bridge at 11 o'clock and was there till 11:30?*

"I say he was not," replied Groves.

The Solicitor General then questioned Groves closely about the missing scrap log, giving rise to the legend of its being deliberately destroyed, the inference being that mention of rockets seen by Stone was thus erased from ***CALIFORNIAN***'s official log, along with ***CALIFORNIAN***'s real position. Much ado has been made over the fact that ***CALIFORNIAN***'s scrap log had "disappeared," further "proof" of Lord's guilt as legend has it. Scrap log sheets were, and are, routinely scrapped each day as the official log is written up, usually by the Chief Officer. That is precisely why they are called "scrap" logs. It is much like an author's first draft of a manuscript, which may contain errors in spelling, grammar, superfluous information which is unnecessary in an official document. There is nothing the least bit sinister in ***CALIFORNIAN***'s scrap log having been "scrapped," yet legend has made it seem so. The sinister treatment of a logbook in this affair is the disappearance of ***TITANIC***'s log.

The last of ***CALIFORNIAN***'s officers, Chief Officer George Frederick Stewart, was interrogated by Solicitor General Sir John Simon, immediately after Groves' testimony. The thirty four year old Stewart was also considered honest and responsible by Captain Lord, according to Leslie Harrison. Stewart's testimony was only hearsay. He had gone on watch at 0400, thus had only heard Stone tell him that he had seen rockets. What did Stewart think a ship would throw up white rockets for, Sir John wanted to know. Stewart finally replied that he believed they had been distress rockets. *"They were from the description just what you would expect if they were distress rockets?"* was Sir John's leading question. *"They were white rockets,"* replied Stewart evasively.

At 0400, one hour and forty minutes after ***TITANIC*** had foundered, but at least an hour before ***CARPATHIA***'s running lights were in view, Stewart, with Stone still on the bridge, had seen a steamer south of them with two white mastlights and a few lights amidships. Stewart asked Stone if this was the ship he had seen, and Stone replied that he did not think she was the same one.

After Stone had gone off duty Stewart called up the master, who came to the bridge about 0430. Stewart pointed out the steamer to Captain Lord, who spoke of getting under way to resume their voyage. Stewart allegedly asked Lord if he would not head south to see why this other ship might have been firing rockets. Lord replied, *"No, I do not think so; she is not making any signals now."* When Stewart indicated that he thought the steamer he now saw, with two mastlights, had either been the one firing rockets, or had seen the other ship firing rockets, but had "drifted" back somehow during the night, Mersey and Sir John ridiculed him and began questioning him about the scrap log. Neither Mersey nor Sir John could comprehend what a scrap log was, and was for. Their questioning of Stewart on the subject contributed to the legend of skullduggery with the scrap log, and consequently with the official log. Sir John could not understand why ***CALIFORNIAN*** had remained on the same parallel of latitude for so long prior to her stopping, which clearly indicates his ignorance of navigation while insinuating again that Lord had lied about ***CALIFORNIAN***'s position.

Dunlop's interrogation of Stewart was somewhat friendlier. The Leyland Line's attorney ascertained that ***CALIFORNIAN*** had come some 30 miles from her stopped position at 10:21 PM on Sunday night to the position in which ***TITANIC***'s alleged "wreckage" and boats were found, 41°33'N, 50°01W, which is just 6 minutes of longitude, or about 5 miles, east, and 32 miles south of ***CALIFORNIAN***'s stopped position. As we have seen in the previous chapter, the set of the surface current had been deflected to the south by strong northerly winds during Sunday's daylight hours. As the wind abated the set would have gone slowly back to its prevailing direction, ENE, but we have no way of knowing whether the wind actually abated or both ***TITANIC*** and ***CALIFORNIAN*** had moved into the lee of a larger ice field to the north. This is important for two reasons. First, every ship in that area would have been somewhat south of her dead reckoning position because the southerly set was not taken into account in figuring that position. Naturally a larger vessel would be more affected by wind and current because she had more area both above and beneath the water's surface for the wind and current to act upon. Today this effect of wind and current is factored into computerized navigation systems, but in ***TITANIC***'s time it was considered impossible to know how much the ship was affected and thus it was not figured in dead reckoning unless an individual master simply estimated it from the known prevailing set during periods of bad weather when celestial observations were impossible. We know from Lightoller's testimony that ***TITANIC***'s officers expected the ice to be moving with the prevailing surface current, which they expected to be east-northeast. Second, ***TITANIC*** and ***CALIFORNIAN***, both stopped, were drifting with the set, but so was all of the material that Murdoch had ordered pitched over ***TITANIC***'s side for use as makeshift rafts. Additionally, the boats had been rowed toward the approaching ***CARPATHIA***, which came from the southeast. ***TITANIC***, then, had to have struck ice west and north of the position in which her boats and jetsam were found, which fits with her official distress position, yet she must have been somewhat south of where her navigators thought she was.

Stewart verified Captain Lord's estimate of 19 1/2 to 20 miles from ***CALIFORNIAN***'s stopped position to ***TITANIC***'s distress position which was *"south, a little west"* of ***CALIFORNIAN***. Stewart also explained that at 6:30 on Sunday evening he had found an error of two miles between ***CALIFORNIAN***'s latitude taken from dead reckoning using her noon sights, and shooting the Pole Star. ***TITANIC***, bound for New York, should have been 30 to 40 miles south of ***CALIFORNIAN***, bound for Boston, said Stewart.

Mersey's mind was made up again, however. He was satisfied that the ship seen from ***CALIFORNIAN*** to "throw up rockets" was the ***TITANIC***, that the White Star liner had been no more than five miles from ***CALIFORNIAN***. And so the legend remained.

But Stewart reiterated that he had asked Stone if the white rockets seen by the Second Officer might have been distress rockets. Stone answered that he did not think so because they made no report. While Stone had been positive when he saw the rockets that they did not signify distress because they contained no color and made no report, if this statement attributed to Stone by Stewart was true, it indicates only that Stone, with the hindsight of knowing that ***TITANIC*** had fired white rockets while she was sinking, now realized that he must have seen ***TITANIC***'s rockets. Hindsight, of course, always has 20-20 vision.

Cotter asked about the ship seen by Stewart and Stone at 0400. Stewart said that when the sun came up he thought she had a yellow funnel. She definitely had four masts, he said.

The only ships on the North Atlantic in that era which had yellow funnels belonged to Canadian Pacific. The only CP liner known to have been nearby, admittedly even closer than ***CARPATHIA*** when ***TITANIC*** sent her first CQD, was ***MOUNT TEMPLE***, with one funnel and four masts. Norddeutscher Lloyd, and Russian American, however, had buff funnels, which in the first rays of the morning sun might have been mistaken for yellow. NDL's ***FRANKFURT*** had two masts, however. Another NDL liner, which passengers later claimed had been near ***TITANIC***, was ***GEORGE WASHINGTON***. She had four masts, but two funnels, and Stewart was positive the ship lying a few miles south of ***CALIFORNIAN*** at daybreak had only one funnel. ***GEORGE WASHINGTON*** was over 25,000 GRT, of a size which should have been easily recognized as a passenger liner. The Russian American liner ***BIRMA***, also known to be in the vicinity, had one

*ABOVE: For over 80 years, **CALIFORNIAN**'s actions, and those of her master, Captain Stanley Lord, have been questioned and debated. However, Captain Lord became a convenient scapegoat for the maritime disaster. (Artwork by James A. Flood)*

funnel and four masts. The logical conclusion, in light of other facts, is that ***MOUNT TEMPLE,*** whose passengers swore in notarized statements that she had been within sight of ***TITANIC,*** was the vessel which had come up during the night to lie between ***CALIFORNIAN*** and ***TITANIC,*** after the first, much smaller tramp had departed. In fact, the first tramp may have been that allegedly seen by ***MOUNT TEMPLE***'s master, Captain Moore. But why investigate when ***CALIFORNIAN*** was such a convenient scapegoat?

There would be many more examples of those who did not believe that white is a color before the Board of Trade inquiry was finished. Raymond Asquith asked Bedroom Steward Charles Donald Mackay if the light toward which Number 11 boat had been rowed was *"colored or white."* Mackay replied that it was a "reddish" light, yet he had judged it to be the stern light of a ship. Number 11 had followed it for two hours. It should be noted that in some atmospheric conditions a white light may appear to have a reddish hue.

Lightoller described the rockets as *"principally white... almost white."* They were all fired from the starboard side as far as he could remember.

On 22 May Boxhall told Attorney General Asquith that the rockets he had fired were *"socket distress signals," which* unfortunately was later wrongly transcribed as *"rocket distress signals."* If Boxhall meant this literally as the socket distress signal approved by the Board of Trade and described as rising to a height of 600 to 800 feet, then we can rely upon the distance between ***CALIFORNIAN*** and ***TITANIC*** being no less than 37 miles and no more than 41 miles, the heights at which a rocket's apogee could have been seen from ***CALIFORNIAN***'s bridge.

Harland & Wolff naval architect Edward Wilding was just as vague as everybody else at describing ***TITANIC***'s rockets. Wilding told Mr. Rowlatt, Counsel for the Board of Trade, that Harland & Wolff supplied the rockets, that they were *"the cotton powder,"* the *"approved pattern of distress signal."* Wilding believed that it was a pattern of signal understood to be restricted to ships in distress, and registered for that purpose. What else would he say? It was not a matter that Wilding routinely dealt with, however. By *"cotton powder"* Wilding apparently meant the aforementioned universal propellant, with nitrocellulose as chief explosive ingredient, which had finally been perfected for safe use and storage in 1886.

For several days in June Sir Walter Howell, one of the Assistant Secretaries to the Board of Trade and Chief of the Marine Department, was interrogated on the matter of bulkheads and lifeboats. When Mr. Clement Edwards, M.P., appearing on behalf of the Dockers' Union, brought up the subject of distress signals Howell said that he "thought" they were contained in the *International Regulations for Preventing Collisions at Sea,* by which he apparently meant the *International Rules of the Road.*

It should be noted that on page 859 of the Board of Trade inquiry there was a discussion of these *Rules,* between Lord Mersey and the Attorney General, Sir Rufus Isaacs, which indicated that neither really understood that the *International Rules of the Road* encompass more than the prevention of collisions at sea. If this was the British attitude in 1912 then it explains the ignoring of proper internationally recognized pyrotechnic distress signals simply because they were not considered applicable to British ships, just as the internationally mandated wireless distress call SOS, which had been accepted by the rest of the world in 1908, was not accepted by the British until the ***TITANIC*** fiasco made it evident that even British vessels might sometimes need "foreign" help. It is doubtful, however, that British sailors themselves misunderstood or ignored the *Rules* as applying only to prevention of collisions. This would mean literally that the *Rules* could be ignored unless vessels were in such close proximity that they were in danger of collision, in which case the right of way and certain obligations by each vessel were mandatory under those *Rules* and that those *Rules* would be upheld in admiralty courts. The other possibility is that Mersey and Isaacs chose to ignore the *Rules* on pyrotechnic signals and thus used the phrase *"Regulations for Preventing Collisions at Sea"* in the same manner they were now using the phrase *"the colour white"* with reference to ***TITANIC***'s rockets... to avoid any discussions or investigations into why ***TITANIC***'s rockets did not conform to the standards of the *International Rules of the Road.* The fact remains, however, that Isaacs flatly stated that the *Rules* were *"**only** for preventing collisions at sea."* They had *"no application beyond that,"* said Isaacs, wondering why the *Rules* said nothing about ice. While the *Rules* were explicit in mandating *"moderate"* speed in situations which obscured visibility, such as fog, mist, falling snow or heavy rainstorms, it was obvious why they said nothing about ice. That was a matter which had to be left to the master's discretion because each vessel had different maneuvering characteristics. It had been found through general practice as well as turning tests that a ship would take less time to turn at higher speeds, thus the equation of time and distance before possible impact was virtually the same at high, or "moderate" speeds.

The discussion of distress signals was cut short by Lord Mersey, who asked what point Edwards was intending to make. Did he mean, asked Mersey, that distress signals were *"not effective, or what?"* When Edwards replied that he meant to bring home the responsibility of those responsible for navigating the ***CALIFORNIAN***, Mersey interrupted again, saying that he had no doubt at all that ***TITANIC***'s signals were seen by ***CALIFORNIAN***, whose officers should have made efforts to get to ***TITANIC***. Edwards declined to pursue the matter further.

In the Board of Trade's summary ***TITANIC***'s rockets were continually referred to as distress rockets, when in fact they were not. Officers aboard ***CALIFORNIAN*** saw ***TITANIC***'s *distress rockets,* declared Lord Mersey. There was no doubt of that, he said. ***CALIFORNIAN*** could have gone to the ship five miles away, ice or no ice, so said Mersey, totally ignoring visibility tables which were in all seamanship manuals. Never once did anyone conducting either the British or American inquiries ask any officer about visibility at sea in reference to anything other than ice or running lights. If ***TITANIC*** had indeed been only five miles from ***CALIFORNIAN*** Stone would have seen her boats in the water, and of course ***CALIFORNIAN*** could have and would have gone to her aid. If ***TITANIC*** had fired distress rockets Stone would have recognized them, heard them if she had really been only five miles from him. It was as simple as that, yet the controversy has raged for over eight decades, controversy where there should have been none in the first place.

Lightoller himself wrote in his memoirs over two decades after the disaster that the B.O.T. inquiry was a "whitewash," an interesting choice of words considering that one of the most important items hidden under that whitewash was the lack of color in ***TITANIC***'s alleged distress rockets. Continued questioning of survivors indicated that not even all of the interrogators believed that white is a color. Had the rockets been red or green there would have been no need for so much discussion about them, and in fact there would have been no need to question ***CALIFORNIAN***'s officers at all... that ship would have arrived at the wreck site long before ***CARPATHIA*** and Captain Lord would have been the hero of the day.

The *International Rules of the Road* are explicit, they were and are international *laws* from which not even British vessels were exempt. United States Delegate Goodrich, in the International Conference Rule of the Road Committee in 1890, said *"I do not want any option in these rules. The minute that you permit a sailor to have an option, whether he will or will not do a certain thing, you introduce confusion in the rules. I want to see these rules, as far as they can be made, as rigid as steel, so that there shall be no doubt what the Conference of Nations mean. They say, 'Obey these rules, and you will be saved from the danger of negligence; disobey them, and the courts will impose upon you the penalties of disobedience to the rules adopted by the nations of the world.'"* Masters, therefore, are bound to obey the rules and entitled to rely upon the assumption that they will be obeyed by others.

The *Rules* apply to all vessels alike. *"The size, importance or speed of a vessel does not give her special rights over small, less important or slower vessels. All are equal under the rules and obligated to the same strict observance of them. Passenger steamers have no special rights."*

Particularly telling regulations under *Article 8,* which clearly show that the men who drafted the *International Rules of the Road* distinguished white from colors, stated that *"Pilot vessels when engaged on their station on pilotage duty shall not show the lights required for other vessels, but shall carry a* ***white*** *light at the masthead, visible all around the horizon, and shall also exhibit a flare-up light or flare-up lights at short intervals, which shall never exceed fifteen minutes. On the near approach of or to other vessels they shall have their side lights lighted, ready for use, and shall flash or show them at short intervals, to indicate the direction in which they are heading, but the* **green** *light shall not be shown on the port side, nor the red light on the starboard side. A pilot vessel of such a class as to be obliged to go alongside of a vessel to put a pilot on board may show the white light instead of carrying it at the masthead, and may, instead of the* **colored** *lights above mentioned, have at hand, ready for use, a lantern with* **green** *glass on the one side and* **red** *glass on the other, to be used as prescribed above."*

Clearly, the men who had drafted the *International Rules of the Road* considered red and green to be *colors,* as opposed to *white.* This message had to get through to the sailors who interpreted those *Rules,* and to them red and green were colors, white was not.

The question still continually arises… why did not Captain Lord, or one of his watch officers, awaken the wireless operator? This is sometimes put into a different context… he *should* have awakened the wireless operator. That is easy to say from hindsight, and is another example of not viewing the incident through the eyes of a *pre-**TITANIC*** 1912 seaman.

In the first place it could naturally be assumed that if the vessel was firing pyrotechnic signals, she did so because she had no wireless. Further, the vessel which actually was in sight, her mastlight and sidelight showing to ***CALIFORNIAN***'s bridge, was a relatively small tramp which appeared to have oil lights, meaning no electricity, thus no wireless.

Nobody seems to have wondered, however, why Captain Smith did not personally go to ***TITANIC***'s wireless room to ask if his operators were communicating with the mysterious vessel two points off ***TITANIC***'s port bow, a curious lack of initiative indeed, considering that the wireless room was certainly close enough to the bridge for quick communication. Smith could as easily have sent an officer on the mission, perhaps Boxhall himself. It had been stated by several ***TITANIC*** crew members that they had been ordered to pull for the lights of that nearby ship and it would have been logical for Smith to have thus tried to contact her by wireless.

When Senator Smith finally asked Boxhall if there had been any attempt to get into wireless communication with this "mystery ship," Boxhall replied, *"I do not know what was transpiring in the wireless room."*

So why did both Captain Lord and Captain Smith seem to forget about their ships' wireless apparatus at a crucial moment?

The answer cannot be comprehended unless one again returns to the mind of a 1912 sailor. Both Captains Smith and Lord had apprenticed in sail, spent many years at sea before wireless was installed in ships. They were, like all shipmasters of their era, quite used to handling every situation with their own judgement based on their own experience. Captain Lord had a better reason to ignore his wireless. His watch officer reported merely a white pyrotechnic signal of some kind, a signal that contained no colors and therefore was *not* a distress signal, whatever else it might be. Because the ship was using pyrotechnic signaling, she presumably had no wireless. ***CALIFORNIAN***'s lone wireless operator had been on duty since early morning, and would arise very early again the following morning. Captain Lord saw no reason to disturb Evans' very short rest period. He repeatedly asked his watch officer if there was any color in the signals, if they were distress signals. The answer was always no.

There is another important consideration, something that was entirely an individual matter in the acceptance of wireless at sea.

Sailors have often written that they go to sea to get away from responsibilities ashore. In so doing they take up, of course, another set of responsibilities, which happen to breed tremendous self confidence and self reliance. The master who can continually best the elements in the eternal struggle against nature's most violent realm becomes assured of handling any situation alone. Many, many shipmasters grumbled about having wireless installed in their vessels, for it took away too much of their independence. They were used to acting entirely on their own in every matter at sea, receiving orders around the world only from land semaphore telegraph stations at various ports. With wireless they were, so to speak, constantly under the watchful "ear" of their owner, who often came up with difficult, virtually impossible orders for their masters to follow.

McFee had some pithy words on that subject, too. Wireless was the beginning of the end of a comfortable sea life. Old-style shipmasters, who enjoyed absolute authority in their seagoing domain, were resistant to the idea of being reached by their owners anywhere on the high seas. They had been bred to accept full responsibility for the voyage, something that may seem strange to those today who are accustomed to abdicating responsibility whenever possible. As a class the old shipmasters, said McFee, were for the most part psychologically averse to the presence of this new element on their ships. The wireless operator, usually a fuzz-faced boy about the age of an apprentice or a mess boy, never kept an "honest watch," and was answerable not to the owners or the master, but to the wireless company who trained and paid him. The average shipmaster of 1912 had yet to become used to engineers and firemen, who had come with the filthy, coal-fired steam engines that fouled the lovely white sails, rendering them obsolete, while intruding upon the master's supremacy. Engineers, confident in their own mechanical world, were also independent, a breed apart from deck officers. Even today in the Merchant Navy the old cliche, *"Oil and water don't mix"* is a way of saying that there is a definite chasm between the psyches of deck and engineering officers.

Many shipmasters naturally took out their resentment on the wireless operator personally. "Sparks" had become the darling of the newspapers and the general public, especially after the ***REPUBLIC*** disaster-fiasco in 1909, when Marconi's Jack Binns became the hero of the day. Egged on by the wireless companies themselves, the publicity-seeking Marconi being involved in more spectacular incidents than any other company. Sparks often got his photograph in the newspapers, usually with the caption "hero" attached, while the routine heroism of deck and engineering officers was ignored. McFee wrote, *"Those of us who sailed with them were not invariably in love with them."* One cartoon of the era showed an anxious and youthful wireless operator looking for his lifeboat on the slanting deck of a sinking ship, with the line, *"Where do I go, please?"* A big, burly deck officer scowled down at him and answered, *"You? You're the bloody 'ero. You go down with the bleedin' ship!"*

No doubt at least some of this antagonism was fueled by the cocky arrogance of many early wireless men, who also quickly became the darlings of the lady passengers on board the liners, much to the disgust of the masters who previously had had their pick of the prettiest. It was a new and glamorous profession, and most of the early operators had actually installed the wireless apparatus that they worked aboard ship. Men who understood a technology that was beyond the knowledge of the average deck officer, and often tried to explain it as if they were talking to infants, did not endear themselves to men who did not want them there in the first place.

As late as 1955 Dutch sailor/author Jan de Hartog wrote *"A Sailor's Life"* (Harper & Brothers, New York), with its tongue-in-cheek description of each crew member in a ship, from master to ship's monkey, rats and stowaways. The wireless operator, being *"neither fish nor fowl,"* that is, neither deck nor engineering department, did not "fit in," and was often suspected of not pulling his own weight. Wireless operators, wrote de Hartog, usually appeared *"in feminine garments at infuriating hours."* Roars of hearty laughter provoked by unseen comedians might emanate from the cozy warmth of the wireless room, to be heard by a disgruntled watch officer miserably pacing the bridge in freezing rain. When asked to explain this strange behavior, the wireless operator's response was usually *"testing."* Only a wireless operator, wrote de Hartog, could really tell whether another operator was *testing*, or *resting*.

The intrusion of radio upon the independence of aviators paralleled the resistance of mariners to the new technology. Within my own experience, I can recall that in the nineteen fifties and sixties, until jets made Instrument Flight Rules mandatory at all times, many of the old captains we flew with would take off in clear weather in their prop-driven aircraft, cancel IFR, shut off their radios, and fly a thousand or more undisturbed miles to their destinations before switching on the radio again to call for the necessary landing clearance. Radios were (and are) annoying, and so were wireless operators to many of the old shipmasters.

And so it was in the early days of wireless at sea, a situation not easily understood by modern researchers, possibly not even by modern mariners who began their careers in radio equipped vessels, and who thus have no more knowledge of a previous era at sea than airline pilots today have of flying the mail in the days of open cockpits, airway marker beacons and flying instruments on nothing but "needle, ball and airspeed."

Any one or all of these factors influenced both Captain Lord and Captain Smith, both men schooled in a pre-wireless age, men used to relying upon themselves rather than a mere snip of a wireless operator who had been put on board primarily for the convenience of passengers who wanted to send paid messages.

Captains Smith and Lord had one other good reason not to call their wireless operators. Both commanders obviously knew of Marconi's restrictions on communicating with other wireless services. If they had any reason to believe that the ships they saw were foreign, they might have hesitated on these grounds, remembering ***REPUBLIC***'s catastrophe when Captain Sealby refused aid from a United-equipped vessel with which Jack Binns refused to communicate. While it is argued that Marconi operators did freely communicate with other services during an emergency, in every recorded instance prior to ***TITANIC*** they did so only when the other fellow was in trouble, and once again, salvage was the name of the game. When a British ship was in distress it seems to have been a foregone conclusion that there would be enough of their own available to take care of them. After all, Britannia did rule the waves, did she not? Most Englishman of ***TITANIC***'s era truly believed that Britain had been endowed with the God-given right to the seas, that others were intruders. At any rate, with Ismay on or near the bridge. Captain Smith was undoubtedly reticent about accepting aid from just anywhere, until it was too late. Ismay definitely wanted a British ship if he could get one.

There is also the question of why Captain Lord did not personally come to ***CALIFORNIAN***'s bridge that night, when his watch officer reported seeing pyrotechnic signals.

Reisenberg answered this, too. *"The master who is not too familiar gets on best,"* he wrote. And, *"The master who interferes with the routine work of the ship is usually a fool."* Reisenberg wrote that one of the best master mariners he had ever known *never* set foot on the bridge except to enter or leave port, or in fog, or other danger. Thus when he did appear on the bridge all hands were immediately on their toes. The wise master, wrote Reisenberg, saw everything *"through the corners of his eyes and did his kicking through the Chief Mate."*

While it has often been written that Captain Lord was an "autocrat," all shipmasters are to a certain extent. It is necessary to achieve the absolute command that the master must have. Merchant seamen say that "the captain stands alone next to God," and as Reisenberg wrote, a good commander stays aloof. If he or she seems to lay too much responsibility upon the chief officer, it is because that individual is a commander "in training," and must therefore accept that responsibility. It has been written that ***CALIFORNIAN***'s apprentice was too timid in trying to wake Captain Lord for this reason. Any apprentice was apprehensive in such a situation, but if Gibson was afraid of Lord it was Gibson's problem, not Lord's, for Gibson would have been shy with any commander. There is no evidence, however, that this was the problem. That, too, is undoubtedly merely one of the myths perpetuated by those who have never been to sea.

Captain Lord, like Captain Smith when he was involved in the ***OLYMPIC-HAWKE*** collision, never lost his certificate, never even had it suspended, a tacit admission that it was known by those involved in the Board of Trade inquiry that Lord was not guilty. The official reason given for this was that it would reflect upon the integrity of the British mercantile marine, something that the B.O.T. investigators certainly did not want. Although Captain Lord did lose his position in the Leyland Line, undoubtedly because the line would not want the notoriety attached to his name, he soon obtained a command with the nitrate carrier Lawther, Latta & Company, where he gained many champions among the men who served under him. Lord served with quiet competence and dependability throughout World War I, and until ill health forced his retirement in 1929. The ***TITANIC*** matter had been forgotten until authors scrambling to get books out on the subject to take advantage of the 50th anniversary of the disaster brought up the subject of the ***CALIFORNIAN*** again, but did no research beyond the official conclusion, thus creating the lingering myths.

Captain Lord passed away on 25 January, 1962, leaving the task of trying to clear his name officially to Leslie Harrison, then General Secretary of the Mercantile Marine Service Association, which represents British shipmasters.

After years of petitioning for a reopening of the ***TITANIC-CALIFORNIAN*** investigation Harrison finally succeeded in this accomplishment. The conclusion reached by the Marine Accident Investigation Branch, Department of Transport, was summarized in March, 1992. While the modern investigators were somewhat more lenient in their appraisal of the situation than Lord Mersey, the Board of Trade and respective attorneys were in 1912, they still failed to see the incident through the eyes of a 1912 merchant seaman, particularly in the matter of distress rockets.

Chapter Seven

The German Connection

In its January/February, 1962, issue the *Belgian Shiplover*, quarterly newsletter of the Belgian Nautical Research Association, carried an article about ***TITANIC*** written by Wilhelm Müller, one time German deck officer turned Canadian farmer.

Müller was born in Stettin, a port city ceded to Poland in the Armistice terms of World War II, and now named Szczecin. He was related to the Rudolph Christian Gribel family of shipowners, who had been running a fleet of small cargo-passenger vessels east into Russia since early in the nineteenth century. Growing up in such an atmosphere, young Wilhelm had a natural interest in ships, and frequently visited the Vulcan shipyard at Stettin, where Gribel ships were built, and where he watched the construction of Germany's first Blue Riband winner, which was also the first fourstacker and the first liner to carry wireless apparatus for regular use on the high seas, Norddeutscher Lloyd's ***KAISER WILHELM DER GROSSE***.

Bill Müller also had a special interest in Harland & Wolff, which had built many of the earlier German liners, and which had many German employees. As noted in an earlier chapter, Gustav Wolff was German.

It was only natural that Bill would go into the shipping industry, and he apprenticed in the Gribel line at the usual age of fourteen. A brilliant young man with the customary Teutonic tenacity and capacity for hard work, he soon had his Second Officer's certificate and was being groomed for management in the family line.

As part of his practical experience, in 1909 young Müller took a position as secretary to one Tjietse Hettema, a Dutch traffic inspector whose job it was to evaluate financial investments in various fields, including shipping. Hettema lacked practical nautical experience which Müller provided along with his secretarial duties. Müller worked for Hettema until the beginning of the Great War. For a short period after the War started he returned to the Gribel Line to run German troops to the Russian front, and then Müller served for the remainder of the War in the German Navy.

After the War Müller returned to the German merchant marine, until Hitler's rise to power in 1933. When Hitler decreed that all German deck officers must join the Nazi Party, Müller foresaw another all-out war coming, and he emigrated to Canada, where he eventually became a farmer in an area just east of Windsor, Ontario, which is heavily populated by German immigrants and their descendants.

I first heard of Müller and his ***TITANIC*** article from German maritime historian Arnold Kludas in 1985. I had in my possession, however, only brief parts pertinent to the ***FRANKFURT*** from the *Belgian Shiplover* article at that time. Kludas and I were surprised to learn that Müller was still living, in a Canadian rest home. Bill was ninety two years young when I first contacted him by telephone from my home in Miami, Florida. His mind was still sharp, his memory excellent, but especially on the telephone were conversations difficult because of his hearing impairment and usually my questions and his answers were relayed through sympathetic nurses and office personnel. I therefore asked him only to verify what he had written about ***FRANKFURT*** and ***TITANIC***. Although I asked if he had known ***FRANKFURT***'s officers, unfortunately I asked nothing more at that time, and I used only a small portion of his article in my first book, ***TITANIC*** *R.I.P.; Can Dead Men Tell Tales?* After that book was published in the summer of 1989 I sent

Müller a copy, and kept in touch with him via letters that I wrote and which he answered in subsequent telephone conversations. He shared a room with two other men, which made writing difficult, Müller explained, and although he could still type he had no typewriter of his own and had to borrow one from the rest home office, a practice which he abhorred.

In September, 1989, John Whitman, founder and CEO of the now-defunct ***TITANIC*** Memorial Museum, Inc., in Sidney, Ohio, drove to Ontario with two of the Museum's officers, to interview Müller. Whitman, like many others who had learned of Müller from my first book, was unclear on how Bill knew about ***FRANKFURT.*** Whitman thought that since Müller had been a deck officer and he was German, then he might have been an officer in ***FRANKFURT.*** When Whitman asked Müller, *"What ship were you in on the night of April 14, 1912?"* he was astonished to hear Bill's simple answer: *"I was in the **TITANIC**."* Not prepared for this startling piece of news Whitman could only think of a few corroboratory questions to ask Müller.

In December of that year I made arrangements to fly to Detroit and drive to the small town in Ontario where Müller resided. For three days, in six periods of one to two hours each so he would not tire, I interrogated him. We had immediately established a rapport which came from the simple fact that I had said in my book, without reading all of his article, exactly what he had said and known for many years. To me, trusting me, knowing it was near the end of his life. Bill Müller confided his deep dark secret with all of its painful details. From the night of 14-15 April, 1912, until his death almost eight decades later Müller carried the self-inflicted guilt and shame that he, a healthy young man, had lived while many women and children had not. When I asked why he had not come forth with this information earlier, why he had not garnered the publicity that other survivors courted over the years, his response was as simple as his first admission to Whitman had been, *"I had to put it out of my mind in order to survive."*

When Whitman sent out a press release saying that a new survivor had been found, he was immediately ridiculed by the ***TITANIC*** establishment. Müller had to be a hoax, they insisted without once interviewing him, because he and his employer Mr. Hettema were not listed on the "official" passenger manifest. Several "researchers" insisted that they had "complete" manifests, and neither "Müller" nor "Hettema" were listed anywhere, let alone in First Class as Müller had said they were.

Buried in the obscure and sometimes tedious summary of the Board of Trade inquiry's transcript lies one reason for that manifest discrepancy. The names of six First Class ***TITANIC*** passengers aboard ***CARPATHIA*** were never sent by wireless. "This matter was not important enough to pursue," said Lord Mersey. It was apparently a deliberate omission rather than an oversight, although it should be understood exactly how the survivors' names were sent and received.

Under the direction of ***CARPATHIA***'s Chief Purser his assistants took the names of ***TITANIC*** survivors, who were already segregated into their proper class aboard the Cunarder as they had been in ***TITANIC.*** The lists from each class were then handed to the Marconi operators, ***CARPATHIA***'s own Harold Cottam and ***TITANIC***'s exhausted and injured Harold Bride. The latter had come to help Cottam who had been at his key for two days without sleep. The names, many of them "foreign," their spelling unfamiliar to English wireless operators, were then sent using Morse code. If an operator was as tired and ill as Cottam and Bride were by then it would have been easy to "slur" his code, that is not give quite the proper break between dots and dashes or whole words, thus facilitating misinterpretation. Somewhere another operator, who perhaps was also on duty for extended periods because of the ***TITANIC*** disaster, filtered those dots and dashes through his fatigued brain, and relayed them to yet another operator, and so on, each of whom could have made an error in receiving or in transmitting. Because there were no frequencies every operator within range regardless of his wireless service picked up the signals and sent them to news media, and thus the newspapers had their published survivor lists from any number of sources, with any number of interpretations. For example, on one of the earliest published lists of ***TITANIC*** survivors was a name spelled *"Kennema."* This was interpreted as "Kennyson," as "Kennyman," as "Kenyon," but it could just as easily have been "Hettema." Interpretation depended upon names known by family or friends to have been on board ***TITANIC***. If the name William Müller (Wilhelm always used the Anglicized "William" when in England) had been written by an English-speaking steward, sent by an English-speaking wireless operator, because the German *ü* sounds very much like *e* to English ears it might have been interpreted as "Meller," or William Mellors, a ***TITANIC*** passenger who was saved, and whose name is on "official" lists. A fatigued and distressed wireless operator might have seen two names so much alike and say *"I've already sent that,"* thus ignoring the second similar name. The point is that every name sent was subject to error several times between first transmission from ***CARPATHIA*** and final reception from the fifth or sixth wireless operator who relayed it.

When Ismay was asked directly at the Board of Trade inquiry to provide a complete manifest he replied that such a thing was impossible. The only complete manifest had gone down with the ship, said White Star's Managing Director. With a ship or airplane the booking manifest is not complete, not even now with instantaneous computerized reservations. There are always last minute revenue passengers, and finally non-revenue passengers, as Hettema and Müller were, who are assigned cabins, or seats, after all revenue passengers are provided for.

In a ship the final, complete manifest is made up by the Chief Purser, whose job it is to have that manifest ready for immigrations and customs agents at the next port of call. That manifest must be complete, it must arrive with the vessel, and the names must be correct, whether the port of entry is the United States or any other country. Heavy fines are imposed if manifests are not accurate. In an airplane, with a fast turnaround time, the correct number of passengers is sufficient in most cases, but taking a correct passenger count in a multi-cabined jumbo jet is difficult enough because passengers like to mill around, moving from one cabin to another until the very last minute. In a ship, especially one as large as ***TITANIC***, where passengers, who do not all speak the same language, can disappear in cabins, alleyways, public rooms, etc., it is impossible to get a complete manifest until she has departed her last port of call, which in ***TITANIC***'s case was Queenstown, and even that is extremely difficult. In the heyday of the transatlantic liners there were always visitors aboard until shortly before sailing time, creating chaos for the harried stewards and stewardesses, another reason for waiting until after departure for completing the manifest. Under such conditions stowaways all too often manage to sneak aboard as well. Thus Ismay explained to his interrogators that the only complete manifest, taken after ***TITANIC*** departed Queenstown, went down with her. There is no such thing as a **complete *TITANIC*** passenger manifest. Newspaper articles of 1912 said it, and I say it again... there is no way to know exactly how many people were aboard ***TITANIC***, how many died... or how many were saved. To reject out of hand Müller's claim to having been in ***TITANIC*** solely on the basis of her known manifest without interviewing him is arrogant, faulty research.

It is also entirely possible that Hettema and Müller were among those names that were deliberately never sent from ***CARPATHIA***. There is nothing illogical about Ismay personally protecting male survivors from the public scorn and ridicule that would eventually destroy him, and that was already apparent aboard ***CARPATHIA***. Neither Hettema nor Müller had any family who knew they were on board the ill-fated White Star liner. Hettema was a bachelor, he had been living in England away from any family members for many years. He and his young secretary had been personally invited by Bruce Ismay to make the maiden voyage in the White Star liner, and Ismay must have felt responsible for putting them in danger. Hettema's job was to evaluate the new ship for potential investors. The arrangements for their passage had been made only the day before sailing in White Star's London office. Müller was eager to compare the English liner with the new German *schnelldampfers,* of course, but he had a soft spot in his heart for the White Star, which was an *"underdog to Cunard,"* and he greatly admired Ismay. But we will use Wilhelm Müller's own words, taken from his 1962 article, *Once Again the* ***TITANIC***, with his permission.

"... Ever since that tragic day in 1912 there has been a flood of books, of articles, of newspaper notices, of movie films and television shows. We have been shown the ***TITANIC*** *affair from everyone's own viewpoint, prejudices, desires to make money or whatever, else yet, in those fifty years we have not come closer to the truth, we are, rather, pushed farther away from it, than we were in the first year.*

"Fifty years, I said. For, in a few months we will celebrate (?) the fiftieth anniversary of shipping's most stupendous case. And, with it, very likely, we will get from all sides a flood of articles, memoirs, shows, and what else, wherein each and everyone will try to sell us their ideas of what has happened. But, will it all bring us closer to the TRUTH?

...

"The Germans, in their treasures of myths and stories have the story of the cobbler who was busy at his daily job, and as the sun shone brightly through the window, his wife heard him singing out: 'You won't bring it to light.' She heard it, and every woman, bored into him, 'What will it not bring to light?' Until he succumbed. Once he had admitted a misdeed, a grave misdeed, and the victim, staring at the sun had cried out, 'You will bring it to light.' And, the sun did, for the cobbler's wife, true to wifely nature, brought it to light and the cobbler to justice, just like this, the never ending stream of ***TITANIC*** *literature will once bring the truth to light. Not the least of the stepping stones may be the recent book by Mr. Oldham, a friend of the Ismay family, who bore some facts about Mr. Ismay, father and son. But, ever since we had heard that Mr Oldham was working on that book, we hoped, the book would bring FULL disclosures of the background of the* ***TITANIC****; but, it did not divulge anything more than we already knew.*

"That failure prompts me to meet the fiftieth anniversary with a set of my own observations, reminiscences, and a few hard facts.

"The reason that all the mystery-hunters in the matter ***TITANIC*** *never come to the truth, forever tread along their own paths is, that no one dares to touch 'political' backgrounds, environments. Because, if one writes for money, as they all do, they have to attract a readership, and they will not find that, if any uncomfortable points are added. Mr. Oldham, in his recent book does not come closer to political entanglements than the telegram the former German Kaiser sent to the family of Mr. Ismay, father, on the occasion of Mr. Ismay's serious illness. It would be well worth to each shiplover, to read that telegram, and have a few thoughts about the true character of that fallen monarch.*

"One cannot claim to be a student of shipping, a lover of ships, if one pursues heads-in-the-sands policy, never dares to say a word about past political intrigues and shortcomings. Shipping is the mirror of every nation's policy, ambitions, and abilities, and without considering those, one simply cannot speak with experience about any matter concerning ships.

*"In the beginning of this article I mentioned the many new, or younger, shiplovers who have enrolled and want something worthwhile, and I write this article especially to introduce them to the shipping of the past, and give them as many items as fit into the '****TITANIC****' story to round out their knowledge of the past. I beg the older members, to keep that intention in mind, in appraising this article.*

∽

"One day in the winter 1909-10 I had to attend a shipping conference in London (on the) Australian trade. Nearing the end of the conference, some delegate, (in our 1962 jargon we would call a 'neutralist') had the nerve to ask, 'If there was anything more to know about the loss of the ***WARATAH****.' The* ***WARATAH****, a brand-new British ship was on the return trip of her second Australian voyage when, near the South African coast, she disappeared without a trace.* (**Author's note:** ***WARATAH*** departed Durban on 26 July, 1909, due Capetown 29 July, but never arrived.)

"A shiver of displeasure covered the brows of all the British shipping men present. Finally one spoke up and said that this loss had been the subject of a thorough investigation that had found no fault whatsoever, and the loss must be considered as some act of 'force majeure.'

"After that conference, there was a banquet for all the great men, while the less important 'juniors' and assistants had their tables decked in an adjoining room. I have no doubts, that the bosses' room was as sanctimonious as they were at the conference table, say, forbidding like the white cliffs of Dover, but at the juniors' tables there was a lively conversation. For theirs was the job to 'fish' for information, listen to others' arguments and bring them next day to their bosses and earn praise for their diligence. That was the world of business then without female secretaries in shipping, and it was a nice life for those able and willing.

"I am no great friend of speaking during meals, too much of a gourmet with the nice things a London hotel s cooking has to offer… until I heard someone pressing the friend sitting next to me for an answer. Then I knew I had to say something to help my friend (who, by the way, was British and later became a well-known shipping personality). The question was, that the experts had proclaimed the ***WARATAH*** *to be of best workmanship and design, meeting every existing rule of shipbuilding. I countered that with the question: 'Is it not well-known that the preceding Lund (the owners of the* ***WARATAH****) ships were pretty weak seaboats, hadn't they a tendency in a heavy sea to have difficulties to "straighten-up" again?' The questioner stopped for a moment, he admitted having heard of that… so I continued: 'And with the* ***WARATAH*** *being a development of those ships, but 60% larger, would you think, that the "danger point" was 60% lessened or enlarged?' I became aware that there was near silence now, almost everyone listening…*

"I recall, having returned aboard the ***WAKOOL*** *in those South African waters, one of the most turbulent, treacherous seas there are, and I know, how I stood there, counting the seconds it took the ship after a deep dip to find herself again, trying to straighten up. For a man knowing ships and their behaviour, a most stirring pastime, I tell you… How then, a few inches of free water spread over the bottom of the ship may so change what the ship designer calls the "metacentric height" of the vessel as to cause it to capsize. Every ship has a center of gravity and a center of buoyancy somewhat below the center of gravity. When the ship heels over in a storm, the center of gravity does not change, but the center of buoyance moves toward the low side. A vertical line drawn from this point until it intersects the center line of the ship, marks the metacenter, and the distance this point is above the center of gravity, is the metacentric height. Therefore a small amount of free water at the bottom of the hull may change the metacentric height, and exert a capsizing force well above the deck line… Finally, you were speaking of the ship being built according to the highest rules of British classification authorities...*

"Let me tell you something. Great Britain depends upon its shipping. That shipping has to prosper, and shipping is highly competitive. The British seaman has to have a pay and living and working conditions that are somewhat higher than some competitors can give. All that has to fit into the ship that is being built. Consequently, a British tramp steamer can stand just so much and be kept in the running, or better

expressed, your shipbuilding rules are not the highest but a compromise of what can be done to have a good ship and still have it built competitive and operated competitively." It took sometime until free conversation returned to the room, for everyone needed sometime to see if further discussion was intended, but no one spoke up.

"However, a few days later I ran into Mr. J. Bruce Ismay, the chief of the White Star Line. We had met before. Somewhat embarrassingly for me. 'I heard you had quite some discussion the other night, my man told me. Would you care to drop in and have a few words with me some time?'

"I promised I would, because I liked him very well. Yes, I liked, I admired Mr. Ismay. When having an examination, I chose to write a paper on 'Management of a Large Shipping Company,' taking as the fleet of that company the White Star fleet. The examination being German, I did not dare use a German firm for fear of showing preferences. I took the White Star fleet and covered with it a world-wide service, without knowing that the General Manager of the White Star Line once had dreams along those lines, dreams that had become utterly frustrated by the domination of White Star Line by the International Mercantile Marine Company, American. Someone had told Mr. Ismay of my 'feat' and he became interested, in that way I had come to know a little more of Mr. Ismay than the rest of the world knew.

"When Mr. Ismay was still a young man, a few ideas began to ripen in him. It is needless to speak of his personal dilemma... the first idea he got from reading Jules Verne's 'Around the World in Eighty Days.' He took his beloved White Star Liners and worked out a sailing-list, and a net of hypothetical services, circling the world, and he found, that with his existing ships, their speed, etc., he could easily maintain an Around-the-World service within eighty days. Mr. Ismay, through his father's strict training, had become a stickler in punctuality, time-tables to set up and adhere to were his 'psychological escapism.' In his later years, he greatly preferred his post at the London & North-Western Railway than being with a steamship enterprise, time-tables are easier to maintain and... there are no icebergs.

"The second great idealism came to Mr. Ismay when he was still in his late twenties... there, in Hamburg had come to rule the Hamburg-Amerika-Linie a young man of nearly the same age, a man who made a great imprint onto the shipping world; a man unhampered by any strict father, a man who in a few years reshaped the weakened Hamburg-Amerika-Linie into a strong, fearless factor. That man, Albert Ballin, fascinated Bruce Ismay, aching under the restrictions of his position. The third idealism was that no British firm existed which had a globe-circling net of services. They all catered for some specialized trade, some to North America, some to the Orient, or some to South America. But the two large German firms extended into every corner of the globe, and the time-table-struck Mr. Ismay loved the thought of such world-wide services. Had not his White Star Line once begun with the South American trade? Had not their sailing ships once flown the flag on almost every sea? Had he not been sent to Australia and New Zealand to get first-hand knowledge of those trades? This Albert Ballin-like service, this world-wide White Star idea, this Around the World in 80 days, all by White Star, this had caught the imagination of J. Bruce Ismay.

"But as the 1890's drew to their end, realities came instead of dreams. Instead of 'escapes' from the restricted presence came the restrictions of duty. His father became sick, and finally died; his White Star Line had to face a grave crisis. We will have to take a look at the developments of shipping during the 1890's, the decade that lies right amidst that 'Golden Era of the Steamship.'

"In 1890 (my chief recording of shipping is a 'Review of World Shipping,' a volume for every ten years, as 1880, 1890, and so on) shipping conditions had reached a certain 'zenith.' On the North Atlantic, for instance, on Bremen to New York the Norddeutscher Lloyd had in mid-summer three sailings a week with its 'express' steamers, in addition came secondary ships and the Baltimore, etc., services. The Hamburg-Amerika-Linie had commissioned their four twin-screw express steamers of the ***AUGUSTE VIKTORIA*** *class, a group of four of uniform type and size, more homogenous than any other firm. The Cunard Line had the still good* ***UMBRIA*** *and* ***ETRURIA****, augmented by Guion's* ***OREGON****, together*

***ABOVE:** The Norddeutscher Lloyd's **KAISER WILHELM DER GROSSE**, launched by Vulcan of Stettin on 4 May 1897, took the Blue Riband on her maiden voyage in September of that year with an average speed of 21.39 knots between the Needles and Sandy Hook. The first fourstacker, at 14,349 GRT, **KWdG** measured 627.4 feet between perpendiculars, with a beam of 66 ft. She was powered by two sets of 8-cylinder triple expenasion engines driving twin screws. The immensely popular **KWdG** was also the first liner to be permanently equipped with wireless for routine use upon the high seas. (Artwork by Ryan Katzenbach)*

***ABOVE:** Hapag's **DEUTSCHLAND** (III), also built by Vulcan of Stettin, made an average speed of 22.42 knots between Eddystone and Sandy Hook on her maiden voyage, taking the Blue Riband from her rival, the **KAISER WILHELM DER GROSSE** in July 1900. Another fourstacker, at 16,502 GRT, she measured 660.9 feet between perpendiculars with a beam of 67.3 feet. Her twin screws were driven by 12 cylinder quadruple expansion engines, giving her a steady service speed of 22 knots. (Artwork by Ryan Katzenbach)*

*with the **AURANIA**, a very well balanced quartette. White Star had the brand new **MAJESTIC** and **TEUTONIC** plus the aging **GERMANIC** (when I say aging, that ship was then not quite through the first third of her life) and **BRITANNIC**. The French Line had that famous quintette of '**LA**' ships. So, five leaders in the field were well equipped, truly the 'Golden Era.'*

*"Ten years later, in 1900, things had changed. In those ten years, the British had only added in 1893 the Cunarders **LUCANIA** and **CAMPANIA**, while the White Star had, and that only in the last year of the decade, added the **OCEANIC**. Three ships in a decade.*

*"On the Continent, the Norddeutscher Lloyd had brought out the **KAISER WILHELM DER GROSSE**, in 1897, the **KAISER FRIEDRICH** in 1898 and the Hamburg-Amerika-Linie was then completing **DEUTSCHLAND**, with the N.D.L. having the still better **KRONPRINZ WILHELM** under construction. With the coming out of the two Cunarders in 1893 it was thought that the zenith was reached, bigger machinery was deemed impossible. Mr. Ismay, the elder, was wary of taking too much of a risk. That the **KWdG** had been built, and had become the largest and fastest of them all, caused a great stir in Britain. I have been asked often about it, and in my manner I dispersed British naivety with this: 'Well, you see, the Germans have a one-track mind (so, at least the Britishers always pretend): they tried to build a ship that could steadily make Atlantic crossings on a 28 day turnaround, and pay for it, so, in their thoroughness, they calculated very precisely, not thinking of any mischief but, as the ship was completed, alas, they found out that they had not only built the biggest but also the fastest ship...' The Britishers liked that explanation, as long as it was a pun… but some did not like it, and we have in our collection a cartoon, taken from a British provincial paper, showing a 'Britannia' sitting on a chair, as awakening, her hand raised to her head, feeling… that her crown was lifted. Far beyond, near the horizon a four funneled steamer, the '**KWdG**' steams away, carrying a long pennant, that famous 'Blue Ribbon' of the Atlantic. Such, then, was the consternation, and the jingoists began their infamous drive, to stir up the British people.*

"Then, in 1900, Williamson wrote his book 'War and Policy,' in this book the author lays down the law: 'With the exception of Italy, England has blocked the path of every nation that pressed toward the sea.' It was the 'Mein Kampf' of 1900. But we have no intent to follow that now, we only try to expound the influence of world politics into the shipping business of Great Britain. Only thus, we can understand, what J. Bruce Ismay took over, when he, after his father's *death, became head of the firm of Ismay, Imrie & Co., the Oceanic Steam Navigation Company. Upon the commissioning of the German record ship, White Star Line had to build a liner, least of all to stay abreast of the two Cunarders of 1893. It was intended to build two ships, but that was given up. The British people, stirred up by the jingoists, expected White Star to beat the Germans. We have a cartoon just expecting that… it shows the young German Kaiser playing with a tub full of water with a model of the **KWdG** floating on it and behind him stands John Bull, with an **OCEANIC** under the arm, saying 'Well, now let me try mine!' White Star was expected to do something it had not bargained for. Mr. Ismay, the elder, had become wary. Ship*'s *machinery had reached the limits of the possible. In Germany, another yard had tried fast ships, that ship, the **KAISER FRIEDRICH**, turned out a dismal failure. It cautioned Mr. Ismay against building any record-ship. Personally, I have always thought of **KAISER FRIEDRICH***'s *misfortune as an act of sabotage caused by family affairs. (Schichau had died in 1896, and the yard passed over to his son-in-law, Herr Ziese, thus eliminating other men of long standing.)*

*"The same yard that had built the **KWdG**, the Vulcan of Stettin, also built Hamburg-Amerika*'s ***DEUTSCHLAND**. And subsequently, the three following NDL ships, all five of them surpassing each other, having no peer anywhere.*

"That was the situation when the younger Ismay took over, he, who had dreamed of giving his country

an 'All-Over-the-World' shipping firm, in fact faced a grumbling Britain that accused the Ismays of 'YOU HAVE LET US DOWN"

"The White Star Line had then just initiated the new Australian service, catered for by five ships of each over 12,000 tons, the largest by far in the Australian trade. For the New Zealand trade three ships of the same size were contemplated. This construction program needed vast sums of money, money that was hard to get in a country with a 'You-have-let-us-down' grudge, in a country that was deep in a tough struggle in South Africa. (One cannot speak of 'War' when on one side the nation that rules the world stands, and on the other two hapless countries of peasants). Young Ismay's idol, Albert Ballin, always spoke full of praise of his four giant 'P' class steamers, each of some 14,000 tons. Compared to the money-wasting express liners, they were the real dividend earners. Ismay heard it, and he heard more. Ballin spoke of that new facility: his 'P' steamers with their many decks and large cargo capacity had been laid-out like a classification yard of a railway. Cargo was at loading-time classified and could, right after arrival, be taken out and hurried off to destination. That feat appealed to Mr. Ismay. Large ships, of reasonable speed, high-class passenger accommodation and this cargo-layout, all this, combined, could turn the tables in favor of White Star.

"Furthermore, taking the Australian and New Zealand ships as a yardstick, those new ships ought to have that certain size... which calculation led to the planning of the four famous **CELTIC** *class ships. From planning to building was another step, the financing. Financing, I have said having its thorns through present British conditions.*

"On the other side of the ocean, the good Americans had their own ideas. The 1890's had seen great numbers of immigrants arriving, nearly all of them on foreign ships, and it was known that most shipping firms had based their existence chiefly on the ability to attract emigrants. Why, then, if America took on all of Europe's castaways, why should America not reap, at least part of that business? Secondly, America had just then had the Spanish-American War, a war that needed much troop transporting, and that war had found America lacking ships. So much so, that the American government had to buy every foreign ship it could get at pretty high prices. Those ships then were kept by the Army, under its Quartermaster Department, instead of being operated by shipping firms at good rates, as the British did in their South African struggle.

"Both of these points were very reasonable, there is no cause whatsoever, as has been done, of accusing the Americans of any unfair proceedings. By then the Americans owned the American Line, or the International Navigation Company, a firm that also owned (however uncomfortable that is) the Red Star Line. White Star Line needed capital, plenty of it, but so also did Cunard Line, which, too, needed something better than the Germans had. There developed a sinister play, a play few have understood, but, as we try to interpret the 'Tragedy of the **TITANIC**' *we have to explain everything. It is known, and has been admitted in our TBS, in that article on Cunard Line, that Cunard had been in discussion with the Morgan people before the White Star did. But, as White Star heard that Cunard had entered golden prospects, they, too, rushed into discussion. As soon as they did, Cunard retracted, and 'free handedly' loudly proclaimed their true British heritage. It paid off well. Cunard was now the darling of the British, the jingoes had a hero to worship, and the British government backed the building of Cunard's 'answer to the Germans' handsomely, in fact so handsomely that Mr. Ismay complained, 'With the subventioning, in a field of paying shipping, the North Atlantic, of one company against all others, the government had upset the equilibrium of the North Atlantic shipping.' For so long every shipping firm had been on its own, as the business warranted, as good as its management did work, but now, one firm had been given full government backing, listening to the jingoists and the man in the street.*

"As to the effect upon Britain's shipping I quote from the book 'Steamship Conquest of the World.'

'One day the ***LUSITANIA*** *and a twenty-knot liner left New York within a few hours of one another. The Cunard boat in round numbers had 1,000 passengers aboard; her slower rival had less than 200. Comment is needless.' I can do still better, I have in my files from New York Port Authority data:* **'SS ADRIATIC** *(White Star Line) for Southampton with 34 passengers and mail' Here I say, 'Comment is needless.'*

"This shows how British chauvinism ruined its own famous 'Merchant Service.' They covered that up by talking about 'foreign competition,' and the book 'Steamship Conquest' *is typical of that smokescreen, that evading the truth. Just as much as the building of the famous battleship* ***HMS DREADNOUGHT*** *in 1906 did not put Britain out of naval competition, but rather forced all other nations to build likewise* ***DREADNOUGHTs****, so the building, with government money, of those two Cunarders forced all shipping firms, British and Foreign, to build something equal. My superior in England, at that time, as we spoke of the battleship and the Cunarders, said, 'Dreadnoughtitis, a sickness of the British,' and, I think he was right. It was not strength, it was a feeling of weakness, an hysteria, that ultimately led to the Great War.*

"And, looking back at that period, having felt the foolishness, the own great losses, the disintegration of the proud British Empire, we know what is meant behind the words, 'For firm patriotic grounds that the less said about ***TITANIC*** *the better.'*

"Let us now return to Mr. Ismay. This unfortunate man, with all his intentions having come between the Scylla and the Charybdis, between his British people's *antagonism and this American management of his family firm, now, as the effects of the 'upset equilibrium' showed up in the yearly returns, his American superiors grumbled, wanted to know, what counter-measures he intended to take! Mr. Ismay was now the General Manager of the whole International Mercantile Marine Company... and his was the duty to come up with counter-measures. What an irony! What those measures were, I found out, when I made good my promise to have* 'some talk some day.'

"Our early 1910 meeting started with the ***WARATAH****. Mr. Ismay had heard that I had made some 'on the spot' investigation in Durban, and he wished to hear what I had found out.* ***WARATAH*** *had steamed from Australia to Durban, roughly 20 days (since bunkering), with a bunker capacity of about 2100 tons, and a daily coal consumption of about 80 tons a day. We will say, that weights within the ship were greatly shifted. At Durban the master found a cable from the owners, saying to 'proceed with least delay' to Cape Town to load a valuable part cargo. Lund*'s *were in some financial trouble, competition on the Australian trade was keen, cargoes were often not sufficient, so, the firm tried to pick up as much as possible in South Africa. Hence, this order. Steamships had been the victors against the sailing ship, but some old traditions lingered on. The masters felt master of the ship after leaving homeport and remained master until arriving home; they did not like orders at every port. I had my own hard experiences along that line. And, as I had my training chiefly to be in the managerial business, not the operation of the ships, but preferred also to thoroughly understand the seaman*'s *job, I had the full training. And as I sat for my examination, I laid before my examiners (captains of the old school who stuck to the privileges of the masters at sea) my thesis, that with business as it had developed, home office any time should have the right to direct the ships what to do at any part of a given passage. They bellowed at me for that, but had to let it pass. For that I was highly interested in Lund*'s *directives to* ***WARATAH***'s *master. That Cape Town consignment could be the difference between a paying voyage and an unprofitable one; to pick up that business could mean the recovery of Lund*'s *from their financial distress. Mr. Ismay fully agreed to that (and he should know the why).* ***WARATAH*** *left Durban not fully bunkered. Possibly, as I had said during the* ***WARATAH*** *debate, that part bunkering might have added to* ***WARATAH***'s *congenital weaknesses. Then there was a second factor at Durban. There were great numbers of gold-seekers from the South African fields, who waited for a ship for fast return to good old England. They are a boisterous lot. Going out, they are more well behaved,*

***ABOVE: TITANIC** bound for Queenstown. It would be almost 80 years later before would learn that Bill Müller and his boss had been on **TITANIC**—a fact that helped shed light on what really happened. (Artwork by James A. Flood)*

and fit fine into any ship, and any company's financial returns.

*"But returning, they are hardened characters, disliked by the passengers that travel between the Cape and England. They also are always accompanied by a good number of shady ladies who sharklike go for their share of the gold findings. Union Castle's agents are careful to book them on the 'intermediate' or 'extra steamers,' but now they want to go cabin, not steerage. So, the agents try the steamers which return from Australia via Durban (besides, the agents receive a higher commission from the Australian ships, which like to return with a fuller passenger capacity). That is, what this crowd was waiting for. The acceptance of those passengers is in the hands of the captain. The master of the **WARATAH**, who with 'least delay should proceed to Cape Town,' had to spend much of his precious time with the passenger booking business, which, however, was done to the full satisfaction of the agents, Lund s Blue Anchor, and… the captain. As only those, willing to satisfy the terms were taken, a good number was left behind, and an angry outburst arose from them, wishing the wrath of heaven down upon poor **WARATAH**; so much so, that one passenger, having had a bad dream, became alarmed, and jumped over board, to stay at Durban. The lone survivor. There certainly was more behind the loss of the **WARATAH** than the official investigation dared to go into.*

"Having told that to Mr. Ismay, I found out the question he wanted to ask me: At the bottom of Hamburg-Amerika-Linie's long fleet-list there stood:

"'.... (under construction) Steamship, 50,000 tons gross.'

"That item fascinated, worried, Mr. Ismay. Now, the author of 'Steamship Conquest,' a man who

*knows, seemingly, everything, an Expert as he would call himself (but when it comes to write of White Star's ill-fortunate **REPUBLIC**, he spells it '**REPUBLIQUE**'!) The author states in his book that the Germans asked British shipyards to produce plans for the ship, and having been supplied with them, built the ship in their yards. Reading that, is the cause for the bulk of this article, which was written in 1913 to rebuke the author's untruths. I went to Stettiner 'Vulcan,' the contractors for building the **IMPERATOR**, and the General-manager, Dr Flohr, and the technical director, Herr L. Schwartz, both well-known, respected men, from whom I learned most that I know, branded that statement as complete untruth, designed to inflame the minds of the readers, the young Britons. They showed me, from the first sketches until the final plans, the full development of **IMPERATOR**'s design.*

*"It had been assumed that Ballin with this '50,000 ton steamer' was repeating his 1900 performance of the lone **DEUTSCHLAND**, largest, fastest, but lone. I told Mr. Ismay, that to the best of my knowledge Ballin intended to build three ships and operate them on a weekly schedule with a 21-day turn-around. Hearing this, Mr. Ismay burst out: 'How can he do it? His ships have to steam a full day more in each direction!' This, then, gave away the great mystery: Ismay intended to operate with three super-liners of moderate speed a service that had needed four ships so far. With his hobby for exact schedules he believed to be able to do that. All the nonsense about 'records,' up until today, is baseless. Yet, for 1911, such an attempt was marvelous, to say the least. But Mr. Ismay was a shipping man, a leader in that industry, and leadership has to be bold, to be successful, especially in view of the Government-created 'upset equilibrium' of the North Atlantic shipping. This, then, was Mr. Ismay's answer. But now Mr. Ismay had learned, that from another party even that scheme ran into heavy competition, and he knew, that the Hapag-trio would show features even his ships did not have.*

"Remains this point of "How can he (Ballin) do it?'

"We have been fed a lot of nonsense by writers on ships and shipping. We have, and again I quote from this book 'Steamship Conquest of the World,' heard so much about rivalry, unfair competition, etc. Now then, I have always thought of the Britisher as a 'sporting fellow,' a fellow who is fairplay, and knows the handicaps. But, the sporting Britisher is nowhere in the field of shipping. In all their writings, British shipping writers never say a word about that tremendous handicap their German competitors work: that 'he has an extra day to steam in each direction.' In that extra day there lies the cause for the German attempt to build a faster, a better ship, the extra effort made to stay in the business.

"It makes a tremendous difference, if one ship has to travel an extra 600 miles, has to carry bunkers for some extra 24 to 30 hours of steaming. And the financial returns sure show that handicap; a tremendous handicap never shown in any book or article. Mr. Ismay, as we saw, fully knew, understood, and banked upon that handicap. I answered him, 'I have no doubt that with their genius for organization and the devotion of each one, seamen as well as harbour workers, that venture will be fully successful.'

*"When I said that, I knew those people, and how right I was proved when the **IMPERATOR** in her first year had a serious fire on board. Then the crew did their utmost, but the second officer, Herr Karl Gobrecht, let himself be locked behind the fire-tight doors, disregarding the pleas and specific commands to come up, and directed the fire extinguishers until he perished, but the ship was saved.*

"The third point of our conversation was on Mr. Ismay's question of what about the threat of war between Great Britain and Germany, a threat constantly in the minds of the British people. On that point I gave him some information that can even now, fifty years later, not be repeated.

*"That conversation left me with great respect for Mr. Ismay. With even greater interest in the outcome of his project... the new **OLYMPIC** and **TITANIC** (of which a picture 'as they will appear when completed' was shown to me by Mr. Ismay). But still more in my thoughts was the third ship, the 1899 **OCEANIC** a great favorite of mine, which, very likely, would have to complete the trio until a third giant... alas, the*

*name **GIGANTIC** was, then, assumed to be given to it.... but, after **TITANIC**, that name was forgotten.*

"A few years ago, in the mid-1950's, two large passenger ships collided on the North Atlantic, near the American coast. The larger one, a new, very modern ship, sank, fortunately with little loss of life. The other ship, badly damaged and in fear her collision bulkheads might give way, took a large number of passengers on board, in addition to her own many passengers. The bulk of passengers and crew, however, were picked up by one of the largest, best known liners on the Atlantic. That liner made off in a rush to land those passengers. The damaged ship sent a wireless asking if the liner would stand by and escort it to port (New York). The liner declined that request, with a long message that ended with the words: 'MY SCHEDULE IS IMPERATIVE.' We took that full report for our archives and were somewhat amiss, looking that up in later reports, in articles, in books, those words were deleted. Now, the act of saving so many lives makes good publicity, for a liner that largely lives on its publicity; but, to admit publicly, that one's ship is on such a strict schedule as not to render more than the most necessary assistance, leaves room for after-thoughts. Somewhat later we read an alarming article (Readers Digest) in which the author stated that our modern aids to navigation are absolutely not foolproof to wit that collision, but also, that ships are nowadays put on such a 'tight' schedule that they actually race the oceans dare-devil style.

"The authors of books, the writers of articles, concentrated a little heavily upon the speed of ships. For well over a hundred years 'speed' has been the catch-word for maritime interest. Beginning with the first steamships crossing, the sporting blood of the Briton looked for and spoke of. speedy crossings. Whether they sat in their parlors and drank tea, or in the pubs, drinking ale, the talk about ships centered on their speed, and good old England could be jolly proud of its ships. And, all those people expected their shipping to remain supreme. We do not object to that, knowing that shipping is Britain's life-blood.

"But, as H. W. van Loon says in his excellent book 'A Story of Mankind' (every shiplover, to understand shipping, its need and its development, should have in his library van Loon's two books: 'Geography,' and 'A Story of Mankind'): 'That curious island on the other side of the North Sea lives by and for just one thing: TRADE. Those who do not interfere with British commerce are, if not exactly "friends," at least "tolerated strangers." Those, on the other hand who, however remotely, might become a menace to the imperial hegemony are "enemies" and they must be destroyed at the first possible opportunity.'

"That is exactly my quotation of Williamson's 'War and Policy,' of 1900. This is exactly what I told Mr. Ismay upon his question as to the threat of war. That I was afraid, that, when those three Hapag giants neared commissioning, the hour for war had struck.

"To make the British minds ready for that hour, such books as 'Steamship Conquest' with such a provoking final chapter as 'WHY GERMANY BUILDS HER LINERS' were written.

*"And that psychology existed already in 1897, when, on the advent of the **KAISER WILHELM DER GROSSE** a cartoonist sketches a cartoon, captioned 'The Rape of Britannia'... (Rape: 'seizing and carrying off by force,' but here speculating upon the effects of the popular meaning of the word).*

*"Had the Ismay built in 1899 an **OCEANIC** that was faster than the **KWdG** they would have been the darlings of the British nation, their failure (?) to do so was a stigma.*

"Yet, slowly Mr. Ismay had worked to assert himself within the I.M.M.Co.; as the years passed, except the American capital, the policy had almost become British. We have another cartoon (cartoons express so well thoughts that are not coined into words) showing a John Bull gorging an oversize I.M.M.Co., an Uncle Sam is standing, watching and muttering: 'He's Swallowed It, Be Gosh!' (New York Globe). Given a fair chance, Mr. Ismay would do well.

*"**LUSITANIA** and **MAURETANIA** entered service in 1907. The depredation of the passenger business of which the author of 'Steamship Conquest' writes rather happily, began. In 1908 the planning for Mr. Ismay's ships started, keel for the first one was laid that same year. The building of the 'unsinkable'*

ships had begun; they were said to be a 'city in themselves,' so safe, they nearly needed no lifeboats.

"Speaking about the ***WARATAH*** *I had said, 'It is the business of the builders and the surveying authorities to supply the ship that is wanted. The shipowner has his hands full of other things; if the shipbuilding industry is worth its salt, and classification rules to ensure the shipowner, then the shipping industry can plan with confidence.'*

"Three ships were intended to run a weekly service, all through the year. I pick out, among the many I could choose, my handbook of the 'Atlantic Transport Line' of 1906. That line operated a regular weekly service London to New York. With 4 steamers. Into that handbook, then, in 1906 I had fastened a note: 'Note that four ships, of very moderate speed, but of immense cargo capacity operate this service, out of a port that is farther away, and of a more complicated access (then anyway, with apologies to the Port of London Authority) than ports like Southampton, Liverpool, Glasgow.' Yet, with all modern navigational aids lacking, with port facilities and load, and that immense amount of coal to bunker, those four ships operated a schedule of a weekly sailing. Out of Southampton, a much easier port, four fast express steamers were needed to maintain a weekly service, and they did not load much cargo.

Note: page 219 has these as tabbed "charts"

"Schedule in 1906: ***MINNEHAHA*** *leaves London April 21 & May 19*

MINNETONKA	"	"	*April 28*	"	*May 26*
MESABA	"	"	*May 5*	"	*June 2*
MINNEAPOLIS	"	"	*May 12*	"	*June 9*

*"**MESABA** was only a single-screw steamer, with a speed of 14 knots at her best and absolutely not in the class of first-grade New York liners. Still, she filled her place in that schedule satisfactorily. Speaking of her, one might assume that she was rather a tough ship, 'for men only' preferably. In fact, on that stated voyage she carried 16 male and 31 female passengers, truly the 'family boat' on the Atlantic.*

"What made this feat, operating such a difficult service with only four ships (under same conditions most other lines would have 5 or even 6 ships attached) was the absolute devotion of everyone to their jobs, the seamen as well as the shore staff never thinking of the hours worked, nor any 'slow-down' policy, but always proud so a ship was again on her way.

"I could have taken other firms for comparison, but A.T.L. for some reason fitted me best.

"Yes, from Southampton, from Liverpool, from Bremen, from Havre and from Hamburg a weekly EXPRESS schedule was always scheduled with four ships.

"There were exceptions.

"For instance, AMERICAN LINE. The two remaining large Inman liners, new ships large and fast, the **CITY OF PARIS** *and the* **CITY OF NEW YORK**, *had been taken over by the Americans, that change of flag made possible by special act of Congress, and from early in 1893 the ships were now sailing under American management, Mr. Griscom at that time being the American General Manager.*

"The schedule, early 1893, was: Southampton to New York on Saturdays:

PARIS	*April 22*	*and again*	*May 20*
BERLIN	*April 29*	"	*May 27*
NEW YORK	*May 6*	"	*June 3*
CHESTER	*May 13*	"	*June 10*

"In mid-summer, on the NORTHERN TRACK, the two fast steamers were put on a 21-day turnaround, as follows:

NEW YORK	*October 21,*	*November 11,*	*December 2*
PARIS	*October 28,*	*November 18,*	*December 9.*

"Into this 'fast' schedule, *the two older steamers were put in between, for instance* **CHESTER** *November 4, and again December 16. The accelerated schedule was made possible by putting the New York departure on Wednesday, instead of Saturday, thus saving 3 days in port. During this accelerated service American Line advertised 'while on the Northern Track passengers frequently can dine in New York on Friday evening' (6 1/2 days after leaving Southampton).*

"You will know by now what I intend by showing sailing schedules beginning with Atlantic Transport, and its cramped days in port to load and bunker. ***NEW YORK*** *and* ***PARIS*** *in order to maintain their 21-day turn-around did not make much faster crossings, but the stay in port, Southampton and New York, practically enabled the 21 day schedule. The whole business of racing ships served publicity and the 'sporting spirit,' and, perhaps, national pride. All that was required from ships of the speed of* ***PARIS-NEW YORK*** *or* ***OLYMPIC-TITANIC*** *was to have a steady good speed that keeps the ship within its schedule, whatever happens enroute. The captain of the* ***TITANIC*** *consequently was in the same position as his fellow-master nearly 50 years later: 'MY SCHEDULE IS IMPERATIVE,' ice warnings, fog, or what else. The two Cunarders of course had such a high speed, that the 21-day turn was easily maintained, especially, as they hardly took time with loading or unloading cargo, which trouble could be spared, because, the publicity gave them, as we had heard, passengers, high-paying passengers at the ratio of 5:1. (Thank you, 'Steamship Conquest.') With that, and the Government subsidy, all services in port could be afforded to speed up readiness for departure.*

*"****LUSITANIA*** *made eighteen round-trips per year that is, each in 21 days. Now, refloating upon the accusations* ***TITANIC*** *had suffered, would you think that during the 18 round voyages* ***LUSITANIA*** *had encountered large ice fields, heavy fog for days, etc., and... how much slowed she down?? If she did, how could she accomplish 18 round voyages??*

"In 1908 Cunard Line issued a folder, arranged like a photographic film, depicting the passing of the ***LUSITANIA*** *on mid-Atlantic. The witness is supposed to stand aboard the* ***IVERNIA*** *(Cunard) and see first only a plume of smoke on the horizon, then the masts, the funnels, finally she passes the* ***IVERNIA*** *and disappears beyond... all that calculated to 'bring home' to the witness the immense speed of* ***LUSITANIA****, a speed enabled by Government payments and now used to corner every possible passenger. Now this passing, within a few minutes is nothing pre-arranged, it is rather a few minutes (that is what the text states) during one voyage, one out of 36 in a year, in an endless haste to speed and gain business by speed. During how much of the year did the ship encounter ice warnings, fog, long periods of fog... and, how much did she slow down, for the safety of her passengers? Thirty six crossings on a 'My schedule is imperative' schedule.*

"Then, there was the day when New York newspaper reporters were busy writing down the stories told by passengers who had just landed, the 'thrilling' voyage they had had, when (now, watch this!) the American liner ***ST. PAUL*** *and the Cunarder* ***LUCANIA*** *'RACED INTO PORT* ***THROUGH TEN HOURS OF FOG*** *TO SETTLE A QUESTION OF SPEED SUPREMACY.' (Comment unnecessary.)*

"While ***LUSITANIA*** *made her 36 speedy crossings, we looked at the log of NDL's* ***KRONPRINZ WILHELM****, under Captain Nierich. The ship had so far a good voyage, then ran into a continued fog, the ship slowed down to 5 knots, which was the lowest possible in order to keep her under control, and consequently arrived in port. New York, not on Tuesday morning but Wednesday afternoon. A slowdown from 20 knots to 5 knots for a lengthy amount of time throws a ship completely out of schedule.*

"For a 25-knot liner running on a tight 21-day schedule a slow-down would be even more impossible. What I am driving at is not to show other people's sins, but bring home the understanding that 'racing' had been going on ever since Collins and Cunard rivaled, secondly, that a set, tight schedule that forces ships to maintain their speed, knocks the 'safety margin' out and simply invites a catastrophe.

"Just an hour or two before ***TITANIC*** *struck that iceberg, two of her passengers. Colonel Gracie and Mr. Charles M. Hayes, President of the Grand Trunk Railway, had a conversation, during which Mr. Hayes said, 'The White Star, the Cunard, and the Hamburg-Amerika-Linie are devoting (sorry, Mr. Hayes, H.A.L. then had not a single high-speed steamer running) their attention and ingenuity in vying with one another to attain supremacy in luxurious ships and in making speed records. The time will soon come when this will be checked by some appalling disaster.' That disaster struck an hour or SO later, and Mr. Hayes died that night. The incident proves that passengers were well aware of the danger, the knocking out of the 'safety margin.'*

"We mentioned when we gave the accelerated schedule of the American liners in 1893, that the general-manager of that line was Mr. Clement A. Griscom. Mr. Griscom was perhaps the outstanding personality of pre-WWI American shipping. He was one of the founders of the American Line in 1871, and that the American flag stayed on the Atlantic was his achievement. During the forty years that Mr. Griscom managed the American Line it is said that it never lost a ship, never lost a passenger or a bag of mail. Despite the few ships in service, compared to the European companies, during some of the years his American Line was the top passenger carrier on the Atlantic. With the formation of the I.M.M. Co., and Mr. Ismay's ascendance as its general-manager, Mr. Griscom became the chairman of the board of directors. When, under the impact of the Cunarders I.M.M.'s business slumped, Mr. Griscom, though already ailing in his health was very outspoken in his criticism and, repeatedly told them, the directors and Mr. Ismay, 'how he had run ships during his years.' To wit, the three-weeks turn of the two ships, or, say, when ***LUCANIA*** *tried to show* ***ST. PAUL*** *(American) that she still was the mistress of the Atlantic ('raced into port through ten hours of fog to settle a question of speed supremacy') well, good that* ***ST. PAUL****'s master took up that challenge, otherwise, it would have been hard to face Mr. Griscom. After the* ***TITANIC*** *tragedy, the 'insiders' were well aware of the real cause, the "tight schedule," and there was one 'inside' senator, at least one, who, as often as questioning went into dangerous waters, always popped the questions about 'speed,' about 'revolutions,' about top speed of the ship, and the witnesses duly answered*

ABOVE: *Cunard's 12,952 ton, 601 ft.* ***LUCANIA*** *was launched in 1893 by Fairfield Company Ltd., Glasgow. She played an important part in the development of wireless at sea, and was destroyed by fire in Huskisson Dock, Liverpool, in August 1909. (Artwork by Ryan Katzenbach)*

that they never ran top speed, no, sir, and there was no thought at all to strive for a 'Blue Ribbon' record. (Silly at all). But, there was no one who told them, that that 'modest' speed ***TITANIC*** *was running, actually was more than any fast liner, from* ***LUCANIA*** *over* ***TEUTONIC*** *to* ***NEW YORK*** *had run. (Except, of course, the two Cunarders, and the five Germans.)*

"And, the other question never put forward, never answered was: 'What difference was there, if ***TITANIC*** *with her 66,000 tons (weight, displacement) ran with 21 or with 23 knots onto the iceberg?' Ballistic experts know the answer (American detractors of Mr. Ismay, and 'certain' authors do well to put the Griscom-factor into their notebooks).*

"All the items I have just related are part of a careful recording of shipping. Let it be said, that the shipping of every nation is closely watched by the other nations. The shipping companies, the shipbuilders, the insurance firms, the cargo brokers, the governments, all have their 'scouts' (what a nice word) at work checking closely what the other fellows are doing. I recall one man, being at work on the Chinese coast for a shipping firm; the Navy had given him two years 'furlough;' in return, being an officer, he sent in his reports. As the two years neared their end, there was no relief in sight, so he wrote to the officer at home, and asked if his furlough could be extended another six months. Reply: 'Try to stay there another two years; your reports are worth more than you being navigation officer aboard a warship that is all the time at anchor.'

"So, we have said that the tight schedule knocked out the safety margin. During the ***WARATAH*** *discussion we had stated that the shipowner had the right to expect from the builders the ship he needs for that particular service. For instance, going around the Cape, coming the long trek from Australia, a ship should be able to stand the seas with bunkers, etc., much depleted. The builders… having their 'scouts' watching everything, should know the particular weakness of a type of ship and remedy it, for instance, develop a type of ship, like Deutsche Australische's freighters, that are safe to pass any seas. Now,* ***OLYMPIC*** *and* ***TITANIC****, long before they came out, had been heralded as the 'practically unsinkable' ships. What may have induced builders and owners to put that emphasis on the word "unsinkable?" Were they aware that the ship was intended to run on such a 'tight' schedule that the 'safety margin' (time to go at low speed if ice or fog makes it necessary) was taken away? What ship did they turn out as an 'unsinkable' one?*

"When Captain Rostron, master of the ***CARPATHIA****, the ship that picked up* ***TITANIC****'s survivors, stood before the United States Senate's Investigation Committee, the chairman asked him: 'How it came that* ***TITANIC*** *had twenty lifeboats only, while* ***CARPATHIA****, less than one-third its size, and only one half its passengers and crew also had twenty lifeboats.'*

"Captain Rostron's answer: 'The ***TITANIC*** *was supposed a lifeboat itself.'*

"Very well. Because ***TITANIC*** *was such a safe ship (everyone was lulled into that belief) she did not carry enough lifeboats. She could disregard ice warnings. Her crew NEVER had a boat drill, her crew, picked together from several other smaller ships, was so unaccustomed to this big ship that there existed no 'feeling' between the different stations. And, because she was such a safe ship, unsinkable, the wireless operators thought nothing of ice warnings, kept them in the pocket, because they were too busy sending off paying messages.*

"And, some writer, in just those days sits down and writes a book, 'Steamship Conquest of the World,' bragging about his country's achievements.

"And, I have another cartoon, showing an iceberg, with the name FACT on it, and a sunken ***TITANIC*** *at the bottom of the ocean with the word THEORY. The theory, that Britain with its ships had conquered the oceans.*

ഗ

"From the 'Chicago Evening Post':

"'America may make, as the London papers have said, 'hasty and often cruel verdicts' but in the ***TITANIC*** *case America is becoming daily more glad that the investigating committee of United States senators had the energy and vision to board the* ***CARPATHIA*** *before she docked. Else, who knows how little of the truth about the wreck we would ever have known? The testimony has taught us that even the wireless, the wonderful instrument for lessening the perils of the sea, may become in unworthy hands an instrument for capitalizing human agony instead of alleviating it. We have learned that this new force must be sternly regulated if it is to perform its due service to humanity.'*

"I quote this fully, because the truth about the miserable part wireless played has been suppressed. But our talkative friend, the author of 'Steamship Conquest' *again gives us a good clue. Writes he:*

"'The result (of Marconi's *system of wireless) was that within a short time every Atlantic liner of importance carried this equipment. The Germans resented this tendency (?). Teuton (!) inventors, following in Marconi*'s *footsteps, developed a system which has become known since as the "Telefunken," whose advance, by the way, has been due to the personal endeavours of His Majesty the German Emperor. Efforts were made by the leading liners to displace the Marconi in favour of the Telefunken system. But it was of no avail"... IN FACT, AT THAT TIME MARCONI STATIONS REFUSED TO ACCEPT MESSAGES FROM THE LATTER... This situation was alleviated by the astute German move at the Radio-Telegraphic Conference of 1906, when it was agreed among the Powers that there should be free trade in wireless telegraphy.'*

"The reader will understand by now, that, with Britain having accepted and organized the Marconi system, it tried to monopolize wireless. The author's *explanations are just to cloak those proceedings. His next sentence literally 'let*'s *the cat out of the bag.' (Read this carefully). 'Curiously enough, it was a German boat that inaugurated wireless telegraphic conversation on the restless ocean. The first liner fitted with this beneficial apparatus was the famous* ***KAISER WILHELM DER GROSSE*** *in 1900. After the* ***KAISER WILHELM DER GROSSE*** *had demonstrated in a very convincing manner, the serviceability of the invention on board in connection with oceanic navigation other vessels in the running for trans-Atlantic patronage were compelled to follow suit. The German flyer was securing a distinct advantage' This sample of propaganda is typical of what had been going on during the years 1902 to 1914. What the author had said about the German attitude in the first part, that they, in straight words were 'copy-cats,' imitators, stealers, (I refer to the claim about* ***IMPERATOR***'s *design) now, suddenly, he declares them to be the first ones, having a 'distinct advantage.'*

"All this may seem trifling, but, we have here the ***TITANIC*** *case to explain, the editorial, I have quoted from the 'Chicago Evening Post.'*

"The reader will have the feeling by now, that Germany's *'astute' move at the Radio Conference had been to safeguard an invention that was theirs. But, British hegemony in shipping and naval affairs did not like that idea, that the enemy of the future had his own wireless system. Could, possibly, compete. The Russian fleet at Tsushima was condemned to death from the start, but the British 'experts' could not do enough to blame 'Telefunken' for its destruction. One is right to assume that the rivalry reached down to the operators on board. We have from those years a good number of 'clippings' telling of mischievous messages, sent to 'razzle' the other fellow. Then, without the regulations that the 'Chicago Evening Post' demanded (all American and Continental European papers were in unison to demand such regulations) had it not been many a time that passengers, especially after some party at night had sent messages into the*

air for the fun of it? Has it? Paid for, of course!

"That night, Norddeutscher Lloyd's *steamship* **FRANKFURT,** *a 7400 ton, immigrant and cargo carrier, on her return trip from Baltimore to Bremen was approximately 24 miles from the* **TITANIC. TITANIC**'s *wireless operator, before the U.S. Senate, testified, that by the strength of her signals he thought her to be the nearest ship. At about the same distance from* **TITANIC** *lay the Leyland liner* **CALIFORNIAN.** *That ship lay still, on account of ice. It lay there till next morning, daybreak. (Yet with that much ice,* **TITANIC** *on her 'imperative schedule' ploughed with 21 knots through the ocean, because, she was an unsinkable ship.)*

"The wireless operator of **CALIFORNIAN** (*with* 'S*teamship Conquest*'s *superior wireless service') had gone to sleep, until next morning. But aboard the 'Teuton'* s*hip, with her 'inferior' wireless service, the operator was on duty. He was not a green boy on an adventure trip; like every German in charge of an important service, he was a man of long training and responsibility. As soon as he had received* **TITANIC'**S *CQD, he brought it to the captain. (The following is recorded in the German journal 'Überall,' a monthly magazine for Army and Navy affairs, based upon the investigations in the U.S.A., in Britain, and the German See-Amt hearing of the* **FRANKFURT.** *That report, in 'Überall' is a pretty fair, unbiased report, without any accusations, compared to the critical time). The Captain of the* **FRANKFURT** *at once set course to the stated location, he gave orders to 'BAKE BREAD and BREAK OUT BLANKETS' (hear that!). HE GOT THE BOAT CREWS ON DECK. Travelling with his best speed through the ice he should reach the scene in about 2 hours. But, there was nothing said about* **TITANIC,** *if she was hurt, not a word, that she was sinking. She might still be steaming ahead, she could by the time* **FRANKFURT** *reached her, be farther away from the scene than* **FRANKFURT** *had been. The captain had a great responsibility. His firm, Norddeutscher Lloyd, has a shining record of savings from the perils of the sea. The most shining one, when NDL*'s **FULDA** *saved the whole crew and all the passengers of Cunard*'s **OREGON**, *saving 880 people, delaying her arrival at New York for 16 hours. Cabled, what claims the NDL made, the answer was: 'Highly gratified having been instrumental in saving so many lives. No claim.'*

"Such, then, were the men, such were the preparations. To keep in touch with **TITANIC** *and her eventual new position, the captain ordered the operator to reach* **TITANIC** *and ask for that information.* **FRANKFURT** *received a curt 'Y.A.A.F' [You Are A Fool].*

"You understand now what 'Chicago Evening Post' meant in its editorial.

*"***FRANKFURT** *had all cause to believe that this had been some hoax, and that there was enough to write into their log without again being told… "YAAF."*

"The testimony has taught us that even the wireless, the wonderful instrument for lessening the perils of the sea, may become in unworthy hands an instrument for capitalizing human agony instead of alleviating it. The men aboard **TITANIC** *strove to have a British ship coming to help, although Phillips (***TITANIC**'s *wireless operator, who had told* **FRANKFURT** *'YAAF') felt certain that* **FRANKFURT** *was much nearer than* **CARPATHIA** *with which communication had been established.*

"Such seeds, as sown in books and magazines, had come to bear fruits.

"The full brunt of Britain's *anger fell upon an innocent man, Captain Lord of the* **CALIFORNIAN.** *The chairman of the British investigation committee branded his attitude with scorching words. And, those book writers, film producers, felt, under that indictment, safe to use even 44 years later, those same indictments, to further their own low capitalization of the tragedy, they even proclaim those products as 'the fruits of painstaking research of many years.'*

"Captain Lord, then 78 years old and ailing in his health, was deeply hurt by these mud-rakers. As I have said, that German cobbler spoke that the sun would bring it to light. Perhaps, these were the thoughts

of Captain Lord.

ᔕ

"After that, there is one more thought. Mr. J. Bruce Ismay.

"In all my recordings of shipping I have always tried to keep the 'MAN' behind the ships in focus, because, no shipping firm is anything unless we consider its leader. I have always been a bit wary of the 'father-to-son' rule in a shipping firm, although my most admired firm, the firm R. C. Gribel, of Stettin, is now for 185 years in a father-to-son succession. My *wariness rests on the thought that a stern father very likely leaves an intimidated son.* A *successor with some 'weak strain' within him. As much I have observed Mr. Ismay, there was no weak strain, but, there was a feeling of responsibility, a duty that underwent severe strain when White Star Line came under American domination, his family being practically rubbed out. Here, then, we have a son, who tried to be able to stand before his father, his stern father, and confess: 'I have tried to keep my inheritance clean and proud. I have not faltered, when the favours of our British people were against me; because, their minds were befogged by unreasonable demands and war-mongering psychosis. I have not given up leadership, but have tried to find another glorious epoch in shipping, as you, in your start, in 1871 had given the British people by introducing White Star Line's superior class of ships. And in doing that, I always have had in mind the hope that by some change of conditions. White Star Line might return to full ownership under the Ismay name. But, you had the British people behind you, and in a sober mind; I had to deal with Americans who did not care of old traditions, and British people that had become disturbed by politics. Both parties expected me to find the remedy... the remedy for something I had not brought about. In your days, a good ship, well built, meant success; in my days, requirements went beyond what shipbuilders could furnish...'*

THE END

Author Frederick A. Talbot's *Steamship Conquest of the World,* one of his *Conquests of Science* series, was published in 1912, by J. B. Lippincott Company, Philadelphia, and William Heinemann, London. Wilhelm Müller took exception, as did his countrymen, to Talbot's freehanded accusations that all of Germany's great liners had been copied from the British, that wireless telegraphy had been invented by Guglielmo Marconi alone, that Germans were "copycats." *"It will be remarked,"* wrote TalB.O.T. in his final chapter. *Why Germany Builds Her Liners, "that the Germans have followed slavishly in British footsteps, but this is only in accordance with Teuton traditions. The German is a magnificent copyist, but a poor pioneer."*

Is it then any wonder that Bill Müller felt compelled to answer Talbot's accusations, or that Talbott's book did fan the flames of already- raging anti-English feelings in Germany?

Bill Müller was an especially important ***TITANIC*** survivor because in 1912 he was nineteen years old and a seaman. He therefore had special knowledge which enabled him to be more aware of what was going on that night than the average passenger would have been. The only survivors left in 1989 were those who had been children when ***TITANIC*** sank, all passengers, most of them female. Unfortunately I was the only ***TITANIC*** researcher to interview Bill, and my deepest regret is that we lived so far apart that I could not see him... again... and again. Bill was a walking encyclopedia of the old ships, and when I asked him why he replied simply, *"Ships were my life."* Bill's career in the German Navy in World War I was a book in itself, he chuckled when he told me that, and I wanted to write it. He passed away two years later, not quite reaching the century mark for which he was striving, and all I had of him were the tapes of our interviews. The questions I should have asked, so many thoughts of too late, could never be answered. Bill's daughter was kind enough to send me a duplicate copy of Bill's ***TITANIC*** article, which you have just read almost in its entirety, printed with Bill's permission, given before he passed away. She knew little of his early life, however. There were no old photos of Bill, unfortunately for in his nineties he was still tall and straight, with twinkling clear blue eyes. Typically Teutonic, he must have been a fine looking young man. I would have liked a photograph of him in one of his uniforms. Unlike most descendants of other ***TITANIC*** survivors. Bill's offspring did not want to talk about him, or the ***TITANIC***. They wanted absolutely no publicity, nor had Bill himself sought publicity, further proof that he was not a hoaxster seeking the limelight.

On 9 April, 1912, the day before sailing, Hettema and Müller had been in London. Müller had gone to the White Star office to make the final arrangements for their passage in ***TITANIC***. They were, in airline parlance, "non revenue" passengers, meaning their trip was "on the house," at Ismay's invitation. They were assigned adjacent cabins on B deck, port side forward. On sailing day they took the boat train to Southampton where they boarded ***TITANIC*** about an hour before departure. When I asked Bill to name a ship or two that he remembered seeing in port that day I expected him to name American Line's ***NEW YORK***, the ship which had been pulled from her moorings as ***TITANIC*** passed her, and the ship which anyone might have named because that story is so well known and is mentioned in every ***TITANIC*** book. If Bill had been a hoaxster I expected him to name ***NEW YORK***. To my surprise Bill mentioned ***EDINBURGH CASTLE***, a Union Castle liner running to Cape Town, built by Harland & Wolff. Checking *Lloyd's Weekly Shipping Index*, ***EDINBURGH CASTLE*** was indeed in Southampton on 10 April. It should not have surprised me that Bill would notice her. He was especially interested in Harland & Wolff vessels. This yard not only built the prettiest ships to come out of Britain, it had built many of the early German liners. At that time I did not know of Bill's interest in the ***WARATAH***, and other liners running to South Africa. Nor should it have surprised me that when I asked Bill directly about the incident with ***NEW YORK*** his reply was a shrug and a reply typical of a professional seaman. *"I heard about it,"* said Bill. *"We were below then."* But only passengers would have been topside waving goodbye to friends on the pier. Hettema and Müller were working. And the ***NEW YORK*** incident has been blown up out of all proportion to its significance. To a sailor, it was all in a day's work, like "losing" an engine is to an airline crew. Passengers love to dramatize.

In his capacity as traffic inspector it was part of Hettema's job to inspect the ship. Müller naturally accompanied his "boss." (He always referred to Hettema as his "boss," and always called him *"Mister* Hettema"). In an astute move to impress the man on whose recommendation investors such as insurance companies, banks, private individuals and even at least one religious institution, would buy shares in Morgan's I.M.M., Ismay assigned a stewardess to show Hettema around the ship. And Ismay naturally picked the prettiest, youngest stewardess on board, Mrs. Lucy Violet Snape. *"See what they choose to show you around, an important man like you... a stewardess!"* Müller teased her rather than Hettema. And he flirted a bit. Lucy, apparently, did her job as assigned, but rejected Bill's shy advances. *"She was the only one I liked in the whole ship,"* Bill told me, *"and she died. When I teased her, she had only two days to live."* Obviously her death still haunted him. He broke down and tears came into his eyes when he told me how, in the lifeboat, they had heard the cries of a woman in the water, cries that became weaker, and weaker, until they were silent. Although he did not say it, it was obvious that he had believed, still believed, that the woman crying so piteously for help which never came, was the stewardess, who had given him as her name only "Gwendolen."

I puzzled over that name for some time. There was no "Gwendolen" on the stewardess manifest, yet Bill's physical description fit Mrs. Snape exactly, even to his saying that "she had good teeth." In fact, Snape's first name was not given until Brian Ticehurst, a founder of the British ***TITANIC*** Society and editor of that organization's newsletter, the *Atlantic Daily Bulletin,* recently unearthed a brief article from the *Surrey Advertiser and County Times* of 20 April, 1912. Further, Mrs. Snape was the youngest stewardess, only three years older than Bill, and very pretty, with a pensive expression in the one photograph extant of her which shows a row of perfect white teeth, in an era when good teeth were rare.

But how might Mrs. Snape, a young widow, be "Gwendolen"?

From my own experience as an airline stewardess I know that it is not unusual to give a persistent passenger a phony name, to get rid of him politely. Before "individual assertiveness" replaced empathetic good manners derived from the Golden Rule, passengers, customers and clients were always treated with polite deference, never antagonized. When Snape was assigned to show Hettema, and his tall, handsome young secretary around the ship, she knew what her job was. She did it, and that was all she was going to do. Perhaps if Bill had not been, as Ismay liked to call him, "that *German* chap," Snape might not have rebuffed him. Or perhaps she sensed his youth, or she rejected him because of her status as widow with child. But why, when Bill asked her name, would she choose *Gwendolen* as a pseudonym?

When I worked as a reservations agent for a Miami-based cruise line I learned that everybody has a "fantasy" name; even men do, surprisingly. We used first names only on the phones, the line's management apparently believing that this created a friendlier atmosphere. Obviously, however, if a newly hired agent had the same first name as one already working the phones then there was only one solution... the new-hire had to choose another name. On the first day of training we were asked to choose two first names other than our own, and it was no problem for any of us. Names came from relatives, from celebrities, and from fictional heroes or heroines. Fantasy names all.

I reasoned that Mrs. Snape, an attractive, obviously intelligent young widow with a baby, who had been married to a sea captain, probably had done a lot of reading while she waited for her husband to come home from the sea. She had lived in Singapore, where she undoubtedly had servants, time on her hands to dream, to romanticize. So I looked for a heroine in a romance novel of the period. I found the perfect match in George Eliot's famous and tragic heroine Gwendolen Harleth from *Daniel Deronda* (William Blackwood and Sons, Edinburgh, 1878) a popular novel of the Victorian-Edwardian period. George Eliot was the pseudonym of late nineteenth century feminist writer Mary Ann (sometimes Marian) Evans whose plots usually revolved around central characters, particularly women, who were forced by circumstances beyond their control to make moral choices and take responsibility for their own lives. Eliot's Gwendolen, like Snape, and Müller's Gwendolen, had light brown hair and blue eyes. Like Snape, Gwendolen Harleth was very pretty, very bright, she wanted to make her own way in the world, and she was a widow at the end of the novel.

If Snape did indeed identify with Eliot's Gwendolen, a Welsh name which means "fair one," there may have been yet another reason for her doing so. All Victorian marriages were not the utopian dream of the modern male, wherein wives were completely submissive and unquestioning of male supremacy. The fictitious Gwendolen Harleth's marriage was extremely unhappy A woman with talent and intelligence that she wanted to use, Harleth was forced by financial circumstances and gender-related restrictions of her era into marriage with an aristocratic, manipulating, abusive husband who had chosen her merely for her beauty, and treated her like any of his other material possessions. When he died, at sea, she was plagued by guilt because she had longed to be free, yet she knew that only if he died could that wish be fulfilled. When he fell overboard from his yacht and called for her help, Gwendolen hesitated for a moment, a moment which was the difference between life and death for him. Perhaps there was such a tragic guilt in Snape's life, in that she, too, longed for freedom but knew it would elude her as long as her husband lived. Perhaps she had had a fleeting moment, or more, when she wished for his death. We can never know. It was an era when marriage was expected, when women were given little choice, when many strong, intelligent women were trapped into roles that stifled their individuality in a world dominated by men. That Lucy Snape was caught in that unhappy, unfulfilling trap was evidenced by her refusal to stay in it after her husband died. She could have chosen to remain at home, with her family and her baby girl, until another "suitable" husband was found, and no doubt even in her circumstances she had many suitors for she was very attractive. Wrote Eliot about her Gwendolen, *"What she was clear about was that she did not wish to lead the same sort of life as ordinary young ladies did; but what she was not clear upon was, how she should set about leading any other, and what were the particular acts which she would assert her freedom by doing."* Eliot might have had her heroine choose a career as a ship's stewardess!

Lucy Violet Leonard had married Captain Lawrence Edward Snape, a British shipmaster commanding vessels which plied Malaysian waters. Stricken with dysentery on a voyage, he had been taken to a hospital near Hong Kong, where he died. Lucy, with their infant daughter, returned to England in December, 1911. Her father, who was employed by Joseph King, MP, used this connection to obtain a position for Lucy as a Second Class stewardess in White Star's new liner ***TITANIC***, although she had no experience at sea, excepting what she might have had as the wife of a master mariner of that era when commanders often took their wives to sea with them. Being a stewardess in a luxury liner was somewhat like being an airline stewardess in the "Golden Age of Aviation," when few had the opportunity, and other women envied their globe-trotting freedom.

And Lucy Snape obviously *chose* to die. As a woman she could have entered a lifeboat. Although she might have been one of the stewardesses turned away by Lightoller, she could have escaped in a boat loaded by any other officer. She is therefore conspicuous by her death, being one of only three stewardesses who perished. It is believed that Mrs. Snape in fact was the stewardess noted by other crew members who personally persuaded many reluctant women passengers to enter lifeboats, thus saving their lives. If Wilhelm Müller had read English romance novels, the fact that Snape had called herself "Gwendolen" would have told him a great deal about her. Perhaps that in itself was her reason for using the pseudonym.

When ***TITANIC*** struck ice it just felt like a "big wave" hit the ship, said Bill. Nothing alarmed him until she stopped, and even then neither he nor Hettema took it seriously, an attitude accepted at first by most passengers, and even by many crew members. As Hettema's employee Bill went to scout around to see what was going on, and returned to report to his boss that orders had been given to don life vests and go to the boat deck. He helped Hettema into a life vest, after both men put on their heaviest clothing. They stuffed a few items into their pockets, but Hettema left most of his cash in the cabin, above that which had been placed in the purser's safe (a fact that worried him not a little while they were in the lifeboat). At that time both men expected to return to their cabins eventually. ***TITANIC*** would be towed to safety, thought Müller, and they would be taken aboard the rescue ship. People were saying they could see a ship's lights only a few miles away.

When they arrived on the boat deck it began to dawn on them how serious the situation was, yet Müller still thought that ***TITANIC*** had not exceeded her floodable length. She was down by the head and passengers were beginning to panic, but Müller was not yet convinced she would founder. He had Hettema to worry about, however. Müller led his boss to the second boat on the port side, the one to which they had been assigned. Captain Smith beckoned to them, no doubt at Ismay's order, and according to Müller, Smith personally placed both men in the lifeboat. In addition to the fact that Ismay felt responsible for Hettema and Müller because he had invited them on the maiden voyage, he wanted Hettema to inform the investors that ***TITANIC*** had been sound in every way, that the collision had been a *force májeure,* something that could not have been avoided. And this Hettema later did. In the boat Bill told ***TITANIC*** crewmen that he was a seaman, and he was assigned an oar. Then, he, too, saw the ship's lights several miles away. It would be over two years, however, before he would come to believe that ship was German… NDL's ***FRANKFURT.***

When he boarded ***CARPATHIA*** Bill looked for Gwen throughout the ship. He had assumed that, being a woman, she would be saved. Her loss precipitated much of the guilt that followed him to his grave, primarily because in the rush of evacuation he had not taken time to look for her.

About two weeks after arriving in New York aboard ***CARPATHIA*** Hettema and Müller returned to England in White Star's ***CEDRIC.*** They stayed briefly in England, then journeyed on to The Netherlands. Later they went to Berlin, where Hettema opened an office and Müller remained as his secretary until the Great War started. Hettema returned to his native country when war became imminent, and Bill lost track of him. He could tell me only that Hettema had come from somewhere around Utrecht, in The Netherlands, and that he was a Frieslander. At that time I knew nothing at all about The Netherlands, and had never heard of Friesland. Through contacts in that country I obtained a list of "Hettemas" and began to write to them. Within my first few letters I received an answer from Cornelis J. Hettema, an amateur genealogist. With a great deal of time and effort, he located Müller's "Boss." Tjietse Hettema had died before World War II, and his only biographer had died in the fifties in an automobile accident. Hettema had spent much time working in England, he was in his mid-forties when he embarked in ***TITANIC,*** and he was a life-long bachelor, which was unfortunate because he left no descendants to facilitate our research. It somewhat explains the "father-son" relationship which Müller said they had, however. Strangely, although Hettema was Protestant, he had willed his entire estate to a Roman Catholic monastery. Probably the monastery was one of the "Dutch religious institutions" which invested heavily in American railroads, including those financed by Pierpont Morgan, and thus invested in Morgan's shipping interests.

The *Boston Globe* of 16 April, 1912, carried an article which stated that ***TITANIC*** had a separate manifest of last minute passengers, which was not produced to make up the official list published in newspapers and books of the period. The *Philadelphia Inquirer* carried a similar article saying that it would never be known just how many people had died because the only complete manifest went down with the ship.

Legend has it that a Liverpool newspaper of the time carried an article about two men who had arrived there in a White Star liner a few weeks after the disaster. White Star officials, says legend, hustled the men away before reporters could interview them. Passengers aboard the ship told reporters that the two men were ***TITANIC*** survivors. This story is discounted on the strange theory that no survivors could have been picked up at sea so long after ***TITANIC*** sank. A search of Liverpool newspapers within the proper time frame given for this legendary article failed to find it. However, it is known that several survivors, those who had arrived in New York the normal way aboard ***CARPATHIA,*** did return in ***CEDRIC,*** but no names have ever been produced from British immigration lists. These were survivors who had testified at the American inquiry, and/or who had

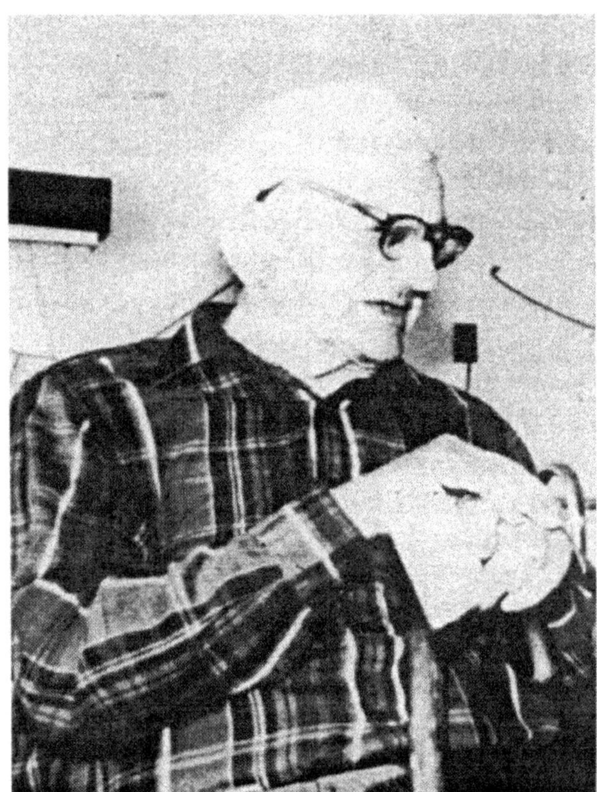

***ABOVE: TITANIC** survivor Wilhelm Müller in 1989. The **TITANIC** 'Establishment' insisted that Müller was a hoax because he was not listed on any of their 'official' passenger manifests. However, the only complete official manifest went down with the ship, according to Bruce Ismay's testimony at the Board of Trade inquiry.*

been hospitalized briefly in New York.

Certainly there have been charlatans who have made false claims about having been in ***TITANIC***, but one of the first ways to spot them is simply that they seek publicity. Neither Hettema nor Müller did, in fact they were ashamed of their survival. Müller did not even tell his family, nor did Hettema tell his apparently. Müller did, however, antagonize the maritime community by his insistence upon "bringing to light" information about ***TITANIC*** that officialdom wanted kept buried. In particular, Müller's insider knowledge of shipping and his friendship with Ismay have been a target of certain members of the ***TITANIC*** establishment, apparently for personal reasons. The fact that Müller lived in virtual seclusion in a rural Canadian village for most of his life made it easy to ignore him. He wrote for the *Belgian Shiplover* only because his friend Alan Deitsch had asked him to, for Deitsch knew well Müller's extensive knowledge of ships and shipping. Müller, a very intelligent man, had little patience with those who did not understand what he wrote.

Two stewardesses, Mrs. Gold and Mrs. Martin, years later told a different story about "two German men" who may have been Hettema and Müller, but their account is about boat number 11, on the starboard side. As this boat pulled away from ***TITANIC***'s side they found the two "Germans' hiding under a seat. One of them did nothing "but cry and moan about his money," the women said. It would have been unusual for an English woman of that era to notice the difference between a German and a Dutch accent. It is entirely possible that the braver story which Bill told me had been his way of compensating, the way of remembering his escape which protected him psychologically, enabling him to carry on with his life. It is also possible that, with anti-German feeling running high in England at that time, the two stewardesses who remembered the two "German men" simply wanted them to appear cowardly and thus embellished their story. We will never know now. Bill did repeat several times, however, that he escaped because it was "his duty" to take care of his "boss," perhaps another way of compensating.

Müller ran into Ismay in London about a year after the ***TITANIC*** disaster. Ismay, said Bill, was "a broken man." This is evidenced by Ismay's self-imposed exile for the rest of his life. Yet here again it would be impossible to blame Ismay personally for the disaster. He made some wrong decisions, but who does not? Ismay really did nothing more, nothing less than any shipowner might have done in similar circumstances. He simply suffered from "maiden voyage euphoria," a syndrome well known to mariners, in this case exacerbated by the phenomenal success of ***TITANIC***'s elder sister ***OLYMPIC***.

Bill Müller never saw Ismay again. Before another year had passed a young German sailor had more important things to take his mind off ***TITANIC***.

Chapter Eight

Sparks Across the Sea

Who invented wireless telegraphy?

If you are Italian, or British, you won't hesitate to answer, perhaps a bit smugly, *"Why, Guglielmo Marconi, of course!"*

But if you're Russian you'll know just as surely that Aleksandr Popov invented radio. If you're German, you might opt for Professor Adolf Slaby, or you might say that Ferdinand Braun was the one who first found a practical way to harness "Hertzian Waves" for the purpose of sending signals, or messages, through the ether from transmitter to receiver. If you're American you might root for Nikola Tesla, the Serbo-Croatian immigrant and "father" of alternating current, who utilized those same "Hertzian Waves" to control his roB.O.T. boats, and who described in detail the principles of wireless telegraphy two years before Marconi began to build his first experimental wireless signaling apparatus. Or, you might call American Dr. Lee de Forest the *"Father of Radio,"* as he titled his autobiography (Wilcox & Follett Co., Chicago, 1950).

TITANIC legend equates wireless telegraphy with Marconi, and he was introduced as the "inventor of wireless" at both the American and British ***TITANIC*** inquiries. Reading the usual ***TITANIC*** books leaves one with the erroneous impression that Marconi was the only provider of shipboard wireless service in 1912, when in fact Marconi's equipment was generally considered, within the industry, inferior to other wireless services, and was aboard fewer vessels than other services. There is no doubt that ***TITANIC***'s survivors owed their lives to Marconi wireless, but there was another side to the wireless story, a far darker side which German deck officer-turned Canadian farmer Wilhelm Müller exposed in his 1962 article for the *Belgian Shiplover,* wherein Müller claimed that ***TITANIC***'s wireless operator had turned away the nearest rescue ship, the Norddeutscher Lloyd emigrant liner ***FRANKFURT*** To correctly interpret Müller's comments, to understand what happened between ***TITANIC***'s senior wireless man, John George "Jack" Phillips, and the German operator aboard ***FRANKFURT,*** it is absolutely necessary to study the worldwide development of wireless communication, the men behind it, the companies which commercialized it and the operators who made it work.

Actually wireless telegraphy and telephony were the culmination of research done by many engineers and scientists, from every major maritime country, over a period of many years. Some of these men preferred to lose themselves in the thrills of extending scientific frontiers rather than becoming involved in the business of commercializing their discoveries; thus their names are known today only in engineering circles. It is beyond the scope of this book to recount the entire achievements of so many… Armstrong, Branly, Braun, Dolbear, Dunwoody, Fessenden, Fleming, Hertz, Hughes, Jackson, Kelvin, Lodge, Marriott, Maxwell, Muirhead, Pickard, Popov, Poulsen, Preece, Pupin, Rathenau, Ruhmkorff, Shoemaker, Slaby, Stone, Strecker, to name only a few. For the sake of brevity only milestones in the histories of the "Big Three" in 1912 marine wireless communication will be discussed, along with pertinent highlights from the careers of some who contributed to the progress of wireless, plus one other, the man who may well have been the first to discover the secrets of wireless communication, but whose name is rarely known today outside professional circles… Nikola Tesla.

Guglielmo Marconi was neither scientist nor engineer. He was an inventor who happened to have the right financial and political connections coupled with tremendous drive and charisma

ABOVE: *Guglielmo Marconi in 1902. (Photographer unknown.)*

which enabled him to commercialize his applications of the discoveries of more learned men.

At the ***TITANIC*** inquiries in America and Britain Guglielmo Marconi testified that the German ***FRANKFURT*** used wireless equipment manufactured under his patents. Marconi further stated that he was on the board of directors of DEBEG, the company that provided ***FRANKFURT***'s wireless service. These statements were made to prove that there was no rivalry between the German and British wireless services, that Marconi and DEBEG operators routinely exchanged messages, thus there could not possibly have been any animosity between the English Marconi operator in the ***TITANIC*** and the German Telefunken-DEBEG operator in the ***FRANKFURT***. Marconi's testimony was never questioned, nor was it elaborated upon. Thus the ***FRANKFURT*** incident was quickly dropped from newspaper reports of the day and has become entirely lost in ***TITANIC*** legend. Marconi's name had become synonymous with wireless telegraphy in Great Britain, due not only to the publicity which he routinely sought for his demonstrations, but also due to such incidents as the dramatic arrest of the notorious wife-murderer Dr. Hawley Harvey Crippen, who fled England in the Canadian Pacific liner ***MONTROSE*** in 1910 and was apprehended through the use of Marconi wireless. A year earlier Marconi operator Jack Binns had garnered a tremendous amount of favorable publicity and become an overnight hero by sticking to his post as White Star's ***REPUBLIC*** sank after collision with the Italian Lloyd liner ***FLORIDA*** off Nantucket. Guglielmo Marconi was handled with great consideration and reverence, especially at the British inquiry where his chief interrogator. Sir Rufus Isaacs, was the brother of the Marconi Company's Managing Director, Godfrey Isaacs. Both Isaacs brothers, plus a third brother, Harry, were at that time caught up in what came to be known as the "Marconi Scandal."

When Marconi indicated that DEBEG used his patents, what he really meant was that he had filed patent infringement lawsuits in every country that had a burgeoning, competitive wireless industry, which of course included Germany. Patent infringement suits go hand in hand with technological development. Winning or losing them, when the subject was such a radically new and rapidly developing technology, often had more to do with an attorney's skill and a judge's lack of technical knowledge than with the prior art claimed by the parties involved. Even when smaller companies, or individuals, had valid patent rights, they often did not have the financial resources to maintain extended legal battles with such a large, financially sound company as Marconi.

On 25 April, 1900, *"The Marconi International Marine Communication Company, Ltd."* was formed as a subsidiary of the parent British Marconi Company The new company's purpose was handling all maritime work of the parent company, except naval contracts.

In 1910 the German Emperor, Wilhelm II, foreseeing the inevitability of war between Germany and England, demanded that all foreign (meaning British) wireless equipment and personnel be taken from German vessels, which included the Hapag and NDL liners built with the expectation of being used as armed cruisers in the event that Germany went to war. On 14 January, 1911, a new company was formed by the amalgamation of the German Telefunken and the Marconi Marine. It was named *"Deutsche Betriebsgesellschaft für Drahtlose Telegraphic,"* and known by its acronym DEBEG, for obvious reasons. DEBEG took over the wireless operations of the entire German mercantile marine. Telefunken, which manufactured the wireless apparatus and equipment used in German ships, held the controlling 55% of the new company's stock, while Marconi Marine held the remaining 45%, and Guglielmo Marconi was given a titular seat on the board of directors.

Theoretically this meant that German ships could now communicate with not only Telefunken but also Marconi shore stations and ships. In fact, DEBEG was a German company, and its personnel, including its marine operators, were German. English operators who had been working in German ships were either out of work, or they displaced more junior men aboard British ships, all of which fueled the already intensely bitter jingoistic rivalry between English and German wireless men. Naturally, the degree of animosity varied from one individual to another. To understand this, it is necessary to know where, why and how the animosity began and what motivated its perpetuation.

The Beginning

Ferdinand Braun was born on 6 June, 1850, in Fulda county seat of the Electorate of Hesse-Kassel, where his father, Johann Conrad Braun, was a civil servant. The fifty-one year old Johann and his thirty-three year old wife, Franzisca, had been married for twelve years. They would have altogether seven children, Ferdinand being their sixth child and youngest son. According to the custom of the time, the Brauns raised their sons in Johann's Protestant religion, while the daughters were brought up in Franzisca's Roman Catholic faith.

In the spring of 1856, the same year that Nikola Tesla was born, Ferdinand began attending the Lutheran elementary school in Fulda. He was a good and serious student, a pleasure for his teachers. In 1859 Ferdinand matriculated at the Fulda Gymnasium, as his four brothers had done before him. Johann Conrad worked day and night, serving as his own secretary to provide educations for his boys, and dowries for his girls.

Young Ferdinand soon proved to be gifted in mathematics and science. One of his teachers was Dr. Wilhelm Gies, who had taught several boys who became professors at the University of Marburg. Gies recognized Braun's talents, and encouraged him to plan for studying at Marburg, too. Gies was very much interested in the science of crystallography and this no doubt influenced Braun to begin experiments which would eventually lead to his discovery of a crystal detector receiver for use in wireless telegraphy. By the summer of 1865 the fifteen year old Braun was skilled enough to write a textbook on the subject, which he illustrated himself. Shortly before his eighteenth birthday Braun graduated, with A's in mathematics, physics, history and religion, with B's in Greek, Latin and French.

Following his favorite professor's advice, Ferdinand entered the University of Marburg that fall. Franz Melde, also a former student of Dr. Gies, was the Director of the Mathematics and Physics Institute at Marburg. At this point in his life Ferdinand Braun had no plan for his future beyond his father's wish for him to become a high school teacher. Perhaps Fate chose him to combine Dr. Gies' interest in crystallography with Franz Melde's interest in acoustics, for both were important to the development of wireless telegraphy and telephony.

After two semesters at Marburg, Ferdinand felt ready to move upward. He chose the University of Berlin, which was the top scientific school in Germany, but very expensive for poor Johann Conrad, who could barely afford to keep his sons at Marburg. As the older boys graduated and shared incomes from their chosen careers, Herr Braun was able to finance two semesters at Berlin, after which he expected Ferdinand to return to Marburg and prepare for the security of a teaching career.

In Berlin, Braun studied under such well-known physicists as Georg Hermann Quincke and Gustav Magnus, both of whom were greatly impressed by the young man's talented brilliance. In December, 1869, Professor Quincke offered the nineteen year old Braun an assistantship in a new physics laboratory which later became part of the Technical University of Berlin. This relieved the elder Braun of some of his financial burden and allowed Ferdinand to continue his specialized studies. On 23 March, 1872, Ferdinand received his doctorate in philosophy. In September of that same year his name first appeared in a research journal when a paper based on his doctoral dissertation was published in *Annalen der Physik und Chemie.* Less than a month later Professor Quincke accepted the Chair of Physics at the prestigious University of Würzburg, and took Braun with him as his assistant.

At Würzburg Braun began to use his natural talent for satirical writing to supplement his small salary. He submitted poetry and articles to various publications under several pseudonyms, yet found time for his research and scientific papers. Quincke's special interest was in the capillary properties of fused substances, while Braun became engrossed in the study of fused salts.

Under Quincke's tutelage Braun matured and began to gain scientific recognition. His salary, however, was still not enough to give him complete independence from his family. After two years at Würzburg Braun accepted a position as teacher of mathematics and science at a Gymnasium in Leipzig. He had finally focused on a goal… he would be a university professor.

It was about this time that Braun's experiments with crystals led to the discovery of the rectification effect (that the magnitude of the flow of the electrical current through certain compounds depends upon the polarity of the voltage imposed upon them rather than following Ohm's Law which stated that the current flowing through a given resistance is equal to the voltage divided by the resistance) which in turn led to the development of transistors and many other devices which are used in modern, solid-state electronics. Braun's first report *On the Conduction of Electrical Currents Through Metal Sulfides* was published in the *Annalen der Physik und Chemie* in 1874, the same year that Guglielmo Marconi was born. It would be almost three decades before Braun's discoveries would be recognized and certain metals and crystals would be utilized as detectors of the electromagnetic waves used for wireless signaling.

In the spring of 1875 Braun passed his probationship at Leipzig and received a permanent position. By the end of the year he had two more promotions, along with much praise from his students who were always delighted by Braun's droll sense of humor and interesting approach to lessons. Otto Spamer, a leading publisher of science books, asked Braun to write a book on mathematics for Spamer's series *New Library for Youth and the Home.* It was just the sort of challenging project that Braun found irresistible, and his book, expanded to include all of the natural sciences, received excellent reviews.

In September of 1877 Braun moved back to Marburg, where he accepted the newly established post of Associate Professor of Physics. Fourteen months later the eighty-year-old Johann Conrad passed away, leaving all of his sons well-educated, with promising careers. Ferdinand was rapidly making a name for himself in European scientific circles. In 1878 he achieved further recognition from his paper showing that British physicist William Thomson (later Lord Kelvin) had erred in his 1851 theory on computing electromagnetic force.

In 1880 Braun was tempted by the challenge of building a new physics department at the University of Strasbourg. Here he began his lectures on magnetism, electrostatics, galvanism, the properties of heat and light, and other topics in theoretical physics. He continued his various experiments, and often proved errors in long-accepted theories. In 1883, when he was not quite thirty-three years old, Braun was appointed to a full professorship at the Technical University of Karlsruhe. One of the men who had recommended him for the post was his old professor and friend, Quincke. At Karlsruhe Braun advocated the introduction of a new department to teach electrical engineering. More and more cities, factories and railways were converting to electricity for light and heat, recognizing it as safer and more efficient than gas. The need for specialized studies in electrical engineering had been endorsed by Wemer Siemens, of the new firm of Siemens and Halske. The Prussian Government had begun to share Siemens' views, and Braun easily won a subsidy of 2,000 marks to establish the special courses, along with the necessary laboratory which featured a dynamo manufactured by Siemens and Halske.

In the spring of 1885 Braun moved once more, this time to the Chair of Physics at the University of Tübingen, another challenge that appealed to him, for the university's Physics Institute needed much improvement. In May of the same year Braun married Amalie Bühler, a niece by marriage of Dr. Carl Engler, professor of chemical engineering at Karlsruhe. Heinrich Hertz moved into Braun's old rooms at Karlsruhe.

While he supervised construction of a new laboratory, Braun chafed at his limited facilities. He returned to his youthful interest in crystallography which required little space for experiments. One of Braun's studies during this period concerned the electrical properties of ordinary rock salt. On 20 May, 1887, Braun's paper containing the first description of his *electrometer*, or electrostatic voltmeter, appeared in *Annalen.* Although such instruments had been in use for some time, Braun was the first to design a practical, relatively inexpensive machine, and he was the first to calibrate his machine in volts.

Wilhelm I died in 1888, and his son Friedrich III, married to Queen Victoria's namesake daughter, inherited the Prussian throne. Friedrich had been suffering horribly with throat cancer, and in just 99 days his failing health forced him to abdicate in favor of his son, who became Wilhelm II. This was a momentous year in German science, too. Not only was Tubingen's new Physics Institute finally opened after two and a half years of construction, but it was also the year of Heinrich Hertz's history-making discovery.

In 1873 Scotland's James Clerk Maxwell had postulated the existence of electromagnetic vibrations above and below visible light. Fifteen years later Hertz tested Maxwell's theory by connecting two ends of a coil of wire to the opposite sides of a gap, across which a spark would jump when he pressed his transmitter key, which had been connected to a high voltage source. A similar coil of wire was placed several yards away from the transmitter, and it was attached to a much smaller spark gap which acted as a receiver. When the longer spark jumped across the transmitter gap, a tiny spark also jumped across the receiving gap, indicating that energy applied to the transmitter had been radiated in the form of electromagnetic waves to the receiver.

Braun completed his treatise *On Continuous Conduction of Electricity Through Gases* in October of 1893. In the following year Hermann von Helmholtz died, leaving the Chair of Physics open at the University of Strasbourg. Again Braun moved. Strasbourg's railroad station had been one of the first in Germany to be lighted by Nikola Tesla. The city was, in 1895, among the first to replace its direct current power station with Tesla's alternating current. The University's electrical engineers were eager to utilize the new system.

Braun's experiments that year were overshadowed by Röntgen's discovery of X-rays. Wilhelm Konrad Röntgen used an experimental device first constructed by physicist Julius Plücker in Bonn in 1858, the first cathode ray tube. It had been merely a curiosity displayed at local fairs and investigated by a number of scientists, including Hertz, until Braun invented the cathode-ray oscilloscope, which he first demonstrated on 15 February, 1897, and which was the direct ancestor of our television picture tube. During Braun's lifetime there would be many versions of the cathode-ray oscilloscope manufactured, and many men, including Tesla, would attempt to prove priority in patents. But Braun never patented the device, and his reasoning for not doing so apparently lay in his scientist's point of view. Because he wanted every scientist to be able to use it, Braun published such an exact description of his cathode-ray oscilloscope that anyone could build it.

From the middle of the nineteenth century when Samuel F. B. Morse's electric telegraph replaced visual semaphore signaling, the best scientific minds in the world had worked to transmit Morse's signals without wires. In 1842 Morse had observed that signals continued to be transmitted for sometime after one of his underwater cables broke. In 1895 and 1896 Dr. Karl Strecker, working for the German Post Office, continued experiments in conduction telegraphy which had originated in the German Navy. Strecker's work inspired Braun to make his own attempts at wireless signaling. In Britain William Preece, and in Germany Erich Rathenau were also working to send signals through water. This would obviously be useful only for communication between ships, and from ships to stations built close to a shoreline. One as yet unsolved problem was that of superimposing detectable signals on the high-frequency electromagnetic waves. Hertz had used a spark gap as his detector, but in 1890 Edouard Branly in Paris found that metal filings encased in a glass tube could be changed from high to low resistance by electromagnetic waves passing through them. Branly's device consisted of a small-diameter glass tube, with metal plugs in each end, which contained loosely packed metal filings. Electromagnetic waves passing through the tube caused the filings to "cohere," or pack tightly together. After each signal the detector had to be tapped to separate the filings and restore the high resistance. British scientist Oliver Lodge named Branly's device a "coherer," although Branly preferred to call it a *radioconducteur,* which was one of the first instances of the use of the word *radio* in connection with wireless communication.

The effects of Branly's coherer had been observed and studied by many scientists, including Braun. In 1894 Lodge attached the clapper of an electric bell to a coherer so that the passage of electromagnetic waves through the metal filings would cause the bell to ring. The clapper then struck the tube, shaking the metal particles into their original loose state, ready to receive another electromagnetic wave which would again *cohere* them. The Russians would later base their claims to the invention of radio on Alecksandr Popov's paper *On the Relation of Metallic Powders to Electrical Oscillations,* written in 1895, and his *Apparatus for the Detection and Recording of Electrical Oscillations,* written in 1896. Popov had utilized Lodge's adaption of Branly's coherer in his experiments.

While Braun was steadily climbing in the esteem of Europe's scientific community, a fey, darkly handsome Serbo-Croatian boy named Nikola Tesla was beginning his education in the city of Gospic in Yugoslavia. Born on the stroke of midnight between the 9th and 10th of July, 1856, in the village of Smiljan, province of Lika, in Croatia, Nikola was the fourth child of the Reverend Milutin Tesla and his wife, Duka Mandic. The Teslas were Serbian, an ethnic minority in Croatia. Reverend Tesla presided over the Serbian Orthodox Church which stood next door to the tiny house in which Nikola was born.

When Nikola was six years old his family moved to Gospic, where he started to school. He was an exemplary student who was already displaying the genius for invention that would one day make him famous. Nikola inherited a talent for writing poetry from his father, while from his mother came a prodigious memory which would allow him to keep plans in his head until he had finished building his inventions. Later Tesla would write that his mother was "an inventor of the first order." He was sure that she would have achieved great things, if she had not been so remote from life's opportunities.

Even Nikola's excellence in the study of languages was surpassed by his amazing skill in mathematics. His genius for inventing seemed to stem from his strange psychic powers, which often plagued him until in later years he began to understand and deliberately utilize them. To this day many of Tesla's accomplishments are not understood by orthodox science. When he was still only a child Tesla became excited by reading about Niagara Falls in far-off America. A vision in which he saw a big wheel driven by the thunderous power of the waterfall convinced him that he would one day go to America and harness that unlimited power.

Tesla was ten years old when he entered the Gymnasium of Gospic, which had a Department of Physics. All of his life he would suffer from bouts with mysterious, severely debilitating ailments. One such illness interrupted his early schooling but it did not stop his insatiable desire for reading, which sustained him until he was well enough to continue his formal studies. By now he had found a new interest... electricity.

In 1875 Tesla enrolled in the Austrian Polytechnic School at Graz, to study physics, mathematics and mechanics. He had a fellowship from the Military Frontier Authority, which paid his tuition for the two years of study that Tesla was determined to cram into one, but at the end of this year the Authority was abolished and Tesla lost his funding. His clergyman father could not afford the tuition, and Tesla had to make the most of what little time he had in this school. It was apparently here that he first conceived the idea of an alternate to the direct current then generated by the world's few electrical power plants.

When his money ran out Tesla turned to gambling. He became skilled at billiards, but his card playing was less than good, and he had to turn to his mother for the necessary funds to go to Prague. There he spent two years, and may have gone to the university unofficially. There is no record of his enrollment in any of Czechoslovakia's universities.

In 1879 he tried to find a job in Maribor. When his quest for employment failed Tesla returned home. His father died that year, and Nikola returned to Prague. Margaret Cheney, author of *Tesla, Man Out of Time,* (Dorset Press, New York, 1981) believes that he remained in Prague, studying in the library and auditing courses, keeping up with the progress of electrical engineering and physics until he was twenty-four years old. Self-teaching would not be unusual in one with such genius as Tesla possessed.

In 1881, through the help of a friend of his uncle, Tesla got a job in the Central Telegraphy Office of the Hungarian Government at Budapest. It was only a drafting position, with very low pay, but Tesla threw himself into his work so industriously that he was soon stricken with another severely debilitating and mysterious ailment, which his doctors finally named a nervous breakdown. The malady caused Tesla's hearing to become so sensitive that even a fly lighting on a table in his room caused a dull thud in his ear. Tesla's senses had always been abnormally acute, but now he claimed to hear the ticking of a watch from three rooms away. His pulse fluctuated wildly, and he trembled uncontrollably.

His physicians, who were naturally intrigued yet helpless before Tesla's bizarre symptoms, gave up, and with the aid of a close friend, Anital Szigety, Tesla decided to manage his own cure. Szigety, who was a master mechanic and an athlete, saw to it that Tesla exercised, and together they took long walks through the city until Tesla's health returned. Legend has it that during one of these long walks with Szigety the solution to producing alternating current came to Tesla "like a flash of lightning." In a frenzy of creativity he seized a stick and drew in the dust a diagram of the motor that he would exhibit six years later in an address before the American Institute of Electrical Engineers.

Alternating current had been used to power arc lights as early as 1878 by Elihu Thomson in the United States. European scientists Lucien Gaulard and John Nixon Gibbs had produced the first AC transformer, to which George Westinghouse had bought American rights, but Tesla was the first to produce a successful, simple and commercially feasible AC motor. In time almost all electricity in the world would be generated and distributed by means of the Tesla Polyphase System, which could produce higher voltages carried over longer distances than Edison's direct current system. Edison's light bulbs could use either alternating or direct current, but Edison himself was totally devoted to maintaining direct current transmission.

In 1882 Tesla's inventions were still largely in his head. He had come out of his latest illness robust and eager to work in his chosen field. Tall, handsome, with thick, wavy black hair crowning a finely-chiseled but pale face in which burned the piercing eyes of genius, Tesla was an imposing figure when family friends got him a job with Edison's telephone subsidiary in Paris. Here he tried to convince Continental Edison Company officials of the enormous benefits of alternating current, only to be told of Edison's strong personal aversion to the subject.

Although blind to his suggestions, Tesla's employers placed enough confidence in the young Serb to assign him the task of troubleshooting Edison's power plants in France and Germany. In Alsace on his first job, Tesla built his first AC motor.

In 1883 Tesla was sent to Strasbourg, with the understanding that he would receive a substantial bonus if he could fix the railroad station's lighting plant after the German Government had refused to accept it when a chunk of the station's wall had been blown out by a short circuit during the opening ceremony. Tesla, whose engineering abilities were matched by his fluency in the German language, made friends as quickly as he repaired the power plant. But when he returned to Paris to collect his bonus his superiors denied it and the angry Tesla resigned. The plant manager, Charles Batchelor, urged Tesla to go to America, which Tesla had wanted to do since childhood anyway. Batchelor and Edison had worked closely together, improving Bell's first telephone, and installing the first self-contained marine lighting plants for ships, so Batchelor felt that he knew Edison well enough to give Tesla the necessary letter of introduction. Tesla's long journey got off to a bad start when he lost all of his money and his tickets. He managed to talk his way aboard ship when nobody claimed the berth he had originally booked. He arrived in America with a few coins, some poems and articles he had written, and drawings of his design for a flying machine. He was twenty-eight years old.

Thomas Alva Edison, only four years older than Tesla, had by this time opened his Machine Works, a generating station on Pearl Street which served all of Wall Street and the East River area, and a big research laboratory at Menlo Park, New Jersey. The Pearl Street station supplied direct current to individual mansions as well as individual plants in mills, factories and theaters located all over New York City. In addition Edison was accumulating more and more contracts for lighting ships. The Inman Line's Blue Riband winner ***CITY OF BERLIN*** had been the first Atlantic liner fitted with electric lights when a small generator and six lamps were installed in 1878.

The first mansion illuminated by electricity belonged to John Pierpont Morgan, who had financed Edison's original enterprise in 1878, The Edison Electric Illuminating Company. In 1882 Pierpont's "Drexel, Morgan and Company" had become the first Wall Street office to be served by the Pearl Street Station.

When Tesla arrived in New York on a steamy summer day in 1884 Edison was juggling numerous complaints, which included demands from the Cunard Line that ***SS OREGON***'s broken dynamos must be repaired at once because the ship made no money while she remained in port. When two crossed wires ignited wall hangings in the Vanderbilt mansion on Fifth Avenue, a hysterical Mrs. Cornelius Vanderbilt, who had posed for a photographic portrait in costume as the "Spirit of Electricity" the previous year, demanded that the whole Edison installation be removed from her home immediately. As if this was not enough, a poorly wired junction box at the comer of Ann and Nassau Streets had emitted a shock which was said to have tossed a ragman and his horse into the air, much to the astonishment of nearby pedestrians. Into this chaos walked Tesla. He presented his introductory letter from Batchelor, and Edison promptly sent him to repair ***OREGON***'s dynamos. By dawn the next day Tesla had them working, and the new Cunard flyer resumed her tight sailing schedule.

Although Edison seems to have appreciated Tesla's skill and knowledge, their opposing views on alternating versus direct current would eventually cause an irreparable rift between them. First,

ABOVE LEFT: *Nikola Tesla, electrical engineer and inventor. (From the Dictionary of American Portraits, Dover Publications 1967.)*

ABOVE RIGHT: *Thomas Alva Edison, inventor. (From the Dictionary of American Portraits, Dover Publications 1967.)*

however, Tesla suggested ways to improve Edison's direct current dynamos. Edison offered Tesla a $50,000 bonus if he could do it. As usual, Tesla threw himself into the project, working night and day for almost a year. When he had successfully completed the assignment he asked for his bonus. Edison fell forward openmouthed, leaned on his desk, and stared in mock surprise. *"Tesla,"* he said, *"you don't understand our American humor!"* (Edison's supporters tell a different version of this anecdote. Tesla offered Edison his patents, they say, for the sum of $50,000, and Edison refused.)

Rejecting Edison's compromise offer of a raise in salary from $18 to $28 per week, Tesla angrily resigned, just as he had when cheated out of his bonus in Paris. The Wizard of Menlo Park surely recognized Tesla's threat to his direct current system. Edison's antipathy for alternating current probably came from the simple fact that he could not understand it. Few engineers understood AC at the time, and Edison was no engineer. He must have been aware of Tesla's superior intellect and understanding of the principles behind all of Edison's experiments, which the Wizard himself lacked. Tesla once commented that Edison would search long and hard for something that a little calculation could have told him immediately. Or perhaps Batchelor's introductory letter put a chip on Edison's shoulder from the beginning. Batchelor had written *simply, "I know two great men, and you are one of them. The other is this young man."*

Tesla had already achieved a reputation which attracted investors. He jumped at the chance to form a company under his own name, believing that at last his alternating current would be presented to the world to benefit mankind everywhere. His backers had other interests. Improved arc lights for streets and factories would produce profits, never mind benefits to mankind.

The "Tesla Electric Light Company" was headquartered at Rahway, New Jersey, with a branch office in New York City. Tesla immediately developed an arc lamp which was simpler, more reliable, safer and more economical than those currently in use. The system was promptly patented, and the first new lights were installed on the streets of Rahway. Tesla was supposed to receive shares of stock for his new patent, but instead he learned how American financiers treated inventors... acquire the patents, then throw away the person whose hard work and inventive genius had won them. The same harsh lesson would be learned by another American closely associated with the development of wireless telegraphy... Lee de Forest.

In 1886 the United States was in the grip of a severe depression, which ended Tesla's budding company. He was forced to labor on New York City's work gangs in order to survive. Four years had passed since Tesla had built his first AC motor. In America he had obtained nine patents for which he had received no remuneration, and now he was as poor as when he had first set foot on American soil.

Always impeccably dressed and aristocratic in appearance despite his financial straits, Tesla stood out like one of his own arc lights among the workmen in his crew. The foreman recognized him and took him to meet A. K. Brown, manager of the Western Union Telegraph Company. Brown was also interested in alternating current, and with his help a new Tesla company was formed, with the specific goal of developing the AC system that Tesla had first conceived in Budapest in 1882. The Tesla Electric Company, which opened in April, 1887, with a capital of $500,000, had its laboratory and shops at 33-35 South Fifth Street, just a few blocks from Edison's workshops.

George Westinghouse, inventor of the railroad air brake, had operated his first commercial alternating current system in Buffalo in 1886, using the Gaulard-Gibbs patents, but Westinghouse had no practical AC motor. Like Tesla, Westinghouse had long dreamed of harnessing the tremendous power of Niagara Falls. They were a natural team. Within two months Tesla had filed his first AC patents, and by 1891 he had acquired a total of forty patents, all so original that he met with no delays in obtaining them. Cornell University Professor of Electrical Engineering William A. Anthony spoke out in favor of Tesla's AC system, and saw to it that the Serbian immigrant, with no university degree, was invited to lecture before the prestigious American Institute of Electrical Engineers, on 16 May, 1888. Tesla's address became a classic and he was delighted to discover that he enjoyed lecturing.

The extraordinarily handsome Tesla had also begun to enjoy a place in New York's high society. Although not affluent, he behaved and dressed as if he were, and indeed his financial prospects should have been excellent. As one of the city's more promising and attractive bachelors, Tesla made the famed "400" party circuit his home. Anne Morgan, the spirited young daughter of Pierpont Morgan, found Tesla interesting. But, as society would later whisper about Anne, so Tesla's detractors began to whisper about his possible homosexuality. Tesla's many eccentricities and apparent celibacy only fueled the fire of gossip.

Reluctantly Tesla put the high life of New York City behind him and moved to Pittsburgh to work as a consultant for Westinghouse. On 30 July, 1891, Tesla became a United States citizen, an achievement he seemed to prize more highly than any of his numerous scientific honors. In September of the same year, having completed his assignment at Pittsburgh, Tesla returned to New York for a brief stay, then sailed for Paris to attend the International Exposition there before going on to Croatia. Collapsing once more from exhaustion, he rested with his widowed mother until he was able to regain his health and vigor.

Meanwhile, the battle of the currents had begun. Edison, enraged by the Tesla-Westinghouse AC system, demonstrated for reporters the dangers of alternating current by using it to gruesomely electrocute neighborhood pets, collected by small boys who were paid 25 cents a head for dogs and cats. On one occasion Charles Batchelor received a severe shock while trying to hold a struggling puppy on the sheet of metal to which wires were attached from an AC generator producing a current of 1,000 volts.

An Edison laboratory assistant named Harold P. Brown managed by subterfuge to buy a permit to use Tesla's AC patents without revealing his intended purpose. Brown then went to Sing Sing Prison and persuaded authorities to "Westinghouse" condemned murderers rather than hanging them. "Professor" Brown took Edison's sadistic show on the road, electrocuting a number of calves and large dogs to prove that Tesla's alternating current was dangerous to have in the home. On 6 August, 1890, the first condemned murderer to be electrocuted with alternating current was William Kemmler. Our electric chairs today, then, are direct descendants of the War of the Currents between Edison and Tesla.

Tesla's scientific and commercial reputation, however, was firmly established on both sides of the Atlantic by this time. Financial battles, waged by bankers who wanted to gain complete control of the new "age of electricity," retarded the advancement of scientific discoveries. Some of the men who invested in electrical companies would go on to invest in wireless telegraphy, among them J. P. Morgan and John Jacob Astor, two names well known to ***TITANIC*** readers.

Tesla was not the only inventor in financial trouble. So were Edison and Westinghouse. When George Westinghouse needed financing for further experimental projects, the bankers told him that Tesla, with many key patents in his name, was a tremendous liability. Westinghouse found himself in the unenviable position of having to tell Tesla that his polyphase system patents could be preserved for world use only if Tesla sold them to the company for a fraction of their worth. Tesla chose to save Westinghouse and accepted $216,000 for his patents, thereby relinquishing past and future royalties which would have been worth millions of dollars. Tesla returned to the lecture circuit.

During 1891 and 1892 Tesla delivered stunning lectures throughout Europe and America. He kept his audiences spellbound with spectacular demonstrations. Among other props, Tesla used gas-filled tube lights, the forerunners of our fluorescent lights. He never patented them or tried to commercialize them, and it would be another fifty years before someone else did. One of his more puzzling props was a set of wireless lamps, which Tesla moved about the room while they continued to glow. Tesla spoke of running motors without any wires at all, and he was convinced that energy could be transported through space, without wires, free for the taking.

Tesla now improved on Hertz's original spark gap experiments with a series of high-frequency alternators which produced frequencies up to 33,000 cycles per second. From this he developed what is still known as the *Tesla coil,* a device for producing high voltages, still used in one form or another by today's radio and television sets. Tesla thus preceded by several years the first Marconi experiments.

By this time Tesla had become obsessed with the wireless transmission of communication signals. He foresaw not only global, but interplanetary communication. In 1892 Tesla accepted invitations to lecture before the Institute of Electrical Engineers in London, and the Royal Society of Great Britain. He then hurried to Paris, where his audiences were the Société Internationale des Electriciens and the Société Française de Physique. While he was in Paris Tesla received word that his mother was dying. He rushed off to Croatia, reaching home in time to spend the last few hours with her, then once more Tesla collapsed from exhaustion. His full recovery took weeks. In August, 1892, he was well enough to return to New York, embarking at Hamburg in Hapag's ***AUGUSTA VICTORIA***.

In the Spring of 1893 Tesla returned to the lecture circuit. At the Franklin Institute in Philadelphia, and at the National Electric Light Association at St. Louis he described in detail the principles of wireless communication. It was in St. Louis that Tesla made the first public demonstration of wireless communication, which preceded Marconi's 1895 demonstration by two years. When Marconi arrived in London with his first wireless apparatus it was exactly what Tesla had described in his widely-published lectures of 1893, which had been translated into many languages. Marconi would later deny that he had ever read of Tesla's demonstrations. A long and bitter patent war between Marconi and Tesla would not be resolved until 1943, when, eight months after Tesla's death, the United States Supreme Court ruled that he, not Marconi, was the inventor of radio.

On 26 August, 1873, while Ferdinand Braun was beginning to make a name for himself in the German scientific community, and a frail, young Nikola Tesla lay ill in bed, Lee de Forest first saw the light of day in Council Bluffs, Iowa, United States of America, where his father. Dr. Henry Swift De Forest, was pastor of the First Congregational Church.

Three years later Dr. De Forest moved his lovely young wife, the former Anna Robbins, and their three children to Talladega, Alabama, where he became the first administrator of Talladega College, a pioneer school which was the first in the United States to accept students without regard to race, religion or gender. The original Baptist college building had been purchased with money donated by Civil War General Wager Swayne. Talladega thus became the first university open to the many slaves freed by the Civil War. Lee's upbringing in this liberal atmosphere assured that for the rest of his life he would lack the prejudices so common in early twentieth century America.

Lee attended Talladega, where he decided to become a mechanical engineer. He would go to Yale, where a distant cousin of his father had established a scholarship for the De Forest men.

Like Tesla, Lee de Forest (who adopted the small 'd' rather than the capital *"D"* heretofore used in the family name) exhibited at an early age a talent for inventing and an insatiable thirst for knowledge. Both boys tried to invent that which had eluded scientists for centuries… a perpetual motion machine. Like both Braun and Tesla, Lee would all of his life write poetry to express his deepest feelings. And Lee de Forest, too, would carve a niche for himself in the history of wireless telegraphy and telephony.

A scholarship did not pay for everything. Like Tesla and Braun, Lee de Forest found it necessary to work as well as study. He invented an underground trolley system, hoping to win the $50,000 prize offered by the Metropolitan Railway System. When the prize money was withdrawn Lee turned his attention to a steam-saver boiler invention, but he lacked the funds to build a working model. At Crittendon Library he began to study telegraphy, driven by the hunch that some day he would be working in that field. Here it was that Lee de Forest first read about Nikola Tesla and quickly decided that he wanted to work for Tesla.

In January of 1896 Lee's father died. While grieving, Lee had to economize even more. His resolve to work for Tesla strengthened and he read all of Tesla's lectures. In September Lee began his first postgraduate year and switched to electrical engineering. And in this year Lee de Forest met Nikola Tesla for the first time.

But Tesla was in the middle of one of his frequent financial crises and was in no position to hire an assistant. In March, 1895, Tesla's laboratory on South Fifth Street had caught fire and destroyed the entire six story building in which it was housed. All of Tesla's research apparatus and much of his rare paperwork were lost. The moody Tesla was justifiably depressed. His closest associates knew that Tesla's work encompassed advanced research in radio, wireless transmission of energy, guided vehicles, robots, and a means of producing liquid oxygen for the first time. Perhaps it was the latter experiment which caused the fire. It was not the first accident in Tesla's laboratory, and it was a wonder that such a catastrophe had not happened sooner. Tesla often worked with millions of volts of his "controlled lightning." All of Tesla's radio equipment, with which he communicated between his lab and various points within the city, was destroyed in the fire.

De Forest had to look elsewhere for work, while he spent his spare time reading the published works of Lodge, Maxwell and Hertz, and studied German. A former Talladega professor, Frederick Reed, encouraged de Forest to continue at Yale until he had his doctorate, but eager for adventure, in 1898 Lee enlisted in the Army as a bugler during the Spanish-American War. Fortunately, the war was soon over and Lee returned to Yale stouter, healthier, and even more eager to resume his studies. That June he graduated again. The subject of his doctoral thesis was *Reflection of Hertzian Waves From the Ends of Parallel Wires.*

Meanwhile, with help from George Westinghouse, Tesla was ready to move ahead again by the spring of 1897. He made wireless transmission tests using a receiver installed aboard a boat on the Hudson River. He was able to detect a signal sent from a transmitter at his laboratory 25 miles away. On 2 September, 1897, Tesla filed his basic patent applications for wireless signaling. Both of these were granted in 1900, as #645,576 and #649,621. They would be bitterly contested by Guglielmo Marconi, but not until after Tesla sued Marconi for infringement.

Unlike many other pioneers in wireless communication, Guglielmo Marconi was never plagued by any serious shortage of funding for his research. Nor was he ever exploited by his financial backers, as were Tesla, de Forest, and Braun. This is undoubtedly the reason why Marconi is so well remembered today, while the others are forgotten and unknown to the general public. Marconi's name has been perpetuated in the company he founded, while the original companies of

Tesla, Braun and de Forest were all swallowed by others, or, in de Forest's case, destroyed by their incompetent or illegal management.

Guglielmo's mother, the beautiful and talented Annie Jameson, was the daughter of a Scot who emigrated to Ireland, where he built a large and successful distillery. Family wealth sheltered young Annie from the horrors of the Great Potato Famine, from which so many Irish peasants fled to America to escape starving to death.

When Annie, who had a fine singing voice, was determined to pursue a career at the Covent Garden opera house, her parents sent her to stay with the family of her father's business associate in Bologna, Italy, hoping that she would settle down and forget her desire to appear on the operatic stage. Little did they dream that Italy would provide Annie with a far more exciting alternative. Annie's host introduced her to his widowed son-in-law, the suave, charming and attractive Giuseppe Marconi. It was love at first sight, for both of them.

Annie rushed home to Ireland to beg her parents' permission to marry the handsome Italian. The Jamesons were horrified. Not only was Giuseppe a foreigner, but he was too old, and he was second-hand, with a son to prove it. They refused their consent, kept Annie at home, and pushed her into a breathtaking round of social activities calculated to interest her in young men of her own age and nationality. These tactics would drive most teenagers into the arms of the forbidden lover, and Annie was no exception. She and the passionate Giuseppe carried on a clandestine correspondence in which they planned their elopement as soon as Annie came of age. They were married on 26 April, 1864, in France, at Boulogne on the Channel coast.

Giuseppe took his young bride to the Palazzo Marescalchi, his town house in Bologna. Within a year they had their first son, Alfonso. Annie and Giuseppe contentedly divided their time between the Palazzo and their country estate. Villa Grifone, just outside the city.

The Marconis were celebrating their tenth wedding anniversary when Guglielmo made his appearance, on 25 April, 1874, in the Palazzo. Giuseppe was by this time forty-eight years old, and settling comfortably into "middle age" as men of that era did. Annie, however, was in her prime, eager to have fun and show off her beauty. Guglielmo's difficult birth, during which Annie nearly died, convinced Giuseppe that his wife's health was delicate. Annie easily persuaded her "aging" husband that she needed to frequently take the waters of a spa at nearby Poretta. She used her feminine frailty as a good excuse to spend winters in the mild climate of Florence, or in Leghorn where her sister, married to a British Army officer, lived with her daughters who were near Guglielmo's age. Giuseppe preferred to stay at home and look after his business and estates while Alfonso and Guglielmo traveled everywhere with Annie. She taught both of her boys to speak English and brought them up in her Protestant religion, in spite of the fact that both had been baptised Roman Catholic. Giuseppe offered little objection. Colonies of British residents at both Leghorn and Florence provided Anglican churches where Annie took her sons for religious instruction. No doubt this had much to do with Guglielmo's later affinity for England.

Perhaps it was this cosmopolitan upbringing which caused Guglielmo to have trouble making friends when he started to school. His classmates found the bilingual boy "different," and generally shunned him. His teachers found no reason to encourage him along any particular academic lines. Young Guglielmo soon realized that he most enjoyed his stays at Leghorn, which was a main seaport of the newly-united Italy. Here he spent much of his time watching the splendid warships anchored in the bay, with smartly-uniformed officers strolling their decks. Giuseppe was pleased with his son's new interest, and encouraged him to study hard so he could enter the Naval Academy. He even bought the boy a small sailboat to further encourage his nautical ambitions. Although

Guglielmo enjoyed flitting around the bay in his little boat, with his cousin Daisy Prescott crewing for him, and although he was always building something and interested in how mechanical things worked, he was not a good student. He failed his entrance exams at the Naval Academy, and the disgusted Giuseppe was convinced that his son's tinkering was rubbish which took too much time away from his studies.

Guglielmo was thirteen years old when he was introduced to the study of physics and electricity at the Technical Institute at Leghorn. In 1894 Heinrich Hertz died, and Professor Augusto Righi, who taught physics at the University of Bologna, wrote an obituary which detailed the German physicist's work with electromagnetic waves. Righi routinely taught his students about the work of Hertz, Braun, Tesla and other scientists of the day.

Professor Righi happened to live near the Villa Grifone. When Guglielmo also failed the entrance examination to the University of Bologna, Annie visited Righi and asked him to tutor her son. Marconi supporters insist that he never actually studied under Righi, and Marconi himself would later deny ever having attended Righi's classes, just as he would deny having known about Tesla's lectures and experiments. There is evidence, however, that Guglielmo did study privately with Righi. One of Marconi's biographers, W. R. Jolly, (*Marconi,* Stein and Day, New York, 1972), wrote of a gardener at the Villa Grifone, one Antonio Marchi, who died in 1948 at the age of 105, and left with his son an account of his work at the Marconi country estate. One of Antonio's duties had been to accompany the fourteen year old Guglielmo as he rode a donkey to his lessons at Professor Righi's home. In 1903 Righi would side with Marconi by saying publicly that the idea of wireless telegraphy had been "born spontaneously" in the mind of the young man from Bologna, rather than from his knowledge of similar experiments made by others before him. With Marconi's patent infringement suits pending in the courts of every major country in the world, a friend and mentor of Marconi would hardly say otherwise. Whether young Guglielmo studied with Righi, or merely used university facilities which Righi was able to make available to him makes little difference. Either way, Righi certainly was an influence on Marconi.

In 1894 Guglielmo began his experiments in two attic rooms of the Villa Grifone. He started by copying Hertz's experiments in order that he could observe for himself the behavior of the electromagnetic waves which so fascinated him. His transmitter spark gap had been somewhat modified by Righi, so that a curved metal reflector placed behind it directed the waves toward the receiver. Marconi improved Hertz's receiver by attaching a Branly coherer to its coil.

Throughout the winter of 1894-1895, and into the following spring, Guglielmo continued his experiments, locked away in his attic rooms, keeping everyone out, even Annie. That summer he successfully sent signals from his transmitter in one room to his coherer-receiver in the other. Now he was ready to move outdoors where he could extend the range of his signals. Antonio Marchi recalled digging ditches deep into the garden for Marconi to bury the mysterious metal plates and wires which were his first antennas. Marconi moved his receiver farther and farther from the house as he extended his signaling range. By the fall of 1895 he had achieved a range of over one kilometer, as far as he could go on the grounds of his father's estate. He now had a wireless telegraph, and he wanted to commercialize it.

Giuseppe, who had been cool to his son's constant "tinkering," now realized that the experiments might be financially lucrative. He began to seek backers through the Italian Government, while Annie wrote to her friends and relatives in Great Britain. But the Italian Government, although wanting assurance that Guglielmo would not forget his Italian heritage, did not consider wireless telegraphy any threat to the cable telegraphs already firmly in place throughout the world. Clearly, wireless signaling had its greatest potential between ships at sea, and between ships and shore stations, particularly lighthouses. The logical place to look for financing was in the country which could benefit the most from wireless, the country with the largest navy and mercantile marine in the world… Great Britain.

The British were quick to realize that equipping their lighthouses and lightships with wireless could reduce the loss of life and property in their hazardous coastal waters. So Annie brought her son to London.

Marconi's biographers, including Jolly, have said that Annie's cousin, Henry Jameson Davis, who was then well established in London business circles, introduced Guglielmo to William Preece, Chief Engineer for the British Post Office. But Jolly wrote in his biography, *Sir Oliver Lodge* (Associated University Presses, Inc., Cranbury NJ, 1975) that it was Campbell Swinton who introduced Marconi to Preece. Even while he experimented at Villa Grifone, Marconi had been afraid of Lodge, conscious that his wireless apparatus was very much like that which Lodge had been using. When Swinton asked Marconi in what way his apparatus might differ from Lodge's, Marconi indicated that his coherer-receiver was superior in its sensitivity. But when F. T. Trouton, a young scientist from Dublin, came to see one of Marconi's first demonstrations he was permitted to carry the closed box which contained the receiver. Trouton was surprised when it picked up clear messages at over 300 feet from the transmitter. After the demonstration Trouton congratulated Marconi, who allowed him a peek into the box. When Trouton remarked that the box contained a Lodge coherer Marconi slammed the lid down again and remarked *"You would steal my invention."*

Preece had been experimenting with wireless signaling by *induction* (current generated through a conductor by another current flowing through a nearby conductor) and *conduction* (current sent through the earth or water). These phenomena had been observed many times since Morse's broken cable in 1842, and Preece was not the only one attempting to harness them for wireless communication. The German electrical manufacturer, Allgemeine Electricitats-Gesellschaft (AEG) had sent its Chief Engineer, Erich Rathenau, to observe some of Preece's induction experiments. Rathenau had then begun his own experiments in a lake near Berlin. He had been able to send direct current through water, with the result that he received a "soft, rumbling noise" up to a distance of 4.5 kilometers.

On 2 June, 1896, Marconi filed his claim to priority of wireless communication with the British Patent Office. On 7 July he demonstrated his system to Preece and other senior officials and engineers at the General Post Office building in St. Martin's-le-Grand, where his wireless apparatus had been assembled on the roof. Marconi successfully communicated with Preece's staff on the roof of another Post Office building less than a mile away.

Not all British scientists were impressed by the young Italian's "invention." Nor were they impressed by Preece's judgement and engineering expertise. Oliver Lodge's dry comment on Marconi's demonstrations was included in a letter he wrote to the *Times*. *"The only important discovery about the matter of wireless telegraphy had been made by Hertz in 1888."* Other British scientists were quick to point out that Preece ought to have been aware of what had already been done in the field of harnessing Hertzian waves for communication.

In 1881 Oliver Lodge had accepted the post of Professor of Experimental Physics and Mathematics at the new University College at Liverpool. The new department would meet the scientific needs of medical students until it attracted students into its own field of experimental physics. Before he set up the new school, Lodge returned to Germany to get ideas upon which to base its curriculum. As a British student Lodge had visited Heidelburg and attended lectures by the famous chemist, Robert Wilhelm Bunsen. Lodge had also spent part of his honeymoon in the lovely German university town.

Lodge had visited the great Helmholtz in Berlin and met the professor's assistant, Hemrich Hertz. Lodge and Hertz got along well, and when Hertz made his famous 1888 experiments with electromagnetic waves Lodge was one of the first to begin his own research to extend the Hertzian frontier. Lodge's 1894 demonstration using Branly's coherer had been completed while the teenaged Marconi was just beginning his own experiments based on the same instruments.

Lodge's good friend, Alexander Muirhead, was skilled in cable telegraphy, and Muirhead had provided the cable telegraph recorder that Lodge had used for his 1894 transmission of Morse signals. Together Lodge and Muirhead acquired a number of wireless patents before Marconi arrived in England. In 1897 the Lodge-Muirhead Syndicate was formed to promote the commercialization of wireless telegraphy. Eventually, Lodge would challenge the Marconi Company in British courts and win, but in the end Marconi would buy the Lodge-Muirhead patents and utilize them as his own.

There is little doubt that Marconi's tremendous success in England stemmed from Preece's early and enthusiastic endorsement of the Italian's wireless system. But why did Preece embrace the foreigner to the exclusion of a highly-respected countryman?

Preece undoubtedly had personal reasons for backing Marconi over Lodge's objections, and his motive was revenge against Lodge rather than enthusiasm for Marconi.

In 1888 Lodge and Preece had clashed publicly over the matter of lightning conductors. The Royal Society of Arts had received a grant in 1887 for a series of lectures to perpetuate the memory of Dr. Mann, one of its members who had worked in Africa, where he had studied the problem of protecting buildings from lightning damage. The Society deemed it appropriate that the first lectures should be on the subject of lightning conductors. Lodge, a highly respected Professor of Physics and Mathematics and an acknowledged authority on electricity, was naturally chosen to speak. Like Tesla, Lodge illustrated his lectures with spectacular displays of artificial lightning.

Electrical engineers of the day understood direct current very well, and the Post Office, with Preece as its Chief Engineer, along with many other British engineers, had endorsed the protection of buildings with lightning rods based on the theory that lightning consists of a simple direct current in one direction, to the ground. Lodge disputed this theory and suggested that a lightning flash consisted instead of an oscillatory current. The charge flowed first one way, and then in the opposite direction, with the amount of current diminishing with each reversal. Lodge's theory, which turned out to be correct, drew derision from Preece's followers, who prided themselves on their practicality. Preece challenged Lodge publicly, confidently boasting that at the Post Office he had under his supervision 500,000 lightning conductors, which obviously made him an authority on lightning. Lodge replied that he had not one lightning conductor under his charge. When Preece's contingent asked why he had none on his house. Lodge answered that he found it cheaper to insure. There followed a heated exchange of words between Preece's "experienced" followers, and Lodge's group of "experimentalists."

The controversy dragged on for months and was thoroughly covered by articles and letters in the *Times* as well as electrical journals. A cartoon of the period depicted Preece as a gladiator, his weapon "*Experience,*" standing over a defeated Lodge, who lay prone on the ground with his weapon, "*Experiment,*" beside him. Oliver Heaviside, who would along with American Arthur Kennelly discover the ionosphere (the layer of electrically charged particles above the Earth's surface which facilitates radio transmission) attacked Preece, suggesting that the Post Office's Chief Engineer was not wholly acquainted with the subject of electricity.

Heaviside and the *Times* agreed that the Lodge-Preece controversy had deeper implications than the subject of lightning conductors. The real issue at stake was the entire new field of the study and use of electromagnetic waves, for 1888 was the year of the discovery of self-induction, and Hertz's experiments which pushed theoretical physicists the world over in new directions.

When current flowing through a wire is increased, or decreased, the change in the magnetic field produced by the current tends to try to maintain the current at its original value. This is called the *"self-inductance"* of the wire, and it is relatively unimportant when dealing with direct current. Alternating current, however, is always changing, as its name implies. It rises to its maximum in one direction, then falls to zero, and rises to its maximum in the opposite direction, and so on. Self-inductance thus becomes important when working with alternating current, which Tesla had caused to supplant direct current by proving it more efficient and economical. Lodge had been experimenting with electricity since he was a boy and was quite familiar with self-induction, but many engineers of his day were not.

In England Preece championed the young Italian inventor to Lodge's detriment, and remained Marconi's best public relations man. Lodge, after hearing one of Preece's lectures on the wonders of Marconi's "invention," wrote to the *Times* Editor explaining again that he had used the same method of transmitting signals via Hertzian waves in 1894. Lodge gave credit to Marconi for the commercial success of the invention, but pointed out that the popular usage of the term *"Marconi waves"* was incorrect, if not absurd.

Marconi's connections made his progress remarkably easy compared to the men who would be his most vigorous competitors... Braun, Tesla and de Forest. Preece was able to convince the Post Office and the War Office to give their valuable support and assistance to Marconi's further experiments. In March, 1897, on Salisbury Plain, Marconi's apparatus achieved a range of 4.5 miles. In May he extended the distance to 9 miles, sending signals between the mainland and the island of Flatholm in the Bristol Channel. This was the same year in which Tesla achieved a signaling range of 25 miles on New York's Hudson River.

Marconi's experiments were reported by conventional communication all over the world. The Italian Ministry of Marine was interested enough to keep track of their native son's work, but not enough to provide financial help. At this time Guglielmo was forced to make a choice between renouncing his Italian citizenship, as his English colleagues urged, or returning to Italy to serve in the military, as all Italian men of his age had to do. Strings were pulled, in London and in Rome, and Guglielmo was enrolled on paper as a cadet in the Italian Navy, his failed entrance examination now forgotten. He was immediately transferred to the Italian Embassy in London as attaché. In return for this dispensation Guglielmo was obligated to return to Italy to demonstrate his wireless apparatus.

While Marconi was in Italy the "Wireless Telegraph and Signal Company, Ltd.," was formed to commercially promote his wireless signaling system. Two years later the company's name was changed to Marconi's Wireless Telegraphy Company, Ltd., with an authorized capital of £100,000 in £1 shares. Sixty thousand shares were given to Guglielmo in return for the exclusive rights to all of his patents. Henry Jameson-Davis became the new company's Managing Director, and Marconi, who was one of the five original directors, was given the right to personally appoint one additional member to the Board. Guglielmo was a relatively wealthy man when he and Annie returned to London in August of 1897.

Ferdinand Braun was in America from July to October, 1897. In August he presented a paper at the sixty-seventh annual meeting of the British Association for the Advancement of Science at Toronto. Braun showed how a cathode ray could be deflected in a magnetic field produced by alternating current. Unfortunately, the American debut of Braum's tube was hardly noticed in the Association's crowded agenda. To Braun the highlight of his trip was the discounted cross-country journey presented to him by the Canadian Pacific Railroad. Like de Forest, Braun would always love nature, and would often need to get away from the stresses of business by hiking in the wilderness. From Canada Braun made a side trip to Yellowstone, where he captured the Park's scenic splendor in the watercolors with which he loved to paint.

In America, Edison had tried to communicate with moving trains by sending signals through wires laid alongside the tracks, and in England Preece had some success in transmitting from a wire laid along the coastline to another wire laid along the shore of a nearby island. But telegraphy by induction and conduction was not as practical as transmitting via Hertzian waves, which Marconi and Tesla were doing. When AEG's Rathenau observed the British conduction experiments, the German Emperor became interested. Wilhelm arranged for his personal advisor on science and technology. Professor Adolf Slaby of the Technical University of Berlin-Charlottenburg, to attend the March, 1897, Marconi demonstration on the Bristol Channel. Marconi was furious, but he had no choice. He was forced to endure Slaby's presence. The German scientist came away from the demonstration with public praise for Marconi, and the determination to match the Italian's achievements. On 7 October, 1897, while Braun was returning from America, Slaby sent his signals an unprecedented distance of 21 kilometers by using balloons to tow his antenna wires to a height of 300 meters.

Albert Zobel, an astute German businessman who realized that wireless telegraphy needed a lot of money to develop its full potential, undertook to raise the necessary funding. Zobel contacted Ludwig Stollwerck, one of five sons of the well-known Cologne chocolate manufacturer Franz Stollwerck. Ludwig had already invested in several scientific projects, including Edison's phonograph and the Lumiere brothers' cinematograph. Zobel and Stollwerck knew of Braun's reputation and experiments with Hertzian waves, so they chose him to evaluate the invention they considered financing. Braun thus was late in entering the commercialization of wireless telegraphy, but as usual it was the tremendous challenge that tempted him. In July, 1898, the Zobel-Stollwerck-backed Friedrich Niess and Gustav Gümbel applied for a patent on their conduction telegraphy, with its range of only 1.6 kilometers, while Slaby, using the Marconi system, had reached 21 kilometers. The reason for patenting a system known to have inferior promise was simply that Marconi's patents blocked any others on transmission of signals via Hertzian waves.

While Marconi was generating worldwide publicity with his frequent public experiments and demonstrations, the apparatus he used was kept carefully locked up, and was never explained although it was patented, quite probably because neither Marconi nor any of the men who worked with him at that time really understood the fundamentals behind their experiments.

In September, 1898, the Braun-approved Niess-Gümbel patent was rejected on the grounds that there had been previous similar experiments. Braun immediately wrote to the German Patent Office, explaining that the earlier tests had failed to achieve any range because they had used direct current, whereas he had used the modern alternating current developed by Tesla. Stollwerck nevertheless asked Professor Slaby to evaluate Braun's work. Insulted by this professional slur, Braun promptly resigned.

Just prior to the split with Stollwerck, Braun had made a thorough study of the competing Marconi system. He observed that in the past year Marconi had made no noticeable improvement in his signaling range. Braun reasoned that because Marconi was using a spark gap inserted between antenna and ground, an arrangement which had proved to be the least satisfactory in water conduction telegraphy, then if Braun utilized his improvement which had so effectively extended the range of conduction signals, then he should also increase the range of Marconi's apparatus. Braun set up a copy of the Marconi device, but with his own modifications, and proved that he was right. Slaby, despite having seen Marconi's experiments, despite having worked to improve them for over a year, had been unsuccessful. The usually passive Braun felt justifiably angered when Slaby was chosen to inspect his work.

Stollwerck, realizing how much he needed Braun, cancelled Slaby's visit. Braun continued improving Marconi's circuits, and successfully demonstrated not only that he had dramatically increased the range of the signals, but that signals could actually go through buildings that were between the transmitter and receiver. Braun's invention, a primary coil in the oscillating circuit with a loosely-coupled secondary coil to transfer the oscillations into the antenna-to-ground circuit, gave the Germans a system independent of Marconi. Braun immediately applied for a patent. Zobel wrote to Stollwerck that Braun had proven scientifically that he could broadcast three times as far as Marconi.

Braun himself was more cautious in his claims, and rightly so. Before the end of 1898 he learned of Nikola Tesla's U.S. Patent #645,576, and realized that Tesla's patent was similar to his own. On 15 December of that year a company using Braun's patent was formed under the title Funkentelegraphie GmbH Koln. In view of the Tesla patent with its drawings similar to Braun's transmitter, the new company's attorney cautioned Braun to keep silent about his invention.

Unfortunately, it was bad advice. Against his better judgement, Braun said nothing for twenty-three months, thus allowing the publicity-seeking Marconi and Slaby to leave in the public mind a legend of priority in wireless telegraphy.

Braun quietly continued his work to extend the signaling range of his wireless apparatus, while Tesla, in lectures and newspaper interviews, spoke of worldwide, even interplanetary wireless communication, and transmission of electrical power without wires.

In April, 1899, without Braun's presence, his assistant, Austrian Mathias Cantor, began experiments at Cuxhaven on the North Sea. By June the range had been extended to the island of Neuwerk, a distance of 12 kilometers from the transmitter. Braun's associates decided it was time to form a new, extended company, which became Professor Braun's Telegraphie GmbH. The company's main purpose was to raise capital for further experiments. In July, 1899, a syndicate was formed with a capitalization of 2 million marks. It soon became known by its cable *address "Telebraun."* In this same month the Kaiser happened to pass the Braun installation at Cuxhaven, in his yacht ***HOHENZOLLERN***, on his way to Helgoland. Finally Wilhelm learned that someone in Germany besides his own Professor Slaby was experimenting with wireless telegraphy.

Lloyd's, the largest marine insurer in the world, with its own signaling and intelligence systems, was considering a switch to the new wireless communication. Marconi had already submitted a bid, but a Lloyd's representative had heard about the professor from Strasbourg who had devised a new circuit that was more efficient than Marconi's, and urged a competitive demonstration. Suddenly, inexplicably, the Lloyd's experts decided that Braun's more complicated system, which used a primary and secondary circuit tuned to each other, was less efficient than Marconi's untuned circuit, and Marconi got the Lloyd's contract.

Even in summer the tempestuous North Sea is unpredictable, and now it kept Braun from extending his wireless range to the goal of 100 kilometers which he and his partners had set. The experiments which had worked perfectly in the confined limits of the laboratory did not work so well when capricious winds tore down antenna guy wires. When Braun wanted two masts, each 45 meters tall, his carpenter could manage only 35 meters in the high winds. Braun's crew barely escaped with their equipment and their lives when an unexpected spring flood knocked down the masts. Racing unimpeded across the water, a September storm struck Cuxhaven with viciously high winds that toppled the transmission mast and tore off the station's roof, although both structures had been strengthened to withstand severe winter weather.

In October, 1899, Jonathan Zenneck replaced Cantor, who had not wished to renew his contract with Telebraun. The excursion steamer ***SILVANA*** was chartered, and Braun crammed her saloon full of wireless apparatus. By December the Braun system had reached a range of 35 kilometers. Again the fickle short seas reminded the experimenters that nature would have the last word. Early transmitter coils were immersed in vats of oil for insulation, a hazardous arrangement at best. On one winter voyage ***SILVANA*** rolled so heavily in the storm-tossed waves that the coils became partly exposed and arced over with a burst of flame that set fire to the container's wooden walls. ***SILVANA***'s next roll submerged the coils again, and the heavy oil doused the fire. ***SILVANA***'s owners were naturally concerned about the peril in which Braun was placing their ship, so he substituted a more viscous and less flammable oil. But again the North Sea mocked the experimenters, and with each of ***SILVANA***'s rolls oil slopped out of its containers and greased the linoleum floor, making it as slippery as an ice skating rink. While the fragile wireless equipment slid from one end of the cabin to the other, Braun's men skidded after it, their feet slipping out from under them as they tried desperately to secure the apparatus.

While Braun's transmitter already surpassed Marconi's for efficiency, the coherer in his receiver was unreliable and drove the usually placid Braun to use strong language. Remembering his early experiments with crystals, Braun built a crystal detector. Unfortunately, it produced no better results than the coherer, with the method then in use of recording incoming code on a moving paper strip. In 1901, when audible signals came into use, the crystal detector proved to be far more efficient than the coherer.

While experiments were continued aboard ***SILVANA***, Telebraun decided to gain publicity by equipping the lightship ***ELBE II*** with wireless, although Braun would have preferred to put this off until after they had achieved their goal of communication with the island of Helgoland. Braun was still busy with his university activities, and it was September of 1900 before the Helgoland link was finally established.

Suddenly, with no notice or explanation, Preece began experiments at Fort Burgoyne, near Dover, which excluded Marconi. Convinced that Preece was angry because he had exchanged his patents for shares in the newly formed Marconi Wireless Telegraphy Company, Marconi wrote privately to Preece, suggesting that he would have to take his work to another country unless Preece, the British Post Office and the Admiralty continued to cooperate with him. But during 1898 and 1899 Marconi's company and the British Government went their own ways.

In 1900 the British Post Office secretly commissioned Sir Oliver Lodge to study the possibility of invalidating the Marconi patents, or somehow getting round them by using legally different equipment. Lodge and his associate, Silvanus Thompson, had always questioned the moral and legal right of the Marconi Company to its patent claims, but the Admiralty advisor was Captain Henry Jackson, a friend of Marconi. Jackson had been working on wireless for the Royal Navy before he became acquainted with Marconi, yet he advised that it was not wise to antagonize the Marconi Company, which might eventually improve its apparatus.

Establishing permanent shore stations for experiments and public demonstrations of wireless telegraphy became the Marconi Company's top priority. The first such station was built in the Needles Hotel, at Alum Bay, on the Isle of Wight. The second station was set up 14 miles away at Bournemouth, on the mainland. Both stations were housed in hotel rooms, which must have greatly disturbed the sleep of other guests. The masts were over 100 feet high, and during transmission the crash of spark could be heard for miles. Marconi was always present, even during the most dangerous experiments. In November of 1898 he was aboard a tug in the Solent during a fierce gale when communication was established with the Alum Bay station 18 miles away.

Experiments were soon undertaken on behalf of Trinity House, and the South Foreland lighthouse, near Dover, was equipped to communicate with the East Goodwin Lightship about 12 miles away. This lightship is generally credited with the first wireless distress call in maritime history. At four o'clock on the morning of 3 March, 1899, the lightship was rammed by the steamer ***R.R. MATTHEWS***. The call was not SOS, which would not be used for another nine years. The ***EAST GOODWIN***'s crew simply reported the incident to the South Foreland lighthouse, and tugs were sent to tow the lightship to safety.

In 1899 Lee de Forest, working in the Western Electric Company's experimental telephone laboratory in Chicago, had already experimented with the Marconi Company's Branly coherer, with its tapping-back device and Morse inker. But Marconi's method did not satisfy de Forest. He wanted a "self-restoring" detector which would permit an operator to hear the actual sound of the transmitter spark through a telephone device.

In 1900 the United States Patent Office finally granted Tesla's basic wireless patents, for which he had applied in 1897. Marconi repeatedly contested these patents, but his infringement suits were rejected by the Patent Office on the prior art of Tesla, Lodge and Braun. After a further rejection on 3 June, 1902, Marconi failed to reply within the year required under the Patent Office rules. Sixteen months later, on 6 October, 1903, Marconi filed a petition for revival of the case. Less than two weeks later the Examiner recommended to the Commissioner that the petition should be denied, stating that Marconi's pretended ignorance of the nature of a "Tesla oscillator" was little short of absurd. He cited Tesla's famous lectures on alternating current of high frequency, which had been delivered in 1891 and 1892, in America, Britain and France, and which had been widely published in many languages, making the term Tesla oscillator" a household word. The Examiner also pointed out that Marconi evidently knew of Tesla's invention in 1897, because Marconi was quoted in an 1898 publication as having used it.

Throughout 1903 Marconi's petition for revival was denied. But suddenly, on 19 February, 1904, Marconi requested a reconsideration of the petition, and it was inexplicably granted on 28 March by the Commissioner of Patents. There was no evidence in the file indicating that the petition had been submitted to the Examiner for consideration, and Marconi's application was granted on 28 June, 1904.

In April, 1900, Lee de Forest left Western Electric and went to work for the newly formed American Wireless Telegraphy Company at Milwaukee. The company's president, Professor Johnson, was the wealthy owner of the Johnson Pneumatic Heat Control System, and had made his fortune from a patented automatic heat-control thermostat. Johnson and his assistant, Fournier, had been working with a coherer utilizing iron filings, which de Forest already knew was impractical.

At Western Electric de Forest had experimented on his own time with a responder device patterned after one he had read about years earlier. At American Wireless Lee again worked on his own time, when Johnson and Fournier were out of the lab, to perfect his responder. When Johnson learned about de Forest's private project, he suggested that Lee should give his responder to the company. Wisely, de Forest refused to give up an invention with such potential, and it was the end of his association with Johnson. Lee returned to Chicago and went to work as an assistant editor for the *Western Electrician.* He renewed contact with a friend from Western Electric, Ed Smythe, and Ed's brother. Will. The three men continued the development of Lee's responder.

Professor Clarence Freeman of the Armour Institute's electrical engineering faculty became interested in de Forest's work and allowed the young inventor free run of the Institute's laboratory. In return Lee assisted students with their lab work. De Forest was now so engrossed in perfecting his responder that he needed to devote his full time to it. Ed Smythe managed to provide Lee with a survival allowance so he could resign from his job at the *Western Electrician.* To supplement the pittance that Smythe could afford, Lee taught at the Lewis Institute two nights a week. In July, 1900, de Forest and Smythe achieved transmissions of half a mile, with the signals received into a telephone rather than the inked paper strip which Marconi used. Soon the distance was stretched to four miles, from the Armour Institute to Ferdinand Peck's Auditorium.

Professor Freeman had a friend who owned a yacht, and the next step was ship-to-shore communication on Lake Michigan. This time Morse code was used, replacing the simple tone signals de Forest had previously used. These tests attracted Lee's first publicity, and he liked it. His goal now was to cover the 1901 International Yacht Races.

Marconi had covered his first yacht race in 1898, for the *Dublin Daily Express,* which saw the publicity value in wireless reporting of the Kingstown race. Queen Victoria had provided more good publicity for Marconi when she wanted to communicate from Osborne House on the Isle of Wight to the royal yacht moored in Cowes Bay, where the Prince of Wales was recovering from a knee injury. The distance between Osborne House and Cowes was only two miles, but the messages between the Queen and her son generated tremendous publicity for the Marconi Company. It soon became the stylish thing for the wealthy to send "Marconi messages" to each other. Marconi began to work on a cross-Channel wireless link, between the South Foreland lighthouse and Wimereux, a village near Boulogne. He also began more ship-to-shore experiments, this time for the French Navy.

In September, 1899, Marconi sailed for New York in Cunard's aging ***AURANIA*** to cover the America's Cup races in October for James Gordon Bennett's *New York Herald.* While in America Marconi was scheduled to demonstrate his equipment to the United States Navy. Before he could report the races Marconi had to contend with a patent lawsuit threatened by the American Wireless Telegraph and Telephone Company, which claimed that their patent, obtained by Professor Amos Dolbear of Tufts College in 1885, covered the entire art of wireless telegraphy. Then, the races were postponed by the arrival of Admiral Dewey, fresh from his victories in the Philippines. Bennett arranged for Marconi to report the Admiral's arrival from a hurriedly equipped tug. But Dewey arrived two days early, before the tug was ready. Aboard a new Puerto Rico Line steamer, the ***PONCE,*** Marconi joined the parade of ships which had assembled to salute Dewey.

Marconi's official tests for the U.S. Navy went well, and as luck would have it, the apparatus was put to practical use when a man fell overboard from the battleship ***USS MASSACHUSETTS****. A* message was flashed to the following ***USS NEW YORK***, and the man was quickly rescued.

Marconi's equipment presented two major obstacles which precluded its purchase for use in United States warships. First, Marconi had not accomplished selective tuning, and when several ships began calling each other at sea the jamming made messages unintelligible. Marconi claimed to have a device which would solve this problem, but he refused to give any details as it was not yet protected by a patent. But there was no getting around the second problem. The Marconi Company's policy was to lease equipment, with its own men operating and caring for it aboard the ships. Marconi offered to lease a minimum of twenty sets to the U.S. Navy at the rate of $20,000 per year for each set the first year, and $10,000 annually for each set thereafter. Obviously, the U.S. Navy could not employ foreign nationals, or civilians, in its warships. Marconi declared that it was a company policy which he refused to change. The U.S. Navy bought German Slaby-Arco equipment. Marconi, however, felt so confident about the future of his wireless development that he formed the Marconi Wireless Telegraph Company of America under the laws of the State of New Jersey. The new American Marconi Company was capitalized with an authorized stock of 2,000,000 shares at $5 per share. Marconi himself held 600,000 shares while the English Marconi Company held 350,000 shares.

By the end of 1905 the U. S. Navy had 45 ships equipped with wireless apparatus, and between the Navy and the U. S. Army there were 40 land stations.

In December of 1899 the Russian Navy's cruiser ***APRAKSIN*** was wrecked in the Baltic Sea, prompting Czar Nicholas II to order that his entire navy must immediately be equipped with wireless. Popov had not yet perfected his wireless system, and like the Americans, the Russians wanted no foreign civilians, especially the British, aboard their warships so the Czar turned to Germany. Slaby, better known than Braun because of his connections to the Kaiser, got the contract. Alarmed because his own navy was lagging far behind in wireless equipment, the Kaiser ordered competitive trials between Braun and Slaby to quickly decide which would equip the German Navy. Although Slaby's circuits were copies of Braun's, and Slaby's latest transmitter was a copy of Braun's patent of 14 October, 1898, Slaby had two years' experience in the Russian warships, while Braun-Siemens was given two days to install their equipment. Braun reached a range of 105 kilometers, while Slaby reached 115. Vainly Braun-Siemens argued that Slaby had infringed the Braun patents. The Kaiser was interested in distance, not patents. Braun-Siemens took AEG-Slaby-Arco to court. Predictably, the Kaiser backed Slaby. The German press began to clamor for a merger between Braun and Slaby that would create a purely German wireless system, as Marconi's was purely British.

Marconi returned to England in November of that year, in the American Line's ***ST. PAUL***. When he set up his equipment to test its range enroute, ***ST. PAUL*** technically became the first transatlantic liner to be equipped with wireless.

On 28 February, 1900, Norddeutscher Lloyd's Blue Riband winner, ***KAISER WILHELM DER GROSSE***, departed Bremen with Marconi wireless equipment aboard. She was the first transatlantic liner to carry a permanent wireless installation for use on the high seas. Marconi had also received the German Government contract to equip the Borkum Riff lightship and the Borkum Island lighthouse, in spite of Slaby's work for the Imperial Navy.

On 25 April, 1900, "The Marconi International Marine Communication Company, Ltd." was incorporated as a subsidiary of the parent English Marconi Company, with offices in Brussels and London, and agencies in Paris and Rome. It was established to handle Marconi's maritime contracts, with the exception of naval installations, which remained with the parent company. Britain's Telegraph Acts of 1888 and 1889 stated that a private telegraph company could send messages for its own use, but not for profit as a public service. A private telegraph company could legally install its own operator and apparatus aboard a vessel for the purpose of communication with shore stations, provided that no charge was made for the messages. But the company would be free to use its equipment to send paid messages, if they were sent and received on the high seas.

The regulations were ambiguous, and to test their limits the new Marconi International Marine Company obtained permission from the Belgian Government to build a shore station for the purpose of communicating with the Belgian cross-Channel packets in the Dover-Ostend service. The first of these ships so fitted was the ***PRINCESS CLEMENTINE***, on 3 November, 1900. The British Post office clarified its position by forbidding the exchange of messages for pay inside its three-mile limit.

On 1 January, 1901, ***PRINCESS CLEMENTINE***'s wireless operator, F. C. Stacey, demonstrated the humanitarian purpose of her new installation by summoning aid for the bark ***MEDORA***, aground on Ratel Bank. Nineteen days later Stacey's distress call was for ***PRINCESS CLEMENTINE*** herself, ashore at Mariakerke in a thick fog.

Stacey was soon transferred to the Elder Dempster-Beaver Line's ***LAKE CHAMPLAIN***, the next transatlantic vessel to be Marconi-equipped. She had not been built with wireless in mind, and Stacey had a small "shack" erected on her boat deck. It was really no more than a lean-to, four and a half feet by three and a half feet, built against an iron bulkhead. Stacey estimated the cost of construction at 5 pounds sterling, or about $25. It is apparently this "shack" which originated the slang term "radio shack" for a ship's wireless cabin.

LAKE CHAMPLAIN's primitive wireless apparatus consisted of a ten-inch spark coil, a straight "earthed" gap, a transmitter key, and two oscillation transformers, all mounted on a green baize table. Two six-volt batteries were installed under the table. The receiver consisted of two coherers and the usual Morse tape. The transmitter key was a long-handled lever, which required muscle rather than the good light touch which came with later, smaller keys.

LAKE CHAMPLAIN sailed from Liverpool on 21 May, 1901, bound for Halifax. Once Stacey was out of range of the Rosslare station he had nobody to communicate with, as the only other wireless-equipped vessel on the North Atlantic was NDL's ***KAISER WILHELM DER GROSSE***, and her schedule kept her far out of Stacey's range. There were no Marconi shore stations in America at that time. But before the Beaver liner had reached the English coast on her homeward voyage, Stacey was surprised to hear the Cunarder ***LUCANIA*** on her first wireless-equipped voyage to America.

Stacey made several more trips in ***LAKE CHAMPLAIN***, and then the wireless apparatus was transferred to another vessel, while the lean-to became a vegetable locker. In 1902 Stacey was transferred to the American Line's ***PHILADELPHIA***, from which he set a record for communicating over 150 miles.

The Second Officer in ***LAKE CHAMPLAIN*** on the first wireless-equipped voyage was that same Henry George Kendall, who, as master of Canadian Pacific's ***MONTROSE*** would use wireless to apprehend the infamous wife-murderer Dr. Crippen. Unfortunately Captain Kendall would be best remembered as master of the ill-fated ***EMPRESS OF IRELAND***.

In September, 1901, Cunard's ***CAMPANIA*** was equipped with Marconi apparatus. She was quickly followed by ***UMBRIA*** and ***ETRURIA***. In these early years the engineer who installed the ship's equipment usually sailed as her wireless operator.

De Forest's success on the Great Lakes convinced him that it was time to move to New York, where he learned that Marconi already had an Associated Press contract to cover the forthcoming International Yacht Races. A former Yale classmate. Max Stires, succeeded in getting the Publishers' Press Association to sponsor de Forest's system. A month before the races Lee and his associates began construction of the radically new equipment they planned to use. A week before the races de Forest collapsed from exhaustion and had to be hospitalized for a short time. It turned out, however, that neither Marconi nor de Forest had the technology to combat deliberate jamming, and the "wireless" coverage of the 1901 races reported by the newspapers was nothing more than old-fashioned semaphore signaling. Contrary to legend which says that Marconi and de Forest jammed each other, in fact it was Harry Shoemaker and Greenleaf Whittier Pickard of the American Wireless Telegraph and Telephone Company who completely drowned out all Marconi and de Forest signals.

Shoemaker was one of the engineer geniuses who contributed so much to the pioneering of wireless telegraphy and telephony, yet whose name is unknown today outside of professional circles. Born in Millville, Pennsylvania, on 11 May, 1879, Harry attended Greenwood Seminary and the Muncy, Pennsylvania, Normal School, where Professor Henry Russell was his teacher for two years. Russell frequently performed scientific experiments for his students that went beyond the normal curriculum. One of these experiments consisted of a demonstration of wireless signaling, in 1894, when little was known about this phenomenon. Shoemaker became so interested in Russell's experiments that he stayed after school to assist him. In 1895 Shoemaker built his own wireless apparatus, setting it up in his father's nearby sawmill. He managed to send signals over a distance of 150 feet. Throughout 1896 he experimented with wireless signaling, using methods learned from Professor Russell, and developing a decoherer of his own design.

Shoemaker's transmitter was a direct-connected spark coil, with the antenna connected to one side of the gap, and the ground connected to the other side. For a receiver he used a series circuit which connected the antenna, coherer and battery to ground. The coherer and battery were connected by a galvanometer, which was arranged so that its needle would hit the coherer, causing the metal particles to decohere, ready for the next signal. This apparatus was almost exactly like that described in Marconi's first patent application of 1896. Seeking a patent never occurred to the teenaged Shoemaker, who simply was fascinated with his experiments.

This same year Harry matriculated at Penn State, where he continued his wireless experiments along with his regular studies, for the next four years. Upon receiving his degree in electrical engineering he went to work for Dr. Gustav Gehring, a mining stock speculator who was primarily interested in promoting wireless stock. Gehring established the first wireless operating companies in the United States, naming his parent company American Wireless Telegraph and Telephone Company, and making Harry Shoemaker his Chief Engineer. American was a holding company which included nine operating companies in different parts of the United States.

De Forest began his coverage of the 1901 races using a Freeman transmitter, which immediately broke down. He tossed it overboard and installed a Ruhmkorff spark coil with an interrupter, which held up, but could not compete with the twenty-inch coil used by Americans Shoemaker and Pickard, who had not been authorized to report the races.

Telebraun, too, had gone to sea, but not yet with happy results. On 29 October, 1900, the lightship ***ELBE II*** summoned aid for the four-masted sailing vessel ***H. BISCHOFF***, which had run aground during a night storm. Unfortunately, the rescue boat capsized and sank with all hands, and 19 of the ***BISCHOFF***'s *21* man crew were drowned.

When word got around that Telebraun was equipping lightships and pilot boats with wireless, requests for information began coming from all over the world, and Marconi no longer had a monopoly. But Telebraun had no funds to continue its production of equipment, nor for conducting additional experiments. German financiers balked at taking chances on the embryonic industry, and governments hesitated on the grounds that transoceanic cables were already in place, forgetting the ease with which an enemy could cut those cables in wartime.

Telebraun tried to interest Albert Ballin, Director of the large shipping firm Hamburg-Amerikanische Packetfahrt Aktien Gesellschaft (Hapag). Reasoning that Slaby had the Kaiser's backing and was therefore a safer investment, in June of 1900 Ballin equipped his new flagship ***DEUTSCHLAND*** with Slaby-Arco wireless equipment.

To compete with AEG's Adolf Slaby and Count Georg von Arco, Telebraun was finally forced to merge with Siemens & Halske. Now Braun was urged to speak about his improvements in wireless telegraphy equipment, for publicity was essential to the merger. In December, 1900, the amalgamation was completed, and the new company was named Gesellschaft fur Drahtlose Telegraphie. Telebraun contributed Braun's patents while Siemens & Halske provided the necessary funding for further development, along with its production capacity and international business connections. Braun now had the prestige to compete with the AEG-Slaby-Arco group.

Braun was sure that Marconi had infringed his British Patent #1862, of 26 January, 1899, which protected Braun's coupling circuit. Allegedly Marconi had admitted this. But Braun-Siemens did not immediately bring suit against Marconi. They were more concerned about their German competition, Slaby and von Arco. Braun's circuits were frequently used by Slaby, and increasingly Slaby's transmitters resembled Braun's.

With the Kaiser's backing, Slaby had the contracts for the German Imperial Navy. Braun-Siemens had the German Army. The first mobile Army wireless installations were in horse-drawn carriages, battery-powered, with balloons carrying antennas to the necessary heights. During the German Army's maneuvers in 1901 ranges of 100 kilometers were routinely reached by the Braun-Siemens equipment. The German generals were understandably not happy with allowing the enemy to tune in on all of the messages they sent, so Braun was given an Army contract in the summer of 1901 to perfect "directional wireless telegraphy."

In December of the same year Marconi finally succeeded in sending his first transatlantic signal from Poldhu, on the coast of Cornwall, to St. John's in Newfoundland. There was no message, just the three dots of the Morse letter "S," which was a long way from the commercial service that Marconi wanted to establish, but the unparalleled feat gave him a lot of publicity.

The nature and purpose of early wireless transmitters and receivers demanded that they be placed in high, windswept areas near vulnerable coastlines, where they were at the mercy of wind and wave. Like Braun at his North Sea base, Marconi had suffered many setbacks from storm damage, with the ensuing frustrations and delays. Tesla's laconic comment on Marconi's transatlantic achievement was, *"Marconi is a good fellow. Let him continue. He is using seventeen of my patents."*

Pioneer wireless engineer and American Marconi shipboard operator, E. J. Quinby, pointed out many years later that while Tesla failed to accomplish his dream of a global wireless communication system, he lived to see it carried out by others who used the system he had so thoroughly described years before their efforts.

During the winter of 1901-1902 Lee de Forrest desperately sought financial backing for his research, while he worried about his frayed, thin overcoat lasting through the bitter cold weather. Lee was acutely aware of Marconi's lead in commercial wireless telegraphy, and he was eager to catch up.

In 1902 de Forest's ambitions seemed about to come true, with the formation of "The American De Forest Wireless Telegraph Company," financed by the Wall Street wizardry of stock manipulator Abraham White. De Forest had one driving, short term goal… to make his name rank with Marconi's. His interest still lay in telephony, voice transmission, which Marconi had apparently not yet considered. In April, 1902, an article in the *New York World* sang the praises of the new, all-American wireless system, and noted that a de Forest operator in New York had exchanged messages with the Hapag liner ***DEUTSCHLAND***, 100 miles at sea. De Forest had no problem in communicating with the rival Slaby-Arco system, while Marconi operators were forbidden to exchange messages with any but their own.

The de Forest company put up two wireless stations on New York Bay, one at Coney Island, and one at Rockaway. These were soon followed by stations at Montauk Point, Key West, Havana and Atlantic City. De Forest had two New York offices, thirteen patents pending, a shop to make his own equipment, and constant competition from Marconi.

Many of the early wireless companies formed in the United States were short-lived because there simply was not yet enough business to pay operating costs and still finance the continual experimenting so necessary to a new technology. Unfortunately, more than a few of these companies were created merely for the purpose of selling worthless stock. As the stock of one company was sold out, a new company was born to take over the remaining assets and sell stock, while the old company was left with the liabilities.

Two of the Gehring group of companies which shared the same officers were the Pacific and the Continental Wireless Telegraph and Telephone Companies. Robert Marriott, an Ohio State graduate who had worked with Harry Shoemaker and Greenleaf Pickard in 1901, was promoted to Chief Engineer of the two companies, whose headquarters were located in Denver, Colorado. Marriott promoted the first two stations linking San Pedro, California, to Avalon, on Catalina Island, about 30 miles off the coast. Catalina's only contact with the mainland had been a ferry which operated two round trips a day. Most island residents were unable to comprehend wireless telegraphy, and became convinced that messages were actually being sent by carrier pigeons. San Pedro and Avalon exchanged the first commercial wireless messages in the United States in July of 1902. They may also be credited with the first apprehension of a criminal by wireless.

Two thieves had been regularly stealing cash and liquor from Avalon's Metropole Hotel, then escaping on the 5PM ferry to San Pedro. Because the earliest contact with the mainland would be the 11AM ferry the next day, the thieves would be safely hidden in Los Angeles by the time police there could be notified of the robbery.

The Metropole's manager, who had been much interested in the new wireless stations, thought he knew the identity of the robbers, so after the next robbery a wireless message to San Pedro preceded the 5PM ferry's arrival. Police met the vessel, arrested the thieves, thus putting a sudden end to the crime spree.

In the summer of 1902 de Forest's successful trials won him a contract with the United States Army Signal Corps. Observing this, the U.S. Navy decided to test de Forest's apparatus against their Slaby-Arco equipment. Meanwhile de Forest was also winning more and more civilian contracts. In February, 1903, de Forest invaded Marconi territory by equipping Sir Thomas Lipton's private yacht ***ERIN*** for her voyage from Clydebank to New York, where she was to act as tender to Lipton's racing yacht, ***SHAMROCK III***.

De Forest's top operator, Harry Mac Horton, went to Glasgow to supervise the installation of ***ERIN***'s wireless equipment. For three long weeks after the little flotilla departed Scotland, three de Forest operators spelled each other on a round-the-clock watch at the Steeple Chase Park Coney Island station, eagerly awaiting the first signal from Horton aboard ***ERIN***. De Forest joined his men as the calculated day of the yacht's arrival at New York grew closer. Never a good sailor, Horton was seasick constantly on the long voyage, and bad weather often made it necessary for him to tie himself to his chair as the little vessel continually rolled through an arc of sixty degrees. Horton optimistically began calling the Coney Island station when he was 1,000 miles out. ***ERIN*** was 90 miles off Sandy Hook when operator Jim Easton finally picked up the weary Horton's signal, sent on a standard 1 KW set.

Two of de Forest's operators at the Coney Island station knew Continental as well as American Morse, and they delighted in setting up the "Limey Sparks" aboard Cunard's ***LUCANIA*** when that Marconi-equipped vessel was in New York. The Marconi coherer-relay outfit with its Morse inker tape was incapable of handling code above 15 words per minute, while de Forest's equipment and operators easily sent and received up to 30 words a minute. The de Forest men would begin sending slowly to ***LUCANIA***'s "Sparks," then gradually they would speed up their transmissions until the Marconi man was completely lost in a meaningless rattle of relay, while the Yanks pounded merrily on. This was undoubtedly the real reason why Marconi operators were forbidden to exchange messages with other wireless services. Technological advances by so many engineers and scientists in other countries had left the comparatively uneducated and monopolistic Guglielmo Marconi far behind. For competitive purposes it was wiser not to let prospective customers for Marconi equipment realize that. At the American ***TITANIC*** inquiry her junior Marconi operator, Harold Bride, sneered at American wireless operators' abilities, but perhaps there was a tinge of envy in his scorn. In the United States virtually unlimited competition had forced rapid technological advances in the new science of wireless communication. But American wireless had another advantage, little known today. All of the early American wireless operators came from either Western Union or one of the many railroads in the United States. Thus they were naturally the best of the wire telegraphers. Their speed in transmitting and receiving was therefore as good as any equipment they used. In other countries, particularly Britain hampered by Marconi's wireless monopoly, there was no similarly driving competitive force, and no readily available pool of experienced telegraphers. The Marconi Company for the most part trained their own operators, thus their transmitting and receiving speed was never any better than Marconi equipment would make it. The top American wireless operators, however, most of whom had run the hot news and stock market wires, could easily send and receive 35, even more, words per minute.

De Forest had been experimenting with a Bunsen burner, into which he inserted two platinum electrodes, which were in turn connected to a telephone receiver and a dry battery. To one electrode de Forest connected an antenna wire which he ran out of the laboratory window to the top of a flagpole on the roof. Connecting the other electrode to a waterpipe which he used for a ground, de Forest listened for signals from the few wireless-equipped ships coming into New York Harbor. He soon received signals which confirmed his theory that incandescent gases would make a sensitive electromagnetic wave detector. De Forest worked secretly for the next few years, adding another electrode which gave his "gas-flame" detector greater efficiency. It would become known as the *"Audion,"* the first three-electrode vacuum tube, for which de Forest acquired U.S. Patent #841,387, on 15 January, 1907.

Wireless coverage of the 1903 America's Cup Races began as inauspiciously as it had in 1901, with frantic wig-wagging replacing the jammed, unintelligible dots and dashes of both Marconi and de Forest equipment.

In 1902 Dr. Gehring had launched another venture, the Consolidated Wireless Telegraph and Telephone Company, which was capitalized at $25 million. It absorbed the old holding company, American, along with the New England, North Western, Federal, and Atlantic operating companies. But stock sales were slow, and in February of 1903 Gehring moved again, to form the International

Wireless Telegraph and Telephone Company, capitalized at $7.5 million. Shoemaker and Pickard remained with the new International, and they put in another unauthorized appearance, covering the 1903 races from a schooner, utilizing its high masts for their antennas. An expert operator aboard the schooner spewed profanities, obscenities and ribald poetry into the ether, completely drowning out Marconi and de Forest transmissions again. Adding to this confusion was a powerful new station constructed at Atlantic Highlands to show the world that Professor Reginald Aubrey Fessenden had the only good system of tuning.

After two days of frustration de Forest, working with Harry Brown and "Pop" Athearn, replaced his original 5-kilowatt, 60-cycle generator and transformer. Failing to find the readymade electrolytic interrupter that he needed, de Forest rigged a collection of long, thin, steel rods and a porcelain tube, which dipped into an earthenware crock containing dilute sulphuric acid, along with a lead plate cathode. This makeshift rig was mounted on top of 100 acid-leaking storage batteries, on the open deck of the tug, where the whole contraption was subjected continuously to conducting salt spray. Brown swore softly as he had to reach gingerly over the acid and gently tap the rod each time the signal became weak and irregular. The jury-rigged apparatus worked well enough that its high-pitched squeal was picked up by eager ears at de Forest's Coney Island station, coming through over Marconi's hammerlike spark and the more musical, 120-cycle notes from the schooner. De Forest proved that even a faint high-frequency spark could get through where a ten times more powerful low-frequency signal was useless.

In 1904 de Forest sent equipment and operators to the Far East to establish a communication network for Captain Lionel James, war correspondent to the *London Times.* Previously, war news had traveled by cable and special courier, often reaching newspapers days after the event. De Forest operator "Pop" Athearn set up his equipment aboard ***HAIMUN***, a fast tug which James had chartered to cover what became the biggest naval battle of the Russo-Japanese War, while Harry Brown set up his land relay station at Weihaiwei, a British lease port on the northeast China coast.

By a stroke of superb luck ***HAIMUN*** happened to be near Admiral Togo's fleet when the Russian battleship ***PETROPAVLOVSK***, equipped with Slaby-Arco wireless, was lured from the safety of Port Arthur by Japanese light cruisers which looked like easy prey for the big warship. But using Marconi wireless, the cruisers quickly summoned fast torpedo boats which made short work of the ***PETROPAVLOVSK***. When Togo hoisted signal flags giving an ultimatum to the remainder of the Russian fleet, James scribbled his report to the *Times,* which Athearn flashed to the waiting Harry Brown, who relayed it to London by cable. James scooped his competitors by days, and de Forest got a tremendous amount of publicity.

The Russians became suspicious of the ever-present little ***HAIMUN***, and sent their cruiser ***BAYAN*** to investigate. As the Russian warship approached the tug, Athearn quickly tapped out a warning to Brown, telling him that ***HAIMUN*** was about to be boarded, and that if Brown heard nothing from Athearn in three hours he must notify the *Times* and the British consul. When the cruiser's officers boarded ***HAIMUN***, Athearn showed them a copy of the message he had just sent. The Russians studied it for a few moments, then quickly departed.

Marconi's first transatlantic transmission alarmed both Braun and Slaby. Braun-Siemens announced that they would file patent infringement suits against Marconi, then did not file. Officials of both AEG-Slaby-Arco and Braun-Siemens met at Kiel to discuss a merger. Slaby wanted the new company to use his name only, and Braun found that totally unacceptable. Nothing came of the merger talks. Braun and Slaby continued their patent fights while Marconi pushed ahead with his plans for a worldwide wireless network that would link the farthest outposts of the British

Empire.

Ever since the ***APRAKSIN*** incident in 1899 public sentiment in Germany had run high for a wireless system that would be strictly German, with the strength to compete against the British Marconi system. Rumors had spread that Braun-Siemens was considering a merger with Marconi, a situation entirely unacceptable to the Kaiser or his subjects. On 15 May, 1903, the first two syllables of the old Telebraun were combined with Slaby's "Funkentelegraphie" to form "Telefunken," the name of the new all-German company. Braun, Slaby, von Arco and Siemens pooled patents, employees and experience to compete effectively against Marconi. The feuding between the two German companies which had given Marconi a good lead, was over. The Kaiser expected Germany to forge quickly ahead in worldwide wireless competition. The business direction of the newly formed company was handled by Georg Count Arco, but Slaby continued to attack Braun's reputation and patents, until he lost favor even with the Kaiser, and died a bitter man in 1913.

Ferdinand Braun was now well-known not only in Germany, but in the international world of science as well. His views on wireless telegraphy included the edict that ships and shore stations must handle one another's traffic regardless of the wireless system used, and he recommended prescribed wavelengths for each. Still primarily an investigative scientist, Braun settled back into his university routine. He sought connections between acoustics and optics. He studied the effects of gravity on plant growth, and he continued and advanced electromagnetic wave experiments begun by Hertz.

In 1902, when the Kaiser's brother. Prince Henry, returned to Germany from America in the Slaby-Arco equipped ***DEUTSCHLAND***, he was furious to learn that he could not communicate with other German ships which were equipped by Marconi and carried British operators. Still smarting from this slight, in 1903 the Germans called the first conference to study the regulation of wireless telegraphy. It was confined to informal discussions and the preparation of an agenda for the next International Convention on Wireless Telegraphy, which would be held in 1906. The Italian delegation was concerned about distress signals from ships at sea, and brought up the desirability of a special and unmistakable signal, which must be granted complete priority over all other communications. The call "SSSDDD" was suggested. The 1903 Conference concluded that all wireless telegraphy stations, regardless of ownership, must give priority to distress calls from ships, but they left any definite regulations to be decided at the next conference in three years.

For several years Braun's crystal detector remained in limbo while Telefunken's Slaby-Arco faction insisted on using their own liquid-detector-earphone receiver. In 1905, after the vacuum-tube rectifier was introduced in America, Braun's crystal detector was revived. It was simple, inexpensive to produce, and it would become a household item in America, where the "crystal set" became the first radio in many homes.

In February, 1905, for the first time the Kaiser heard someone other than Slaby lecture on the subject of wireless telegraphy, when Braun addressed the Institute of Naval Architects m Berlin. Braun pointed out the fact that although distance communication was no longer a problem, transmitting in only one direction was still impossible. The Kaiser was impressed enough to see to it that Braun was offered a chair at the University of Berlin. But Braun much preferred Strasbourg, and there he stayed. Later that year he was diagnosed as having rectal cancer. Newly developed surgical techniques cured him, but left him greatly fatigued. Even though he was exhausted, Braun continued to contribute suggestions for Telefunken's technical development.

On 10 December, 1905, the first American wireless marine distress call was sent, from Relief

Ship No. 58, on Nantucket Shoals Station, after she had been trapped for several days in gales which intermittently reached hurricane force. Hammered repeatedly by heavy seas, the little vessel began to leak. Although all pumps operated to capacity, it became impossible to keep the water out. At 9AM Second Class Electrician William Snyder broadcast the call for aid to the Lighthouse authorities. He sent the simple word *"HELP,"* in both American and International Morse, and added *"Send aid from anywhere!"* Although the lightship finally sank, all thirteen of her crew were rescued by the Lighthouse Service Tender ***AZALEA***, responding to Snyder's wireless call for help.

As a result of de Forest's work for Sir Thomas Lipton the British Post Office invited the American inventor to demonstrate transmission across the Irish Sea in competition with their own system. De Forest and Mac Horton packed up their equipment and traveled eastward in White Star's ***MAJESTIC***. But when de Forest equipment with Horton at the key ripped off a fast 35 words per minute, the British decided that the American system could not possibly be as safe and reliable as they wanted. Nevertheless, de Forest considered it a personal triumph to prove his system's superiority.

There were still no regulations controlling wireless transmissions, except the unwritten code of courtesy among operators... of the same company! De Forest wrote in his autobiography, *"if a good old Yankee wireless jammed a Marconi lime-juicer... that was just too bad!"*

Marconi's magnetic detectors and coherers could not keep up with the carborundum detector invented in 1906 by former United States Army Signal Corps General Henry C. Dunwoody, who had become a de Forest vice president. Carefully wrapped in cotton batting and hidden in the pocket of many a "Limey Sparks," was a small chunk of "coal," as the Dunwoody carborundum came to be called, for the operators' personal improvement to Marconi's shipboard stations. In the same year Greenleaf Pickard discovered that silicon, galena and other minerals also acted as detectors, and some of them were more sensitive than carborundum. Operators from every company each had their own ideas about which mineral was the most sensitive, and consequently carried their own personal crystals, despite company regulations to the contrary which were imposed to prevent patent infringements.

In the Marconi Company "*CQ*" was the "all stations" call. Every station receiving *CQ* was to immediately stand at attention and reply. It became standard procedure for an operator to throw out the *CQ* call every two hours if no ships were being worked. By this method the operator could know if any vessels were within range, to be relied upon in an emergency. The Marconi Company issued charts to each of its shipboard operators, on a monthly basis, giving the expected tracks and positions of all Marconi-equipped vessels which he could expect to encounter in his area of the ocean. By perusing his charts an operator could know when he might reach another ship within his range. But ships, like airplanes, do not always stick to planned courses and schedules. They have mechanical problems and run late, and they go off course to avoid bad weather. The charts were therefore not always accurate. A chart was published, and is still used by ***TITANIC*** researchers to prove that ***FRANKFURT*** was 140 miles from ***TITANIC*** when she picked up and answered the White Star liner's first distress call. At the British Inquiry, however, Guglielmo Marconi admitted that this chart was made up *after* the disaster, and it was not one of the standard charts issued to Marconi's North Atlantic operators for the month of April, 1912. In fact, the *real* charts have always been conspicuous by their absence, yet there must have been many of them which might have been saved for posterity, for each operator was assigned a chart at the beginning of a voyage.

"*CQ*" being merely a standby signal, the Marconi Company realized that something more definite was needed to denote a distress call. In 1904 the third letter *"D"* was added, and "*CQD*" became Marconi's call *"to be given by ships in distress,* ***or in any way requiring assistance.*** *"* This meant that a vessel which was not necessarily in danger of sinking, yet needed some kind of assistance, perhaps a tow if her propeller shaft or engines had failed, or if she had run out of coal and was left powerless at the mercy of the sea, would use *"CQD"* to get attention. ***TITANIC*** legend erroneously parrots the official reckoning that *CQD* was a *distress* call specifically meaning that the ship was sinking, but in reality it was no such thing. Officially, however, it could not be admitted otherwise. Because ***TITANIC***'s Jack Phillips sent *CQD* first, the call heard by the German ***FRANKFURT***'s operator, asking what was wrong with ***TITANIC*** was a perfectly legitimate question, in spite of inference to the contrary by Harold Bride at both inquiries. And because the first call heard by the ***FRANKFURT*** operator, who answered Phillips immediately, was Marconi's *CQD* and not the international distress call *SOS,* the German operator had every reason to believe that ***TITANIC*** was not in dire straits, every reason to believe that the White Star liner wanted a *British,* Marconi-equipped ship and no other.

A romantic public immediately assumed that the letters *CQD* must stand for something, and assigned the phrase, *"Come Quick, Danger."* The letters meant nothing of the sort. They were merely a convenient extension of the normal *"Q"* code. For example, *"QRT"* meant *"Stop Sending." "QRU" meant "I have nothing for you." "QRL"* meant *"I am busy, please do not interfere,"* and *"QTC"* meant *"I have a message for you,"* or, *"How many messages have you to send?"* depending upon what the following transmission might be. *"QTH"* meant *"What is your location?"* or *"My location is...,"* again depending upon the context of its usage. *"QTR"* meant *"What is the exact time?"* or *"The time is..."* The "Q" code remains in aeronautical language today, particularly in international weather reporting, where *"QNH,"* for example, is followed by the altimeter setting at the given airport, while *"QFE"* is followed by an enroute altimeter setting.

German ships were accustomed to using *"SOE"* in the same way that Marconi used *"CQ."* When the 1906 Wireless Conference convened the German delegation suggested that *SOE* would do well as the new international distress call, but other delegates pointed out that the final "E" was only a dot in Morse code and could easily get lost through interference, or transmission by a nervous operator. The American delegation, headed by Admiral Manney and Ambassador Charlemagne Tower, suggested the letters *"NC,"* which were already used in the International Signal Code for visual signaling. The code flags for "N" and "C" meant "in distress" when flown from a vessel's signal halyard.

A modification of the German "SOE" was then suggested. The three dots, three dashes, and three more dots of "SOS" could not be mistaken for anything else. They could be sent and understood by the most inexperienced or nervous operator, and it was an attention-arresting, distinctive signal. The •••---••• was actually to be sent as one unbroken signal and could have signified the letters "VYB," "IJS" or "SMB" in Morse code. "SOS," however, was simpler. Again a romantic public believed the letters must stand for something, and assigned such phrases as "Save Our Ship," "Save Our Souls," and "Send Out Succour" to the signal. "SOS" meant none of these things. It was merely a conveniently-coupled, easily sent, easily understood series of dots and dashes.

Article 3 of the 1906 wireless treaty dealt specifically with allowing free traffic among all wireless systems, so that *"the monopolistic ambitions of some systems would be subverted for the good of all, at least where traffic between shore stations and ships" stations was concerned."* From 1 July, 1908, when the treaty went into effect, all public ship and shore wireless telegrams were to be handled between competing wireless systems when necessary. This did not mean just distress messages.

There were times when only a rival company's station had the range to relay messages, especially between ships at sea. Part of the international agreement mandated a standard frequency of 600 meters for ship-to-shore work, with 300 to 450 meters being used for short-range work.

It was in this same year, 1908, that the U.S. Government could not communicate with a party of Congressmen bound for the West Indies and the Canal Zone, because a young Marconi operator named Jack Binns obeyed Marconi Company regulations and refused to accept messages for the Americans aboard his ship because those messages were routed through the United Wireless station at Key West, Florida.

No wonder, then, that the United States delegates were not satisfied with the treaty's watered-down version of message relays. The Americans advocated completely free intercommunication between rival wireless firms, with mandatory free traffic between ships. De Forest had been doing it for years with no problem. Great Britain, Italy, Montenegro, and other countries committed to agreements with the Marconi Company, opposed the American suggestion. It was finally held that the objections to mandatory ship-to-ship traffic between rival systems made by Italy and England were justified. The Conference agreed, however, that it could not be denied that traffic between ships was growing rapidly, and that a situation where one ship might refuse to communicate with another in a very important matter was untenable. Therefore a settlement was reached wherein, with the *exception* of England, Italy, Japan, Portugal, Mexico and Persia, all Marconi territory, all the member states of the Treaty signed an added agreement, after which every ship's station, regardless of system, was obliged to conduct routine traffic with all other ships' stations. The Marconi Company continued to instruct its marine operators not to accept messages from ships using competing wireless systems, unless it was an emergency call. When Guglielmo Marconi indicated at the American ***TITANIC*** inquiry that the United States was not a party to the international wireless convention he was absolutely incorrect. Actually it was Great Britain and other Marconi dependent countries which were not parties to the treaty.

The "SOS" call was officially adopted by international ratification in July, 1908, but Marconi operators continued to reject it, possibly because it seemed in their minds that "SOS" was too close to the German "SOE." Marconi men continued to use "CQD," until Jack Phillips finally sent SOS from ***TITANIC***, an indication of his desperation, or possibly a direct order from Captain Smith who must have known full well the difference between "CQD" and "SOS." It has been erroneously written so often that ***TITANIC*** sent the first "SOS" in history that it has become firmly entrenched in ***TITANIC*** legend. This, too, is absolutely incorrect. ***TITANIC***'s Phillips sent the first "SOS" from a *British* vessel, but certainly not the first SOS in history. Operators from other wireless systems had no problem with accepting the 1908 treaty adoption of "SOS," just as they had no problem with intercommunication between rival systems.

Spark transmitters in use by United Wireless in the summers of 1907 and 1908 bore the insignia of American de Forest, and had been designed by Harry Shoemaker. These transmitters were known among shipboard operators as superior to the spark-coil transmitters that the Marconi Company was then using, because they used alternating current derived from motor-alternators and an open core transformer, which gave more transmitting power. Here was one more reason why Marconi operators found it difficult to communicate with other wireless services. Undoubtedly this rather than monopoly was the real reason behind Marconi's refusal to accept the terms of the 1908 wireless treaty. While there can be no doubt but what Marconi was working hard to catch up with such a rapidly advancing technology, it was one thing to fit out new ships with a competitive apparatus, but it was quite another, and very costly matter to retrofit those already carrying the older equipment.

The first actual use of "SOS" from an American ship was sent by United Wireless operator Theodore D. Haubner, on 11 August, 1909, from the Merchants and Miners ***SS ARAPAHOE***, a single screw freight and passenger liner bound for Charleston, South Carolina, and Jacksonville, Florida, from New York, when her shaft broke 21 miles southeast of Cape Hatteras. ***ARAPAHOE*** was helpless, adrift in a gale which was driving her toward the infamous Diamond Shoals, an area that mariners called "Graveyard of the Atlantic." Haubner sent both "SOS" and "CQD" so there could be no possibility that the new call would be lost on an operator unfamiliar with it. ***ARAPAHOE*** was rescued by two company ships, ***HURON*** and ***IROQUOIS***. *A* few months later Haubner's role was reversed, and ***ARAPAHOE*** answered an SOS sent by the ***IROQUOIS***. At the age of nineteen Haubner was the first operator to send, and the second operator to receive, the new SOS call.

The first SOS sent on the Great Lakes came from the sinking Pere Marquette Car Ferry No. 18, on 9 September, 1910. In the early part of this century the Pere Marquette Railroad, as did other railroads of the area, operated a fleet of assorted vessels to cut rail travel time and thus save money by crossing Lake Michigan instead of going all the way around it. The main eastern terminus of the Pere Marquette fleet was Ludington, Michigan, located in the center of the Lake's long north-south shoreline. The largest units of the fleet, which had been one of the first to be equipped with de Forest wireless, were railroad car ferries.

Pere Marquette No. 18 had been launched from the American Shipbuilding Company's Cleveland yard in August, 1902. She was a combination passenger and car ferry, built of steel, with a length overall of 358 ft., and a breadth overall of 56 ft. No. 18 departed Ludington at 11:40PM on 8 September, 1910, bound for Milwaukee with 29 loaded railroad cars. The wind was freshening out of the north, and a heavy sea was running. At 3AM an oiler on routine rounds discovered that the after compartments were flooding fast, and immediately reported this startling piece of news to his Chief, who lost no time in reporting it to the bridge. Pumps were started and 12 cars were jettisoned to lighten the load, but it was in vain. Wireless operator Stephen Szcpanck, who doubled as purser and freight clerk, was routed out of bed to send the SOS. At 4:15 Operator Durffe at Ludington heard the distress call and dispatched rescue vessels to the scene.

No. 18's sister ship, No. 17, was enroute from Milwaukee to Ludington when her operator picked up the SOS. She arrived on the scene at 6:30AM, just as No. 18's bow rose high in the air, and the ship paused for a brief moment before her final plunge. Boats were quickly lowered from No. 17 and 32 people were rescued from the water. The master, 23 other crew members and Operator Szcpanck were lost. Legend has it that Szcpanck's radio receiver washed ashore near Manitowoc, Wisconsin, and was displayed in a local store window for some time. If this is true, it was the only piece of wreckage ever found from No. 18.

Still working to establish his planned commercial transatlantic wireless service, in May, 1905, Guglielmo Marconi sailed with his new bride in the Cunarder ***CAMPANIA*** to New York. After being chased by many women for years, the charming and attractive Italian had proved himself a chip off the old block. At the age of thirty three he married twenty-year old Beatrice O'Brien, the lovely daughter of an Irish peer in the House of Lords. Now Guglielmo took his young bride to Glace Bay, on Cape Breton Island, in Nova Scotia, where he hoped that his newly completed station would be the western half of a commercial wireless link between Europe and America. Bea was extremely unhappy when Marconi devoted most of his time to work instead of her. After a few weeks he returned to England in the ***CAMPANIA***, leaving Bea to be miserable at Glace

Bay while he checked the signal strength of the Cape Breton and Poldhu transmitters as the Cunarder steamed eastward. The results were not as good as he had hoped, and he was forced to make quite a few modifications to the Poldhu station before he got good signals during the day as well as at night. While making these adjustments Marconi discovered that results were better if he used a long wire aerial set up so that it pointed toward the distant transmitter. He filed for a British patent on his "horizontal directional aerial" in July, 1905. De Forest claimed to have made the same accidental discovery in 1903, but he did not file for a United States patent on his horizontal antenna until 20 June, 1906. His Patent #1,101,533 described horizontal receiving and transmitting antennas, as well as a method for utilizing railroad trackside telegraph wires as a "wave chute" between transmitter and receiver, with the rails used as the earth connection.

Cuthbert Hall, the Marconi Company's Managing Director, had been trying to get the Admiralty to underwrite the cost of moving the Poldhu station to a safer position, as it was thought that the Cornish coast would be particularly vulnerable to wartime naval attacks. Hall had no success with the Admiralty, and Marconi decided to build the new station with company funds. He chose Clifden, in Galway, on Ireland's west coast, for the site of the new station. On 15 July, 1907, the transatlantic wireless link was established between Glace Bay and Poldhu, which was used temporarily for the tests. In September regular commercial service was finally inaugurated between Glace Bay and Clifden.

Tesla's years had been filled with lectures, development of his roB.O.T. boats and torpedoes, and the experiments he carried out in his Colorado Springs laboratory which brought him ridicule and hostility from local residents. In Colorado Tesla had heard "radio signals from outer space," and he was convinced that they came from intelligent beings, perhaps from Mars. He became obsessed with finding a way to answer them, while he continued experiments aimed at establishing global transmission of electrical power without wires.

Early in 1903 Tesla had returned to New York, again impoverished, seeking backers who would finance his proposed worldwide wireless telegraphy network. He wrote to Westinghouse, urging another collaboration, for his experiments had convinced Tesla that global communication would be possible, using machinery he had developed in his Colorado laboratory. Westinghouse suggested that Tesla should turn again to the bankers. Tesla wrote to J. P. Morgan, begging the great financier to back his international wireless system. Morgan advanced $150,000 with 51% interest in Tesla's wireless patents to be used as collateral. Tesla purchased 200 wooded acres on Long Island for the site of his first station. He would employee 2,000 men, who would be housed with their families on the tract, which Tesla named "Wardenclyffe." He engaged famous architect Stanford White, who had designed many impressive New York City buildings, to construct the grandiose establishment. Tesla expected to get a United States Navy contract for his radio-controlled coastal defense system which would help finance the Wardenclyffe project. Unfortunately, the Navy contract never materialized.

Wardenclyffe's lofty towers reached skyward, while Tesla poured the $150,000 and more into his project. Hampered by lack of funding, perhaps unwilling to take one small step at a time as Marconi was doing, Tesla begged Morgan for more money. Morgan refused. To economize, Tesla moved his New York lab facilities to Wardenclyffe, then wrote more letters to Morgan, some angry, some beseeching, which Morgan refused to answer. Word got around the financial community that Morgan had dropped out of the Wardenclyffe project, and other bankers steered clear of Tesla.

But worse was to come. Tesla was sued by the City Power Company of Colorado Springs for payment on the electricity he had used in his experiments there. He had gone to Colorado with the assurance from one of the power plant's owners that electricity would be provided free for his laboratory. The City of Colorado Springs also sued Tesla for payment on water he had used, and the lab's caretaker sued for back wages. Tesla was forced to take time off from the Wardenclyffe project to return to Colorado and settle his debts. A little money came in from the sale of his "therapeutic coils," being manufactured at Wardenclyffe for sale to hospitals and medical researchers, but it was hardly enough to pay his employees' wages. Tesla invented a revolutionary turbine which he expected to restore his fortune and reputation, but again the bankers failed to back him. All of this sidetracked Tesla from the original purpose of Wardenclyffe, while Marconi forged resolutely ahead.

Tesla still had many friends, many who believed in his genius, and who did all they could for him, but the big money men had permanently forsaken the man whose flamboyant schemes were probably beyond their intellectual comprehension and conservative financial practices. On 25 June, 1906, Tesla received an even greater blow. His friend and designer of Wardenclyffe, Stanford White, was shot to death on the roof of Madison Square Garden by Harry K. Thaw, in a dispute over showgirl Evelyn Nesbitt.

Wardenclyffe was finally abandoned. Vandalized after Tesla could no longer afford a caretaker, what was to have been the world's first global wireless communication center fell into disrepair. Tesla signed the deed to Wardenclyffe over to Waldorf-Astoria, Inc., so that he could continue to live in his customary luxury at the Waldorf.

In 1905 President Theodore Roosevelt, aboard the battleship ***USS WEST VIRGINIA*** off Cape Hatteras, received a message from the Governor of Ohio, sent from de Forest's transmitter at Cleveland. Roosevelt's enthusiastic recommendations soon got de Forest a contract to equip the entire United States Navy. The Mallory Clyde, Savannah, Red D, New York and Puerto Rico steamship companies, all U.S.-flagged Standard Oil tankers and Atlantic coastal vessels carried de Forest equipment.

New shore stations had to be built to keep up with the seagoing wireless traffic, which now exceeded that provided by Marconi. De Forest masts soared above Bridgeport, Boston, New Haven, Portland (Maine), Montauk Point, Navesink Highlands, Atlantic City, Key West, Havana, Southwest Pass and Galveston. Great Lakes vessels equipped by de Forest also needed more shore stations. Detroit, Port Huron, Buffalo, Cleveland, Michigan City and Chicago joined the de Forest network. In addition to new offices at 42 Broadway, New York City, where a 2-kilowatt station with call letters "NY" was built atop Lee's penthouse laboratory, his crowning achievement in 1905 was the completion of America's first 50-kilowatt wireless station, "DF," at Manhattan Beach, Coney Island. In October that year de Forest operators set a new distance record, 2,150 miles between Manhattan Beach and Colon, in the Canal Zone, almost the distance of Marconi's transatlantic signals.

In May, 1905, Ferdinand Braun was elected Rektor for the 1905-1906 academic year at the University of Strasbourg. Braun looked ahead to the future of physics, when matter would be divided into particles 2,000 times smaller than the atom. In the same year Braun warned about the malevolent use of wireless in wartime. He pioneered the development of phased antennas, while his dry sense of humor continued to delight his students, for it kept his lectures lively.

De Forest's successes in America, Captain James' highly lauded coverage of the Russo-Japanese War, and the growing number of de Forest-equipped vessels arriving in England persuaded a group of London financiers headed by Lord Armstrong to attempt an introduction of de Forest service in England, the heart of Marconi territory. In February, 1906, de Forest once more headed for the

British Isles, this time aboard the aging Cunarder ***LUCANIA***, his hopes for a new transoceanic wireless link bolstered by the Colon-Manhattan Beach record.

De Forest's first Yankee wireless stations on British turf were at Oxford and Cambridge, and they employed British operators. The stations were equipped with alternating current transformers, and electrolytic detectors with headphones connected to three-coil slide tuners. They differed radically from Marconi equipment, but were exactly like de Forest stations on the American Atlantic coast.

First, de Forest attempted to build a station at Glengariff, on the Bay of Bantry, in Ireland. He planned to utilize heavy-duty kites, tethered with special cable developed by the United States Army Signal Corps, to carry his antennas to new heights, which he expected would give tremendous range to the wireless signals. His goal was to "bring in" the de Forest station at Manhattan Beach.

High winds sweeping across Bantry Bay proved too much for the kites, so de Forest moved his site to Cahermore, some thirty miles west of Glengariff. There, on the night of 11 April, 1906, with the kite at an altitude of 2,000 feet, de Forest was sure that he received the Long Island station. But the New York operator was sending too fast for de Forest to copy. Mac Horton, who had already left Cahermore to supervise work on the British stations, could easily have read the message, but de Forest lacked practical Morse experience. Before leaving New York he had arranged with operator "Driver" Harris to send nightly messages at specified times. Too late de Forest realized that he should have stuck to something simple like Marconi's first "S." He did recognize, however, the strictly American style of sending, and the spark frequency was much higher than that of any British ships, and decidedly different from the "splashy plop-plop" of Poldhu. De Forest's transatlantic achievement came almost five years after Marconi's first "S" transmission, but several months before Marconi established regular commercial transatlantic service.

Upon his return to Castletown two days later de Forest was greeted with a demand from His Majesty's General Post Office to know if he had been receiving telegraphic signals across "their" Atlantic Ocean, and if so, by whose authority? On 1 January, 1905, The Wireless Telegraphy Act of Great Britain had gone into effect. It stated that the Post Office must grant permission for all wireless stations operated in Britain, and de Forest had failed to apply for permission. Promptly and politely, de Forest wrote to the Postmaster General, explaining that his experiments had been with receiving equipment only, and suggesting that work of such scientific value should be encouraged rather than frowned upon.

In 1906 a young woman named Anna Nevins left the Western Union to try her hand at the new wireless telegraphy The De Forest Company hired her to handle traffic at its "NY" station atop 42 Broadway in New York City. Nevins had no problem working the cumbersome key used in those days to break the crashing open gap spark, and she was soon clearing NY's ship traffic as competently as any male "brass-pounder." In July, 1910, Nevins married H. J. Hughes, manager of "NY," and "retired." A young Florida woman, Miss Graynella Packer, came to United from Western Union in 1910, and had the distinction of becoming the first female seagoing wireless operator when she was assigned to the Clyde Steam Ship Company's ***SS MOHAWK*** in November of that year. There was naturally a good deal of opposition from ships' officers, as a female operator brought up the question of gallantry... could they properly leave a woman at the wireless key of a sinking ship, thus violating the "first law of the sea," meaning women and children first? Packer insisted that "ladies first" did not apply to her, but as it turned out her brave words were never put to the test. She left the sea shortly after that to study music. During her brief tenure at sea, however, male operators who had at first treated her with polite deference, began using profanities and "burning her up," that is sending too fast for a novice to receive, after Packer made the mistake of telling reporters that a life at sea was a good life for a woman. Male operators well remembered that many of them had lost landline telegraphy jobs to women who did the job just as well, at half the pay of men.

Also during 1906 de Forest patented what he called his "Aerophore signaling device," which automatically warned mariners of "approach to a point of danger, giving direction therefrom." Lee foresaw land stations like lighthouses warning ships of their proximity when lights would be obscured by fog or storms. Aerophore sets on ships would "absolutely" warn mariners of the approach of a vessel fitted with a similar device, and would give the direction of approach.

During the summer of 1906 the relationship between Lee de Forest and his company's managers began to deteriorate. While de Forest was in England, Abraham White organized the United Wireless Telegraph Company. After overselling de Forest stock. White had transferred all of the assets of the American De Forest Wireless Telegraph Company into United, leaving American De Forest with nothing but the debts. White then announced to the press that the new company was soon to be merged with the American Marconi Company, which the latter firmly denied. Angrily, Lee de Forest resigned, turning back all of his personal stock shares into the empty De Forest Company treasury, and demanding full rights to pending Audion and Aerophone patents, $1,000 in cash, and a general release. Philip Farnsworth, the company's patent attorney, advised White to accept de Forest's demands because the patents were worthless anyway, and de Forest's contributions to the company had been negligible! Attorney C. C. Higgins demanded half of the $1,000 settlement as his fee for representing de Forest. Out of the remaining $500 Lee bought a 5,000 cycle generator from the old company for $150. Thus he started over again with a capital of $350. But Lee de Forest had no trouble attracting investors, and late in 1906 he designed and built his first carbon arc transmitter for the new De Forest Radio Telephone Company.

It had been noted for sometime by several different scientists that bundles of weakly magnetized iron wire exposed to a field produced by high frequency alternating current could receive radio signals. In 1904 Marconi began using his version of the *magnetic detector*, replacing the bundles of wire with a slow-moving band of fine insulated iron wire. The band moved around two rotating discs, one of which was driven by clockwork. The band itself was about 1/8 inch in diameter, and it passed through a small glass tube, which was bound by fine copper wires, one end of which was connected to ground, the other to an antenna. The Marconi Company used magnetic detectors from this time until after World War I, although they were not as sensitive as a good crystal detector, then being used by de Forest, Telefunken and United Wireless.

During the week of 15 to 20 July, 1907, de Forest equipped W. R. Huntington's yacht ***THELMA*** at Put-In-Bay on Lake Erie with the first marine radio-telephone, excepting that which de Forest had recently tested in a Lackawanna Railroad ferry. From ***THELMA*** Lee broadcast news of the Interlakes Association races to shore stations. The greatest signal range achieved was only four miles, but that was remarkable considering the low height of ***THELMA***'s masts. De Forest predicted that in five years' time voice/radio range would be 500 miles. In fifteen years it would reach across the Atlantic. He was wrong. In less than nine years radiotelephony had gone transatlantic. Still, even an old friend from Lee's Western Electric days, W. W. Dean, president of the Dean Telephone Company at Elyria, Ohio, was skeptical. Dean predicted that there would be little market for wireless telephone equipment!

In September, 1907, de Forest began to equip the United States Navy with radio-telephones. Tests between the battleships ***USS VIRGINA*** and ***USS CONNECTICUT*** had reached a range of 22 miles, and convinced Navy officials that sixteen battleships, six destroyers and two auxiliary vessels commanded by Admiral Evans should be equipped with radio-telephones before starting their globe-circling cruise. The Fleet was no more than hull down on the horizon when de Forest turned his attention to equipping the United States Army Signal Corps with a shore installation at Fort Monroe, and he installed another set aboard its minelaying tug ***RINGGOLD***. But all did not go well that year for Lee. Just after Christmas he

suffered a serious setback due to fire, which destroyed his laboratory, along with all of his original Audion tubes.

In the early morning hours of 3 February, 1908, the White Star liner ***CYMRIC*** was struggling through a blinding snowstorm and raging seas about 200 miles east of Cape Sable, when her watch officer spotted the fiercely burning cargo steamer ***ST. CUTHBERT***, out of Antwerp for New York. Realizing that no small boat could live in the mountainous seas, ***CYMRIC***s master, Captain John Lewis, could do no more than stand by hove-to until 2 o'clock the following afternoon. By then the storm's fury had slackened enough that Lewis could order the launch of one boat manned by five seamen and one officer. ***ST. CUTHBERT***'s entire crew of 38 men was then shuttled to safety aboard ***CYMRIC***. The liner's Marconi operator flashed an account of the dramatic rescue to New York newspapers, which gave the Marconi Company much favorable publicity, although wireless had not actually contributed to the rescue. ***ST. CUTHBERT*** had no wireless, and ***CYMRIC***'s proximity to the burning freighter was merely lucky chance. There would be a great deal of discussion at both ***TITANIC*** inquiries about the practice of Marconi operators selling their eyewitness accounts of maritime disasters to newspapers. The Marconi Company had never discouraged this, and for good reason... it was free publicity. In fact, it was fantastic publicity which could not have been purchased at any price.

Uncharacteristically, Marconi refrained from publicizing his new transatlantic wireless link. Cuthbert Hall suggested that it would be better to let the new service announce itself rather than have ceremonial, publicity-seeking messages followed by periods of failure, like the earlier attempt to establish the service. Marconi, too, was having problems attracting financial backers. In 1908 he succeeded in selling two coastal stations to the Government of South Africa, but his plans for an Empire wireless system fell on deaf ears.

On 11 September, 1908, Marconi's daughter Degna was born, but there were signs of a strain in his marriage.

Also in 1908 Cuthbert Hall resigned and Marconi was appointed temporary Managing Director, with Jameson-Davis and Flood-Page to assist him. Late in 1909 the transatlantic service was interrupted when the Glace Bay station was almost completely destroyed by fire. It did not come into full operation again until April, 1910.

Bea was pregnant again, and Marconi sent her, with her sister Lilah, to Villa Grifone to await the baby's arrival. Annie had seen little enough of her son; in fact she had to beg others to keep her informed of his whereabouts. She seemed only too glad to have her daughter-in-law and grandchild in Italy, staying so close to her own home in Bologna.

Also in February, 1908, Lee de Forest married Nora Stanton Blatch, Cornell University's first female civil engineering graduate, and granddaughter of Suffragette leader Elizabeth Cady Stanton. De Forest combined business with his honeymoon trip to Europe, where he introduced his radio telephone to ***Parisian***s by broadcasting from the Eiffel Tower. All night he and Nora played phonograph records into a microphone. In the morning they were delighted to learn that they had been heard as far away as Marseille, on the Mediterranean coast, a distance of 500 miles.

From France the newlyweds traveled to Germany, where they met such prominent German scientists as Dr. Georg Seibt, who was working with the new "quenched-spark" wireless telegraphy. When Seibt showed de Forest his experiments utilizing the quenched spark combined with a high-frequency alternating current source, de Forest realized that his Radio Telephone Company could easily enter into the telegraphy field, and suggested that Seibt come to America to work for him.

The next stop on the honeymoon-business trip was Italy, deep into Marconi territory. Despite strong protests from Marconi Company officials, the Italian Government installed four de Forest radio telephone instruments on battleships at Spezia. Then it was back to Paris where de Forest demonstrated his "radio knife," or "cold cautery" as he preferred to call it, which was beginning to revolutionize surgical procedures. Aggravating Marconi further, Lee and his bride traveled to England, where he installed a radio telephone aboard the Royal Navy cruiser ***HMS FURIOUS***. During the Admiralty tests Lee worked the apparatus aboard the cruiser, while Nora, who had returned to college for a special course taught by Professor Pupin so that she could assist her husband, handled the equipment aboard the school ship ***VERNON***.

De Forest's proposal to broadcast opera from Covent Garden to every home within a radius of thirty miles elicited a response from Marconi himself. *"I want to say that we shall not have long to wait for the wireless telephone. De Forest and his colleagues are doing great things in that direction."*

Returning to the United States, de Forest continued with his experiments in radiotelephony, his goal to broadcast opera for all to enjoy as he did. It was not long until he knew he had succeeded. Wireless operators at sea and at the Brooklyn Navy Yard were surprised to hear music coming through their earphones instead of the familiar harsh staccato of Morse.

The strain of working together, for a woman as independent as Nora Blatch de Forest, would eventually cause a rift in their marriage. Lee was ecstatic when their daughter, Harriet, was born on 19 June, 1909, but two years later he and Nora agreed to part, while Nora pursued her engineering career.

Dr. Seibt came from Germany with his quenched-spark, new inductive couplers and variable condensers, among other improvements. By the middle of 1909 reports were coming in from remarkable distances, from ships and even from United Wireless stations, which heard de Forest's 1,000 sparks per second notes, read through static and interference which completely obliterated the old low-frequency sparks.

In 1909 the Junior Wireless Club Limited was formed by a group of New York schoolboy amateur wireless operators, with Professor Reginald A. Fessenden as their advisor. The Club's fourteen-year-old president, W E. D. "Weddy" Stokes, Jr., went to Washington to argue against the first attempt by Congress to regulate amateur operators out of existence. Eloquently young Stokes attacked the "wireless trust" and declared that the "inventive genius of America's dedicated young wireless amateurs must be protected." Three years later at the ***TITANIC*** inquiries amateur operators would be vilified by investigators and the press, blamed for spurious messages and for "jamming" legitimate messages concerning the ***TITANIC***.

American freedom and ingenuity had teamed up to foster the development of amateur wireless in the United States, as in no other country. Freedom of the airwaves extended to small boys who claimed the right to send "GTH" (Go To Hell) to exasperated Navy and commercial operators. "Tin-can" amateurs blithely gossiped or did their arithmetic homework via wireless. With no wavelengths prescribed, the ether became literally a chaotic free-for-all. U.S. Navy operators at Newport claimed that amateur interference prevented important messages from reaching President Roosevelt aboard the battleship ***USS MAINE*** off Cape Cod in 1906, losing many hours when the dispatches had to be carried by a destroyer.

Amateurs were quick to retort that the Navy used antiquated equipment and that most Navy operators could profit from more training. While "Weddy" Stokes was lobbying in Washington, amateur operators deluged their Congressmen with mail protesting any form of Government control of the airwaves. The Army, Navy and Coast Guard were naturally in favor of regulations, while the commercial companies were divided. Records were produced to show how amateurs had falsely sent distress messages from fictitious ships at sea. The Revenue Cutter Service complained that amateurs not only broadcast profanities, but also filled the airwaves with music from their gramophones. In the early days of wireless not many professionals thought beyond the transmission of paid messages as the future of wireless. Commercial broadcasting of music, plays, opera, speeches, and advertising was far in the future.

In rebuttal, amateurs were quick to point out that not all Navy traffic was important, or even official. Trivial, social correspondence, which ought to have been handled by telegraph, telephone or mail, was filling the ether with sometimes embarrassingly personal, even compromising messages better left to the privacy of the boudoir. One dashing officer had used Navy wireless to cancel plans with a lady friend when his wife had come home unexpectedly early. Navy wives routinely used wireless to plan their teas and cocktail parties. Amateurs painstakingly copied all of these incriminating messages. One especially enterprising California boy sent some of these spicy messages to the press, while admitting that he often had fun at the expense of Navy operators by interrogating ships at sea and signing the name of some high-ranking officer to his messages. Experienced Navy and commercial operators were well able to recognize an amateur "fist" and transmitter, when they heard it often enough, and that was their only defense. It was not uncommon to hear a pro pounding out *"You kids shut up!"*

With no prescribed wavelengths wireless anarchy was common at sea, too. Everybody heard everybody else within range, which was usually from 100 to 150 miles. Occasionally ranges were extended, especially at night, to as much as 500 miles, by the radio phenomenon which is known today as "skip." The tone emitted by the standard key of this era was broad and interfering, and while it was transmitting it blocked all signals within its range. Operators might carry on personal conversations, usually about amorous adventures in their last port of call, or they might even play chess via wireless. Operators within their range who had legitimate messages to transmit had to rely entirely on the courtesy of those already sending to allow them to break in. A favorite method of retribution was to drop a book on the key and go outside for a smoke, thus effectively ending all traffic within range for as long a period as suited the whim. Arguments between rival company operators were frequent. *"GTH"* was the usual transmission in such cases, but stronger ones, such as *"FU,"* were also used. Every operator had at his fingertips a long line of abbreviated epithets, which occasionally brought two operators into fisticuffs when they met at a saloon or pub ashore. One legendary and lengthy transmission to a German operator was *"God damned Slaby-Arco rotten louse and humpbacked monkey!"*

But there are two sides to every story, and on the other side of the amateur wireless coin were boys like Edwin Howard Armstrong. He was an excellent example of the dedicated amateur who rose to the top of his field as a professional.

Edwin Howard Armstrong was born a week before Christmas in 1890, in the Chelsea district of New York City, to a financially comfortable, educated and intellectual family. Howard's mother, Emily, was a graduate of Hunter College. She had taught school for ten years before her marriage to John Armstrong, who became a vice president of the American branch of Oxford Press. In 1902 the Armstrongs moved to Yonkers. Two years later, returning from his annual trip to London, John brought his thirteen year old son a book titled *"The Boys' Book of Inventions."* John's London trip the following year added a second book, *"Stories of Inventors."* Howard was hooked. He *would* be an inventor. By 1905 he had entered high school and focused on the exciting new field of wireless telegraphy.

Like the young Marconi, Howard worked in the attic of his family's home. And like so many American youngsters, he painstakingly built his own wireless apparatus. Part of the fun of being an amateur wireless operator lay in experimenting, tinkering, improving, extending the range and strength of signals, reaching farther and farther away for new wireless friends. Howard Armstrong, typical of the majority of young American wireless amateurs, went on to study electrical engineering at Columbia University, and became a wireless professional. While still a student at Columbia, Howard began to study Lee de Forest's Audion, and he discovered the Audion's *regenerative, or feedback,* effect.

De Forest himself had apparently not understood what Armstrong learned from exhaustive analysis of currents and voltages in the Audion's circuits. Aided by Professor Morecroft and the school laboratory facilities, Armstrong discovered that some alternating current was being produced in the plate current, where it had been assumed that only a diminishing direct current existed. It was common practice in electrical engineering to increase an alternating current by tuning, but Armstrong placed a second tuning coil in the Audion's output, or *"wing"* circuit. The results were astounding. Distant signals, which had been only a whisper under even the most favorable circumstances, came in loud and clear with Armstrong's regenerative circuit. From his Yonkers attic Howard pulled in Glace Bay, Clifden, and other European stations. He could receive not only Marconi's spark, but also Poulsen-arc continuous wave stations as far away as San Francisco and Honolulu. No commercial station had that ability when teenage amateur wireless operator Howard Armstrong made his startling discovery in 1912. There were so many amateurs who improved upon commercial equipment that it was not uncommon for amateur operators to relay messages for even the big commercial stations. The majority of amateurs, then, were competent, inventive, conscientious and reliable. Armstrong himself would go on to discover "frequency modulation," the basis of the FM radios that we know today with their greater immunity to static and superior sound fidelity. Unfortunately, Armstrong would later become locked in a bitter patent struggle with the Radio Corporation of America, then headed by one-time Marconi office boy and close friend of Howard's, David Sarnoff. In 1954 when Armstrong's personal funds had been exhausted and there seemed no hope of ever winning, he who was always enamoured of heights leaped to his death from his thirteenth floor apartment overlooking New York City's East River.

Late in 1909 the United States Army Signal Corps contracted for de Forest's wireless telephones. In the same year Lee's mother-in-law, Harriet Stanton Blatch, delivered a speech on women's suffrage from a radio-telephone transmitter atop the Metropolitan Life Building in New York City. On the ninth floor of this lofty building de Forest opened a sub-office, which was the first store in the world devoted entirely to the display and sale of amateur radio apparatus and parts, which his company manufactured.

About this time de Forest opened a Philadelphia station on the top of the Land Title Building. It was equipped with a quenched-gap transmitter and steam-arc telephone, and designed to work with his New York station in the upper dome of the Manhattan Life Building at 52 Broadway. This new station was located in an area of the most complete and hostile radio interference, but de Forest was willing to accept the challenge as a chance to test the anti-interfering circuits he was developing. He effectively broadcast through United's old-fashioned spark gap and carborundum detector, and through the Marconi Company's three slide tuner in its Waldorf-Astoria station. While deliberate interference for the sake of suppressing competition was normal in those days before regulations, it promoted the development of selecting tuning devices, and the shielding of receiving apparatus, which might not have been achieved so rapidly under more amicable relations between wireless systems.

This was the year, 1909, in which Braun and Marconi jointly received the Nobel Prize for Physics. In his speech introducing the two recipients Hans Hildebrand, President of the Royal Swedish Academy of Sciences, declared, *"The development of a great invention seldom occurs through one individual man, and many forces have contributed to the remarkable results now achieved. Marconi's original system had its weak points. It is due to above all the inspired work of Professor Braun that this unsatisfactory state of affairs was overcome."*

Marconi and Braun met for the first time on this occasion. Personally they had never been rivals, and each had acknowledged the importance of the other's work. Braun, the scientist, was too easygoing to find it difficult to share the coveted Prize. If Marconi resented having to share the limelight with another, particularly a German, he was gracious enough not to publicly show his displeasure.

The most important wireless event of 1909 had nothing to do with technological advances. It was the sinking of the White Star liner ***REPUBLIC***. It raised Marconi's popularity to new heights, and made a young man by the name of Jack Binns famous, the same Jack Binns who had refused to accept messages from the Government of the United States when they were relayed through a rival company's station. If anyone had paid attention, these two unrelated acts foreshadowed a far worse marine disaster that would take place three years later, and they set the state for the greatest loss of life yet in maritime history. The ***REPUBLIC*** sinking is so important to understanding the ***TITANIC*** tragedy that it will be dealt with in a separate chapter, rather than digressing from the history of wireless at this point.

By 1910 the many smaller wireless operating companies in the United States had begun to disappear, merged with, or absorbed by the larger companies. The Gehring group, mentioned earlier, had been absorbed by American de Forest. At the time Abraham White formed United Wireless to take over de Forest assets, it included 39 land stations and over 100 marine installations.

Along with the Gehring group, de Forest had acquired the young genius Harry Shoemaker. But due to policy disagreements with de Forest and White, Shoemaker resigned in 1904, and with John Firth as manager, formed the International Telegraph Construction Company, which supplied equipment to commercial and government stations. International was absorbed by United Wireless in 1908, after Firth's expertise was lost when he resigned in February to form the Wireless Specialty Apparatus Company with Greenleaf Pickard. In July of the same year United's Wilson gained control of International and acquired Shoemaker, who became United's Chief Engineer.

By 1910 United had 88 stations on the United States mainland, plus 9 in Alaska and 34 in Central and South America. United also equipped 262 ships. United's major competitor was American Marconi, which was still using ten-inch spark coils in their standard 1½ kilowatt shipboard installations, while United used more effective 2 KW sets.

The Marconi Company's financial situation took an upward turn in 1910, after the appointment of Godfrey Isaacs as Managing Director on 10 January. In March of that same year Isaacs sent a proposal to the Colonial Office for Marconi's long-coveted Empire wireless system. In the same month Godfrey's brother, Rufus, was appointed Solicitor General to His Majesty's Government.

Sir Rufus would play a key role in the Board of Trade inquiry into the sinking of the ***TITANIC*** two years later.

The big wireless event of 1910 also gave Marconi a great deal of favorable publicity. On Wednesday, 10 July, the 5,431 ton Canadian Pacific steamer ***MONTROSE***, Captain Henry George Kendall commanding, cleared Antwerp bound for Canada with two notorious passengers listed on her manifest. Disguised as John Philo Robinson and his sixteen-year-old son were wife-murderer Dr. Hawley Harvey Crippen with his former mistress-now-new-wife Ethel Clara LeNeve. ***MONTROSE*** was still steaming down the River Scheldt when Captain Kendall happened to glimpse the odd couple standing near a lifeboat, holding hands in a manner that suggested they were more than father and son. His curiosity aroused, as soon as ***MONTROSE*** reached the open sea Captain Kendal sent an invitation to the strange pair to dine at his table. Kendall had heard all about the murder of Crippen's wife, actress Belle Elmore, and had saved newspapers containing their photographs to read when he had a bit of spare time at sea. He took a piece of chalk and whited out Crippen's glasses in one of the photos, and then drew a beard to resemble Mr. Robinson's. Satisfied that he did indeed have Dr. Crippen aboard his ship, Kendall turned to Ethel LeNeve's photograph, altering it to fit the apparel and short hair of Robinson's "son." Still, worried that Canadian Pacific would be unhappy, to say the least, if he falsely accused two passengers, Kendall waited until ***MONTROSE*** was almost to the 150 mile limit of her wireless range. One hundred and thirty miles west of the Lizard, Kendall handed to his Marconi operator the message that would keep the world buying newspapers for the next eleven days, a simple "Crippen and Miss LeNeve are in the ***MONTROSE***."

It was 8 o'clock in the evening, after a long day's work when Scotland Yard's Chief Inspector Walter Dew, who had had the dubious pleasure of discovering Belle's decapitated and decaying remains buried in the cellar of Crippen's house at No. 39 Hilldrop Crescent, London, was handed Kendall's wireless message. It had been known for sometime that Crippen was on the run with Ethel disguised as a boy. Belle's friends in America had even staked out incoming liners, expecting to recognize the pair when police might not. Both Crippen and Belle were Americans, and it was expected that Crippen might contact his son, Otto, in California, who was by coincidence a lineman for the Pacific Telegraph and Telephone company.

Inspector Dew immediately phoned Sir Melville Macnaghten, The Yard's Criminal Investigation Division chief. Dew rushed to Macnaghten's residence by cab, and showed his chief the Marconigram. They agreed that Dew, who had interviewed Crippen early in the investigation, must board the faster White Star liner ***LAURENTIC***, which could make the passage to Quebec in seven days, while the ***MONTROSE*** required eleven. Under the unimaginative alias of "Mr. Dewhurst" the good inspector sailed aboard ***LAURENTIC*** the following morning.

Wireless sparks literally flew across the Atlantic, relayed from ship to ship, keeping the press informed of the sea chase. Captain Kendall played out the charade, dining pleasantly with the "Robinsons," all the while sending descriptive messages to various newspapers about even such mundane matters as Ethel's trousers being held together with safety pins after her voluptuous figure had split them down the back.

Aboard ***LAURENTIC*** Inspector Dew's alias failed to save him from questions continually wirelessed to him by the fascinated press. At midnight, 27 July, ***LAURENTIC*** passed ***MONTROSE*** in mid-Atlantic.

Disguised in the uniforms of pilots, Dew and local police officers boarded ***MONTROSE*** at Father Point in the St. Lawrence River. Crippen recognized Dew immediately. Captain Kendall ordered three blasts from ***MONTROSE***'s siren, the signal pre-arranged by wireless for the pilot boat ***EUREKA***, loaded with reporters, to approach ***MONTROSE*** in order that the eager journalists could interview passengers and crew. Legend has it that Crippen shouted a curse on Captain Kendall as he and Ethel were dragged off the Canadian Pacific steamer by police. Whether there was a curse or not may depend on how one views such a coincidence as Captain Kendall's later command, ***EMPRESS OF IRELAND***, in collision with the Norwegian collier ***STORSTADT*** off Father Point on 29 May, 1914. ***EMPRESS*** foundered quickly, in less than half an hour, with the loss of 1,062 lives, which, contrary to legend, did not include Captain Kendall, who retired in 1939 from his post as Canadian Pacific's Marine Superintendent at Surry Commercial Docks. Kendall outlived his wife by twenty five years, living to the ripe age of ninety one, when he died peacefully in a London nursing home on 28 November 1965. He had received a reward of £250 from the Home Office for his part in apprehending Crippen. Inspector Dew retired at the early age of forty seven, then lived to be eighty four, dying at his home in Worthington in 1947. Sold out by his attorneys, having lost his life's savings in a bank failure, and after an alert warden foiled his last-minute suicide attempt, Crippen was hanged at Pentonville Prison, at 0900 on 23 November 1910. Among his last words to his beloved "wifie" were, *"I cannot believe otherwise but that we shall be together in that other life I am going to soon."* On the same day as the execution a heavily veiled woman dressed in black boarded White Star's ***MAJESTIC*** in Southampton, bound for New York. On the manifest as "Miss Allen," Ethel LeNeve Crippen disembarked at New York and traveled immediately to Toronto, whence she and Crippen had been bound when apprehended. Unhappy and lonely without Crippen there, she soon returned to England, eventually married again, raised a family, had grandchildren and died a widow at the age of eighty four. ***MONTROSE*** herself had a tragic end. In December of 1914, after her holds had been filled with cement preparatory to her sinking as a barrier ship off Dover Harbor, ***MONTROSE*** broke her moorings during a gale and grounded on the notorious Goodwin Sands, perhaps a better end for a staunch ship than in ignominious scuttling.

The Marconi Company gained a lot of favorable publicity over the Crippen incident, which is still touted as the first instance of a criminal being captured through the use of wireless, although this is not accurate as we have seen. The Metropole Hotel criminals may not have attracted the world's attention as the tragically romantic Crippen and LeNeve did, but their apprehension by use of Mariott's Pacific and Continental Wireless Stations preceded the Crippen-Marconi incident by several years.

Although de Forest and Shoemaker had tried to convince United's management to concentrate on the lucrative marine traffic, the company's corrupt officials were more interested in selling watered stock. During the summer of 1910 the United States Government finally made its move. Postal Inspectors raided United's offices at 42 Broadway in New York City on 15 June and arrested President "Christopher Columbus" Wilson and Vice President Samuel Bogart, charging them with using the mails to defraud and selling worthless stock.

Remaining United officers immediately began a drastic cost-cutting program which included a cutback to 51 land stations in the United States, while they concentrated on acquiring more marine contracts. By 1912 United equipped over 400 ships. American Marconi at that time had 5 U.S. land stations, and 40 marine installations.

On 29 May, 1911, the defendants were found guilty on all counts of mail fraud and conspiracy to defraud the United States Government. Wilson was sentenced to the Federal Prison at Atlanta, Georgia, for three years, where he subsequently died. Two United officials, Parker and Butler, were sentenced to two years each in the Atlanta prison, while two lesser officers, Tompkins, and Wilson's nephew, Treasurer W. A. Diboll, were sentenced to one year each in the New York County Penitentiary. Samuel Bogart's original fine of $2,500 was later reduced to $2,000. United was ripe for Marconi's picking.

In the United States there had been many wireless systems, most short-lived, many ending in prison terms for their stock-manipulating founders. Some had been legitimate, and the talent of their engineers had been quickly absorbed into larger companies. In 1910 the Continental Wireless Telephone and Telegraph Company was formed to amalgamate four wireless operating companies, including Pacific Wireless Telegraph System, founded in 1903.

The Massie Wireless Telegraph System was founded by Walter Wentworth Massie in May, 1905, under the laws of the State of Rhode Island, after Massie had in 1904 equipped the entire Fall River Line of steamers with wireless. This line was the first in the world to be 100% wireless-equipped. Massie, who had studied both civil and mechanical engineering at Brown and Tufts, had become interested in wireless when, as a junior engineer for the city of Providence, he had been commissioned to repair the de Forest masts at Block Island and Point Judith after a severe storm in the summer of 1903 had toppled them. Massie then resigned his city engineer's position and devoted his full time to wireless. He built stations at Providence, Rhode Island, and Norwalk, Connecticut. In 1906 Massie built 10 complete stations for the United States Navy.

Thomas E. Clark was born in Canada, but moved to Detroit when he was a child. He was about thirty one years old when he became interested in wireless, in 1900, and set up a small experimental laboratory. Using a ten-inch spark coil, in 1902 he sent a message across the city of Detroit, a feat which prompted him to found the Thomas E. Clark Wireless Telephone and Telegraph Company under the laws of the State of Michigan. Clark built stations at Detroit and Cleveland, with an eye on Great Lakes ship traffic. Senator James McMillan, whose family had owned the Detroit and Cleveland Navigation Company line of Lakes passenger steamers since 1850, was approached by Clark. McMillan gave Clark a coded message to be sent from one of his ships in the middle of Lake Erie to the Detroit station. In spite of heavy static the test was successful, and McMillan gave Clark the contract to equip all D & C liners with wireless. By 1909 Clark had a total of 8 stations at Lakes ports, from a 2-kilowatt at Toledo to 15-kilowatt stations at Duluth, Buffalo and Milwaukee. When United Wireless was formed from the American de Forest Company in 1907, it was too aggressive for Clark, and in addition United could provide service to the East Coast, while Clark stations were confined to the Lakes area. Desperate for strengthening allies, Clark joined Continental late in 1909 as Vice President and General Manager. By mid-1910 Clark had lost most of his business, including the D & C liners, and was reduced to building "jamming" stations at Erie and Buffalo. These transmitters, when turned on, could send a continuous and meaningless jumble of dots and dashes that obscured signals from United stations in the area. On 21 September the D & C Liner ***WESTERN STATES*** sent out an SOS after breaking a high pressure connecting rod off Erie, Pennsylvania. The United operator at Erie answered at once, but the nearby Clark operator turned on his jamming transmitter. The United operator had to call the Clark station on a land telephone line to inform him that an SOS was being worked. Clark's operator turned off the jammer long enough for the distress message to get through, then turned it on again. Later United sued Clark and its Erie operator over the incident. Based on information in United operator Ken Richardson's station log, United won the case, and the Clark operator was jailed for interfering with an SOS.

In May, 1903, A. Frederick Collins formed the Collins Marine Wireless Telephone Company under the laws of the District of Columbia. Collins concentrated on experiments to improve marine wireless telephony, rather than on the service of transmitting messages. He toured the United States, demonstrating his wireless telephones, and collecting money for stock in his company. Unfortunately the money was not used to build the company to the benefit of stockholders. Collins, however, did build a reputation as a wireless expert, and wrote one of the first good textbooks on the subject, published by McGraw Hill in 1905. In 1909 he published the *Manual of Wireless Telephony and Telegraphy*. In the same year his *Design and Construction of Induction Coils* was published, and is still considered an excellent text for reference. In 1909 Collins Wireless became part of Continental, with the understanding that a Collins wireless telephone would be installed in each Continental station.

In December, 1911, Continental's officers, excepting Walter Massie, were indicted for mail fraud and selling worthless stock. Most of the charges were concerned with the Collins wireless telephone, and Collins was charged with fraudulently demonstrating his wireless telephone in Madison Square Garden on 14 October, 1909.

In January, 1913, four Continental officers were convicted and sentenced to prison terms of up to four years. The individual companies which had comprised the Continental group had not long to survive. By April 1912, American Marconi had taken over what was left of Pacific and Massie.

Under the laws of the State of California the Poulsen Wireless Telephone and Telegraph Company was formed in October, 1909, with Standford University graduate Cyril F. Elwell as Director and Chief Engineer. Elwell had been experimenting with arc transmitters for both telegraphy and telephony, but his system of damped waves generated by a spark coil was disappointing. Elwell had gone to Denmark to study Valdemar Poulsen's "singing arc" system and negotiated a contract to buy Poulsen's U.S. patent rights by selling stock in the new company.

Poulsen Wireless built two demonstration stations to promote stock sales, one at Sacramento, and one at Stockton, California. The stations failed to increase stock sales, and the company built a third station at Ocean Beach, San Francisco, in July of 1910 to prove that more than two arc stations could operate at the same time without interference because of the fine tuning made possible by the use of continuous waves. A fourth experimental station was opened at Los Angeles, 350 miles to the south, in October, 1910. The opening of this station was attended by Beach Thompson, a San Francisco financier who was impressed enough by Poulsen's performance to invest, proposing the formation of a new company to provide enough stock sales for expansion. In February, 1911, the new Poulsen Wireless Corporation absorbed Elwell's company, with Thompson as president and Elwell as Chief Engineer.

A new agreement was reached with Valdemar Poulsen, wherein all of his U.S. patents were transferred to another newly-formed group, the Wireless Development Company. In July of the same year this name was changed to Federal Telegraph Company.

Federal successfully expanded to both the east and the west, building stations as far apart as Chicago and Hawaii. In August, 1912, Federal opened a press service between San Francisco and Hawaii. By the end of World War I Federal had racked up an impressive reputation, built the most powerful wireless transmitter in the world, and proven the superiority of continuous wave over Marconi's spark.

In May, 1910, Marconi's son Guilio was born, while he was returning to Europe from Glace Bay. In September Marconi sailed for Buenos Aires to test long distance reception. Flying kites from the ship to carry his antennas aloft, Marconi pulled in signals from Clifden up to 4,000 miles away during the day, and later up to 7,000 miles away at night. Marconi's marriage was rapidly failing, but in August, 1911, when Italy declared war on Turkey, he had more pressing problems. He returned at once to his homeland, and volunteered his services.

While Guglielmo Marconi was blessed with managers who realized that the inventor himself was the nucleus around which their company must be built, Dr. Lee de Forest was twice cursed with managers who saw wireless telegraphy and telephony only as new gimmicks for promoting quick stock sales.

De Forest's first Radio Telephone Company was capitalized at only $200,000, insufficient funding for the experimental work which de Forest needed to do. Consequently, de Forest and James Dunlop Smith, who had been an outstanding stock salesman for the original American De Forest Wireless Company, launched The Radio Telephone Company on 15 May, 1907, capitalized at $2,000,000, with Smith as President. Even this was not enough funding for de Forest's work in "aerophony," as he called his radio telephony. It was then decided to adopt the policy which had worked so well for the original telegraph company, as well as for others in the field. In early 1908 the Great Lakes Radio Telephone Company was formed and the building of a chain of land stations to circle the Great Lakes was proposed, and advertised as a means of selling stock in the company. Actually, no stations were listed in the Call Book for 1909, while only 15 were listed for 1910 and 14 for 1911. None were listed for 1912. Two more companies were formed in 1909, the Atlantic Radio Telephone Company, which handled East Coast business, and the Pacific Radio Telephone Company, which would handle traffic on the West Coast. A total of 11 short-range Great Lakes stations were built, 5 stations were built on the Atlantic Coast, and none on the Pacific Coast.

At the director's meeting late in 1909 Smith announced that Radio Telephone Companies were bankrupt, although their capitalization within the past twelve months had totaled $6 million. There was no cash to pay debts totaling $40,000, said Smith. After he left the meeting a number of options were discussed, including reporting Smith to the Federal authorities for raiding company treasuries. In the end it was decided that the bankrupt companies would be replaced by a new company, which was named the North Atlantic Wireless Corporation, founded under the laws of the State of Maine, with a capitalization of $10 million. Elmer E Burlingame, of the Great Lakes Company, was behind this new scheme. De Forest turned over all of his stock in the Radio Telephone Companies, losing clear title to his Audion patents in the transaction.

Using a ½ KW radiophone transmitter, de Forest realized one of his favorite dreams by broadcasting from the Metropolitan Opera House on 13 January, 1910. Unfortunately, he broadcast on a wavelength of 850 meters, the same as the busy United Wireless spark station, "DF," in New York City. Much of the broadcast was lost through DF's legitimate interference, but de Forest did not give up. He continued to broadcast opera, and in May he broadcast from his Radio Telephone Company station, "XAW," in Newark, New Jersey.

Early in 1910 the United States Army Signal Corps became convinced of the superiority of quenched-spark wireless telegraphy, which de Forest and Seibt had been perfecting. De Forest went to the Pacific Coast to install sets on two Army transports, the ***DIX*** at Seattle, and the ***BUFORD*** at San Francisco. When the installations were completed the two transports could work each other regularly, and when the ***DIX*** voyaged to Honolulu, her messages were heard on the West Coast. De Forest fell in love with California and when his Radio Telephone Company collapsed in March, 1911, he was still on the West Coast, but without a job. Realizing he could salvage nothing from the ruins of his second company, he looked up old friend Cyril Elwell, of Federal Telegraph. Many of de Forest's patents had been lost with the demise of his American de Forest Wireless Telegraph Company, and others were at risk with the bankruptcy of Radio Telephone. Worse was to come. In

March, 1912, de Forest was served with a warrant for his arrest on charges of mail and stock fraud, along with Smith, Burlingame, and Samuel Darby, all officers of the company. Being innocent, Lee [de Forest] later claimed that he did not worry about anything other than the added expense and how his arrest would affect his loved ones. His worries were well-founded, for the harmful publicity put an end to the Radio Telephone Company.

By this time in early 1912 although radio telephony was used by the armed forces for shortrange work, wireless telegraphy, Morse Code, was used almost exclusively aboard merchant ships, including the big transatlantic passenger liners, simply because it had a much longer range. Each letter came to the operator's earphones as a series of dots and dashes, and as the operator heard them each letter was scribbled on a piece of paper until the message was finished. Most company regulations forbade anticipation of words which gave too much chance for error, so at sea a pencil became literally an extension of an operator's fingers, while at land stations typewriters came into general use as a speedy means of copying letters as they were heard. For this reason, because no operator was good enough to keep the whole sequence of dots and dashes in his or her head and not make errors, the statement by Guglielmo Marconi at the British ***TITANIC*** inquiry that ***CARPATHIA***'s wireless log was made up later from logs of other ships because her wireless operator Harold Cottam had no time to keep notes made absolutely no sense. From his scribbled series of letters, and/or from his Morse inker tape, Cottam would have made up his scrap log, from which he would have later made up the official wireless log. He certainly would not have thrown any of this away until that official log was made up, for this was the way he did his work, meticulously, accurately, as the Marconi Company and every other major wireless company demanded. There has to be, then, something very suspicious about the original ***CARPATHIA*** wireless scrap log not being used to make up ***CARPATHIA***'s official wireless log. Mindful of Jack Binns' sale of ***REPUBLIC***'s foundering, Cottam would have sensibly kept every scrap of paper with an eye to selling his story later. While a great deal of attention has been paid to ***CALIFORNIAN***'s "missing" scrap log throughout the past eight decades, nobody ever asked about ***CARPATHIA***'s missing wireless scrap log.

In fact, Cottam was the wireless operator to testify at the American inquiry, on the night of 19 April. When Senator Smith asked Cottam what he did on Monday and Tuesday after ***CARPATHIA*** had picked up ***TITANIC***'s survivors and was on her way to New York, Cottam replied that he had no record of the whole work, he had "*only memorized it.*" Smith verified that statement then asked, "*Was there no written record of those messages?*" Cottam then reversed himself and replied that there was, that he had made up that record as the messages were sent and received. The records, said Cottam, were in the Marconi house on the ***CARPATHIA***.

If you are not familiar with code it may be impossible to understand, but the dots and dashes were not heard by an experienced operator as dots and dashes; they were instantly, automatically converted it that first and most marvelous of computers, the human brain, and "heard" as letters, which were written on paper very quickly as the signals came in. Still, there was a great deal of room for human error depending upon the experience and expertise of the individual operators and the technology of the wireless equipment, as the sending operator might rattle them off so fast that dots and dashes could run together, just as the same three dots, three dashes and three more dots of SOS could have indicated several other letter combinations. Additionally, punctuation had its own dots and dashes which could easily be confused into letters. The receiving operator might be tired, might be interrupted while taking the message, or might anticipate a letter he copied, whether company regulations forbade it or not.

There were no assigned wavelengths in April of 1912, only the one common 600 meter shipboard frequency, nor was there selective tuning. Jamming was still common, whether accidental or planned. Much of an operator's work was done in spite of conditions over which he, or she, had no control, a situation which created stress in itself.

By the time ***TITANIC*** sank the United Wireless Company, successor to the American de Forest Wireless Telegraph Company, had more wireless telegraph installations, both ship and shore stations, than any other wireless company in the world. Many of the hardworking, conscientious de Forest Company engineers and operators who had remained to build United were still there when United filed for bankruptcy in 1911. Most remained to work for American Marconi, which in this way acquired the genius of that same Harry Shoemaker who had so effectively jammed the official wireless reporting of the 1901 and 1903 America's Cup races.

The April, 1912, issue of *Modern Electrics* explained that after the American Marconi Wireless Telegraph Company had filed a lawsuit against United for infringement of Marconi's famed 7777 patent, a merger agreement was reached between the two companies in which United, with no funds to fight the financially solvent Marconi Company, entered no defense, and consented to a decree in favor of Marconi.

By this time Telefunken, thus Germany, already had its global wireless system intact, with stations in virtually every country excepting those deeply committed to Marconi. Telefunken even had one land station in England, however, and was deeply ensconced in China and South America. In 1913 Telefunken began building near Sayville, Long Island, what would be the first wireless station with the power to consistently span the Atlantic, under the operating name "The Atlantic Communication Company." Because Sayville could communicate on a regular schedule with the powerful Telefunken land station at Nauen, near Berlin, as well as German ships traversing the Atlantic, this raised much concern among the pro-English factions in the United States, who believed that the station was built to communicate intelligence messages. This was allegedly proven in 1915, and the United States Navy took over the Sayville station.

But the acquisition of United Wireless, along with Marconi's contract from His Majesty's Government to build at last the Empire wireless system, precipitated what came to be known as the Marconi Scandal, which came close to ending the company and toppling Prime Minister Asquith's Liberal Government.

Chapter Nine

The Frankfurt Scandal

First, The Marconi Scandal

Britain's Minister of Posts and Telegraphs Mr. Herbert Samuel, together with Attorney General Sir Rufus Isaacs and his brother Godfrey Isaacs who was the Marconi Company's Managing Director, had entered into an agreement to purchase shares in the American Marconi Company at the published low price, allegedly with the prior knowledge that Marconi would soon own the majority of the world's wireless stations through acquisition of the American United Wireless Company, and that Marconi's tender for the Empire wireless system would be accepted, both of which would raise the price of shares tremendously. This transaction had taken place a few days before Marconi's tender was actually accepted by the British Government, on 7 March, 1912. Because Samuel, as Minister of Posts and Telegraphs, had to give his approval before the Marconi tender could be accepted, there were many who believed that the whole deal looked very much like a bribe. Various tabloids in England, such as the *Morning Post,* the *Outlook,* the *National Review,* the *Eye-Witness* and the *Spectator,* jumped at the chance to expose these members of Prime Minister Asquith's Liberal government. Prominent authors H. G. Wells, G. K. Chesterton and Rudyard Kipling found time to write on the subject, the latter composing one of his popular verses about the sordid affair. But none of the men involved filed libel suits until the private stock transaction came to international public attention when the French newspaper *Le Matin* published an article originating from its London office in February, 1913. Tenders for the Empire wireless system had also been submitted for the Danish Poulsen-arc transmitters and the German Telefunken with its quenched-gap system, both claimed superior to Marconi's equipment. The Danish system was at once ruled out as not having been sufficiently proven, and naturally Telefunken was dismissed on the grounds of patriotism. The de Forest system was also considered, but United Wireless, which had taken over de Forest and still used his equipment, was in its financial death throes with no capital to fight patent infringement litigation and a subsequent takeover by American Marconi which gave Marconi all of its biggest rival's assets, including better equipment and some of the top engineers in the business. The contract awarded to Marconi for the Empire system included building and operating five long-range wireless telegraph stations in the worldwide network, at about $300,000 each building capitalization, with long-term operating contracts. As it turned out only two of these stations were built by the parent company, one at Leafield, England, and the other at Cairo, Egypt. The remainder were built by the American Marconi Company using standard Marconi equipment. The Marconi spark transmitters, however, were never reliable. No condensers were found that could hold up under the impact of the damped waves generated by the high-power spark. Nikola Tesla's radio frequency alternator which generated continuous waves, invented in 1895, improved upon first by Fessenden, and later by Ernst Alexanderson of the General Electric Company, turned out to be the solution. When this high-frequency alternator replaced the Marconi spark transmitter at the New Brunswick, New Jersey, station WII, the first continuously reliable transatlantic wireless service was established. Marconi's attempts to acquire the patents controlling this technology were thwarted by the interest of the U.S. Navy. At the Navy's suggestion, a conference of the top officials of the many American wireless companies, which had until that time been frustrated and financially exhausted by continual patent infringement litigation, emerged with the idea of pooling valuable patents and paying the patent owners with stock in the proposed new Radio Corporation of America, which would be built around the nucleus of the American Marconi Company. The entire American radio business thus became unencumbered and able to progress rapidly, while the British Marconi Company's offer of $5 million for the valuable patents was rejected. On 17 October, 1919, the company that would become familiar to millions of Americans as RCA was incorporated in the State of Delaware, U.S.A. The new company would always remain under American control, no more than 20% of its stock could be owned by foreign investors, its executives must always be citizens of the United States, and a representative of the U.S. Navy would be allowed to sit in on meetings of its board of directors. One-time American Marconi office-boy David Sarnoff, a Russian Jewish immigrant who rose through the ranks of various wireless operator's positions while he studied electrical engineering, and whose mentor and idol was Guglielmo Marconi, was appointed RCA's new commercial manager, his salary raised to $11,000 per year. While ***TITANIC*** legend has it that Sarnoff was a Marconi operator who heard ***TITANIC***'s distress signals at his post atop Wanamaker's department store in New York City, this was a fable later promoted by Sarnoff himself as well as RCA's publicity department.

In March, 1912, Guglielmo Marconi, Godfrey Isaacs and Percy Heyburn, a member of the London Stock exchange, went to America to oversee Marconi's takeover of United Wireless. While in America Isaacs and Marconi successfully negotiated contracts with Western Union and with the Canadian Northwestern Telegraph Company, both of which would henceforth act as forwarding agents for Marconi's future westbound transatlantic wireless traffic, and would accept messages throughout the North American continent for eastbound transatlantic transmission by Marconi. This relieved the Marconi Company of the financial burden of maintaining separate facilities on the American continent. Although this information was kept secret for some time, insiders knew that these contracts, too, would raise the price of Marconi shares both in England and in America.

Herbert Samuel and Sir Rufus Isaacs immediately filed a libel suit against *Le Matin*. In a lengthy statement made in rebuttal of the accusation. Sir Rufus explained that on 17 April, 1912 (which happened to be coincidental to the phenomenal rise in value of Marconi stock due to news of the ***TITANIC*** disaster), he had purchased from another brother, Harry Isaacs, a London ship and fruit broker, 10,000 shares in the American Marconi Company. Sir Rufus then sold 1,000 of these shares to Mr. Lloyd George, Chancellor of the Exchequer, and 1,000 shares to the Master of Elibank (later Lord Murray), at the same price he had paid for them. He suggested to his friends, Sir Rufus declared, that the American Marconi stock would be a good investment, although he was sure that they had never heard of the company. It turned out to be an even better investment after the ***TITANIC*** disaster. Marconi stock went up so fast after the publicity which inferred that all survivors owed their lives to Marconi wireless that all hell broke loose on the London stock exchange. A virtual embargo had to be placed on the public sale of American Marconi stock in London, which had been $5 a share on 17 April, and went up to $16 the next day. On 19 April the price had gone to $20, but no more shares were available. Godfrey Isaacs' stockbroker, Charles Edwin Fenner, could not deliver any more shares even at $20 so he skipped town, leaving £100,000 worth of indebtedness to the Liberal party and others. Frantically other brokers cabled New York for a new issue of American Marconi stock. It was apparently Fenner's hasty departure which triggered the investigation and tumbled the whole mess before the public through *Le Matin*.

Sir Rufus insisted that he had no idea that the American Marconi Company was any part of the British Marconi Company, or that the American firm would have any benefit from the British

Government wireless contract, such a fantastic piece of naiveté that it was incredible that anyone believed it, and not many did. It was unlikely that brother Godfrey would have kept Sir Rufus in the dark about the English Marconi Company owning 350,000 shares in American Marconi.

Lloyd George insisted that of his 1,000 shares, upon the advice of his broker, on 20 April he sold 500 shares, and on 3 May Sir Rufus sold another block of 314 shares for him, making a profit of about £750. However, on 22 May Lloyd George and the Master of Elibank had bought between them another 3,000 shares in the American Marconi Company. He went on to answer allegations that he was a wealthy man, and could not have become so by his £5,000 a year salary alone. He had only one house to his name, declared the Chancellor, a house worth only £2,000, which had been photographed by the press from an angle to make it look like a mansion.

A select committee was appointed by the House of Commons to investigate the allegations. Their findings were made public in June, 1913. The majority report found little to criticize. The minority report, however, found that the stock purchases on 17 April, 1912, were made when the shares could not have been bought in the ordinary way on the Stock Exchange, and at prices which were not available to the ordinary person. Sir Rufus was able to buy these shares on such favorable terms because he bought them from his brother Harry, who had them on even more favorable terms from brother Godfrey of the Marconi Company. It was also found that the American Marconi Company *did* have a material interest in the conclusion of any agreement between the British Marconi Company and His Majesty's Government. Unfortunately, said the official story, the rumors had abounded because of the reticence of the ministers to speak publicly of the matter. Asquith reported to King George what some of his ministers had confessed, and the resultant field day of the press can be imagined. Even Winston Churchill had been accused at one point, and he indignantly replied that he had never been involved in such shady deals, which he had not. Asquith passionately proclaimed the innocence of his ministers, admitting that they had been indiscreet but not criminal. His Majesty's Government had been hard hit, and it took the Great War to make the public forget about what had been dubbed the *Marconi Scandal.* How different the outcome might have been had the ***TITANIC-FRANKFURT*** incident been publicly explored. As it was, with the latter incident hushed up, the conclusion was that although Marconi wireless had saved the lives of ***TITANIC*** survivors, obviously more wireless would have saved more lives. ***CALIFORNIAN***, for example, had only one wireless operator, as did all smaller vessels. If the Leyland liner had had two operators, with one always on duty, or if there had been some sort of warning device set off by a distress call to awaken a sleeping operator, then everybody aboard ***TITANIC*** might have been saved. This set new legislation in motion in England as well as in America, and immediately raised the prestige of Marconi companies all over the world. Because no wireless companies except Marconi's were mentioned at the American and British ***TITANIC*** inquiries, Marconi prospects rose along with the price of its stock.

Except for those in the profession and the enthusiastic American amateurs, nobody in 1912 knew anything about wireless, and unfortunately nobody but Marconi and his employees were ever called to testify at either ***TITANIC*** inquiry. If Lee de Forest, Reginald Fessenden, Harry Shoemaker, Oliver Lodge, Ferdinand Braun, Nikola Tesla, even young "Weddy" Stokes, for example, had been subpoenaed, as should have been done in a thorough investigation, an entirely different picture of wireless at sea would have emerged. As it was, Guglielmo Marconi had it all his own way, especially at the British inquiry where his chief interrogator was his Managing Director's brother and a stockholder in his company who was prominently involved in the Marconi Scandal, hardly an impartial investigation. Even in the United States, however, where the senators should have known better. Senator Smith addressed Marconi, saying, "*You, being the leading and most active figure in the field of wireless telegraphy, probably the most prominent man in the world in that work, and your offices being in every part of the world and on most of the ships at sea...*" What a statement to make in a country that was home to Nikola Tesla and Lee de Forest, just to name two wireless pioneers who had gone far ahead of Guglielmo Marconi.

When Bill Müller wrote about the ***FRANKFURT*** *incident* in 1962 he was writing from first-hand, personal knowledge, not just from the *Überall* as he stated. But that, too, was a part of the deep, dark secret which Müller hid from friends and family alike.

In the summer of 1914, soon after the Great War started, Müller was Second Officer in a Gribel ship running troops to Libau. He happened to be in that port when ***FRANKFURT*** arrived. Knowing of the rumors about ***FRANKFURT***'s involvement in the ***TITANIC*** disaster, and obviously having an intense personal interest in the matter, Müller went aboard the NDL ship for a chat with her officers. The wireless operator happened to be the same man who had been at ***FRANKFURT***'s DEBEG wireless key the night ***TITANIC*** sank. From him directly Müller learned how Phillips had arrogantly dismissed him, calling the German a fool with his curt "*YAAF.*" With anti-English feeling running high in Germany, it was no wonder that the German operator yanked off his earphones with a few well-chosen expletives and went to bed. It was past midnight, the operator was accustomed to rising at 4AM to begin his work day, and even a Teutonic wireless operator needed some sleep. What he reported to Captain Hattorff was simply that the English were calling them fools again. Hattorff naturally assumed that ***TITANIC***'s master wanted an English ship to stand by, to tow her if necessary. Every shipmaster knew that salvage fees were the name of the game here, and the fees in ***TITANIC***'s case would be tremendous because they were predicated upon the monetary value of the vessel and all that she carried, excepting human life.

But a British ship, or in fact any vessel coming under the aegis of Morgan's IMM, would not charge one of her own any towing or salvage fee, although the courts could, and usually did, later award monetary remuneration to crew members involved. Salvage fees were and are awarded in order to stimulate the desire to aid in distress. It is all very well to romanticize about humanitarian instincts as ***TITANIC*** legend does, but money talks louder. This is entirely fair considering that the rescuing crew very often risks their own lives in order to save others, and the rescue ships naturally burn extra fuel as well as putting ship's boats and other equipment under additional stress which may necessitate costly repairs or replacement.

When the Cunard flyer ***OREGON*** sank off Fire Island in 1886, NDL's ***FULDA*** happened to come along at the right time to see ***OREGON***'s distress rockets and the Germans saved everyone from the British liner. Although Norddeutscher Lloyd, as Müller had correctly reported in his 1962 article, had responded to Cunard's query by waiving any remuneration, ***FULDA***'s master, Captain Ringk, and her Chief Purser, H. Eich, filed to claim a salvage fee for themselves, Norddeutscher Lloyd and the entire crew of the ***FULDA***, against diamonds saved from the ***OREGON***. They asked that the diamonds be condemned and sold, and a portion of the proceeds be distributed among the officers and crew of the ***FULDA***. The ***OREGON***'s value pales at comparison to ***TITANIC***.

Neither ***FRANKFURT***'s master, Captain Hattorff, nor his wireless operator had any notion that ***TITANIC*** might be sinking. Why would they? Within their own memory at least three German liners had struck ice and not foundered. Only four days earlier the CGT liner ***NIAGARA*** had struck ice, sent out an SOS and then canceled it, proceeding to port under her own power. Why would Hattorff expect any less of the mighty, brand new ***TITANIC***? From the beginning ***FRANKFURT*** was within sight of the apogee of ***TITANIC***'s rockets, but the German officers, seeing the all-white signals, were assured that ***TITANIC*** was signaling to one of her own, for her rockets were not the proper internationally recognized pyrotechnic distress signals. Nor were any other proper distress signals, such as "flames on the vessel," emanating from ***TITANIC***'s bridge deck. Müller emphasized that the problem lay between wireless operators, *"not between shipping men."* If Captain Hattorff had seen a shower of brilliant red or green stars glowing on the horizon he would have sped with all haste to their source, in spite of the wireless rebuff. Captain Fenlon, master of the Standard Oil tanker ***CITY OF EVERETT***, had sped to ***REPUBLIC***'s aid in 1909 in spite of the fact that his United wireless operator could not communicate with ***REPUBLIC***'s Marconi man, Jack Binns. ***FRANKFURT***'s master knew as well as ***TITANIC***'s Captain Smith did that Marconi operators were notorious for their arrogant dismissals of other wireless companies' operators. With Phillips' abrupt YAAF all direct communication between ***TITANIC*** and ***FRANKFURT*** was effectively ended because Phillips had literally refused to communicate with the German.

While Müller gave ***FRANKFURT***'s itinerary as Baltimore to Bremen, and others have written that she was bound from Galveston to Bremen, calling at Philadelphia, either of which were her normal routes, according to NDL's newspaper advertisements in Galveston, ***FRANKFURT*** *was* on a long nonstop voyage from that Texas port on the Gulf of Mexico, to her home port, Bremen. She had little coal to spare. With no reason to waste time and fuel by staying in the area, seeing the lights of other ships nearby, Hattorff properly resumed his course, but apparently not before ***FRANKFURT***'s lights had been seen from ***TITANIC***'s boat deck, or so Müller always believed. Captain Hattorff, very correctly although his wireless operator had been contemptuously dismissed by Phillips, had continued toward the distress position given in the first CQD call. This is very important because it was the only distress position that Hattorff ever had directly from ***TITANIC***. ***FRANKFURT***, however, was within sight of the rockets, all of them, but to Captain Hattorff and his watch officers ***TITANIC*** appeared to be moving, just as she had to ***CALIFORNIAN***'s Herbert Stone. Coupled with that apparent movement was the fact that the rockets were emanating from a position about 10 miles east of the wirelessed distress position, furthering the illusion that ***TITANIC*** was slowly steaming away.

Rescue, Wireless and Salvage

In his fascinating autobiography ***IDA*** *Was a Tramp _ and Other Reflections* (Exposition Press, Hicksville, NY, 1975) Commander E. J. Quinby, USN (Ret). gave an excellent example of a scramble to win a salvage fee from a ship in trouble.

In February, 1920, Quinby was the lone wireless operator aboard the Barber Line's tramp steamer ***IDA***. Out of Nagasaki, Japan, for San Francisco ***IDA*** crossed the international date line and gave her Chief Engineer two consecutive birthdays, which happened also to be Valentine's Days. The extra-long double celebration got out of hand and began to smack of mutiny when the deck officers joined in. The whole engineering department was inebriated and belligerent, and as the Chief drank more he became increasingly morose. He determined to get even for all imagined wrongs perpetrated by ***IDA***'s master, Captain Magee, by stopping the ship. All right, agreed the master, who could do nothing anyway. *"We'll stop right here until you fellows get ready to proceed."* While Captain Magee locked himself in his cabin, Quinby was forced to barricade himself in the wireless cabin. Realizing that ***IDA*** was probably going to need help, Quinby switched on his receiver to find out what ships were within range. The first thing he heard was *"SOS SOS KDKN KDKN."*

With no power Quinby could not answer the SOS. He managed to get a hastily scribbled message to Captain Magee, by wrapping it around a bar of soap and tossing it out the wireless shack's window and down the ventilator shaft into Magee's cabin. The master persuaded his Mate and Chief Engineer to talk with Quinby. ***IDA***'s "Sparks" thus ended the mutiny when the Chief ordered his men to get steam up and go to the stricken vessel's aid.

"KDKN" turned out to be the call sign of another U.S. Shipping Board-registered tramp named ***WEST HEPBURN***, which had lost her propeller and was wallowing helplessly and shipping water in the trough of heavy seas about 300 miles from ***IDA***. Captain Magee estimated that he could be alongside the stricken ship in about 24 hours.

Meanwhile, a Japanese freighter had been monitoring the wireless exchange between ***IDA*** and ***WEST HEPBURN***. The Japanese operator in ***OSAKA MARU*** called Quinby, saying that his ship could get to ***WEST HEPBURN*** faster. He asked for ***IDA***'s position and speed. Quinby responded by asking for ***OSAKA MARU***'s position and speed, but the Japanese operator refused to give it. Quinby at once reported this exchange to Captain Magee, who remarked that the Japanese just wanted to get a line on ***WEST HEPBURN*** first so they could claim salvage. Magee told Quinby to ask ***WEST HEPBURN***'s master which ship he preferred to have come to his assistance. ***WEST HEPBURN***'s operator, Redmond Scribner, quickly replied that his captain wanted ***IDA***, and added that her signals were much stronger than those of ***OSAKA MARU***, therefore ***IDA*** must be closer. The rescue mission had developed into a race for salvage rights. ***IDA***'s mutineers were now sober and knowing that ***OSAKA MARU*** was trying to beat them to the salvage, they exerted every effort to drive ***IDA*** at her best speed. Periodically the Japanese operator would inquire about ***IDA***'s progress, without giving any details of ***OSAKA MARU***'s position or speed. Note especially that *neither **IDA** nor **OSAKA MARU ever** gave their positions to the vessel in distress. **IDA**'s master had only given his estimated time of arrival alongside **WEST HEPBURN**.*

When ***IDA*** got close to the position ***WEST HEPBURN*** had given, by mutual agreement the two operators began gradually cutting down on their power. Even with minimum output they could hear each other clearly, proving that they were very close, but in the overcast darkness they could not see each other. Quinby had Magee change ***IDA***'s course so that he could determine if ***WEST HEPBURN***'s signals would increase or decrease in strength, indicating whether ***IDA*** was steaming closer to her or farther away from her. ***WEST HEPBURN***'s searchlight had been sweeping the horizon all this time, but finally Magee requested that it be pointed straight up, and it was near midnight when ***IDA***'s officers spotted the searchlight's reflection on a cloud. It was daylight when ***IDA*** finally came alongside the distressed ***WEST HEPBURN***. *A* whole gale lashed seas dangerously high for both ships which now wallowed perilously near each other, with ***WEST HEPBURN*** rolling on to her beam ends. It was almost noon when ***IDA***'s crew succeeded in getting a line aboard the stricken vessel, and ***OSAKA MARU*** hove into view just as this feat was accomplished. The Japanese freighter circled the American ships a couple of times, her officers observing the rescue progress. Then ***OSAKA MARU*** resumed her eastward course with no more comments from the Japanese "Sparks." By this time wireless operators across the Pacific, in ships and shore stations, knew of the dramatic race for ***WEST HEPBURN*** and had been cheering ***IDA*** on. Finally ***WEST HEPBURN***'s pumps were able to contain the water pouring into her, her cargo was again trimmed and she became more docile on the tow line. The little ***IDA*** towed ***WEST HEPBURN***, equal in size to herself, all the way across the Pacific to San Francisco. Magee had elected not to put into Honolulu for coal, but in the end he had to fuel ***IDA***'s furnaces with her mahogany deck cargo.

And The Carpathia

The first wireless operator called to testify before the U.S. Senate subcommittee in New York City was ***CARPATHIA***'s Harold Thomas Cottam. He was questioned by Senator William Alden Smith at 8:30PM on 19 April.

Cottam was twenty-one years old, called Liverpool his home, and had been with the Marconi Company for three years. He had gone to sea, then worked as a telegrapher for the British Post Office for about sixteen months, then gone to sea again in White Star's ***MEDIC*** on the Australian run. In response to Smith's question Cottam answered that ***MEDIC*** had a 1 1/2 KW set. This was the standard power of Marconi seagoing equipment of that era. From ***MEDIC*** Cottam had gone into ***CARPATHIA***, having joined her the previous February in Liverpool. Smith's questions were mostly confined to ascertaining the power and range of ***CARPATHIA***'s wireless set along with confirming Captain Rostron's dramatic assertions to the press that Cottam had caught ***TITANIC***'s *CQD* "providentially," having at the time been disrobing for bed. Cottam denied that he had been disrobing, that he had removed his shoes as the press had reported. He had removed just his coat, said Cottam, and he was waiting for further contact with ***PARISIAN*** to confirm an earlier time rush message he had communicated to her on Sunday afternoon. (Time Rushes, or TR's, were an accumulation of messages to be relayed as ships or shore stations came within range). While he was waiting he heard Cape Cod calling ***TITANIC***. He picked up ***TITANIC***'s distress call only when he called her to ask Phillips if he knew that Cape Cod had messages for him.

The first testimony about ***FRANKFURT***'s proximity to ***TITANIC*** came from the White Star liner's junior wireless operator, Harold Bride, on 20 April. Bride's statements must have come as a horrible surprise not only to Ismay but to Guglielmo Marconi, who happened to be in New York along with his Managing Director Godfrey Isaacs, to oversee his company's takeover of

ABOVE: Rendition of the rescue ship ***CARPATHIA*** *which earned* ***TITANIC*** *fame for rescuing the survivors of the disaster.* ***CARPATHIA***'*s career would endin in World War I, when she was struck by a torpedo and foundered 170 miles from Bishop's Rock on July 17, 1918. (Artwork by James A. Flood.)*

ABOVE:** John George "Jack" Phillips, Senior Marconi Operator,* ***TITANIC

United Wireless and therefore was available for the Senate inquiry. Marconi had already testified that he had spoken only briefly with ***CARPATHIA***'s wireless operator, Harold Cottam.

Bride had been hailed by the press as ***TITANIC***'s exemplary hero, and the dead Phillips was being posthumously lionized as the savior of those who had survived to be rescued by ***CARPATHIA***. Bride presented a pitiful and heroic sight, carried into the hearing room with his frostbitten and injured feet swathed in bandages. To the general public in England and America Bride could do no wrong, but to Guglielmo Marconi, listening for the first time to his employee's account of the disaster, it was obvious that wrong had been done and must, at all cost, be shut up. To tamper with Bride himself after the fact of his public statements about ***CARPATHIA*** and Phillips, was unthinkable not only in view of Bride's popularity, but the last thing Marconi wanted was to discredit one of his own operators.

Bride's heroism was the greater because he had actually gone down with the ship, remaining at his post with Phillips until the end, just as wireless operators were supposed to do. Bride told the senators how Captain Smith had released them from their duty a few minutes before ***TITANIC***'s final plunge. Bride and Phillips had then come out of the wireless cabin, which was just aft of the Sixth Officer's cabin on the port side. The two men naturally looked for a lifeboat, only to find that the one boat remaining on board was the Engelhardt that Murdoch was trying to launch. The final surge of water over ***TITANIC***'s bridge deck not only freed the Engelhardt, but washed Bride and Phillips overboard. Bride surfaced underneath the upturned boat.

"I got on top of the boat eventually," Bride said. *"There was a big crowd on top when I got on. I had to get away from under the bottom. The boat had gone over the port side. I heard afterwards that the senior operator was on board."*

Lightoller was the one who said that Phillips had been on the upturned collapsible boat, but he had died and slipped off into the water during the night. Bride, however, thought that Phillips' body had been taken aboard ***CARPATHIA*** and buried at sea.

Bride was twenty-two years old. He had been with Marconi since July of 1911, and had served in ***HAVERFORD***, ***LUSITANIA***, ***LANFRANC***, and ***ANSELM***. In ***LUSITANIA*** he had been junior operator, but in the smaller ships he had been the only operator. Prior to going to sea Bride had spent eight months training at the British School of Telegraphy.

ABOVE:** Harold Bride, Junior Marconi Operator,* ***TITANIC

He held a government certificate and earned £4 per month as ***TITANIC***'s junior operator. He had not met Jack Phillips until the two men joined ***TITANIC*** at Belfast.

Bride's first startling answers were to questions about ***TITANIC***'s trials in Belfast Lough. Ismay had already testified on the inquiry's first day that he had not been present for the speed trials of his new ship, but Bride had not heard Ismay's testimony. Senator Smith had heard the rumors that Ismay had directed the speed and course of ***TITANIC*** from Queenstown, conspiring with Chief Bell to bring her into New York ahead of schedule, as they had done with ***OLYMPIC***.

"Did you see him (meaning Ismay) *during that voyage?"* Smith asked, referring to the voyage out of Queenstown up until the impact with ice.

Bride answered that he knew Ismay was on board, but he did not know the line's Managing Director by sight. Bride was new to the White Star Line.

"Did he send or receive messages through you during the voyage?" Smith asked.

"I believe there were some transmitted for him, sir."

"Official messages?"

"They would rank with us as official messages," Bride answered.

"Did they have to do with the direction or the speed of the ship?" Smith pursued his line of questioning.

"Coming around from Belfast there were messages transmitted for Mr. Ismay regarding the speed of the ship." Bride voluntarily changed the subject to a more interesting line of questioning.

"He was not then aboard?" Smith, remembering that Ismay said he had not been at Belfast, seemed taken aback. *"Was he aboard the ship from Belfast to Southampton?"*

"I believe so."

"He was?" Smith asked incredulously.

"Yes, sir," Bride answered firmly.

"That was on the trial trip?" Smith asked.

"Coming around from Belfast to Southampton," Bride corrected.

"That is, the trial tests were made in what waters?"

"Belfast Lough," Bride replied.

"And then the ship was put underway for Southampton?" Smith pursued.

"Yes"

"And while she was underway these messages were sent?"

"Yes, sir."

"And received? Did you get any reply?" Smith asked.

"I could not tell you, sir," Bride answered.

"To whom were they sent, do you remember?"

"They were sent to the White Star offices at Liverpool and Southampton."

"Liverpool or London?"

"Liverpool and Southampton," Bride corrected.

"Can you recall what was contained in the messages?"

"No, sir."

"Generally, do you know what they said," Smith pressed.

"Generally, sir, that the trials of the speed of the ship were very favorable." Bride affirmed.

It may be argued that Bride was confused, that the messages were actually sent *to* Ismay at a White Star office in either Liverpool or Southampton. Because ***TITANIC***'s speed was an important consideration in proving or disproving White Star's liability, it is a moot point whether Ismay had *sent* word that ***TITANIC***'s speed trials were better than expected, no doubt better than

OLYMPIC's, or whether Ismay, in either Liverpool or Southampton, had merely *received* the messages from someone aboard ***TITANIC***, possibly Captain Smith himself. The point is that the trials did indicate that ***TITANIC*** could better ***OLYMPIC***'s speed and that was what Ismay needed. There is little doubt but what Smith would have prudently slackened speed in the ice zone if Ismay had not been on board to push him into taking chances. Ismay knew this and that was precisely why he was on board. Ismay, in his testimony, naturally denied that he had expected ***TITANIC*** to be faster than ***OLYMPIC***. Given known information, however, about ***TITANIC***'s performance from the time she departed Queenstown until she struck ice, it is easy to figure that had she lived, with her engines properly run in she could have worked up to 24 knots as her steady sea speed, with possible bursts of speed even faster. ***TITANIC***, of course, was running on ***OLYMPIC***'s schedule, but if the younger ship happened to be faster then she had more reserve speed to help her maintain the tight schedule. And on the maiden voyage she could make a noticeably earlier arrival in New York than ***OLYMPIC*** had made less than a year earlier.

Senator Smith returned to his attempt to prove that Ismay had sent or received messages between ***TITANIC***'s departure from Queenstown and the point of impact with ice. Bride could not recall any, but he was sure that Captain Smith had not received any messages from any White Star official regarding the speed or direction of ***TITANIC*** on the maiden voyage itself. He would have seen such messages. Bride said, because he was delivering them to the bridge for Phillips. With Ismay aboard. Captain Smith hardly needed to confer with lesser White Star officials ashore.

Bride then answered Senator Smith's questions about wireless ice warnings received on ***TITANIC***'s bridge. On Sunday afternoon Bride had ignored the Leyland liner ***CALIFORNIAN***'s warning of three icebergs sighted near her track, because he was busy with his accounts. About thirty minutes later, Bride said he had heard the same message transmitted from ***CALIFORNIAN*** to White Star's ***BALTIC***. He had copied the message, acknowledged its receipt not to ***BALTIC***, but to ***CALIFORNIAN***, and delivered the message to ***TITANIC***'s bridge. Bride, apparently, was wrong about the name of the ship in this case, because later ***CALIFORNIAN***'s wireless operator said it was ***ANTILLIAN***, not ***BALTIC***.

He had been asleep when ***TITANIC*** struck ice, said Bride, while Phillips had been at the key clearing paid messages, to and from passengers, with Cape Race. The operators' sleeping quarters were in a cabin adjacent to the wireless cabin. Bride insisted that he had not been awakened by the impact, but had awakened a few minutes later of his "own accord" because he had intended to relieve Phillips early. When Bride relieved Phillips, the senior operator told him that ***TITANIC*** had apparently been damaged enough that they would probably return to Harland & Wolff's at Belfast for repairs. As Phillips was preparing for bed Captain Smith came into the wireless cabin and told Phillips to send a call for assistance. Phillips immediately sent *CQD* about half a dozen times, followed by ***TITANIC***'s wireless call sign, *MGY*, half a dozen times. Within two or three minutes, said Bride, Phillips received an answer from NDL's ***FRANKFURT***. Bride could hear what Phillips was sending, but he could not hear the replies from ***FRANKFURT*** because Phillips was wearing the earphones.

There then ensued a lengthy questioning about the meaning of the call *"CQD,"* during which Guglielmo Marconi confirmed Bride's assertion that it was a "conventional" call, but Marconi explained that did not mean it was the distress call decided upon at the Berlin convention. That call was *"SOS,"* said Marconi, which Phillips had also sent.

Bride said he had relieved Phillips at about midnight ship's time. Allowing about five minutes for Phillips briefing Bride on what little he then knew of the situation, for Captain Smith's entry into the wireless cabin after Smith had evaluated the impact damage and conferred with ***TITANIC***'s designer, Thomas Andrews, and Phillips again taking over the key, a conservative estimate puts the first CQD call at about five to ten minutes past midnight, at the very earliest. Therefore ***FRANKFURT***'s alert operator, the only operator aboard the small emigrant liner, was up late. The German responded immediately to the call for assistance.

Phillips sent Bride to Captain Smith with the message that ***FRANKFURT*** had answered ***TITANIC***'s *CQD,* and Smith asked for ***FRANKFURT***'s position, then had Boxhall work up ***TITANIC***'s position. Boxhall should have been able to figure ***TITANIC***'s coordinates by dead reckoning in less than five minutes, certainly no longer than that. The Fourth Officer himself took the coordinates, scribbled on a piece of paper, to Phillips, who sent it immediately to ***FRANKFURT.*** Boxhall reworked the position and found that he had erred. He returned to the wireless cabin a few minutes later with the corrected coordinates. Phillips was still waiting for ***FRANKFURT***'s position when ***CARPATHIA***'s Harold Cottam called ***TITANIC,*** asking Phillips if he knew that Cape Cod was calling him. Phillips immediately answered Cottam with, *"Come at once; it is a distress message C. Q. D."* and then Phillips gave Cottam ***TITANIC***'s position, *the second, corrected coordinates.* It should be noted that this was a rather lengthy message which could have been abbreviated simply *"SOS, MGY, sinking"* and position. There was at this time in radio chronology no particular protocol for distress messages, the wording was left up to the operator's discretion.

It is extremely important to note that Phillips had sent ***FRANKFURT*** the first set of coordinates, 41°44'N, 50°24'W. He never sent the second, corrected position, 41°46'N, 50°14'W, to ***FRANKFURT,*** while he sent only the second position to ***CARPATHIA,*** according to Bride's *first* testimony.

Cottam promptly ran to the bridge, and quickly returned to send ***CARPATHIA***'s position to Phillips. He added, at Captain Rostron's orders, that the Cunarder was speeding with all haste to ***TITANIC***'s aid. Bride took this message to Captain Smith, who was then in the wheelhouse. Smith returned to the wireless cabin with Bride, and asked Phillips what other ships he was working. Phillips had just established contact with ***OLYMPIC,*** and he so informed Captain Smith. The master roughly estimated the distance between ***CARPATHIA*** and ***TITANIC,*** then returned to the bridge.

Phillips exchanged a few messages with ***OLYMPIC,*** then Bride took the earphones while Phillips went outside to see what was going on.

"I understand from you that the first response to the CQD call of distress was from the ***FRANKFURT?****"* asked Senator Smith.

"Yes, sir," answered Bride.

"What line of boats?" Smith asked.

"German line as far as I can remember, sir," Bride responded.

"The North German Lloyd," Marconi interrupted.

"Did you receive any other communication from the ***FRANKFURT?****"* Senator Smith asked.

"Not then, sir," Bride answered. "We *had transmitted to the* ***FRANKFURT*** *our position, but we had received nothing from him in return."*

"You transmitted to the ***FRANKFURT*** *your position in the sea?"*

"Yes, sir."

"And never received any further acknowledgment?" Smith asked.

"He told us to stand by, sir. That means to wait."

"The ***FRANKFURT*** *told you to stand by?"*

***ABOVE:** The Norddeutscher Lloyd **FRANKFURT**. (Photo courtesy of HAPAG-Lloyd, Germany.)*

"Yes, sir "

"Does that mean 'I am coming'?" Smith asked.

"It means wait; he is coming back again," Bride explained.

*"Where was the **FRANKFURT** headed for?"* Smith asked.

"I believe she was bound east, sir; but I can not say for certain."

*"Had you been in communication with the **FRANKFURT** during that day or the preceding day?"* Smith wanted to know.

"I can not say, sir, as to that," Bride answered.

"What is your best recollection about it?"

"I can not say, sir We were in communication with several ships during the afternoon and evening."

*"Is it impossible for you to recall whether you had any communication from the **FRANKFURT**, or sent any to her, at any time during the voyage from Southampton to the place of this collision?"* Smith asked.

*"I do not think there was any communication established with the **FRANKFURT** before we sent the distress signal, sir,"* was Bride's answer.

*"Did you pick up any message from the **FRANKFURT** intended for any other operator?"*

"No, sir."

*"Do you know what the **FRANKFURT**'s position was when she received the CQD call?"* Smith asked.

"That is what we were waiting for, sir," Bride answered.

"Did you ever ascertain?"

"No, sir." Bride answered.

"Did anyone say in your hearing that they thought the ***FRANKFURT*** *was in closer proximity to the* ***TITANIC*** *than any other ship?"* Smith asked. Unfortunately there is no way to know now just what prompted Senator Smith to ask this question, but he must have heard rumors. Surely he would not have thought of it entirely on his own. We also have no idea now of Senator Smith's foreign allegiances, if any, which were already being formed in American political circles, with the impending war between England and Germany in mind. It is certain, however, that if Smith had never asked this question and pursued this subject it would quite probably never have attracted attention. It also indicates that there was a great deal going on behind the scenes of this investigation, and that Senator Smith may have been so interested because he had anti-German pro-British leanings, or some of his more powerful constituents had such leanings.

"Yes, sir; Mr. Phillips told me so," Bride answered.

"Who said that?"

"Mr. Phillips told me that, judging by the strength of the signals received from the two ships, the ***FRANKFURT*** *was the nearer,"* Bride answered.

"Did Mr. Phillips tell you that he was trying to establish such communication with the ***FRANKFURT*** *as would bring that ship to your relief?"* Smith asked.

"Well, Mr. Phillips was under the impression that when the ***FRANKFURT*** *had heard the CQD and got our position, he would immediately make it known to his commander and take further steps. Apparently he did not."*

"Did the captain of the ***TITANIC*** *make any personal reference to that matter to you, or within your hearing, or to Mr. Phillips?"* Smith asked.

"No, sir; he asked us where the ***FRANKFURT*** *was, but we told him we could not tell him."* Bride's answer was not ambiguous. ***FRANKFURT*** had *never given Phillips her position.*

"But from the force of the current Mr. Phillips gathered that the ***FRANKFURT*** *was the nearer ship?"* Smith asked.

"Yes, sir."

Wireless operators were accustomed to judging the proximity of ships by their signal strength, as we have seen in the ***IDA-WEST HEPBURN*** rescue, provided they knew the power of the sending station.

John George "Jack" Phillips was twenty-four years old. He was from Francombe, Godalming, Surrey, and he had begun his career as a telegraph learner in the Godalming Post Office. In March, 1906, he had joined the Marconi School at Liverpool. He had served in James Gordon Bennett's yacht, in Peninsular & Orient ships, in White Star's ***OCEANIC***, and had then been posted to ***TITANIC***. Phillips had been an operator long enough to know what type equipment German ships used. In addition, as we have also seen in the preceding chapter, each system had its own peculiar sound, easily recognized by an experienced operator. Phillips, and even the less experienced Bride, should have been able to pick out the sound of Telefunken, or United Wireless spark, as distinct from the sound of Marconi's spark, which de Forest had described as "hammerlike."

"And the fact that it was the first to respond was rather confirmatory of that?" Smith asked.

"No, sir: it would not be," Bride answered.

The fact of rapid response indicated not proximity, but an alert operator on duty.

"It would not be?" Smith asked again.

"No, sir."

"Did you have any other communication with the ***FRANKFURT*** *after that ship responded to the distress call?"* Smith asked.

"Yes, sir," Bride answered.

"What was it?"

"He called us up at a considerably long period afterwards and asked us what was the matter."

"How long after?"

"I should say it would be considerably over 20 minutes afterwards," Bride answered.

"Twenty minutes after the message giving your position, the position of the ***TITANIC****..."*

"And the CQD," Bride interrupted.

"And the CQD distress call," Smith continued, *"you got another message from the* ***FRANKFURT*** *saying, "What is the matter?""*

"Yes, sir."

"Did they say anything else?"

"He merely inquired, sir, as to what was the matter with us."

"To that message what did you say?" Smith asked.

"I think Mr. Phillips responded rather hurriedly."

"What did he say? I would like to know."

"Well, he told him to the effect that he was a bit of a fool," Bride hedged.

"Just give it in his language."

"Well," said Bride, *"he told him he was a fool, sir."* ***TITANIC***'s junior wireless operator could not have said it any more plainly.

There is, unfortunately, no record of the expression that must have passed over Guglielmo Marconi's face upon hearing the bombshell that Bride had just dropped. Phillips, calling for help from a sinking ship, had not only dismissed the wireless operator of a vessel that Phillips judged to be closer than any other to ***TITANIC***, Phillips had also insulted the German operator. And Marconi knew why. This obviously was the first that Guglielmo Marconi had heard of the ***FRANKFURT*** *incident* or he would naturally have warned Bride to keep quiet about it.

"Is that all?" Smith asked, as if that were not enough.

"Yes, sir."

"Did he preface that word with anything more severe?"

"No, sir."

"Did Mr. Phillips then tell him what was the matter?"

"No, sir."

"Did he have any further communication with the ***FRANKFURT?****"*

"No, sir. He told him to stand by, sir... finish."

What Phillips had sent was *"YAAF,"* wireless slang for the phrase *"You Are A Fool."* The German operator had heard it before, from Marconi men. He knew perfectly well what it meant.

"In the interim you had got into communication with the ***CARPATHIA****?"*

"And the ***OLYMPIC****,"* Bride replied. Communication with the ***OLYMPIC***, 560 miles away, and Phillips' subsequent messages telling the sister ship to *"have her boats ready,"* indicated that Phillips at that time did not understand the urgency of ***TITANIC***'s situation. Why would he? On his mind surely was the ***FLORIDA-REPUBLIC*** collision only three years earlier. The 570 ft. ***REPUBLIC*** had lived for *39 hours, over a day and a half,* after her mortal wound, which must have seemed much worse than the damage that ***TITANIC*** had just sustained for ***REPUBLIC***'s wound could be clearly seen, and in fact her wireless cabin had been damaged by the impact. It could never have occurred to Phillips at the moment when he turned away the ***FRANKFURT*** that ***TITANIC*** would do less,

that she could founder before any other ships arrived alongside. It was impossible. So many ships had come to ***REPUBLIC***'s aid that there was fear of striking her again in the fog. Phillips, and Bride, had no idea of the extent of ***TITANIC***'s damage, they probably knew nothing of the coal bunker fire, and even if they had heard of it through the ship's scuttlebutt they would not have understood the fire damage to the bulkhead. Wireless operators of those days generally kept to themselves aboard ship, they fraternized little with the deck officers, not at all with engine room staff, particularly the lowly stokers. Officers had sense enough to keep quiet about such matters unless talking among themselves. Above all it must be understood that Phillips did not have any idea when he rebuffed the ***FRANKFURT*** that he would thereby cause so many deaths. The only criteria Phillips had in the matter was ***REPUBLIC*** and Jack Binns, and he no doubt saw himself in Binns' shoes, being lauded as the exemplary Anglo-Saxon hero, selling his story for a good sum of money, being chased by the ladies, ending up with a better job. It must also be understood that Phillips was a product of his time and occupation, not a malicious man, as was perhaps the wireless operator of the ***MORRO CASTLE*** over two decades later. When Phillips sent YAAF to the German it was an instinctive reaction. It may be argued that he was under great stress. While this is true, if he could not handle stress he should not have held such a position. The very fact that he had gone to sea for several years indicated that he usually managed stress very well. While it has become customary to look for someone to blame in the ***TITANIC*** disaster, it must be remembered that it was not one single incident or person who caused the tragedy with its great loss of life. Phillips was only one more link in the chain of disaster.

Senator Smith pressed Bride further.

"To what line did the ***OLYMPIC*** *belong?"*

"White Star, sir," Bride answered.

"And the ***CARPATHIA*** *belongs to the Cunard Line?"*

"The Cunard; yes, sir."

Both British, one the same company that owned ***TITANIC***. No salvage fees. The first choices of any master calling for help, and Phillips had to know it as eight years later Quinby knew it.

Second Officer Fosgate's comments: *"Clearly, if the crew did not feel that the ship urns in imminent danger, they would not have sought help from any but a company or federal vessel. Salvage is payable under international civil law to compensate for the extraneous expenses of the salvor, and divvied up to the owners, cargo owners, and crew under terms to compensate for out of pocket costs, lost time, etc., and only limited by the value of a salvaged ship and her cargo. No one gets anything if the salvage is not successful and the ship and cargo salvaged with a value afterwards. No value has ever been put on human life. No compensation is given for the rescue of life at sea."*

"Did you ever learn the position of the ***FRANKFURT?****"* Senator Smith asked

"No, sir."

"After she had first responded to your call?"

"No, sir."

"Did Mr. Phillips ask for it?"

"Yes, sir."

"How often?"

"When she first answered our CQD he said, 'Go and get your position.' The ***FRANKFURT*** *replied 'Stand by.'"*

"Did the ***FRANKFURT*** *at that time know your position?"* Smith asked.

"Yes, sir."

FRANKFURT's master knew only the first position, 41°44'N , 50°24'W, which Boxhall had hastily worked out. When Phillips later began sending the second, corrected position, 41°46'N, 50°14'W, ***FRANKFURT***'s operator had already gone to bed. This discrepancy in ***TITANIC***'s coordinates is repeated because of its importance. In fact, it is the primary clue in disproving any testimony about communication between ***TITANIC*** and ***FRANKFURT*** *excepting* Bride's first statements on the subject.

"What was your interpretation of 'stand by,' in that connection?

"To wait for his position and what he was going to do about the matter," Bride replied.

*"Did you ever get the position of the **FRANKFURT?**"*

"No, sir."

" Did Mr. Phillips?"

"No, sir."

"Did you and Mr. Phillips talk about it?" Smith wanted to know.

"Yes, sir."

This puts the lie to the explanation of Bride's testimony accepted by the ***TITANIC*** establishment. Bride, they say, just did not hear ***FRANKFURT***'s response because he was running messages to the bridge at that time. But Bride, remember, could not hear anything but Phillips' transmissions because Phillips was wearing the earphones. Bride and Phillips *discussed* the ***FRANKFURT***'s not sending her position. Bride could have checked the Morse inker tape, but there was no reason to if Phillips told him that ***FRANKFURT*** had never sent her position.

"What did you say to one another about it?"

*"We expressed our opinions of the operator on the **FRANKFURT**."*

"Was it critical?" Smith asked.

"Yes, sir."

"And uncomplimentary?"

"Very."

"Was it based upon any knowledge or suspicion that the operator was personally derelict in his duty?"

"Yes, sir."

*"Was it based upon any suspicion that the **FRANKFURT** had not responded to this distress call as that ship should have done?"* Smith pushed.

"Yes, sir."

"Was it a matter of deep regret between you and Mr. Phillips?"

*"Well it was at the time when the **FRANKFURT** asked us what the matter was with us, because we realized then that we were getting into… we realized what had happened to the ship."*

While Bride's wording is a bit confusing, it is still clear that sometime after Phillips had rebuffed the German operator he and Bride realized that ***TITANIC*** was probably going to founder, yet they could not have guessed how quickly. ***REPUBLIC***, again, would have been their only criteria for judging ***TITANIC***'s life expectancy. ***REPUBLIC*** had lived long enough to transfer her people to ***FLORIDA***, and transfer them again to ***BALTIC***. Why should Phillips expect the much larger ***TITANIC*** to do less? ***REPUBLIC*** was also being towed toward safety when she finally foundered. If ***TITANIC*** had been towed less than 100 miles part of her superstructure could have remained above water, although probably neither Bride nor Phillips realized that fact.

"But you realized at that time that all the lives on that ship depended upon getting relief from some other vessel?"

*"At the time the **FRANKFURT** asked us what was the matter with us; yes, sir."*

"After you told him that he was a fool, did you tell him the ship was going down?"

"No, sir; we told him to stand by, sir; to keep out of it."

"Keep out of what?"

"Not to interfere with his instrument, sir; because we were in communication with the ***CARPATHIA****, and we knew that the* ***CARPATHIA*** *was the best thing going."*

"Did you tell that to the operator of the ***FRANKFURT?****"* Smith pursued this line of questioning further.

"No, sir."

"When you said 'Keep out of it,' could that be interpreted as in any way changing the first distress call?" Smith asked.

"Merely told him not to interfere with our communications," Bride answered.

After the German had been called a fool, it is to his credit that he did not simply drop a book on his key and go to bed, thus effectively rendering ***TITANIC***'s wireless silent. In fact, although the German operator did go to bed in something of a huff, ***FRANKFURT***'s master continued to approach the position given to him in ***TITANIC***'s CQD message. Müller did not mention Captain Hattorff's motives for doing so, and what his motives were, monetary or humanitarian, is not important. The fact that he did continue toward ***TITANIC*** for a short time *is* important because when Captain Hattorff first learned of the CQD call ***FRANKFURT*** was already within sight of the apogee of ***TITANIC***'s rockets. ***FRANKFURT*** *was,* by the time Phillips sent YAAF, less than 20 miles from ***TITANIC***'s first distress position, less than 30 miles from her corrected distress position, allowing for state of the art navigational errors.

It is obvious in Bride's answers that he did not understand the serious consequences of Phillips' arrogant response to the German. It is also obvious that Bride was absolutely convinced of the superiority of Marconi operators and he wanted everyone else to be convinced, too. The allegation that ***FRANKFURT*** had refused to answer a "distress" call, however, was a very serious matter, a criminal matter in fact. Yet Bride's first testimony on this subject clearly indicates that he was completely convinced that Phillips' behavior had been correct, the German's had not, and ***TITANIC***'s only surviving wireless operator wanted the world to understand how derelict the Germans had been in their duty.

It is interesting to note that just seventeen months later, in October, 1913, when the Uranium Steamship Company's ***VOLTURNO***, Rotterdam for New York, Captain Inch commanding, wracked by explosions, burning fiercely, sent *SOS* the first ship to answer was NDL's ***SEYDLITZ***. Almost immediately the Marconi operator aboard Cunard's ***CARMANIA*** broke in and told the German DEBEG operator in ***SEYDLITZ*** to "stand by" so that he, the Marconi operator, could get the distress message, in spite of the fact that the message itself went out on one frequency that every wireless system could receive. Obviously Marconi operators had not learned anything from the ***TITANIC*** disaster, but how could they when everything in the media ignored the truth about ***FRANKFURT?*** It is, however, quite possible that DEBEG operators had been cautioned about such an incident happening again, for the ***SEYDLITZ*** operator stuck to his key and the German liner was one of numerous vessels of all types which surrounded the flaming ***VOLTURNO*** with what for many hours were would-be rescuers frustrated by raging seas. The wireless services represented, were the English Marconi, DEBEG and the former United which was now American Marconi, while vessels registered in Britain, Germany, France, The Netherlands, the United States and Russia responded to the SOS.

Senator Smith continued relentlessly to set the record straight. *"Now CQD was the strongest language that you could use under your wireless regulations to apprise any station that you needed help immediately; is that right?"*

It was not right, of course, as we have seen in the preceding chapter. But Bride defended *CQD*, saying, *"Any operator hearing a CQD, giving a ship*'s *position, when on the job, would immediately, without inquiring further into the matter, go to his captain and inform his captain. It would be a waste of time asking anything about it. The less time spent in talking, the more time can be spent in getting to the ship."* In fact, this is precisely what the German operator had done. It must be noted that the German operator would not have answered the Marconi call if he had not interpreted it as a distress call because he knew that in any other circumstance the Marconi operator probably would not answer him.

No prudent master would send his ship, full of passengers, speeding over the ocean at night knowing that ice was all around, toward what might have been a fictitious distress call. He was, however, obligated to respond to a legitimate call for help, after he had ascertained that it was legitimate, and this ***FRANKFURT***'s master tried to do. Captain Hattorff had every right to ask for more details, to know just what role ***FRANKFURT*** might play, simply so that he could better prepare for it. The German commander had to know, among other things, would he need to launch his lifeboats quickly, or would he need to have a tow line ready, or both? In fact, this is information required by a rescue ship in any case. For that the Germans were abruptly, haughtily dismissed.

But Phillips did do a lot of talking with Marconi-equipped, British ships. Why did he not do the same with the German ***FRANKFURT,*** Senator Smith wanted to know.

The court reporter read the last question to Bride, who finally answered, "We *could not send anything more than CQD."* Phillips could have, should have, and allegedly finally did send *SOS*. But by the time the international distress signal SOS, prescribed by the Berlin Radio Conference, had flashed through the ether, if it ever did, ***FRANKFURT***'s operator had shut down his wireless apparatus for the night.

It should also be noted that Phillips did a lot of useless sending which blocked other ships from answering him. Many years ago this author had the good fortune to walk into the cockpit of a Boeing 727 in performance of duties as a senior flight attendant, immediately after the flight deck crew had caught a *"Mayday,"* the radio-telephone equivalent of *SOS*, from the pilot of a light plane preparing to ditch off the Florida coast. At the time I, of course, did not realize how relevant the event would eventually be to my ***TITANIC*** research. Keeping silent during such important communication, I overheard the captain assign radio duties to the Second Officer. *"Acknowledge you've heard him, call the Coast Guard with his position* (on another frequency), *then listen to him but keep quiet so he can continue to send and receive until he*'s *down,"* ordered our captain. This is the proper way to respond to a Mayday, or an SOS. With the airliner's higher altitude and superior radio equipment we naturally had a range far greater than the light aircraft could reach, thus the U.S. Coast Guard was alerted to the emergency and was able to save the pilot.

"After you told this operator he was a fool, and twenty minutes had gone by, did you tell him that your ship was sinking?"

"No, sir," Bride answered.

"Did you give him any additional information?"

"He ought not to have wanted any in the first place," Bride answered. Again, Bride was absolutely wrong. The German's question about ***TITANIC***'s condition was perfectly logical. Hattorff knew that he might have to steer an intercepting course if ***TITANIC*** was proceeding slowly, which she did for a short time after impact. Remembering ***BALTIC***'s SOS after collision with the German

tanker ***STANDARD***, which was subsequently cancelled as ***BALTIC*** proceeded to New York under her own power, and the similar situation in the French Line's ***NIAGARA*** only a few days earlier, surely no one could blame Captain Hattorff for believing that ***TITANIC*** would do the same. This was one more misunderstanding, one more link forged in the chain to disaster.

"Upon the information you did give him, are you ready to say whether the ship responded or not?"

"There ought not to have been any doubt about the information we gave him at all, sir; he ought to have known what to do with it immediately."

*"So far as you know, the **FRANKFURT** did not respond?"*

"No, sir."

*"Will you tell us what confirmation you have that the operator of the **FRANKFURT** received your CQD distress call correctly?"*

*"Mr. Phillips had the telephones on at the time, sir. He called 'CQD.' The **FRANKFURT** answered. He gave the **FRANKFURT** our position. He said, 'Come at once.' The **FRANKFURT** said, 'Stand by.' We waited, and that is the last we heard of the **FRANKFURT** until he said, 'What was the matter with you?' a considerable period afterwards."*

"After he said, 'What was the matter with you?' then what was said?"

"We told him he was a fool, sir"

"Was that the last thing you said to him?"

*"To the **FRANKFURT**, yes, sir."*

You recall that you said later to him to keep out, not to interfere with your insulation [sic] or..."

"We told him to keep out and not interfere with our communication."

"Was that all in one message?" Smith asked.

"That was all in the one message."

"You are a fool. Keep out and do not interfere with our communication"

"Yes, sir."

"That was all in the one message?" Smith asked again. Bride had not told him of the wireless slang, *YAAF*, a simple -•-- •- •- ••-- which said it all very briefly, and ranked with *GTH* and *FU* for dismissal of a rival company's operator. Could anyone honestly be naive enough to expect the German operator to continue calling ***TITANIC*** after that? Just think about it, to borrow a favorite phrase of Lord Mersey's... what would the German say? Would he waste time apologizing, and for what? Would he beg Phillips to answer him? Hardly.

Here Senator Smith switched his line of questioning slightly, and fortunately for posterity asked one very important question.

*"Now, did you see the **FRANKFURT** in the vicinity of the wreck of the **TITANIC**, or after you were taken on board the **CARPATHIA**?"*

*"The only ship I saw, sir, was the **CARPATHIA**."*

*"Do you know whether the **CARPATHIA** had any communication of any kind from the **FRANKFURT?**"*

"No, sir; I can not say."

"You could not say?"

"No, sir."

*"While you were at the key, or at the apparatus, no message was received from the **FRANKFURT?**"*

"No, sir."

Smith then recalled ***CARPATHIA***'s wireless operator, Harold Cottam.

*"Did you receive any message from the **FRANKFURT?**"* Smith asked Cottam.

"No, sir; none whatever." Cottam's answer was emphatic and positive.

"At no time?" Smith pressed.

"No, sir."

"Do you know of any being sent from the ***CARPATHIA*** *to the* ***FRANKFURT****?"*

"No, sir."

"You did not pick up any stray messages?"

"No, sir."

This testimony in particular was extremely important, as we shall see, because other wireless operators allegedly heard much jamming by ***CALIFORNIAN*** and the DEBEG-equipped ***FRANKFURT***, as well as the United-equipped ***BIRMA***.

It could not have been plainer. Neither Bride nor Cottam knew of ***FRANKFURT***'s alleged proximity to ***CARPATHIA*** on Monday morning. This could be explained by the simple fact that both wireless operators never had time to go topside and look at other ships. Bride, being injured, had not taken over the key until late Tuesday when fatigue began to wear Cottam down. But after that they spelled each other, watch on watch. One or the other of them was always at ***CARPATHIA***'s wireless key, so they had to know of any communication between ***FRANKFURT*** and any other vessel within radio range, which meant at least 150 miles. Because Bride knew of ***FRANKFURT***'s rebuff by Phillips and the German's alleged dereliction of duty in the matter of a distress call, it is logical to assume that Bride would have told Cottam of the incident. Therefore any transmissions overheard from or to ***FRANKFURT*** would have been of special interest. This early testimony that neither Bride, nor Cottam, had heard any communication from or to ***FRANKFURT*** is extremely significant, as we shall see.

Further questioning of Harold Bride revealed Bride's arrogance in the matter of the use of *CQD*. Senator Smith asked ***TITANIC***'s junior operator if he knew whether the German operator in the ***FRANKFURT*** *understood* English. There was no necessity for him to understand English, Bride asserted, because the *CQD* was *"an international call which meant the same in any language."*

While it was true that other wireless services recognized Marconi's CQD from experience, the fact that ***TITANIC*** was still sending *CQD* until ***FRANKFURT*** was summarily dismissed with the *YAAF*, coupled with the all-white rockets, indicated to the Germans one thing... ***TITANIC***'s British master wanted a British ship, a perfectly logical conclusion in view of the fact that *CQD* was strictly Marconi, and Marconi was identified with Great Britain. The fact that Phillips had sent CQD and not SOS was apparently recognized as a grave error by Marconi himself as we shall see in attempts to prove that Phillips had sent SOS.

When Senator Smith asked Bride if *CQD* was the distress call under the Berlin convention. Bride evaded by answering, *"I can not say, sir."* Bride surely knew that this was not true, that *SOS* was the recognized distress call under the Berlin convention, *and had been for almost four years.* In fact. Bride later claimed that he had suggested to Phillips jokingly that he send *SOS* because it might be *"the last chance to use it."* Bride continued to say that *CQD* was recognized by all ships' operators as being a signal of distress, that *CQD* meant the ship was sinking, when in fact it did not necessarily mean that at all. As we have seen in the preceding chapter, *CQD* was an extension of Marconi's "Q *code,"* an extension of the CQ "all stations" call, and *CQD* was to be sent by any vessel in need of assistance, and did not specifically mean the ship was sinking. *CQD* merely commanded attention and the sending operator had to qualify its meaning as briefly as possible.

Senator Smith wanted it in the record why *"after a message was received from the* ***FRANKFURT*** *asking 'What is the matter' you did not reply 'We are sinking and the lives of our passengers and crew are* *in danger.'"*

"You see," said Bride, *"it takes a certain amount of time to transmit that information, sir. If the man had understood properly, as he ought to have, CQD would have been sufficient, sir CQD is the whole thing in a nutshell, you see."*

It was not, of course, and Phillips had the patience to transmit lengthy and irrelevantly dramatic messages to other Marconi-equipped vessels. Senator Smith had noticed this and asked Bride why a message similar to the one sent by Phillips to ***CARPATHIA***, to the effect that the boiler rooms were filling with water, could not have just as well been sent to the closer ***FRANKFURT.*** Bride did not see how such a message could have been sent to ***FRANKFURT*** under the circumstances. Smith was surprised that Marconi regulations gave operators such discretionary power that they could dismiss an inquiry from the ***FRANKFURT*** *when* ***TITANIC*** was in such dire straits.

"You use your common sense," Bride interjected. *"You use your common sense and the man on the* ***FRANKFURT*** *apparently was not using his at the time."* Again we have Bride's assertion that only Marconi operators knew what they were doing.

"I know," responded Smith, *"but the theory upon which you were angered was that the* ***FRANKFURT*** *was closer to you than any other ship?"*

"The ***FRANKFURT*** *was the first one. We had not got the position. We could not say he was nearer. The signals were stronger."* Bride changed his story about ***FRANKFURT***'s known proximity to ***TITANIC***, possibly because it had finally dawned on him that he had just implicated Phillips in the deaths of at least 1,400 people. But once again Bride reiterated... they *never* received ***FRANKFURT***'s position.

Suddenly and inexplicably Smith gave Bride an out. *"Now, Mr. Bride, I would like to ask you whether your dismissing the somewhat tardy inquiry of the* ***FRANKFURT*** *was due to the fact that you were in constant communication with the* ***CARPATHIA***, *understand me?"*

"Well, it appeared to Mr. Phillips and me, sir, that the ***CARPATHIA*** *was the only thing we could hope for at the time we told the* ***FRANKFURT*** *to keep out of it."*

"In other words, you held on to a certainty rather than an uncertainty?" Smith's phrasing of this question would later be used by Harold Cottam in Phillips' defense.

"Yes, sir," affirmed Bride.

Smith then asked if Phillips and Bride had known that ***FRANKFURT*** was 20 miles closer to ***TITANIC*** than ***CARPATHIA*** was, would they still have confined their communications to ***CARPATHIA?***

"Had we known the ***FRANKFURT***'s *position, having already got the* ***CARPATHIA***'s *position, we should have used our judgement, and had the* ***FRANKFURT*** *been any reasonable distance nearer we should have informed the* ***FRANKFURT*** *of the whole business and repeated each word we sent to him about a dozen times, to make sure he got it."*

The inference here is that Germans spoke only German, as most English and Americans spoke only English in 1912. According to Müller, however, in 1912 all German wireless operators spoke English, as did most German deck officers, although usually with an accent. Certainly the German understood *CQD* and *YAAF.* He had occasion every minute that he was on duty at his wireless apparatus to read Morsed conversations in English. He understood English, there can be no doubt about it. There was at this point in time a general but definite contempt for "foreigners" who did not speak English, a belief that somehow English was a "superior" language. This is evident in many statements given by British crewmen at both inquiries.

There is a more sinister aspect, however, to Bride's statement. It should never have been the wireless operator's responsibility or prerogative to decide which ships would be answered, which might be turned away. That was the master's decision to make. Perhaps Captain Smith would have chosen ***FRANKFURT*** *had* he been apprised of all the facts. If the wireless operators had been ship's employees rather than employees of the wireless company they might have worked more closely with the ship's officers. But, in any case, Ismay was on board to veto Smith's choice if he had chosen a foreign over an English rescuer. Ever mindful of cost, White Star's Managing Director probably would have chosen ***CARPATHIA***, or any English ship, taking the chance that she would arrive soon enough. In fact, that is undoubtedly exactly what Ismay did. Most lines gave their masters discretionary powers in such matters, with so many cautionary statements about unduly paying salvage fees that they reacted as Captain Sealby had done in ***REPUBLIC***, risking his ship to save the $20,000 fee asked by Captain Fenlon, master of the ***CITY OF EVERETT***, and losing that ship worth more than $2,000,000. Captain Sealby was in a no-win situation, as was ***TITANIC***'s Captain Smith. If the matter had been left to Captain Smith's decision, he no doubt would have chosen not one vessel, but every ship he could get, regardless of flag, because Smith knew the urgency of the situation, as did all of his officers. Yet, sixteen years later. Captain Carey, master of the ill-fated Lamport and Holt Line's ***VESTRIS***, held to his company's strict admonition to be "absolutely sure" that his ship was "really" sinking before he sent a very tardy SOS that was the direct cause of many deaths. *(See Chapter 13; Other Shipwrecks.)*

"Her position, however, was an object of some speculation?" Senator Smith asked again of the ***FRANKFURT.***

"Yes, sir."

Smith then asked Bride to explain how an operator could judge a ship's position by signal strength.

"When a ship is working wireless, there is no trouble whatever in reading her signals. You can read the signals through the telephone. When you have one telephone off, you can read them through one telephone. When a ship gets 100 miles off, you have to have both telephones on and devote your attention to it; and as the ship gets farther and farther away the difficulty in reading the signals increases and the strength of the signals decreases."

Almost everyone knows that now, but in 1912 only professionals understood it. It was the basis of the radio direction finder which Marconi, de Forest and others were at that time proposing. As we have seen, ***IDA*** found ***WEST HEPBURN*** in the same manner, and in 1912 wireless operators the world over were in the habit of judging a vessel's proximity, and direction, by her signal strength. The Radio Direction Finder, or RDF, a manually-timed loop antenna, and its descendant, the Automatic Direction Finder, utilized that same principle and were standard equipment in ships and airplanes by the beginning of World War II. If ***TITANIC*** could have been turned while Phillips was working ***FRANKFURT***, he could have determined the NDL liner's bearing from ***TITANIC*** with a reasonable degree of accuracy. If Phillips and the German operator in ***FRANKFURT*** could have cooperated amicably perhaps Chief Bell and Captain Smith could have run ***TITANIC*** dead slow ahead, or astern, toward ***FRANKFURT*** as the German liner sped toward ***TITANIC***, thus bringing the two ships within rowing distance of each other, perhaps alongside, before ***TITANIC*** foundered. Like ditching an airliner near a ship, even though ***TITANIC*** might have taken on more water when she was moved, the risk could have been more than worth it.

When Senator Smith ascertained that Bride allegedly did not know anything about ***FRANKFURT***'s wireless equipment, including what company provided it, the Senator asked Guglielmo Marconi, who no doubt had listened intently to Bride's testimony.

The ***FRANKFURT*** *is, I believe, a ship belonging to the North German Lloyd. She is equipped by a German company, called the Debed [sic] Co. It means a lot of things in German, each letter, which I will not go into, of which I am a director,"* Marconi explained smoothly.

"You are a director in the German company?"

"Yes."

"And you are familiar with the wireless equipment or apparatus?" Smith asked.

"I am not familiar with the wireless equipment of that particular ship," Marconi answered evasively.

"So that you would be unable to make a comparative statement... to make a comparison between the equipment or apparatus on the ***CARPATHIA*** *and the apparatus on the* ***FRANKFURT?"***

"I would be unable, sir, to do it," answered Marconi. Actually he should have been able to compare them, for he should have been aware of technological developments in German wireless telegraphy, especially since he would claim that all German wireless equipment was manufactured under Marconi patents.

Would the fact that the ***FRANKFURT*** *is equipped with an apparatus of German type in any way lessen their interest in calls made through the Marconi machine or apparatus?"* Smith asked.

No, because it is a Marconi apparatus. It is made in Germany, but it is made under my patents under an arrangement which we have with German interests," Marconi replied. This was not true as we have seen in the preceding chapter.

Smith then asked if German wireless regulations were in "perfect harmony" to the Berlin convention, and Marconi replied, *"Absolutely. They were enacted at Berlin and most of them were inspired by the German Government."*

Smith asked again if the *CQD* call was prescribed and recognized by the German convention. Marconi explained that the Berlin convention's call was *SOS*, but that *"Marconi companies have used and use the CQD call. The* ***FRANKFURT,*** *which was equipped with wireless, belonged to one of what I may call the Marconi companies, because I would not be a director of the company if it was not associated with us."* This also was not entirely true, as we have seen.

Smith wanted to know what, if any, confusion might have arisen out of using *CQD* rather than the Berlin convention-mandated *SOS*.

"I should state that the international signal is really less known than the Marconi Company's signal," replied Marconi. Again, not true at all. Marconi ship stations were outnumbered by both DEBEG and United Wireless stations at that time.

While every wireless operator afloat was aware of Marconi's CQD, and their refusal to use SOS, it should be remembered that Marconi wireless stations, shipboard and shore, were in the minority until American Marconi acquired United Wireless. That deal was being consummated when ***TITANIC*** sank. The American United operators, who had been used to communicating with other services continued to do so after they came under Marconi regulations. Even American Marconi operators were never as rigid about non-communication with other services as were the British Marconi operators. And after ***TITANIC***'s loss even British Marconi operators were not so belligerent about refusing to communicate with other services. The equipment used by United was superior to that used by Marconi at the time of the takeover, thus Marconi quickly acquired the ability to send and receive at speeds comparable to other services when it acquired United's equipment and engineers. Marconi's technological advancement was rapid after this period, and commensurate with the advancement of wireless services worldwide.

It should be noted, for the benefit of readers who know little of the caste system at sea, that in "the golden age" of transatlantic travel, that is the heyday of the big express liners, the officers and masters of the major passenger lines, for example Cunard, White Star, Hapag, CGT, NDL, Holland-America, were at the top of the prestige heap. Next came the intermediate liners' officers, and the lesser-known passenger lines which catered primarily to second and third classes. At the bottom of the totem pole were the men who crewed the cargo tramps. Marconi operators appeared to use the same caste system. Those operators in the express liners were senior men who took precedence over all below them. While it is considered heresy to suggest any flaws in Bride's, or Phillips' behavior or character. Bride's testimony particularly at the American inquiry indicates an arrogance that resulted from this seniority-caste system and was not necessarily indicative of the operator's individual skill. It is mentioned here not to denigrate either ***TITANIC*** operator, but to point it out as one of the many heretofore unnoticed links in ***TITANIC***'s chain of disaster. I cannot say it often enough… Jack Phillips and Harold Bride were products of their time and occupation, as were all others involved in the disaster which need not have been. We cannot, must not, judge them from our point in time.

As we have seen, other wireless company operators had used both *SOS* and *CQD* in distress calls so that Marconi operators would understand it. While in the United States Congress had not fully ratified the international terms of the Berlin conference agreement, American wireless companies had been complying with the agreement completely, and had been using SOS for distress calls. The pertinent fact in ***TITANIC***'s case was that Phillips used *CQD* first, and that was the *only* call ***FRANKFURT***'s operator had heard before he was rudely dismissed with Phillips' *YAAF.*

Smith next asked the logical question, could ***FRANKFURT***'s operator have heard the conversation between ***TITANIC*** and ***CARPATHIA***?

"Certainly," replied Bride. *"He ought have heard every word that passed between us."*

But Smith asked another question, did Bride have any reason to believe that the German *had* overheard the conversation between ***TITANIC*** and ***CARPATHIA***?

"No, sir," replied Bride.

*"No messages came, involved or otherwise, that would indicate that the **FRANKFURT** had gotten any other information than the information you first gave her?"*

"No, sir," Bride answered again.

And why should ***FRANKFURT***'s operator have remained on duty listening to a British operator who had so rudely dismissed him? It was enough that Captain Hattorff continued to steer ***FRANKFURT*** toward the CQD position. Had ***TITANIC*** been in or near that position, had she displayed proper internationally recognized pyrotechnic distress signals, Hattorff most certainly would have continued to approach ***TITANIC***, whether he could communicate with the White Star liner by wireless or not. Bill Müller always emphasized the fact that it had been a matter between wireless men, not between shipping men.

Again Smith logically pursued the matter of Phillips taking time to apprise other vessels of ***TITANIC***'s situation, while refusing to send the same information to the German. Was there any code word for *"fool,"* Smith wanted to know.

No, sir," replied Bride. This was not true, as we have seen. Phillips, said Bride, assumed that if the German did not get the first *CQD*, which *"was sent slowly and carefully by Mr. Phillips,"* he would not get anything else.

But obviously the German had caught the *CQD* message and understood it. And here Bride again mentions the speed of Marconi operators as superior to all others, when in fact it was not. DEBEG's Telefunken crystal detectors and Harry Shoemaker's Type D receiver featuring a carborundum detector, operational with United Wireless after 1908, were superior to Marconi's standard shipboard installation's magnetic detector and coherer-Morse inker receiver. Bride's assertions that Marconi operators had to send "slowly and carefully" to other wireless services' operators was a coverup for this technological gap.

Continuing with Bride's original testimony. Senator Smith then asked if ***TITANIC*** had reserve power after her *"boilers were submerged,"* as indicated by the dramatic message Phillips had sent to ***CARPATHIA*** and ***OLYMPIC.***

"The customary power was not submerged," replied Bride. Phillips' plaintive message, which has become part of ***TITANIC*** legend, was merely drama and not true at all. Simple logic should have sunk that myth years ago. By the time all boilers were "submerged" ***TITANIC*** was on her way to the bottom, and both Marconi operators had been gone for ten minutes at least.

The motor and alternator that was working our wireless set were running when we left the cabin, 10 minutes before the ship went down," Bride explained.

Phillips had again gone outside to see what was going on, and Bride tried to establish communication with the ***BALTIC.*** It is interesting to note that ***TITANIC***'s wireless men, even in the final moments of ***TITANIC***'s life, called only their own, no matter how far distant they were, further confirmation of wanting a British, Marconi-equipped vessel. Had they been in free communication with other services throughout the voyage, they would have known all ships which might have been within range to aid ***TITANIC.***

Even as Phillips and Bride donned life vests and gathered up Phillips' spare cash, they continued trying to contact other British ships with the signal *"CQD, MGY."* Finally, Captain Smith entered the wireless cabin one last time, and released Phillips and Bride from duty, about 15 minutes before ***TITANIC***'s final plunge.

Bride could not have been more clear, more positive of the facts in his original testimony, taken just one week after the disaster. ***FRANKFURT*** had answered the *CQD* first, and although Phillips had sent ***TITANIC***'s position (the first coordinates that Boxhall had worked out), ***FRANKFURT***'s operator had *never* sent hers.

Two days later Bride was recalled before the Senate subcommittee in Washington. Senator Smith here asked Bride whether he had seen Captain Smith wearing a life preserver. Bride said he had not seen the master with a life preserver, and he had seen Smith go overboard from the bridge about three minutes before Bride had gone into the water. Bride explained that he and Phillips had not immediately left the wireless cabin when Smith came to release them. Several minutes had elapsed between that release from duty and their actual departure, minutes during which Phillips sent a final *CQD* and was answered.

"Phillips gave another call of CQD, I believe, and had an answer to it," Bride said.

"From whom?" asked Senator Smith.

"I could not say whom the answer was from. I could hear what Mr. Phillips was sending, but I could not hear what he was receiving."

"And he did not state to you from whom the answer came?" Smith persisted.

"No, sir."

"And you had no means of fixing the source of that message?" Smith asked.

"No, sir. I do not think there was an answer, because he would have told me if there had been," Bride answered

"Was your CQD confirmed by any other ship's operator?" Smith asked.

"Phillips called CQD and listened for an answer, but whether he got one or not I can not tell. He did not tell me he had an answer He did not say he had not got an answer "

"And you never talked with him about it after that?" Smith asked.

"No, sir."

"Did you ever see him alive after that?"

"I saw him walking aft as I was helping to get the collapsible onto A deck," Bride answered.

"And he got aboard the collapsible, too?" Smith asked.

"So I am told."

*"As I recollect, you say he died before you got to the **CARPATHIA**?"* Smith continued.

"Yes, sir."

"So you are unable to fix, by any means, the source of this answer that he got?" Smith fortunately was persistent in this line of questioning.

"I think he would have stated it if he had had an answer."

"Was that last CQD all you said, or all he said?"

"That was the last, because we were of the opinion at the end that we were not getting a spark, owing to the poor supply of power"

"The power had been impaired?"

"The power was impaired all the time," Bride answered.

Smith asked if ***TITANIC*** had been in communication with ***MOUNT TEMPLE*** at any time on Sunday evening, and Bride did not recollect it.

"I want to fix this fact in the record, so that there can be no question about it," Smith continued. *"What was the hour when the **CALIFORNIAN** tried to get you Sunday evening?"*

"With the ice report?" Bride asked.

"Yes."

"It was in the vicinity of 5 o'clock. It may have been before or it may have been after that time," Bride answered.

"And at that time you were figuring up your accounts?" Smith asked.

"Yes, sir."

*"And did not reply to the **CALIFORNIAN** for 30 minutes?"*

"I should not say it was 30 minutes. It was nearer 20 minutes," Bride replied.

"And when you did reply, what information did you get?"

*"The **CALIFORNIAN** transmitted the ice report to the **BALTIC**, and when the **BALTIC** had acknowledged to the **CALIFORNIAN** the receipt of the ice report I did the same."*

*"Then the **CALIFORNIAN**, that had been trying to get you about 5 o'clock to give you these ice reports, was unable to give you directly a warning about the ice?"* Smith asked.

*"No, sir; I read it as it was being sent to the **BALTIC**,"* Bride insisted.

*"I understand, but I think the record shows that the message was sent out by the **CALIFORNIAN** on Sunday about 5 o'clock to the **TITANIC**, or communication was undertaken with the **TITANIC** about that time, to warn you of ice. Am I right?"*

"Yes, sir," Bride affirmed.

This was an earlier ice warning, in which ***CALIFORNIAN*** reported passing three large icebergs south of her track, a warning which was also reported to the U.S. Navy Hydrographic Office. Bride reaffirmed that he had taken this message to the watch officer on the bridge.

*"Did you receive any other messages on Sunday warning the **TITANIC** of ice?"* Smith continued.

"Not to my knowledge, sir," Bride answered.

Senator Smith returned to the ***FRANKFURT.***

"Now let us fix exactly the first message you received after you sent out your first CQD call. What was

the first reply you received?"

"The first reply we received was from the ***FRANKFURT,"*** Bride reiterated.

"Was that an immediate reply?"

"I should think so, sir," Bride answered.

"Did the ***FRANKFURT*** *give her position?"*

"No, sir."

You are positive of that?" Smith persisted.

"Yes, sir "

"Did you or did Mr. Phillips take the ***FRANKFURT*** *message?"*

"Mr. Phillips," answered Bride.

"Were you present at the time?" Smith asked.

"Yes, sir."

"What was the reply?"

"Mr. Phillips told me to write in the log the result of the replies as he told me, and the reply was, "O.K.- Stand by." That was the reply the ***FRANKFURT*** *gave to our C.Q.D and position."*

"What is the meaning of 'Stand by'?" Smith asked.

"It tells you that he has not finished corresponding with you," Bride answered.

"Did you infer from that that he had not enough information?"

"You infer from 'Stand by' that he is going to report, or he is getting something for you, and he will call you again in a minute or so," Bride explained.

"Does that mean, 'Hold on; I will talk with you later'?" Smith summarized.

"Yes, sir."

"Did he talk with you later?"

"Yes, sir."

"What did he say?"

"He said, 'What is the matter?'"

"And that is all. I do not think I shall ask you to repeat what you said to him. You do not wish to change it, as I understand. You did not hear from him again." Smith left the ***FRANKFURT*** for a moment and asked, *"What ship did you next hear from?"*

"The ***CARPATHIA****, sir."*

"How long after this last message from the ***FRANKFURT?"***

"Mr. Phillips just called 'C.Q.D' and gave our position and the ***CARPATHIA*** *responded immediately."*

"At that time you did not know, and you do not know now, how far the ***FRANKFURT*** *was from you?"*

"No, sir."

"Did the ***CARPATHIA*** *give you her position?"* Smith asked, and his line of questioning became clear.

"Yes, sir."

"With the first response to the C.Q.D?"

"No, sir: we waited about two minutes for the ***CARPATHIA****'s position."*

Let us pause to examine this answer of Bride's. Would Captain Rostron or one of his watch officers have been able to figure ***CARPATHIA***'s position any faster than Captain Hattorff in ***FRANKFURT,*** or Boxhall in ***TITANIC***, when all computations were by hand? It must have taken at least five minutes, allowing time also for Cottam to run to the bridge, give the message to the watch officer, who then roused the master, who figured the position and either took it to Cottam in the wireless shack, or gave it to the watch officer to take to Cottam. All of this in two minutes?

Because Smith emphasized that ***CARPATHIA***, and subsequently ***BALTIC*** and ***OLYMPIC***, gave their positions to ***TITANIC*** immediately, it was obvious that the Senator's line of questioning was directed at condemning ***FRANKFURT***'s master for not sending her position instantly.

Let us put ourselves on the bridges of ***CARPATHIA***, and ***FRANKFURT.*** Rostron might have worked the position first, then given his orders to make ready for the rescue, knowing that he had a few hours in which to perform the latter duties. But Hattorff, realizing quickly how close he was to ***TITANIC***, might very well have given his orders to turn out the boats, bake bread, gather blankets, etc., even as he turned his ship toward ***TITANIC***'s distress position, a logical sequence of events under the circumstances. In this case, Hattorff, after everything was being made ready, realizing that he had only two hours, or less, to prepare to take on at least 2,000 survivors, thinking that ***FRANKFURT***'s position given to ***TITANIC*** was not quite so important that it must take precedence over the other duties, then quickly figured ***FRANKFURT***'s position, but asked his operator first to find out ***TITANIC***'s situation. His time for preparation was much more limited than ***CARPATHIA***'s was. But Captain Hattorff was never called upon to explain all this.

Smith asked once again, *"At that time did you know, or did you have any means of knowing, or were you advised by the captain or anyone else, which one of these ships was in closest proximity to the* ***TITANIC****?"*

"Yes, sir. We were told that the ***CARPATHIA*** *was the nearer; but the captain did not express any opinion on the* ***FRANKFURT,*** *because he had not got their position. It was Mr. Phillips who expressed the opinion that the* ***FRANKFURT*** *was nearer, and he was judging by the relative strength of the signals."*

"How do you account for the fact that the ***TITANIC*** *was not in communication with the* ***CALIFORNIAN*** af*ter about 5 o'clock Sunday afternoon?"* Smith asked.

"The ***TITANIC*** *had not been in communication with the* ***CALIFORNIAN*** bec*ause there was no necessity for it,"* was Bride's explanation.

Mr. Bride, did you receive, or did Mr. Phillips to your knowledge receive, a wireless message from the ***CALIFORNIAN*** at *11:15 ship*'s *time, or about 10 o'clock New York time, Sunday evening, saying 'Engines stopped.* We *are surrounded by ice'? Now, think hard on that, because I want to know whether you took that message."*

"Mr. Phillips was on watch at the time."

"Do you know whether he received a message of that kind?" Smith persisted.

"He did not say so, sir."

"And you have no means of knowing?"

The witness did not answer.

What do you mean by saying there was no necessity for keeping in communication with the ***CALIFORNIAN****?"* Smith asked.

"If the ***CALIFORNIAN*** *had anything for us he would call us, or if we had anything for the* ***CALIFORNIAN*** we *would call him; and there was no necessity for us to call the* ***CALIFORNIAN*** *unless we had business with him, or vice versa, because it would then interrupt other traffic,"* Bride explained.

Obviously, ***CALIFORNIAN*** carried no passengers who might send a message to, or receive one from, a passenger in ***TITANIC.*** Nor would ***TITANIC*** need to relay any messages through ***CALIFORNIAN*** with her much less powerful wireless set. The most forgotten wireless information in ***TITANIC*** research is simply that wireless in this era was primarily for paying passengers, not yet for navigational purposes. In other words, the installations had to pay for themselves, and they could do that only with commercial traffic. That was simply the way it was. The fact that lesser, smaller vessels were beginning to carry wireless installations was simply because they were part of the vast relay network, and some enlightened shipowners had begun to realize their value in distress... to passenger ships. To the owners of the vast numbers of tramps plying the world's oceans, however, wireless was an expensive and unnecessary commodity. They paid their masters to handle everything themselves, why should they need wireless? This was the fallacy in ***TITANIC***'s heavy reliance upon wireless for aid, because there were many tramps near ***TITANIC*** without wireless, as we have seen.

Smith pointed out that ***CALIFORNIAN***'s wireless log showed this transmission, but Bride, who had been writing ***TITANIC***'s wireless log, did not remember seeing any such entry. Phillips would have logged ***CALIFORNIAN***'s interruption, said Bride, only if ***CALIFORNIAN*** persisted in breaking in.

Smith returned to trying to pin down times, and asked again just how long it had been after impact until they had sent out the CQD call. Bride estimated, to the best of his recollection, that it had been about ten minutes after impact when the master had come into the wireless cabin and ordered the call for assistance. Bride estimated this from the fact that he and Phillips had been discussing the time rushes exchanged with Cape Race, and what Phillips thought was wrong with the ship. This is not a realistic figure, however. No master sends out a call for help until he is *absolutely sure* he needs help. Smith had first to send for the carpenter to sound the ship, to send Boxhall not once, but twice, to ascertain the damage forward. Smith had to consult with Chief Bell, and most certainly with Thomas Andrews. All of these people except Boxhall who was on watch had to be roused, or come to the bridge after being asleep. This was most certainly not done in ten minutes, especially considering ***TITANIC***'s size.

Smith pointed this out, saying that Rostron had testified that he received the CQD call at 10:45PM New York time, 12:35AM ship's time. Bride attributed this to the confusion in times due to keeping two clocks in the wireless cabin, one on New York time, and one on ship's time.

"Assuming that the message was received a few moments before it was handed to the captain... and they seem to have responded very promptly... they did not get your message until 10:45 New York time, or 12:35 ship's time. Fifty-five minutes elapsed between the time you say you gave the signal and the time Captain Rostron says he received it," Smith summarized.

"There must be a mistake in the time somewhere," Bride explained.

Obviously, Bride, under great stress at the time, and without ***TITANIC***'s written log to prompt him, could not estimate time with any degree of accuracy. In an emergency situation time can seem to stand still. You can accomplish a great deal more in a specified time than you would think, and it can seem as if you are moving in slow motion. In ***TITANIC***'s era there was no such thing as studying human reaction in disasters, so nobody had any way of understanding this, therefore they continued to belabor the times. Again, in the wireless chronology the exact times were not too important. The *sequence* of calls was very important, however.

Boxhall, who had already testified that the first CQD went out about 35 minutes after impact, was asked again to confirm that time, which he did. He explained that the differences in time were probably caused by the various times kept by east and westbound vessels, and whether they set their clocks back or ahead at noon or midnight. The pertinent fact, however, is not the clock time stated by each witness for the first distress call, but the probable elapsed time from impact to first CQD call. Boxhall's estimate of 35 minutes is logical. Bride's estimate of 10 minutes is not.

The important information is that ***CARPATHIA*** was not the first ship to answer. ***FRANKFURT*** was the first ship to answer, and somewhere between the German's first answer and his second call to ascertain what had happened to ***TITANIC***, Cottam in ***CARPATHIA*** had answered Phillips in ***TITANIC***. When the German came back, then, Phillips knew that he had an English ship within a reasonable distance from ***TITANIC*** and an English ship would be preferable as a rescue vessel for many reasons, including salvage and jingoism. It could never have occurred to Phillips, or Captain Smith, or Ismay, that ***TITANIC*** could founder before ***CARPATHIA*** could arrive. By the time the severity of ***TITANIC***'s damage had been thoroughly understood, ***FRANKFURT*** had been dismissed and it was too late to call her back. Even then, however, there is little doubt but what Ismay continued to hope, holding on to Chief Bell's statement that he thought the pumps could contain the water inflow.

Twice Bride had testified that ***FRANKFURT*** had answered first, and she had never given her position.

On 4 May Harold Bride gave additional testimony before Senator Smith at the Waldorf Astoria Hotel in New York City. Bride proceeded to read a report of the ***FRANKFURT*** incident which he had allegedly addressed to the Marconi Company, dated 27 April, a week after his first revelation concerning the proximity of ***FRANKFURT*** to the sinking ***TITANIC*** and Phillips' curt *YAAF* to the German operator, but *two days before his second testimony recounted above in which he confirmed his first statements of 20 April.* It is interesting to note the differences in Bride's stories, and speculate on what prompted those differences. Those differences are so great and the dates on which each of Bride's three statements concerning the ***FRANKFURT*** are so contradictory that it seems quite possible that Bride had not written the letter to the Marconi Company at all, but that someone had written the letter for him.

Writing to W. R. Cross, Esq., Bride began his new version of events by regretting that his memory failed him with regard to the times of occurrences and incidents, but otherwise he was "sure of his statements." He explained how stressed he and Phillips had been on Saturday night, because they had worked for six hours repairing the wireless set's transformer. Because of Phillips' extra work on Saturday, Bride promised to relieve the senior operator early on Sunday night, thus allowing Phillips to turn in at midnight instead of his usual 2AM.

Bride confirmed that early on Sunday evening, around 5PM, he had been working up the abstracts when he heard ***CALIFORNIAN***'s ice report. He did not answer immediately, said Bride, because it took some "considerable time" to start up the motor and alternator, *"it not being advisable to leave them working, as the alternator was liable to run hot."* (Note that Bride had not used this excuse in his other two versions of the incident). He did however, acknowledge receipt of the ice message when ***CALIFORNIAN***'s operator sent it to ***BALTIC***, and Bride insisted that he had taken that message to the bridge. Neither he nor Phillips had received any other ice reports, said Bride again, an amazing statement considering how many ice warnings were known to have been sent and received by other ships as well as by ***TITANIC*** in the two days preceding the accident.

Bride's report began by repeating that he had awakened on his own accord at midnight. He reiterated that Phillips, who had continued sending his paid messages to Cape Race for a short time after ***TITANIC*** struck ice, told him that they had evidently struck something and would probably have to return to Belfast. Bride routinely took over the earphones and Phillips was preparing to retire when Captain Smith came into the wireless cabin and told the Marconi men to get assistance immediately. Bride's story began to change when he recounted how Phillips again took over the earphones and asked the master if he should use the *"regulation distress call 'CQD.'"* Captain Smith allegedly answered *"Yes."* With this statement any blame for using *CQD* instead of *SOS* was shifted on to Captain Smith's very broad and very dead shoulders, while at the same time Bride was reiterating the assertion that CQD was "the regulation" distress call.

Having already obtained ***TITANIC***'s position, Phillips sent CQD, along with the coordinates. This is in direct opposition to testimony already given by Fourth Officer Boxhall, and by Bride himself. The master had not brought the ship's position with his first visit to the wireless cabin, it had been brought by Boxhall a few minutes later, *after* Phillips had sent Bride to the bridge to tell Captain Smith that ***FRANKFURT*** had answered the distress call. Thus although ***FRANKFURT*** had answered the first *CQD* immediately, a few minutes had elapsed between that answer and Phillips' sending ***TITANIC***'s coordinates to the German operator, who had then to take that information to his commander. This in itself would today be considered poor planning, as the position is the most important part of a distress call. We must remember, however, that they had no navigation computers in 1912. Nothing was automatic, all computation was done by hand. The master had first to ascertain the extent of impact damage, and Smith's hands were full in that respect, before he could send a distress message if necessary. And it is important to also note again that in the position report to ***FRANKFURT*** Phillips had known only the first coordinates worked up by Boxhall. A few minutes had elapsed between the sending of the first coordinates, and Boxhall again entering the wireless cabin with the second, corrected coordinates. After Boxhall had given Phillips the second coordinates, it was another ten minutes at least before the German operator asked what was the matter, and Phillips responded with YAAF. In the meantime, however, although unknown to Phillips and Bride, ***FRANKFURT***'s course had been changed and she was pounding toward ***TITANIC***'s first distress position.

FRANKFURT was first to answer the first CQD call, Bride still admitted, while continuing his otherwise changed story. Phillips gave the German ***TITANIC***'s position, and the German operator replied *"stand by."* At this point ***CARPATHIA*** answered the *CQD*, giving her position and saying that she was coming to ***TITANIC***'s assistance. ***OLYMPIC*** and ***BALTIC*** also quickly answered, but according to Bride, Phillips did not engage in any lengthy conversations with them.

Now Bride's timing was completely changed. At this point. Bride now said, Captain Smith once again came into the wireless room and told Phillips and Bride that ***TITANIC*** was sinking fast and could not last more than half an hour. Phillips went outside to see what was happening, and returned to tell Bride that the forward well deck was under water. Phillips began sending *SOS* along with *CQD* for "nearly five minutes" when suddenly *both* ***FRANKFURT*** and ***CARPATHIA*** replied, while *at the same instant* Captain Smith returned to the wireless cabin for the last time and told Phillips and Bride, *"You can do nothing more; look out for yourselves."* Phillips resumed listening for a few seconds, then suddenly jumped up, exclaiming, *"The __ fool. He says 'what's up, old man?'"* Bride asked, *"Who?"* and Phillips answered *"The* ***FRANKFURT.****"* At that time, Bride allegedly wrote, Phillips was sure that the German had either taken no notice of, or had misunderstood ***TITANIC***'s call for help. Under this duress, Phillips had lost his temper and sent the *"YAAF"* which told the German to keep out.

It is important to note the sequence. Phillips sent the first CQD at about 0010. It was answered immediately by ***FRANKFURT.*** According to Bride's earliest statement about 20 minutes elapsed between ***FRANKFURT***'s first response and the German operator coming back to ask what was the matter. This puts the time of Phillips' dismissal of ***FRANKFURT*** at about 0030, or half past midnight. Yet Rostron claimed that he had not received his first knowledge of ***TITANIC***'s distress call until 0035 ***CARPATHIA***'s time. ***CARPATHIA*** was east of ***TITANIC***, therefore her clock was ahead of ***TITANIC***'s, and this slight discrepancy can therefore be explained. It should be noted, however, that originally Bride had said that Phillips had never told him about the last answer to his final CQD sent after Captain Smith released the operators from their duties, but now in this alleged report to his employer Bride said that final transmission had come from ***FRANKFURT.***

The remainder of Bride's report concerned the reason that he and ***CARPATHIA***'s Marconi operator, Harold Cottam, refused to answer queries from United States Navy ship and shore stations. They had hundreds of messages from and to ***TITANIC*** survivors aboard the ***CARPATHIA***, explained Bride. As an afterthought in his report. Bride stated that the U. S. Government had sent out the ***USS CHESTER*** to obtain a list of survivors. Bride had sent over 300 names three times to the "inferior" operator aboard the ***CHESTER***, he claimed, although he had sent to the Navy operator "slowly and carefully." Bride felt compelled to defend himself against charges that he and Cottam had kept information to themselves in order to sell it to newspapers later. This is such a trivial matter, and in itself took up so much time at the inquiries that should have been spent on more profitable testimony. There was absolutely nothing morally wrong with the two young operators selling their stories. In fact. Bride did sell his story for $1,000, Cottam sold his for $750, and Marconi got the free publicity. To have tied up the airwaves with accounts of the disaster would have been superfluous and unconscionable, as it would have interfered with normal traffic that had to continue in spite of the disaster. In fact the ***CHESTER***'s operator was primarily concerned with learning the fate of President Taft's friend and aide, Major Archibald Butt. But discussion of money paid for the eyewitness stories may have been deliberate, for it did take the public's mind off of the more important issues... for example, why were spurious messages sent all of Monday to the effect that ***TITANIC*** was still afloat, and why did ***CARPATHIA***'s Marconi operators refuse to converse with U. S. Navy wireless operators, ashore and afloat? The answer to those questions was, obviously, it gave time to reinsure ***TITANIC***, which was done after she had foundered, and It kept I.M.M.'s stock prices from plunging rapidly. It also gave Marconi investors with inside information time to buy stock at the original low price before its phenomenal rise.

Comparing this testimony to his first statements a week earlier, made in front of Guglielmo Marconi and J. Bruce Ismay, note that Bride had just compressed the events of over two hours into a few minutes. In his first statement before the Senate subcommittee Bride said that ***FRANKFURT*** had immediately answered the first distress call, then had called back about twenty minutes later asking *"What is the matter?"* This concurs with the information given to Müller by ***FRANKFURT***'s wireless operator in 1914. But Bride's report, allegedly written one week later, but two days before his second recall when he confirmed his first testimony about ***FRANKFURT,*** the written report allegedly given to the Marconi Company and then to the subcommittee, has changed the elapsed time between the first distress call and ***TITANIC***'s actual sinking. From half past midnight when Phillips sent YAAF to ***FRANKFURT*** until ***TITANIC*** slipped beneath the waves at 0220 is 1 hour and 50 minutes. But Bride was now saying that Phillips had sent YAAF to ***FRANKFURT*** only minutes before ***TITANIC*** sank, when Captain Smith had released them from their duties. Something happened, then, in that week between Bride's first story and the second, written report to his company. The only logical answer is that the second story, the "official" report to the Marconi Company exonerated not only Jack Phillips but the Marconi Company as well. The question then becomes: why did Bride confirm his first testimony *two days after* his alleged written report to his employer gave a different version of events? The only logical answer is that Bride was then unaware of the written report because *he had not written it.* This is one more question that will never be answered because nobody asked it when those who could have answered it were still living.

Bride's alleged report continued with a sordidly dramatic tale of a stoker trying to steal Phillips' life vest even as the heroic senior operator sent the final messages from ***TITANIC***. Phillips and Bride, said the junior operator, had "skirmished" with the stoker, leaving him to die in the wireless cabin. Whether this was true or not, it made a good story, and once again the lowly stokers were condemned as something less than animals.

One of the more significant statements contained in this letter, and in Bride's testimony as well, is the repeated assertion that Marconi operators, in this case Bride and Cottam, had sent "slowly and carefully" to the U.S. Navy operators. It will be impossible for those not familiar with Morse telegraphy to understand, but it would have been difficult for an operator used to sending and receiving at higher rates of speed, for example the 35 words per minute standard of American operators using United or de Forest-designed equipment, to slow down to the Marconi-equipped standard speed of 15 to 20 words per minute. There is a certain rhythm to Morse that an experienced operator gets used to. In this accustomed rhythm lies the subtle distinction between letters, punctuation, numerals and abbreviations. It must be clearly understood that an operator did not hear dots and dashes, as such. The operator "heard" *letters,* which ran quickly into words with punctuation and numerals where necessary. Alleged difficulties in transmissions were explained by Marconi officials by the fact that American operators used only American Morse, while British operators used International, or Continental Morse code. There was actually very little difference between the two codes, but any American operator who routinely dealt with ships at sea knew both codes perfectly well.

There was well within wireless range at this time another vessel, the Russian-American liner ***BIRMA***, equipped with a de Forest-United Wireless apparatus. ***TITANIC*** had no communication with ***BIRMA***, either, and the reason was obvious. If Marconi operators tried to communicate with other services, they simply could not keep up with the rapid Morse used by American and German services with their superior equipment. United Wireless at that time used 2 KW sets in their shipboard stations, while Marconi was still using ten inch spark coils and 1 1/2 KW sets as standard shipboard installations. While some sources give this standard set as being used aboard ***TITANIC***, Bride and other Marconi employees claimed that ***TITANIC*** had a 5 KW set, an unusually powerful seagoing station for that period.

Also on 4 May at the Waldorf-Astoria, Senator Smith questioned Gilbert William Balfour, a traveling inspector for the Marconi Company who had been in White Star's ***BALTIC*** the night ***TITANIC*** sank. ***BALTIC***, said Balfour, had been 243 miles southeast of ***TITANIC***'s distress position, when he first caught the CQD at about 11PM New York time. Captain Ranson had been immediately notified, had gone to the bridge himself, and ***BALTIC*** had headed for ***TITANIC***'s position. About nine minutes later an officer came from the bridge to verify ***TITANIC***'s position and see if Balfour had picked up any additional information. At 11:10 according to ***BALTIC***'s wireless log, Balfour had written, *"Jamming bad, but hear* ***TITANIC***, *very faint, calling* ***OLYMPIC***. *Latter strong; freaky. Hear* ***CARONIA*** *calling. He tells me* ***TITANIC*** *requires immediate assistance."* ***CARONIA*** was at that time about 600 miles east of ***BALTIC***, said Balfour. Through ***CARONIA*** Balfour told ***TITANIC*** that ***BALTIC*** was coming to her rescue. This is strange, and may well indicate that distances given between ships were typographical errors, considering that ***BALTIC*** allegedly had her message relayed to ***TITANIC*** through a ship that was even farther away than ***BALTIC*** was. It is interesting to note that the masters of all these ships expected ***TITANIC*** to live long enough for them to be of assistance.

At about 11:45 Balfour received Phillips' legendary message about water reaching the engine room. According to Balfour ***TITANIC***'s transmissions ended there, and he assumed that water had flooded out the dynamo.

At 12:10AM Balfour said that he had transmissions from ***AMERIKA*** and ***PRINZ FRIEDRICH WILHELM***. He told both German ships to "stand by." *"We had to tell them to stand by, to give us a chance of getting at the* ***TITANIC****,"* Balfour continued. Then, he said he told the operator in ***PRINZ FRIEDRICH WILHELM*** *not to touch his key!* Was it any wonder that Phillips instinctively told ***FRANKFURT***'s German operator to keep out, and that the German did just that without waiting to hear it again? What gave the right to a Marconi operator, however, to tell operators from other services not to touch their keys? Thus at least three German ships had answered the distress call in perfectly good faith but had been rebuffed by Marconi operators who found time to converse at length among themselves.

At 3:05AM Balfour had written that the station at Eastport, Maine, call letters WQ, was asking ***FRANKFURT*** about the CQD calls. *"This station had been jamming all the night. Jamming is a term we use to indicate interferences, trying to get in; trying to get the way through. They were talking about things not really having to do with the rescue,"* said Balfour.

"How far was Eastport, Maine, from you?" asked Senator Smith.

"I could not exactly say. It is on the Bay of Fundy. It is very far and it is a very freaky station. You can hear it almost halfway cross the ocean," replied Balfour.

Eastport, Maine, was a powerful 5 KW United Wireless station. It was not "freaky" that it could be heard halfway across the ocean, it just had the power to transmit a great distance. But Balfour's inference was again, as Bride's had been, that anyone else sending messages was interfering, or "jamming" Marconi's ether.

At 5:05 AM ***BALTIC*** had the first exchange of signals with ***CARPATHIA***, but, said, Balfour, he could not work the Cunarder because of jamming from ***CALIFORNIAN***. ***BALTIC*** was then about 130 miles from ***TITANIC***'s distress position, a very good range for a standard 1 1/2 KW shipboard station.

At 5:30 AM ***CALIFORNIAN*** persisted in talking with ***BIRMA***, said Balfour. *"It was impossible for us to work,"* declared Balfour. This was a direct slap at ***CALIFORNIAN***'s Marconi operator, Cyril Evans, who either dared to communicate with other wireless services, or was accused of it because it also served to implicate ***CALIFORNIAN*** even further into her officers' alleged error in not responding to ***TITANIC***'s calls for help. At 0545 ***ANTILLIAN*** called *CQ* and was told to stand by. At 0630 ***BALTIC*** received an unofficial message from ***CARPATHIA*** saying that ***TITANIC*** had gone down with all hands, *"with the exception of 20 boatloads"* which ***CARPATHIA*** had picked up. Captain Ranson then asked if ***BALTIC*** could be of any assistance in taking survivors from ***CARPATHIA***. Captain Rostron replied that ***BALTIC*** might as well be on her way to Liverpool, that he was proceeding to Halifax or New York, with about 800 survivors aboard. At 0655 Balfour again attempted to contact ***CARPATHIA*** *"but could do nothing for jamming by the* ***CALIFORNIAN*** an*d the* ***BIRMA****."* According to Balfour, ***CALIFORNIAN*** and ***BIRMA*** persisted in jamming everybody by communicating with each other constantly until about 1 PM.

When Senator Smith asked Balfour if he had communicated any message conveying the fate of ***TITANIC*** and the number of survivors, Balfour's answer contradicted his earlier statements to the effect that ***BALTIC***'s primary interest had been in ***TITANIC***.

"We refused all information to all ships," said Balfour. When Smith asked *"why?"* Balfour replied, *"We were not directly interested in the* ***TITANIC****, and it is against the regulations to give that information. Another thing, it is very undesirable to give the information to all ships coming along."*

Again Smith asked, *"Why?"*

"There is no use giving it to strange ships," replied Balfour. *"It would be of no use to them."* What Balfour really meant was that Marconi wanted all the publicity connected with ***TITANIC***.

Balfour's statement that the information concerning ***TITANIC*** would be of no use to all ships coming along overlooked one important factor. Other ships steaming anywhere near ***TITANIC***'s distress position could have, would have, should have been alerted-to the fact that there might be survivors clinging to wreckage in the vicinity. The very fact that there was never any proper search for stray survivors is highly suspicious, and in fact was criminal.

Balfour then read from the Marconi Company's list of regulations.

"Another general obligation which is imposed on all stations alike, and which is regarded as of the highest importance, is that they shall interfere as little as possible with the working of other stations. The rules of working are largely designed to prevent such interference.

"Failing any mention of a particular station in the signal of distress, any station which receives the call is bound to answer it.

"In doing this ships must beware of interfering with each other, and not more than one ship should answer if it is found that confusion results. ***A ship which knows from the strength of the signals of distress that she is near the ship requiring assistance should take precedence in answering and taking the necessary steps with regard to the distress signal."*** (Emphasis by the author.) Here we have further proof that not only did Phillips know ***FRANKFURT***'s proximity to ***TITANIC*** by the strength of ***FRANKFURT***'s signals, but ***FRANKFURT***'s *operator also knew it from the strength of* ***TITANIC***'s *signals, and the German operator knew that he should take precedence, by Marconi's own regulations, over* ***CARPATHIA*** *or any other ship.*

"That is the regulation," said Balfour. *"Therefore, under that regulation, as I had no definite information to give, the next best thing was to stand by."* Suddenly Balfour had silenced his key, and refused communication with other ships, including ***AMERIKA*** and ***PRINZ FRIEDRICH WILHELM***, *both Ge*rman DEBEG-equipped, and ***BIRMA***, equipped with United Wireless apparatus. But neither he nor ***OLYMPIC***'s operator had been silent during ***TITANIC***'s final travail, although they were both hundreds of miles away from the sinking ship.

Balfour, in answer to Smith's standard question about wireless operators selling their stories to newspapers, made his personal position on the subject quite clear. He did not approve of it, and had in fact refused to sell his story of the ***REPUBLIC*** disaster, during which he had been at ***BALTIC***'s key, although he had been offered from $1 to $5 per word.

Balfour again read from his log, and reported that the Eastport, Maine, station (United Wireless) had called ***FRANKFURT*** at 3:05AM on 15 April. This was his only reference to ***FRANKFURT*** although Smith brought up the subject again. Four very important things had occurred that night, said Smith, and he wanted Balfour to know of them. First was ***FRANKFURT***'s quick response to ***TITANIC***'s first CQD, but the German ship did not give her position. Second, Cottam accidentally caught the CQD as he was preparing for bed. Third, the belated inquiry from ***FRANKFURT*** asking "what was the matter," and Phillips' subsequent hasty reply, "You are a fool; keep out." And fourth, when ***CALIFORNIAN*** had called ***TITANIC*** to tell her of her proximity to ice. Bride had been working on his accounts and delayed taking the ice warning to the bridge for thirty minutes. Smith believed that regulations should be changed to prevent such oversights as ***FRANKFURT***'s not being required to give her position immediately. Bride's not being required to take an ice warning message immediately to the bridge while his accounts took precedence over ship's business, and in the case of Cottam's providentially catching the CQD, Smith, and others, had proposed some type of automatic warning to alert a lone operator off watch to a distress call. All admirable suggestions, of course. Balfour finished his testimony by asserting that he had never communicated with ***MOUNT TEMPLE,*** she was too far away.

In Washington, D. C., on 25 April, Harold Cottam was recalled for testimony before Senator Smith.

Smith had two important concerns, first that Cottam and Bride at ***CARPATHIA***'s wireless key had refused to answer the ***USS CHESTER*** and ***USS SALEM,*** sent by President Taft to expedite news of the survivors because ***CARPATHIA***'s wireless range was limited. The second matter concerned Guglielmo Marconi's personal approval of Bride and Cottam's exclusive sales to New York newspapers of their accounts of the disaster. Tied in with this wireless silence from ***CARPATHIA*** were the spurious messages sent to the effect that ***TITANIC*** was still afloat and was being towed, with all passengers safe, to Halifax on Monday. Senator Smith had received no satisfactory answers from Marconi, and he turned now to Cottam. To have it all in the record. Smith asked again about Cottam's wireless background and experience, then he asked Cottam to repeat the first wireless contact he had with ***TITANIC*** after her collision with ice. It had come, said Cottam, at about 11:20PM New York time; he had not noted either Greenwich or ship's time. (Marconi operators on transatlantic voyages worked on Greenwich time east of the 40th meridian, west of that meridian they worked on New York time). According to Cottam, then, he did not catch ***TITANIC***'s distress message until about one hour before she foundered, while ***FRANKFURT***'s operator had caught it roughly half an hour after ***TITANIC*** had struck ice. During this questioning Senator Smith seems to have become confused over who was in what ship. When he asked Cottam to whom on ***CARPATHIA***'s bridge he had reported the wireless communications of the day, Cottam answered, *"To the officer on watch on the bridge."*

"Who was it?" Smith asked.

"Mr. Bisset, the second officer."

"He did not survive, did he?" Smith was completely confused.

"Yes," replied Cottam, *"he is on the **CARPATHIA**."*

"Oh, yes. Murdock [sic] was the officer on watch that night, was he not?" Smith remained confused.

*"No, Dean. Murdock [sic] was on the **TITANIC**."*

"Pardon me. You reported this information to the officer you have named?" Smith finally gave up trying to unravel the names.

Phillips had sent ***TITANIC***'s position with the first CQD, said Cottam. (That is, with the first CQD that Cottam heard, not the first CQD which ***FRANKFURT*** *had* answered). He had taken this at once to the bridge, and Captain Rostron had given him ***CARPATHIA***'s position to send to Phillips. Cottam had then stood by to assist Phillips with relaying messages to other ships. Once more, it must be noted that Cottam heard only the second, corrected position, 41°46'N, 50°14'W.

*"Did you assist him in communication with the **FRANKFURT?**"* asked Smith.

"No, sir."

*"Did you have any communication with the **FRANKFURT?**"*

"No, sir."

Cottam had assisted Phillips in communicating with ***OLYMPIC*** and ***BALTIC,*** both White Star ships, and that was all.

Smith next asked if Cottam had any communication with the Canadian Pacific liner ***MOUNT TEMPLE.***

*"I had a communication with the **MOUNT TEMPLE** about half-past 10; gave him good night,"*

replied Cottam.

"That night?" Smith asked.

"Yes."

"Before the accident occurred?"

"Yes," Cottam replied again.

*"Did you know the position of the **MOUNT TEMPLE?**"* Smith asked.

"No, sir."

This exchange, too, is extremely important, as we shall see.

Smith then asked if Cottam had any information at 10:30 that night about ***MOUNT TEMPLE***'s position, or any communication from the ***MOUNT TEMPLE*** about her proximity to ice. Cottam replied *"No, sir, I do not remember"* to both questions.

On that same day, 25 April, newspapers across Canada and the United States had broken the story of ***MOUNT TEMPLE***'s passengers accusing her master, Captain James Henry Moore, of taking his vessel to within sight of the sinking, rocket-firing ***TITANIC***, then stopping his ship and putting out her lights. Senator Smith had read the newspaper reports, and was now asking Cottam about ***MOUNT TEMPLE***'s position. From Cottam Smith received no help.

Nor did Cottam's testimony now confirm Bride's assertion that ***FRANKFURT***'s signals were stronger, thus she was closer to ***TITANIC*** than ***CARPATHIA***. Smith asked Cottam again if there was any way to tell by what Smith called the "impact," meaning signal strength, the proximity of a ship or coastal station.

"Not after dark, sir," was Cottam's strange reply. This was not true, as we have seen with ***IDA*** and ***WEST HEPBURN*** at near midnight, approximately the same time of night that ***TITANIC*** and ***FRANKFURT*** were communicating. The only difference between night and day transmissions was that wireless signals generally had greater range at night. The strength of signals would still indicate proximity, day or night. Cottam had apparently not been apprised of the Marconi Company regulations concerning this matter, which had been read into the Senate records by Marconi's Traveling Inspector Balfour. But Senator Smith, knowing nothing about wireless at all, depending entirely upon Guglielmo Marconi and his employees, was easily misled, as have been all ***TITANIC*** researchers since then who rely only upon official testimony for wireless information, and who believe that Guglielmo Marconi was "the inventor of wireless telegraphy."

Smith returned to questioning Cottam about the lack of communication with ***USS CHESTER*** and ***USS SALEM***. Again Smith's ignorance of wireless allowed Cottam to easily fool him. Cottam and Bride simply did not want to communicate with Navy operators. The operator at the U. S. Navy Yard in New York had also sent Senator Smith a note avowing that he had offered to relay messages for ***CARPATHIA*** at 5:30PM on 18 April, when Cottam and Bride were trying to contact Marconi's New York stations. Only the Navy Yard operator could hear them, yet they refused his aid. In addition, Cottam had received a personal message signed "Marconi" telling him to keep quiet, that he could receive remuneration in "four figures" from New York papers for his exclusive ***TITANIC*** story. Guglielmo Marconi denied sending the message, but admitted that he had asked Cottam to meet him after landing in New York. All of this is perfectly logical, hardly criminal, and not at all relevant to the cause of ***TITANIC***'s demise or subsequent high death toll. The most sinister thing involved was Marconi's great desire for publicity, for which he could hardly be blamed. Wireless telegraphy was still a highly cutthroat business, and it was conducted any way commensurate with profit. Cottam did deny that he had met Marconi. He had gone to the Strand Hotel, he said, but Marconi never showed up. In later testimony Cottam admitted that he had received $750 from the *New York Times* for his story, a large sum of money for that era, and Marconi admitted that he had indeed sent the message that he wanted to meet with Cottam. It is interesting to note that the operator who had intercepted the message, John W. Lee, identified the sender as Marconi's Sea Gate station, not only by its call sign *MSE,* but by the peculiar sound of its spark, which had a rising tone at the beginning of sending and a falling tone at the end. No other station around New York, said Lee, had that peculiarity, which was caused by the operator's sending while his spark gap was changing speed.

Senator Smith then returned to the matter of *CQD* as opposed to *SOS,* and ***FRANKFURT***'s allegedly negligent wireless operator.

"I would like to ask whether, from your observation and experience, there is any rivalry or hatred among wireless operators using the Marconi system against those who do not use the Marconi system?" Smith asked.

Cottam's reply is significant. *"There used to be a certain amount, before the Marconi Company amalgamated with the Telefunken. There used to be a certain amount of rivalry between the two... the Telefunken system and the Marconi system."*

Smith had not specified the German system in his question, yet Cottam immediately assumed that the Senator could mean only the German Telefunken was Marconi's rival. The facts of the Marconi-Telefunken amalgamation have been recounted in the preceding chapter. The facts were also that DEBEG was German, Marconi was English, and propaganda was already preparing both countries for the inevitable war between them. Anti-German feelings ran high in Britain, and anti-British feelings were rampant in Germany, both fueled by newspapers and certain jingoistic politicians and military men on each side of the North Sea, as well as by books such as Talbot's *Steamship Conquest of the World,* as recounted in a previous chapter. But by now Guglielmo Marconi had had plenty of time to meet with Cottam, who obviously by now knew what to say to his Senate interrogators. The real question, however, becomes: was Senator Smith a party to this, and if so, as it certainly appeared, at what point, why and how was the Michigan senator so influenced? Unfortunately there can never be an answer to that question now.

Smith continued to question Cottam about Phillips' confrontation with ***FRANKFURT***'s DEBEG operator. Cottam naturally supported Phillips all the way, saying that he, too, would have dismissed the German by telling him he was a fool.

Once again Smith asked Marconi if ***FRANKFURT*** was fitted with Telefunken or Marconi equipment. Marconi evasively replied that he really did not know.

And once again Smith asked Cottam if ***FRANKFURT*** had given her position.

*"I am not positive... absolutely positive. I can not remember I did not take much notice of it. I was helping the **TITANIC.**"* Cottam had suddenly changed his story.

Smith continued, *"Under the regulations of the Berlin convention the **FRANKFURT** was obliged to give her position, was she not, upon receipt of this CQD call?"*

"If he had used any common sense he would have done it," interjected Cottam.

Smith insisted that what he was trying to get at was *"whether it is the duty of any ship whose country is a party to the Berlin convention to respond to that call, and whether when that response is made the ship's position is given as a part of the regulations. Do you see my point?"* Smith asked Marconi.

"Yes," replied Marconi.

The Germans had now effectively been put on the defensive. It was ***FRANKFURT***'s fault if her position was not given to ***TITANIC***.

Smith asked Cottam why Phillips had told the German he was a fool and to keep out.

"Because if he had not done it he would have been a nuisance, as we were in good satisfactory communication, and as he could not get satisfactory communication with the ***FRANKFURT*** *he tried elsewhere then,"* replied Cottam.

"What would you have told him if you had been the operator on the ***TITANIC****?"* asked Smith.

"I should have told him the same."

Smith pursued the subject further. "Do *you not think it would have been just as well, not knowing the position of the* ***FRANKFURT****, for the operator on the* ***TITANIC*** *to have said, "We are sinking?" It would not have taken any more words to say that than it did to say 'You are a fool'."*

And Cottam's amazing reply, *"CQD is sent out with the position. When a man sends his position and CQD the first thing to do is to turn right around and steer for that position. The position of the* ***FRANKFURT*** *to the* ***TITANIC*** *did not matter at all."*

Smith told Cottam that he was a little sorry to hear him say that he would have made the same answer, and Cottam defended himself with the statement that he and Phillips were trying to work the ***OLYMPIC*** at the time ***FRANKFURT***'s operator came in with *"what is the matter?"* and interfered with the sister ships' communication. ***OLYMPIC***, hundreds of miles away, was in absolutely no position to offer anything but moral support to ***TITANIC***, yet Phillips decided that ***OLYMPIC***'s communication was more important than answering a logical and simple question from a ship that might have saved almost everyone aboard ***TITANIC***, and Cottam supported Phillips' decision, which had just cost 1,400 or more lives.

But Smith finished by asking Cottam, *"Suppose this boat that Boxhall and Lightoller and others seem to have seen ahead of the* ***TITANIC*** *had replied, after a CQD had been received, 'What is the matter?' and that you had ignored them altogether?"*

"I should not give up a certainty for an uncertainty when I was working the certainty," replied Cottam, using Smith's earlier words.

"Hold on until I get through. Suppose you had ignored them altogether and told the operator he was a fool, and suppose it had turned out that that ship you were talking with could have reached the side of the ***TITANIC*** *and saved those 1,400 lives; do you not think your curt dismissal of the second inquiry would be a pretty big responsibility for you to assume?"* asked Smith a bit impatiently.

"Perhaps it would; but if a man was making a nuisance of himself… if he had been a nuisance in the case, as you say, and he could not have got that CQD from the ***TITANIC*** *with the insulation [sic] he had, the best insulation [sic] in a merchant ship, he did not deserve to go to sea as an operator"* (The Senate stenographer seems to have had a bit of trouble with the shorthand for the word "installation.")

Here again was Cottam's arrogant assertion that Marconi equipment was superior to all others, when in fact at that point in time it was inferior.

All right," responded Smith. *"Let us go a little further than that. Suppose this ship that was just ahead of the* ***TITANIC****, the* ***MOUNT TEMPLE,*** *and was in sight of its officers from its deck, was itself stuck in a field of ice and could not at that moment move, would that change your view of your duty?"*

"You mean in sight of the ***TITANIC****? I do not understand it. I do not understand the question."*

Smith had the stenographer repeat the question, and still Cottam did not understand it, which was not surprising considering how ambiguously Smith had worded it. Or, Cottam as yet genuinely did not understand the role played by ***MOUNT TEMPLE*** in the drama.

Smith explained his own previous question, and finally Cottam's equally ambiguous reply was, *"The operator on the ship has no duties on the bridge to perform, with regard to keeping a lookout or anything like that. His duty in a case of that description is to keep a constant watch…"*

"Wait a minute now," Smith interjected. *"Suppose that this ship was stuck in the ice herself and he*

was taking business for his captain."

"I know he was not, sir," Cottam replied.

"How do you know he was not?"

"Because, as I say, when the communication with the ***TITANIC*** *was going on there was not a sound otherwise,"* Cottam replied.

But you were passing from your room to the deck delivering these messages, along about half past 10 Sunday night?"

"About 5 minutes..." Cottam began.

Suppose that during the time you were temporarily absent from your apparatus a call had gone out from the ***MOUNT TEMPLE*** *that they were in the ice, and having a little difficulty, you would have missed it?"*

"If I had not been in the room, certainly I would have missed it," Cottam answered.

And therefore you would not know all that was taking place; and when you came back you might get the second message instead of the first one. And, as a matter of fact, the only one you did get was the good-night message from the ***MOUNT TEMPLE."***

"That is right, sir. That was at 10:40 o'clock."

"I want to get into your mind the fact that there are people who were on the ***MOUNT TEMPLE*** *who say they saw the lights of the* ***TITANIC*** *when it went down, and there are people who were on the* ***TITANIC*** *who say they saw the lights of a boat ahead when the* ***TITANIC*** *was sinking, and in that situation it is no time to be flippant or discourteous, in such a responsible position as you held."* Smith almost seemed to have forgotten that he was questioning ***CARPATHIA***'s wireless operator, not ***TITANIC***'s.

"I was not flippant. Nobody was flippant with the ***MOUNT TEMPLE.*** *The* ***MOUNT TEMPLE*** *was off watch,"* replied Cottam defensively.

"I understand that; you were not discourteous to the ***MOUNT TEMPLE.*** *But you say you would have made the same answer to the* ***MOUNT TEMPLE*** *that you made to the* ***FRANKFURT*** *if the* ***MOUNT TEMPLE*** *had asked the same question the* ***FRANKFURT*** *asked.*

"I do not think I will pursue this any further. The only purpose I have is to call the attention of the wireless people to the necessity for some regulation which will insist that even a second call is entitled to respectful reply."

Smith's reference to ***MOUNT TEMPLE*** having been the primary mystery ship is interesting. Did he know something about the Canadian Pacific liner that he let slip during this interrogation of Harold Cottam? This is one more question that can never now be answered.

Could it have been plainer? ***FRANKFURT*** had *never* given her position after her operator had been dismissed as a "fool" But Senator Smith had also effectively given an excuse to the ***MOUNT TEMPLE*** for not going to ***TITANIC***'s aid, yet ***CALIFORNIAN***, even farther from ***TITANIC*** than the Canadian Pacific liner, was afforded no such defense. One must ask: *why?*

For a moment let us digress, going to ***FRANKFURT***'s bridge, into the mind of Captain Hattorff. ***FRANKFURT***'s DEBEG operator had immediately taken the news to Hattorff that he had picked up a CQD from the new British liner ***TITANIC*** on her maiden voyage, one of the two largest ships in the world. The operator also handed the scribbled coordinates to Hattorff, 41°44'N , 50°24'W. Hattorff went into the chart room, and by dead reckoning quickly figured his position relative to ***TITANIC***'s coordinates. Realizing that he was less than 25 miles away, Hattorff gave the appropriate orders, knowing that there might be no time to lose. Full steam at once, a new heading for the helmsman, orders to cooks, bakers, stewards, seamen, firemen, engineers, quickly

Hattorff rousted them out of bed and sent them scurrying. Then Hattorff picked up his binoculars, peered through them toward the position given in the CQD call, to which ***FRANKFURT*** was now pounding furiously. Very faintly, on the horizon he saw a flash of white, which might have been a shooting star. Patiently he watched for several more minutes, and saw another white flash, unaware that at the same moment another watch officer, in ***CALIFORNIAN***, was watching the same pyrotechnic display from a different perspective. As Hattorff swung his gaze across the horizon he could see other lights... white lights, mast lights, stern lights no doubt. Hattorff, like every other master on the North Atlantic that night in that area knew that the atmosphere was unusually clear, that visibility was unusually good. By this time Hattorff had guessed that the white flashes were rockets, emanating from ***TITANIC***, he wondered? Or from a vessel beyond her, answering her distress call? The flashes seemed to come from farther away than the position given in the CQD call, and they were white. What could they mean, Hattorff pondered. He discussed it with his watch officer, while together they watched more white rockets go aloft. And Hattorff sent to his wireless operator, possibly forgetting that he had not sent ***FRANKFURT***'s position to ***TITANIC***. *"Call her up again,"* ordered the German master. *"Ask the British what is the matter with them."* Minutes later the operator ran back to the bridge. *"They told me I was a fool... we are fools,"* he reported. Hattorff turned again, focused his night glasses on the area of sky where he had seen the faraway white flashes. It was dark, still, quiet. There were no more flashes. He re-entered the chart room, quickly figured how far he had run toward the CQD position. He was only a few miles from there now. There should be signs of ***TITANIC***, her lights, distress rockets, signal bombs, something. Remembering the white flashes, again Hattorff recalled that they seemed farther away than the position he had been given by wireless. Still, he let ***FRANKFURT*** run on toward the position in which he had last seen the flashes. He called up his chief engineer, they consulted on the coal supply. The British had sent CQD, not SOS, they were not firing distress rockets. The British operator had sent YAAF to the German operator. ***TITANIC*** was not where her wireless operator had said she was. It was either a hoax, or they wanted a British ship. Hattorff asked his operator, were there British ships nearby? Yes, replied the DEBEG operator. He had been listening to them all night. He had heard ***CARPATHIA, BALTIC, MOUNT TEMPLE, VIRGINIAN, CALIFORNIAN, PARISIAN***, and he had been conversing with the nearby Russian-American liner ***BIRMA***. *They obviously do not want or need us."* Hattorff shrugged. One last time he studied the now dark sky in the direction of the CQD coordinates.

It must also be noted that Cottam did not hear any transmissions from ***MOUNT TEMPLE*** after 10:40PM, nor had he heard any lengthy exchange of messages between ***FRANKFURT*** and ***TITANIC***, an exchange that ***MOUNT TEMPLE***'s master and wireless operator would testify to under oath, an exchange which would effectively put ***FRANKFURT*** 140 miles from ***TITANIC*** and officially establish ***FRANKFURT***'s coordinates for posterity.

Four days later an entirely different wireless scenario was presented by ***MOUNT TEMPLE***'s Captain Moore, who had been accused by his passengers of taking his ship within sight of ***TITANIC***, yet refusing to render aid. Amazingly, in spite of all its discrepancies Moore's version of the lengthy wireless conversation between Phillips and the ***FRANKFURT*** operator has never been questioned. Because Senator Smith accepted Captain Moore's word wholeheartedly, it remains firmly entrenched in ***TITANIC*** legend in spite of all evidence against it.

Senator Smith had received a letter from the Vice Consul at Toronto, Ontario, Canada, enclosing an affidavit made by Dr. F. C. Quitzrau, who had been a passenger in ***MOUNT TEMPLE.*** The affidavit read:

"Dr. F. C. Quitzrau, being first duly sworn, deposes and says that he was a passenger, traveling Second Class, on steamer ***MOUNT TEMPLE,*** *which left Antwerp April 3rd, 1912; that about midnight Sunday, April 14th, New York time, he was awakened by the sudden stopping of the engines; that he immediately went to the cabin,* [sic] *where were already gathered several of the stewards and passengers who informed him that word had been received by wireless from the* ***TITANIC*** *that the* ***TITANIC*** *had struck an iceberg and was calling for help. Orders were immediately given and the* ***MOUNT TEMPLE*** *changed course, heading straight for the* ***TITANIC.*** *About three o'clock. New York time, two o clock ship time, the* ***TITANIC*** *was sighted by some of the officers and crew; that as soon as the* ***TITANIC*** *was seen all lights on the* ***MOUNT TEMPLE*** *were put out and the engines stopped and the boat lay dead for two hours; that as soon as day broke the engines were started and the* ***MOUNT TEMPLE*** *circled the* ***TITANIC'***s *position, the officers insisting that this be done, although the Captain had given orders that the boat proceed on its journey. While encircling the* ***TITANIC'***s *position we sighted the* ***FRANKFURT*** *to the northwest of us,* ***BIRMA*** *to the south, speaking to both of these by wireless, the latter asking if we were in distress; that about six o'clock we saw the* ***CARPATHIA,*** *from which we had previously received a message that* ***TITANIC*** *had gone down; that about 8:30 the* ***CARPATHIA*** *wirelessed that it had picked up twenty lifeboats and about 720 passengers all told, and that there was no need for the* ***MOUNT TEMPLE*** *to stand by, as the remainder of those on board were drowned."* This affidavit was subscribed and sworn to on 29 April by William James Elliott, Notary Public for the Province of Ontario. Dr. Quitzrau had the times wrong but a passenger could be excused for that. His statement that ***MOUNT TEMPLE*** had put out her lights would turn out to be extremely important, although there was probably nothing sinister in Moore's order to do so. Moore, on the bridge himself by this time, and within sight of the apogee of ***TITANIC'***s white rockets, would have wanted no stray light rays to interfere with his viewing ***TITANIC'***s lights or pyrotechnic displays.

On ***TITANIC'***s boat deck fifteen-year-old Edith Brown saw the lights of a ship so close that she was sure they would all be rescued soon. Edith called her father's attention to the ship, and as he turned around to look in the direction she was pointing, Edith saw the deck lights of the other ship go out.

From Spokane, Washington, on 27 April, another ***MOUNT TEMPLE*** passenger, W. H. Kenervorst of Nelson, British Columbia, said that ***MOUNT TEMPLE*** was within five miles of the ***TITANIC*** half an hour before the liner went down. Kenervorst declared that *"he saw the lights of the* ***TITANIC*** *and that although Captain Moore had received wireless messages that the White Star liner was sinking and that the women and children had been put off in the boats, he hove to his ship in spite of the entreaties of his officers that he rush to the aid of the* ***TITANIC."***

Kenervorst said that officers, clothed in high boots and heavy overcoats, were ready to lower the ***MOUNT TEMPLE'***s boats, and had urged Captain Moore to make an attempt to reach the ***TITANIC,*** but Moore replied that it was too dangerous and he would not risk the lives of his own passengers. He had learned all this, said Kenervorst, through a friend of the Marconi operator on board ***MOUNT TEMPLE,*** John Durrant.

In his book, *A* ***TITANIC*** *Myth, The* ***CALIFORNIAN*** *Incident* (William Kimber & Co., Ltd., London, 1986; Second Edition, Revised, The S.P.A., Ltd. Hanley Swan, Worcs., 1992) Leslie Harrison quotes a letter from Canadian Pacific deck officer W. H. Baker to Captain Stanley Lord of the ***CALIFORNIAN.*** Baker had been assigned to ***MOUNT TEMPLE'***s eastbound voyage immediately after the ***TITANIC*** incident when one of her officers had been assigned to a shore billet. Baker told Lord that ***MOUNT TEMPLE'***s officers told him that she was not more than 14 miles from the sinking ***TITANIC.*** Captain Moore himself had put her closer.

On 25 April Moore had told *New York Times* reporters: *"Furthermore, what do the people who were on board my steamer know what I was doing or where I was going? How could they tell in what direction I was sailing? It was past midnight and they were below. The statement was absurd. Leaving humanity out of the question, do you not think that I would have liked to have been the lucky one to pick up those people?"*

The official explanation for Dr. Quitzrau's accusations, which has become part of ***TITANIC*** legend, is that he was traveling in Second Class, had demanded to be upgraded to First at no extra cost to him, and had been refused. He was therefore disgruntled and chose this way to get revenge. This has always been a standard excuse to dismiss passenger complaints in the airline industry as well. Until I read it in ***TITANIC*** legend I had no idea that flight crews had not invented it.

As noted in a previous chapter, on 24 April ***CALIFORNIAN***'s Second Donkeyman Ernest Gill had his accusation against Captain Stanley Lord notarized for the Senate subcommittee. Gill accused Lord of being within sight of ***TITANIC***'s rockets and doing nothing to render aid. Captain Lord was firmly hooked and reeled in while ***MOUNT TEMPLE***'s master, Captain Moore, was slipping away. Why was no action taken to investigate the passenger complaints against Captain Moore? Why was Captain Moore's word taken as absolute truth, while Captain Lord was branded a liar? Why were ***CALIFORNIAN***'s officers and even her Second Donkeyman called upon for testimony, while ***MOUNT TEMPLE***'s officers were never questioned? In fact, it is extremely rare for any but the master to be asked to testify in such an inquiry, as we may see by studying the remainder of the American and British inquiries. The master's word is always taken, unless it is an accident of such magnitude that the officers and seamen of the vessels directly involved are called upon for testimony.

The answer to that important question lies in Captain Moore's testimony at the American inquiry. Moore provided two very important items... the alleged position of the ***FRANKFURT,*** and coordinates for the field ice which made it appear that ***TITANIC*** struck a lone iceberg east of the main field, thus supporting White Star's claim that she had been on the proper Southern Track. The Southern Track's comer coordinates at that time were 42°N, 47°W. The rhumb line from the comer to New York passed right through the ice field in question. If ***TITANIC*** was on the proper Southern Track rhumb line, then she had to have struck ice on the eastern side of the field. If she struck ice on the western side of the ice field, then she could not have been on the Southern Track because she could not have run full speed through field ice. It was that simple.

After Ernest Gill's first American testimony was finished Captain Lord was sworn by Senator Smith. Smith wanted to know why Lord had tried to warn ***TITANIC*** of the ice he had encountered.

"It was just a matter of courtesy," said Lord. *"I thought he would be a long way from where we were. I did not think he was anywhere near the ice. By rights, he ought to have been eighteen or nineteen miles to the southward of where I was. I never thought the ice urns stretching that far down."*

Lord described the ice field as reaching as far as he could see in either direction, but that would have been just over 7 miles either way, in a north-south direction. The field was 1 1/2 to 2 miles wide in the east-west direction, said Lord, and as we have seen, the field had curved back upon itself in a shape something like the letter "S." Therefore, when Gill reported having seen the big passenger liner she could well have been beyond these limits and still have been visible to Gill. It would have been difficult for Gill to know whether he had seen a large vessel farther away, or a smaller one slightly closer at that range, without night glasses. A large passenger ship like ***TITANIC*** was unmistakable at night, usually having several rows of lighted ports in her crew quarters, as well as in First and Second Class and public rooms, even at that late hour. Yet, at a distance, although a Deck Department crewman could better judge what she was. Gill probably could not. He may very well have seen ***TITANIC***, and she simply disappeared over the horizon before she struck ice. Or, Gill may have seen the passenger liner described by the master of the ***LENA***, as noted in the preceding chapter.

Chief Officer Evan Elias had calculated that at the time ***TITANIC*** sank ***LENA*** was 30 miles to the northeast. But Elias had said that earlier in the evening three westbound steamers had passed the slow-moving ***LENA,*** and Elias was sure that one of the three, a fairly large passenger steamer, could have been near ***TITANIC***.

Elias had described a four-masted passenger ship which passed ***LENA*** 3 miles to the south. ***MOUNT TEMPLE*** had four masts and was about twice the size of ***CALIFORNIAN***. Her rated sea speed was 13 knots. She would hardly have looked like a "big German," but there are other points in favor of her being one of the mystery ships.

Captain John Dudley, master of the tramp freighter ***DULWICH,*** was only one of many masters interviewed by reporters who could not understand how ***TITANIC*** had escaped the most dangerous points and was wrecked as she was passing from the ice fields. In fact, ***FRANKFURT***'s officers would later tell German reporters exactly the same thing.

On 17 April the Allan liner ***PARISIAN*** arrived at Halifax, where her officers heard the first reliable news that ***TITANIC*** had foundered three days earlier. ***PARISIAN***'s wireless operator, Donald Sutherland, estimated that his ship had been only 50 miles southwest of ***TITANIC*** when she struck ice, but he had been off watch for the night. Sutherland had been at his key all day Sunday, trying to get assistance for the DAPG tanker ***DEUTSCHLAND*** which had run out of coal and needed a tow. At 10PM ***PARISIAN***'s master, Captain Haines, had ordered Sutherland to bed. Haines had been steering ***PARISIAN*** in the direction of the disabled ***DEUTSCHLAND,*** while Sutherland had been sending ice warnings to other ships, including ***CALIFORNIAN***, all day. Captain Haines wanted Sutherland to be back on duty at 4AM to find out what had happened to the ***DEUTSCHLAND***. This information supports the belief that ***TITANIC***'s Captain Smith did not know that ***DEUTSCHLAND*** had been rescued earlier on Sunday, for obviously ***PARISIAN***'s master did not know it. It also indicates that in all probability the western limits of the ice fields were pretty much as Captain Lord gave them, and as the diagrams prepared by ***BORDERER***'s master and ***LACKAWANNA***'s chief officer pictured them. In other words, water to the west of these described ice fields was clear. If ***TITANIC*** had headed south just a few miles farther west she would have been home free. Haines' interest in ***DEUTSCHLAND*** was undoubtedly the reason he had come so far south to go to a Canadian port, and an interest in ***DEUTSCHLAND***'s salvage was probably the reason ***MOUNT TEMPLE***'s Captain Moore had strayed so far south.

There were many ships whose masters admitted to being in ***TITANIC***'s vicinity, some without wireless, some with lone operators who had gone off watch for the night. All of which brings us full circle to two major questions, why was ***CALIFORNIAN*** singled out for censure, and why did none of the watch officers in other ships hear ***TITANIC?*** The answer to the first question is undoubtedly hidden within Captain Moore's testimony before the Senate subcommittee, testimony that was never questioned although it contradicted everything said by wireless operators Harold Bride and Harold Cottam. The answer to the second question is simply that only ***CALIFORNIAN*** was hove to.

A ship under way is noisy. Sailors, like aviators, often lose their hearing as an occupational hazard. Outside the wheelhouse, on the open bridge wings and in the open crow's nests of ***TITANIC***'s era, the wind created by the way on the ship whistled past a watch officer's, or a lookout's ears, while the water crashing under the bow could obliterate many other sounds. In the background always was the rumbling throb of the main engines as well as the auxiliaries. Bells sounded from time to time. Even at night a cacophony of voices and music could emanate from the public rooms of a speeding liner, adding to the background noise. Of course, the faster the speed the louder the racket. Any ice in the water could increase the noise. (Second Officer Fosgate's comment, *"They aren't called growlers for nothing!")* While in the relative silence of ***CALIFORNIAN***'s bridge wings screams and steam blowing off might have been heard... *if* ***CALIFORNIAN*** ha*d actually been no more than 5 miles away as legend has it...* on the open bridges of ships under way they would necessarily have to have been much closer for ***TITANIC***'s death throes to have been heard. In fact, it was common practice when navigating in ice areas to stop the engines periodically and listen for sounds that indicated the proximity of ice... in tramps which had no "imperative schedule" to maintain. Although there is no evidence either way, logically ***FRANKFURT*** was never hove to, and possibly ***MOUNT TEMPLE*** was not, either. Captain Hattorff might have stopped his engines briefly, and allowed the way to run off ***FRANKFURT*** for a short period, but probably he simply ran briefly at "dead slow ahead" while he studied his situation relative to ***TITANIC***. *A* ship's steam whistle is required to have an effective range of only 2 miles in fog, for example. Exhausting steam from ***TITANIC***'s relief valves would have made no more noise than her steam whistle. The primary mystery ship off ***TITANIC***'s port bow briefly displayed at least one sidelight, which theoretically could be seen for 2 miles. It might have been seen farther on such a crystal clear cold night, however. But this primary mystery ship was *moving,* as ***FRANKFURT*** and ***MOUNT TEMPLE*** were. This mystery ship was *not* hove to, as ***CALIFORNIAN*** was. Therefore, from the bridges of ***FRANKFURT, MOUNT TEMPLE,*** and any other nearby ship without wireless equipment, or with a wireless service which could not communicate with Marconi, the only indication of distress was visual... ***TITANIC***'s rockets. As we have seen in a previous chapter these rockets were all white, there were only 8 of them fired, and rather than indicating distress they signaled *"Keep clear.* "

At the American inquiry Senator Smith asked Captain Lord, *"Captain, did you see any distress signals on Sunday night, either rockets or the Morse signals?"*

No, sir; I did not. The officer on watch saw some signals, but he said they were not distress signals."

"They were not distress signals?"

"Not distress signals," Lord repeated.

But Smith also asked Captain Lord if he had seen the ***FRANKFURT.***

"I met him 5 or 10 minutes past 12, after I was leaving the **TITANIC**, *the scene of the disaster. He was running along parallel with the ice, apparently trying to find an opening, and he saw me coming through, and he headed for the place I was coming out, and as we came out he went in. He went through the same place toward the scene of the disaster."*

"Where was the ***FRANKFURT*** *headed?"* Smith asked.

He was running about south-southeast, when I saw him, coming away from the northwest," Lord answered.

"For what port?" Smith asked.

Lord's answer was very strange. *"I saw in the papers since, he had arrived at Breton Harbor. I did not know then."* Perhaps the court stenographer confused his shorthand notes for Bremen and translated them to "Breton Harbor" a more familiar name to an American. Or, did Captain Lord confuse ***FRANKFURT*** with another ship? A Canadian vessel, perhaps... ***MOUNT TEMPLE,*** for example? The yellow funnels of Canadian Pacific and the buff funnels of Norddeutscher Lloyd could have been confused in the early morning light.

"Had you any means of fixing his position at any time between 10 and 12 o'clock Sunday night?" Smith asked.

"Oh, no; none whatever."

"Or between 10 o'clock Sunday night and 2 o'clock Monday morning?"

"None whatever."

*"Do you know the captain of the **FRANKFURT**?"* Smith asked.

"I never met him," Lord answered.

When Smith asked Lord if he ever had the ***FRANKFURT***'s position on Monday morning with reference to distance or longitude and latitude, Lord's reply was, *"I do not know; he did not give us his position."*

Shortly after 0500 ***CALIFORNIAN***'s Marconi man had allegedly received a message from ***FRANKFURT*** saying something like *"ship sunk,"* said Lord, *"But I understand between the German and English operators they do not always grasp one another's messages; there is a little confusion about it. Apparently we did not get it. The first report I got to the bridge that morning, after I had sent down and had the operator called, the chief officer came back and said, 'He reports a ship sunk.' I said, 'Go back and wait until you find out what it is. Get some news about it.' So he went back, and I suppose 10 minutes afterwards he came back and said, 'The **TITANIC** is sunk, and hit an iceberg.'"*

Captain Lord had promptly given orders to get ***CALIFORNIAN*** under way and proceed to the position given as the wreck site. At daylight, said Lord, he had seen a *yellow-funnel steamer* to the southwest, beyond where ***CALIFORNIAN***'s mystery steamer had been seen, about 8 miles away.

Immediately after Captain Lord's testimony ***CALIFORNIAN***'s Marconi operator, Cyril Furmstone Evans, was sworn in by Senator Smith. Evans was twenty years old, from Seaforth, Liverpool. He had been a wireless operator a scant six months; he had been trained at the Marconi school, the same school, Evans pointed out proudly as Bride, the junior operator in ***TITANIC***. Evans had made one trip in White Star's ***CEDRIC***, then had joined ***CALIFORNIAN*** for three trips. He had met ***TITANIC's*** senior operator, Jack Phillips just once, in Marconi's London office.

Evans began by relating his schedule on Sunday 14 April. At 5:35PM New York time he had sent an ice message to another Leyland ship, the ***ANTILLIAN***. ***TITANIC***'s operator had overheard it and called Evans, who said, *"Here is a message; an ice report."* ***TITANIC***'s operator (Evans did not know whether it was Bride or Phillips) had come back with *"It's all right, old man. I heard you send to the **ANTILLIAN**."*

At 9:35PM New York time Evans had attempted to call up the ***TITANIC***, at Captain Lord's instructions, and had begun casually, *"Say, old man,* (wireless abbreviation OM) *we are stopped and surrounded by ice."* ***TITANIC's*** operator Jack Phillips had snapped back *"Shut up, shut up, I am busy; I am working Cape Race."* At 11:25PM Evans had heard Phillips still working Cape Race, sending paid messages from passengers to be relayed through Marconi's land station there. Phillips had ignored the final and most significant warning of ice ahead of ***TITANIC***. The warning never reached ***TITANIC***'s watch officer, and in fact Evans had never sent ***CALIFORNIAN***'s position because Phillips had cut him off too quickly. Evans had expected ***TITANIC*** to be "very much south" of ***CALIFORNIAN***, which was bound for Boston. Therefore, Evans had not considered his ice warning any more than conversation, and Phillips was too interested in his paid messages to ask for further information. Evans put down his earphones, undressed and went to bed.

At 3:30AM New York time Evans was awakened by ***CALIFORNIAN***'s Chief Officer, George F. Stewart, who told him, *"There is a ship that has been firing rockets in the night. Please see if there is* *anything the matter."*

"I jumped out of bed, slipped on a pair of trousers and a pair of slippers, and I went at once to my key and started my motor and gave 'C.Q.'" Evans continued, *"About a second later I was answered by the* ***FRANKFURT,*** *'D. K. D., D.F.T.' The 'D.F.T' is the* ***FRANKFURT***'s *call. He told me the* ***TITANIC*** *had sunk."*

"He told you the ***TITANIC*** *had sunk?"* Smith asked.

"Yes, sir," replied Evans.

"You went to your operating room?"

"My bunk is in the same room as the apparatus," Evans explained.

"You put the telephone on your head?" Smith asked.

"Yes, sir."

"And received from the ***FRANKFURT*** *..."*

"I started my motor first," Evans interrupted, *"and called. I called 'C.Q.'... C.Q. means all stations, some one answer... and gave my own code signal. The D.F.T answered me. He said, 'Do you know the* ***TITANIC*** *has sunk during the night, collided with an iceberg?' I said, 'No; please give me the latest position.' He gave me the position. I put the position down on a slip of paper, and then I said, 'Thanks, old man,' to the German operator, and then the* ***VIRGINIAN*** *started to call me. 'M.G.M.' He started to call me up, and I told him to go. I answered him and told him to go. He said, 'Do you know the* ***TITANIC*** *had sunk?' I said, 'Yes, the* ***FRANKFURT*** *just told me.' I sent them a message of my own, what we call a service message, that an operator can always make up if he wants to find out something. I sent a service message, and said, 'Please send me official message regarding* ***TITANIC,*** *giving position.'"*

"Have you got with you the message you received from the ***FRANKFURT*** *at 3:40 Monday morning?"* Smith asked.

"No, sir; that was not an official message; that was only a conversation. But a few minutes after that I got an official message from the ***VIRGINIAN.****"*

"I would like any message, if you have it, that you received from the ***FRANKFURT,****"* Smith told Evans.

"No, sir; I have none."

"You have none at all?" Smith asked.

"No, sir. The only thing he gave me was the position of the ***TITANIC.*** *He did not send me an official message."*

"He gave you more than the position of the ***TITANIC.*** *He told you the* ***TITANIC*** *had sunk,"* Smith remarked.

"He simply told me the ***TITANIC*** *had sunk."*

"Then he gave you her position?"

"Yes, sir," Evans replied. *"The chief officer was in the room, and I said, 'Wait a moment; I will get an official message.' I got the official message and the positions were both the same. The position I got from the* ***VIRGINIAN*** *and the position I got from the* ***FRANKFURT*** *were both the same. I sent that up to the skipper. I did not have time to date the message. I dated my own copy of the message, but I did not get the name of the ship on either, or the date, or who it was addressed to, in my hurry."*

Again, there is something very suspicious in the disappearance of Evans' scrap log, the notes he was required to make as each message came in, as well as the inker tape which was standard equipment on Marconi receivers at that time. He did not need to fill out an "official message" form to have a copy of all items sent and received. They were written as a matter of course and regulation. So what happened to them, why did they disappear from so many ships... unless they were incriminating in some way, perhaps because there never was any communication from ***FRANKFURT*** at all?

*"Did you have any difficulty whatever working with the **FRANKFURT** operator?"* Smith asked.

"Not then, sir," Evans replied.

"Did you afterwards?"

*"He was jamming a little afterwards, and interfering when I was trying to get the **CARPATHIA**."*

Again, reference to any other service's operators "jamming" Marconi.

*"Did the **FRANKFURT** operator say anything to you about his having received a C.Q.D. call from the **TITANIC** immediately after she had struck the iceberg?"* Smith asked.

"No, sir."

*"Did he say anything to you about having received a rebuff from the operator of the **TITANIC**?"*

"No, sir."

*"Did you understand that the operator of the **TITANIC**, after he had given the **FRANKFURT** the C.Q.D. call, had waited 20 minutes before he had received any reply and then received a reply from the **FRANKFURT**, asking what was the matter and that he then said to the **FRANKFURT** 'You are a fool, keep out?' Did you hear anything of that kind from the **FRANKFURT** operator?"*

"No, sir."

"Or from anyone else?" Smith asked.

"No, sir; only from the papers when I got in," Evans replied.

*"Did you know the **FRANKFURT**'s position when she gave the message that the **TITANIC** had sunk?"*

"No, sir. He told me he was about 30 or 40 miles off. I remember that. He did not give me the official position, no, sir."

"Did he give you an unofficial position?" Smith asked.

"No, sir."

"That is, the longitude and latitude?"

"No, sir."

"But he said he was about 30 or 40 miles off," repeated Smith.

"Yes, sir "

"How did he happen to say that?"

"I asked him," Evans replied. *"I forget how it happened, now, but he said, 'We are 30 or 40 miles off. We are steaming as fast as we can.' But this was after I had taken the message up, and we were under way. I said, 'We are steaming full speed, now.'"*

"I understand you perfectly," Smith said. *"He told you that after he had told you the **TITANIC** had sunk?"*

"Yes, sir."

*"Did he tell you from whom he obtained the information that the **TITANIC** had sunk?"*

"No, sir."

"Do you know from whom he obtained it?"

"I did not know until I got in, sir I only knew from the newspapers and what I said just now," Evans answered.

Senator Smith, and then Senator Bourne asked Evans about his wages, which were £4 per month and board. The senators also wanted to know about Phillips telling Evans to keep out when the latter had tried to warn ***TITANIC*** of ice ahead. *"Can you take more than one message at the same time?"* asked Senator Bourne.

"No, but my signals were the loudest," replied Evans, who had not been able to hear Cape Race calling ***TITANIC***.

There ensued some testimony about ***FRANKFURT***'s hypothetical position, and confirmation that at no time had ***FRANKFURT*** given any coordinates to Evans, only that she was, as Evans was allegedly communicating with her, about 30 or 40 miles from the wreck site. But if ***FRANKFURT*** truly was 140 miles from ***TITANIC*** when she first answered the CQD call at about midnight, which is her official position accepted by the ***TITANIC*** establishment, ***FRANKFURT*** could not possibly have been 30 or 40 miles from the wreck site at about 0400 on Monday, but this figure may have been simply an estimate by the German wireless operator at this time. She could have reached the wreck site by 1000 on Monday, which is the official time of her arrival there.

Evans was questioned at great length about conversations aboard ***CALIFORNIAN*** on Monday morning. Everyone was talking about the rockets, said Evans, but his only interesting statement was about Donkeyman Ernest Gill.

Has anyone told you that he was to receive $500 for a story in regard to these rockets… anyone on your boat?" asked Senator Burton.

"I think the donkeyman mentioned it," replied Evans.

"What did he say?" Burton asked.

"He said, 'I think I will make about $500 on this.'"

"Did he say that to you?"

"Yes, sir."

"That is the man who was a witness here this morning?" Burton asked.

"Gill, the second donkeyman," replied Evans.

"He said he thought he would make $500."

"Yes."

"When was that said?" Burton asked.

"The night before last."

Senator Smith continued to press Evans for details on his being awakened early Monday by ***CALIFORNIAN***'s Chief Officer Stewart, who wanted Evans to get more information about the ship which had fired rockets during the night. At the time Evans thought that Stewart believed they might have come from the tanker (DAPG's ***DEUTSCHLAND***) which had been asking for a tow.

The most significant part of Evans' testimony was that he *never* had any coordinates from ***FRANKFURT***. Nor did Evans give the coordinates which ***FRANKFURT***'s operator had allegedly given him as ***TITANIC***'s distress position. Evans merely said that they were the same coordinates given by the ***VIRGINIAN***. These coordinates from ***VIRGINIAN*** had already been given by Captain Lord, but they are of no use because of an apparent transcription error made by the Senate inquiry's stenographer. The coordinates were given as *"41°46,' longitude 10°15',"* which put ***TITANIC*** aground on the western Irish coast, and as *41°56'N, 50°14'W*. It is, however, fairly clear that ***VIRGINIAN*** gave the second set of coordinates, not the first set that Boxhall had given to Phillips. The first set of coordinates was the only position ***FRANKFURT*** had for ***TITANIC***, having been rebuffed by Phillips before Phillips began sending the second, corrected position which was about 10 miles farther east. This is proven by Norddeutscher Lloyd's official statement from ***FRANKFURT***'s master, Captain Hattorff, given out from Bremen on 24 April. It is significant that in his official statement Hattorff gave ***TITANIC***'s position as 41°44'N, 50°24'W, the first coordinates sent by Phillips before Boxhall had corrected the position. This was the only position

Captain Hattorff would have had if his wireless operator had hung up his headset in disgust after the YAAF.

But Evans testified that he had received the same position for ***TITANIC*** from both ***VIRGINIAN*** and ***FRANKFURT***. *This is impossible because* ***FRANKFURT*** *had only the* **first** *coordinates,* ***VIRGINIAN*** *had only the* **second**, *final coordinates. It is therefore significant that Evans had no written record of his alleged conversations with either* ***FRANKFURT*** *or* ***VIRGINIAN***.

Three days later, on 27 April, one week after Bride's first startling testimony about Phillips' rebuff of the ***FRANKFURT***, on the same day that Bride had allegedly written his report to the Marconi Company telling a different story of Phillips' sending *YAAF* to ***FRANKFURT***'s wireless operator. Captain James Henry Moore, master of the Canadian Pacific intermediate liner ***MOUNT TEMPLE***, gave some of the strangest testimony to come out of the American inquiry. Moore gave the first, the only coordinates ever presented for the enigmatic ***FRANKFURT***. The position was accepted officially without any corroborating information from ***FRANKFURT***'s log or her wireless log, and none of ***FRANKFURT***'s officers or crew were ever called upon for statements although the ship continued to voyage regularly to the United States. Nor was ***FRANKFURT***'s wireless operator ever asked to give his side of the incident although pages allegedly taken from ***FRANKFURT***'s wireless log, as well as the logs of English Marconi-equipped vessels, were later produced to support Moore's testimony. These pages, however, were conspicuous in that the information which supported Captain Moore's version of the conversation between ***FRANKFURT*** and ***TITANIC*** contained entries which had been doubled up on one line, as if inserted later. This is not, and was not, the proper way to keep an official log. Had an error been made which required an additional entry in such a manner the proper procedure would have been to tear out that page and write it up properly.

If ***TITANIC***'s Jack Phillips had turned away the nearest ship to the sinking ***TITANIC*** because that ship was German, it was a politically sensitive issue. In 1912 it was known quite well by statesmen from most nations that war between England and Germany was imminent. The United States, a country founded by English colonists and heavily populated by German immigrants, was the key to winning the coming war. Both sides wanted American raw materials and industrial production. England needed American industry and manpower to win a war against a country with the largest standing army in the world. Germany knew full well that England allied with the United States was an unbeatable team, simply because of the vast size of the United States and the large numbers of men available to serve in the Army. The Kaiser, knowing as Hitler knew a generation later, that the United States would not join forces with Germany, could only hope that the Americans would remain neutral. Several of the wealthy and influential Americans who died in ***TITANIC*** had important financial and industrial connections, in England and Germany as well as in the United States. Neither the English nor the Germans wanted to antagonize the friends, relatives, or business associates of these men, but imagine the fury aroused if it had been discovered that a German ship could have saved all of those lost, but she had been turned away by ***TITANIC***'s English wireless operator. Would you blame the English wireless operator, or would you blame the German operator and shipmaster? In retrospect it was easy to say that the latter should have continued to monitor ***TITANIC***'s transmissions, that Captain Hattorff should have gone to ***TITANIC***'s rescue whether her owner and master wanted him or not. But here again hindsight always has 20/20 vision. And imagine what might have happened to Marconi's takeover of the American company, United Wireless, his deals with the American Western Union Telegraph Company.

After Captain Moore was sworn in Senator Smith asked the usual preliminary questions, ascertaining that Moore called Liverpool home, he had been going to sea for 32 years, 27 of which had been spent in the North Atlantic trade. Moore was quite familiar with ice and icebergs. In answer to Smith's direct question on the subject, Moore explained that it was generally accepted among mariners that 7/8 of a berg was submerged. He estimated that the largest bergs he had seen were from 300 to 400 feet long and just as high. He affirmed that taking the water temperature at frequent intervals when approaching the known parameters for field ice would give an indication of its proximity. Bowditch, however, and other experts of this era denied that there was any reason to believe that water or air temperature would drop at any distance great enough to give warning of field ice, particularly in areas where there was an intermixture of cold and warm currents, for example where the cold Labrador current joined the warmer waters of the Gulf Stream. Bowditch recommended that large bergs might be detected by an echo from the ship's steam whistle, and the American senators frequently asked the British officers about this. Moore replied that he had never tried this method except when approaching high cliffs.

In response to Smith s question about his whereabouts on Sunday, 14 April, Moore began, *"At 12:30 on Monday morning ..."*

"Give the date," Smith interrupted.

The 15th, sir. I was in latitude 4°25' and longitude 51°15', sir. I believe that is correct."

"What time of day was that?" Smith asked.

"At 12:30 a.m.," Moore repeated.

"Was it New York time or ship's time?"

That was ship's time, sir," Moore answered, then consulted a memorandum *"4°25' north and 51°41' west was my position."*

"What hour was this in the morning?" Smith asked yet again.

"12:30 a.m., sir," Moore gave it for the third time.

"Ship's time?" asked Senator Newlands, who apparently had not been paying attention.

"Ship's time," repeated Moore.

"What date was that?" asked Senator Fletcher.

"The 15th," repeated the patient Captain Moore.

"Kindly give the longitude at that time," requested Senator Fletcher.

"The longitude was 51°14' west," answered Moore, who had either given three different longitudes, which nobody questioned, or the court stenographer had unfortunately transcribed three different longitudes for posterity. The last was apparently correct, as later Moore gave ***MOUNT TEMPLE***'s position at 0030 as 41°25'N, 51°14'W to the Board of Trade inquiry. The position of ***MOUNT TEMPLE***, however, was never corroborated by her logbook. Captain Moore's word was taken for her position at the time he allegedly heard ***TITANIC***'s distress message, just as his word alone was taken for ***FRANKFURT***'s position, and the position of the ice field.

"When was your ship's clock set?" asked Smith.

"At noon the day before, sir," replied Moore.

Finally Smith asked Captain Moore to tell in his own words what had happened on Sunday and Monday, *"Just tell what you did, what you saw, and where you saw it,"* said Smith.

"At 12:30 a.m. on the 15th I was awakened by the steward from my sleep with a message from the Marconi operator, sir"

"On your ship?" asked Smith.

"On my ship; yes, sir. I immediately switched on the light and took a message that the operator sent

*up to me which said that the **TITANIC** was sending out the C.Q.D. message, and in the message it said 'iceberg.'"*

"Have you the message?" Smith asked.

"Yes, sir."

"Just read it, please."

*"**TITANIC** sends..."* Moore began.

"Kindly give the date line, if any; the hour, if any; and to whom that message is addressed, if to anyone," Smith interrupted again.

"It was a general message, sir." Moore read, *"TITANIC sends C.Q.D. Requires assistance. Position 41°44' north, longitude 50°24' west. Come at once. Iceberg.'"*

"Who signed that, if anybody?" Smith asked.

"This was just a message he picked up, sir. He happened to hear it. He was sending this up at once to me."

MOUNT TEMPLE's Marconi operator, John Durrant, had not replied to Phillips, and Moore read Durrant's note at the bottom of the message, *"Can't hear me."*

If ***MOUNT TEMPLE***'s position was at that time 41°25'N, 51°14'W, her latitude was 21 miles south of ***TITANIC***'s final distress position, her longitude was about 45 miles west of ***TITANIC***'s final distress position, well within range of the standard Marconi shipboard wireless installation. This puts ***MOUNT TEMPLE*** about 49 miles from ***TITANIC***, as Moore estimated. The Cunarder had answered later, but Phillips had no trouble hearing her, and he should have heard ***MOUNT TEMPLE*** equally well. Moore had, he said, immediately notified his watch officer to steer N 45°E, while he got dressed. Then Moore went to the chart room and figured out that he had to change course to due east by compass to ***TITANIC***'s CQD position. The question must arise... why was a ship bound for Saint John, New Brunswick, so far south of ***TITANIC***, bound for New York? One answer, again, might have been the drifting DAPG tanker ***DEUTSCHLAND***. Captain Moore in fact said that he was bound for the same corner as ***TITANIC*** which was the Southern Track corner for vessels bound to American ports... 42°N, 47°W. Captain Moore effectively covered that question by saying that he had encountered the ice field and run south, going around the southern end of it. If that was true he should have known the extreme coordinates of the field and been able to find his way back to ***TITANIC***'s distress position, around the ice field if she had really struck ice east of the field. But Moore's answer also puts her safely southwest of ***TITANIC*** when in reality she was probably the second vessel which lay between ***CALIFORNIAN*** and ***TITANIC***, the yellow-funneled steamer seen from ***CALIFORNIAN***'s bridge at daybreak, the four-masted passenger liner seen from ***LENA***'s bridge. Unfortunately, there are no routine position reports extant for ***MOUNT TEMPLE*** prior to news of ***TITANIC***'s striking ice, as there are for ***CALIFORNIAN***, although Moore was obligated to report the ice field and its position to the U.S. Navy Hydrographic Office, just as Captain Lord had reported it from ***CALIFORNIAN...*** *if indeed Moore had run his ship south to avoid the ice.* By saying that he, too, had used the Southern Track corner to avoid ice and admitting that he was near ***TITANIC*** Captain Moore effectively validated White Star's Southern Track defense and concealed any connection to the ***DEUTSCHLAND*** salvage.

Either the court reporter bungled it again or Moore changed his course again to N 65°E true. This was not actually made clear, but later, at the British inquiry, Moore would give the course as N 65° E true. By this time Durrant had heard Phillips sending Boxhall's second, corrected position, 41°46'N, 50°14'W, about 10 miles farther east than the first position. Moore estimated ***MOUNT TEMPLE***'s speed at about 11 1/2 knots, and added, *"Perhaps she would have a little of the*

Gulf Stream with her, too," although her rated sea speed was 13 knots and in answering a distress message he should have made his best speed. At about 0300 ***MOUNT TEMPLE*** began to meet the ice, said Moore. ***MOUNT TEMPLE*** was now running on dead reckoning, without taking into consideration the southerly set.

When Senator Smith asked Moore if he had the messages received from and sent to ***TITANIC***, Moore's strange testimony began. While allegedly nobody else called upon for testimony at the Senate inquiry had kept any written record of ***TITANIC***'s distress message exchange with other ships. Captain Moore had supposedly ordered Durrant to monitor all of these messages and keep a written record of them without saying a word himself, in spite of Marconi Company regulations to the contrary, a peculiar precaution under the circumstances, especially considering the fact that ***CARPATHIA***'s operator Harold Cottam had already testified that ***MOUNT TEMPLE***'s operator had gone off watch at *half past ten* ***CARPATHIA***'s *time, or well over an hour before* ***TITANIC***'s *first CQD call.* The very peculiar thing about Moore's statements was that nobody questioned them, nobody seemed to notice the discrepancies, nobody questioned ***MOUNT TEMPLE***'s watch officers ruthlessly like ***CALIFORNIAN***'s watch officers were grilled. There had to be a reason for this. The logical reason is simply that Moore exchanged something the investigators wanted in return for his amnesty.

When Senator Smith asked Captain Moore if he had made any reply to ***TITANIC***'s CQD message, Moore replied, *"None whatever. We did not want to stop these messages from going out, sir. He makes a remark at the bottom, 'Can't hear me.'"*

Marconi regulations did recommend remaining quiet when a vessel was sending out a distress call, otherwise the call could be jammed, but absolute silence was ridiculous. When you pick up a distress message you acknowledge it, although briefly, so the sender knows that somebody has heard the call for help and is responding to it. Moore's reasoning in not replying is therefore very strange. Two possibilities come to mind... either Moore did not hear these messages at all, or he had no intention of responding to them. Only the former makes any sense.

When Moore told Senator Smith that *"at 3 o'clock we began to meet the ice,"* Smith immediately asked, *"Where? From which direction?"* Moore's answer was ambiguous to say the least. *"We were passing it on our course. We met ice on our course."* The questions deteriorated to Smith's asking how Moore had doubled ***MOUNT TEMPLE***'s lookout, always a safe subject. He had, said Captain Moore, rung his engines to stand by, put the fourth officer on the forecastle head, another lookout on the forward bridge, in addition to the lookout in the crow's nest. At 0325 Moore stopped ***MOUNT TEMPLE.*** He estimated his original distance from ***TITANIC*** as about 49 miles, and when he stopped ***MOUNT TEMPLE*** was a mere 14 miles from ***TITANIC***'s position, but by then the White Star liner had gone down, according to Moore. Before he had stopped, however, Moore said he had seen a schooner, had starboarded his helm and passed her green to green.

Moore also saw what he described as "a tramp steamer" of about 4,000 to 5,000 tons, which appeared to him to be foreign, not English, and he thought she had no wireless. Her funnel was black with "some device" in a white band. There were several shipping lines in 1912 which had black funnels with a "device" in a white band, the Standard's German subsidiary DAPG being among them. DAPG had some of the few tankers with engines and bridges amidships, thus they looked much like any cargo tramp. ***NIAGARA*** and her sisters had, indeed, been designed to carry general cargo as well as oil, and were thus equipped with cargo derricks. They could easily have been mistaken for tramps.

When Senator Smith told Moore that some of his passengers accused him of being within sight of ***TITANIC***'s rockets, Moore denied it by assuring Smith that no passengers were on deck at all. Yet Moore claimed that he had made preparations similar to those made aboard ***CARPATHIA*** as she approached ***TITANIC***, preparations which had awakened passengers, causing them to think that there was danger to the Cunarder. It is hard to believe that nobody aboard ***MOUNT TEMPLE*** had the same reaction and decided to investigate, if for no other reason than curiosity. Moore also said that his bridge was 50 ft. above the waterline, thus the apogee of ***TITANIC***'s rockets should have been visible to him very quickly.

"Do you wish to be understood as saying that you did not see, on Sunday night or Monday morning, any signal lights from the ***TITANIC****?"* Smith finally asked directly.

"I can solemnly swear that I saw no signal lights, nor did my officers on the bridge see any signal lights," replied Captain Moore, but his officers were never asked the same question.

At a distance of about 30 miles ***MOUNT TEMPLE***'s officers should have clearly seen the apogee of ***TITANIC***'s rockets. But it would have taken ***MOUNT TEMPLE*** almost 2 hours to cover half the alleged mileage between her and ***TITANIC*** when the first CQD was received at about half past midnight. The probability, then, is that ***MOUNT TEMPLE*** was closer to ***TITANIC*** originally than Moore admitted. If ***MOUNT TEMPLE*** was indeed the four masted passenger ship which had passed ***LENA*** earlier on Sunday she should have been very near ***TITANIC*** by midnight, according to ***LENA***'s officers. If ***MOUNT TEMPLE*** was north of ***TITANIC*** as she should have been, bound for Saint John, then she could very well have been the yellow-funneled ship seen from ***CALIFORNIAN*** at daybreak lying between ***CALIFORNIAN*** and ***TITANIC***.

Next Smith asked about ***MOUNT TEMPLE***'s wireless apparatus. It was Marconi, replied Moore, with one operator. He did not know why his operator was still on duty at 0030, and he thought they were in communication with the Russian-American liner ***BIRMA***. Moore then proceeded to read from the wireless messages copied by his Marconi operator. *"Has got* ***CARPATHIA****, and tells him position 41°46' longitude, 50°14'."* Moore pointed out that this was a different position, about 10 miles farther east than the first one sent by ***TITANIC***, and said that he had received this message almost immediately after the first one. *"'We have struck iceberg. Come to our assistance at once.' That is the message he gives the* ***CARPATHIA****,"* Moore explained.

The next message read by Moore was from ***OLYMPIC***. *"Position 40°22'N, 61°18'W. Are you steering southerly to meet us?"* This message was signed by ***OLYMPIC***'s master, Captain Haddock. Note that Phillips was not offended by such a "stupid" message, yet he had responded to a similar question from ***FRANKFURT***'s operator with the abrupt YAAF. According to Moore, Phillips simply replied to ***OLYMPIC***, *"We are putting the women off in the boats."*

"Then what did you pick up, or what did you send next?" Smith asked.

*"I did not send anything at all, sir. This is a message that we caught: '****TITANIC*** *says engine room flooded.* ***OLYMPIC*** *sends, am lighting up all possible boilers as fast as can.' But he was a day's sail away from him, sir."*

"The ***OLYMPIC*** *was a day's sail away from the* ***TITANIC****'s position?"* Smith asked.

"I dare say a little more than that," replied Moore. *"Then, there is another message that the Marconi man sends to him: 'Still calling distress.'"*

"That is your operator?" Smith asked.

"Yes, sir."

"He sends a message to you at the bridge that he is still calling distress?"

"Still calling distress, sir. ***CARPATHIA*** *asks if he wants any special boat to wait on him.* ***TITANIC*** *says, 'We want all we can get.' I do not think anybody realized at the time that it was so bad, sir,"* added

Moore.

Captain Moore then told Senator Smith that he had received all of these messages between 12:30 AM, ship's time, and the time that ***MOUNT TEMPLE*** received word from ***CARPATHIA*** in the morning that nothing more could be done, that ***MOUNT TEMPLE*** need not stand by. He added that ***TITANIC*** had told ***OLYMPIC***, *"Captain says get your boats ready; we are going down fast by the head."*

It seems to have struck no one as the slightest bit peculiar that Moore could be so close to a large passenger ship sending such urgent distress messages to a vessel several hundred miles away, and do or say nothing. While ***CALIFORNIAN***'s master Captain Lord was condemned for not waking his wireless operator, ***MOUNT TEMPLE***'s operator was allegedly not only awake but listening to every word ***TITANIC*** sent. Captain Moore received no censure whatsoever, and in fact was commended for not risking his ship in the ice. Moore's name is unknown to any but hardcore ***TITANIC*** enthusiasts, while over eight decades later the name of ***CALIFORNIAN***'s master, Captain Stanley Lord, is still bandied about in the media.

He seems to have got hold of the **OLYMPIC** *and kept on with him, sir,"* said Moore.

"His communications were running with the **OLYMPIC** *at that time?"* Smith asked.

"Yes, sir; and we picked them up."

"Go ahead," Smith ordered.

Captain Moore referred to his memorandum. *"**SS FRANKFURT** (German) gives **TITANIC** his position at 12 p.m.* [sic] *39°47'N, 52°10'W. **TITANIC** asks 'Are you coming to our assistance?' **FRANKFURT** asks 'What is the matter?' **TITANIC** replies, 'We have struck iceberg and sinking. Please tell captain to come.' **TITANIC** still calling distress. **FRANKFURT** seems nearest to him according to strength of signals."*

"What are you reading from? " asked Smith.

"This is what my operator sent up to me. These are the messages he sent up to me, the original messages."

"Received by your wireless operator on the **MOUNT TEMPLE?"**

"Yes, sir."

"And taken to you at the bridge?"

"Yes, sir."

"Is that signed?" asked Smith.

"This is signed 'J. Durrant.' He was my operator," replied Moore.

Let us pause to examine the above exchange. First, of course, it is extremely bizarre that Durrant would copy all of these messages without replying to Phillips in ***TITANIC***, especially under the circumstances. But Durrant could not tell that ***FRANKFURT*** was closest to ***TITANIC*** from the "strength of the signals" that were coming through Phillips' earphones in ***TITANIC***. Only Phillips could tell that, and nobody had that information except Phillips and Bride, until Bride testified to that effect at the U.S. inquiry. Phillips never sent that information to anybody, he only discussed it with Bride. There was only one other way that Durrant in ***MOUNT TEMPLE*** could know that ***FRANKFURT***'s signals indicated that she was close to ***TITANIC***, and that was if Durrant knew that ***MOUNT TEMPLE*** was very close to ***TITANIC***. He could know this by getting ***TITANIC's*** position relative to ***MOUNT TEMPLE*** from ***MOUNT TEMPLE***'s officers, as passenger Kenervorst had said, or by actually seeing ***TITANIC***'s lights. In view of all other evidence, however, this whole exchange, which includes the information about ***FRANKFURT***'s signal strength, appears to have been fabricated to fit Bride's original testimony and refute the fact that Phillips had turned away ***FRANKFURT***.

Finally Senator Smith asked the crucial question. *"Did you know of the* ***FRANKFURT****'s position?"*

"He gives his position there, sir," replied Moore.

"He does not give his position, does he?" asked Smith as if playing a part.

"Yes, sir," answered Moore.

"Not the ***FRANKFURT?****"* Was Smith feigning incredulity?

"The ***FRANKFURT*** *says that at 12 o'clock his position is 39°47', sir,"* replied Moore.

"But this wireless message says that he judges by the strength of his signals or messages that the ***FRANKFURT*** *is nearest."*

"But he gives his position, sir," Moore insisted.

"That is the position at the time this last message was sent, which you have handed over; at the time that was delivered?" Smith asked.

"The ***FRANKFURT*** *gives his position as 39°47'N, 52°10'W, sir,"* replied the deferential Captain Moore, giving the first and only "official" position for ***FRANKFURT.***

In spite of the fact that Durrant's allegedly overheard communication between ***FRANKFURT*** and ***TITANIC*** directly contradicted everything that Bride had said, in spite of the fact that Durrant's version made absolutely no sense, it has been accepted as unadulterated truth for over eight decades.

"You must excuse me for being so minute about it," Smith continued, *"but I want to find out whether the* ***FRANKFURT*** *made any effort at all to reach the* ***TITANIC****'s position."*

"Of course, this is by the operator, his personal statement, that he seems to be the nearest on account of the strength of the message. As a matter of fact, you see he was one degree to the westward of my position, or pretty near it, when I first turned around," Moore explained.

"The testimony shows that from the strength of the wireless impact, if it may be called that, he judged that the ***FRANKFURT*** *was nearest?"* Smith asked again.

"Yes, sir."

This exchange indicates without doubt that Moore meant that it was Durrant who had allegedly judged ***FRANKFURT*** to be the nearest ship to ***TITANIC,*** that Durrant had made that decision on his own, and only corroborated Bride's statement to that effect. *But let me emphasize again that Durrant could not have known what Phillips heard through his earphones aboard* ***TITANIC,*** *unless* ***MOUNT TEMPLE*** *was almost on top of* ***TITANIC.*** *This means that the messages that Captain Moore was reading to Senator Smith had to have been faked… and/or that* ***MOUNT TEMPLE*** *was in sight of those on* ***TITANIC****'s bridge. Moore was saying that Durrant had copied these messages on the night of 14–15 April, yet nobody knew about* ***FRANKFURT****'s proximity to* ***TITANIC*** *until Bride broke that news at the Senate inquiry on 20 April.* And we must remember that Durrant, according to Captain Moore, had already written on one of the messages allegedly overheard from ***TITANIC,*** that ***TITANIC*** *"can't hear me."* If Phillips could not hear ***MOUNT TEMPLE,*** which should have had the same 1 1/2 KW set that ***CARPATHIA*** had, the standard Marconi shipboard installation of the period, and ***MOUNT TEMPLE*** was at first less than 50 miles from ***TITANIC,*** then how could Phillips have heard ***FRANKFURT*** booming into his earphones as ***CALIFORNIAN*** ha*d* done, if ***FRANKFURT*** was indeed about 140 miles away? Telefunken had good wireless sets, but not that good at that time, in an emigrant ship.

"But the testimony also shows that the ***TITANIC*** *operator, when the* ***FRANKFURT*** *asked what was the matter 20 minutes after receiving the C.Q.D., replied "You are a fool; keep out." Now, I am asking you in detail about the* ***FRANKFURT*** *because I desire, if possible, to get some authentic information regarding her conduct after receiving that C.Q.D. call."* Smith was now putting the Germans on the

defensive.

"Yes, sir."

"Now, proceed," ordered Smith.

"This is another message (indicating). This is a note to me from the Marconi man: ***OLYMPIC*** *sent that message at 1:30, this ship's time. That means the time of my ship. '****TITANIC*** *acknowledged it, but has not spoken since, although* ***OLYMPIC, BALTIC*** *and* ***FRANKFURT*** *calling him.'"*

"That is one hour after I received my first message that we caught the C.Q.D.," continued Moore.

"Let us see what other vessels..." Smith began.

"Perhaps I had better read it through," Moore continued. He repeated the above message, then added, *'American ship...'* Moore interrupted himself with, *"Which proved to be a Russian ship, sir...'name unknown, tells* ***FRANKFURT*** *he is 70 miles off* ***TITANIC.****'"*

"This Russian ship is that distance?" Smith asked.

"It says here American ship, but it turned out to be a Russian ship named the ***BIRMA****, 70 miles off, a much faster ship than our vessel,"* replied Moore. In fact, the Russian-American Line's ***BIRMA*** was rated at the same sea speed as ***MOUNT TEMPLE,*** 13 knots.

Moore then continued by reading from what he called *"a copy of the operator's book,"* and by which he apparently meant Durrant's wireless logbook. Moore began by saying that at 10:25 New York time Durrant had picked up ***TITANIC***'s CQD, had answered immediately, but Phillips had allegedly replied *"Can not read you, old man, but here is my position... 41°46'N, 50°14'W. Have struck berg."* Durrant had then written, *"Informed captain."*

At 10:35 PM New York time ***CARPATHIA*** had answered ***TITANIC***, and Phillips had repeated, *"Struck iceberg. Come to our assistance at once."* Phillips had then given the position again.

At 10:40 Durrant had allegedly written, *"Still calling C.Q.D.. Our captain reverses ship and steams for M.G.Y.* (***TITANIC***'s wireless call sign) *We are about 50 miles off."*

Moore explained that was the position he had given to Durrant, and he had afterwards found that he was only about a mile off in his estimate.

At 10:48 (New York time) Durrant had allegedly written, *"****FRANKFURT*** *answers M.G.Y.* ***TITANIC*** *gives his position and asks, 'Are you coming to our assistance?'"*

Then, according to Moore, Durrant had written, *"Asks, 'What is the matter with you?' M.G.Y. replies, 'We have struck iceberg and sinking. Please tell captain to come.'"* This exchange was said to have taken place at about 0040 ***TITANIC***'s time.

This alleged exchange between ***TITANIC*** and ***FRANKFURT*** compresses the two exchanges described by Harold Bride (i.e., ***FRANKFURT***'s first call up and the second call twenty minutes later which was rebuffed with YAAF) into one exchange, and also puts ***FRANKFURT***'s first answer to the CQD as being *after* that of ***CARPATHIA***. While there will naturally be a difference in times given as ship's times, when New York time is given we can translate it easily into ***TITANIC***'s time. It is the sequence of calls that is important, however. Therefore the 10:48 exchange between ***TITANIC*** and ***FRANKFURT***, as allegedly recorded by Durrant, establishes ***FRANKFURT***'s answer to the distress call as coming *after* that of ***CARPATHIA***, thus rendering it relatively unimportant. But... and again this is extremely important... if this were true then ***FRANKFURT*** *would* have had the second, corrected coordinates. If Captain Hattorff had the second coordinates, then why did he give only the first coordinates to his company to be used in NDL's official statement?

Senator Smith responded to this revelation with, *"Let me see. 'M.G.Y.' was the message from the* ***TITANIC****?"*

"Yes, sir," Moore answered. *"He has given me the code here, according to each ship, sir."*

"That indicates that the second message was a further call of distress?" asked Smith.

"Yes, sir. of course, the distress signal was going. We first caught it at 12:30 by our ship's time, sir," Moore replied.

*"You think we are getting what the **FRANKFURT** got?"* Smith asked ingenuously.

"These are the messages that crossed between the two ships, sir, which we caught," Moore answered.

*"The **TITANIC** and the **FRANKFURT?**"* Smith asked again.

"Yes," replied Moore. *"I have a code here. Perhaps I had better give the names."*

"I wish you would."

*"**FRANKFURT** asks, 'What is the matter with you?' **TITANIC** replies, 'We have struck iceberg and sinking. Please tell captain to come.' 'O.K. Will tell the bridge right away,'"* Moore read from the messages he had allegedly stuffed into his pockets on the night of 14-15 April. Then he interpreted this last message for the Senate committee. *"That means that the **FRANKFURT** asked if the **FRANKFURT**'s operator should tell the captain of the **FRANKFURT** right away, and the other man says, 'O.K. Yes; quick.' That is, the **TITANIC**'s man said, 'Yes; quick.'"*

*"'10:55 **TITANIC** calling S.O.S.,' which is the other distress signal… the new distress signal,"* Moore explained.

"The signal of the Berlin convention?" Smith asked.

"Yes, sir; I suppose it is," Moore replied casually.

"10:57 Ditto. 10:59 Working M.R.A.," Moore read.

"Who is that?" Smith asked.

Here the testimony deteriorated briefly into the explanation of the code "M.R.A." At first Moore interpreted it to mean that Phillips was not working with the regular current. *"Perhaps he is on his auxiliary,"* Moore mulled this over. Eventually Moore, and Smith, realized that this was a typographical error and it was actually ***CARPATHIA***'s wireless call sign *M.P.A.*

Moore continued to read. *"11:00 Calling M.G.N. (the **VIRGINIAN**) and C.Q.D" That is the distress signal,"* Moore explained.

At 11:20 Durrant had written, *"Gets **OLYMPIC** and says, 'Captain says get your boats ready. Going down fast by the head.' **FRANKFURT** says, 'Our captain will go for you.'"*

At 11:55 Durrant had allegedly written, *"**FRANKFURT** and Russian liner **BIRMA** calling **TITANIC**. No reply."*

At 12:10 AM *"**OLYMPIC, FRANKFURT, BALTIC** calling **TITANIC**. No reply."* At 12:35 *"**BIRMA** tells **FRANKFURT** it is 70 miles from **TITANIC**."* And at 12:50 the ominous message, *"All quiet now. **TITANIC** has not spoken since 11:47 PM."* (New York time.)

By his own admission Captain Moore had just said that he had come to only 14 miles from ***TITANIC*** after listening to her final desperate messages, knowing that she was sinking, and had in all probability already foundered, surely realizing that she had not enough lifeboats to accommodate all souls on board. And Moore had done nothing! Somewhere in the darkness ahead of him 2,000 people struggled desperately in the water, or were freezing in the ship's too few boats, or were clinging to bits of wreckage, possibly had taken refuge on ice floes that Moore allegedly knew were all around, yet Moore stopped his ship and *did nothing!* Senator Smith's comment on this startling news was, *"I think it was very thoughtful of you, Captain, to bring the operator's notes. It is the most complete information we have had concerning messages from the **TITANIC**, their records all being destroyed. Have you anything further to read?"*

"Yes, sir; I have a lot, sir," Moore replied.

MOUNT TEMPLE's master continued to read, and comment. At 0125 ***CARPATHIA*** had sent. *"If you are there, we are firing rockets,"* to ***TITANIC***, which no longer was there.

*"Let me ask you right there, did you see the rockets from the **CARPATHIA**?"* Smith asked.

"I never saw any rockets whatever, sir," Moore replied.

*"Is it possible that this passenger from Toronto, who claims to have seen rockets, may have seen the rockets from the **CARPATHIA** at that time?"* Smith asked.

*"I do not think it possible, sir, because if the **CARPATHIA** was farther away it is not likely you would see her rockets. But you see, this ship says she is sending rockets up. So it is possible that other ships may have seen them. I do not know. I thought of sending rockets up, but I thought it far better to let it alone, because if other ships... they thought they saw them... might be coming to me, and I had not seen anything of the **TITANIC** and did not know exactly where she was; because I think, after all, the **TITANIC** was further east than she gave her position, sir. In fact, I am certain she was,"* Moore answered.

"East or south?"

"East, sir." Moore added, after a further query from Senator Smith, *"I should think at least 8 miles, sir, of longitude."*

"What makes you think so?"

*"Because when I got the position in the morning I got a prime vertical sight; that is a sight taken when the sun is bearing due east. That position gave me 50°9'30"W. I got two observations. I took one before the prime vertical and also on the prime vertical. We were steering north at the time, steering north to go around this pack again, to look out, to see if we could find a hole through the ice, and we took these two positions, and they both came within a quarter of a mile of each other; so that the **TITANIC** must have been on the other side of that field of ice, and then her position was not right which she gave."*

Moore had just excused himself from going to ***TITANIC***'s rescue, and he had put ***TITANIC*** east of the ice field as well, thus confirming White Star's Southern Track defense. Smith asked if ***TITANIC*** might have drifted east after she struck the iceberg, and Moore did not think she could have drifted that far east in such a short time. Nor did she move under her own power that far, said Moore.

At about 0600 on Monday Moore had sighted ***CARPATHIA*** picking up ***TITANIC***'s boats… east of the ice field.

So, was ***TITANIC*** east, or west of the field ice?

If Moore's other statements had made sense it would be easier to believe everything he said. ***MOUNT TEMPLE***'s master then made a very strange statement. *"I had no idea that the **TITANIC** had sunk. I had not the slightest idea of that."*

But Moore had just finished reading the alleged wireless messages flashing between ***TITANIC*** and other ships, including ***FRANKFURT,*** which certainly indicated that she was going down rapidly, and then an ominous silence which should have indicated to all but the densest listener that she had indeed foundered. Moore had not given up hopes of seeing ***TITANIC***, he claimed, until about 0900 when he had word from ***CARPATHIA*** that she had picked up the boats and ***TITANIC*** had sunk. Moore had seen both ***CARPATHIA*** and ***CALIFORNIAN*** to the east of the ice field, which he estimated as 5 to 6 mile wide. He had seen the tramp steamer, and at about 0800 he had sighted ***BIRMA***. Oddly, Moore described ***BIRMA***'s funnel as "yellow," like his own ship's funnel, rather than buff. Did he do this to explain the "yellow-funneled" ship which had been seen between ***CALIFORNIAN*** and ***TITANIC*** at daybreak on Monday, thus exonerating himself still further?

Before we examine Durrant's allegedly overheard messages, let us examine Captain Moore's behavior, or lack of it. He had supposedly just listened to ***TITANIC***'s final and desperate distress messages, indicating that she was sinking fast, and then silence. Any shipmaster ought to know what this meant, and be able to form a mental picture of struggling people in the water, clinging to wreckage, in this case possibly clinging to ice floes. Any reasonably sensitive commander would have immediately taken his ship toward that position to offer succor to those drowning, freezing souls, as well as to those which Moore knew were in lifeboats, knowing that because of the water and air temperatures time was of the essence in saving lives.

We also have the question, quite naturally, why would Moore and Lord stop their ships, with Moore refusing to go near any ice at all, while ***CARPATHIA***'s master, Captain Arthur Rostron allegedly dodged icebergs at full speed with a ship full of passengers on his way to aid ***TITANIC***'s victims? The answer is simple. It is the same reason why some airline captains will fly through thunderstorms, while most will fly around them. Hans de Mierre provided the real answer, however, in his *"Clipper Ships to Ocean Greyhounds."* De Mierre had been Second Officer in ***MAURETANIA*** with Captain Rostron commanding, immediately after World War I. Of Rostron's performance, de Mierre wrote, *"Captain Rostron handled his ship as though she were a destroyer and so had others before him."* That was the stuff of which topnotch express liner commanders were made. Some men had it, most did not. In Captain Lord's case he had stopped prudently for the night, to find his way through or around the ice in daylight. But Lord had not been listening to ***TITANIC***'s desperate wireless cries for help as Moore had allegedly been listening. Thus who should have been blamed for not going to aid these victims? Who really should have been investigated?

As for Durrant's alleged messages copied from ***TITANIC***'s transmissions, not only their content but the times given for each are suspect because they do not match anything Bride or Cottam had said in their earliest statements. According to Moore, Durrant had first caught ***TITANIC***'s CQD with her position at half past midnight ship's time, and this was the first distress coordinates. But by this time ***FRANKFURT*** had called and been rebuffed, and the second, corrected coordinates were being sent, according to Bride's first testimony.

Senator Smith asked Captain Moore if the ice field might have drifted over ***TITANIC***'s grave after she had sunk. Moore replied, *"It is just possible, sir, and nothing more. of course, that ice had been in the Gulf Stream and was going with the Gulf Stream. The Gulf Stream, as we know, is always flowing to the east-northeast, and it is just possible that when he struck he might have been in that ice pack. I do not know whether he got into it or not. Do the officers say they got into any field ice?"*

"They say they saw field ice all about them. Do you mean the officers of the ***TITANIC****?"* Smith asked.

"Yes."

"They saw considerable ice... field ice."

"Did they see field ice or icebergs?" Moore had now turned interrogator.

"Both," answered Smith.

TITANIC's officers had seen field ice and bergs at daybreak, although Boxhall had reported hearing water breaking against the ice during the night. Major Peuchen had reported departing ***TITANIC***'s port side and rowing toward the light two points off her port bow. She was heading north, and Peuchen had seen the Northern Lights, as recounted in an earlier chapter. The starboard lifeboats had been rowed toward the light seen off ***TITANIC***'s starboard quarter. While ***TITANIC*** was still afloat those in the lifeboats had some reference as to direction from her. But after she had disappeared for most of those survivors there was no sense of direction. Generally they tried to keep together and rowed to keep warm. The officers, Lightoller, Pitman, Boxhall and Lowe, should have noted direction by the stars. These officers had been taking celestial observations from these stars every few hours. As Second Officer Fosgate has explained, the watch knows which celestial bodies are visible just above the horizon. Perhaps the confusion over direction was deliberate. It is difficult to believe that a deck officer of this era had already forgotten the common sense first item of seamanship in a lifeboat... note direction, with compass or by the visible celestial bodies. If ***TITANIC*** *had* indeed been east of the field ice, and had struck either the pack ice or an outlying berg, then those boats lowered on the port side which rowed toward the primary mystery ship, were rowed toward the north-northwest, and the boats' occupants should have seen ice very quickly. Those which rowed in an easterly direction should have seen none. After ***TITANIC*** was gone and all boats began to keep together, then were rowed toward the lights of the oncoming ***CARPATHIA***, they should not have encountered ice, nor should ***CARPATHIA*** have encountered ice, coming as she was from the southeast. Yet ***CARPATHIA*** did encounter ice, a lot of it, and survivors said that they found themselves surrounded by ice at daybreak, indicating that the ice was east of ***TITANIC***, between the spot where she foundered and ***CARPATHIA***, pounding toward her from the southeast.

As was pointed out in an earlier chapter, the set had been deflected to the south by strong northerly winds earlier in the day and evening, as well as during the two preceding weeks. Every bit of testimony indicated that Murdoch's evasive action had been to miss a growler, not an iceberg, not field ice. There was no way that Murdoch could have missed seeing such a large quantity of field ice dead ahead. On clear nights the sky along the horizon in the direction of the ice is markedly lighter than the rest of the horizon. This effect, called "ice blink," can be seen by the watch officer long enough before the ice is sighted to take evasive action, as Captain Lord in ***CALIFORNIAN*** did. We are left, therefore, with one of two possibilities... either ***TITANIC*** struck an outlying growler well east of the field ice reported by wireless, or she came around the northern edge of the ice field and struck a growler west of the field. All evidence points to the latter. Lightoller had cautioned his lookouts to be especially alert to spot "small ice and growlers," exactly what would be expected to trail field ice moving in an east-northeasterly direction, as ***TITANIC***'s navigators expected the ice to move. The fact that the ice was actually moving in a more southerly direction has no bearing on the coverup, because it was not yet realized in April, 1912, although it does have a bearing on the actual cause of the accident.

Captain Moore, then, had effectively fed four very important pieces of information to the Senate inquiry which cleared the White Star Line of any wrongdoing. Moore had effectively put ***TITANIC*** where she should have been if she was "exactly on the Southern Track," i.e., east of the ice field, and Moore had established for posterity that ***FRANKFURT*** and ***TITANIC*** had exchanged wireless messages at great length, thus exonerating Phillips for his allegedly turning away the closest ship, the German ***FRANKFURT*** which could probably have saved almost everyone aboard ***TITANIC***. Moore had also effectively put ***FRANKFURT*** too far away to have been of any help to ***TITANIC***, thus confirming that the German operator and Captain Hattorff had not been negligent in any way. And Moore had convincingly recorded for posterity that Phillips had correctly sent the Berlin convention distress signal *SOS*, rather than only the Marconi signal *CQD*, whether Phillips actually did or not.

But what did Moore receive in return? Obviously, he received deferential treatment at both inquiries, and his own conduct was never questioned.

Moore continued to read Durrant's messages. ***CALIFORNIAN*** ha*d* worked ***VIRGINIAN***, ***FRANKFURT***, ***BIRMA***. ***BALTIC*** had allegedly sent a message to ***CALIFORNIAN***'s operator, Cyril Evans, to "stand by," a message that warned Evans that he was "jamming."

Smith asked Moore what precautions a shipmaster should take when in the ice zone. This was a standard, safe subject, as Bill Müller noted in his 1962 article. *"The less said* (about anything else) *the better,"* wrote Müller. Moore explained about the usual extra lookouts, and said that his company (Canadian Pacific) warned its masters not to enter field ice. Moore, therefore, had allegedly gone south, around the southern edge of the reported field ice, after hearing from the Allan liner ***CORSICAN*** that Allan's *CORINTHIAN* had sighted ice in 42°25'N, 50°30'W.

When Senator Smith remarked that he had not noted any report from ***FRANKFURT*** after "12PM," an erroneous way of stating time, Moore repeated that ***FRANKFURT*** had been in communication with "these other ships."

"But this is the time when she gave her position?" Smith asked.

"Yes, sir."

"The ***FRANKFURT****'s position?"* Smith asked.

"Yes, sir."

"She did not give her position at any other time?" Smith pursued.

"No, sir," Moore replied.

"Did you see or hear anything of the ***AMERIKA*** *on Sunday, Sunday night, or Monday?"* Smith asked. ***AMERIKA*** was another German, DEBEG-equipped liner.

"I do not know. I did not see personally..." Moore began. And suddenly Smith changed the subject.

Senator Smith's conclusions after Captain Moore's testimony were astonishing. Bear in mind that Smith had just listened to Moore read off the final, tragic wireless messages from the huge, sinking passenger liner, Moore had just admitted that his ship had been at least 6 miles closer than ***CALIFORNIAN***'s alleged distance from ***TITANIC***, while Captain Moore did nothing. The Michigan Senator's comments, *"I am very much obliged to you for your kindness in responding to our request to come here."*

Moore replied, *"I was only too glad to come, sir."*

I do not want any wrong impression to get out concerning the course of the ***MOUNT TEMPLE*** *after receiving this warning,"* Smith apologized.

I assure you that I did everything that was possible, sir, consistent with the safety of my own ship and passengers," replied the obsequious Moore.

I want to compliment you upon your care and solicitude for the passengers and property that have come under your care," fawned Smith.

"I thank you, sir," responded Moore.

A sickeningly sweet exchange at best… how different from Captain Lord's treatment.

On 2 May Senator Smith privately took testimony from the American Marconi Company's vice president and general manager, John Bottomley. Smith began by covering again the fact that Bride and Cottam had been paid rather large sums of money for their stories concerning ***TITANIC***. Eventually Smith came to something far more interesting and pertinent.

"A passenger on the Russian ship ***BIRMA****, fitted with another wireless system* (United) *reported on reaching London, that the ship's offers to help care for the survivors on board the* ***CARPATHIA*** *were met by repeated signals to 'Shut up.' Were those answers in consonance with the general orders of the Marconi Co.?"* Smith asked.

"Most certainly not," replied Bottomley. *"The absolute order is that everything must be communicated with, ships or anywhere, in any time of danger or distress. That is one of the first provisions of our general orders."*

However, as noted earlier, this procedure had not previously been followed when a Marconi-equipped vessel was in distress, nor had it been necessary prior to ***TITANIC***'s demise. In every other incident involving Marconi-equipped ships in distress there had been a plethora of Marconi-equipped vessels available for the rescue.

"That passenger gave the London Daily Telegraph a statement, attested by the officers and wireless operators of the ***BIRMA****, that on the day of the disaster and on days following the ship was refused any information whatever with regard to the wreck survivors. Was that refusal in obedience to orders or instructions given by the Marconi Co.?"* Smith continued.

"Most certainly not," replied Bottomley.

Senator Smith then brought up the subject of operators "chatting" among themselves. Bottomley explained that "chatting" was against all Marconi regulations and operators who did so and were caught were severely reprimanded, in some cases discharged. Smith asked, "Do *you not think this practice should be regulated by law; that it ought to be made the subject of inquiry by the Berlin convention, in order to insure the proper transaction of public business?"*

Bottomley concurred, and said that he thought the matter would be brought up at the next Berlin convention. Again Smith's questions turned to the Marconi operators who had been offered money for their stories, another safe line of questioning. Finally he questioned Bottomley about the wireless equipment in ***MOUNT TEMPLE, CALIFORNIAN, OLYMPIC, BIRMA*** and ***FRANKFURT.*** Bottomley appeared to know very little for a man who held such a prominent position with American Marconi. In fact, Bottomley was an attorney who had become interested in wireless telegraphy. Guglielmo Marconi met Bottomley in New York in 1899, and when American Marconi was reorganized in 1902 Marconi tapped Bottomley to be his American General Manager, Secretary and Treasurer. In 1913 E. J. Nally took over the position of General Manager, but Bottomley continued as Secretary/Treasurer through 1918.

On 15 May ***CALIFORNIAN***'s wireless operator, Cyril Evans, was interrogated by Sir John Simon. Evans' testimony in England was essentially the same as that given before Senator Smith in the United States. He had, said Evans, received ***TITANIC's*** position and the news that she had foundered from ***FRANKFURT*** *first,* then from ***VIRGINIAN.*** The two positions given were the same, Evans reiterated without giving the coordinates.

No effort was made by Sir John to clarify the position of ***TITANIC.*** The Solicitor General simply remarked that it was the position that had been mentioned several times previously. As we have seen, however, that position was extremely important because the only position ***FRANKFURT*** heard was the first one, not the second corrected position sent by Phillips. Evans then mentioned that ***FRANKFURT, VIRGINIAN*** and ***BIRMA*** said they were going to ***TITANIC's*** distress position to see if they could be of any help. He told Sir John that ***BIRMA*** did not use Marconi wireless, but in a case like that they all united. It does seem extremely odd that Evans would communicate with ***FRANKFURT*** and ***BIRMA*** when Bride and Cottam in ***CARPATHIA*** would not, plus the fact that neither operator in ***CARPATHIA*** admitted even overhearing communications *with* ***FRANKFURT*** and anybody else during their earliest statements. But astonishingly Evans also said that he knew ***FRANKFURT*** *had* passed ***CALIFORNIAN*** *the day before.* This is in direct opposition to Captain Moore's position for ***FRANKFURT,*** about 140 miles southwest of ***TITANIC.*** If the eastbound ***FRANKFURT*** had indeed passed ***CALIFORNIAN*** sometime on Saturday, then ***FRANKFURT*** should have been well east of ***CALIFORNIAN*** and ***TITANIC*** on Sunday night. If, by "the day before" Evans meant Sunday, the German liner should still have been too far east to arrive at the wreck site by 1000 on Monday. But Moore had already put ***FRANKFURT***'s official position 140 miles *west,* not east, of ***TITANIC.*** In fact, figuring ***FRANKFURT***'s departure time from Galveston, using GPS, she should have been just where her wireless operator told Bill Müller she was… about

24 miles from ***TITANIC***'s first distress position.

FRANKFURT departed Galveston, Texas, at 4PM on 6 April. Her schedule varied. On some trips she was scheduled to call at either Baltimore or Philadelphia, but on this particular voyage she went nonstop to Bremen, her home port. From Galveston ships head for the Straits of Florida to pass close to the Florida Keys, then swing north, taking advantage of the swift, northerly flowing Florida Current and Gulf Stream all the way to Cape Hatteras. Then they pick up a great circle for the shortest track to the Channel, exactly as a vessel departing New York does. ***FRANKFURT***'s sea speed was 13 knots. She picked up about 1 knot from the Loop Current coming across the Gulf of Mexico, past the Dry Tortugas, staying close to Key West, swinging on to a northerly course and picking up at least 2 1/2 knots from the Florida Current. Passing Miami, staying with the Gulf Stream, ***FRANKFURT*** picked up a steady 1 1/ 2 to 4 knots all the way to Hatteras. From there the set added slightly less to her speed, but the set coincided with the great circle, the shortest track to the Channel. Captain Hattorff was familiar with the route, and we can bet that he knew every trick to keep his schedule and lessen his coal consumption.

TITANIC's Second Officer, Herb Lightoller, was also familiar with the Galveston-Channel route. He had served in White Star ships calling at Galveston, and in fact while guarding the gangplank for disembarking passengers there he had once "decked" an overly enthusiastic American prize fighter who had tried to push his way aboard ship. With Lightoller's navigation experience it took but a few moments to work out a position right on the Galveston-Channel track, but far enough away from ***TITANIC***'s position to clear not only Phillips and Marconi but also ***FRANKFURT*** and NDL of any negligence in not rendering aid to ***TITANIC***. Norddeutscher Lloyd, as mentioned earlier, had a profit-sharing agreement with Morgan's I.M.M..

If she was 140 miles west of ***TITANIC*** when she caught the first CQD, ***FRANKFURT*** must have been dragging an anchor. If she was over a day's steaming time east of ***TITANIC***, (Evans had not been specific about the time of passing) then she must have acquired jet propulsion for part of her passage. ***FRANKFURT***, declared Evans, had turned back to the scene of the disaster. Obviously Evans had not been apprised of Captain Moore's "official" coordinates for ***FRANKFURT***. Unfortunately, nobody asked for times, and again, nobody asked ***FRANKFURT***'s officers or master or subpoenaed ***FRANKFURT***'s logbook. But if ***FRANKFURT*** *had* been a day's steaming time, or over 300 miles east of ***TITANIC***, she could not have arrived at the wreck site at 1000 on Monday, as officialdom and legend has it, because ***FRANKFURT*** did not hear of ***TITANIC***'s collision with ice until shortly after midnight between 14 and 15 April, according to Harold Bride. Eastbound she had the Gulf Stream with her, but westbound it was against her. If ***FRANKFURT*** *was* indeed that far east of ***TITANIC***, Captain Hattorff surely would not have risked steaming back over his course for such a great distance, knowing that so many other ships, and British ships at that, were near ***TITANIC***. Higher speeds require higher hourly coal consumption, thus steaming at full speed over such a distance (600 miles round trip) would have consumed enough coal that ***FRANKFURT*** might have ended up in the same position as DAPG's ***DEUTSCHLAND***... needing a tow. In addition ***FRANKFURT*** was a passenger ship, equipped mostly for Third Class with few Second Class accommodations. Passengers, like steam engines, need "fuel." Hattorff would have taken all this into account when making a decision to retrace his route at top speed on the off chance that he might not be rebuffed again. Considering all of this, Evans' story is not at all logical.

Sir John asked if Evans had known the position of any of the aforementioned ships, but Evans had not. He knew only that ***VIRGINIAN*** was coming up "from Cape Race way." In answer to further questions put by Sir John, Evans explained that the best range he could get for ***CALIFORNIAN***'s wireless installation was 250 miles.

Mr. Scanlan, on behalf of the Sailors' and Firemen's Union of Great Britain, asked Evans what basis he had for saying that ***TITANIC*** was near ***CALIFORNIAN***. Evans replied that he knew by the strength of the signals, then later said that "you cannot judge a distance accurately" (from signal strength), which of course is true. An operator could judge comparative proximity, and through experience could "guesstimate" mileage, but could not give mileage accurately. There then ensued a peculiar exchange. Scanlan asked Evans if ***TITANIC***'s operator, upon hearing Evans sending the ice warning shortly before 11PM on Sunday night, could tell that ***CALIFORNIAN***, thus the ice, was nearby? Lord Mersey broke in with, "*The ice?*" and Scanlan suddenly changed the subject. Evans never answered the question. Obviously the subject of ice proximity was taboo. But yes, Phillips should have realized ***CALIFORNIAN***'s proximity from her signal strength. Had he been alert, rather than preoccupied with his paid messages, Phillips should have realized that if ***CALIFORNIAN*** was nearby, then so was the ice which surrounded her. It was not Phillips' job, however, to understand the significance of this proximity, for he had no way of knowing in which direction the ice and ***CALIFORNIAN*** lay from ***TITANIC***; it was not his job to take it upon himself to warn the watch officer. Wireless had been installed in ships primarily for the convenience of passengers who wanted to keep in touch with friends and business associates ashore during the long transoceanic passages. The realization of the value of wireless as a navigational tool came later. Wireless operators were in a very new profession in 1912. They would learn as their profession matured, and those who came after Phillips and Bride would learn from ***TITANIC***.

Possibly Phillips figured that ***CALIFORNIAN***, bound for Boston, should have been considerably north of ***TITANIC***, bound for New York. Scanlan quickly steered Evans to another subject, that of his having been asleep by the time ***TITANIC*** called for help. Much emphasis had been put on that fact, and it was a safe subject.

Mr. Thomas Lewis, on behalf of the British Seafarers' Union, did dare to ask if Marconi regulations forbade communicating with other systems, and he specifically asked about de Forest. Evans replied that under ordinary circumstances Marconi operators were not allowed to communicate with other systems, although there were no written instructions to that effect. When asked if he had had any communication with ***FRANKFURT*** and ***BIRMA***, Evans apologized. He had made a mistake, he said. ***FRANKFURT*** was equipped with Telefunken, which had "amalgamated" with Marconi, therefore they could communicate. Yet, if he had routinely communicated with ***FRANKFURT***, and other German ships, why would Evans have to think about it twice? But they were not allowed to exchange messages with the Americans. While Evans claimed to have exchanged messages with both ***FRANKFURT*** and ***BIRMA*** on Monday morning, he said that on other occasions operators from those systems had jammed Marconi operators a great deal in the "ordinary course" of transmissions. Of course they had. As Lee de Forest had written, it was common practice to "jam" the other fellow in the spirit of free enterprise competition in the new industry. But considering some of Evans' illogical answers, his mention of ***FRANKFURT*** and ***BIRMA***, along with Durrant's mention of the same vessels, was simply to cover up the fact that both ships had been rebuffed by Marconi operators at a time when they should have all cooperated.

Mr. Cotter, appearing on behalf of the National Union of Stewards, questioned Evans about the charts that Marconi used in every ship upon the North Atlantic to give operators an idea of the proximity of other Marconi-equipped ships. Evans described the charts, but said he had none on this particular voyage. When Cotter wanted to see one of the charts, Evans replied that ***CALIFORNIAN*** was not marked on it because she had no regular run. In his hurry, Evans said, he had picked up a South Atlantic chart rather than the proper one for the North Atlantic. Thus no working chart constructed *prior to **TITANIC**'s loss* has ever been available for research.

Examined by Leyland Line attorney Dunlop, Evans was reminded of his statement to Senator Smith that it was impossible to judge proximity by signal strength, in spite of the Marconi Company's regulation to judge proximity by signal strength when a distress signal was sent, and give precedence to the nearest ship. Evans stood by that statement, and again declared that he thought ***TITANIC*** must be very much south of ***CALIFORNIAN***, because the Leyland liner was bound for Boston and was north of the Track. Evans insisted that Captain Lord had told him to expect ***TITANIC*** to be "away to the southward of us."

Sir John Simon returned to question Evans further about signal strength and proximity. Evans explained how the sound of spark from various types of installations was easily recognizable. The bigger, faster ship had the right of way, said Evans, meaning that ***TITANIC***'s Philips was senior to him and thus had the right to tell him to shut up. Sir John then displayed a sample of the Marconi chart that Evans had mentioned. It should be noted that only Marconi-equipped vessels were drawn into the chart ordinarily, but this one did show ***FRANKFURT*** as being at the official coordinates given by Captain Moore. This chart was made up after ***TITANIC***'s demise, according to Marconi's later testimony.

Captain Moore of the ***MOUNT TEMPLE*** was next to testify, questioned by Mr. Butler Aspinall, Counsel on behalf of the Board of Trade. Moore's testimony was essentially the same as he had given in the United States, excepting that he did give the coordinates for his corner... 41°20', 50°W. He had come that far south, declared Moore, after a warning from *CORINTHIAN* of ice from 42°15'N, 49°48'W to 41°25'N, 50°20'W. He had been steering, said Moore, S65°W. Examining this statement while studying a chart one finds that ***MOUNT TEMPLE,*** out of London, was taking an extremely long and southerly course to Saint John, and in effect seemed to be wandering all over the North Atlantic. ***MOUNT TEMPLE*** should have been well north of the reported ice. ***MOUNT TEMPLE***'s position when he received ***TITANIC***'s distress call, said Moore, was 41°25'N, 51°14'W. This appears to clarify the confusion generated by the multiple positions given by Moore to Senator Smith. Moore told Aspinall that he had immediately turned around and steered east, although later he clarified that statement, too, by repeating what he had said in America, that he had steered N65°E true, and then due east. At a distance of about 15 to 16 miles from ***TITANIC***'s distress position Moore saw the aforementioned sailing vessel, which he passed green to green. Then he saw first a stern light, then two mastlights of the ship which had a black funnel with a white band, and a device of some kind in that band. He had kept this ship's lights in sight the whole time, said Moore, and at daybreak saw her near ***TITANIC***'s position. This "mystery ship" was eastbound and south of ***MOUNT TEMPLE*** .

Moore was taken back over the same questions asked by Senator Smith, with the exception of several questions about the strength and maneuverability of lifeboats under adverse conditions, always a safe subject for the interrogators. While ***MOUNT TEMPLE*** was heading toward ***TITANIC*** Moore said they had taken an hour to get 18 of her boats ready for lowering. ***MOUNT TEMPLE***'s other 2 boats under davits were the emergency boats, already prepared for lowering.

MOUNT TEMPLE's wireless operator, John Durrant, came next. Durrant explained his late hours by saying that he always took a three-hour nap after his midday meal so that he could stay up until 1AM. He affirmed that he had caught ***TITANIC***'s CQD at about 12:30AM. Contrasting this statement with Moore's answers to Senator Smith's questions about Durrant's late hours, ***MOUNT TEMPLE***'s master did not seem to know that Durrant was in the habit of napping

MOUNT TEMPLE PASSENGERS SAW SIGNALS FROM TITANIC

Dr. Quitzrau Positive He Beheld Masts of Foundering Titanic, While Members of Crew Allege They Heard Officers Discussing Distress Messages Which They Saw

STATE SHIP DELIBERATELY DECLINED TO GIVE AID TO PEOPLE ON BOARD TITANIC

Strathcona, Alberta, Canada, April 25.—E. W. Zurich, who crossed from Antwerp to St. John, N. B., on the Canadian Pacific Railway steamer Mount Temple, has made a statement here concerning what was observed from the Mount Temple at sea the Sunday night the Titanic went down. According to Mr. Zurich passengers on board the Mount Temple heard of the Titanic's distress at 12:15 o'clock Monday morning, when a wireless call for help was caught. Captain Moore changed his vessel's course at once and headed for the Titanic, life boats being swung from davits meanwhile, and other preparations being made for landing assistance. The northern course was not held long, however, says Mr. Zurich, because a great field of ice loomed up ahead. It was reported among crew and passengers, according to Mr. Zurich, that Captain Moore made no further efforts to penetrate the floes, asserting that he could not afford to take the risk of endangering the two thousand passengers on board his ship.

SAW TITANIC LIGHTS.

The statement of Dr. Quitzrau to the effect that passengers and crew believed they could see the lights of the unfortunate Titanic is borne out by Mr. Zurich. With two companion passengers he disobeyed the captain's orders, which forbade passengers entrance to the upper deck at any time. He is fairly positive that they saw the masts of the Titanic, and he says he is not ready to accept the assertion that their ship was at least 40 miles from the wrecked liner at the time. At any rate, he thinks the Mount Temple might have reached the spot before the Titanic sank, and his supposition, he says, seems to have been entertained by others on board.

Their vessel sighted the Carpathia next morning, Mr. Zurich says, and keeping in touch with wireless communications to land, they were conversant with the story of the wreck. Mr. Zurich says also that the Mount Temple sighted immense fields of ice during Sunday and Monday.

MOUNT TEMPLE CREW SAW DISTRESS SIGNALS

New York, April 25.—Special dispatches received here from St. Johns, N. B., carry allegations to the effect that certain members of the crew of the steamer Mount Temple saw the distress signals from the Titanic. A dispatch to the Tribune sets forth that members of the crew of the Mount Temple deliberately sailed away after reading the Titanic distress signals, and did not attempt to give assistance."

The dispatch further states "Sailors, firemen and others, declare that they sat on deck for hours and watched the Titanic sending up rockets and burning red and blue light, until the Mount Temple steamed so far away that these signals were lost."

OFFICERS DISCUSSED SIGNALS.

"One of the sailors, who says he was on watch Sunday night, states that he heard Notley, third officer, tell the captain of the distress message, and that instead of the steamer heading directly to the wreck, she steamed away on her own course, so that the lights were soon lost. An oiler named Pickard, who was on duty at the time, declared that the second engineer came below and asked the men to 'keep her fired up to the limit,' as it was a case of life or death.

"Another engineroom hand adds that when his watch was over he

TITANIC NEWS NOT HELD UP SAYS CHIEF OF THE WIRELESS

Witness Before Senate Committee States There Is No Alarm On Shipboard by Which Wireless Operators May Be Aroused—Discusses Message to Carpathia That Vessel "Hold Out Its News of Disaster For Four Figures"—Tells of the Strength of the Wireless Instruments.

Washington, April 25.—Officers of the Titanic, who have appeared before the senate investigating committee were urging early today that they be permitted to go back to their homes in England at the earliest possible moment. All of the surviving officers have testified, but the committee is loathe to let ony of them return until the testimony of all the ship's crew has been taken. Counsel for the White Star company urged that the officers be permitted to return under the promise that they could be recalled and would respond if necessary. It was contemplated that a decision in the matter would be reached some time today.

When the Titanic hearing was resumed at 10:26 o'clock this morning Senator Smith called to the stand Guglielmo Marconio, president of the Marconi Wireless Company.

Guglielmo Marconi, head of the Marconi company, who testified at the hearing in New York, came to Washington today at the request of Chairman Smith, and was the first witness. Before taking the stand, Mr. Marconi frankly discusser the message sent from New York to the wireless operators on the Carpathia by Chief Engineer Sammis of the Marconi company, asking them to hold out their news when they reached port for "four figures."

"Yes, that message was sent by Sammis," said Mr. Marconi," but I know nothing about the message until afterward. There is this about it that I want to say: "The message was not sent while the Carpathia was at sea. It was not sent until the Carpathia

wages," he said, "because the sea is attractive to young men."

The wages in America, Mr. Marconi said, were slightly higher.

"Where were you on Sunday and Monday night, April 14 and 15?" asked Senator Smith.

"New York."

HAD NO COMMUNICATION.

"Did you have any communication personally or by your order with the Carpathia Sunday or Monday?"

"No." The witness said he learned between 7:30 and 8 o'clock Monday evening, April 15, that the Titanic had sunk. Tuesday evening he learned about the rescue by the Carpathia.

"I asked for further information," said the witness, "and was told by my operator that it would probably be impossible because the Carpathia would be extremely busy with the messages of the captain and the passengers aboard."

He made no further attempt to reach the Carpathia because he did not care to exercise his authority to interfere with the operation of the wireless. The captain and officers of the Carpathia, he felt, were the best judges of the situation. Mr. Marconi told of going aboard the Carpathia when it docked in New York.

"I went directly to the wireless room," he said, "and congratulated Bride, the Titanic's operator, on what he had done. Cottam, the Carpathia's operator, was not there. He called me later on the telephone and asked me whether he might give out a report of the wreck. I told him he might do so under the circumstances."

Mr. Marconi added that there was an ironclad rule in his company's regulations prohibiting operators from acting as reporters. He said that under

in the forenoon, and remaining on duty until 0100, a strange admission in view of the fact that Durrant was the only operator on board, and according to Marconi regulations he was subject to the master's orders.

Durrant had his *procés-verbal*, a copy of the messages he had overheard to and from *TITANIC*. He read the same messages that Captain Moore had read to Senator Smith. Finally the Solicitor General specifically asked Durrant about hearing ***FRANKFURT.*** Durrant repeated everything Moore had told Senator Smith. Phillips had answered the German operator, ***FRANKFURT*** had responded with "O.K. Will tell the bridge right away." Sir John then asked Durrant if he had heard ***TITANIC*** sending SOS. Durrant affirmed that he had, and in response to Sir John's next question Durrant insisted that CQD would be more quickly "jumped at" than SOS because it had such a good name because of Jack Binns and the ***REPUBLIC*** disaster. The public knew that CQD was a distress call, insisted Durrant. This is not entirely true, and is also irrelevant. Although

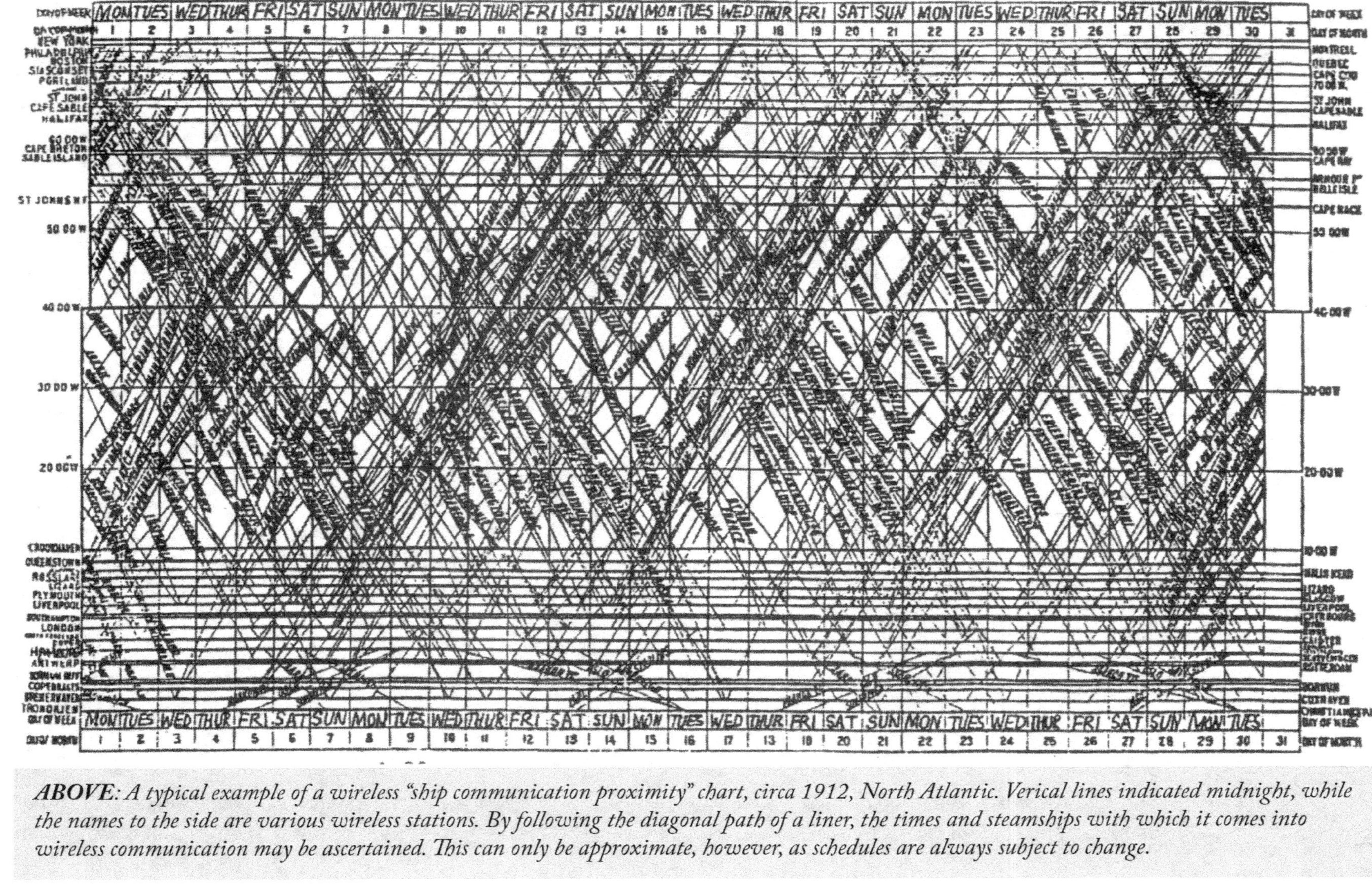

ABOVE: *A typical example of a wireless "ship communication proximity" chart, circa 1912, North Atlantic. Verical lines indicated midnight, while the names to the side are various wireless stations. By following the diagonal path of a liner, the times and steamships with which it comes into wireless communication may be ascertained. This can only be approximate, however, as schedules are always subject to change.*

the public may have recognized CQD because Marconi always courted publicity, other wireless services abided by the Berlin convention and used SOS. German and American operators knew the difference between CQD and SOS, whether the general public did or not.

After a discussion about other ships which were in communication with ***TITANIC***, Lord Mersey stated flatly that ***MOUNT TEMPLE*** *was never in a position to render aid to* ***TITANIC***. Sir John agreed, saying that ***MOUNT TEMPLE*** was 49 miles away, while Captain Moore had already said at the American inquiry that he had stopped just 14 miles away from ***TITANIC***. ***MOUNT TEMPLE*** could not possibly have reached ***TITANIC***, declared Mersey. Sir John affirmed that if Durrant had broken in and called ***TITANIC***, then he would have stopped ***TITANIC*** from calling others.

As we have seen, this statement makes little sense. Surely it would have been great comfort to ***TITANIC***'s officers to know that an essentially British vessel was closer than ***CARPATHIA*** and making every effort to reach the sinking liner. Moore may have been afraid to go near the ice, but did he know, as did Durrant, of Marconi Company regulations which declared that the ship known to be closest to the stricken vessel by the strength of her signals should take precedence in the rescue? If Durrant had transmitted (assuming that Durrant really was awake and listening to ***TITANIC***'s calls for help) Phillips would have known that ***MOUNT TEMPLE*** was closer than ***CARPATHIA***. And Captain Moore would have been obligated to do something.

The remainder of Durrant's testimony was essentially the same as Moore's testimony had been in the United States. Durrant affirmed that ***TITANIC***'s Jack Phillips had communicated freely with ***FRANKFURT*** and ***BIRMA***, the two ships which had been nearby but which used rival wireless services with whom Marconi did not routinely communicate. Sir John's final comment was that he knew ***MOUNT TEMPLE*** did her best, but could not get to ***TITANIC*** in time.

On 22 May Solicitor General Sir John Simon questioned George Elliott Turnbull, Marconi's Deputy Manager in England. The guaranteed wireless range of ***TITANIC***'s wireless set was 300 miles, said Turnbull. It could be considerably more, especially at night, but 300 miles was promised by the Marconi Company.

Turnbull affirmed that the *procés-verbal*, the log of the messages sent and received during the voyage, as well as the official messages on special forms were sent to Marconi's head office when the ship returned to England. He provided the *procés-verbal* from ***LA TOURAINE, CARONIA, BALTIC, CALIFORNIAN, MESABA***, the German DEBEG-equipped ***AMERIKA***, and a "reconstituted" record of ***TITANIC***'s communications, allegedly just as Phillips would have recorded them. Of particular interest to the inquiry board was the ice warning sent from the Hapag liner ***AMERIKA*** to the U.S. Navy Hydrographic Office via Cape Race and ***TITANIC***. The call sign for the relaying station listed on the Master Service Message form was MGV, which was a Canadian Pacific liner named ***MONMOUTH***, rather than ***TITANIC***'s call sign MGY. Turnbull could not understand how such an error could have been made, he was sure that ***TITANIC*** had relayed the message. This is very important because it was obviously introduced to indicate that Marconi and DEBEG routinely exchanged and relayed messages. ***MONMOUTH*** appears to have been in port on the date in question, 14 April, not on the high seas, therefore the message was apparently relayed through ***TITANIC***. The Board adjourned until the following day at 1030 when Turnbull was recalled.

The questions were mainly concerned with ice warnings sent to ***TITANIC*** and other ships, and whether or not they reached ***TITANIC***'s bridge. Turnbull confirmed that Marconi operators were required to write down every letter as it came through their earphones. A great deal of time was spent on confirming that ***AMERIKA***'s message to the Hydrographic office via Cape Race was indeed relayed by ***TITANIC***.

Harold Bride was then called to testify. Bride was questioned at length about his rejecting an ice warning at about half past five from ***CALIFORNIAN***. Bride now reiterated that he had been busy writing up his accounts. In New York, however, in his written report to the Marconi Company related earlier. Bride had said that he did not answer ***CALIFORNIAN*** at once because it took "some considerable time" to start up the motor and alternator, it not being "advisable to leave them working as the alternator was liable to run hot." At any rate. Bride had caught the message later when ***CALIFORNIAN*** had sent it to ***ANTILLIAN***, and about two minutes later Bride had delivered the ice warning to an officer on ***TITANIC***'s bridge.

Bride was taken through his previous testimony in America. He repeated that ***FRANKFURT*** *had* been the first to answer ***TITANIC***'s first CQD. Bride reiterated that ***FRANKFURT*** had *never* given her position, that ***Frankfurt*** had been "interfering" with Phillips' communication with ***CARPATHIA*** and Phillips had told the German operator to "keep out." Bride also confirmed Phillips' statement to him that by the signal strength he was sure ***FRANKFURT*** was the closest ship. But Bride's statements to this effect were never pursued at the British inquiry.

On 24 May ***CARPATHIA***'s wireless operator, Harold Thomas Cottam, was sworn. The Marconi Company had provided ***CARPATHIA***'s *procés-verbal*, and copies were handed out to the Court. Sir John Simon explained, however, that this was not a copy of the actual document, but had been made up later by the Marconi Company. The reason for this, explained Sir John was that Cottam had been too busy to keep records of his exchange of messages with ***TITANIC***. This makes no sense considering that Cottam had to write down the letters as they came into his earphones, and he had the inker tape as well. Mindful of Jack Binns, Cottam would surely have saved every scrap of paper in this case, from which he should have completed his *procés-verbal*. In New York both Cottam and Captain Rostron had told the Senate subcommittee that the Marconi log had remained in ***CARPATHIA***, yet the original was never produced, anywhere.

At 7PM New York time, or about 8:50PM ship's time, Cottam had traded time rushes with ***TITANIC***. For the next 2 hours and 45 minutes Cottam had exchanged messages with Phillips, merely to "keep in touch." Cottam now said it was 10PM when he had bid "goodnight" to Durrant in ***MOUNT TEMPLE***. He had also received a private message from a passenger in ***TITANIC*** to a ***CARPATHIA*** passenger.

In New York Cottam had said he received the first CQD from ***TITANIC*** at 11:20PM, New York time, but now he said that was a mistake and the first CQD had been received at 10:35PM New York time, or about 12:25AM ship's time. Cottam knew of the error "by a chit of paper" which he had scribbled out at the time. This was a copy of the *procés-verbal*, but it was the last message to be in the PV, according to Cottam and the Court.

Durrant's PV was compared with the reconstructed PV of ***CARPATHIA***. At 12:21AM (0021) Durrant had entered in his PV the fact that ***TITANIC*** "was still calling CQD" and was answered by ***CARPATHIA***. ***MOUNT TEMPLE*** was then out of range, or nearly so, of ***CARPATHIA***, but ***TITANIC*** with her much more powerful wireless set was easy to read.

At this time Cottam was waiting for confirmation of an earlier TR message sent to ***PARISIAN***, and he had taken off his coat preparatory to turning in for the night. He called ***TITANIC*** to ask if Phillips knew that Cape Cod had a lot of messages for him, and Phillips replied, "We have struck a berg; come at once," and gave ***TITANIC***'s position.

But, while Bride had already testified that any operator who was "on the job" would have immediately taken this information to the bridge, Cottam instead asked Phillips if he should take the message to the bridge immediately and get the ship turned around. Phillips did not lose his temper with Cottam as he did with the German operator. Phillips replied. *"Yes, quick."* Cottam ran to the bridge, gave the CQD message to the watch officer, who in turn quickly roused Captain Rostron. The master gave Cottam ***CARPATHIA***'s position, turned her to a northwesterly course, and Cottam told Phillips they were on their way to ***TITANIC***.

Cottam then aided Phillips with his communications because ***TITANIC*** was blowing off steam, and there was a rush of air from the expansion joint which was near the wireless cabin. This was caused, said Cottam, by air being forced out of the "hollow of the ship" by inrushing water. The air thus had no place to go at that time but through the expansion joint. The combined noise of the steam and escaping air made it extremely difficult for Phillips to hear even through his earphones, although Cottam explained that it was not just the noise, it also made the whole ship tremble. Just how he would know that if he had never been in a sinking ship was not made clear.

At this point Cottam introduced ***FRANKFURT*** into his testimony. When he had returned from the bridge, said Cottam, he found that Phillips was in communication with ***FRANKFURT.*** Durrant's copy of the wireless exchange between ***TITANIC*** and ***FRANKFURT*** was quickly read to Cottam, who corrected the timing somewhat. Cottam confirmed Bride's earliest statement about ***FRANKFURT***'s lapse of 20 minutes between the first and second (and last) exchange with ***TITANIC***. Surprisingly, Cottam insisted that as far as he knew all exchange between ***FRANKFURT*** *and* ***TITANIC*** ceased at about 10:45PM New York time, which would have been 0035 ***TITANIC*** time, although he admitted that he could not be sure about times. Cottam did confirm Bride's earlier statement that communication with ***FRANKFURT,*** in other words when Phillips sent YAAF to the German operator, ceased sometime prior to ***TITANIC***'s foundering rather than the few minutes before as Bride's letter to the Marconi Company had said. *"You have told us what you know about the* ***FRANKFURT***," said Sir John, and that was the end of that. At the British inquiry there were no more questions about ***FRANKFURT***'s conduct or position, and the reasons were obvious. In addition to liability there was an extremely sensitive political climate involved.

Cottam, however, discounted several messages that are part of ***TITANIC*** legend, and which came from Durrant's allegedly overheard messages, and from ***CARPATHIA***'s *procés-verbal* made up by the Marconi Company There was no message, said Cottam, about ***TITANIC***'s people being put into lifeboats, and no message telling ***OLYMPIC*** to get her boats ready. The legendary message about ***TITANIC's*** signals being blurred, ragged, then silent, at 0020 New York or 0210 ***TITANIC*** time were false, said Cottam. Her signals had been clear to the end.

On 18 June Sir Rufus Isaacs, brother of the Marconi Company's Managing Director Godfrey Isaacs, interrogated Guglielmo Marconi.

Marconi first answered questions about Marconi Company regulations regarding CQD and SOS. He confirmed that CQD was strictly a Marconi call, but insisted that both CQD and SOS were used since the Berlin International Radio-Telegraph Convention of 1906 had mandated SOS as the recognized distress call, which was to be implemented in July, 1908. Marconi pointed out, as his operators had done, that CQD was better known, however.

Isaacs then asked about ***TITANIC***'s wireless installation and Marconi confirmed that it was a 5 KW station with duplicate apparatus, or a backup system as we would call it today. It was powered under normal circumstances by the ship's dynamos, and in an emergency by a storage battery provided with the installation by the Marconi Company, which enabled its use even if the ship's normal power source was submerged.

Isaacs next introduced a sample of the communication diagrams issued each month to Marconi operators which enabled them to know when to expect other Marconi-equipped vessels to be within range. Obviously this was necessary for the time rush message relay system. Marconi believed that ***TITANIC*** had one of the diagrams on board. She would have in the ordinary course of events, but not like the one presented to the Board of Trade inquiry. This one, said Sir Rufus, was "worked out after the accident." Mersey confirmed that he knew this, saying, *"This is later than the accident."*

While ***FRANKFURT*** was plotted into this diagram presented before the Board of Trade inquiry, *it is useless in proving **FRANKFURT**'s position because this diagram was worked up **after** the accident to show what happened, where **TITANIC** had foundered and what vessels were close to her.*

Sir Robert Finlay, Counsel on behalf of the White Star Line, however, insisted upon seeing one of the "ordinary" diagrams. Isaacs and Marconi promised to produce one after lunch.

A copy of the Marconi Company's *Handbook for Wireless Telegraph Operators* was then produced. This spelled out the rule in force for giving distress calls precedence over all other traffic, regardless of wireless system. But reading Rule 73, which said that ships in distress must make use of "the following signals," Sir Rufus asked if that meant the SOS. Marconi replied that it would be the SOS, but it is not exactly the SOS as shown in the handbook, "but it is practically." This conversation was never explained, nor was a copy of Rule 73 printed with the inquiry transcript for posterity. There was some discussion over the date of printing for the *Handbook,* which was finally established as *pre-**TITANIC*** 1912. Bride was asked if he had such a copy aboard ***TITANIC***, and he replied that their *Handbook* had been a 1911 issue, but Rule 73 was the same in both.

Finally Sir Rufus asked the big question. Had any vessels been prevented from going to ***TITANIC***'s assistance owing to messages received from ***TITANIC***, or owing to any erroneous messages being sent or received? As far as Marconi himself knew, had any vessel been prevented by any such message from going to the assistance of ***TITANIC?***

What could Guglielmo Marconi answer but, *"As far as I know, none."*

There followed a discussion of the ice messages and warnings probably received by ***TITANIC***. Then Sir Rufus suggested amending the International Wireless Telegraph regulations by making a mandatory long dash of a period of from 15 to 30 seconds. This would in turn cause a bell to ring which would be a signal denoting that a ship was in distress somewhere. The operator, whether on duty or not, could hear the bell ring and immediately be at his key. Eventually, of course, an automatic device did give such a warning and we have ***TITANIC*** to thank for that.

Mr. Cotter then asked Marconi about the fact that Evans said he had no communication diagram aboard ***CALIFORNIAN***. Everyone seemed to have forgotten Evans' testimony to that effect, so Cotter repeated his questions and Evans' answers. It was merely the boy's oversight, said Mersey. But should not someone see to it that these operators were always supplied with the proper charts. Cotter asked. *"I think that is always done,"* replied Marconi.

One of the original diagrams was never produced. Did Evans in fact have one, but had to say he had not? If he had admitted to having one, then it might have been produced. And what might have been on the original diagram made up prior to ***TITANIC***'s loss? We will never now know.

At the British inquiry Leyland Line attorney C. Robertson Dunlop said that two German vessels were known to be near ***TITANIC***. One was a "German petroleum ship," the other a "Hansa liner." But Dunlop declined to name the vessels on the grounds that doing so would violate "the loyalty owed by one shipowner to another." The puzzling clue here lies in the term "Hansa liner." There was a Hansa Linie, running vessels of about this size from Germany to the Far East, and that line's ***TRAUTENFELS*** has been implicated by some investigators as the primary mystery ship. But in investigating ***TRAUTENFELS*** the funnel described by witnesses as being black with a white band and some device in the band, was suddenly transformed to a black funnel with a red top, yet Hansa's funnel colors were something like Moore had described… black, with red, white and red bands, and a black Maltese Cross in the white band. A letter from the U. S. Customs Service in Boston, to which ***TRAUTENFELS*** had been bound, discounted the ***TRAUTENFELS*** theory. She probably could not have been in ***TITANIC***'s vicinity, because she arrived at Boston early on the morning of 18 April, said Customs officials. Unfortunately no exact times are given. Other steamers were mentioned, but no funnel colors came as near to matching the description of witnesses as those of Deutsche Amerikanische Petroleum Gesellschaft, DAPG, Standard Oil's German subsidiary. As mentioned earlier, however, there were many lines with similar funnel colors.

But Dunlop declined "to name" the shipowners involved, if he knew. If he had truly meant a vessel of the Hansa Linie, then he did in fact name the shipowner after he had refused to do so. What is far more likely is that Dunlop used a generic term, common among the British when referring to Germans in that era. ***FRANKFURT***'s home port was Bremen… one of the original Hanseatic League ports, thus a "Hansa port," therefore a "Hansa liner."

Unfortunately we will never know ***FRANKFURT***'s position when she received the first CQD message flashed from ***TITANIC***. We have Bill Müller's word for his conversation with ***FRANKFURT***'s wireless operator in 1914. This would mean nothing in itself, but Bride's early testimony authenticates the German wireless operator's statements. In view of the discrepancies in Moore's and Durrant's statements, however, it makes more sense that the German operator told the truth, and so did Harold Bride in his earliest testimony If ***FRANKFURT*** approached ***TITANIC*** from the west, which is likely, and Captain Hattorff steered for the first distress position, 41°44'N, 50°24'W, then stopped or slowed as he neared that position and saw ***TITANIC***'s rockets, then ***FRANKFURT*** would have been lying off ***TITANIC***'s port side and would have been within sight from ***TITANIC***'s bridge… if Hattorff had let her run on toward where he had seen the rockets… while he tried to appraise the situation and decide what to do. Hattorff knew there was no use trying to get into direct wireless communication with ***TITANIC*** again because Phillips had refused to exchange messages with the German. It is possible that Hattorff did try to answer

ABOVE: *Canadian Pacific Liner* ***MOUNT TEMPLE****, Captain James Henry Moore. (Artwork by Ryan Katzenbach.)*

TITANIC's Morse light, but his message was not understood by ***TITANIC***, or the lights were out of range which was generally 2 miles. We can picture the final scene:

On ***FRANKFURT***'s bridge Captain Hattorff spoke quietly to his watch officer. *"Steer south five east. We are going home."*

FRANKFURT's head swung slowly around to the south while Hattorff peered through his binoculars one more time at the huge English liner. Satisfied that she was not in dire straits, she had not fired distress rockets, her wireless call was not the internationally accepted SOS, she was showing all of her normal lights, Hattorff never looked at her again. He took up a station on the bridge wing opposite that of his watch officer. They would need all the eyes available tonight, Hattorff knew. Probably the speeding ***TITANIC*** had glanced against a growler, and she would be late arriving in New York on her maiden voyage. A pity, he thought, then knew he did not really mean it. It served the arrogant British right. Hattorff shrugged, sniffed the icy air and stared into the blackness ahead of his ship. The British might be reckless, thinking they were invincible upon the seas. But he had no desire to cost his company extra money for repairs, or worse. He could smell the ice, see its faint blink to the east. His safest course was to run south for a few miles, then head straight for the Channel which the English insisted upon calling theirs, and keep the extra watch until they were well east of the ice reported by ***AMERIKA*** and ***GEORGE WASHINGTON***. Then maybe he could finally get some sleep. It had been a very long night.

Chapter Ten

Fire Down Below

When ***TITANIC*** foundered many armchair "experts" refused to believe that a mere iceberg could have sunk such a large, new vessel. In particular the 1912 press, wildly dramatic even at its most conservative, literally ran amok with descriptions of a "mountain of ice," and stock photographs were liberally used to illustrate this Arctic goliath. One of them purported to show the very iceberg she had struck, with an incriminating streak of red paint along its side. Because ***TITANIC***'s only red paint was on her bottom, which struck a submerged ice spur, it was explained that impact force had caused the berg to capsize, thus bringing its telltale underwater portion into view.

Nor were reporters deterred by figures. Like the legend of ***TITANIC***'s "unsinkability," the myth of the 300 ft. gash in her hull actually began with overzealous reporting. Three hundred feet was over one third of ***TITANIC***'s 850 ft. length between perpendiculars. Had water entered her hull at impact for that length, she would have been flooded as far aft as Number 4, perhaps even Number 3 boiler room immediately, and would have foundered within minutes. It was, of course, expedient for the White Star Line (meaning I.M.M.) to promote this illusion of a *giant* berg which had torn a *huge* gash in ***TITANIC***'s hull. Nothing less could have sunk such a mighty vessel. Unfortunately the illusion persists in spite of evidence presented at both inquiries to the contrary.

One oft-touted theory to explain ***TITANIC***'s rapid sinking has been that a coal bunker fire generated an explosion of coal gases which tore an immense hole in her side. A similar theory was espoused by armchair sailors when Cunard's ***OREGON*** sank off Fire Island in 1886, simply because nobody wanted to believe that collision with a mere sailing vessel could sink the North Atlantic's fastest liner. In 1886, however, coal was the only means of firing the steam engines which drove ships over the seas. In 1912, as we shall see, there was another very important reason to conceal anything that had to do with the fire in ***TITANIC***'s bunker, and it had nothing to do with explosions. This coverup has generated over eighty years of theorizing about the "real" cause of ***TITANIC***'s sinking. The truth, however, was known in 1912, the truth is much simpler, yet far more interesting than any theories put forth in the past eight decades.

Many survivors did report hearing "explosions," either shortly before or shortly after ***TITANIC*** foundered. Some of these eyewitness accounts were "prompted" by British inquiry officials. Rather than explosions, these sounds may have come from failing bulkheads, the ordinary noises made by tortured, tearing metal, the shrieks and cries of a ship in her death throes. A sinking ship is subjected to tremendous stresses for which she was not designed, all of which contribute to her breakup on the way to the bottom, and all of which are perfectly normal. Not many people have watched a large steamship in her final moments, going down with engine rooms in full running order, other than those who served in a navy or merchant marine during the two World Wars. Certainly ***TITANIC***'s survivors had no such experience to judge what they were hearing and why.

Some theorists go so far as to deny that an iceberg was present at all. This is impossible in light of all the witnesses who saw ice. Many of these witnesses were passengers, and it would have been very difficult to tamper with their testimony. Passengers are, at best, unreliable when giving statements about any technical matters, yet their ingenuous veracity and uncontrollability may have been the real reason why Lord Mersey refused to interview any passengers other than the Duff-Gordons at the British inquiry. The Duff-Gordon lifeboat case was made a great scandal in itself by the ever-dramatic Edwardian press, a fact which was useful in concealing other, more important information.

One fairly recent theory suggests that ***TITANIC***, and her sister ***OLYMPIC***, were built of an "inferior steel" which shattered upon impact because it had been made "brittle" by prolonged exposure to the extreme low temperatures of water in the North Atlantic. ***TITANIC*** did suffer from "brittle" steel, but only in one crucial place and not where she suffered the impact with ice. If, as suggested, Harland & Wolff had built ships of inferior steel, or state-of-the-art steel was inferior, then why were so many ships able to withstand striking icebergs and each other without shattering and sinking? ***OLYMPIC***'s collision with ***HMS HAWKE*** and the liner's "unusually severe" impact damage has been cited as an example of the 1912 state-of-the-art inferiority of mild steel. ***OLYMPIC***'s subsequent ramming of a submarine in World War I, and her ramming and sinking of the Nantucket Lightship in 1934 with little damage to herself indicates that her hull plating was not as fragile as some theorists would like to assume. Much of the damage inflicted upon ***OLYMPIC*** by ***HMS HAWKE*** was caused by the warship's bow-ram, which was *supposed* to inflict extensive damage upon any ship she struck. In fact, ***HAWKE*** lost her ram in the collision. When ***HAWKE***'s bow was rebuilt she was modernized and the ram was not replaced. In addition, the ***OLYMPIC-HAWKE*** collision took place in the warmer waters of the Solent, not the frigid winter waters of the North Atlantic. (See Chapter 3)

When Senator Smith marshaled his inquiry committee so quickly, literally meeting the incoming rescue ship ***CARPATHIA*** with subpoenas for many ***TITANIC*** crewmen. White Star (I.M.M.) attorneys had little time to discuss the situation with those men who would be testifying, to tell them what statements would be detrimental to the line, what was best left unsaid. Therefore statements made to the press immediately after ***CARPATHIA*** docked, and testimony taken during the early days of the American inquiry were more reliable than anything said later. A newspaper editorial at the time contained words of wisdom worth repeating:

"Many of the later statements of ***TITANIC*** *survivors, especially those which are filled with details, are obviously colored by much reading of the early printed matter."*

This is perfectly normal behavior. Police detectives and intelligence officers know that it is wise to question witnesses as soon as possible after an incident, while they remember rather than rationalize what happened. There is also the normal human behavior of "remembering" as survivors *wanted* to remember the disaster. Those who had exhibited behavior which was downright, or even nearly cowardly did not want to remember themselves that way, while others may have subconsciously shut out memories too horribly painful to bear. Thus they recalled events and actions in the way they wanted to believe them, telling their versions so often that they actually *did* believe them. It became obvious as the inquiries went on for weeks in the United States and Britain that some witnesses changed their stories, whether because of coercion or genuine lack of memory can never be known. Some later statements seemed to be made only after very careful consideration, undoubtedly after crewmen were made to understand exactly what picture of the tragedy they were to convey officially to the public. This is perfectly normal procedure with any investigation into a transportation accident. Although today we have more knowledgeable media and instantaneous news coverage via television, the causes of transportation accidents which remain in the public mind are still often quite different from the real causes, uncovered after months, even years of investigation, and published long after the public has forgotten the original incident. No transportation company, be it concerned with ships, airplanes, buses or trains, can afford to lose the traveling public's confidence by allowing that public to believe that the company was in any way at fault in an accident. Such lack of confidence quickly shows up in falling profits and dividends that turn away investors and may result in bankruptcy. While the ***TITANIC*** inquiries were investigations, not trials, every bit of information uncovered was subject to later use in liability lawsuits. Ultimately the general public, especially in the waning age of chivalry which characterized the pre-World War I twentieth century, would always rather believe a romantic, heroic version of a disaster than the bloody, inept truth. Britain had a great political and patriotic stake in ***TITANIC***'s coverup... Britannia must rule the waves at all cost. Her life depended upon it. Any visible weakness, any chink in the armor of maritime supremacy, gave her enemies their needed opportunity to enlarge that crack into an entry through the barricade of ships which Britain needed to protect and maintain the Empire.

In proving the Harter Act's terms that White Star (I.M.M.) had sent ***TITANIC*** to sea in an absolutely seaworthy condition, it was necessary to downplay any importance that might have been attached to the fact that ***TITANIC*** had a smoldering fire in a forward coal bunker which began soon after her departure from Southampton. This story, incidentally, has often been told with the fire starting soon after the ship left *Belfast*.

Leading Fireman Charles Hendrickson apparently began the Belfast legend, with statements to his interrogators at the Board of Trade inquiry on 9 May, 1912. Hendrickson had only *heard* that the fire started in Belfast, however, as he had not been aboard then. During his first watch after departing Southampton Hendrickson and his mates had begun to empty that bunker. They had not extinguished the fire until all of the coal had been removed during their watch, the 4 to 8, on Saturday evening, the day before ***TITANIC*** struck ice. Hendrickson himself had removed the last bit of coal, had seen where the bulkhead plating was red hot. The steel was dented, warped, said Hendrickson. He had rubbed "black oil" into the spot to make it less noticeable.

Earlier in Hendrickson's testimony Lord Mersey had made one of his many disparaging remarks about lesser-ranking crewmen. Hendrickson, said Mersey, did *"not appear to know much."* Unfortunately the bulk of Hendrickson's testimony came in answer to questions about the Duff-Gordons, for Hendrickson had been in the infamous "millionaire's boat," a fact which tended to discredit him as a witness to anything else in the eyes of the press and the public.

There can be no doubt, however, that the fire began shortly after leaving Southampton, not Belfast. Because the run from Southampton to Cherbourg was only a few hours, the fire may not have been detected until after ***TITANIC*** departed that French port. ***TITANIC*** lay at her berth in Southampton for nearly two weeks during which steam was kept up to power auxiliary engines and dynamos while workmen completed last-minute details, plenty of time to move the coal, thus extinguishing the fire before bunkering for the transatlantic voyage, *if* the fire had started at *Belfast*. It is also unlikely that ***TITANIC*** would bunker for the entire voyage at Belfast, especially in view of her hasty completion of steaming trials and departure for Southampton. In fact, a coal strike in Great Britain had put coal in such short supply that ***TITANIC*** had been bunkered with coal from other I.M.M. vessels in Southampton in order to meet her maiden voyage sailing schedule.

Coal bunker fires were not uncommon, despite the fact that Hendrickson claimed he had never seen one during his five years in the White Star. Other witnesses had seen many of them. Still in the minds of older mariners was White Star's ***ATLANTIC***, which had fatally run aground in March, 1873, while trying to make Halifax after an unusually slow passage had seriously depleted her coal supply. Seamen knew that ***ATLANTIC***'s engineers and firemen had been fighting a bunker fire when she ran aground, and it was known that at least some of ***ATLANTIC***'s coal had been of inferior quality.

Indeed, many wooden-hulled sailing vessels had survived coal fires in their cargo. One of the

***ABOVE: TITANIC** leaves for her sea trials. There was speculation that the fire in her stokehold began around this time. However, the fire likely started after **TITANIC** departed Southampton on April 10th.*

more spectacular of these took place in ***TWIN BROTHERS***, a sailer engaged in the wheat trade between San Francisco and Liverpool at the turn of the century. She was returning from England with 1,000 tons of coal in her hold as cargo-ballast, when just after rounding Cape Horn fire was discovered deep in the piles of coal.

TWIN BROTHERS happened to carry a steam pump. Her crew secured the lower hatches, then used the pump to flood the cargo hold until the vessel rode about four feet lower in the water than she normally did. In this condition the ship made her regular call at Valparaiso, and not a man deserted, so confident were they that she could reach San Francisco safely in spite of the fire.

Lumbering along with hardly any freeboard, it took ***TWIN BROTHERS*** *72* days to reach San Francisco, where her master promptly grounded her on mud flats, thus flooding her holds almost to the top deck and finally extinguishing the fire. For over two months her crew had lived with the sight of smoke rising ominously through cracks in the deck planking. Although in at least a dozen places the ship's wooden bottom was burned through, the thin sheet of copper sheathing around her hull was intact, and it was all that stood between her crew and the sea. The weight of coal and water inside the hull just about equaled the water pressure outside the hull, which kept the copper plating from giving way, although it was not much thicker than an ordinary tin pan.

In his *Reminiscences of a Sailor* (John Menzies & Co., Edinburgh and Glasgow, 1894) Captain William R. Lord of Liverpool (possibly distantly related to Captain Stanley Lord) wrote of battling

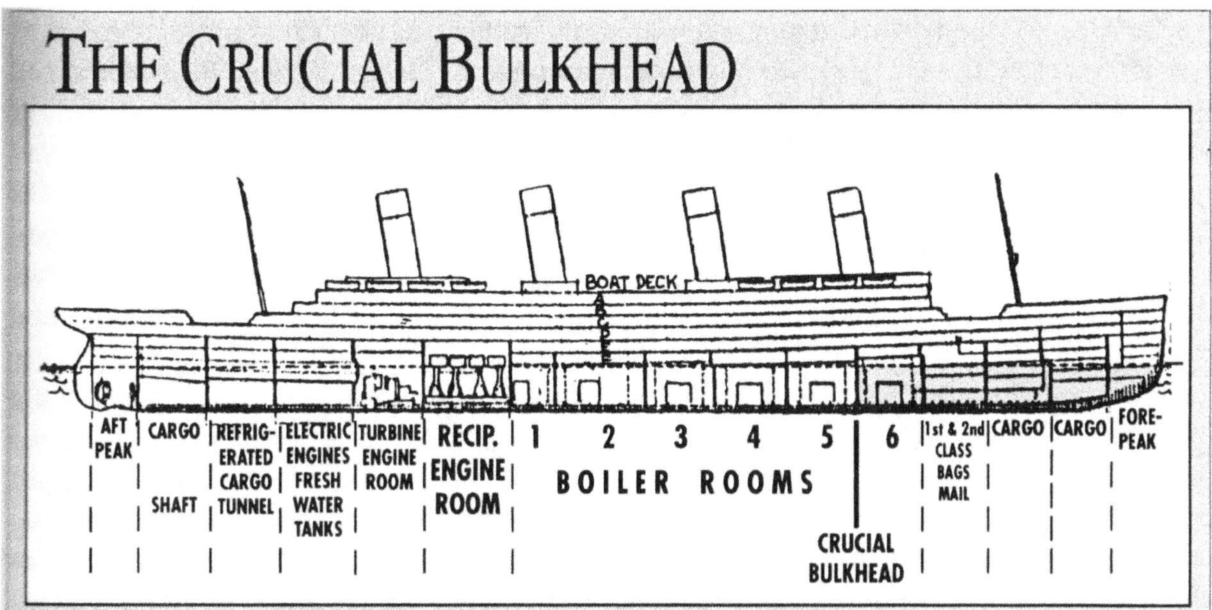

ABOVE; Side view of TITANIC showing compartmentation. Solid vertical lines define watertight bulkheads; vertical dotted lines define cross bunker areas. Shaded areas indicate extent of impact flooding. There was no 300 ft. gash as legend has it.

bunker fires on two occasions in one vessel he commanded. He noted that pouring water on the fire actually generated heat, and that the burning coal had to be literally dug out, amid dense volumes of sulphurous smoke. The fires in each instance were not extinguished until all the coal had been used. Captain Lord had seen the bunker plates red-hot, *"a sight that at once suggested disaster of a direful nature,"* he wrote.

Hans C. de Mierre, in his memoirs *Clipper Ships to Ocean Greyhounds,* mentioned in an earlier chapter, told of far more harrowing circumstances when, in April, 1912, he was Second Officer in ***SUTLEJ***, a Nourse liner out of Suva for Calcutta. The crew had just heard of the loss of ***TITANIC*** four days earlier, when de Mierre went to the bridge to take cross-bearings of two prominent hills which would give a good position as point of departure. Puzzled because as he stood by the standard compass atop the wheelhouse he felt a hot blast of sulphurous fumes, de Mierre walked to windward, to the starboard bridge wing, and sniffed the air. In a flash he knew what had happened. ***SUTLEJ*** had taken on additional coal for the round trip from Calcutta. It was stored in a part of the hold partitioned by a temporary wooden bulkhead. The coal had ignited by spontaneous combustion, and when the ship rolled to leeward the part of the hull which had been underwater was exposed, and from it came a hissing noise and a great cloud of steam, which vanished as she rolled her lee side under again. The fire had evidently been smoldering for days, and the ship's efficient cowl-ventilators acted as a set of bellows, fanning the blaze into violent life. ***SUTLEJ***'s side plating was red-hot.

Second Officer de Mierre immediately roused the master, Captain Brown, who gave the appropriate orders for moving passengers out of the way and fighting the fire. The heat was so intense, however, and the fumes so poisonous that the only thing to do was shut off the ventilator cowls on the main deck and pump water down their shafts. ***SUTLEJ*** was a "coolie ship," transporting indentured servants from one British colony to another, and many of these hapless people were ill. Captain Brown, realizing that fighting the fire was ineffective, decided to run his vessel as close to

***ABOVE**: Boiler room watertight doors typical of the* ***TITANIC**.*

the beach as possible and transport his human cargo in the ship's boats to land. ***SUTLEJ*** carried no wireless, so Captain Brown sent his Third Officer ashore in the seaboat to find a telephone and report to the Harbormaster at Suva that they needed a boat to rescue the passengers.

SUTLEJ, like ***TITANIC*** and all other ships of their time, had not enough boats to transport all passengers at once, so the sickest, along with the ship's Surgeon, were landed first and makeshift shelters were built for them. The healthier ones came ashore in the second trip. Eventually all were safe on the beach, Third Officer Farrow had found a planter who was a retired sailor, and the distress message was telephoned to Suva. The coal fire was not extinguished, however, until the bulkhead burned through and collapsed, a rush of water drowned the fire and almost drowned Chief Engineer Potter and his men. Thus, within the one week in April, 1912, two coal fires in ships on opposite sides of the globe had very different endings. There are many more tales of coal fires told in the memoirs of sailors who went to sea in sail and made the transition to steam, tales too numerous to mention here. Rarely, however, were the fires fatal in steel-hulled steamships.

Spontaneous combustion in coal was expected, cautioned against in every seamanship manual, and still is. It was caused by oxidation of the coal surface, which in itself generated heat. If the heat was not dissipated, the temperature continued to rise, in a self-aggravating process until the coal caught fire. It was believed that coal shipped from Virginia, New South Wales, Calcutta, or the River Clyde was especially vulnerable to spontaneous combustion.

During bunkering in ***TITANIC***'s era coal tumbled down chutes into the ship's yawning bunkers, and was shoveled by hand into proper trim. Because freshly broken surfaces of coal recently handled were most susceptible to spontaneous combustion, fires were most apt to break out soon after coal was taken aboard. For this reason it was recommended that the first loads of coal taken aboard should be carefully lowered rather than dumped into the bunkers or cargo holds. Contrary to ***TITANIC*** legend, it was not general practice to wet down the coal before or during bunkering. For one thing, this would have made the bunkering process even messier than it normally was. But coal was paid for by weight, and wetting it made it as much as 2 1/2 to 3 per cent heavier. Penurious shipowners were not going to pay one extra penny for anything. Chief engineers and masters who bought coal in foreign ports were frequently warned about buying coal that was wet. And wetting not only did absolutely nothing to prevent spontaneous combustion, in some types of coal it appeared to cause it.

The best method of prevention was to keep a constant check on the temperature at the bottom of the coal pile. This was occasionally done with a thermometer, but usually by thrusting iron rods, preferably with perforated ends, deep into the pile, then feeling the rods with the hand. When the temperature rose above 140℉ it was time to keep a close watch on the pile. When it rose above 150℉, it was time to move the coal. Smoldering coal also gave off an unmistakable sulphurous odor which an experienced officer could readily identify.

In steel-hulled vessels these fires were not generally considered dangerous as long as the fire was confined to a bunker and not near flammable cargo, although as Captain William Lord noted, the heat could damage a watertight bulkhead's mild steel plating. Considering a liner's "imperative schedule," more than a few of them had sailed with at least one smoldering bunker.

The best way to stop the heating was simply to move the coal as quickly as possible to a place where it could cool off. It was, of course, preferable and most economical to discharge the coal into the nearest of the vessel's yawning furnaces. The use of water poured directly on the coal in a bunker was not practical, because to work at all the water had to reach the coal that was actually burning, which would naturally be at the very bottom of the pile. Anthracite was rarely available and too expensive anyway, but bituminous coal "cokes" on heating, so that a shell of tar-like material forms around the hottest spots and prevents water from reaching them. This necessitates hand-shoveling into the pile to turn the coal. It is therefore better to simply use the coal, and this is what ***TITANIC's*** Chief Engineer Joseph Bell undoubtedly ordered. It also was undoubtedly not the first bunker fire that Chief Bell, his watchkeepers, and ***TITANIC***'s senior deck officers had seen in their long careers at sea. In fact, ***TITANIC's*** Second Officer Lightoller would later write in his memoirs ***TITANIC*** *And Other Ships* of a coal cargo fire at sea in Greenshield, Cowie & Company's four-masted barque, ***KNIGHT OF ST. MICHAEL***, in which he had been Third Mate. In his inimitably cheerful style, Lightoller made light of the incident, although he likened it to "sitting on a volcano." ***TITANIC***'s Second Officer did not mention her bunker fire in his memoirs. He did, however, make much of fire control in modern liners, meaning those of the mid-thirties, the time period in which his memoirs were published.

It had been necessary to take the coal out of sections two and three, on the starboard side, forward, and when the water came rushing in after the collision with the ice, the bulkheads would not hold because they did not have the supporting weight of the coal," an unidentified firemen told reporters in New York. *"Somebody reported to Chief Engineer Bell that the bulkhead had given way, and the Chief replied,* 'My *God, we are lost!*'" This particular item was quickly squelched and never mentioned again in the newspapers.

That the bunker was empty when ***TITANIC*** struck ice on Sunday night was confirmed by several witnesses. Under normal conditions the fact that this particular watertight bulkhead had glowed red hot for at least 70 hours would have made little difference. This was a calculated risk, of the sort taken every day in every transportation business. The odds that this particular bulkhead would ever become crucial to ***TITANIC***'s survival before she returned to Belfast for her next routine drydocking were probably a billion to one.

But Fate sometimes surprises by choosing the longest odds, which is after all, the very factor that keeps lotteries going.

When ***TITANIC*** was bilged on her starboard bow, water immediately poured into the forepeak and the forward cargo holds. That she was bilged in No. 6 boiler room was known because there fortunately were witnesses from that area who survived.

Legend has it that upon impact *six major* compartments were immediately flooded. In fact, five relatively small compartments were flooded soon after impact. These were the forepeak, considered negligible as far as buoyancy is concerned, the three small cargo compartments and the No. 6 boiler room. Apparently it is the number of that boiler room that fostered the myth of *six* flooded compartments. Because in ***TITANIC*** boiler rooms were numbered from the engine rooms forward. *No. 6* was *the forwardmost* boiler room. It was, however, the *fifth* compartment from the stem counting the forepeak, and it was smaller than the other boiler rooms because the ship was narrower at that point. Contrary to legend. No. 5 boiler room was *not* flooded by impact damage. Being new, ***TITANIC***'s bulkheads had not wasted, were strong enough to have confined water to this initially flooded area for many hours. She should have remained afloat, though precariously, with her forward decks awash, long enough to evacuate all passengers and all but a skeleton crew, possibly long enough to tow her to Cape Race, or at least to shallow water less than 100 miles to the north.

On 7 May, in the Wreck Commissioner's Court, Scottish Hall, Buckingham Gate, London, the first survivor from No. 6 boiler room was interrogated. George William Beauchamp had been a fireman in No. 10 stokehold on the 8 to midnight watch. Number 10 was the aftermost stokehold in No. 6 compartment.

In response to questions asked by Raymond Asquith, Counsel on behalf of the Board of Trade, Beauchamp said that steam pressure on ***TITANIC***'s final watch had been 210 pounds. Her boilers were built for a maximum working pressure of 215 pounds per square inch. (Two days later Trimmer George Cavell would testify that in No. 4 boiler room the steam pressure had been 225 psi.)

The shock of impact had been *"like thunder,"* said Beauchamp. (One can imagine how the sound must have reverberated inside that all-steel, non-soundproofed "box" which was the hull). The engine telegraph had rung to *"Stop."* The warning bell had rung and the watertight door had closed as Beauchamp rushed to comply with the order to *"shut the dampers,"* an order which Beauchamp said was shouted simultaneously by the leading stoker and the engineer. Beauchamp could not be pinned down to times, and rightly so although his interrogators unfortunately insisted upon hearing exact times for every action, but he and other firemen had been drawing fires as water poured through the hull plating and, seeking its own level, fell, and then rose under the floor plates. In response to questions from Asquith and Lord Mersey, Beauchamp insisted that water was coming through the bunker door and over the plates, then qualified that statement somewhat with, *"Yes, coming through the bunker like."* Nobody ever asked him to explain that final statement. When all the fires had been drawn, which Beauchamp estimated took about 15 minutes, the order was given, *"that will do."* Beauchamp and the other men then scrambled up the escape ladder. He had not looked back to notice how much or how fast water was coming in.

Beauchamp went immediately to the boat deck. Not knowing his boat assignment, he went to the nearest boat, which happened to be No. 13. After assisting in its loading, when an officer asked if he could pull an oar and Beauchamp answered *"yes,"* he was assigned to crew the boat.

When asked if he had heard explosions as ***TITANIC*** foundered, Beauchamp answered again that he heard a sound *"like thunder."* The Wreck Commissioner, Lord Mersey, was not satisfied with that answer. He told Beauchamp to apply his mind to the question, and asked again, *"Did you hear any explosion?"* This time Beauchamp simply answered, *"Yes,"* even though as one who had never witnessed a shipwreck he had no way to judge what he heard. For the benefit of historians. Lord Mersey would have done better to keep out of it. It was one of many instances where Mersey unfortunately influenced testimony. We can only guess now whether this was prompted by ignorance or arrogance, or was deliberate manipulation as part of the coverup. Far from conducting an impartial investigation to get at the facts, Mersey manipulated facts and interpreted them his way, the way they have remained firmly embedded in the public mind for over eighty years. While the British press made great fun of Senator William Alden Smith's investigation in the United States, they ignored Mersey's often ridiculous statements and questions. It was also unfortunate that the remainder of Beauchamp's interrogation was conducted by several attorneys representing passengers and seamen's unions, who were interested merely in his experiences in the lifeboat with the by then infamous Duff-Gordons. Lifeboats were always a safe subject, impact damage and water inflow from that damage were not.

Aboard the ***OLYMPIC*** at New York on 25 May Leading Fireman Frederick Barrett showed Senator Smith exactly where he had been standing in No. 6 boiler room when water poured into ***TITANIC***'s hull. Barrett, like Beauchamp, had been on the starboard side of No. 10 stokehold.

"I was standing talking to the Second Engineer," Barrett said. *"The bell rang, the red light showed. We sang out shut the doors,"* Barrett indicated the ash doors to the furnaces, *"and there was a crash just as we sung out. The water came through the ship's side. The engineer and I jumped to the next section. The next section to the forward section is Number 5."*

"Where did the water come through?"

"About two feet above the floor plates, starboard side."

"How much water?" Smith asked.

"A large volume of water came through," Barrett replied.

"How big was this hole in the side?"

"About two feet above the floor plates," was Barrett's ambiguous and repetitive answer.

"You think it was a large tear?"

"Yes, I do."

"All along the side of number six?"

"Yes," Barrett affirmed.

"How far along?"

"Past the bulkhead between sections five and six, and it was a hole two feet into the coal bunkers. She was torn through Number 6, and also through two feet abaft the bulkhead in the bunker at the forward head of Number 5 section. We got through before the doors broke, the doors dropped instantly, automatically from the bridge. I went back to Number 6 fireroom and there was eight feet of water in there. I went to Number 5 fireroom when the lights went out. I was sent to find lamps, as the lights were out, and when we got the lamps we looked at the boilers and there was no water in them. I ran to the engineer and he told me to get some firemen down to draw the fires. I got fifteen men down below."

"Did you not have fires in Number 6?" Smith asked.

"Yes, the fires were lit when the water came in."

When the engine telegraph rang through *"Stop"* to *"Full Speed Astern,"* that was the crash back order given with the engines running at full steam pressure. There was, as Barrett had described in his British inquiry testimony, *"like a clock rigged up in the stokehold."* The face of this indicator showed a white light when the ship was running *"Full Speed Ahead."* But with the crash back, the indicator changed to red as a piece of red glass dropped over the face. At this point the first thought in the minds of engineers and firemen was to relieve the steam pressure before the boilers were damaged, or worse. Therefore, as relief valves were opened and steam began blowing off, the crewmen were striving to extinguish all fires simply to stop heating the water which made the steam. According to Beauchamp's testimony there was a time lapse of at least a few seconds between the time Murdoch rang the reciprocating engine telegraphs through "Stop" *to "Full Speed Astern"* and the turbine telegraph to "Stop," and the actual impact with ice. In the interval between the sudden engine order and impact the verbal order had been given to shut all dampers, and this was being done as ***TITANIC*** struck. The crash came, according to Barrett, before all dampers could be shut. But as we shall see, the men in No. 6 did have time to continue with shutting the dampers and pulling the fires prior to the compartment's flooding. Contrary to the legend of a "wall of water" spewing through this puncture in No. 6 compartment, which drove Lead Stoker Barrett and Junior Second Engineer Hesketh to leap into No. 5 as the watertight doors dropped, as we have seen from Beauchamp's testimony men remained in No. 6 drawing fires for at least a few and possibly fifteen minutes after impact. The fact that these men in No. 6 had been shutting the dampers when the crash came, indicates that Murdoch had pulled the lever to drop the watertight doors immediately after he had rung the engine telegraph to *Full Speed Astern,* which would have been the normal sequence of events. According to Barrett's own testimony, which compressed the time during which events happened, he and Hesketh had not jumped into No. 5 until impact, and therefore there was a time lapse between the *"Full Speed Astern"* order and the impact accompanied by the dropping of the watertight doors. Beauchamp's testimony indicated that he and other crewmen had remained in No. 6, continuing to comply with orders, shutting the remaining dampers and drawing fires as water came in, until the job was finished. According to Barrett, the only man saved from those who had remained in No. 6 was Beauchamp.

The water would have initially entered at such a low height that it would have immediately fallen below floor plate level, then risen gradually. Unfortunately nobody asked Beauchamp simply how deep water had been while they were drawing fires in No. 6. Was the water ankle deep, knee deep, waist deep, or what? We may study other shipwrecks and learn that engineers could remain below and work desperately with water up to their shoulders if necessary. The fact that Beauchamp did not volunteer such information seems to indicate that the water had not immediately been very deep, certainly it took sometime for water to rise above the floor plates.

Senator Smith wanted to know how many boilers were lit, and Barrett answered that five boilers were not lit. Twenty four boilers were lit, including three that had been lit Sunday for the first time, but Barrett did not know if those three had been connected up or not.

"This tear went a couple of feet past the bulkhead in Number 5. How were you able to keep the water from reaching..." Senator Smith began.

"It never came above the plates," Barrett interrupted, *"until all at once I saw a wave of green foam come tearing through between the boilers and I jumped for the escape ladder."*

There had been no explosion, Barrett said, but a volume of smoke had come up as the ship sank.

Barrett's testimony for Senator Smith in New York seemed terse, rehearsed, and revealed little, *unless it is compared with his earlier testimony at the British inquiry.* No doubt the leading fireman had told his story so often he was sick of it. No doubt he just wanted to get on with the painful process of forgetting, of shoving the horrible memories deep into his subconscious where they could not continually haunt him. This is a normal symptom of post-disaster syndrome. There is also little doubt that British crewmen resented being questioned by Americans over something that had happened to a vessel which flew the Union Jack. But there is also an obvious discrepancy in Barrett's description of the impact damage given earlier at the British inquiry and his testimony aboard ***OLYMPIC*** given to Senator Smith in New York. In fact, as we shall see, Barrett repeated to Senator Smith Lord Mersey's conclusion that ***TITANIC*** was torn all along No. 6 and into No. 5 boiler compartments.

Barrett had told a different version of damage to ***TITANIC***'s hull when questioned by the

Solicitor General, Sir John Simon, on 7 May at the British inquiry, his testimony beginning on page 53 of the transcript.

Barrett began by insisting that Sir John use his proper title. Leading *Stoker,* explaining that a stoker was *"a little higher"* than a fireman. He had held that position in Section 6 on the night of 14 April. At this point Barrett explained that there were two *stokeholds,* the area between furnaces and bunkers, to each section, one stokehold being at the forward end, one at the aft end of each compartment. (In American ships the term "fire room" was generally used instead of "stokehold.')

Remembering that boiler rooms with their stokeholds and bunkers were numbered from the reciprocating engine rooms forward, when Barrett spoke of stokehold No. 10, in compartment No. 6, he was speaking of the boiler room farthest forward, its aft stokehold and bunker being numbered 10, its forward stokehold and bunker being 11.

TITANIC's bunkers consisted of a 'tween deck space on each side of the ship, between the lower and middle decks, into which coal was first poured via the coaling ports in the ship's side. From these "wing" bunkers coal was distributed by gravity to the cross bunkers which extended athwartships the full width of the vessel in each boiler room, then shoveled by hand into proper trim. The White Star Line did not favor the standard forced draft system by which fans created an artificial draft in the furnaces themselves. Rather, White Star officials preferred the closed stokehold system, which required two huge Sirocco fans for each boiler room, placed at the middle deck level. The fans drew air in through ventilating shafts from the boat deck and conveyed it through trunks to the level of the furnaces. This system, which literally pressurized each individual boiler compartment, had first been fitted with success in the Inman liners ***CITY OF NEW YORK*** and ***CITY OF PARIS***, of 1888 and 1889 respectively. Two ash ejectors of standard design were fitted in each of ***TITANIC***'s five large boiler rooms. Ashes were shoveled by hand into a hopper on the stokehold floor, were then drawn by the rush of air into a water jet which was discharged at a pressure of about 150 lb. maintained by pumps. The water jet carried the ashes up an inclined pipe until they were discharged well clear of the hull when the ship was at sea.

Running athwartships through each cross bunker was a watertight bulkhead, its watertight door stepped to fit flush with the aft bunker bulkhead. This made each boiler room a self-contained entity, capable of keeping up its fires and thus running engines and auxiliaries even though an adjoining compartment might be flooded. It also helped maintain the "pressurized" closed stokehold system of creating air flow through the furnace combustion chambers. But it also meant that when working, even though running full speed in ice or fog, watertight doors remained open to facilitate working coal out of the bunkers into the adjacent stokeholds. (***TITANIC*** and her sisters had transverse watertight bulkheads only, unlike the Cunarders ***LUSITANIA*** and ***MAURETANIA*** which had longitudinal as well as transverse watertight subdivision. The merits of the two systems were hotly debated after ***TITANIC*** foundered. It was never proven that longitudinal bulkheads would have saved her, but that lack of proof was predicated upon the myth of her hull being torn open at impact for at least 300 ft. Probably a longitudinal bulkhead system would have saved her). In addition to the watertight door in each transverse watertight bulkhead, crewmen had a backup means of emergency egress in an escape ladder which slanted up over the boilers in each compartment, to the next deck above, terminating through a hatch into the working alleyway. (Much has been made of the fact that this alleyway was dubbed "Scotland Road" by crew members, but that was merely one of the names given to the working alleyways in every British merchant ship). These escape hatches, however, were in the bulkhead deck, thus the deck was vulnerable to water entry if any hatch was left open. It is doubtful that a crewman would have left a hatch open under the circumstances, but

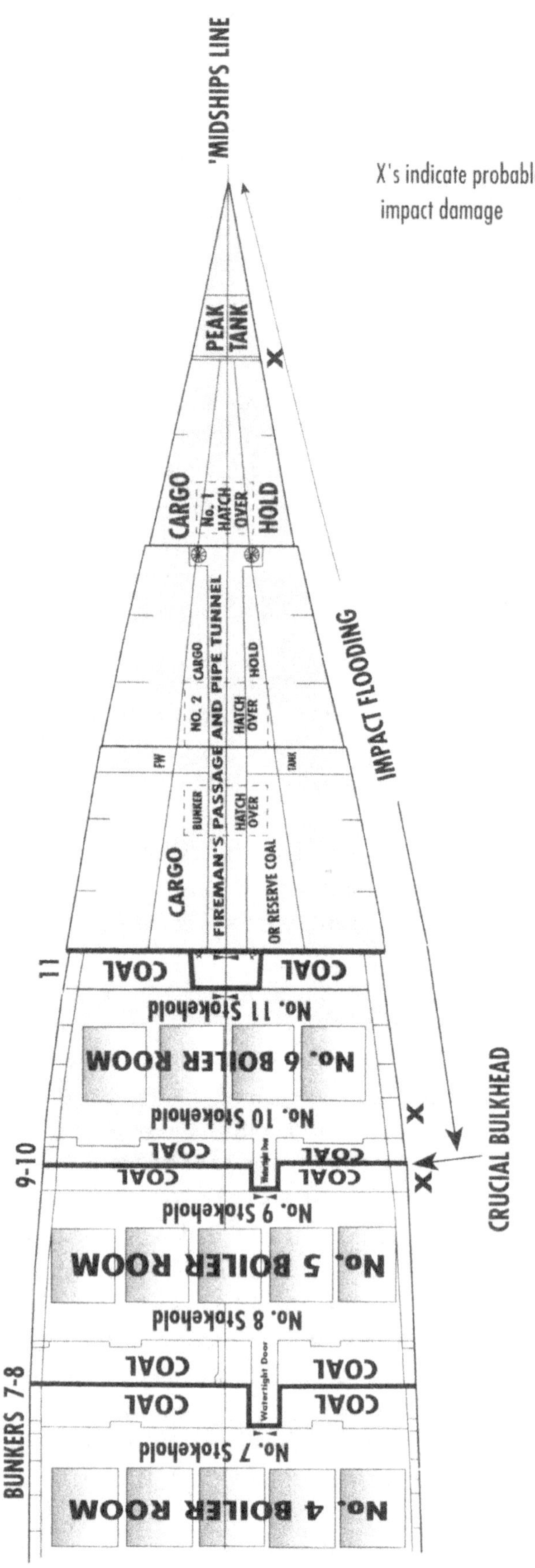

it remains a possibility. By the time they used the hatch as a means of escape their minds were strictly upon personal survival.

The No. 1 boiler room contained only five single-ended boilers, and thus had only one bunker from which trimmers wheeled the coal into the adjacent stokehold, from whence firemen shoveled it by hand into the furnaces. All other compartments had five double-ended boilers, excepting the narrower forward compartment. No. 6, which had four double-ended boilers. Each of the double-ended boilers was 15 ft. 9 in. in diameter, 20 ft. long, and was heated by 6 furnaces. Each single-ended boiler was the same diameter, but was only 11 ft. 9 in. long and was fired by 3 furnaces. Boiler rooms were 57 ft. in length, excepting No. 1, which was 50 ft. This shorter boiler compartment was necessary because of the length of the reciprocating engine rooms, 69 ft., just abaft No. 1, because bulkhead spacing was required to assure that any two adjacent compartments could be included in the floodable length.

The confusion over this numbering of compartments has led some researchers to conclude that there were two fires, but the "Number 2" bunker, when counting from the stern, as described by firemen talking to reporters in New York, was the same as the No. 10 bunker, counting from the reciprocating engine rooms forward, named properly by Frederick Barrett.

In each watch in No. 6 there were eight firemen, four trimmers, one leading stoker, and one engineer. In Barrett's watch the engineer in No. 6 was Jonathan Shepherd, who was the

Junior Second Assistant.

Barrett explained how he had been standing in No. 10 stokehold, starboard side, talking with Junior Second Engineer James H. Hesketh, when they were surprised to see the white indicator light which signified *full speed* suddenly change to red, which indicated *stop.* According to Barrett, as the lead man he immediately shouted, *"Shut all dampers,"* but Beauchamp had already testified that the order was given simultaneously by Hesketh and Barrett, and in fact Barrett would say the same thing to Senator Smith aboard ***OLYMPIC*** in New York. Hesketh, like all the engineers, had died and therefore was not there to give his story, which may have emboldened Barrett to claim priority in giving the order. This shut off the draft to the furnaces, or as Barrett put it, *"shut the wind off the fires,"* which in turn would extinguish the fires.

According to Barrett, they were still shutting the dampers when there was a crash and water poured through a hole in the starboard hull plating. Barrett's first statement about the inrush of water was that *"the ship*'s *side was torn from the third stokehold to the forward end."* The third stokehold would have been No. 9, or the forward stokehold of No. 5 compartment. Sir John then told Barrett to take it slowly, because this was very important. The Solicitor General began by asking Barrett, at Mersey's prompting, where the water had come from. This question should have become more famous than Senator Smith's asking Fifth Officer Lowe in New York what an iceberg was made of. When Sir John asked where the water came from, Barrett replied, *"Well, out of the sea, I expect."*

But Sir John was not put off nor did he lose his patience, fortunately, for he managed to drag many details from Barrett, slowly, *"by degrees,"* details which Senator Smith had not the time nor the expertise to uncover.

Water had come in, on the starboard side of No. 10 stokehold, about 2 feet above the floor plates, that is 2 feet above Barrett's own feet. The floor plates were about 6 feet above the tank tops. The tanks were subdivisions in the ship's double bottom, which was 5 ft. 3 in. deep, increasing to 6 ft. 3 in. under the reciprocating engine rooms. The tear, declared Barrett, had extended 2 feet aft of the watertight bulkhead which separated No. 10 and No. 9 bunkers. But Barrett said that he and Hesketh had not stopped to see if the tear was continuous from No. 10 bunker into No. 9, meaning that it went right through past the watertight bulkhead separating No. 6 compartment from No. 5. If this had been the case, then the bulkhead itself must have been damaged. When Barrett and Hesketh jumped into No. 5 as the warning bell rang and the watertight door between these compartments came crashing down there had been no time to stop and make observations for posterity. In fact, it was actually not a very smart move for Barrett and the Junior Second due to the distance between them in stokehold No. 10 and the watertight door which was actually part of the aft bunker bulkhead of No. 9. With each bunker 9 ft. deep it meant that the two men had to sprint at least 20 ft. to safety, with the chance that they would not make it through fast enough to avoid being crushed by the door as it closed. Legend has it that, many years later, an engineer was crushed by a closing watertight door in ***QUEEN MARY*** when he ducked back to retrieve a spanner after the warning bell had rung. Fortunately Barrett not only made it safely into No. 5, but he survived to tell about it, thus giving us the only witness to events in No. 6 as well as No. 5.

But Barrett was now adamant about one thing... ***TITANIC***'s hull had *not* been breached *anywhere aft* of the tear in No. 9 *bunker,* not No. 9 *stokehold,* an entirely different matter. Additionally, there is the possibility that under the duress of the moment, and in his haste, Barrett confused No. 10 bunker with No. 9. Beauchamp had said that water came into No. 6 through the "bunker door." Did Barrett, then, actually see a puncture in No. 6's aft bunker rather than No. 5's forward bunker? Surely he and Hesketh noticed the water coming into the bunker out of the comer of their eyes as they sprinted through the bunkers. We can never now know for sure. The important information that we do have, however, tells us about how long No. 5 remained dry, and how water finally did enter No. 5.

In spite of assertions that every word of the inquiries is absolutely accurate, there are several errors in the original transcription and typographical errors as well. One of these errors occurs unfortunately in the extremely important testimony of Harland & Wolff naval architect Edward Wilding, who was first called as witness at the Board of Trade inquiry on 6 June. Wilding had been Thomas Andrews' assistant in designing and building ***OLYMPIC*** and ***TITANIC***. He thus knew more about the ships than anyone living, and his statements were more than theories. They were backed by professional expertise and experience as well as mathematical calculations. But Wilding's testimony with its subsequent transcription errors has been misinterpreted for over eight decades.

Wilding had listened carefully to the testimony of Engine Department survivors. Answering question #20422 when he was recalled on 7 June, Wilding acknowledged that there was *no damage* in the fore and aft line *abaft* the small puncture to which Barrett had referred in No. 5's forward bunker. Unfortunately an error in transcription first gave the distance from the stem to that puncture as *500* ft., and this error may have come from a court reporter hearing the number *"five"* referring to the compartment's number. A glance at the deck diagrams, and mathematical calculations to support Wilding's figures prove that the figure *"500"* is an error.

Wilding had stated that the aftermost damage was the small puncture mentioned by Barrett in the starboard side of No. 9 bunker. But damage *500 ft.* abaft the stem would have been over half ***TITANIC***'s *length overall,* somewhere in the vicinity of the bulkhead between No. 1 and No. 2 boiler rooms, under ***TITANIC***'s third funnel, yet Wilding had made it clear that he was *definitely* referring to the forward end of *No. 5 compartment* as the aftermost damage, and he later gave this distance from stern to aftermost impact damage as *200 ft.*

But Wilding elaborated, supported his statements with mathematics. Knowing from the statements of eyewitnesses that within 40 minutes after impact the forepeak, Nos. 1, 2 and 3 cargo holds, and No. 6 boiler room were flooded, and knowing that the combined capacity of these compartments was about 16,000 tons of water, Wilding could compute the area of water inflow by using the mathematical formula for figuring the flow of liquid through an orifice. This worked out. Wilding said, to mean that the area of water inflow from impact damage was only about 12 square feet. Thus, if the hole had been continuous it could have been only 3/4 of an inch wide. Wilding therefore concluded that the hole was not continuous, but a series of holes. Multiplying 3/4 in. X 200 ft. gives very nearly the correct figure of Wilding's conclusion, about 12 square feet. Multiplying 3/4 in. X *500* ft. gives a figure just over *30* square feet. Therefore the figure *"500"* can only be an error in transcription, a later typographical error in printing the transcript, or a deliberate error inserted later to support the myth of a lengthy gash in ***TITANIC***'s hull, necessary to conceal the damage done to the crucial bulkhead by the bunker fire.

Reworking Wilding's figures, John Bryant Williams, P. E., who has master's degrees in both industrial and mechanical engineering, and who has contributed greatly to the technical information in this book, has this to say:

> The equation for liquid flow through an orifice is:
>
> $Q = A\ C_d\ [2\ \Delta P/\rho]$ where:
> Q is flow in cubic feet per second;

A is the area of the orifice in square feet;

C_d is a dimensionless factor called the discharge coefficient and, for a sharp-edged orifice is 0.61 (reference: Page 239, *"Mechanical Engineers' Handbook,"* by Lionel Marks, McGrawHill, New York.)

ΔP is the net pressure in pounds per square foot; for seawater the pressure is 64 lbs/sq-ft for each foot of depth below the surface.

ρ [Rho] is the density of the liquid in slugs/cubic-foot. For seawater the density is 64/32.2 = 1.99 slugs/ft^3 (Reference Page 6-04, *"Handbook of Engineering Fundamentals,"* by Ovid W. Eschbach, published by John Wiley, New York.)

Thus on per square foot of orifice area basis, and taking the value of C_d 0.61, the flow equation becomes:

$Q/A = 0.61\ [2 \times 64\ h/1.99]^{1/2}$ or $4.89 \times \sqrt{h}$

Assuming that after 40 minutes the Nos. 1 ,2 and 3 cargo holds and No. 6 boiler room were flooded and the combined capacity of these compartments was 16,000 tons of water, and the head below the waterline was 10 1/2 ft…

16,000 tons = 16,000 x 2,000 = 32,000,000 pounds of water this corresponds to 32,000,000/64 = 500,000 cubic feet.

This flooding occurred in 40 minutes, so the average rate of influx of seawater was: 500,000/(40 x 60) = 208.33 cubic feet/second.

But $Q = 208.33 = A \times 4.89 \times \sqrt{10.5}$, or $15.845 \times A$

so A = 208.33/15.845 = 13.14 sq. ft.

(Wilding had apparently rounded off the figure to 12 sq. ft., or he had figured the depth of flooding to be less.)

Thus if the average width of puncture in the hull had been 3/4 in. (0.0625 feet), the length of the puncture would have been:

13.14/0.0625 = 210.24 feet long (Wilding estimated or rounded off to 200 feet.)

Evidence from Barrett's testimony told Wilding that the vertical position of the damage indicated that the head (of incoming water) was about 25 ft. above ***TITANIC***'s bottom. Her loaded draft was 35 ft. 6 in., making the head only about 10 ft. 6 in. below the waterline. The height of the boiler room was 44 ft. above the tank top, and the watertight bulkhead was capped with a watertight deck above. As the water rose inside the ship the rate of inflow would have been somewhat reduced after the water level inside the ship reached the level of the puncture in the hull through which the water entered. While diagrams have often been published showing the entire area of these forward compartments flooded, it must be remembered that initially these compartments could be flooded *only to the waterline.*

We may take Wilding's figures one step further. Applying the same formula to No. 6 boiler room only, assuming conservatively that boilers, machinery, ducting, coal in the forward bunker and so forth, occupied 60% of the cubic area in No. 6, meaning that water could enter only 40% of the total cubic area, and assuming that within 15 minutes after impact water had reached its outside level and there was 10 1/2 feet of water in No. 6, we may assume that the orifice area of inflow was 0.96 square feet, *less than one square foot.* Because water inside the hull could be no deeper than water outside the hull, and there was about 30 ft. of air space between water level and bulkhead deck, the water level could not rise inside the ruptured compartments until ***TITANIC*** sank further by the head, pulled down by additional inflow of water somewhere forward.

TITANIC was designed to stay afloat with any two *major* compartments flooded. Watertight bulkheads are spaced so that compartments are divided with floodable length in that area of the vessel taken into consideration, so that two adjacent compartments may be in free communication with the sea and the vessel will remain afloat. This provides for a collision which may have its point of impact directly on a watertight bulkhead. It is considered highly unlikely that any collision could involve two watertight bulkheads so far apart. Contrary to legend, ***TITANIC*** was not unusual in any way in this construction. It did not make her safer, or less safe, than other vessels of her day.

The forward holds and forepeak cubic area combined did not add up to the buoyancy capacity of a major compartment, and No. 6 boiler room was smaller than a major compartment, smaller than other boiler rooms. The buoyancy of a compartment is figured by subtracting anything, engines, boilers, cargo, etc., which takes up air space in that compartment. Cargo, if it is not permeable, may actually add to a compartment's buoyancy factor because it takes up space that cannot therefore be filled by incoming water, and may weigh less than the water it displaces. The fact that ***TITANIC*** was down by the head rather than having two 'midships compartments flooded did make her situation more precarious, as we shall see.

Sir John pursued his interrogation of Leading Stoker Barrett until he had been satisfied that water had come into No. 9 bunker, but not into No. 9 stokehold. This meant that the nonwatertight bunker bulkhead between No. 9 bunker and No. 9 stokehold would contain any water entering that bunker for some time, and the forward bulkhead of that bunker was the watertight bulkhead, which was stepped aft 9 feet, to starboard of the 'midships line. This was necessary because having a watertight door in the center of a transverse bunker where coal was constantly being worked was awkward, spilled coal being apt to impede the working of the door. We can readily see from the deck diagram, however, that stepping the watertight bulkhead aft and to starboard of the 'midships line literally made two separate bunkers, the smaller of the two being on the starboard side where the flooding due to impact had begun. This accounted at least partially for ***TITANIC***'s early list to starboard because there was initially no water in the port bunkers until water rose high enough that it could level off by entering bunker escape holes on the port side. When the port side bunkers flooded that brought more weight into the port side, thus she righted herself, then began to list to port. Wilding believed that her inherent transverse stability would have righted her had she been able to stabilize her longitudinal stability.

But the crucial, damaged watertight bulkhead was the one that separated boiler rooms 6 and 5. It should be noted that a *watertight* bulkhead is one in which there are no openings. When the bulkhead is fitted with a "watertight door," the actual watertight integrity of the bulkhead is compromised, and the term "watertight" becomes a delusion, entirely dependent upon the proper function of the door, and the human factor which assures that proper function. In this case it was known that Murdoch had immediately closed the watertight doors from the bridge at almost the same time he rang the engine telegraphs to *Full Speed Astern*. Barrett's testimony indicates that Murdoch had acted prior to impact, thus all watertight doors were dropping at the moment of impact.

However, a watertight door will never be as tight as riveted and caulked steel plates. Water will spurt in around the door seam to a certain extent, but it will be a negligible amount of water which should be easily handled by the ship's pumps, *as long as the bulkhead and the door itself hold fast.*

As soon as Barrett and Junior Second Engineer Hesketh were in No. 5 boiler room, Hesketh shouted an order for the men to stand by their stations. Because Barrett and Engineer Shepherd were posted to No. 6, they tried to re-enter that compartment, by going up the escape ladder from No. 5, intending to come down the ladder into No. 6. Their entry, however, was blocked by what Barrett estimated as 8 feet of water in No. 6. Barrett estimated that ten minutes had elapsed from the time he and Hesketh had jumped into No. 5 as the watertight door closed between 6 and 5. This was, then, roughly ten to twelve minutes after impact.

When recalling an emergency situation it is virtually impossible to accurately give times, unless the witness happened to look at a clock or watch at a crucial moment, and it is not a natural instinct to do so under such circumstances. Barrett testified that firemen rarely wore watches when on duty. This makes sense considering that watches were relatively expensive, and men of this era wore pocket watches, which were usually carried in vest pockets. Stokers and firemen were thinly clad in singlets and trousers only because of the heat in stokeholds. Their job demanded much stooping and bending, movement which could jeopardize the safety of a watch and its chain which might have cost at least a few months' pay. As an example of not being able to judge time during an emergency, surviving crew members of the ***HERALD OF FREE ENTERPRISE*** capsize at Zeebrugge, Belgium, in March of 1987, recalled how they estimated ten minutes for an action that they learned later had taken an hour or more to accomplish, and vice versa. It is therefore futile to try to pin down witnesses who are catastrophe survivors to exact times, yet in ***TITANIC***'s era this was not really understood. Hence, particularly at the British inquiry, efforts were made to have exact times and posterity clings to those efforts as absolute to the minute. We do need some basis upon which to reconstruct the sequence of events during ***TITANIC***'s final two and a half hours, and all we have for that now is the testimony of a few survivors from the engine room.

The bunkers between No. 6 and No. 5 compartments were empty, Barrett said, supporting Hendrickson's statement that the coal had been removed to extinguish the fire. There would have been no other reason for those particular bunkers to be completely empty at that time, for it meant that furnaces in that area were being fired with coal brought from other bunkers, an inefficient operation. Each compartment's bunkers under normal circumstances contained exactly enough coal to fuel that compartment's furnaces for the entire voyage. With the bunkers empty the shoring support of the coal was gone, and coal would have displaced the incoming water as well. In addition, coal would have prevented the water's sloshing and surging against the bulkheads, thus lessening pressure on the crucial bulkhead. With the bunkers empty nothing stood between the inrushing water and the next dry compartment aft except the relatively thin mild steel plating, 0.56 inches thick at the tank top, and 0.30 inches thick at the overhead, stiffened every 29 7/8 inches, slightly better than the 30 inch stiffening limit set by Lloyd's. But part of this plating was damaged, and no doubt heat from the fire had also started some of the rivets, further weakening the bulkhead.

Finding No. 6 flooded. Shepherd and Barrett returned to No. 5, again using the escape ladders.

Barrett never explained how or when Shepherd departed No. 6 in the first place, although later when Sir John and Lord Mersey were discussing Barrett's testimony they recalled that the leading stoker had named Shepherd as the engineer who jumped with him from No. 6 to No. 5. Barrett, however, had given a name which the court reporter spelled as "Hescott." Barrett specifically said that "Hescott's' rank was "Second Engineer." Brian Ticehurst and Geoffrey Whitfield, officers of the British ***TITANIC*** Society, in their book-in-progress *"The* ***TITANIC*** *- The Doomed and the Delivered,"* which encompasses the most complete information yet compiled on those aboard ***TITANIC,*** list James H. Hesketh as Junior Second Engineer. In fact, when Barrett later had the opportunity as he was questioned by Mr. Roche, who named Hesketh correctly, Barrett set the record straight by saying, *"That was the man who jumped through the watertight door, not Mr. Shepherd."* The Senior Second Engineer was W. Farquharson, and he would have been the watchkeeper, in charge of the entire Engine Department on that watch. The Chief Engineer, like the master, never keeps a watch. Technically, the Chief, like the master, is always on duty.

When they returned to No. 5 Barrett and Shepherd found Junior Second Assistant Engineer Herbert Gifford Harvey and Senior Second Assistant Engineer Bertie Wilson attending to the pumps. Barrett affirmed that there were pumps in each section. At this time there was still *no water in No. 5.* Barrett explained that by saying that the hole in No. 5 was not so big as the one m No. 6, and *"by the time the water had got there she had stopped."* Apparently he meant that ***TITANIC*** herself had stopped, reducing water pressure in the area of the hole. When Sir John asked if water was not coming in fast enough to flood No. 5, Barrett replied, *"No."* There was *no water* above the floor plates in No. 5 at that time. The puncture in No. 9 bunker at the forward end of No. 5, then, was negligible in size and incoming water was kept under control by the pumps. In fact, when later pressed to describe the flow of water coming into No. 9 bunker, Barrett likened it to "an ordinary fire hose." A fire hose in 1912, when fire wagons were still horse-drawn and water was hand-pumped, had nothing like the pressure of a fire hose today. This evidence indicates that the hole in No. 9 bunker at the forward end of No. 5 boiler room was entirely separate from the bilging in No. 6 because it had not damaged the watertight bulkhead between 6 and 5. If that bulkhead had been damaged at impact, then No. 5 would have been flooding almost immediately and No. 9 bunker would have been flooding as fast as No. 6 boiler room was flooding. Unfortunately nobody ever asked, nor did any witnesses volunteer to say whether they had seen any fire damage to nonwatertight bunker bulkheads, yet there must have been some. Nor did anyone ever say in which bunker, No. 9 or No. 10, the fire had started. Obviously if the coal in one bunker ignited, the heat it generated would eventually ignite the coal in the adjacent bunker. As witnesses said, coal had been removed from both bunkers.

It is also unfortunate that there were no survivors from the forward end of No. 6 who could report on the condition of the watertight bulkhead which separated No. 6 from No. 3 cargo compartment. It is entirely possible that ***TITANIC*** was bilged right at that bulkhead, yet even this should not have sunk her so quickly.

At this moment an order came through via telephone from the engine room for all stokers to go topside, except for Barrett, the lead man, who was to remain on duty. All the stokers then went to the boat deck, leaving Harvey, Wilson, Shepherd and Barrett in No. 5, *which was still dry.* This indicates that the watertight bulkhead was still intact.

It should be understood that at this time each boiler room had become a separate entity, with an engineer in charge in each compartment, and none of the men in one compartment would know exactly what was going on in the compartment adjacent to theirs, with the exception of the men in No. 5 who had tried to enter No. 6 and been blocked by 8 feet of water there. With the watertight doors closed, none of them had any means of egress excepting the emergency ladders. While they could, with release of the master system from the bridge, deactivate the watertight door controls individually and raise the doors by hand, they were not going to do that without an order. Senior Second Engineer Farquharson, however, might have been going from one compartment to another via the escape ladders to keep an eye on events, under Chief Bell's direction. Chief Bell, and no doubt Thomas Andrews and his Harland & Wolff men, should have been doing the same, but concentrating on checking the bulkhead between No. 6 and No. 5 for the first signs of rupture.

The lights then went out, and Harvey sent Barrett for lamps. At the top of the escape ladder, in the working alleyway where the lights were still on, Barrett encountered two firemen. He sent them aft to the lamp room, which was near the engine rooms, and a few minutes later they returned, carrying over a dozen lamps. By the time Barrett returned to No. 5, however, the lights were on again, powered by the emergency dynamo. He estimated this had taken ten minutes. *No. 5 was still free of water.*

Barrett checked the water gauges in the boilers, found them dry, and reported this fact to Harvey, who ordered him to get some men to pull the fires. Barrett rounded up about twenty men to pull fires in the thirty furnaces. He estimated it took them 20 minutes to accomplish this task. *No. 5 was still dry,* approximately *45 minutes after impact,* by Barrett's estimation.

Sending these men up to the boat deck immediately after the fires had been pulled, Barrett remained in No. 5. Harvey ordered him to lift a manhole plate on the starboard side so the engineers could get at the pump valves. But nobody had told Shepherd about the open plate, and the Junior Second Assistant fell into the hole, breaking his leg. Harvey and Barrett carried Shepherd into the pump room. Although the compartment was still dry, Barrett said it was now filled with steam from water thrown on the fires to put them out, making it difficult to see.

No. 5 was still dry until an estimated 15 minutes later, or at least one hour after impact, when a rush of water came through the pass between the boilers from the forward end of the compartment. Sir John asked Barrett if the bulkhead had given way, would water come through it and through the pass between boilers? *"Yes,"* replied Barrett. He had naturally not stopped to look, however.

Lord Mersey's ingenuous response was, *"It would not come over the top of the bulkhead, I suppose?"*

This line was pursued until Barrett responded with, *"I do not see how it could come over the top."*

As in any ship, ***TITANIC***'s watertight bulkheads rose to a watertight deck called the *bulkhead deck.* Again, however, this deck was watertight only if all openings in it were secured shut, and they had to be dogged by hand. If water was flowing over the top of bulkheads as Mersey suggested, this was the way it was going to do it. In other words, as ***TITANIC*** went down by the head and submerged one of these openings which might have been aft of a watertight vertical bulkhead which was maintaining its integrity, then it might have seemed to a landsman like Mersey that water was "flowing over the top of the bulkhead." But in this scenario water would not come "through the pass with a rush of green foam." It would spill from above through an open hatch, which would have been obvious, and efforts should have been made to close the hatch. According to some survivors air ports had been left open in crew quarters, and possibly in forward steerage passenger quarters, which allowed water a means of ingress above the bulkhead deck. Additionally, portlights are not stressed to withstand the same pressure as the hull plating. This was the danger to ***TITANIC*** in her forward compartments being flooded. Therefore, while her eventual demise was virtually assured, her life expectancy is the point in question here. She should have lived long enough to wait for rescue ships alongside with time enough to transfer all of her people to safety, if that had been her only problem.

In Lord Mersey's question, however, lay the foundation for the myth of water "flowing over the top of each bulkhead," progressively flooding each compartment "like water flowing from one compartment to the next in a tray of ice cubes," an oft-used analogy which gives the erroneous impression that there was an open space between the top of the bulkhead plating and the bulkhead deck plating above.

On 8 May Barrett was asked directly if anything had been done to stop the water from coming into No. 9 bunker. He had not seen anything done, Barrett replied. He was then asked if he had seen whether water came into No. 5 through a failure in the watertight door or in the bulkhead. Barrett replied that he had not noticed. The next questions concerned the bunker fire. They were not uncommon, declared Barrett. The proper order was to empty the bunker as soon as possible, Barrett affirmed.

Mr. Laing then asked Barrett again about extinguishing the fire. *"Was it fire or only heat?"* asked Laing. *"It was fire,"* replied Barrett. There had been 8 to 10 men fighting it the whole time, playing the hose upon it, Barret explained.

Unfortunately nobody ever asked Barrett exactly which boilers he had seen the rush of water come through into No. 5. If he had remained on the starboard side, however, as he had been standing in the starboard side of No. 6 at impact, and as he had sprinted through the watertight door with Hesketh, and the door was on the starboard side of the 'midships line, then it would seem logical that the rush of water came through the pass between the two boilers on the starboard side. If that was indeed the case it indicates clearly that the bulkhead, not the door, had failed.

It has often been recounted how Thomas Andrews, immediately after impact, gave ***TITANIC*** one hour to live. However, with times always so vague in surviving crew members' statements, we really do not know exactly *when* Andrews made that prediction, or even *if* he did. It is entirely possible, indeed probable, that he did not make this dire prognosis until *after* he knew that the bulkhead between No. 6 and No. 5 had failed, just as Chief Bell had declared *"My God we are doomed,"* after he learned of the failure, for as soon as No. 5 began to flood ***TITANIC*** had exceeded her floodable length. Prior to that failure, *if everything had maintained absolute watertight integrity from the watertight bulkhead between No. 6 and No. 5 on forward,* ***TITANIC*** *should have survived.* In fact, ***TITANIC*** survived little more than an hour after the bulkhead failure.

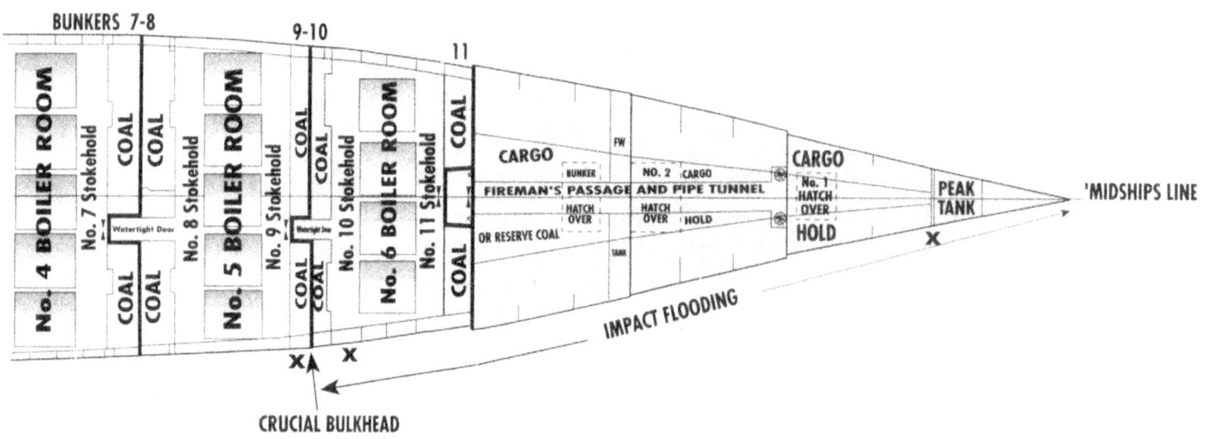

Testimony that fires were drawn in No. 5 when the water rushed into that compartment, and quickly drawn even in No. 6 when that compartment was bilged at impact, offers proof that boilers had no reason to explode. In fact on 10 June, when Edward Wilding was asked explicitly about the possibility that ***TITANIC***'s boilers had exploded, he replied that it was very unlikely. Of ships which had been examined after they had sunk. Wilding said there had been very few cases of boilers having exploded. When water reached the hot boilers the ensuing cloud of steam might give the impression of explosion, he said. Additionally, the sudden cooling and contraction of hot metal would cause a rumbling sound which, along with the steam, might suggest explosion. A landsman would surely think of explosion as Lord Mersey had done, but a marine engineer or naval architect would be more cautious in the assumption of exploding boilers. Wilding also stated that when ***TITANIC*** reached a point about 35° by the head, the boilers might have come unseated. He doubted, however, if her machinery had broken loose.

Sir John asked if the water had come through the pass with a rush, to which Barrett again replied, "*Yes.*"

Lord Mersey asked Barrett if something that had been holding the water back had given way. Barrett replied that had been his idea, but he and the other men had simply jumped once more for the escape ladder, and never looked back. Barrett was asked, however, when he had first noticed that ***TITANIC*** was down by the head. That had not been noticeable, declared Barrett, until they were drawing the fires in No. 5. Thus her forward impact flooding had not been serious until water began to find a means of entry other than her impact damage.

Sir John apologized and explained that he had not been able to follow the testimony on this subject. Mersey explained it, repeating that he had asked Barrett if the *nonwatertight bunker bulkhead* between No. 9 stokehold and No. 9 bunker had been holding back the water and that was the bulkhead which had failed. The Wreck Commissioner turned again to Barrett and asked if that was possible. Barrett replied that he thought it was, and explained again about the watertight bulkhead running athwartships through the bunker, separating No. 10 from No. 9 bunkers and No. 6 from No. 5 compartments. This comment by Barrett makes it unclear whether Barrett and Mersey were talking about the same bulkhead. Possibly Barrett was referring to the watertight bulkhead while Mersey was definitely referring to the nonwatertight bunker bulkhead. Was the bunker door shut, asked Mersey. Barrett replied that he had shut it himself. There is, however, no indication on the available deck diagrams of a door in this bulkhead. Bunkers of ***TITANIC***'s era rarely had doors in bunker bulkheads. They had openings called merely "escape holes," through which the trimmers wheeled the coal in barrows. However, in order to maintain the closed stokehold system of ventilation there had to be at certain intervals bulkheads with no such openings, and this we see on the deck diagrams. The Inquiry was adjourned until the following morning, at which time Barrett was recalled, after a discussion about Barrett's testimony on the previous day. Edward Wilding was asked how far the waterline was below the top of the watertight bulkheads. About 13 or 14 ft., said Wilding. And when the ship sank 13 ft. at that point the water would go "over the top of the bulkhead," declared Mersey in his usual simplistic manner, without any explanation as to how such a thing could have happened. There then ensued a discussion about why the lights had gone out and come on again. The conclusion was that the power had been switched from the main dynamos to the emergency dynamo, which was connected only to necessary power supplies for emergency lighting and wireless operation.

Sir John resumed his questioning of Barrett. He tried to pin the leading stoker down to the exact length of the gash extending into No. 9 bunker. It was 9 ft. from the watertight bulkhead to the bunker bulkhead. Water was coming in, said Barrett, about 2 ft. abaft the watertight bulkhead, or in the bunker itself. Had there been coal in that bunker, had it not been removed to extinguish the fire, it could have greatly impeded the inflow of water as well as provided shoring support for the bulkhead. Water was coming in only from the ship's side, the bulkhead itself was not damaged, declared Barrett. This was further testimony that the tear in No. 6 and the tear in No. 5 were separate, that ***TITANIC*** must have bumped just the once in No. 6, bounced off, struck again lightly at the forward end of No. 5, and then her stern had swung away from the ice, supporting evidence that Murdoch had indeed given that second command... *"Hard Aport."*

Then Lord Mersey made one of his stranger comments. He did not think the witness could answer the questions, and he would place very little reliance upon Barrett's evidence! In the circumstances Barrett would not have noticed where the water came from, declared Mersey emphatically. But if Barrett, the only survivor who had actually been at one point of impact, did not know, who would? Barrett no doubt was disgusted and frustrated by Mersey's comments, but he obviously was in no position to argue. He simply shut up. Thus the best evidence that there was no lengthy gash in ***TITANIC***'s hull, that the crucial bulkhead's premature collapse had in fact caused her rapid demise, was effectively squelched.

Lord Mersey had already made up his mind, then, that the tear in ***TITANIC***'s hull was continuous. No testimony from an eyewitness, nor even testimony from a naval architect supported by mathematical calculations was going to change the Wreck Commissioner's mind.

When Mr. Thomas Lewis, on behalf of the British Seafarers' Union, persisted in questioning Barrett about the bunker fire. Lord Mersey asked how that could be relevant to the inquiry! Fortunately Lewis did not back down, he asked Barrett what condition the watertight bulkhead was in after the fire had been extinguished. Barrett replied that Chief Bell had given him orders... the builders' men wanted to inspect the bulkhead. It had been damaged from the bottom... the *"bottom of the watertight compartment was dinged aft and the other part was dinged forward,"* said Barrett, indicating that the bulkhead had been heated clear through. Mersey asked if Barrett meant to say that the coal fire would dinge the bulkhead? *"Yes,"* replied Barrett.

In response to questions put by White Star attorney Mr. Laing, Barrett said that when he came up from No. 5 into the working alleyway for the last time he had seen "just a little" water in the alleyway. When Laing asked if Barrett knew where that water had come from, Barrett replied that in his idea some of the lower deck ports had been open and when the water level reached them water had begun to come in. That would have been above the bulkhead deck, said Laing. Barrett withdrew.

Modern ***TITANIC*** enthusiasts may argue against the idea of open ports in the near-freezing temperatures of a North Atlantic April. We must think 1912, however. These were hardy souls who preferred fresh air to the stuffy confines of heated quarters. There would have been nothing unusual about open ports, both in crew quarters and forward steerage. In later years, after lessons learned from ***TITANIC***, when ships ran in fog, ice, or heavy seas, ports would be checked to make sure they were dogged shut and watertight. In ***TITANIC*** there was apparently no one who thought to look for open ports. When Boxhall made his initial checks of forward compartments he in fact did not go into all compartments. Exiting crewmen, realizing the urgency of the situation, apparently simply thought only of personal survival, when thinking of the ship's survival would have been far more important, and in fact might have assured their own.

Barrett remained adamant about one thing, and he certainly would have noticed if his feet had been wet. No. 5's floor plates remained dry until the wall of water came rushing through the pass between boilers. But Lord Mersey was just as adamant. Water came into No. 6 and No. 5 from the same wound, declared Mersey emphatically, in spite of Barrett's statements to the contrary. Period. Lord Mersey would have it no other way, and the legend of the 300 ft. gash gathered momentum.

On 9 May Trimmer Thomas Patrick Dillon was sworn in and questioned by Raymond Asquith. Dillon had been assigned to engine room duties until the boilers in his section were lit. It is interesting to note that when Asquith asked him if he had been working in the compartment marked "reciprocating engines," Dillon answered, *"That is where I understand I was."* ***TITANIC***, then, was so big that a man could work in one compartment and never have any idea what went on in the rest of the ship. In fact, in a ship of ***TITANIC***'s size, dreadful things might happen in one end of her, while men working below decks a couple of hundred feet away would never know about it until the subject might be discussed over dinner or during their watch below.

Dillon testified that he had heard the engine telegraph ring on the starting platform, then a few seconds later he had felt only a slight shock as ***TITANIC*** struck ice. The engines were stopped, then went slow astern, then slow ahead, said Dillon. Immediately after impact the engineers on duty had instinctively rushed to the pump valves.

It was Dillon who began the legend of Chief Engineer Bell's order to raise the watertight doors to haul "big hoses" into forward compartments to facilitate pumping. Careful scrutiny of Dillon's testimony, however, indicates that this was done *after* the crucial bulkhead between No. 6 and No. 5 had failed, and water was already seeping into No. 4 as No. 5 flooded.

OLYMPIC and ***TITANIC***, like all vessels of their day, were equipped with the standard common manifold connected to the bilge and main condenser pumps, by means of which any compartment could be drained independently. The main condenser circulating pump was fitted with an emergency bilge suction in the engine room so that it could be used as an emergency bilge pump if the hull was breached. Chief Bell had only to open the great bilge injection valves and his main engines were turned into giant pumps hurling thousands of gallons of water back into the sea every minute. When asked why Chief Bell chose to haul hoses, or pipes, forward for auxiliary pumping, Edward Wilding explained on page 500 of the Board of Trade inquiry transcript.

Wilding believed that Chief Bell had found that water was rising against the pumps in No. 4 boiler room, where there was only one pump, with a capacity of 150 tons per hour. Section 3 had two pumps, one with the capacity of 250 tons, and the ash ejector pump with its capacity of 150 tons per hour. This, according to Wilding, prompted Chief Bell to rig auxiliary connections to increase the pumping capacity for No. 4 section. This was a desperate, last ditch stand. The engineers under Chief Bell's experienced direction were fighting for time… time to save passengers' lives. By this point in the sequence of disastrous events to a man the engineers must have known that ***TITANIC*** could take her downward plunge at any moment, with all of them trapped below.

Legend suggests that the opening of these aftermost watertight doors contributed to ***TITANIC***'s foundering, but it was perfectly proper procedure, and Wilding concurred with this. He explained that the speed with which water would come through the opening left by the raised watertight door would be dependent upon the head of water, which could not exceed the height of the door, or just over 6 ft., and probably was less. The speed and distance of the water's entry into the next compartment could therefore be calculated mathematically. It would not carry more than about 12 or at most 15 feet across the stokehold from the bulkhead, and by the time it had traveled that far the water level would have fallen below the level of the floor plates.

When the watertight bulkhead between No. 6 and No. 5 failed, it could not be known exactly how large an aperture was created and therefore the head of water entering No. 5 could not be calculated as accurately as that which came through an open watertight door the size of which was known. However, the bulkhead would not have failed entirely at the same moment. It was bound to have small apertures appearing at first, then the rush that Barrett described. The initial depth of water in forward compartments, including No. 6, was about 10.5 ft. The water would have spilled into No. 5 at the height of the bulkhead's first break, probably in the area of fire damage which would have been greatest near deck level, where the pressure was also greatest. Seeking its own level the first inrush of water would have sunk beneath the floor plates, then it would have gradually risen against the pumps. But after the initial surge its rise would be slow enough that pumps could contain it for some time, possibly several hours, possibly many hours. The initial surge of inflow into No. 5, however, could have been as high as 10.5 ft., well over a man's head and frightening to say the least. The next watertight door and bulkhead aft, that between No. 5 and No. 4, then became the crucial bulkhead.

In the proper sequence, while the bulkhead between No. 6 and No. 5 was the crucial one holding back all the water which had already entered the forward compartments, then only the next watertight door, that in the bulkhead between No. 5 and No. 4 compartments, needed to be closed to protect against the failure of the bulkhead between No. 6 and No. 5. In sequence, then, the watertight doors need not have been closed excepting for each one at a time which was aft of whatever was the crucial bulkhead. Similarly, fires need not have been drawn excepting in the compartment immediately aft of an already flooded compartment. ***TITANIC***, sinking by the head, filled progressively, in an orderly fashion, bound by known physical laws. There was nothing mysterious about her sinking, no reason to speculate on theories for over eighty years.

It was also correct to concentrate first on pumping the least damaged compartment, then those compartments with the next smallest damage and so on until the limit of the pumps was reached. In other words, No. 6 being the most severely damaged after the forward cargo compartments, could be abandoned if necessary, while pumping capacity was not thrown away on damage beyond its ability. This appears to have been exactly what ***TITANIC***'s engineers did.

Because the four steam-reciprocating-engine-driven generators were located in their own watertight compartment aft of the turbine room, and two 30 KW auxiliary generating sets also powered by the reciprocating engines were located in their own compartment within the engine casing on the saloon deck, the engineers were able to keep lights on and power for the wireless apparatus until the very end. They had to, at all cost, keep fires in No. 1 at least, although they knew that when No. 2 began to flood they probably no longer had time to exit... they would go down with the ship.

On 10 May Greaser Frederick Scott confirmed that he and his mates, acting upon orders from the engineer of the watch, had opened all of the watertight doors aft of the reciprocating engine rooms. This was about one hour after impact, or about a quarter to one as Scott estimated it. Scott could not see if the watertight doors forward of the main engine rooms were open, but he said they must have been, or the engineers could not have carried a big suction pipe through to the stokehold, which has been discussed above. Scott recalled that after the engines had been stopped and put *Full Speed Astern,* they had again been stopped, run *Slow Ahead,* stopped again, and run *Slow Astern* for a few minutes before they were finally stopped for good. (It must be understood that the reciprocating engines had to be run through the "Stop" position on the annunciators because the shafts had to be braked to a full stop before they could change direction.) If this is true, then it meant that Captain Smith and Chief Bell had tried a desperate effort to back ***TITANIC*** toward land, not an unheard of accomplishment in such situations. Even the backing movement had apparently put too much pressure on the crucial bulkhead because any movement of the ship created surges of pressure as the confined water's free surface sloshed against the already weakened bulkhead. With Chief Bell and Captain Smith talking on the telephone from engine room to bridge while the ship was moving slowly ahead or astern, Bell could immediately apprise the master of any dangerously extra pressure on the compromised crucial bulkhead. All efforts to move ***TITANIC*** thus ceased.

Two greasers, said Scott, had answered the engine telegraph, and had rung back to the bridge. It is, however, highly unlikely that two greasers would have answered such an unusual and important order from the bridge. That they would have ignored the chain of command and communicated directly with the watch officer on the bridge before consulting an engineering officer would have been insubordination. That there was no watch engineer immediately available to answer the telegraph order was absurd, and no watchkeeping deck officer was going to communicate with a mere greaser.

Scott also heard no warning bell when the watertight doors closed. Other witnesses had testified that the doors were closing prior to impact, so it would seem that what Scott actually heard first was not the engine telegraph bell but the door warning bell, and that he had simply missed hearing the engine telegraphs prior to the doors closing, or more likely, that the stress of the moment had blurred his memory. Knowing that the watertight doors were suddenly closing would have been a great shock, portending disaster in Scott's mind, and erasing his memory of the proper sequence of events. It is, of course, a highly unusual event for an engine telegraph to ring in mid-ocean when the ship is traveling at full speed. The sudden clang of the telegraph could only portend disaster.

One of the greasers had been trapped in the after tunnel, declared Scott, when the watertight door had closed. Scott and his mate from the other side of the engine room freed the greaser by *"heaving up"* the door. They had not asked permission to raise the door, nor had they needed any release from the door mechanism on the bridge, said Scott, indicating that the doors had already been released from the bridge. The engineer on duty in the turbine engine room then told Scott and his mate to raise all of the watertight doors. The engineer must have cleared this with the bridge, Scott explained, to release the clutch and allow the doors to be raised. These two statements contradicted each other, but they were not the only contradictory statements made by Scott. It was his conflicting statements about the engine orders which gave rise to the erroneous belief held by some ***TITANIC*** researchers that it took a full ten minutes for ***TITANIC***'s engines to be reversed.

On page 123, question 5609, Scott summarized what he had heard and seen. The bridge had rung down *"Stop."* The two greasers answered this order. Then the bridge had rung down *"Slow Ahead."* Then *"Stop,"* and according to Scott "*she went astern for five minutes.*" Because none of this makes any sense in the context of Murdoch's emergency engine orders, Scott must have become confused when he tried to recall what had happened. When reciprocating engines are given the crash back order they must first be stopped, then reversed to start the screws backing, which in turn stops the ship, but not until she has run on for several of her lengths before all way is lost. From the time that Murdoch rang *"Full Speed Astern"* on the reciprocating engines until the outboard screws actually began backing should have taken no more than 90 seconds, not 10 minutes, but ***TITANIC*** herself would not have stopped at that moment. She had way on her for another few minutes, and in fact had steerageway down to a speed of 6 knots. If, however, her reciprocating engines had been rung to an astern speed, and remained in that position for some time, she would have lost all forward way, stopped momentarily, then gathered sternway which would have continued for a short period even after the engines were stopped altogether. This is a very unlikely scenario, however. It is unlikely that a watch officer with Murdoch's experience and expertise would have forgotten to ring the engine telegraphs to *"Stop"* after impact, thus allowing ***TITANIC*** to continue going astern indefinitely. Murdoch knew perfectly well that without first assessing damage below the waterline, the ship should not move in either direction.

Finally the order came to evacuate the engine rooms. Scott and his mates went to the boat deck, along with all of the engineers and firemen from his section. At this time the engine rooms were still dry, putting the lie to Jack Phillips' dramatic wireless message that the engine rooms were flooding. Scott and the other men found all boats on the starboard side had gone away, but on the port side boats 14 and 16 were being lowered. Fifth Officer Lowe was in charge of one boat, however, and he fired his revolver between the boat and ***TITANIC***'s side, shouting dramatically, *"If any man jumps into the boat I will shoot him like a dog!"* No. 4 boat had returned alongside because there were only two men to crew it. When they shouted for two more men Scott and Greaser Thomas Ranger climbed the davits and slid down the falls into the boat.

Scott then recalled seeing ***TITANIC*** begin to break up. She broke just aft of the fourth funnel, he said, while other witnesses claimed that they saw her break between the first and second funnels. Scott's boat was close astern of ***TITANIC,*** however, where he would not have had a good view forward. Scott's testimony indicates that at least some of the engineers did get as far as the boat deck, but probably none of them wore lifebelts, the big cork flotation devices being too cumbersome to permit a man to work. Scott testified that the life vests had made it extremely difficult to get up on the davits and slide down the falls.

Examined by Mr. Roche, who appeared on behalf of the Chamber of Shipping of the United Kingdom, Scott said that he saw about eight engineers on the boat deck, but the only one he knew by name was the Senior Second, W. E. Farquharson.

There has been much speculation about ***TITANIC***'s being bilged at impact as far aft as No. 4 boiler room. Trimmer George Cavell had been working in the starboard side of No. 6 bunker, the aft bunker in No. 4 compartment. When ***TITANIC*** struck ice Cavell was nearly buried in falling coal. He struggled out of the bunker into the stokehold, where he was when the lights went out. He had heard the warning bell for the closing of watertight doors, and knew that the door just aft of him had dropped. Cavell climbed up to the working alleyway on the port side and found Third Class passengers scurrying aft, clutching lifebelts along with their personal belongings. The passengers were *"wet through,"* said Cavell. Lights were on in the alleyway, and Cavell went to get lamps, but by the time he returned to the stokehold the lights had come on again there, too.

Cavell had seen no water coming into No. 4 at impact, nor did he see any after returning to the stokehold. The order was given to draw fires, however.

During the time that Cavell and the other men were drawing fires in No. 4, water began to seep in and rise above the floor plates. It had reached a depth of about one foot above the plates when Cavell decided it was time to leave. He climbed again to the working alleyway, saw nobody and decided to come back down into No. 4, a very strange decision under the circumstances. Finding no one there either, he did not descend all the way to the bottom, therefore was not sure how much water was in No. 4 at this time. Cavell then climbed to the boat deck, went right aft and found only two boats still on board, one of which was in the process of being lowered.

When Cavell said that steam pressure in No. 4 had been kept at 225 psi although design pressure was 215 psi. Lord Mersey wanted to know if there was no better evidence on this point.

During Cavell's early statements he makes it seem as if everything he described had happened in a matter of a few minutes. But when asked directly, in question number 4400, how much time had elapsed between impact until he first saw the Third Class passengers crowding aft in the working alleyway, Cavell estimated an hour and a half. He now said it was about two hours after impact, or only about 40 minutes prior to the final plunge, when he had seen the passengers *"wet through."*

It had been somewhere between an hour and a half and two hours, then, before water began to seep into No. 4 in appreciable quantities. By this time the bulkhead between No. 6 and No. 5 had failed, and ***TITANIC*** was doomed. Water seeking its own level progressed aft as ***TITANIC*** sank further by the head. There was, however, absolutely *no evidence that **TITANIC** was bilged as far aft as No. 4 upon impact.*

Lamp trimmer Samuel Hemming had been in his watch below, asleep, when ***TITANIC*** struck ice. He was awakened by the jar, got up and went to the nearest port where he stuck his head out and looked around to see what the ship had hit. Hemming did not say whether the port was open or he opened it, nor did he say whether he had then closed it, and nobody asked if he did. Not seeing anything at all, he heard a hissing noise and went to find its source. He followed the sound to the storeroom directly forward of the chain locker, and found that a hatch cover was billowing upward. In ***TITANIC***'s era hatch covers were secured against pressure from above, as when the sea broke over the weather deck, but not against pressure from below. Hemming and the storekeeper, probably H. Rudd, had gone all the way down to the tank top and found it dry. Hemming, still following the hissing sound, went up again to the forecastle head, and found that the hiss was coming from an exhaust pipe in the forepeak tank. Water was coming into the tank, forcing air out. Hemming then came across Boatswain's Mate Albert Haines, who had been in charge of the starboard watch. Haines, too, had heard the hissing noise and followed it to its source. Hemming and Haines were joined by Chief Officer Wilde and reported this information to him. Hemming also told Wilde that the store rooms were dry clear through. Wilde asked about the forepeak itself, and when he was told it was dry the Chief Officer merely replied, *"All right,"* according to Hemming. No doubt Wilde reported all of this to the master immediately.

Next Hemming ran into the carpenter, probably J. Maxwell, who told him that holds No. 1, 2 and 3 were making water fast, as was the Racquet Court, which was directly over No. 3, which housed the mail, baggage and specie rooms.

The next person that Hemming came across was Boatswain Nichols, who told him that the crew was to turn out, that Thomas Andrews had given ***TITANIC*** half an hour to live, but they must keep it among themselves. In other words, the passengers were not to know in order to avoid panic.

One of the most interesting parts of Hemmings' testimony which has been entirely overlooked, was his statement that he had "stuck his head out of the port" to look around. This is the only direct statement that ports in forward crew quarters, and probably passenger quarters as well, might have remained open after the collision. While this possibility was addressed at the American inquiry, with ***TITANIC***'s officers not appearing to know what an "air port" was, it has never been seriously addressed by researchers. Obviously open ports would allow water to enter. The forward part of a ship does contain apertures which allow water to enter the vessel when submerged. The hawsepipes are one such means of entry. Hatches are another, and open ports would be still another means of water ingress. This is the reason why having forward compartments bilged will be the most precarious flooding a ship can acquire. Hemming's testimony, however, concurs with Barrett's theory of open ports forward, above the bulkhead deck.

It appears from Hemming's testimony that ***TITANIC*** was bilged right at her collision bulkhead. This bulkhead was just abaft the forepeak, and the chain locker ran straight down to the forepeak tank top. Impact with a submerged ice spur at this point could have damaged the forepeak tank without damaging the forepeak compartment itself. The force of impact could have moved the starboard chain, allowing it to spill into the cofferdam, thus damaging the collision bulkhead.

This is further borne out by the testimony of Able Seaman Ernest Archer, who was interrogated by Senator Bourne on behalf of the Congressional Subcommittee. Archer was 36 years old, had been going to sea for 20 years. Senator Bourne asked Archer to describe in his own way what had occurred immediately preceding and following the accident.

"I was in my bunk, asleep. I heard a kind of a crush, something similar to when you let go the anchor; it sounded like the cable running through the hawse pipe," Archer replied. It was more of a grating sensation than a shock, he continued. Archer jumped out of bed, put on a pair of trousers and ran up on deck to see what was going on.

"I saw some small pieces of ice on the starboard side, on the forward deck," Archer continued.

"Which deck?" Bourne asked.

"The fore well deck," replied Archer.

A.B. George Moore had been in his watch below, and was not yet asleep when, at about a quarter to twelve he heard *"a noise like a cable running out, like a ship dropping anchor. There was not any shock at all,"* Moore told Senator Newlands at the American inquiry.

If ***TITANIC*** came close enough to the growler to strike an overhanging ledge of it, which she apparently did or she would not have had ice on her fore well deck, then possibly her starboard bower was dislodged at this time.

Toward the end of Edward Wilding's testimony he had changed his mind, or it had been changed for him. He stated that there had been impact damage to the watertight bulkhead between No. 6 and No. 5, and that the wound in No. 6 continued into No. 5 although all witnesses gave evidence to the contrary, and Barrett's testimony of the sudden wall of water coming into No. 5 did not fit the scenario of bulkhead damage caused by impact. But Lord Mersey had already made up his mind that damage was continuous, in spite of evidence to the contrary, *or Mersey's mind had been made up for him. As* part of the coverup to conceal the coal fire's damage to the bulkhead Wilding would have had to change his story, too.

In the Board of Trade summary, when each attorney presented his case, Mersey and the rest of the Board concluded that Barrett had closed a door between bunker No. 9 and stokehold No. 9 at the forward end of No. 5 compartment. This non-watertight bulkhead and door had contained the water for some time, but when the door gave way it had allowed the water to enter No. 5 with a "wave of green foam" as Barrett had described it, thus driving Barrett and the other men up the escape ladder. So Lord Mersey concluded.

This theory is flawed for one reason. This was a relatively small space, 9 ft. between watertight bulkhead and bunker bulkhead, 44 ft. in height but less than half the breadth of the ship. (See illustrations of preceding pages) If the watertight bulkhead remained intact and the nonwatertight bulkhead gave way, then only that water confined in that small area was released into No. 5 and the pumps could have handled it. In this scenario the watertight bulkhead remained firm and ***TITANIC*** should have lived hours longer, until that crucial watertight bulkhead did eventually give way. There should have been time to save all of ***TITANIC***'s people, possibly to tow her to safety or a salvageable depth.

If, however, Lord Mersey's assertion meant that the nonwatertight bulkhead between No. 9 bunker and No. 9 stokehold was containing *all of the water which had entered the ship at impact forward of that bulkhead,* then that literally meant that the watertight bulkhead between No. 6

and No. 5 compartments had *already* given way, thus the nonwatertight bulkhead was containing all water forward of it, for which it had not been stressed. We are therefore back to square one, with the coal fire and its subsequent damage to the watertight bulkhead being responsible for ***TITANIC***'s failure to remain afloat until rescue vessels arrived.

Edward Wilding alone of all men now alive could theorize just how much the fire had actually damaged, and weakened, the bulkhead. He could only theorize, however, because he had not been there to see it. The men who had seen the fire and its damage and had the expertise to know what it meant, were dead. Thomas Andrews and his Harland & Wolff crew knew. Captain Smith surely understood, so did Murdoch, Wilde and Lightoller. But of these men only Lightoller survived and he knew when to keep quiet. Andrews no doubt took this damage into consideration when he estimated ***TITANIC***'s survival time at one hour to one and a half hours, and in fact Andrews probably made that estimate *after* he knew that crucial bulkhead had failed, or was close to failing. In fact, Andrews, as Barrett had testified, had inspected the damaged bulkhead and should have had the knowledge to estimate about how long it would hold before failing.

Barrett and Beauchamp could only have guessed how much damage the fire had done, ow much the bulkhead had been weakened. No doubt Wilding listened carefully to their descriptions of the color of the glowing steel, for it told him much. Any coverup, however, would have been predicated on what Wilding, the Board of Trade and Admiralty officials *believed* had happened, and the worst case scenario at that.

The pressure on the bulkhead of a flooded compartment depends upon the depth of flooding, whether or not that compartment is open to the sea, and whether there is additional pressure caused by the ship's forward movement. The pressure is greatest along the deck, and least along the overhead, owing to the depth of water in the compartment. Pressure is increased by the ship's rolling or pitching movements. And pressure is increased as the depth of water increases in the vicinity of the hole which opens the compartment to the sea. If the compartment contains a layer of trapped air, that air will be compressed until it assumes the same pressure as the column of water. It is obvious that a bulkhead built of ductile mild steel plating will give, will stretch and even bulge as the pressure varies. And if it has lost some of its ductility, if it does not give and stretch, it has to break.

TITANIC was fortunate in having a calm sea. It is a commander's first instinct to move a sinking ship toward land, to beach her if possible, at the very least to get her into shallow water where she might be salvaged. Indeed this is the subject of one question asked on the Board of Trade examination for a master's certificate. Obviously Captain Smith, who had, according to some witnesses, run his engines *Dead Slow Ahead* for a few moments shortly after impact, had been apprised by Chief Bell that the pressure exerted upon that weakened crucial bulkhead by the ship's forward movement was too much of a risk. This lessened chances of moving ***TITANIC***, even under tow, to land or shallow water, but it is impossible to believe that hardy and desperate seamen would not have tried a tow, had any of the nearby vessels realized ***TITANIC***'s dire straits. Stranger things have been accomplished at sea under greater duress. With engines not needed for forward movement, all of ***TITANIC***'s engine power was thus concentrated on her pumps within a few minutes after impact.

At best the crucial bulkhead between No. 6 and No. 5 boiler rooms was bound to give way eventually. But the life of ***TITANIC*** and the human life that she carried depended upon this bulkhead holding until help in the form of other ships arrived alongside.

Ships of ***TITANIC***'s era were constructed of *mild steel*, an alloy containing several elements in addition to the basic iron ore. It is the element carbon which transforms iron into steel, and at the bottom of the spectrum the softest mild steel differs little from chemically pure iron. It contains less than one tenth of one percent of carbon, and its tensile strength is about 20 tons per square inch. The hardest, high carbon steel, such as that found in the finest swords or razor blades where a cutting edge is essential, contained about 1.4 per cent of carbon, and its tensile strength was about 100 tons per square inch. Between these two extremes lay the mild steel used in ships of the early part of this century.

In ***TITANIC***'s era the usual shipbuilding steel alloy consisted of iron, 99.185%; carbon, 0.180%; silica, trace; sulphur 0.045%; phosphorus 0.045%; manganese, 0.500%; copper, 0.045%; slag, etc. 0.000%. The carbon content of steel controls its strength, hardness and ductility. Increasing the percentage of carbon, while increasing hardness and decreasing its tendency to warp and crack, will also decrease its ductility and malleability, its toughness and resistance to corrosion. In low-carbon steel phosphorus and copper were added to increase resistance to corrosion, but above 0.05% the addition of phosphorus tends to produce *cold shortness,* or brittleness when the steel becomes cold, usually below 31°F. Much of the sulphur in steel comes from the coke used during the refining process. Sulphur causes brittleness at high temperatures, known as *hot shortness.* Manganese is added to the alloy because it combines with sulphur to produce manganese sulfide which forms strengthening fibers when the steel is rolled.

Although the pioneer of the open-hearth system was an English metallurgist named Heath, it was the German William Siemens, who became a British subject in 1849, who invented the regenerative system in 1860 which produced enough heat to make the open hearth process workable.

It is important to understand the atomic structure of solid metals in order to understand the theory of heat treatment. The simplest and fairly accurate way to describe the atom is to depict it as a miniature solar system. The "sun" is the core, or nucleus, which is composed of positively charged protons, and uncharged neutrons. This dense core is surrounded by the "planets," an orbiting cloud of negatively charged electrons. The whole system is held together by the balance between the negatively charged electrons and the positively charged nucleus. But the loosely held outer electrons can be attracted to the nucleus of other atoms, too. In metals, in the liquid state the atoms move freely, but as the temperature drops they become sluggish, moving ever more slowly until the freezing point is reached. At that point the atoms move into a definite, orderly pattern called a *space lattice,* where they remain, held in place by the mutual attractive and repulsive forces which act between them, until they are disturbed by a change of temperature, or the application of some form of stress. Heated, the lattice expands, is loosened, and disintegrates at the melting point. If stress is moderate, the lattice expands or contracts, but as the amount of stress increases some of the bonds may rupture, electrons shift their loyalties, and a deformation in the metal results.

An engineer or naval architect is interested in the *compressive* strength of a steel, or its ability to withstand squeezing or pressing without failure. *Tensile* strength, also called *ultimate,* or *maximum* strength, is the maximum load on a given area that the metal can stand without breaking. *Toughness* is the ability to withstand sudden shock, such as impact, without breaking, and is the opposite of *brittleness,* which is the tendency to fracture suddenly under low stress, without appreciable deformation. *Ductility* is the property in steel which allows permanent deformation without rupture.

Heat treatment of steel changes its carbon distribution and content by transforming the lattice structure. Heat treatment falls into three categories, *normalizing, annealing,* and *hardening.* Each process is used for some specific industrial purpose. In the mill these treatments are accomplished in a controlled, orderly and known fashion for a definite purpose. The metal is heated to known temperatures, and quenched at known rates to produce the desired change in the structure which gives the selected attributes to the steel. The maximum temperature used, the time taken to achieve it and the time the metal is held at that temperature, as well as the cooling rate are all extremely important. Different temperature levels achieved, with different rates of cooling, produce different characteristics. Cooling may be accomplished by allowing the steel to cool at room temperatures, or by quenching with water or oil.

The temperatures at which changes occur in a metal being heated from room temperature to melting point are known as *transformation* points, or *critical* points. Between *decalescence,* which is the sudden absorption of heat when metals are in the process of being heated, and *recalescence,* which is the sudden release of heat while cooling, lies the critical range of temperatures in which steel is seen to redden and deformation takes place. ***TITANIC*** survivors from the Engine Department said only that the steel had reddened, but there are various stages and shades of reddening, from the dark cherry of about 1100°F to 1200°F, through the bright red between the 1500°F to 1600°F range. Thomas Andrews and his men would necessarily have been familiar with this.

The rate of cooling of steel which has been heat treated is extremely important. Unfortunately no witness gave an exact time for the removal of the last bit of smoldering coal in ***TITANIC***'s bunker on the day before she struck ice, except that it was in the 4 to 8PM watch. The steel plating would have cooled from the outside, but perhaps did not have time to cool completely through to room temperature, in spite of the relative thinness of the plates. In that case it would have been quenched suddenly by the inrush of frigid sea water. The desirable rate of cooling is about 50°F per hour. Anything faster may result in warping or cracking. We have no way of knowing how fast ***TITANIC***'s reddened bulkhead plating was quenched, whether or not the sudden exposure to icy water after it had been cooling gradually over a period of hours did any further damage. But we must remember that any coverup concerning the coal fire was instigated with the worst possible scenario in mind because those involved in the coverup did not know exactly what had happened either.

In ***TITANIC***'s era the strength of the various steel components used in a ship's construction was generally a matter of theory based upon practice, and the experience of the shipbuilder. Andrews and his men considered the *compressive* strength, the ability of the steel to bear compression loads, *shearing* strength, when a metal is subjected to a load exceeding its elastic limit, and *torsional* strength, the ability to resist external forces which tend to twist the metal around an axis. They knew the *elastic limit* of the steel they used, that is the maximum stress it could sustain and still return to its original form. The *factor of safety* is the figure that represents the number of times the ultimate resistance of material exceeds the working load for which it is designed. About twelve times the estimated stresses were usually provided for in the design of a ship.

TITANIC's steel was made by the open hearth process, and cold rolled, meaning that the plates were subjected to a continued rolling after they had cooled below a red heat. Admiralty specifications strictly forbade reheating of cold rolled plates after they had left the mill, for reasons which should now be obvious.

Stress may be defined as a force acting upon a structure. Those stresses to which a ship will be subjected are generally known to seamen as *bending, buckling, compression, panting, pounding, hogging, sagging, heaving, racking, shear, tension* and *torsion. A* seaman in tune with his ship will hear and feel all of these.

Panting, when plates work in and out, is the stress arising from waves beating against the bow and sides. *Pounding* results from a head sea when the ship is light and her bows descend like a hammer upon the waves. *Heaving* is the vertical motion of a vessel, which increases and decreases her draft. *Racking* is the force which tends to distort the shape of a section. *Sagging* is caused when a ship is lifted by her ends, as on the crests of succeeding waves in a head or following sea, leaving little support under her 'midships area. *Hogging* is just the opposite of sagging. *Stress,* then, is a force, while *strain* is the result of the stress imposed. A vessel that has hogged or sagged, for example, has been strained. Her longitudinals may be permanently distorted.

When ***TITANIC***'s bulkhead plating was seen to redden it had been reheated far beyond the boundaries of safety, and the composition of that steel was actually changed. On 10 June Wilding was challenged for an opinion on how much change had taken place.

Wilding had listened carefully to descriptions of the color of the glowing steel, for it told him much. He knew perfectly well that the drastic, uncontrolled temperature change had rearranged the steel's space lattice, altering the known tensile strength and ductility to an unknown factor. It may have been much change, it may have been little, but the deformation was there, and Wilding knew it.

Wilding hedged when Mr. Thomas Lewis, representing the British Seafarers' Union, asked directly about damage to the crucial bulkhead from its being heated red hot. Would this have made the bulkhead very brittle, Lewis wanted to know. Wilding countered by asking what Lewis meant by the term "very brittle." It did not convey anything definite to him. Wilding said.

Lewis persisted. Would a blow cause damage much easier than if it had not been brittle?

It depended on the force of the blow. Wilding evaded again. It would not be brittle like glass, of course, but it might be more brittle than if it had been undamaged.

"More brittle than in an undamaged condition?" Lewis pressed.

"It might be a little more... yes, somewhat more," Wilding finally admitted.

Given testimony from surviving crewmen, coupled with the known factor of the steel damage, the only answer to ***TITANIC***'s quick demise was a failed bulkhead, a bulkhead which failed prematurely because it had been damaged by uncontrolled heating for over three days, followed by uncontrolled cooling.

The watertight doors set into the bulkheads between the various lower compartments in ***TITANIC*** were of Harland & Wolff's special design, but they were similar to the conventional Stone-Lloyd watertight doors of the era. Each door weighed three quarters of a ton, and it was held in the open position by a friction clutch which could be instantly released by an electric switch located on the bridge. Each door could be manually closed or opened individually by means of a lever connected to the clutch, and there was a lever on each side of the bulkhead. As a final backup system, a float beneath each door would activate the closing mechanism if water came into that compartment and became deep enough to touch the float. An electric bell near each door warned of its closing in time for crewmen to escape being crushed or dismembered as the door dropped into the closed position. The warning bells could be activated from the bridge all at once, along with the door mechanisms, as Murdoch activated them. Or, each individual closing mechanism activated its own door warning bell. That the warning allowed enough time for a jump to safety was proven by Frederick Barrett's survival. It allowed no time for procrastination, however, and the jump had to be fast and instinctive. When closing a watertight door it is always better to sacrifice crewmen rather than the ship with everyone in her. An indicator panel on the bridge showed by means of electric lights for each door whether the door was open or closed. The door was actually a section of the bulkhead cut out and fitted on enclosed slide rail guides. It was as close to being watertight as it could be, but any time there is a seam between door and bulkhead there is bound to be some leakage due to the tremendous pressure put upon it.

To a man ***TITANIC***'s engineers went down with their ship. Very little has thus been written in ***TITANIC*** lore about the last two hours of these brave officers. The only way to understand what the engineers were doing and how they met their end, is by studying other shipwrecks. One of the best documented wrecks, wherein all engineers survived to tell the tale, was that of the Union Steamship Company's ***TSS TAHITI***.

On 15 August, 1930, the 7,585 ton ***TAHITI***, Captain A. T. Toten, was 460 miles south of Rarotonga, out of Wellington, New Zealand, bound for San Francisco. She carried 103 passengers, her crew numbered 149. Her holds contained general cargo and mails, while her specie room carried gold bullion. From jackstaff to oxter plate, ***TAHITI*** was as smart as any transatlantic liner. She was a strong, comfortable ship and she rode easily in a seaway. Her officers were British, among the most experienced in the Merchant Navy.

According to her log the weather was *"moderate to fresh southerly winds, with a heavy southwest swell."* She had just crossed the 180th meridian. Her Senior Second Engineer, Archibald Thompson, had taken over the watch from the Senior Third at four o'clock in the morning. Thompson had made his initial inspections, and settled down to enjoy his cup of tea at half past four when he was startled by a series of sharp explosions which seemed to come from all around him. He sprang toward the starboard main engine, which was actually lifting from its foundations, while the thrust block seemed to be exploding. Every man on duty froze in horror as the starboard engine began to race.

Marine steam engines never raced unless the ship pitched her stern so high that her propellers came clear out of the water. Most ships were fitted with safety devices to stop runaway engines. No doubt ***TAHITI*** had such a device, but for some reason it failed to work. When ***TAHITI***'s starboard shaft broke, the engine, freed from its connecting drive to the propeller, raced uncontrolled. The noise was horrendous. Galvanized into action by years of experience. Mister Thompson immediately stopped his engines, knowing by now that his ship had a broken tail shaft. Fireman Geddes ran to shut off some of the oil fires.

Intent upon learning where the starboard shaft had broken, Thompson managed to get through the watertight door into the shaft tunnel. The port main engine idled, keeping electric lights on.

One broken shaft on a twin screw vessel should not be fatal. Mister Thompson knew full well that ships had been canted while their engineers had fitted new tail shafts at sea. It did not occur to him that ***TAHITI***'s engineers could fail to repair her. Even if they could not, ***TAHITI*** should have made port, a bit more slowly of course, on one engine and one screw. It never for a moment occurred to Mister Thompson that his ship was about to commit suicide. Intent upon his mission, Thompson was startled when he saw a wall of water rushing through the tunnel toward him. He had two doors to get through to safety, with the good chance that a conscientious junior had shut at least one of them, in which case Thompson was a dead man. Aware of all this in less time than it takes to blink an eye. Senior Second Engineer Thompson moved faster than he ever dreamed that he could. He would later swear that it was "positively under one minute" from the time he put down his tea cup until he and the ocean burst into the engine room in a dead heat.

Meanwhile, far up on the bridge, the watch officer, one Duncan MacKenzie, heard muffled rumblings from the bowels of his ship, accompanied by strange vibrations which he could feel through the deck plating and the soles of his feet. Before he could comprehend what these unusual occurrences might mean, the starboard engine telegraph rang *"Stop."* This reversal of the usual order had to mean an accident in the engine room. MacKenzie called the master, who had already been awakened by his ship's thunderous squeals. To the ship's carpenter, a man named Borthwick, whose berth was immediately over the starboard propeller, the noise was something like a railroad train rumbling through his quarters.

The Chief Engineer, another Scot named MacPherson, had also been aroused from slumber by the dreadful din. Clad only in his pajamas the Chief ran down the ladder into the engine room, and after a quick appraisal of the situation he ran to the master. Chief MacPherson wanted the carpenter. He wanted spare timber, booms and extra hands. The after bulkhead, which separated the engine room from the No. 3 hold, was already bulging inward. The watertight door had been shut, and water spurting in around its edges was no problem. But the whole steel wall was giving, stretching, bending before the tremendous pressure of the inrushing sea. Water boiled upward from fractures under the starboard shaft, and it was already even with the floor plates although Mister Thompson had the pumps going at full speed. The Chief knew that if the bulging, crucial bulkhead was not shored immediately they would all go to the bottom in minutes. So MacPherson called for the carpenter, and all the wood he could find.

Working together Carpenter Borthwick, Chief MacPherson and their men put up cross pieces between the thrust blocks and laid struts against the bulkhead. They drove wedges and set up screw jacks against the wood planks. In spite of their efforts water was now up to their waists, and it had reached the dynamos. The ship was in total darkness.

For the next 12 hours Chief MacPherson and his men struggled valiantly to hold back the sailor's ancient enemy. They worked in water that was sometimes up to their knees, sometimes to their necks, as ***TAHITI***, now dead in the water, rolled in the southwesterly swell. Surging water lifted the floor plates, and every once in a while a man would fall through them, to be pulled out by his comrades in misery, their flashlights held high. As the ship rolled, every man received cruel blows, bruising head, elbow, knee, whatever came in contact with unseen metal projections. Mister Thompson struggled to ship a spare armature in the dynamo so the wireless operator could get more range than battery power could give while he pounded out ***TAHITI***'s SOS. It was five

***ABOVE**: The final dramatic moments of the **S.S. TAHITI**. Her bow raises from the water exposing the waterline while black smoke rolls from the sinking stern. **TAHITI** was older than **TITANIC** when she met disaster, however, her crucial bulkhead held while **TITANIC**'s did not. (Artwork by Ryan Katzenbach)*

o'clock in the afternoon before Thompson got the generator running, and the Chief could see what progress had been made in their battle against the bulging bulkhead.

Now ***TAHITI*** was in wireless contact with the outside world. She was no longer alone as her "Sparks" conversed with operators as far away as New Zealand. More important, he had raised the Norwegian freighter ***PENYBRYN***, which ***TAHITI*** had passed before the accident, another Union liner, ***TOFUA***, and the American Oceanic Steamship Company liner ***VENTURA***.

But in the engine room the enemy was winning. Every roll of the ship put more weight on the bulkhead and minute breaks in the heavy steel began to spurt water. Topside the Chief Officer removed hatches, rigged winches with steel barrels on slings, and got his crew bailing. Still the sea was winning. Water spurted in around the "watertight" door, it shot through rivet holes, it bubbled and boiled about the sweating, struggling men who slid and slipped on the broken plates.

Time stood still in the hellish eternity of their struggle against the hungry sea. Later Chief MacPherson dimly recalled sending up for lunch, to be told that it was evening. Throughout the night the Chief and his men struggled, fighting for more time. Dawn came and, cheated of their prey, the seas grew angrier. ***PENYBRYN*** was pounding toward them at full steam. So as ***TOFUA***. ***VENTURA*** was farther away but faster. Everything depended upon that after bulkhead. More beams and jacks were set up and the sleepless, exhausted men continued their fight for survival.

Finally, ***VENTURA*** was on the horizon and passengers were in the boats when Chief MacPherson called for volunteers to go down with him and shore up the bulkhead where it had cracked in new places. And these men went back down into that stygian maelstrom. With water up to their shoulders they managed to put up fresh shoring. MacPherson reported that he could give ***TAHITI*** one more hour. He did better than that, but not by much. As ***PENYBRYN*** and ***VENTURA*** stood by, the bulkhead gave way.

Captain Toten and his senior officers left in the last boat. The purser had safely carried the bullion to ***VENTURA***. The chief steward had saved the beer and whisky, and Mister Thompson had saved his two parrots. Every passenger was safe, of course. And so was ***TAHITI***'s logbook.

But no master abandons ship easily. One must be absolutely certain that she is doomed, that she won't be found still afloat and towed into port by a vessel which can then claim huge salvage fees from her owners. Captain Toten, seeing his people safely aboard ***VENTURA***, returned to his command. Perhaps Chief MacPherson was an alarmist, perhaps she was not sinking after all!

TAHITI was very much down by the stern when her master climbed over her rail for the last time. The Second Class was under water. Captain Toten looked into the engine room once more, and it was enough to convince him. Water was over the main engines and rising rapidly. He left her and pulled back to ***VENTURA***, with what must have been a heavy heart, for a ship becomes part of her master, and losing her is like losing part of himself.

TAHITI's engine room was in running order when she was abandoned, as ***TITANIC***'s would have been. ***TAHITI***'s pumps throbbed under full steam, her oil fires roared, her fuel pumps shuttled slowly back and forth. While her bows rose high in her final agony her signals still flew proudly from the foremast halyards, and oily smoke still spewed from her funnel. As the forepart of the ship stood clean out of the water, the fireroom flooded and smoke no longer belched from her stack. Rending metal generated sparks that ignited fuel oil, and plumes of white steam and black smoke hissed from her submerged gratings. Like ***TITANIC*** allegedly had done, ***TAHITI*** poised for an instant in the vertical position, but she was silhouetted against a sunlit sky and sparkling sea before she plunged silently stern first forever from the sight of humankind.

Did ***TAHITI***'s engineers, who stood by their posts as ***TITANIC***'s engineers had done, think during their long travail of those other men who had died so horribly at their posts just over eighteen years before them?

Of course they did. Merchant Navy engineers still remember ***TITANIC*** and speculate upon how Chief Bell kept his men below while all knew their probable fate. On their uniform sleeves their rank stripes were, and still are, mounted on a field of purple cloth to honor ***TITANIC***'s engineers. The men who fought to keep ***TAHITI*** afloat did exactly what ***TITANIC***'s engineers should have done, might have done, probably did to the extent that they could. And every one of ***TAHITI***'s engineers was frighteningly aware that his fate could have been the same, at any moment. But not one man deserted his post. Only fickle Fate decreed which would die and which would live.

TITANIC's engineers had that one strike against them, and probably ***TAHITI***'s engineers knew of it, for sailors, like aviators, like to discuss wrecks, their causes and what might have been done to prevent them, over fine whisky, or pints of beer in pubs and saloons the world over. They knew perfectly well that ***TITANIC***'s weakened bulkhead collapsed earlier than it might have had there been no fire. And they must have speculated over the question of whether or not ***TITANIC***'s engineers had done anything to shore up that bulkhead. And if they did, how did they do it?

TAHITI was launched in April,1904, by A. Stephen & Son, Glasgow, as ***PORT KINGSTON*** for the Elder Dempster subsidiary Imperial Direct West India Mail Company. She was 460 feet long with a beam of 55 feet, about half ***TITANIC***'s size. Her sea speed was a mere 16 knots, although she had done 18.5 knots in her trials. In August, 1911, the Union Line bought her, renamed her ***TAHITI***, and upgraded her accommodations to 277 First, 97 Second and 141 Third Class. She served the company well, with but one blemish on her career. On 3 November, 1927, she rammed and sank the Sydney harbor ferry ***GREYCLIFFE***, killing 42 people, among whom were many schoolchildren. Although ***GREYCLIFFE*** had crossed ***TAHITI***'s bows when the ferry's master thought the liner was moving at the harbor speed of 8 knots, legend has it that ***TAHITI*** committed suicide in her shame over this incident.

But ***TAHITI*** had made up for her transgression in Sydney harbor. She lived for *60* hours, from the time Second Engineer Thompson put down his cup of tea, until she slipped forever beneath the waves. *Sixty* hours, *2 1/2 days,* time enough to save every soul, the pets, the precious cargo of gold bullion and the booze as well! And ***TAHITI*** was 26 years old! Why, then, should the new and larger ***TITANIC*** live but 2 hours and 40 minutes? There is only one answer. ***TAHITI***'s crucial bulkhead was shored, it had not been previously damaged, and it held firm over 57 hours longer than ***TITANIC***'s crucial bulkhead held.

Dillon's testimony might suggest that the watertight doors had been opened as far forward as the one between No. 4 and No. 5 not just to increase pumping capacity, but for another reason, to facilitate shoring the bulkhead. Every scrap of wood they could round up had to be carried by the engineers through those open doors.

American merchant marine officers were and are taught to shore crucial bulkheads. Were British officers less efficient in this respect? Not according to their seamanship manuals, which teach the same thing. Did ***TITANIC***'s engineers stand around and wring their hands? Did they, like ***TITANIC***'s passengers and apparently her deck officers, excepting Murdoch, put too much faith in the new technology... wireless? Did ***TITANIC***'s officers *really* believe she was "unsinkable"? Did ***REPUBLIC***'s experience only three years earlier lull them into complacency, while ***TAHITI***'s engineers eighteen years later fought for the life of their ship because ***TITANIC***'s experience had jolted them into reality?

In the context of ***TITANIC***'s excessive publicity was it considered politic to conceal the fact that a watertight bulkhead, in which passengers put so much faith, might need a little extra help when it was put to its final test? Admittedly, 2 hours and 40 minutes was not time to do much in the way of shoring. But at the beginning, immediately after impact flooding, they might have at least begun some shoring procedure, especially knowing of the crucial bulkhead's weakness. In an emergency you do not wait to see if your airplane is going to burn or your ship is going to sink. Your survival depends upon first assessing the damage, then visualizing the worst possible scenario and acting upon it immediately. You think first, calmly but quickly, then you move... *NOW.* You do not wait. ***TAHITI***'s engineers did not wait, and probably ***TITANIC***'s engineers did not wait, either. If they relied entirely upon pumps and made no effort to shore that crucial bulkhead, then that was one more link in the chain to disaster, one more dependency upon technology like their dependency upon wireless, when they should have depended upon human intelligence and effort. This would necessarily have been concealed in the coverup, however.

Shortly after ***TITANIC***'s collision with ice Captain Smith dispatched Quartermaster Olliver with a note to Chief Engineer Bell. When Olliver was questioned by Senator Burton about the contents of that note, the quartermaster revealed nothing, unfortunately. He had not read the folded note, as he should not have. But very possibly Captain Smith, in that note, did order Bell to do his best about shoring the damaged bulkhead. It would have been a logical order, although probably unnecessary with Thomas Andrews and his Harland & Wolff men on board. Andrews of all people knew that the crucial bulkhead needed all the help they could give it.

Some theorists have postulated that ***TITANIC*** could have been saved if Chief Bell had simply opened all watertight doors and allowed the water free access to every compartment, thus leveling her off and keeping her from sinking further by the head. While closing watertight doors to her shaft tunnels and flooding them would have been a relatively safe procedure and would have given her some extra weight aft to balance the weight forward, allowing water to run freely into empty compartments of an unstable vessel would seriously affect her metacentric height with disastrous consequences.

Imagine one line drawn through the center of the ship from stem to stern along the line of the keel. Think of this line as representing something like a teeter-totter, which has a board mounted on a center point, or fulcrum, with equal sections of the board on each side of this point. As long as no weight disturbs either end, the board can be balanced, each end is the same distance from the ground, and weighs exactly the same, therefore the board is in a state of *"equilibrium."* But if one child sits on one end of the board, that end tilts quickly downward, bumping the ground. Let another child of exactly equal weight sit on the other end of the board, at exactly the same distance from the fulcrum as the first child, and the board can once more be made to balance. It is again in *equilibrium. Stability* is the power a ship has of righting herself when her equilibrium is disturbed by outside forces, such as a huge wave, shifting cargo, or an inrush of water.

A ship is acted upon by the resultant of two forces: *gravity,* the downward force of her own weight, and *buoyancy,* the upward flotation force of the water she displaces. When these two forces are equal, the ship is in *equilibrium* and she floats, evenly, like the undisturbed teeter totter. The two forces, buoyancy and gravity, may be plotted as acting through two centers, the *Center of Buoyancy,* or *CB,* and the *Center of Gravity,* or *CG.* In a submarine the Center of Gravity lies below the Center of Buoyancy, but in a surface vessel the opposite is true... the *CB* lies below the *CG.* Gravity, of course, acts downward; buoyancy acts upward.

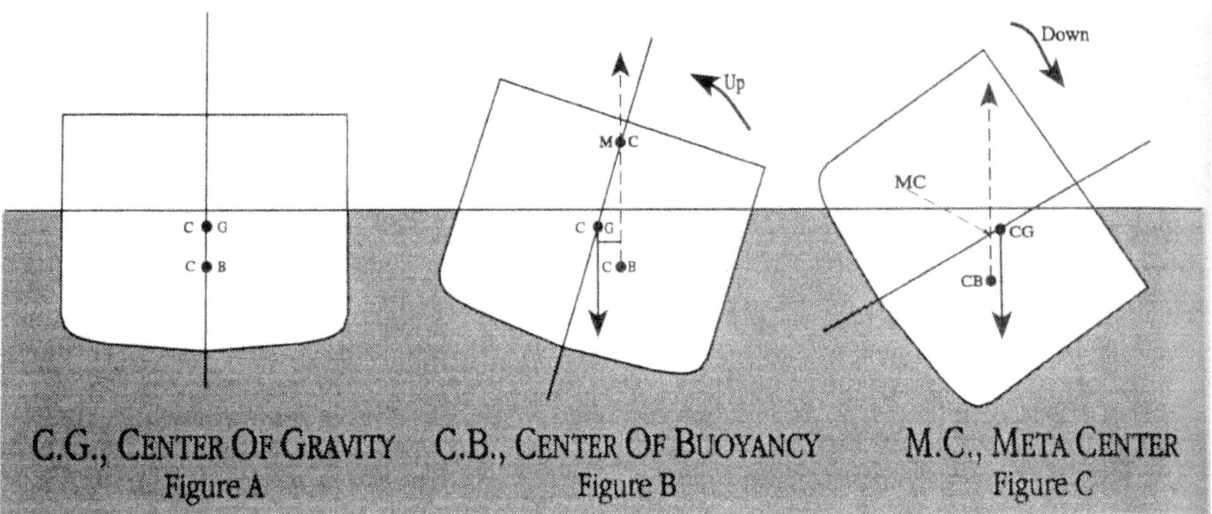

In order for the ship to float in equilibrium the upward force of buoyancy must equal the downward force of gravity; therefore the total buoyancy considered as acting upward through *CB* must uphold the weight of the vessel acting downward through the *CG*. Thus the *CB* and the *CG* lie in a vertical line when the ship is floating at rest on an even keel.

A ship rotates about two axes, her *longitudinal axis,* which runs fore and aft in line with her keel, and her *transverse axis,* which runs athwartships. When she rotates around her longitudinal axis she *heels,* and it is said that her transverse stability has been disturbed. When she rotates about her transverse axis she *pitches,* she is down by head or stern, and her longitudinal stability has been disturbed.

The *CG* is the center of the mass of the vessel, the point at which, if the ship could be suspended from it, she would rest perfectly balanced, because equal weight lies at each side of the point indicated. The *CB* is the center of the submerged portion of the ship, her *underwater body.* As a vessel heels over her *CG* remains the same, but the shape (not the volume) of her underwater body changes, and the *CB* shifts toward her lower side, or end if she is down by the head as ***TITANIC*** was, or by the stern as ***TAHITI*** was. The *Center of Buoyancy* is also known as the *Center of Flotation,*

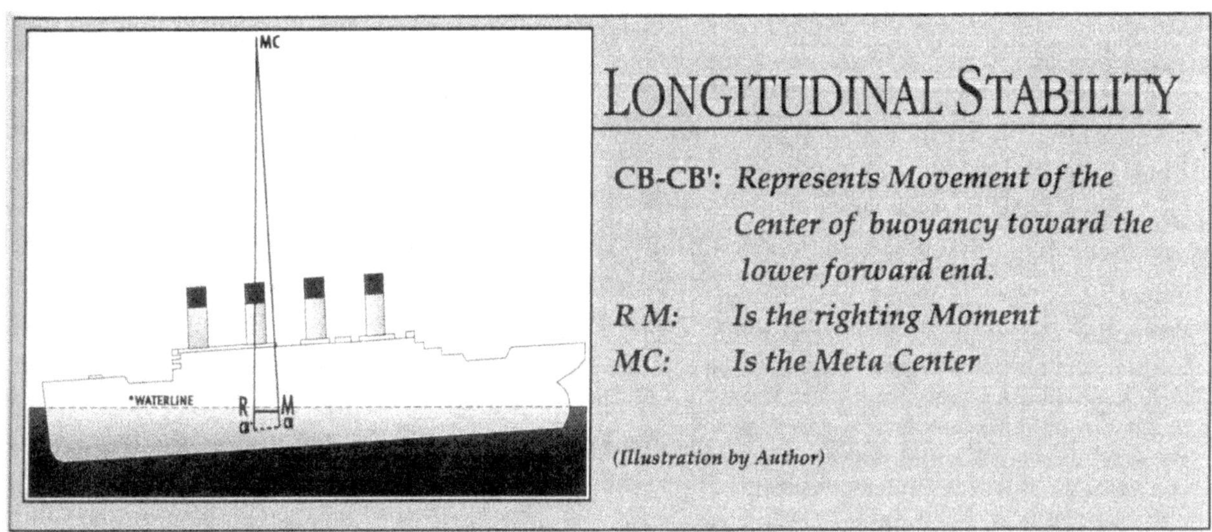

MC
*WATERLINE
R
M
Longitudinal Stability
CB-CB': Represents Movement of the Center of buoyancy toward the lower forward end.
R M: Is the righting Moment
MC: Is the Meta Center

(Illustration by Author)

or *Tipping Center.* The *Moment of Inertia* about the waterplane's axis is the measure of the tendency of the waterplane area to resist motion. The *waterplane* is the plane of an imagined saw cut of the ship severed from her underbody along her waterline. It is therefore the plane of her waterline.

The *metacenter,* or *meta center, MC,* is the point on the center line of the vessel where an imaginary line drawn from the *CB,* passing straight upward, cuts the center line. The meta center is located only when the ship heels to one side or the other from some external force, such as cargo shifting or a great number of passengers moving as one body, water entering, a big wave hitting her, cargo loaded unevenly or fuel either loaded or used unevenly. The *metacentric height* is the distance from *CG* to MC.

The *Moment to Change Trim One Inch,* abbreviated to *inch-trim-moment,* or *I.T.M.,* is the value, in foot-tons, of the moment about the transverse axis passing through the *CG* of the waterplane which will cause a change of one inch in the difference between the forward and after drafts. This would be a half-inch increase in draft at one end of the vessel, and a half-inch decrease in draft at the other end.

The *Righting Moment,* or the buoyant force which tends to restore the vessel's equilibrium and bring her back to an even keel, is the amount of buoyant force acting upward times the horizontal distance between the vertical lines passing through the *CG* and the *CB.* In Figure A we see the vessel on an even keel, floating in equilibrium. In Figure B she has heeled over to starboard (we are looking forward) and the *CB* has shifted to starboard of the *CG.* The two forces, gravity and buoyancy, form a couple and the righting moment is seen. (Edward Wilding testified that ***TITANIC*** would heel about 2 degrees if about 800 people moved 50 feet across her boat deck.) But in Figure C we assume that some external force has caused her to go over so far that the *CB* has passed to port of the *CG,* then the metacenter has passed below the *CG* and the righting moment is gone. The two forces now act as an upsetting couple, and over she goes.

The same calculations apply to a vessel down by head or stern, as in Figure 4, where the line CB – CB^1 represents the shift in the Center of Buoyancy to the down end, and *RM* represents the righting moment. MC is the meta center. Due to the comparatively enormous value of the moment of inertia of the waterplane about the transverse axis, however, there is greater *"stiffness"* when a vessel's longitudinal stability is disturbed than there is if her transverse stability is disturbed. *A stiff* vessel, when the term is applied to her transverse stability, means that she has a comparatively low Center of Gravity and great length of *RM.* She has a short, sharp roll in a seaway, thus is not comfortable to passengers and her cargo may shift easily if not properly secured. The famous CGT liner ***NORMANDIE*** was known for her stiffness. If a vessel is *tender* she has a long, easy roll, the opposite of stiff, her *CG* is comparatively high, her *RM* is short, and if she has not enough freeboard she is in danger of capsizing in heavy seas. (This is what Bill Müller saw in ***WARATAH***). If she has a good freeboard, however, she might have a greater range of stability than a stiff vessel would have. Obviously, the perfect vessel lies somewhere in between these extremes.

THE FINAL PLUNGE

A Likely Scenario

[Since the discovery and exploration of the ***TITANIC*** in the mid-1980's and the expeditions that would follow to retrieve artifacts from the ocean floor, there have been several theories for why the ***TITANIC*** broke in two when she sank. "Researchers" have debated endlessly about whether the ship broke in two at the surface or after she had slipped beneath the waves. Below is a qualified scenario given by an experienced Second Officer, Larry Fosgate.]

"The chances are that as ***TITANIC*** settled by the bow, and the weight of the stern came out of the water, some of her rivets began to pop near the center of gravity, tearing her in two from the gunwale to the keel and across the deck as the weight of the stern came out of the water. The fulcrum of that lever would be at the center of buoyancy and the greatest stress would be at a point where the aft section was not supported by much or any water. Torn metal will snap like the end of a rubber band. Compression fractures will look like the steel was pleated before it broke.

"As for the legend that the falling forward stack floated, stacks are only tack welded. Any shear force at the deck level would unstep a funnel in a microsecond. Stacks, unlike masts are not stepped through the deck below, so when they break they do no great structural damage. Stacks are hollow and bottomless, thus have no buoyance from trapped air and therefore, cannot float.

"After the bow's weight was released from the stern section, the stern section would have settled by its heavier forward end, even though it had more buoyancy. Many stern sections float after the bow breaks off, as the least buoyancy is aft, and they go forward and up, cutting the further flooding enough to stay afloat. Bow sections have done that also when the hull is nearly cut in two 'midships or close to it. The watertight integrity of the transverse bulkheads in the stern section would have been greatly compromised, of course, and she rapidly filled with water through the boiler room, and shaft alley passages, which were not closed in the panic of abandoning ship. The stern would have then settled deeply until the main deck was shipping water, and would have either capsized or plunged beneath the waves at that point. The weight of the entire population still aboard her would have only immersed her about two inches. My guess is that the vastly greater buoyancy of the amount of air still in ***TITANIC***'s stern caused it to separate AFTER it plunged below the surface, and the stern never did resurface, it only rolled and let out a big air bubble.

"As for her being gashed along her whole length, had the berg rubbed solidly down the starboard side, everyone would have heard it, and none would have been so stupid as to try and retrieve a cube for a drink."

—Second Officer Larry Fosgate's scenario on what happened to ***TITANIC*** as she sank.

When ***TITANIC*** struck ice she immediately listed slightly to starboard due to incoming water on the starboard side, which disturbed her transverse stability. But Wilding believed that while the water was contained for sometime on the starboard side forward by a longitudinal nonwatertight bulkhead, when that bulkhead failed and the water gained free access to corresponding space on her port side, then ***TITANIC*** began to list to port. As we have seen however, the probable cause of ***TITANIC***'s initial list to starboard was the fact that water was for a while contained in the starboard side of the two forward bunkers. The important factor here is that ***TITANIC*** could have righted herself as far as her transverse stability was concerned.

All of the above figures are calculated and provided by the shipbuilder in the form of a stability curve chart. Theoretically all deck and engineering officers should know their ships' stability curves.

In practice, however, that often was not the case. Master Mariner Felix Reisenberg tells an amusing anecdote in his *"Standard Seamanship for the Merchant Service."* A certain shipmaster, when handed the stability curve chart for his vessel, asked, *"What am I to do with this?"* The enlightening reply was, *"I don't know, but be sure to receipt for it!"* In practice experience generated the common judgement necessary to properly distribute cargo weights so that a given ship maintained her ability to right herself. When green water poured over the weather rail and fore deck, figures were not so important as feel for the ship, and that came only from experience.

ABOVE: *Thomas Andrews, Harland & Wolff naval architect, designer of the* ***OLYMPIC*** *class ships.*

In ***TITANIC,*** Thomas Andrews must have had the figures in his head, and he would have had a feel for the ship he designed. He knew how many tons of water had disturbed ***TITANIC***'s equilibrium at impact. A quick diagram sketched out, some figures jotted down, and Andrews knew about when ***TITANIC***'s righting moment would turn into an upsetting couple, *after* the crucial bulkhead failed and No. 5 boiler room flooded.

The one thing that might have been done, should have been done, to prolong ***TITANIC***'s life was exactly what ***TAHITI***'s engineers had done. Andrews and Chief Engineer Joseph Bell could have collaborated on shoring the damaged, exposed bulkhead, with whatever materials they could find. It is known, in spite of legend to the contrary, that Andrews did go below immediately after the collision. He was the one man aboard who knew how to save ***TITANIC,*** or how to prolong her life if saving it was impossible, and he went where his expertise was needed. Andrews, his men from Harland & Wolff, and every engineering officer knew immediately that they had to move very quickly, and surely they did because that is what marine engineers do.

When the skin of a ship is ruptured and internal flooding results, the hydrostatic pressures which had been exerted on the shell plating are transferred to bulkheads of the flooded compartments. Because there is considerable upward pressure on the overhead deck of the flooded compartment, attention should be directed to shoring it downward. There is no direct evidence that ***TITANIC***'s engineers considered this, but there also is no evidence that they did not. Probably, however, this was something that engineering officers of ***TITANIC***'s day simply did not know, although Andrews might have known it. Much of what seamen and marine engineers would later know about sinking ships came from war experience, when they had ample opportunity to observe all too many foundering vessels.

Because a bulkhead, its supporting frames and their connection to the hull plating form a sort of spring, the whole structure will move with the varied pressure from the sea. Therefore the

***ABOVE:** The **TITANIC** at night as it might have been on April 13 or even April 14. Captain Smith, J. Bruce Ismay, and Thomas Andrews can be seen just to the left of center walking toward the viewer. (Artwork by James A. Flood.)*

pressure on shoring will increase and decrease, ever changing, ever forcing the shoring away from the bulkhead. The shoring, which is only a support system, is never quite complete. It must always be watched, checked, reinforced, as ***TAHITI***'s engineers did. Shoring will not, nor is it intended to, return the stretched bulkhead plating to its original shape. In fact, excessive shoring pressure may cause the bulkhead to rupture. Props must be placed against the side tightly enough to prevent sagging, not tight enough to exert undue force. If the ratio of length to thickness of the shoring material is greater than 30 to 1, the shore will buckle, and may break. Therefore if a 4 inch by 4 inch support is used, it must be 10 feet long. A 6 inch by 6 inch shore must be 15 ft. long. Experience taught this. In ***TITANIC***, however, as in any coal-burning vessel with transverse bunkers, the bunker bulkheads themselves were placed in such close proximity to the watertight bulkheads that shoring would have been difficult, if not impossible, simply because there was not enough room. Shoring must be spread out to take up pressure over a wide area, not just at one or two points. Shores must form a considerable angle with the bulkhead, and the usual method is triangulation. Because there is obviously danger that the shored bulkhead may carry away, the next bulkhead aft or forward of the crucial bulkhead, as the case may be, should also be shored as quickly as possible. If the shore begins to bend, or bow, it may break at any moment. The bunker bulkhead was only 9 ft. from the watertight bulkhead that needed shoring. Bunkers No. 9 and No. 10 were empty, but those farther aft were not, thus although they had some shoring support from the coal there was no room to do anything else to support them. ***TAHITI*** was oil-powered, therefore her engineers had more room to work.

The point to all this is that when your ship is sinking in mid-ocean and help is not at hand, you do not stand around and say, *"ah, yes, the ship is sinking and I am going to die,"* as ***TITANIC*** legend romantics would have us believe. In a passenger ship it is the engineers' duty to fight for the vessel's survival while the deck officers evacuate passengers. The engineers do everything they can to keep the ship afloat until help does come. In the days of hand-pumping passengers joined crewmen at the pumps, as in ***ARCTIC*** and ***VEENDAM*** for example. False romanticism in her legend has it that ***TITANIC***'s people did not fight at all. They remained calm, it is said, and waited to die. It is more likely, however, that just as we saw in the ***ARCTIC*** disaster, it was expedient for those who had lost loved ones to believe that they had died calmly, happily resigned to a peaceful death.

There was one more very important reason for concealing the fact that a coal-fire-weakened bulkhead had led to ***TITANIC***'s rapid demise. Strange as it may seem, that reason was OIL.

Oil for Progress, Profit and Power

Oil had been known as an illuminant from the earliest times. Primitive humans quickly discovered that the curious, tarry substance bubbling up from the ground, filming the surface of pools and streams somewhere on every continent, would ignite easily. They soon learned to make simple torches that were soaked in the thick, smelly stuff, and found that these torches burned brightly for long periods.

In the eastern part of the United States, particularly the states of Pennsylvania, Ohio, Kentucky and West Virginia, oil was a nuisance that interfered with the commercial value of salt wells, until in the 1840s one Samuel M. Kier, who operated salt wells at Tarentum, a village in Alleghany County, Pennsylvania, decided to turn the nuisance oil into profit. Kier skimmed the oil off the top of his wells, bottled it and sold it in 8-ounce quantities for medicinal purposes under the unimaginative name of *"Kier's Petroleum, or Rock Oil."* "Rock Oil" was used primarily as a liniment, but taken internally, three teaspoonfuls three times a day, it was touted as a cure for everything from liver disease to consumption.

Kier believed that his rock oil should have other uses. It was known to be an illuminant, and had been used in a crude way for lubrication as well, but it contained too many impurities. Kier was astute enough to send a sample of his rock oil to a chemist in Philadelphia, who advised that the oil might be distilled and then burned in lamps. Kier's first batch of lamp oil was "refined" in a five-barrel still, and sold for 62 1/2 cents a gallon to be burned in ordinary coal-oil lamps.

It was soon obvious that oil could be obtained in large quantities only by drilling into the ground for it. The drilling of the first successful Pennsylvania oil well was supervised by "Colonel" Edwin L. Drake, a former railroad conductor, who completed the project derisively called "Drake's Folly" on 1 February, 1860. Although it produced a scant 25 barrels a day, which sold for $18 a barrel, the American oil boom had begun.

Anybody who could come up with a bit of cash bought oil rights, drilled, and distilled the crude, often with disastrous results. But money was to be made and the dangers of handling the flammable stuff were ignored. Often the new "kerosene" produced by the many trailblazing, wildcatting oil entrepreneurs in their primitive stills was of poor quality and dangerous to use in the home. Rivalry was intense and money was the name of the game. Fortunes were made quickly, and just as quickly lost when over-production dried up oil fields in one locality, while those who salvaged a little of their capital moved into new drilling areas.

Cleveland, Ohio, the Great Lakes seaport which was also a great railroad terminus, quickly became the refining center of the new American oil industry.

John Davison Rockefeller was thirteen years old when his family moved to Cleveland from a farm in central New York State, where the boy had been born on 8 July, 1839. Industrious, thrifty, astute, and practical, young John found a job as a clerk and bookkeeper, where he earned $50 in three months. In 1857 John D. Rockefeller was first listed in Cleveland's city directory as a bookkeeper. The following year Rockefeller and his new friend, Englishman M. B. Clark, pooled their money and entered the produce business. In 1862 Clark and Rockefeller invested $4,000 in a new oil refinery built by another Englishman, Samuel Andrews, who had devised new and better methods for refining crude. Within three years oil refining was one of Cleveland's biggest industries, and Rockefeller was on the way to establishing his new empire, the great Standard Oil trust.

But oil's use was still limited to illumination and lubrication. Its medicinal use was already waning, and something had to be found to profitably use all of the crude that was being discovered in so many parts of the world. Electricity was rapidly taking over illumination technology, thanks to Nikola Tesla's new alternating current.

The salvation, and the real beginning of oil's power came along in the form of the gasoline-powered internal combustion engine, used commercially toward the end of the nineteenth century to power the new "horseless carriages." In 1903 gasoline and lubricants for the engine that powered the Wright Brothers' first airplane flight at Kitty Hawk, North Carolina, were delivered by Standard Oil salesmen.

Rudolph Diesel was born in Paris of German parents in 1858. He patented his "Diesel" engine in 1892, and in 1893 he published his *"Theory and Construction of a Rational Heat Engine."* The gasoline-powered internal combustion engine had never been a practical means of propelling ships and gasoline was far more volatile than the fuel that Rudolph Diesel used. In fact, the first Diesel engine was designed to run on coal dust. The Diesel engine was heavier than gasoline-driven engines, but lighter than steam engines, and its heavy-oil fuel had a lower flash point than gasoline. The Diesel's fuel ignition was accomplished by the rapid compression of air in its cylinders to about 500 pounds per square inch, which raised the temperature to incandescence, thus igniting the fuel which was injected into the cylinder in a fine spray at the top of the compression stroke. The gasoline-powered engine depended upon electrical spark for ignition, a spark which could become dangerous when used in confined spaces such as submarines, or near the lifting hydrogen used in Germany's great airships, the turn-of the-century invention of Graf Ferdinand von Zeppelin.

The Diesel engine's possibilities for marine propulsion were immediately recognized. In Copenhagen a young engineer named Ivar Knudsen became so enthusiastic over Diesel's invention that he persuaded the firm of Burmeister and Wain to hire him to investigate the new engine. Knudsen went to the Krupp works in Essen and the Maschinenfabrick at Augsburg, where experimental Diesel engines were being built and tried. Knudsen's glowing reports of the new type engine caused Burmeister and Wain to appoint him a sub-director with the power to negotiate a contract with Rudolf Diesel for manufacturing rights to his engine. On 10 December, 1897, the contract was signed in Munich by Rudolph Diesel. On behalf of Burmeister and Wain, Knudsen and Knud Nielsen signed in Copenhagen on 28 January, 1898. That same year successful oil-fueled Diesel engines were exhibited at the Munich Exposition. By 1904 the Diesel had proven its reliability as a stationary engine, and its fuel consumption was far lower than that of any known type of heat engine.

In 1903 the small Caspian Sea freighter ***WANDAL*** was fitted with Diesel-electric drive, the engine being connected to a generator which furnished current to a motor on the propeller shaft. In 1906 the Lake Geneva freight barge ***VENOGE*** was equipped with a reversible Diesel engine. In 1910 the Dutch brought out their seagoing tanker ***VULCANUS***, of 2,080 tons displacement, fitted with a 480 horsepower Werkspoor Diesel which drove her at a seaspeed of 6 knots.

In the autumn of 1911 the first long-range motorship was launched, for the East Asiatic Company. She was ***SELANDIA***, a Burmeister and Wain Diesel-powered freighter of 4,950 GRT. ***SELANDIA*** had an overall length of 370 ft., a beam of 53 ft., and twin screws, each driven by a vertical single acting four cycle Diesel having eight cylinders and delivering 1,250 horsepower at 140 revolutions per minute, giving ***SELANDIA*** a respectable seaspeed of 11 knots. ***SELANDIA*** departed on her maiden voyage on 22 February, 1912, from Copenhagen, bound for Bangkok via London and Antwerp.

At London ***SELANDIA*** attracted much attention when she was visited and carefully inspected by Winston Churchill and other Royal Navy officials. Here was, for the first time, a vessel which could run 26,000 nautical miles without refueling, with an engine room force of only 8 men, compared to the 25 which were needed in a coal-burning vessel of comparable size and speed.

This efficiency and economy were not lost on Churchill and other Admiralty officials. In the summer of the same year ***SELANDIA***'s new intended running mate, ***FIONIA***, visited Kiel while on her shakedown cruise. The German Kaiser inspected ***FIONIA*** as Churchill had inspected ***SELANDIA***. ***FIONIA*** was accordingly, and immediately, purchased by the Hamburg-South American Line, and renamed ***CHRISTIAN X*** in honor of the Danish king. In 1936 ***SELANDIA*** was still running with her original machinery having traversed her 22,000 mile route a total of 55 times in 25 years. During all of this time she had spent only ten days in port for machinery repairs, a truly remarkable record. If ***TITANIC*** had not foundered on her maiden voyage, the ship which would be remembered for her maiden voyage in 1912 would be the innovative ***SELANDIA***, for she began a new era in marine propulsion.

The following year, 1913, Rudolph Diesel was tragically and mysteriously lost off the Antwerp-Harwich mail steamer sometime during the night of September 30th. Legend has it that he was bringing to England plans for equipping British submarines with his engines. Diesel's biographers are divided over the possibility of suicide or foul play causing his untimely death.

Churchill had been greatly impressed by the new motorships, although it was soon to become obvious that the Diesel engines could never develop the power of steam engines, with the speeds attained by the Parsons turbines. Speed, of course, was the top priority for warships no matter what the cost. Merchant vessels necessarily reach a point where they must sacrifice speed for profit.

In the United States, Germany and Japan, as well as in England, warships had been built which could utilize both coal and oil for steam power. But they lacked the efficiency of pure oil fueling. Churchill knew of the German experiments with oil-firing steam turbines, and after inspecting ***SELANDIA*** on her maiden voyage he knew that future marine propulsion lay with oil, and oil only. Joined by Admiral Fisher, Churchill tried to convince naval authorities and Parliament to equip the new British dreadnoughts with oil-fired steam turbines, as the Germans were doing. But the British were wary of a fuel supply which depended upon foreign countries during war time, when good Welsh coal was plentiful at home. In addition, the mine owners, the miners' unions, and the seamen's unions lobbied against oil power, for they saw a bleak future with so many of their members jobless because of ships which required no stokers, firemen or trimmers, and fewer engineers.

Until the Agadir crisis in June, 1911, Churchill, unlike Fisher, had honestly believed that war with Germany was not inevitable. Churchill preferred to spend money on social reforms rather than preparation for war. When the Germans sent their warships to Agadir, however, with the gunboat ***PANTHER*** carrying a complete Telefunken wireless station in her hold, Churchill joined Admiral Fisher in his conviction that Germany planned to expand commercially, threatening England's colonial enterprises, thus Britain's supremacy at sea. A German naval squadron based at Agadir, a port on the northwest coast of Africa, could have been a serious threat to Britain's supply lines to all of her colonies except Canada, and Germany had already acquired the necessary North Sea bases from which to harass British shipping on the North Atlantic. British merchant ships bound for Gibralter and the Mediterranean, to Egypt and the Suez, for Britain's Caribbean, Central and South American colonies, for Australia, New Zealand, India, Burma, Hong Kong, Singapore, South Africa and those ever important Falkland Islands which guarded both Cape routes, would necessarily come within easy range of German warships based at Agadir, warships whose range would be greatly extended by oil fueling their steam turbines and/or equipping them with Diesels. British merchantmen would need naval escorts, cutting deeply into the number of Royal Navy vessels needed to guard Britain's long coastline, requiring heavy expenditures for laying down new warships. Churchill saw this and he knew at once that the German threat to Britain was very real.

If war was inevitable, then Britain needed to keep pace with the newest in warship technology, and that was oil-firing. Still, British naval authorities and politicians vacillated and risked the loss of Britain's tactical advantage at sea.

Toward the end of the nineteenth century oil was used experimentally to enhance the fires which produced steam in marine boilers. Spraying jets of oil on burning coal was found to make coal burn better and hotter, thus driving marine engines to new efficiency and power.

As early as 1907 John D. Rockefeller's great Standard Oil Company had begun fitting its tankers for liquid fuel. Not surprising, for it was logical that the world's leading oil company would pave the way for more efficient fueling of ships, while acquiring a vast new market for its product. Among the first to be converted to liquid fuel were several DAPG tankers. The Standard quickly convinced the Kaiser and German naval authorities of the practicality of oil-firing in warships. Aside from the obvious advantage of eliminating about three fourths of the engine room staff, there was the tactical advantage of easier refueling at sea, for oil could flow quickly through a hose while coal had to be hoisted in bags from the collier to the warship, a laborious and time-consuming practice which made naval vessels sitting ducks to the enemy while being coaled.

Oil had another major tactical advantage in its smokeless burning. Black coal smoke belching from the stacks of maneuvering warships was a dead giveaway of their position, even when the ships themselves were hidden over the horizon. In a well-managed, well maintained vessel, oil burns virtually without smoke, making it a better fuel for warships than even the good clean-burning Welsh coal on which the British relied. Oil also burns hotter, has more thermal efficiency, thus giving more steam pressure, thus more speed. And when dreadnoughts slugged it out in a free-for-all sea battle oil, flowing through pipes, could keep up speed for maneuvering when stokers might be killed by direct hits from gunfire or torpedoes, thus reducing the ships' speed and safety factor.

Germany had no oil reserves of its own, but it had the Standard subsidiary with its huge refinery at Hamburg. British Intelligence kept a sharp eye on German shipbuilding. In 1909 the Germans laid down the battleship ***KAISER***, the first of her class, at Kiel's Imperial Dockyard. She was completed and delivered in 1912, as was the ***FRIEDRICH DER GROSSE***, laid down at AG

Vulcan, Hamburg, in 1910. Also laid down in 1910, and delivered in 1913 were the remainder of the ***KAISER*** class dreadnought-type warships, ***KAISERIN*** at the Howaldtswerke, Kiel, ***KONIG ALBERT*** by F. Schichau of Danzig, and ***PRINZREGENT LUITPOLD***, from the Germania Dockyard at Kiel. ***KAISER*** and ***KAISERIN*** were each powered by three sets of Parsons turbines driving three 3-bladed screws, driven partly by oil-firing. ***FRIEDRICH DER GROSSE*** was driven by three sets of AEG Curtis turbines; ***KONIG ALBERT*** by three sets of Schichau turbines. Both of these vessels were equipped with supplementary oil-firing and three 3-bladed screws. ***PRINZREGENT LUITPOLD*** was powered by two sets of Parsons turbines driving two 3-bladed screws, fitted for supplementary oil firing. Original plans had provided for the last of the class to have one Germania 6-cylinder 2-stroke Diesel engine, but such a large Diesel was not yet ready for operational use and was not installed at that time. ***KAISER*** was the fastest of her class, with a maximum speed of 23.4 knots at 270 rpm.

John Arbuthnot "Jacky" Fisher, in spite of his lack of aristocratic antecedents, had become Britain's First Sea Lord in 1904 after his rapid rise and brilliant career as a line officer in the Royal Navy. As early as 1901 he had written that oil fuel would revolutionize naval strategy. Speed, declared Fisher, was the first of all necessities in naval warfare. Speed allowed commanders to fight when, where and how they liked. And oil produced superior speed in ships, especially when combined with Parsons' new turbines.

In 1903 Fisher happened to meet William Knox D'Arcy at Marienbad. Born in Devon, England, in 1849, D'Arcy had emigrated to Australia where he had become a solicitor and entrepreneur known for taking chances, one of which was organizing a syndicate to put an allegedly played out gold mine back into operation. It turned out that D'Arcy was right, the mine was still productive, in fact more so than even he had expected. D'Arcy accordingly returned to England a very wealthy man. He maintained two estates in the country and entertained lavishly while he continued to organize syndicates to exploit new investments. It was D'Arcy who founded the Middle Eastern oil industry.

Many years earlier Fisher had been cured of chronic dysentery at the famous spa, and he had been a frequent visitor ever since. Fisher had just been disappointed in the first test of oil fuel in the ***HMS HANNIBAL***. She had departed Portsmouth powered by clean-burning Welsh coal. When she had been switched over to oil fuel in what was to be a dramatic proof of the liquid fuel's superiority, ***HANNIBAL***'s stacks had suddenly emitted a cloud of thick, black smoke, embarrassing Fisher as well as Marcus Samuel, designer of the first bulk tanker, and founder of Rockefeller's biggest rival, Shell Oil Company, which was based primarily upon rich oil deposits in the Far East. Marcus was the one who had promoted the ***HANNIBAL*** demonstration.

It was thus a very depressed and discouraged Fisher who had set off for Marienbad, and a very optimistic, enthusiastic admiral who returned to his beloved England after the chance meeting with D'Arcy, who had just invested heavily in Persian oil. It was a fated meeting destined to save England in more ways than one.

By the time ***OLYMPIC***'s keel was laid oil had been used in smaller warships, in destroyers and of course in submarines and torpedo boats for several years. In fact, oil-firing had been suggested to Ismay for the pretty triplets. But taking the oil plunge so quickly, so grandly, was not something that Ismay was prepared to do. Perhaps, if the War had not come along, if other things had not happened, Ismay would have oil-fired ***BRITANNIC*** from the beginning, using lessons learned from ***TITANIC***'s demise. Again, however, it was a matter of economics. Civilian marine engineers who understood turbines were still few and far between. Engineers familiar with oil-firing large marine steam engines were nonexistent outside the Royal Navy, and few enough there. By the same token firemen and trimmers were experienced and cheap, but support crews for oil-fired steam engines were as nonexistent as marine engineers with oil experience. Many German engineers already had oil experience, but in Diesels. Early German submarines, from the U-1 which entered service in September, 1906, to be used mainly as a research and training vessel, through U-18, were driven on the surface by gasoline engines. Beginning with the U-19 all subsequent German submarines were powered on the surface by Diesels.

The Germans were relying upon their *Unterseeboots* for offense, while the British still saw the silent, underwater warfare as "unsporting." The British relied on their "dreadnoughts," which carried powerful new guns capable of firing fifteen inch shells. But the great battleships needed more speed... speed which First Lord of the Admiralty Winston Churchill and former First Sea Lord "Jacky" Fisher knew could come only from oil fuel. The United States Navy already had its oil-fueled ***OKLAHOMA*** class battleships, laid down in 1911, but the United States had plenty of oil, with the huge Standard trust to push hard for progress.

While Fisher had resigned and been replaced as First Sea Lord by Sir Arthur Wilson in January, 1910, he still had tremendous influence on the Royal Navy through his many proteges and friends, one of whom was Churchill. Needing advice, enthusiasm, moral support and facts for his arguments, Churchill wrote to Fisher. He needed his old friend, said Churchill, because no one else could solve the problem of liquid fuel for the Royal Navy. Fisher still belonged to the Navy, Churchill wrote beseechingly. He must jump back into the fray because his beloved Navy needed him. And jump Fisher did.

At Churchill's request Fisher headed a Royal Commission on Oil Supply. Britain had two major problems with liquid fuel. First, there was no known oil in the British Isles. For oil Britain was dependent upon foreign supplies, and while much of it came from her colonies, its transport was still a major consideration in wartime. As Fisher knew, and Churchill had finally learned, war with Germany was not only inevitable, it was imminent. Second, there was a seemingly inexhaustible supply of good, clean-burning Welsh coal. Mine owners and miners' unions fought to save jobs, while in the big liners seamen's unions fought to save thousands of jobs which would be eliminated with oil-firing in merchant ships. Yet the British Empire was entirely dependent upon not only Britain's naval supremacy but upon the superiority of her mercantile marine as well if Britannia would continue to rule the waves. For her industry Britain needed all kinds of raw materials which must come from the colonies. After the raw material was turned into manufactured goods it must be shipped to buyers around the world. But British bottoms needed to carry more than Britain's needs, they must carry foreign goods as well, and that included human cargo... passengers. Passengers demanded speed and what they imagined as safety. And oil would, in the public mind, be equated with safety if ***TITANIC***'s coal fire had been made publicly known as a major cause of her rapid demise. The general traveling public would not understand that oil, too, had its flammability problems for that is the nature of fuels. Oil, however, requires less bunker space than coal for a given steaming range, thus more cargo, human or otherwise, could be carried in one vessel. Oil can be carried in double bottoms, in places where coal or cargo will not fit. As noted earlier, bunkering with oil is not only cleaner than coal, it is faster, more efficient, thus cutting a liner's turnaround time. No extra labor was needed simply for handling ashes, for trimming or stoking. Oil possesses greater thermal efficiency than coal, thus greatly reducing fuel costs. But, argued the politicians, particularly those of the Labor party, the Socialists, the Liberals, so many jobs would be lost that the country's economy would for sometime take a tremendous downturn at a time when the industrial revolution had already put too many people into the streets to live. One solution to that problem, of course, was war. And warships needed oil despite the cost of changeover. So it was back full circle. Technology, like social reform, has a way of progressing whether it seems comfortable at the time or not.

Fisher's Commission quickly evaluated the situation, and recommended that the advantages of oil fueling Royal Navy ships of the line so far out-weighed any disadvantage in logistics that facilities for storing a four-year supply of oil must be built, and the oil must be acquired in time to thwart German attempts to meet the Royal Navy in combat. Parliament authorized £10 million for building storage tanks, while Churchill sent experts to the Persian Gulf to estimate the supply of oil in that region. An additional £2.2 million was authorized to acquire controlling interest in the Anglo-Persian Oil Company, assuring that its oil would be British. At the outbreak of war in 1914 Fisher in fact returned as First Sea Lord and the first order he gave was to refit warships then building for oil-firing. Germany, too, needed a stockpile of oil, even more than Britain would need.

But, in April, 1912, ***TITANIC*** gave Churchill and Fisher an argument that they needed to expedite the Navy's conversion to oil. If the War had not intervened, Britain's prestigious express mailboats, too, would have been converted to oil firing very quickly. The Germans had been first to install wireless equipment in a liner, in their Blue Riband winner ***KAISER WILHELM DER GROSSE*** in 1900, an accomplishment not dimmed in the public mind by its being a British, Marconi, installation, with a British operator. Nor did the public care that its range allowed little more than 50 miles advance notice of arrival time, that there were no other ships and few shore stations to relay paid "Marconigrams." It was the thought that counted and Britain, after all, had Marconi, and Britain must not just keep up, Britain must lead. Germania must not beat Britannia at oil firing.

At all costs, then, the fact that ***TITANIC***'s *coal* fire had contributed to her high casualty count had to be concealed. Every naval architect who participated in or monitored the ***TITANIC*** inquiries must have seen at once that coal was the cause of her early demise and thus her high casualty count for more reasons than one. The giant liners needed so much coal to keep up their speed that 'thwartships bunkers were mandatory, and so therefore were transverse watertight bulkheads. It was cheaper, easier to build and work transverse bunkers without longitudinal subdivision. Watertight doors inside bunker spaces were impractical, thus Harland & Wolff, and other builders, solved that problem with the watertight bulkheads stepped aft to accommodate the doors. But coal had to be continuously wheeled from bunker to stokehold, thus the watertight doors must always be open when the ship was at sea. With the advent of oil firing ships could run through fog and ice zones with the added safety factor of closed watertight doors and engines at "maneuvering combinations" to allow for quick maneuvering if necessary. It was a lot easier, thus faster, to shut off the flow of oil to furnaces than to extinguish the coal fire in a furnace when water poured in. And, as in the case of the oil-fired ***TAHITI***, with no encumbering coal bunkers a crucial watertight bulkhead could be shored, supported if necessary after a collision. There were many advantages to oil over coal, and they were all pointed out to those astute enough to see them, by ***TITANIC***. The Germans, who had been first with range lights and wireless telegraphy at sea, were already turning to oil-powered cargo and passenger vessels. The Lloyd and Hapag, constant threats to Britain's recently recaptured Blue Riband, needed only well-written, well-placed advertisements stressing the safety of oil-propelled ships and passenger traffic would leave British liners, flocking to their German competitors, for Hapag and the Lloyd could quickly convert to oil firing with this added incentive.

It should be no surprise, then, that so many tankers were plying the North Atlantic on the night ***TITANIC*** sank, carrying American crude to Germany. There were therefore many important men on both sides of the Atlantic who preferred not to let that information go public.

With yet another reason to divert public attention from the real causes of ***TITANIC***'s great loss of life, ***CALIFORNIAN***'s master, Captain Stanley Lord, and the Board of Trade's scanty lifeboat requirements were handy scapegoats. Blame the whole tragedy on ***CALIFORNIAN*** and the Board of Trade and get it over with. The less said, the better.

Chapter Eleven

Lower Away!

For over eight decades a debate has raged within the ***TITANIC*** community about why many of ***TITANIC***'s lifeboats were lowered away with so few occupants. Like many other questions asked about ***TITANIC***, the answer to this one is so obvious that it is a wonder the question was ever asked in the first place.

To begin with we will return to aviation analogies because most if not all of my readers have seen at least once on television newscasts the dramatic moment when an airliner touches down safely... without wheels. A gear-up landing is usually a "planned" emergency, that is the crew knows the problem in advance of the emergency landing, the airport crash crew has been notified, they are in place and have layered the runway with foam to prevent fire. A jet aircraft is relatively easy to land on its belly because there are no propellers to strike the concrete first. Sometimes, however, the gear problem is asymmetrical. Perhaps only the nose wheel deploys, possibly only the main gear, or part of the main gear comes down and locks in place. Then extremely skillful hand-flying is called for and in our age of increasing automation that skill is waning rapidly with each new generation of pilots and automated aircraft systems. What the television cameras show is a shot of the aircraft touching down, usually after sometime has been devoted to trying to get the gear down, dumping or burning off fuel and preparing the cabin for an emergency landing and evacuation. The captain lands the aircraft as gently as possible, it slides along the runway until it comes to a stop. While it is sliding, however, metal is rubbing against concrete in spite of the layer of foam, generating sparks which can ignite fuel spilled from broken lines or tanks. During the slide it also kicks up a tremendous amount of dust which enters the cabin and obscures vision. No wheels means no steering and thus no braking action, thus the aircraft will usually slide off the runway into the grass, which is quickly torn up, throwing more obscuring dust or mud. In fact, in any crash and many emergency landings one of the major evacuation problems will be that passengers and crew alike cannot see and must feel their way out of the aircraft. Flight attendants train for evacuations by wearing smoked goggles to simulate a cabin filled with smoke and/or dust and debris. Watching your television screen safely at home you note that as the airplane finally skids to a stop the evacuation slides immediately pop out of every door exit, excepting those which have been damaged by impact. I have already mentioned the ninety second evacuation time limit. Again the reason for this should be obvious, and it is the same reason ***TITANIC***'s earliest boats got away less than half full. Inside the aluminum tube that is an airliner's fuselage you cannot see what is going on outside. You do not know if fuel has spilled, you do not know whether the airplane will explode into flame at any moment. But you assume that it will. If it does not, you have lost nothing, but if it does, you have saved your life because you got away from it quickly. When the flames erupt it may be too late, and in fact, it will be too late for many.

When a ship sinks and you are on her boat deck you do not know what is going on below, where the water is coming in or how fast it is coming in. Once the master has ascertained that she will founder, and the abandon-ship order has been given, you may hope that she will not go down too quickly; but because you do not know at what moment she will take her final plunge, you do not wait to find out because when she goes it is too late. In any emergency evacuation time is of the essence. In an aircraft accident you immediately deploy your evacuation slides, which become rafts if the landing is on water, and in a ship you deploy your lifeboats, but both are done with the

assumption that you have no time to lose. We have learned a lot since ***TITANIC***'s loss about emergency evacuations, but even ***TITANIC***'s crew, who had no formal evacuation training as airline crews have it today, knew that they had no time to lose. The only difference in evacuating an airplane and a ship is size, and therefore time and number of people involved. Passengers are always reluctant to leave something they know for something they do not know. One of the greatest hazards in evacuating an aircraft is that passengers often do not quickly comprehend the danger of the situation, unless they see flames of course. They inevitably try to take their personal belongings with them. The fewer possessions they have in life the harder they will try to bring them along, as ***TITANIC***'s steerage passengers did while First Class passengers did not. Flight attendants are taught to forestall this instinctive behavior by firm commands and force if necessary. You do not have time to be polite. It is better to offend someone then to let him, or her, burn to death, along with the people trapped behind that person. ***TITANIC***'s crewmen instinctively knew all this. When your job is to deal with passengers you have to know it. This is why women and children were literally thrown into lifeboats when they balked. Lifeboats that went down with the ship still hanging in their davits were of no use to anyone. Boats floating in the water could be of use to those agile enough to climb into them. It had become survival of the fittest, ***TITANIC***'s officers were forced to play God, and well they knew it. Fortunately for those who did survive, ***TITANIC***'s master and senior officers were up to it, as any mailboat officers would have been, or they should not have been on the bridge of an elite transatlantic liner.

TITANIC's officers also knew that there were not enough boats for everyone. Murdoch ordered everything that would float, doors, chests of drawers, deck chairs, over the side to be used as makeshift rafts for those who found themselves struggling in the water. In the first minutes of evacuation, when passengers still groggy with sleep did not comprehend the situation and refused to get into the lifeboats loading at the rails, it was better to get those boats safely away from the ship than to lose their refuge altogether. As even passengers began to understand that the boats were their only hope of survival, and as more passengers from Second and Third Class found their way on to the boat deck, it became easier to persuade passengers to enter the boats and they were filled to capacity before lowering. Although ***TITANIC***'s officers testified that they did not know the boats could be loaded to capacity at the rail because they were afraid the boats might sag in the middle or break the falls, and they testified that they had not realized at first that she was going to founder, they were covering up the fact that they, at least the senior officers, knew full well the urgency of the situation. It is likely that the senior officers understood the urgency because they knew of the weakened bulkhead. When that bulkhead failed, ***TITANIC*** was doomed, but nobody knew just how long it would take that bulkhead to fail.

Despite their unprecedented size ***OLYMPIC*** and ***TITANIC*** each carried only fourteen full-sized lifeboats under davits. Their other two boats under davits were the smaller cutters, or emergency boats, which on every ship afloat were and are carried swung out and ready for instant lowering to rescue anyone who falls overboard. Lifeboat capacity is usually figured in cubic feet, but translated into human capacity ***TITANIC***'s full-sized lifeboats should have carried from 60 to 65 people, probably more if many were children or women. Both ***OLYMPIC*** and ***TITANIC*** carried the same boat capacity, which actually exceeded the Board of Trade regulations, the excess being four Engelhardt "collapsible" boats, with pontoon bottoms and canvas sides. These four were carried lashed to the top of the deckhouse which contained the officers' quarters, wireless cabin, chartroom and wheelhouse. They should have each carried about 40 to 45 people, again depending upon how many were women and children, in relative safety provided the sea remained calm. In heavy seas they were, however, virtually useless, being not much more than rafts. Two of these Engelhardts were nested on each side of the forward funnel, inboard of the emergency boats. The Engelhardts had to be lowered after the emergency boats were away for they used the same davits, making them difficult to launch at best. They had to be uncovered, then literally manhandled into position, one at a time, then attached to the falls before they could be made ready for loading at the rail. Considering these factors it is miraculous, and owing entirely to the superb seamanship and courage of ***TITANIC***'s officers and crewmen that the Engelhardts did save so many people. The last of the Engelhardts floated off, inverted, as ***TITANIC*** went down.

By the time World War I was over it had become obvious that rafts could prove very useful on ocean-going vessels, including the elite liners, but only for temporary refuge and only under certain conditions. The problem with rafts was simply that people could not be put aboard them before the rafts went into the water. Rafts are jettisoned, or tossed overboard, and the current may carry them some distance from the ship, away from the passengers who need them for refuge. People with properly adjusted life vests could then jump after the raft, but unless they were trained, strong and agile, and were swimmers, as for example sailors, the life-saving capacity of a raft was considered conditional. When a ship went down quickly, leaving hundreds of people in the water, experts of the era believed that although rafts floating among them would be of great value, so would any floating wreckage to which they could cling until they were rescued. If a ship was on fire and had to be abandoned before she had sunk to any degree, then rafts had to be thrown from a fairly great height and people had to jump, or be pushed, after them, and many people would be lost in this process. This brought us again full circle... the bulkhead system which would keep the injured vessel afloat, and wireless to call for help were still the only methods available for increasing chances of shipwreck survival. It may surprise readers to know that even today, with all of our modern equipment, if an airliner, or a ship, goes down in the same spot where ***TITANIC*** foundered, people will wait just as long as ***TITANIC***'s people waited for rescue, and probably longer. Ships do not move any faster than they did in ***TITANIC***'s time, and aircraft can do no more than drop rafts to those shipwrecked so far from land. In fact, shipping traffic today is less than it was in 1912 because of the loss of passenger liners, thus the chance of having any help nearby is today far less than it was in 1912.

Some historians have tried to brand Ismay a murderer because evidence indicates that he alone may have made the decision not to carry the three thirty-foot lifeboats which each set of Welin quadrantal davits could accommodate. Had those extra boats been on board there would not have been time to launch all of them. In fact, it is doubtful that any more than the twenty which were launched from ***TITANIC*** could have been utilized, making it a moot point whether or not the extra boats were on board. Second Officer C. H. Lightoller gave a conservative estimate of 15 to 20 minutes to load each boat with passengers and enough crewmen to handle it properly in the water. Figure, then, 10 minutes to strip off the canvas cover of each boat, free it from its chocks, crank the davits outboard and position the boat for loading, plus 15 minutes for loading, another 15 for lowering and freeing the falls, yet another 15 minutes to untangle the falls and attach them to the next boat, with the loading and lowering process repeated, and you have a minimum of 2 hours and 10 minutes to empty each pair of davits, *if* all went perfectly, without a hitch of any kind. And all this is assuming that after seamen were assigned to crew the first boat lowered from a pair of davits, there would still be enough seamen left aboard to lower and crew the second and third boats from the same davits. In Britain, in ***TITANIC***'s era, there were no regulations that demanded lifeboat drill and rowing expertise from trimmers, stokers, stewards, etc. Only seamen were required to have boat skills.

In ***TITANIC*** add to all the boat launching time the approximately 30 minutes that it took to assess the damage and make the decision to abandon ship, and the time is then 2 hours and 40 minutes from impact, which is exactly the time it took ***TITANIC*** to founder after striking the ice. But this equation leaves out three very important variable factors… human nature, Murphy's Law and the fact that ***TITANIC*** was sinking by the head, meaning that toward the end it might have been impossible to launch any boats from davits near her stern due to the extreme slant of her boat deck. This scenario does not include the four Engelhardts, which probably would not have been there if the number of full-sized lifeboats had been tripled.

To utilize all of these hypothetical boats would have required the utmost cooperation from passengers, as well as enough crewmen and officers to lower the boats at every pair of davits *simultaneously*. Passengers gripped by the fear of death do not cooperate well. ***TITANIC*** was a perfect example of the fact that shipping disasters usually happen at night, when visibility is poor, and passengers suddenly awakened are still groggy from sleep. There was no public address system in 1912, and passengers had to be awakened individually, by the stewards and stewardesses assigned to their area of the ship. In this particular case because ***TITANIC*** appeared stable for sometime after impact many passengers refused to accept the fact that she was indeed sinking until it was too late. In addition the weather was unusually calm. There was no shrieking wind, there were no crashing waves, no heavy precipitation to quickly awaken passengers and stimulate the flow of adrenaline.

As ***TITANIC***'s stern rose and her bows settled deeper into the water, it would have been progressively difficult for passengers and crew alike to keep their footing on the increasingly slanting deck, while the boats would no longer lie parallel with the rail. Launching the last boats, particularly those toward the stern, would have been extremely perilous, probably impossible. Actually it was due only to the heroism of First Officer Murdoch that the last Engelhardt was freed in time to float off the top of the deckhouse when ***TITANIC*** made her final plunge.

After ***TITANIC***'s loss mandated that every vessel carry boat space for every soul on board it became the custom for lifeboats to be stacked and chocked under each pair of davits. It was well known among mariners, however, that the possibility of being able to launch *more* than the outside and the upper of these nested boats was very remote. The inside and lower boats were usually so chocked and griped down that it took hours rather than minutes to release them for use. These extra boats may have looked reassuring to passengers, but the odds were that they would go down with the ship and every sailor knew it. And, presuming that all passengers and crew members did get into those hypothetical boats for everyone, if the vessel foundered in mid-ocean with no other ships in sight, just where were the boats going to go? Lifesaving would remain dependent upon other vessels which answered the distress call, bringing us right back to that good bulkhead system which would keep the ship afloat long enough to bring aid and take off her people.

Lifeboats were not and are not meant for anything more than ferrying passengers and crew to a rescue ship or ships, or to the beach if a ship runs aground. They are virtually useless as davits, in heavy seas or when a ship is listing sharply. ***ANDREA DORIA***, for example, lost the use of half her boats when she listed heavily to starboard immediately after impact, and then rolled on to her beam ends before foundering. When there is fire the boats, even all-metal boats, are usually quickly destroyed in the fire area. If seas are heavy and winds are strong the boats may be torn loose because of weather damage, or they probably will capsize at launch. Even modern lifeboats require a lengthy amount of time to fill and lower, and they require full cooperation from passengers as well, something which cannot be expected in emergency situations. Except for wartime scuttlings, maritime history does not record many, if any, vessels which obligingly settled quietly, evenly, slowly into calm seas with no fire. In 1912 lifeboats were wooden, heavy, cumbersome, difficult to launch in the best of conditions. Adding extra lifeboats could easily make a ship top-heavy. Shipmasters naturally balked at anything which might make their vessels so "tender" that rolling would be excessive, making them uncomfortable for passengers, and dangerous in a seaway. Passengers themselves had to bear some responsibility for ***TITANIC***'s "lifeboat shortage," for they preferred their promenades uncluttered, just as today's cruise ship passengers complain when lifeboats obstruct their view from expensive upper deck suites.

ABOVE: *Lifeboats nested under the Quadrant Davits after* ***TITANIC's*** *loss.*

The Board of Trade regulations relied on a good system of watertight bulkheads which was supposed to keep a liner afloat long enough to transfer her passengers and crew. Experience had proven this system to be reliable. Two passenger liners which had sunk within the memory of every ***TITANIC*** crewman and most of her passengers were Holland-America's ***VEENDAM***, which foundered in mid-Atlantic on 7 February, 1898, and White Star's own ***REPUBLIC***, which sank after collision with the Italian liner ***FLORIDA*** in 1909. ***VEENDAM*** had apparently bilged herself, that is, her propeller shaft had broken and torn a hole in her stern plates. This was a decade before wireless was installed in most Atlantic liners, and ***VEENDAM*** had to rely upon rockets and signal cannon to summon aid. Passengers worked hand pumps alongside of crewmen, for her engine had immediately been put out of commission. ***VEENDAM***'s last distress rocket and last signal shell had been fired and her people had given up hope. But just over the horizon, officers on the bridge of the American Line's ***ST. LOUIS*** saw the flash of brilliantly colored stars and set their course toward them with all speed. In the middle of winter, in heavy swells, every person aboard ***VEENDAM*** was ferried to the nearby ***ST. LOUIS***, using boats from both ships.

Wireless had summoned so much aid so quickly and ***REPUBLIC*** had stayed afloat so long after her collision that everyone had become complacent. Yes, the whole system obviously worked very well, now that every *liner* was equipped with wireless.

While the public, falling for the lifeboat "shortage" excuse, clamored for more boats on passenger ships, the United States Navy released a statement on 25 April avowing that boat accommodations for three fifths of the men aboard each ship was ample. *"As the ships seldom go to sea alone, the Navy Department deems that there is no probability of a serious accident without help near at hand, and therefore, does not consider it necessary to provide boats to take off all on board at one time."* The battleship ***USS DELAWARE***, for example, had a crew of 945 officers and men, with lifeboat accommodations for 545. The fallacy in this analogy lay in the fact that Navy sailors were trained in abandon-ship drill. Civilian passengers were not. In the airline industry we always said that if passengers studied our manuals our jobs would have been a lot easier, and safer!

Every major maritime country had essentially the same lifeboat regulations. ***AMERIKA***, owned by Germany's Hamburg-Amerikanische Packetfahrt Aktien Gesellschaft (Hapag), at 22,621 gross registered tons, could carry a total of 3,434 persons, crew and passengers. Her boat capacity was 1,776. White Star's ***CELTIC***, at 20,904 GRT, carried 1,437 souls, with boat capacity for 1,222. Hapag's ***CLEVELAND***, at 16,960 GRT, carried 3,400 persons, and could save but 1,354 of them. ***LAPROVENCE***, owned by Compagnie Generale Transatlantique, the French Line, at 14,744 GRT, carried 1,528 persons, with boat space for 1,099. Cunard's flagship, ***MAURETANIA***, at 31,937 GRT, could carry 2,972, with boat space for 982. The American Line's ***ST. PAUL***, at 11,629 GRT, could carry 1,596, and save 962. Norddeutscher Lloyd's ***KAISER WILHELM II***, at 19,361 GRT, could carry a total of 2,379 persons, and save 1,825. White Star's ***OCEANIC***, at 17,273 GRT, could have 2,121 souls on board, with boat space for 1,175. ***TITANIC***'s sister ship, ***OLYMPIC***, at 45,000 GRT, when filled to capacity had 3,447 souls on board, and could save 1,171, if all had to take to the lifeboats at one time. The majority of passengers in every liner were in Third Class, or steerage, and had little chance of survival in any case. The Board of Trade, then, should never have been a scapegoat for ***TITANIC***'s high casualty count, but like ***CALIFORNIAN*** it was convenient.

Jane and John Q. Public accepted the myth that too few boats had been the sole cause of so many deaths, yet what in the world did they know of lifeboats? The Board of Trade, an agency of His Majesty's Government, was safe from lawsuits. It was clear that White Star could not be held responsible for damage or loss because it had complied with Board of Trade regulations that *"made the said vessel in all respects seaworthy and properly manned, equipped, and supplied,"* according to existing regulations.

Seamen's union attorneys at the British inquiry pointed out that ***TITANIC***, as well as other liners, did not carry enough seamen to man the boats already supplied, let alone any extra ones.

But these lawyers were merely laughed at and accused of trying to acquire more members for their respective unions. It was, as usual, a matter of economics. The whole matter was quietly dropped, with one point sticking in the public mind... ***TITANIC***'s people had died because she carried too few lifeboats.

Casual ***TITANIC*** readers are surprised to learn that the majority of ***TITANIC***'s dead did not drown. Those who were not injured by jumping into the sea while wearing a cork life vest died of exposure, although many did not expire within the legendary few minutes. There were many more than legend tells us who died slowly, over many hours, waiting and hoping for a rescue that never came because no proper search was ever made to find them. Those who managed to take refuge on wreckage and who were in good physical condition to begin with undoubtedly survived for some time, as did those who may have taken refuge on the ice itself. As noted in earlier chapters, two crewmen apparently did survive although they were not in lifeboats taken aboard ***CARPATHIA***. More than one crewman and steerage passenger was actually in the water from the time ***TITANIC*** foundered until ***CARPATHIA*** arrived the following morning, thus defying all odds and logic. ***TITANIC***'s cork life preservers were so efficient that bodies were found floating in them weeks, even months later, but it is not generally known that the cumbersome vests were extremely dangerous. This type of life vest was still in use in World War II, when shipwrecked sailors quickly learned that limbs, jaws, ribs, even necks were broken when men leaped into the water while wearing the so-called lifesaving device. Seamen learned to tie the vests down if there was time, to hold them down otherwise, to keep them from riding up on impact with the water, but it is doubtful if sailors of ***TITANIC***'s time knew this. Certainly passengers did not. Those who put their blind faith into the cork vests and leaped from the sinking ship were undoubtedly injured upon striking the water, and in many cases the injuries were fatal. Second Officer Lightoller, who said he wore a vest, was washed off the boat deck as ***TITANIC*** went down, was sucked under with her, and popped to the surface because of the vest's buoyancy. In retrospect it seems strange that Lightoller, a powerful swimmer, would have worn a life vest at all. They were cumbersome things which made it difficult for a man to work, and swimmers usually disdain wearing them because even modern life vests restrict mobility in the water. In fact, not only in ***TITANIC*** with the cork vests, but with modern life vests now, anyone trapped below in a sinking ship or aircraft will undoubtedly not be able to escape because the buoyant vest holds the person to the overhead as water comes into the compartment, making it impossible to swim downward to an open door or port which might be used as a means of egress from the flooded compartment.

TITANIC's officers all knew that lifeboats belonged in the water to do anyone any good, and getting them there was a must, whether they were loaded or not. There was no time to wait for finicky ladies who were afraid to get into a small boat when ***TITANIC*** still looked so solid. There was no time to wait for passengers who wanted to run back to their cabins for this or that. The boats had to be in the water as quickly as possible, full, empty or in between. It was as simple as that, hardly a question to be discussed endlessly for eight decades and more.

For centuries the small boats carried by merchant vessels were woefully inadequate as lifesaving devices, and every sailor knew it. Life was cheap then, the average life expectancy being little more than five decades, and far less than that at sea. Women counted for very little other than childbearing, and they were expendable. In shipwrecks it was survival of the strongest, which meant men, who could always find other wives to make other children for them. So passengers, particularly emigrants, were jammed into sailing vessels, with boat space for no more than the crew and maybe a few male passengers. The wreck of ***HMS BIRKENHEAD*** in 1852 was a harbinger of change in that respect, but it did little to change public opinion or force any changes in nautical lifesaving equipment. ***BIRKENHEAD*** was, after all, a troop ship, not a passenger liner. Soldiers and their families were expected to endure hardships, even death, in the line of duty to their country.

Knowing that their boats were inadequate, small, difficult to launch at best, sailors took little interest in maintaining them, or stocking them with emergency supplies. In fact, for many years merchant vessels went on long voyages with their boats lashed to skids, bottoms up, or perhaps they were used as convenient chicken coops. Falls were stiff, frayed and worn, burned by the sun, smeared with paint. Few sailors even knew how to pull an oar, and most eschewed learning how to swim, preferring a quick death by drowning to a slow, probably painful death from exposure, shark bite, dehydration, starvation. Rarely was there any such procedure as "lifeboat drill" even in the transatlantic liners. In the United States The Passenger Act of 1882 began to address the matter of lifeboat drill, station bills, and general training of crew members for emergencies, thirty long years after the loss of ***HMS BIRKENHEAD***. Similar laws were enacted in other major maritime countries at about the same time. The master, however, was still given a great deal of latitude in all of these respects. The master could, and can, lose his or her certificate for not adhering to the regulations pertaining to passenger safety, and it is the master's duty, always, to ascertain that the vessel is in every way seaworthy before departure, just as the captain of an airliner may lose his or her certificate for failing to make certain that the airplane is airworthy before taking off. But companies did and do pressure masters and pilots-in-command to cut corners, to maintain schedules and save money. If one captain is too "chicken" there are plenty who are not and again it is a matter of economics. When jobs are scarce we guard them most carefully, taking chances when necessary if we want to keep food on the table and a roof over the heads of our dependents, particularly when we have a job that we really love. In fact, safety regulations at sea and in the air have largely come about because of union agitation to enact them. This is one of the major reasons why so many ships today fly "flags of convenience." In ***TITANIC***'s era it was understood that each master might have individual ideas of the method of conducting drill and making crew assignments. Aboard ***TITANIC*** there had been no boat drill for passengers. Every member of the crew, in particular the officers, should have known their jobs, but many did not.

TITANIC legend has it that the alleged shortage of lifeboat space was the sole cause of her high casualty count, thus it was ***TITANIC's*** loss that changed the amount of boats carried aboard every passenger ship. The truth is simply that the same thing had been happening in every passenger ship loss for centuries. ***TITANIC*** was a turning point only because with her some very wealthy and prominent men died, and some token had to be made to account for their death. If there had been no Astor, no Guggenheim, Thayer, Stead, etc., if those lost had been poor, European emigrants, nothing would have been changed. Proof of that lies in the simple fact that nothing had been changed until ***TITANIC***.

Prior to ***TITANIC***'s demise, in the transatlantic liners especially, it was not considered wise to alarm passengers by placing any emphasis on boat drill, or any other emergency drill. It detracted from the notion that passengers were in a traveling hotel. The same thinking prevailed in airliners up until the 1960s. Prior to that it was believed that any suggestion that life vests were under the seats might frighten passengers. Only when the jets arrived and it became mandatory to explain the use of oxygen masks if cabin pressure was lost, did pre-takeoff emergency briefings become normal procedure. But it was a difficult change for the airlines to make, until it was proven the hard way that it did make a tremendous difference in crash survival.

Lifeboats used in passenger liners of ***TITANIC***'s era were built of wood, although metal boats had been built, and were beginning to be used in most of the world's navies. Wooden boats were *clinker-built,* meaning that the planking was generally thin with the lower edge of the plank overlapping the upper edge of the plank next below, a light, flexible, but surprisingly strong method of construction; or they were *carvel-built,* with the planking lying flush, edge to edge and made watertight by caulking; or they were *diagonal-built,* with two layers of planking worked in from the keel to the gunwale, striking away from the keel at a 45 degree angle, the inner layer usually running from the keel aft, the outer layer running the opposite direction, the two layers crossing each other. ***TITANIC***'s boats were clinker-built, of the whaleboat, double-ended type, excellent, sturdy seaboats which curved gracefully from a low 'midships freeboard to a high bow and stern. In fact, they were probably the most sturdy, efficient type of boats then available. Whaleboats could be pulled with double-banked oars, as ***TITANIC***'s were (two oarsmen to a thwart) or single-banked oars (one oarsman to a thwart) or they could be sailed by standing lug or ketch rig. The early metal lifeboats were patterned after wooden whaleboats.

Boats were carried in davits along each side of the boat deck, lashed securely against wind and wave, covered with heavy canvas also lashed down securely. Usually each boat had two drainholes, with their plugs secured by lanyards. Otherwise when heavy seas were shipped lifeboats would have become giant water scoops, adding further to precarious topside weight. In fact, a method of righting a damaged and badly listing vessel was to fill her boats on the high side with water, and lower those on the low side, even jettisoning them if the situation was desperate enough to warrant it. Prior to launch, of course, it was necessary to be sure these plugs were in position or a geyser of water would come up through each drainhole, quickly sinking the boat.

The Welin quadrantal davits used in ***OLYMPIC*** and ***TITANIC*** were the most modern and efficient davits in use in 1912. With quadrantal davits each davit arm was fitted with a traveling gear, which moved outboard on a worm shaft operated by a crank. The falls must be set taut and belayed before cranking out begins, then the davit heads move outboard in the arc of a circle, and as they rise the boat lifts off its chocks. The chocks were timbers under each end of the boat, shaped to fit around the portion of the boat's hull on either side of the keel. The outboard half of each chock was hinged so that it could drop flat to make way for

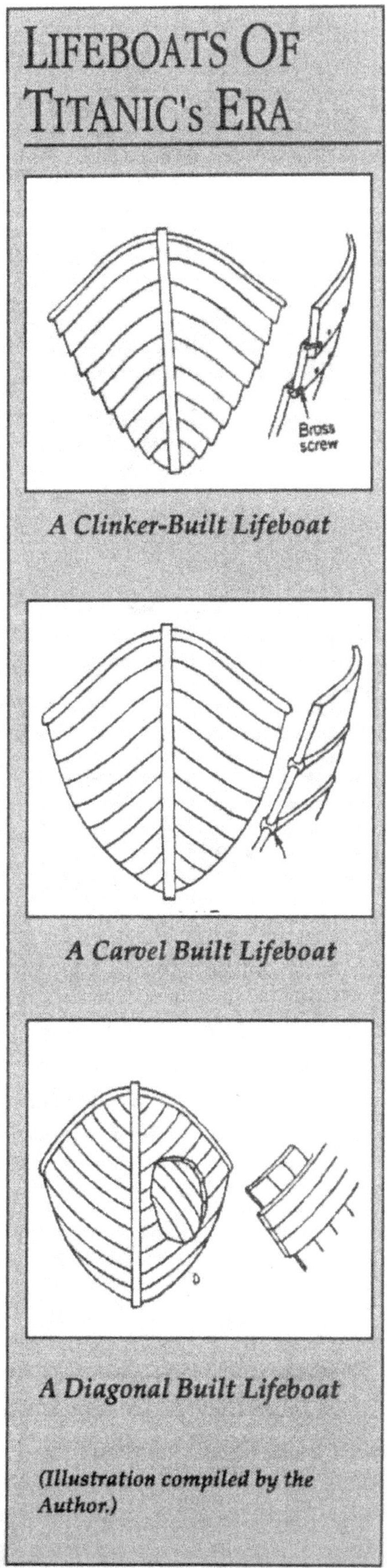

A Clinker-Built Lifeboat

A Carvel Built Lifeboat

A Diagonal Built Lifeboat

(Illustration compiled by the Author.)

***ABOVE: TITANIC, OLYMPIC, & later BRITANNIC** would possess state-of-the-art Quadrant davits. These illustrations give a clear idea of how a boat station looks with a boat swinging out. **OLYPMIC** and **BRITANNIC**'s boat system would be revised after **TITANIC**'s loss to allow the carriage of a larger number of lifeboats.*

the boat to swing out. Davit heads had to be cranked out at an even rate. If one got ahead of the other, one end of the boat could fly off its chock before the other and the end which did not lift off could be damaged.

In heavy weather, or when the ship was listing badly, *frapping lines* were rigged around the falls, one end of the frapping line being bent to something solid on deck, the other end passed around the falls and tended by a turn or two, then taken around something solid on deck. The purpose of a frapping line was to keep the boat from swinging wide and crashing back against the side if the ship rolled, or as in ***TITANIC*** with her list to port frapping lines might have kept the boats closer to her rail, making it easier for passengers to step into the boats. A frapping line would also keep a boat from swinging athwartships during lowering or hoisting.

Boats should go into the water on an even keel, or a little by the stern. The crew must see to it that the boat is fended off the ship's side as the boat goes down. If the sea is very rough the boat should be held above the water, at the order "hold her fore and aft," until a low point appears and the order is given to drop the boat into the water. Legend has it that ***TITANIC***'s falls were too short and boats were dropped into the water. It is more likely that the boats were dropped gently, deliberately, stern first into the water by some boat crews.

The lower block of a boat fall was provided with an automatic, quick-releasing hook which was designed so that it could not open while the boat's weight was on it, but when the boat touched water and became buoyant, the hook tumbled and rejected the hoisting ring. If the boat struck the side of the ship, as may have happened in some of ***TITANIC***'s starboard boats with her list to port, this, too, could have released the weight on the hooks and allowed the boats to fall. In ***TITANIC***, however, according to several boat crews, the releasing gear did not work as it should have and falls were cut away. In an emergency, of course, this was the only way to do it as nobody was worried about hoisting the boats back on board again.

While legend has it that although all of ***TITANIC***'s officers were armed, not one of them fired a weapon directly at any person. Fifth Officer Lowe, who seemed more trigger-happy than any of them, insisted that he fired into the air or between his lifeboat and ***TITANIC***'s hull, warning shots only.

It may surprise modern readers who read every day of the horrors of handguns and the political struggles to outlaw them, that in 1912, and not only in the "uncouth" United States, every man and many women who could afford a handgun frequently carried them for protection. One needs only to read newspapers of ***TITANIC***'s era, and earlier, to note the crimes committed with guns, the adults, and children, accidentally shooting each other. The only difference between then and now in this respect lies in the greatly increased population and the instant, all-too-graphic media coverage today. In fact, passengers in transatlantic, and other liners often used innocent seals, dolphins, whales and other marine life for target practice. Polar bears, sighted on ice floes, were a favorite target of passengers and sailors alike. Ships always carried weapons chests, necessary for defense against pirates in certain parts of the world, or mutinies anywhere, particularly in cargo ships. Sailors were generally quite familiar with handguns.

TYPICAL BOAT DETACHING GEAR OF 1912

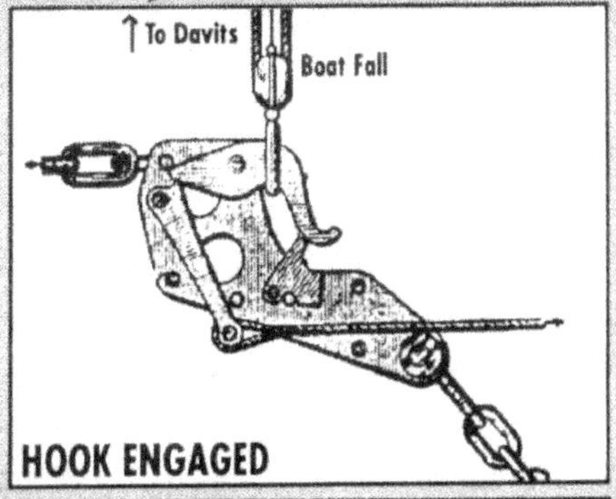

To Davits

Boat Fall

HOOK ENGAGED

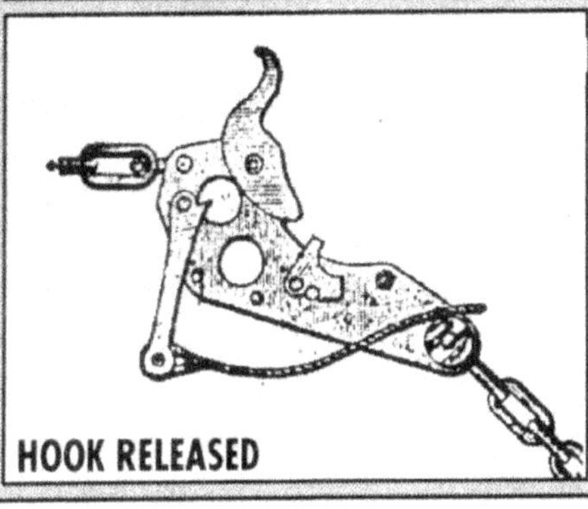

HOOK RELEASED

TITANIC's weapons chest contained Webley automatic pistols, probably the 7.65mm model of 1906, possibly the .38 calibre model offered to the Royal Navy in 1909. Fifth Officer Lowe carried his own Browning automatic, possibly the 7.65mm model of 1910. Several male steerage passengers told newspaper reporters of their being held below at gunpoint until the boats were loaded, but none of these men were asked to testify at either inquiry. Lightoller returned to tell his and Murdoch's friend and former shipmate Captain James McGiffin, then still Marine Superintendent at Queenstown, that Will had been forced to shoot a crewman who led a rush on a lifeboat. The bullet struck the man in the jaw, and he was left on the deck to die while Murdoch quickly loaded mostly Third Class women and children into one of the last boats to leave the sinking ship. There would be nothing unusual about such an anecdote and it is well-documented by other witnesses. No doubt Murdoch was not the only officer forced into such a hard decision. First Class passenger Hugh Woolner testified at the Senate inquiry that Murdoch had used only his fists to throw men out of one boat he was loading, but there can easily come a time in such a situation when one man's fists are simply not enough, no matter how tough he is. Murdoch knew perfectly well how desperate the situation was and his driving goal at that point was to save as many women and children, the helpless ones, as possible. He certainly cannot be condemned for his action, yet just as certainly White Star would never have admitted such a thing.

While in a warship every person on board is skilled and subject to discipline, in a passenger ship it is an entirely different scenario. In an emergency, with at least 85% of the souls on board being unskilled, of every age from very young to very old, and diverse physical conditions, the few officers and seamen on board will have their hands full to enact a semblance of orderly evacuation. In reality what actually takes place is that relatively few lifeboats are successfully launched, and as many people as possible pile into these few regardless of their capacity. Many people end up in the water and they naturally try to climb into the nearest boat even at the risk of capsizing the whole boat load. This is what ***TITANIC***'s boat crews naturally feared because they knew the horrors of previous shipwrecks. Many, many ships have been wrecked and decisions have had to be made about going back to aid those struggling in the water, and in fact the tough decision of fending off survivors in the water is a common problem in shipwreck, whether theoretically there is boat space for all or not. When a boat is overturned only the hardiest and the best of swimmers will have any chance of survival. This is the real, harsh world of survival of the fittest and nowhere is there an environment so cruel as the sea. ***TITANIC*** has been so dramatized, so romanticized for so long that the hard truth has been lost, if indeed it ever was understood by landsmen.

When passengers, and crewmen, rush a boat which is being launched responsibly, they invariably destroy the boat by lowering it improperly, dumping its human contents into the sea to die. Every officer aboard ***TITANIC*** knew this. Felix Reisenberg wrote that passengers should never be allowed to swarm up on the boat deck while boats were being readied. Crew members should be in position to avoid this and they should be armed if necessary, wrote Reisenberg. That was exactly why ***TITANIC***'s armed officers were at first stationed in positions to prevent this first rush while seamen were readying the boats. Passengers must be kept away from davits and falls until the boat is positioned for lowering. Even under conditions of acute danger caution must be exercised, for the old cliche "haste makes waste" is all too true in emergency situations. It is always better in the long run to keep a cool head and do things right. The boats are quickly checked for proper supplies, chocks knocked down, gripes off, covers cleared out of the way, crew assigned to the falls with one sailor in bow and one in stern of boat, boat gear in order, and plugs in. When boats are at rail level, the sailor in each end of the boat steadies her while her quota of passengers is boarded.

All of ***TITANIC***'s boats were launched safely, with the exception of the one Engelhardt which floated off inverted as she went down. Much has been written on what time which boat was launched, and who went in each boat. It is my position that these exact times cannot be accurate, that only a reasonable assumption of the sequence of launching can be reconstructed for reasons already stated. Nothing that happened in ***TITANIC***, or any other disaster, can be frozen into a static picture as posterity would like to see it. As for the manifest of each lifeboat, it seems obvious that if a complete passenger manifest was never available, as explained in an earlier chapter from testimony given by Ismay at the Board of Trade Inquiry, then it would naturally be impossible to know exactly how many people were in each boat, excepting crew members. Some survivors, but not all by any means, knew which boat they were in and even passengers made a point of learning the names of some other occupants of their boats. Not even all crew members, however, were certain of their boat numbers, nor were they always sure of the sequence in which their boat was launched. ***TITANIC*** was so big that a crew member who was, for example, on the port side forward, would have absolutely no notion of what was happening on the starboard side aft. In fact, with deck houses obscuring vision nobody on the port side knew anything that was happening on the starboard side and vice versa. This is the main reason why we have so many different versions of what happened. While in one area there may have been no panic and few people to board a lifeboat, one hundred feet away it was an entirely different scenario with panic reigning until shots were fired. There is very little record of boats launched by the officers who died, i.e., Captain Smith, Chief Officer Wilde, First Officer Murdoch and Sixth Officer Moody. Many crewmen did not know any of the deck officers by name. And many of the men who crewed lifeboats came from the Engine Department. They were firemen and trimmers, not seamen. White Star officials insisted that firemen refused routine lifeboat drill, thus few of them knew anything about boathandling, but that was, of course, not the company's fault. It was sheer luck that weather was good, the sea was calm when ***TITANIC*** was evacuated. Otherwise the loss of life would have been closer to 100% of those on board.

The "Millionaire's Boat"

On 17 May Sir Cosmo and Lady Duff Gordon testified before the Board of Trade inquiry. Much ado had been made by the press of No. 1 emergency boat, with its aristocratic "cargo." Sir Cosmo and his lovely wife had been in the greatly underloaded starboard emergency boat which should have held over six times as many people as it had. Allegedly Sir Cosmo had bribed the crewmen in that boat to take him, his wife and her secretary to safety, everyone else be damned. The interrogation of Sir Cosmo and Lady Duff Gordon seems, in retrospect, to have been one of the biggest farces of the two major investigations. While the press, and many authors over the years, portrayed Lady Duff Gordon as a flighty, nervous, selfish and pampered aristocrat, the truth is quite different. Only the third adjective may come close to the truth, yet considering Lucile's early life her self-centeredness seems more a matter of self-preservation than a serious character flaw.

"Lucile" was Lady Duff Gordon's professional name. She had not been born into the aristocracy. Far from it. Unless one counts her father's very distant claim to an ancient, and extinct earldom.

Lucy and Elinor Sutherland were the impoverished daughters of Douglas Sutherland, a civil engineer of Scots descent, born in Nova Scotia in 1838. Their mother, Elinor Saunders Sutherland, was also born into a pioneering Canadian family, who traced their origin to the owner of substantial estates in Buckinghamshire. Lucy Christiana was born in 1862. Elinor, who would in time become the famous novelist and motion picture writer and director Elinor Glyn, was born in October, 1864, just five months before Douglas Sutherland died of typhoid which he had contracted while working on the building of the Mont Cenis tunnel in Italy. Elinor Sutherland was thus left a young widow with two high-spirited, very intelligent and talented daughters to raise... on almost nothing. Mrs. Sutherland did the only thing she could do. She returned to her family in Canada to raise her daughters in as genteel a manner as possible.

An attractive young widow, Elinor was soon courted by David Kennedy, a man old enough to be her father, who was persistent, and reasonably well off financially. Kennedy finally won Elinor's hand in marriage, but she also won in that she persuaded him to take her and her daughters to England. Elinor was quite sure that they all belonged in the land of their ancestors, and that they deserved a life in London society, impoverished though they were. David Kennedy's older brother, Peter, owned Balgregan Castle on the Mull of Galloway, which became the little girls' first home in Britain. It was not the fairy-tale castle of their dreams, however.

David Kennedy seems to have been penurious, to say the least. While he crushed the spirits of his young wife, and Elinor withdrew into the fantasy world which begat her writing career, the strong-willed Lucy rebelled. Eventually Kennedy gravitated to Jersey, and the Government House set. The mild climate suited his chronic chest problems. As was normal in Victorian families, Elinor and her two girls were forced to live their lives revolving around Kennedy, his physical complaints and bad temper.

It was at Jersey that young Lucy and Elinor, or Nelly as the family called her, met Lily le Breton Langtry, one of the most celebrated beauties of her day who would become mistress to Queen Victoria's son, Prince of Wales and eventually King Edward VII. There is little doubt but what the famous beauty's life and loves influenced both Lucy and Nelly greatly.

While tomboy Lucy was considered the beauty of the family, Nelly was called ugly because she was tall and had red hair, both undesirable qualities in a Victorian woman. While Nelly wrote her stories, Lucy designed and made first doll clothes, and then clothes for herself, her mother and

Nelly.

Lucy married James Stuart Wallace in September, 1884, on the rebound from a man she really loved, with whom she had had a quarrel. She was too proud to apologize. Her daughter, Esmé, was born in August the following year. While James Wallace was at first eager to show off his lovely young wife, he soon returned to his wayward, womanizing, alcoholic ways. He was generous financially with Lucy, when he had money. But he ran up debts he could not pay, living beyond his means. Five years after their marriage he ran off with a dancer, leaving Lucy with a young daughter to raise, an impoverished mother to care for, and Wallace's debts to pay. She turned to her dress-making talent to earn a living. As it turned out she had tremendous talent for design and as her reputation increased, so did her remuneration.

After her experience with Wallace, Lucy was naturally reluctant to marry again. By the time she and Sir Cosmo Duff Gordon became friends and business partners in 1895, Lucy was already famous in the *haute couture,* her firm Maison Lucile making gowns for debutantes, duchesses, princesses and even queens. Margot Asquith was a favorite client who had walked into Lucy's shop saying, "I hear you design the most beautiful dresses in London." Margot sent her friends to Lucy, among them the famous "Souls" hostess Ettie, Lady Desborough, who would be Elinor's lifelong enemy

The décor in Lucy's couture house was as elegantly feminine as her gowns. She favored pale, floral colors, but used discreet touches of vivid colors for accent, and often, when the client's coloring warranted it, used black for accessories. She designed for the individual woman's personality. Lucy did away with restrictive corsets in favor of the natural feminine form. She designed the first "naughty" lingerie, which rapidly became a favorite of duchesses, courtesans and *nouveau riche* Americans alike. Her clothes were shocking for their time. Lucy brought to the haute couture a dainty, yet sexy for its time, appeal which was first to show a little leg peeking out of draped, split skirts and voluminous sheer chiffons. Her garments were characterized not only by soft fabrics and pale colors, but by extravagant and beautifully made silk flowers, ruffles, ribbons, elaborate laces and gilded embroideries. Lucy paid no attention to the Old Guard who accused her of introducing the "cult of immoral dressing." She attracted the attention of yet another famous client, the Duchess of York, later Queen Mary. It was said that the Queen Mother's style of dressing in later life, the soft floral colors with grays, the lace and slim, straight skirts with tunics worn over them, all came originally from Lucile's designs.

By the time Sir Cosmo met Lucy she was a successful, confident, elegant, sophisticated and beautiful woman in her prime. He wanted to marry her almost from the moment he met her, but his mother's High Church of England antipathy to marriage with a divorceé prevented Cosmo from following his heart for fear of escalating his mother's delicate health. He settled for investing in Lucy's business until his mother died in 1900 when he felt free to defy the Church. After quarreling with her previous suitor, Cosmo finally won Lucy's hand. On 24 May of that year Lucy Sutherland Wallace became Lady Duff Gordon. She who created the loveliest, most elegant of wedding gowns, chose an "old frock" for her own second marriage. Lucy later wrote that they were "very much in love."

An artist first, businesswoman last and least, Lucy had been accustomed to receiving needed financial aid from her many masculine admirers, and freely spending most of the money she earned. Sir Cosmo, a fine looking man who had been noted in his younger days for his magnificent singing voice, was also a superb athlete, a member of Lord Desborough's Olympic fencing team. Unlike her sister Nelly, Lucy was little interested in titles, excepting that they were good business for her. She preferred the theatrical crowd, possibly a result of her early friendship with professional beauty-turned actress and royal mistress, Lily Langtry. Lucy began designing gowns for theatrical productions, and as sister Elinor would later create the *"It Girl,"* American movie actress Clara Bow, in 1928, so Lucy "created" the beautiful Lilie Elsie by designing not only gowns but also makeup, hairstyle and a whole new personality for the star of the international hit production of *The Merry Widow* in 1907. Lucy's extravagant and flattering "Merry Widow" hat became the latest style in millinery for women on both sides of the Atlantic. Both Lucy and sister Elinor, who was by then famous as well as infamous as a writer of risqué romantic novels, would acquire coteries of tall, handsome toyboys, which would eventually cause a greater rift between Lucy and Sir Cosmo than even ***TITANIC*** had done.

Lucile had many friends in America by the time she returned there in 1909 to set up the American branch of Lucile, although the ever-cautious Cosmo advised against it.

Lucy had made friends with Elsie de Wolfe, actress, socialite, friend of Anne Morgan, Pierpont's fiercely independent daughter. Elsie persuaded Lucy that New York's socialites were ready for Lucile's naughty, glamorous, feminine styles. With Elsie's help Lucy hired a publicist and embarked on an ambitious promotion campaign. Elinor Glyn had preceded Lucy to fame in America and there was some jealousy between the sisters, possibly because Lucy garnered much publicity because of her title. Americans were, and are, enamoured of English titles, and many American heiresses had married those titles.

Lucy returned to England to prepare her next collection. Her presentations were theatrical productions of the first order, stunning, always with the most beautiful models to show her new line. She originated the concept of the runway model and theatrics accompanying each designer's showing of a new collection.

By the end of February, 1910, Lucy was on her way to New York again, in ***LUSITANIA***. Her collection had been shown to 1,000 guests in London, including the Queen of Rumania and Margot Asquith, whose husband Herbert Asquith was now Prime Minister. The leaders of New York society were eager to acquire gowns by the most popular couturiere in England. The fact that Lucy was an "English aristocrat" attracted women whose husbands had made fortunes in railroads, steel, and other new American industries. Placards on New York street corners announced that the *"Titled Dressmaker and Her Golden Girls Arrive Today to Show Americans How to Dress."* Lucy had discovered a lucrative new sideline as well... she charged $500 for an individual personal consultation to teach New York's society women how to dress like English aristocrats.

Lucy returned to London to ready her next collection, but the following May, after the death of Edward VII, she returned to New York and to one of the worst experiences of her life, second only to ***TITANIC***. She was accused of smuggling dresses and "fripperies" into the United States to avoid customs duties. Elsie de Wolfe insisted that Lucy hire a good lawyer and suggested Bainbridge Colby, who recommended that Lucy go to court and defend herself. This she did, looking fragile in black, and swayed a jury to the extent that her fine was reduced from $50,000 to $10,000. She was now determined to open a branch of Lucile in Paris, where she would compete openly with her greatest rival, Paul Poiret, the rising young designer who favored vivid colors 20 years after Lucy had done them, and who had recently introduced the "Oriental" look. In 1910 Margot Asquith had created what came to be known as the "Gowning Street Scandal" when she invited Poiret to show his collection in London at a time when British rather than French industry should have been boosted, thus making more enemies for her husband.

In March, 1912, Lucy was in Paris expanding the new branch of Lucile when urgent business called her to New York. Allegedly the only berths available were in the new liner on her maiden voyage, ***TITANIC***. Lucy was, as she wrote later in her autobiography, reluctant to travel in a new ship, and hesitated to make the bookings, telling Cosmo of her fears. He volunteered to travel with her, something he rarely did. With her faithful secretary. Miss Francatelli, and Cosmo, Lucy embarked from Cherbourg in ***TITANIC***. She would write in her autobiography years later that although Captain Smith, as well as her "merry Irish stewardess" did their best to reassure her, Lucy felt so apprehensive that she refused to undress completely at night. She claimed that she kept a "warm coat and wrap" always at hand, and her little jewel case was always "on a convenient table" within easy reach. An expensive pearl necklace which she had on approval from a jeweler in Venice was unfortunately locked up in the Purser's safe, neither insured nor paid for.

On Sunday night so Lucy later wrote, she and "Franks," the affectionate nickname she gave to her secretary, had not dressed for dinner, but dined in the same warm clothes they had worn all day. Everyone at neighboring tables were "making bets on the probable time of this record-breaking run." She had been in bed in her First Class cabin on A deck for about an hour when she was awakened by "a funny rumbling noise" and then "heard people running along the deck" outside her cabin. "We must have hit an iceberg," she claimed they had said, citing the fact that there was ice "on the deck.'

Lucy ran across the alleyway to Cosmo's cabin, but he had heard nothing and was annoyed because she had awakened him. Even if they had hit an iceberg, Cosmo told her, it would not do much damage because of the watertight compartments. Lucy went to the rail and looked over the side, but saw nothing. She returned to her cabin, but the noise of steam blowing off alarmed her and she ran again to Cosmo's cabin. This time he got up and went to investigate. When he encountered Colonel Astor the two men agreed that they must have their wives get dressed and prepare for the worst. As Lucy was donning the warmest clothes she had, including a fur coat, Franks came in, agitated because there was water in her cabin and she had seen seamen taking covers off the lifeboats.

According to Lucy's memoirs everything had seemed orderly until they came to the boat deck. There pandemonium reigned. The boats were being lowered hastily, with people fighting for places in them, while officers shouted "women and children first." She heard the "sharp bark of a revolver."

While at least three times officers tried to force Lucy and Franks into a lifeboat, Lucy refused to leave Cosmo, and Franks would not leave her employer. The three of them huddled together, watching "with amazement" American wives leaving their husbands. According to Lucy, and Sir Cosmo, in the story they later told at the British inquiry, suddenly there were no more people on the boat deck in their vicinity, and there was but one boat left, the starboard emergency boat which Murdoch was loading. Murdoch allowed Cosmo to join Lucy and Franks in the boat, and he put A. B. George Symons in charge of the boat. It is known that Murdoch did indeed allow men into lifeboats when women were not available to fill it up.

The arguments against Sir Cosmo, and Lucy, were not so much that they had survived, but that the boat had so few occupants, it had not gone back to try to rescue those struggling in the water after ***TITANIC*** went down, and Sir Cosmo had given a "fiver" to each crew member (actually Franks had written the checks for £5 on note paper for Cosmo to sign because his checkbook had been lost with ***TITANIC***). The suggestion was made that it had been a bribe to keep the boat to themselves without trying to save anybody else.

It boiled down to the word of Sir Cosmo and Lucy against the word of the men who had crewed the lifeboat. The Attorney General, Sir Rufus Isaacs, suggested to Sir Cosmo that this boat could have saved "a good many" if they had gone back, to which Sir Cosmo replied, "I do not know that." In retrospect Sir Cosmo made more sense than Sir Rufus. To take a boat as small and relatively light as the emergency boat in amongst hundreds of drowning people was suicide. And that was assuming that these people, who had relatively no experience in navigation or boathandling, could have found the spot where ***TITANIC*** went down after she had disappeared from their view. None of them seems to have had any notion of studying stars and planets to find their position, or their position relative to ***TITANIC***. They had no compass, and probably no knowledge of using it if they had had it. In view of the fact that none of the other boats went back, either, with the exception of Fifth Officer Lowe's boat, the question should be asked "why were the Duff Gordons singled out for this persecution?" Lowe, in fact, had waited until the cries had died down, in other words until he knew that most of the struggling people had drowned, before he ventured back to look for survivors.

After the interrogation had skirted all around the real question. Lord Mersey finally brought it out in the open. *"Why do you not put it in plain words?"* asked Mersey. What everyone really wanted to know was *"did sir Cosmo promise the men a £5 note if they would row away from the drowning people?"*

There was more than a hint of class antagonism in the brutal interrogation of Sir Cosmo Duff Gordon by attorneys for various unions and the Third Class passengers. Sir Cosmo was merely a passenger, he was not in charge of the boat in spite of his social position and he never should have been questioned on the subject at all. Again, however, a scapegoat was needed and the interrogation of these two "aristocrats" was a show worthy of the media's, therefore the public's, rapt attention. Even the ***CALIFORNIAN*** was forgotten when Lucy and Cosmo testified. No. 1 emergency boat carried to safety only 12 people, A. B. George Symons who was in command of the boat, 5 firemen and 6 passengers. The boat could have comfortably held another 20, another 30 with crowding which would have reduced her freeboard dangerously had any seas come up. Neither Cosmo nor Lucy should have been held responsible for the boat's not going back but firemen in the boat blamed her, saying that she had been fearful the boat would be swamped among the drowning throng. Undoubtedly it would have been. But in each and every underloaded boat crewmen tended to blame "the ladies" who were "fearful" as the reason why they rowed away from the cries of the dying victims. Unfortunately we will never know who was really frightened, but in retrospect it seems very strange indeed that crewmen would allow women passengers to tell them what to do. It also seems more likely that the women, most of whom had left husbands aboard the sinking liner, would have been the ones who would want to go back, hoping to save their husbands.

Actually Sir Cosmo had promised the fivers to replace the crewmen's kits after they complained that their pay stopped when ***TITANIC*** went down and they had lost their kits which went down with her. Thirty pounds or so meant nothing to Cosmo, but £5 was a good sum of money to a man who fed his family on less than that per month. All of the crewmen from No. 1 boat wrote their names on Lucy's life vest before they disembarked from ***CARPATHIA***.

When Lucy and Cosmo arrived in New York they were met by anxious friends, and Lucy's attorney, Bainbridge Colby. Elsie de Wolfe, Bessie Marbury and Mr. Merritt, editor of the *Sunday American,* met the Duff Gordons as they arrived with their only baggage… their life vests. At dinner that night Merritt listened as Lucy, giddy with champagne, told the dramatic tale of their survival. The following morning Merritt phoned Lucy, telling her that Mr. Hearst had called him and wanted her story for the next morning's paper. Merritt asked if he could tell it as he had heard it from her. Lucy gave her verbal permission, but after Merritt told it to an eager reporter the story was embellished far beyond the truth when it was published in the *New York American* under Lucy's by-line.

Rumors were rampant about what was quickly dubbed the *"Millionaire's Boat."* A ***TITANIC*** crewman named Robert Hopkins, who had not been in No. 1, told reporters that another passenger in No. 1, identified only as an "American millionaire," had offered the crew money to pull away from those struggling in the water. Sir Cosmo told his Board of Trade interrogators reluctantly that Mr. C. Stengel, one of the American passengers, had made many remarks such as *"Boat ahoy!"* until Sir Cosmo finally asked Stengel to keep quiet. Stengel told the Senate subcommittee that he and "Sir Duff Gordon" had "directed the boat." Evidence was conflicting, as was to be expected. Immediately after Lucy's testimony the Board of Trade attorneys questioned Fireman Samuel Collins who seemed to have kept a calmer head than anyone. Collins said that no one in the boat had proposed going back to look for survivors in the water, that nobody had countered that proposal with the fear of being swamped, which Lucy was supposed to have done. In fact Collins believed that they had pulled back toward the place where ***TITANIC*** had disappeared, and they saw nothing. The cries had lasted only about ten minutes after ***TITANIC*** went down, said Collins. He had seen the white light for which they had pulled, and he believed that it was either a stern light or a mastlight. Murdoch had loaded the boat, and he had ordered them to pull for the light, which they had tried to do, until they saw ***CARPATHIA***'s lights, when they turned around and headed for the Cunarder.

It was Fireman Robert Pusey who had overheard Lucy say to Franks, *"There is your beautiful nightdress gone,"* and responded with, *"Never mind about your nightdress, Madam, as long as you have got your life."* Lucy would later say that she had been trying to make light of the situation to cheer Franks, but the statement was naturally turned against her as an example of her shallowness.

Those who had been safely by their firesides when ***TITANIC*** had foundered were quick to condemn the Duff Gordons, perhaps out of jealousy. Their many friends stood by them, however, and that included Margot Asquith.

Those who knew them well knew that Lucy's was the dominant personality in their relationship. If Lucy refused to board a lifeboat without Sir Cosmo, then her mind had been made up and she would not have left him. If he wanted her to survive he would go, too, if he could. It was not surprising that Murdoch allowed men into the boats that he loaded. If there had been more women present, Murdoch would have filled the boat with them, and probably Lucy would not have been one of them.

To escape from the publicity Lucy and Cosmo went at once to Paris where she continued with arrangements for Maison Lucile and her new collection. Lucy felt at home in Paris, surrounded by the *demi-monde* in the closing days of the lavish *Belle Epoque.* She could forget ***TITANIC*** in her new success, with her ever-increasing cortége of toyboys. Sir Cosmo had no such shield.

When Lucy continued with her plans to open a branch of Lucile in Chicago, she was suddenly taken ill and required surgery. When doctors forbade her traveling for three months she, Cosmo, their dogs, servants and Lucy's new toyboy, a young Russian she called "Bobbie," rented a house at Mamaroneck. Cosmo at first tolerated Bobbie, but eventually he rebelled. He returned to England without Lucy. Lucy defended the stocky, Russian immigrant, whose real name was Genia d'Agarioff. Lucy and Sir Cosmo never lived together again, although they continued to be business associates. He had never really been a part of his wife's world of high fashion, the one world where women of her time could wield power. ***TITANIC*** haunted him until his death in 1931. He left the income from his estate to Lucy for life.

Lucy again escaped to Paris, where she dressed socialites, actresses and courtesans, where her friends could help her forget ***TITANIC***. But when the War finally started Lucy ran to America, with her four top models, Dolores, Hebe, Phyllis and Arjamand. Her list of clients included stars of stage, screen and musical theater such as the Dolly sisters, Fanny Brice, Irene Castle, Norma Talmadge, Isadora Duncan and old friend Lily Langtry. Mary Pickford modeled a Lucile creation, and went on a bond-selling tour in 1917 wearing a special khaki uniform created for her by Lucy.

In 1916 Lucy departed from the usual lavish presentation of her Spring collection and did a series of *tableaux vivants* starring her special models instead to raise money for a French village which had been in the center of some of the War's most brutal fighting. Billie Burke, actress/comedienne wife of showman/producer Florenz Ziegfield, was a regular Lucile client. She brought her husband to the tableaux, where he immediately wanted to hire Lucy's top models for his new *Follies*. When Lucy told Flo Ziegfield that her models could not sing, dance or act, he said that did not matter in the least because they were so beautiful. Thus Lucy was responsible for another American tradition, the showgirl. She dressed the girls in Ziegfield's *Follies* through 1920, her last theatrical production.

But the Great War was the beginning of the end for Maison Lucile. Lucy had taken to Paris with her a young Irishman named Edward Molyneaux. He, too, had tremendous talent for design, and he possessed great loyalty as well. Lucy's nickname for him was "Toni." During the War women's clothes reflected their new wartime roles and skills. Clothes became austere, practical, with few fabrics available, completely the opposite of Lucy's feminine ribbons, flowers, laces and flowing chiffons. Toni enlisted in the Army, rising to the rank of captain. After the War he stayed with Maison Lucile until 1920 when he opened his own couture house. Lucy never adapted to the changes in fashion brought about by women's changing role in society. The world of couture changed drastically, and the new designers, like Captain Molyneux, were ready for the change. Lucile was not. Her house declined as did her fortunes. She was impoverished, dependent upon friends when she was diagnosed as having cancer in 1934. She went into a nursing home in Putney, which was paid for by a friend. Toni Molyneaux sent flowers often, Elinor visited nearly every day. In April, 1935, Lucy died peacefully, Elinor by her side, 23 years after she had nearly died in ***TITANIC***. Their mother was still living, but Elinor had not the heart to tell her of Lucy's death. Until the end Lucy believed that she would one day again be "Lucile."

It seems a shame that Lucy should be remembered more for being Lady Duff Gordon of ***TITANIC***'s "Millionaire's boat" than for the vibrant, talented, interesting person she was in her own right. She was an individual in an age when women were not supposed to have individuality. She lived life to the fullest, as she wanted to live it, when women were supposed to be nothing more than extensions of their husbands' personalities. "Lucile" is the one who should be remembered, not "Lady Duff Gordon."

Chapter Twelve

Morgan & His IMM

John Pierpont Morgan was born in grandfather Joseph Morgan's house in Hartford, Connecticut, on 17 April, 1837, a year of financial panic in the infant United States of America. The rather pompous-sounding "Pierpont" was quickly shortened to "Pip" while the boy was growing up. Pip's father, Junius Morgan, had wed Juliet Pierpont, the daughter of Boston's fiery Congregationalist preacher, the Reverend John Pierpont, who frequently angered his congregations by preaching against strong drink and slavery. From his maternal grandfather young Pip received the religious training which provided a lifelong moral code and service to his church.

Joseph Morgan's home was not nearly as grand as Morgan homes would later be, but it was a substantial, three-story house in the city, and Grandfather Morgan was comfortably well off, thus Pip was hardly a model for one of Horatio Alger's rags-to-riches stories.

Pierpont's paternal grandfather had moved from a Massachusetts farm to Hartford in 1817. Joseph began the family fortune by running a hotel, buying up real estate, and founding the Aetna Fire Insurance Company in Hartford. When a disastrous fire raged through New York City's business district from Canal Street to the Battery in December of 1835, Aetna promptly paid all its claims, thereby enhancing the company's reputation and tripling its new business.

Joseph's son, Junius Spencer Morgan, had been born in 1813, before the family moved to Connecticut. Instead of going to college, a very rare thing in those days for even the wealthiest young Americans, Junius went to work first in New York City, and later in Boston, where he became a partner in James M. Beebe & Co., a financial firm which specialized in selling American cotton to European buyers.

This was the era of Horace Greeley's popular admonition to "go west, young man," when "west" meant Ohio, Indiana, Illinois, maybe even as far away from New York as Missouri. After the War for Independence, industry had sprung up all along the eastern seaboard of the infant country, and with industry towns had begun to grow into cities. Residents of those cities needed food, and as population and industry spread, they pushed farmers ever farther to the west. Because land was cheap, often free for the taking. European immigrants braved the tremendous hardships to follow Greeley's advice and seek new lives in the new land. The 1830s saw the beginning of the railway boom in America, when immigrant labor was cheap and the new railroad barons took advantage of it. But America had as yet no steel mills to make rails and rolling stock, thus American railroad men turned to Europe, especially to the "mother country," England. In 1834 the last installment of the federal debt was paid off and the young United States had accomplished what no other had done. A wave of optimism swept the country. There were no limits to its expansion.

A man who epitomized the rough and ready pioneer type of American had been elected president in 1829. Andrew Jackson, "Old Hickory," hero of the Battle of New Orleans, had destroyed the Second Bank of the United States when he attacked its policy of prudently denying speculative loans to the men who were scrambling to purchase land newly released for sale by the U.S. Government. By doing this, Jackson killed all remaining restraint on the money supply of the new United States, and unleashed a flood of failed businesses and banks, the result of easy credit which fostered unpaid loans. Neither investors nor would-be farmers had foreseen the problems of bad weather and tremendous distances to be conquered before the land could be made to pay off in food to support even the new settlers, let alone the produce they expected to ship to cities back east. The panic spread to England where bankers had been quick to invest in the railroads and canals being built to carry supplies to America's newly developed West. Much of the financing for this westward drive in America came from British bankers, who scoffed at their former colony's "independence," knowing full well that a country so heavily in debt to its former sovereign was not independent at all. Many of the smaller British financial houses failed when Americans defaulted on their loans.

Throughout this financial chaos Joseph Morgan prospered. He knew that the middlemen who linked British capital and the vast untapped American West would be the ones to thrive and that the bond between British and American banks would eventually create a force even more powerful than the governments in Washington and London. In 1844 Joseph moved with advancing technology. He switched his investments from stagecoaches to railroads, and became a director of the new railroad which linked Hartford to Boston. Grandfather Morgan immediately took the seven-year-old Pip on his first journey by train. Boy and man, Pierpont never forgot its fascination.

In 1850 Junius first brought the Morgan name directly into British banking circles when he set up contacts with London banking houses, including the prestigious Baring Brothers. While his father was in London the teenaged Pierpont kept him informed of political and economic news at home.

In Boston, where Junius soon moved his growing family, and where Pierpont started to high school, the good schools were naturally in the areas where the older and wealthier English immigrants resided. The Irish, German and Italian immigrants were forced by poverty to stay in their ghettos, where schools were as poor as the inhabitants. Pierpont thus was shielded from any contact with the masses of working men, women and even children, who toiled twelve, or more, hours a day, seven days every week of each year, so that a few men like Morgan, Astor, Vanderbilt, Guggenheim, Rockefeller, Carnegie, and Gould, could amass the fortunes that allowed their families to live like royalty. Labor unions had not yet brought vacations, holidays, sick leave, eight hour work days and five day work weeks. The lower classes accepted their lot in life, usually turning to religion for solace. If there was nothing but hardship here, then they would have their riches in the afterlife. Pierpont mingled only with his own kind, all of his life. He never saw the laboring class, never understood their problems. Yet, surprisingly, when the time came that he had to deal with labor leaders, he dealt with them fairly. If Pierpont felt that their demands had merit he granted them.

With good old Yankee conservatism, Boston financiers generally remained aloof from the wild speculation that gripped Wall Street during the new country's rapid growth. Junius taught his son common sense, and Pierpont learned early the concept of sound business practices. The boy's education was typical of the era, practical and thorough. Arithmetic and legible handwriting were deemed as important as the classics or European languages. Pierpont was taught to keep thorough and accurate accounts of his weekly expenditures, and he carefully kept track in writing of each penny spent for pencils and other necessities.

Suddenly, when he was fifteen, the first of many incapacitating and mysterious illnesses forced Pierpont to drop out of school. He remained bedridden for months, and it was a major turning point in his life. It was then usual to send sickly boys on sea voyages, and it did very often restore health. So weak that he had to be carried aboard the barque ***IO***, Pierpont was packed off to the Azores, where the American consul, a family friend of the Morgans, cared for him. Pip enjoyed the mild climate, and by winter's end he was able to travel to London to meet his parents who had gone to England on business. The illness had left Pierpont with one leg shorter than the other, and he had aged physically beyond his years.

Junius then took his recuperating son on his first trip to the Continent. They toured Belgium, France and Germany, and returned to England, where Pierpont visited Windsor Castle for the first time. After a short side trip to Scotland and Ireland the Morgans returned to America. Pierpont's lifelong interest in Europe, his love of traveling, was born in that first excursion to Europe.

Pierpont had lost a year's schooling, but he quickly made it up, and graduated near the head of his class. His education was quite ordinary, and there was nothing in him then to stand out from the crowd, no inkling of greatness to come except, perhaps, his seriousness, his avid interest in commerce. He was an attractive young man, robust and well built in spite of his recent illness, with intense dark eyes that already invoked the piercing, direct gaze which would dominate many a future boardroom. His sensuous mouth gave promise of the libido which would lead him in later life to acquire many attractive mistresses. His ears and nose were fairly prominent, but the latter as yet gave no hint of its future disfigurement.

George Peabody, the eccentric, Socialist-sympathizing American millionaire banker who had spent £500,000 to build homes for the poor of London, along with Baring Brothers' Joshua Bates and the Rothschilds' New York representative August Belmont, were the vital links between British and American capital prior to the Civil War. Peabody was a bachelor, but he wanted a partner to share the burden of his many financial holdings, and he wanted an heir. He was impressed by Junius Morgan's abilities. In 1854 he offered Morgan a partnership in his firm, George Peabody and Company, if Junius would be willing to move to London. Peabody not only controlled millions in American bonds of various kinds, but he worked hard to promote Anglo-American relations by writing pro-American letters to various British newspapers and by contributing to American political campaigns, notably to support the Whigs in Maryland. Peabody, and Baring Brothers, were especially concerned with state bonds, the latter controlling bonds of Massachusetts, Ohio, South Carolina and Maryland. By the late 1840s Peabody and other British investment firms had turned to heavy investments in American railways. George Peabody was exporting iron for rails to America, although the United States had begun the manufacture of heavy rails in Maryland in 1844.

Junius agreed to move to London, but first he sent Pierpont on a trip via the many little, competing railroads that operated throughout New England and upstate New York. Pierpont saw first-hand the inefficiency of competition run amok, another lesson he never forgot.

When his parents moved to London, Pierpont was sent to finishing school in Switzerland. From there he went to the University of Göttingen for a year, where he studied trigonometry and chemistry, and joined the Hannovera, one of the popular German student corps which specialized in drinking and dueling. Pierpont's nose was beginning to show the swelling and redness that would lead to its total disfigurement. Sensitive to any further marring of his features, he carefully avoided dueling, but not the social life of the corps. Although he was at this time strongly attracted to a young Swiss girl, he had promised himself to take an American wife, and already he was showing the iron will for which he would become famous.

In 1857 Junius decided that it was time for his son to return to New York, and go to work. He obtained a position for Pierpont in the office of Duncan, Sherman and Company, a correspondent of Peabody's. Junius Morgan and Alexander Duncan had been friends for years.

As it had been in Pierpont's birth year. Wall Street was again in a panic. Banks were failing, credit too freely given and used was causing businesses and individual fortunes to collapse. Naturally the financial chaos spread to England through British investments in America. But the Morgan companies survived, although 900 other companies did not. Peabody, as well as Duncan, Sherman & Company, survived. Once again Pierpont Morgan learned lessons that he would never forget.

After the crash of 1857 Pierpont followed his father's advice and lived austerely, sharing quarters with another young man, and walking to work, while he learned bookkeeping from Charles Dabney, another family friend. Pierpont was not paid while he learned, and he lived on the small allowance given to him by his father. In return for this pittance he continued to be Junius's intelligence agent in New York. Pierpont knew the sailing schedules of all the transatlantic steamers, and timed his letters to Junius for the quickest passage to England. Pierpont actually remained his father's agent for fifty years, always accountable to Junius, although he did increasingly exert his independence in American dealings.

Quiet, serious, in his youth never one to party or waste time in frivolous activities, Pierpont finally fell in love, with pretty, fragile Amelia "Mimi" Sturges, who was older than he was. Pierpont's parents approved of Mimi, however, and invited her to visit them in London in 1859, while Pierpont traveled to Cuba to study the sugar industry. He suffered more often now from the disfiguring skin eruption which would soon make his nose so enlarged and inflamed that it would be the first thing anyone noticed about him. He also had bizarre fainting fits and painful indigestion. Junius frequently chided his son for eating too fast.

When the Civil War began Pierpont decided that he could best serve the Union by arranging loans in England to finance the fighting. Unfortunately he became involved in a scandalous deal to sell obsolete weapons to the Union Army. Although Pierpont got out of the deal relatively unscathed financially, it was one of the moral low points of his career, a lesson learned and never repeated.

Pierpont decided to marry Mimi, although she was suffering from tuberculosis and probably had not long to live. They were married quickly and quietly, in the Sturges town house, with none of the Morgan family present. As Pierpont had once been carried aboard ship, too weak to walk, so he carried his beloved Mimi aboard the Cunarder ***PERSIA***, bound for Liverpool.

Pierpont took his ailing bride to the sunny Mediterranean, hoping that the mild climate would invigorate her, as the Azores had done for him in his first serious illness. But Mimi was too sick, and in February, 1862, not yet twenty five years old, Pierpont became a widower.

He returned to New York and threw himself into business affairs to take his mind off his debilitating grief. Morgan thus became involved in the fever of gold speculation which prompted Congress to pass the ineffective gold bill of 1864. This served only to drive the price of gold even higher, until Union victory caused the bottom to fall out of gold prices. Morgan was no different from other budding American capitalists, professing sympathy for the North, yet hiring a proxy to fight, and using the war for his own financial gain.

Junius refused to sanction his son's behavior, and arranged for Charles Dabney to join the New York branch of J. S. Morgan & Company, ostensibly as senior partner, but primarily to keep an eye on his errant son. By 1864 Pierpont's annual income had reached $50,000 a year, a substantial sum for those days. He was enjoying an active social life, and was naturally much sought after by society matrons with eligible daughters. Young, virile, wealthy, still attractive in spite of his bulbous nose, he soon found a new partner, Frances Louisa Tracy, always "Fanny" to those close to her, daughter of a prominent New York attorney. They were married in May, 1865, and Pierpont immediately took his bride to Europe to meet his parents. After a short honeymoon in Paris and Switzerland, the young Morgans returned to New York and set up housekeeping on Madison Avenue. Pierpont settled down. He was soon elected to the vestry of the local Episcopal Church, and the gold and arms speculation which had tarnished his reputation during the War was quickly forgotten.

Frances would bear four children, Louisa Pierpont, John Pierpont, Jr., known as "Jack" to avoid confusion with his father, Juliet Pierpont, and Anne Tracy Morgan. Pierpont moved his growing family farther up Madison Avenue, and rented a summer home at Buttermilk Falls, in upstate New York. He settled comfortably into domesticity. While his fortune was growing by leaps and bounds, Morgan became a member of the Board of Managers of St. Luke's Hospital; he helped organize the Metropolitan Museum of Art and the Museum of Natural History; he promoted the Y.M.C.A., and became a vestryman of St. George's Episcopal Church in Stuyvesant Square.

The railroad consolidation wars were just beginning when Pierpont met Samuel Sloan, who had been president of the Hudson River Railroad before Vanderbilt grabbed it. Dabney, Morgan & Company was already dealing heavily in railroad stocks, with British investments increasing. In 1869 one third of all American Government bonds were owned by Europeans, most by the British.

The railroad wards began to look like extensions of the Civil War as men who worked for Fisk, Gould, Vanderbilt, and other railroad barons were encouraged to fight openly, with knives, guns or any weapons they could find. When weapons failed, they rammed each other's locomotives. Nobody thought of the passengers who wanted to use the lines at this point, except Pierpont, who clearly understood that railroads were necessary to the economic growth of America. While Daniel Drew, Jay Gould and Jim Fisk wrecked railroads and ruthlessly destroyed their rivals to line their own pockets, Pierpont and Junius pushed for organization and consolidation. They wanted to run the roads at a good financial profit, but with a stability that would assure future business and stockholders' dividends. They wanted to eliminate competition, but they wanted to do it by buying it out, and running what they had efficiently.

Pierpont had what the other railroad men lacked... international financial backing through J. S. Morgan & Company in London. He learned valuable lessons from the railroad wars. He learned to fight dirty when it was the only way to win. And when he won, he won big.

That redoubtable old steamboat entrepreneur, "Commodore" Cornelius Vanderbilt, had conquered the Atlantic with his 1,867 ton wooden paddle steamer ***NORTH STAR*** in 1853. In February, 1855, Vanderbilt submitted his proposal to the United States Postmaster-General to provide a semi-monthly service between New York and Liverpool. Vanderbilt's line would alternate with the other American flag carrier, the Collins Line. The Commodore requested a subsidy of $15,000 per voyage to carry the mails, provided that his ships equaled the speed of the rival British Cunard liners, and $19,250 if they came up to the Blue Riband holders of the Collins Line. The bid was refused. Vanderbilt then placed the ***NORTH STAR*** and a smaller paddler named ***ARIEL*** in service between New York and Le Havre, under the name Vanderbilt European Line.

In 1857 the Vanderbilt Line did get a one-year mail subsidy, for thirteen round trips between New York and Bremen. In May of that year the new 3,360 ton wooden-hulled paddle steamer ***VANDERBILT*** was added to the service. In 1858 the ***NORTH STAR*** was transferred to the company's New York-Panama run while two new wooden paddlers, ***OCEAN QUEEN***, of 2,801 tons, and ***NORTHERN LIGHT***, of 1,768 tons joined the ***VANDERBILT*** in transatlantic service. In February, 1860, Vanderbilt bought the 2,100 ton ***ILLINOIS*** to run as consort to the ***VANDERBILT***, while ***OCEAN QUEEN*** and ***ARIEL*** were transferred to the Panama service. When his mail subsidy turned out to be less than half of what he had hoped for, Vanderbilt refused to carry any more mails. When the Civil war broke out ***ILLINOIS*** and ***VANDERBILT*** were chartered by the Federal Government, and the Vanderbilt Line's transatlantic service was never revived. The Vanderbilt Line had, however, cut into the profits of the Collins Line, and together

ABOVE: *The founding father of the Morgan banking dynasty, Junius Spencer Morgan, and father to J.P. Morgan (From the Dictionary of American Portraits, Dover publications, 1967)*

ABOVE: *John Pierpont Morgan (From the Dictionary of American Portraits, Dover publications, 1967)*

ABOVE: *John "Jack" Pierpont Morgan (From the Dictionary of American Portraits, Dover publications, 1967)*

ABOVE: *John Davison Rockefeller (From the Dictionary of American Portraits, Dover publications, 1967)*

with the loss of Collins' ***ARCTIC*** and ***PACIFIC***, had assured that line's demise. Pierpont noted all of this, watching attentively from the sidelines.

The Civil War set off a new chain of industry in America. New England's still-famous boot and shoe manufacturing plants had been started to provide boots for Civil War soldiers. New meat packing plants had sprung up in Chicago to feed the Union Army. Of course the manufacture of guns had proceeded at a frantic pace. But cutthroat entrepreneurs had loyalty only for themselves. Union soldiers ate tainted meat from diseased animals, they wore boots made from paper and uniforms made from reclaimed rags. All too often their guns would not shoot, and the horses sold to the cavalry had been drugged to make them perform well only until the "marks" had handed over their money.

This was the atmosphere in which men like Daniel Drew, Jay Gould and Jim Fisk thrived. Observing Commodore Vanderbilt's success with ferry boats. Drew bought an old tub, painted her smartly, and announced that he would carry a passenger from New York to Albany for 25¢, undercutting Vanderbilt's fare considerably. Vanderbilt capitulated, as Drew had planned. The Commodore bought Drew out at a good price and Drew turned his talents to Wall Street and railroad stocks. Again Pierpont observed and learned.

Jay Gould, born in Roxbury, New York, in 1836, had been a surveyor before he went into the tanning business in Pennsylvania. Gould promptly borrowed money from a leather merchant named Leupp in New York City to buy out the tannery. But the enterprising Gould soon became a leather merchant himself, undercutting his benefactor's prices, bringing about Leupp's financial ruin, and subsequent suicide. Like Drew, Jay Gould was drawn to railroad stock speculation.

The nimble wheeling and dealing of Jim Fisk, the Barnum of Wall Street, had made him so overconfident that he set himself up as an independent broker in Boston. But when he went to Wall Street to play the stock market he learned that he was not so smart after all. Fisk lost all the money he had invested, but rebounded quickly, chalking his losses up to experience. Fisk had heard of Daniel Drew, and knew that Drew owned a small railroad called the Stonington, in Connecticut. He went to Drew with a scheme to dump the line on a group of Boston investment speculators. Drew liked the idea, and Fisk proceeded to carry it out, making a nice profit very quickly. Fisk got a big commission and his company became Drew's front for stock speculation.

Drew introduced Fisk to Jay Gould in October, 1867. At the age of seventy eight. Drew was going up against the most formidable rival he had ever encountered… Commodore Vanderbilt. Drew wanted the two smartest young men he knew, Fisk and Gould, on his side. The ensuing battle would come to be known as the "Erie War," and it would eventually involve control of several of the nation's largest railroads, at least two state legislatures, as well as numerous courts and local officials. And it would bring Pierpont Morgan directly into the railroad wars.

By the Summer of 1851 the Erie's new tracks connected New York City and Dunkirk, in western New York State. The Erie had become famous by a stroke of phenomenal good luck and one Mrs. Silas Horton, who lived near the Erie tracks in Oswego, New York. One day Mrs. Horton was hanging out her laundry when she noticed that a tree had been blown down across the tracks, even as she heard the whistle of a train approaching the blind curve which concealed the obstacle from the engineer. Grabbing the first thing which came to hand, Mrs. Horton raced down to the track, waving a pair of her red flannel drawers, flagging down the train which would otherwise have been derailed, with disastrous results. Whether or not it was this publicity which called Drew's attention to the Erie is unknown, but it was shortly after this memorable event that Daniel Drew began very quietly to invest heavily in Erie stock.

Before Erie's management realized what had happened. Drew owned so much of their stock that he was a board member. Within three years he was the Erie's treasurer. Drew then advanced $3.5 million to the company in return for 28,000 shares of unissued stock and $3 million in convertible bonds. Quickly Drew sold short, dumping 58,000 shares. While Erie's stock dropped from $95 to $50, and common stockholders lost their shirts, Drew made enormous profits.

Vanderbilt began to take notice of the Erie, as a possible competitor to the system of railroads that he planned to create. Seeing how railroads might be far more profitable than steamship lines, the Commodore studied first the New York & Harlem, then the New York & Hudson line, which ran into Poughkeepsie. The Harlem ran as far as Chatham, then connected with another line to Albany. Beyond Albany ten small lines had recently been combined to form the New York Central, which connected Albany with Buffalo. The Commodore saw a way to create one big railroad with New York City as its main terminal, and he set out to do it.

Historians are still not clear on how Vanderbilt manipulated the Harlem's stock down to $9 a share, but when he did, he bought controlling stock. He was not so successful with the Hudson, which he had to buy at $25 a share. Then he went after the New York Central.

Vanderbilt's first move was to halt his Hudson line trains at East Albany, making passengers who wanted to connect to the Central walk two miles to the Albany depot. The Central's management promptly complained to the State legislature. But Vanderbilt had outfoxed them all. He had discovered an old law which forbade Hudson Line trains to cross the River into Albany. The law had been pushed through by the then new Central management to stop any competition west of Albany. The crafty old Commodore apologized profusely, regretting that the Hudson had been breaking the law all those years. He promised that his line would not do it again.

Without the connecting traffic at Albany, the Central's traffic and then its stock began a downhill plunge. When it had fallen to Vanderbilt's price, he invested $18 million in it, and made himself president of his third railroad. He named his new line the "New York Central and Hudson River Railroad," and leased the Harlem to it at a stiff price. Then, Vanderbilt went after Daniel Drew's Erie.

It was obvious to everyone that Drew was running the Erie not as a transportation system, but as a means to line his own pockets. He manipulated its stock into quick gains, and depressions, and made personal profit from each fluctuation in price. But in spite of Drew, the Erie was a fairly sound road. While Drew's takeover methods were always covert, Vanderbilt openly announced that he was going to buy control of the Erie. Drew's henchmen, Gould and Fisk, promptly "found" some hitherto "unknown" Erie stock. Vanderbilt and Drew traded injunctions, each having local politicians and judges on his payroll. Wall street went mad. Not only Erie stock tumbled, but so did many other stocks. Vanderbilt ordered his judge to arrest Drew, Fisk and Gould, and to declare the Erie Railroad bankrupt and name a receiver known to be friendly to Vanderbilt interests.

Gould went public, calling Vanderbilt a monopolist. Monopoly was un-American, cried John Q. Public, never noticing Gould's duplicity. Gould pointed out that if Vanderbilt gained control of all the railroads in the area he could manipulate prices of all commodities carried on those roads at his will, but never mentioned that he could do the same. Vanderbilt finally capitulated and sent for Drew. The Commodore accused the Erie men of stealing $4.5 million from him, and he expected to be reimbursed. Drew replied that he'd have to discuss it with his partners.

But Gould and Fisk quickly ousted Drew from control of the Erie. They approached Vanderbilt, and made a deal. Vanderbilt lost more than a million dollars, while Gould made himself president of the Erie, and Fisk was made vice-president and comptroller. Erie stockholders complained in vain, while Erie tracks and rolling stock deteriorated and employees naturally became demoralized. In 1868 an Erie wreck killed scores of people, driving the price of Erie stock to new lows.

The next railroad target for speculators was none other than the federally sponsored and funded Union Pacific. The scandalous method of takeover involved corrupt members of Congress, cabinet officers, the Vice President, and a future President.

Oakes Ames, a Representative from Massachusetts, and his brother Oliver were prominent members of the Credit Mobilier, a company originated by Union Pacific vice-president T. C. Durant specifically to take over the contract for building the Union Pacific, which was being financed by the United States Government. For every mile of Union Pacific track creeping westward toward the Pacific Ocean, the men of the Credit Mobilier collected the money granted to build it by the government. While poor men (mostly Irish immigrants) died to keep that track moving westward, stockholders in the Credit Mobilier got rich at the taxpayers' expense. Eventually public outcry prompted a Congressional investigation, and Oakes Ames was made the scapegoat.

While the Credit Mobilier had been raiding Union Pacific and the public. Jay Cooke, a financier with an untarnished reputation, was financing another transcontinental railroad, the Northern Pacific, which stretched all the way from Lake Superior to Puget Sound. He hired a press agent named Sam Wilkerson, who was able to convince the public that Northern Pacific's route would run through a tropical land lush with orange groves and banana plantations. The unsophisticated new Americans flocked to buy Cooke's railroad stocks with their hard-earned, salted-away savings. When that wasn't enough, Cooke went to Germany to solicit investments from the Teutonic aristocracy. But the outbreak of the Franco-Prussian War squelched Cooke's hopes for German funds. Cooke returned to the United States, with a new plan. He needed a revision of the Northern Pacific's charter from Congress which would double the railroad's land grant. Cooke had already paid off Senator Blaine and Vice-President Colfax, and others who had agreed to help him win the new revision.

Unfortunately for Cooke, the Credit Mobilier Scandal broke while he was in the middle of his negotiations. No politician dared to get caught in more scandal. Cooke's fortunes were dwindling, his overdrafts now amounting to $5.5 million, while Northern Pacific's bonds were going at discounted prices.

Pierpont Morgan moved into the postwar world of finance with a philosophy he would always embrace... if bankers could not control themselves, government would have to do it for them. It was the beginning of an era when a few men would control Wall Street. With the Street, they controlled America, and eventually the world. Their money already controlled politicians and judges where needed. Now their corporations moved to control whole legislatures, while Junius Morgan began to intervene in European politics. It was an age when every American looked at men like Morgan, Vanderbilt, Gould, Cooke, Astor, Carnegie, and thought, "That might be me some day." It would not be, of course, but it was, and is, the American Dream. The American public had not yet become disenchanted with corruption in government led by those same financial manipulators they hoped to emulate.

Dabney, Morgan and Company specialized in railroad stocks. Vanderbilt had used Morgan to arrange the purchase of iron rails from Britain when he wanted to improve the Central's tracks. Dabney, Morgan had acquired an excellent reputation in financial circles, thanks to Junius in London. British railroads are and always have been quite different from American railroads, because of the distances involved. America can obviously accommodate many rail lines, while one is sufficient for Britain. But in this period of expanding U.S. rail systems British investors were not yet aware of the major differences, especially the destructive, unlimited competition, and Junius Morgan was able to sell them American railroad stocks quite easily. Morgan also bought $5 million worth of bonds in Andrew Carnegie's Allegheny Valley Railroad. Through this transaction Morgan became involved with Drexel and Company in Philadelphia, a banking house connected with the Pennsylvania Railroad.

In the summer of 1869 Gould went after the Albany and Susquehanna Railroad, a short line that linked Albany and Binghamton, New York. The Erie was one of three roads competing for coal-carrying contracts, and Gould needed the Albany and Susquehanna to link the Erie with New England. He sent his agents to buy stock which was held by towns along the right of way, and he secured injunctions to prevent the Albany and Susquehanna from issuing new stock to protect itself. Gould even got his paid judge to force the suspension of the short line's president, Joseph Ramsey, and to appoint the Erie's Jim Fisk as a receiver until the Albany and Susquehanna's ownership could be settled. Ramsey got his own judge to reverse all of the decisions favorable to Gould and the Erie. Fisk and his gang of railroad "detectives" and thugs seized as much of the line's rolling stock as he could find at one end of the line, while Ramsey commandeered the rest of it at the other end. Ramsey's men captured one of Fisk's locomotives. One of Fisk's hooligans promptly rammed it with another engine. An armed melee ensued, which at one point involved 12,000 men.

Ramsey's judge and Fisk's judge traded injunctions, until Ramsey, who had bought additional company stock using company bonds as security, with only ten per cent in cash, did not have enough money left to bribe the state legislature. A mutual friend advised Ramsey to go to Pierpont Morgan.

Pierpont deplored the tactics of Gould and Fisk. The young Yankee from Connecticut preferred a civilized approach with sound business tactics, instead of the continuing wars which destroyed both sides. Morgan promoted organization and consolidation, not the chaotic devastation that Fisk and Gould had caused. The churchgoing, family man that Pierpont had become deplored the immoral lifestyle maintained by the flamboyant Fisk, who openly kept so many mistresses, and the greedy, covert Gould, who had thought nothing of destroying Daniel Drew, his former mentor. So Pierpont came into the ring on Ramsey's side. Dabney, Morgan and Company bought 600 shares of Albany and Susquehanna stock to acquire a stake in the fight. The Erie's judge promptly issued an injunction to block the sale. Morgan called a stockholders' meeting at Albany, and had himself made a director of the short line. Fisk held his own meeting. Then Morgan pulled a brilliant coup. The Erie's directors sent a request to the governor to appoint a nominee to run the company until the matter was settled. Morgan persuaded Ramsey and his men to lease the railroad to him through the Delaware and Hudson Canal Company. The lease was drawn up and signed before the Erie forces could stop it.

Eventually the state supreme court upheld Morgan's lease, and Ramsey was confirmed as the legal president of the Albany and Susquehanna. Morgan had won his first railroad victory. Pierpont had learned all the dirty tricks and used them well. Gould was so impressed that he asked Morgan to join the Erie board. Perhaps Gould would not have given in so easily if he had not already been plotting his most infamous transaction ever, cornering the United States gold market.

President Ulysses S. Grant had been in office only two months when Gould began courting the favors of Grant's brother-in-law, Abel Rathbone Corbin, a successful New York attorney and lobbyist. Gould had conceived an idea that other men had no doubt thought of and dismissed as impossible. He would buy all the loose gold in the United States on the open market, but he needed an accomplice in government to make sure that the Treasury did not release any of its huge gold supply. Gould had known Corbin in New York, and must have realized that the attorney was not above cooperating in such a wild scheme. He pointed out to Corbin that the country's economy would be much better off if gold were scarce. Besides, Corbin's cut of Gould's take would be $1.5 million.

Gould, and Fisk of course, quietly began to sell their stocks and buy gold, while Gould began a propaganda campaign to convince the public that greenbacks need be covered by only a minimum gold reserve. President Grant appointed General Daniel Butterfield as Assistant Treasurer of the United States, and Gould promptly purchased a substantial amount of gold in Butterfield's name.

By September Gould had purchased $40 million in gold. The price of gold had gone up to $144 an ounce when Gould, Fisk and a number of their colleagues who were now known as the "Goldbugs," met to congratulate themselves. When the price of gold reached $200, they planned to unload and make a killing.

But President Grant had become suspicious and severed relations with his brother-in-law. Butterfield warned Gould, who was already beginning to unload his gold. The next day, Friday September 24, 1869, known ever after as Black Friday, gold opened at $145 and was pushed up to $162. Railroad and industrial stocks slipped, then skidded downward. Grant suddenly ordered the sale of government gold until the cornering of the gold market was completely foiled. The price of gold immediately plunged to $135. Corbin was ruined by the scandal, while Butterfield was allowed to resign without public disgrace. Gould came out of the Goldbug Scandal with nothing lost but honor. In fact, Gould had sold out his partner and cleared $11 million, while Fisk appeared to be bankrupt. Actually they had broken no laws. No federal law then forbade a private citizen from buying all the gold he could afford.

Fisk and Gould continued to raid the Erie's coffers, with Fisk spending much of his share on showgirl mistresses. On 6 January, 1872, Fisk was shot to death by Edward S. Stokes, at the Grand Central Hotel where Fisk had gone to keep a rendezvous with a Mrs. Morse, allegedly the widow of an old friend. Stokes had become a lover of Fisk's mistress, Josie Mansfield, and through her encouragement he had allowed Fisk to take over management of the Stokes Oil Refinery in Brooklyn. Stokes claimed that Fisk had libeled and "slickered" him, and he had filed a libel suit against Fisk. Although the younger Stokes had supplanted the dissipated Fisk in Josie's affections, he had just lost his libel suit against Fisk and sought revenge. Fisk had not lived to see forty. Stokes spent four years in Sing Sing; there were many on Wall Street who said that Fisk's death had been good riddance.

The Erie's stockholders finally forced Gould to resign, but all of this manipulation and infighting had left the Erie with a crippling $64 million debt, a fact that Pierpont Morgan noted with great interest.

Pierpont had wisely stayed out of the Black Friday debacle, although many of his friends were involved. Junius, now proud of his son's maturity and sound business sense but still unable to say it directly, released Pierpont from Dabney's watchful eye.

Now thirty four years old, when he should have been in his prime physically, Pierpont went into one of his physical breakdowns, which were now always accompanied by the disfiguring skin eruption, known today as *rosacea.* He became depressed about his health. He was perpetually tired, and he had severe headaches. His old fainting spells returned, and he briefly considered retiring, but Junius got involved in the Franco-Prussian War, and Pierpont learned that there was more to life than simply making money.

After Bismarck's Armies captured Napoleon III in 1870, and went on to surround Paris, the

French Government asked Junius to finance the war with a $50 million loan. Junius offered them harsh terms but the desperate French accepted. When the French regained Paris, Junius had cleared $5 million from the sale of discounted bonds in England and America.

A new era had opened up in international banking. It would be known as "dollar diplomacy," and the Morgans, who bridged the gap between their rapidly developing New World country and old European money, invented it. Their aim was not just wealth, it was power.

Junius arranged for Pierpont to join forces with Anthony Drexel, of Drexel and Company, a firm second only to Jay Cooke and Company. The new alliance became known as Drexel, Morgan and Company on 1 July, 1871. Among Drexel's assets was the *Philadelphia Ledger*, which now began a propaganda campaign against Cooke. Articles in the *Ledger* proclaimed loudly that Cooke's plea for a new Union Pacific charter stemmed from the loss of his own money and that of his bondholders.

Drexel, Morgan began distributing United States Government bond issues. Teamed with Levi Morton in New York, a firm allied with the Rothschilds in Europe, Morgan did not at first do well in competition with Cooke's banking firm, which had previously monopolized the Government bond business. But in the Panic of 1873 Cooke went into bankruptcy, and Drexel, Morgan no longer had a worthy rival. The propaganda campaign had worked well. Cooke closed his doors at midday on 18 September. That afternoon the domino effect closed 37 banks and brokerage houses in New York City alone. Railroad construction stopped immediately, not only on Cooke's Northern Pacific, but on railroads throughout the country. Steel mills, sawmills, big and little industries all over the United States shut down. Mobs of frightened, hungry, angry, suddenly unemployed men rushed banks to withdraw their savings. Before the year was out over 5,000 businesses had failed. Daniel Drew was perhaps the hardest hit. When it was over his assets included only his watch, his fur coat and a few other clothing items, his Bibles and prayer books. He was eighty years old. The predators of Wall Street knew no loyalty. Gould and Fisk had dumped the old man who had given them their start, and raped his fortune.

Now Gould kept a wary eye on the downward spiraling Union Pacific stock. He found a new partner to replace the dead Fisk. Russell Sage was not so flamboyant as Fisk, but he was smarter and wealthier. Gould and Sage waited patiently for Union Pacific stock to hit rock bottom.

There were other men who waited patiently, knowing that financial panics are the best time to make money, provided the capital is handy for investment at the right time. Andrew Carnegie was thirty eight years old. He had bought stocks here and there at low prices and expanded his iron making business. The twenty four year old Henry Clay Frick had cornered the coke and coal market in similar fashion. And way out west in Cleveland, Ohio, John Davison Rockefeller's Standard Oil Company weathered the financial storm well. The economic tempest had eliminated at least 20 of the Standard's competitors.

Rockefeller and Morgan had quickly seen that unlimited competition was destructive, not only to the individual, but to the government, to the entire economic structure. Morgan saw himself as a patriot, who could make his money while saving his country from greedy speculators. The slick old rapscallions of American wealth, Vanderbilt, Drew, Gould, Fisk, Carnegie and Frick were fast going out of style. The new way, the Morgan and Rockefeller way, of an economy kept stable by a handful of money manipulators who believed as they did, would have to win in the end, for the good of all.

There were far more wealthy investors in Europe than in America. With J.S. Morgan and Company in London, Drexel, Harjes and Company in Paris, and an alliance with the Rothschilds,

Pierpont Morgan was suddenly one of the key figures in American finance, although at that time his name was virtually unknown to the average American citizen.

Pierpont's offices were now at the corner of Broad and Wall Streets. His family occupied a brownstone house at 6 East Fortieth Street, near Fifth Avenue. And at Highland Falls, near West Point, the Morgans had their own country place, called Cragston.

Pierpont suffered, however, from frequent colds and headaches, along with the recurring skin inflammation which became increasingly disfiguring as he grew older. *Rosacea,* an enigmatic skin disease which features engorged blood vessels, can be treated now with antibiotics and laser surgery, but untreated it produces raised clusters of swollen veins, pustules and the inflamed, bulbous *rhinophyma* nose which disfigured Morgan. Its cause is still unknown, however, with suspects being stress, and *H. pylori,* a bacterium that causes peptic ulcers. Pierpont's tendency to digestive problems and the tremendous amount of stress in his life suggests either or both as the cause of his rosacea. While, especially in Morgan's time, heavy drinking was thought to be the cause of rosacea, a belief capitalized upon by the late comedian W. C. Fields who also suffered from it, alcoholism appears not to be involved.

Pierpont and Fanny, and the children, frequently traveled abroad, often to England where they would stay at one of his father's homes, either the city house at Prince's Gate, near London's Hyde Park, or at Dover House, the country estate at Roehampton. When they came home to Cragston, the Morgans entertained often and lavishly. Pierpont enjoyed long walks with his mastiff, Hero, when he could find the time and was well enough. He began to breed dogs and a gift of one of his pedigreed collie pups was a favor bestowed only upon those he liked and trusted completely.

William H. Vanderbilt, son of the old Commodore who had made his fortune in shipping, had formed the New York Central Railroad by consolidating several small competitive roads. Vanderbilt owned 87% of the Central, which reached all the way from New York to Chicago. Vanderbilt knew that he was not popular with the general public, who greatly resented these rich men who owned so much and made a mockery of honest competition. With the New York state legislature breathing down his neck, questioning his vast inheritance and wanting to impose controls on railroad management, Vanderbilt decided it would be wise to shed the appearance of monopoly. He consulted Morgan who was known to have English investors at his fingertips.

Morgan and Vanderbilt made a secret agreement to sell 250,000 shares of New York Central Stock to English investors. Morgan wanted the Wabash, St. Louis and Pacific Railroad, to connect with the Central. Vanderbilt agreed, and the Central and Wabash were joined. This maneuver forestalled the legislature's attack on monopolies, but it also put an end to one of the freight wars which was destroying railroad profits. Morgan now had a line that stretched from the Atlantic coast halfway across the country, and he had cleared $3 million in profit to boot. Pierpont insisted upon having a seat on the Central's board of directors, while his firm, Drexel, Morgan & Co., were agents for the rival Pennsylvania Railroad. His next move was even more astute… Morgan leased the newly acquired Wabash to Jay Gould's Missouri Pacific.

While the Astors and the Vanderbilts competed for top place in the pecking order of the New World's aristocracy, and finally joined forces so neither would reign without the other, Pierpont Morgan and his family kept quieter company. Morgan was not able to bring himself to spend money like Vanderbilt, on what he considered frivolous, ostentatious items. Pierpont kept his eyes on the future, on the power that he was building, and left the showy extravagance for others. At home he maintained absolute rule over his household, as men did in those days, except for his daughter Anne. She had inherited his intelligent, piercing eyes, and strong will. When he asked her one day what she wanted to be when she grew up, her reply was typical of her independence, *"Something better than a rich fool, anyway,"* was the child's quick retort.

The Morgans, father and son, had needed to persuade the English investors that American railroads could be turned away from their headlong race to destruction through irresponsible competition. In December, 1881, Junius took Pierpont on a business trip, a pilgrimage to the Holy Land during which they discussed the railroad wars while they traveled aboard a chartered British steam yacht named ***PANDORA***. It inspired Pierpont to cable his order for the 165 foot yacht ***CORSAIR***, the first of his yachts to bear the name derived from his alleged ancestor, the infamous buccaneer Henry Morgan. ***CORSAIR*** was slow, but comfortable in a seaway. With her glossy black hull she looked like a pirate ship, and pirates of industry held many secret meetings in her saloon. Many a Morgan contract was signed and sealed far out at sea, away from the prying eyes of newspaper reporters and business rivals.

Pierpont went home to Cragston, where his headaches returned, probably caused this time by the din of construction on a new railroad nearby. Gandydancers, the itinerant track workers, were too close to home for the Morgans, whose lives had always been carefully sheltered from the travails of the lower classes.

The West Shore Line was a "blackmail line," a new railroad built solely for the purpose of driving down prices and putting another road out of business. In this case a personal vendetta was involved. George Pullman was a director of the West Shore, and Pullman was ready to destroy Vanderbilt and the Central, because Vanderbilt had refused to use his "hotels on wheels," the new Pullman luxury cars.

Vanderbilt struck back in similar fashion. He began building the South Pennsylvania railroad, to link up with the Philadelphia and Reading, and break up the Pennsy's freight monopoly to Andrew Carnegie's steel mills and Henry Frick's coal mines. John D. Rockefeller joined Vanderbilt. Not one mile of track was ever laid, although forests were cleared, land was leveled, and reputedly two thousand men died to build another "blackmail" railroad.

The Morgans, Junius and Pierpont, already had a reputation for financial stability in times of economic crisis. Cyrus Field cabled Junius on his own pioneering transatlantic cable, suggesting that more English money, funneled through Drexel, Morgan & Co., might ward off another American economic collapse caused by the endless railroad wars. Junius gave the project to Pierpont.

It took months of negotiating, but Pierpont had decided that harmony between the Central and the Pennsy was the key to success. He easily persuaded Vanderbilt, who was already in his debt. But the Pennsy's George Roberts was another story. As stubborn as Morgan, Roberts was talked into coming aboard ***CORSAIR*** for a secret conference with Morgan and Vanderbilt. ***CORSAIR*** steamed from New York harbor to Sandy Hook, and back. Still the men glowered, threatened, complained, and settled nothing. ***CORSAIR*** steamed to West Point, and back to Sandy Hook again while Morgan wheedled, cajoled and intimidated.

Roberts was the last to capitulate. Morgan had won, and in so doing, had come very close to breaking the laws of Pennsylvania which forbade railroad mergers, and monopolies. The whole transaction was investigated, and Morgan was called upon to explain and justify his actions. He was adroit at avoiding answers which might incriminate him. When asked if the deal had been made aboard ***CORSAIR*** because it was a place of secrecy, Morgan replied simply that *"it was a convenient place."* By the time the Pennsylvania supreme court ruled in 1892 that the Permsy could not acquire its rival, the Central, by virtue of an intermediary sale to Morgan, thereby creating a railroad monopoly, it was too late. Vanderbilt was dead and his heirs were indebted to Morgan. Although there were two railroads, ostensibly rivals, they were controlled by the same man. Competition was anathema to Morgan, unless he competed with himself. It would be almost eight decades before the Central and the Pennsy would openly merge into the now defunct Penn-Central Railroad.

Pierpont was now forty eight years old, and had pulled off his first really big deal without any help from his father, who had just been widowed. He sincerely believed that not only railroads but all industries should be combined into associations, or conglomerates, that could prevent the financial fluctuations that caused economic panics, and would provide better goods and services for the public.

The small, but profitable, Philadelphia and Reading Railroad was now thrown into financial difficulties by Morgan's Pennsylvania Railroad monopoly. The Reading was losing about $6 million each year, and Pierpont assumed the task of making it profitable again. He succeeded, but not without attracting the attention of Congress, which, in 1887, passed a bill establishing the Interstate Commerce Commission. Prior to a United States Supreme Court decision in the case of the Wabash vs. The State of Illinois, states had claimed the right to regulate railroad traffic within their boundaries, a chaotic situation at best. The ICC was established to enforce a Congressional act which was supposed to end the railroads' price-fixing collusion, spawned by the monopolies built by men like Vanderbilt and Morgan.

In December, 1888, Morgan took it upon himself to form a self-regulating group run by the owners instead of the government. This would keep the railroad owners in line and prevent further destructive rate wars. Morgan, of course, would benefit from the growth of a "railroad trust," but so would stockholders and workers.

Once again the Pennsy's George Roberts balked, pointing out that the "gentleman's agreement" urged by Morgan was illegal. Roberts reminded the bankers that it was they who had financed the "blackmail railroads" and created the rate wars which had almost destroyed the industry, and much of the rest of the country with it. But even Roberts eventually capitulated, saying *"but I can stand it, I suppose, if the others can."*

The meetings were held in secrecy, in Morgan's home on Madison Avenue. Reporters clamored for information, egged on by the public which considered the ever-growing trusts to be evil and un-American. All of the big railroad men were there. Each had built his empire with his own combination of guts and greed, and now each was reluctant to hand over even a small measure of authority to an association of men he did not trust. Managers of the western roads especially had no use for the Wall Street bankers, and all was overshadowed by the public fear of conspiracy. In the end it was Morgan's personal charisma which kept the owners reluctantly in his Interstate Commerce Railroad Association. Morgan used several tactics to keep these powerful railroad men in line. There were the voting trusts, in which shareholders handed over voting rights to Morgan's men. Drexel, Morgan and Company obtained the majority of shares in the companies; and Morgan himself sat on the boards of a dozen railroads, while his men sat on the boards of the rest of them in a vast interlocking directorate.

Unexpectedly, in 1890, in the south of France, Junius was mortally injured. He was thrown from his carriage when its horses bolted, ironically after being frightened by a train. He never regained consciousness, and died a few days later. The aging Junius had been wintering on the French Riviera for several years. Pierpont was enroute to make his annual report to his father when news of Junius's death reached him. Messages sent to him in series were supposed to prepare him gradually for the shock, but the impatient Pierpont read the last one first, and collapsed. His daughter Louisa was with him, and continued on to Monte Carlo to comfort him. Pierpont returned to New York with Junius's body, which was interred in the Morgan plot at Cedar Hill Cemetery. In Connecticut, flags on all state government buildings were flown at half-mast. Such was the importance of the Morgan family in that state.

Junius left the bulk of his nearly $10 million estate to be divided among his daughters. He knew that Pierpont had his own wealth, and would be acquiring much, much more. To his son Junius he bequeathed $1 million, and his two London homes. Pierpont was finally the undisputed master of the family fortune. Like his contemporary-in-waiting, England's Prince of Wales, Pierpont was well-prepared for his new position.

Recovering quickly from his grief as usual, Pierpont returned to London, leaving his son. Jack, in New York to collect economic intelligence and forward it to London. Jack was now cast in the role that Pierpont had played for so many years.

But before he sailed eastward, Pierpont ordered a new ***CORSAIR***. He gave the new yacht's designer carte blanche with a book of signed blank checks. He stipulated only that the yacht must be as large as possible and still be able to turn around in the Hudson River at Cragston. ***CORSAIR II*** was 241.5 ft. long overall, (204 feet at her waterline). Her hull was glossy black like her predecessor, but with three engines she was faster than the first ***CORSAIR***. She was a fine sea boat, as large as the early transatlantic liners had been, but shorter than Willie Vanderbilt's ***ALVA***, which was 285 feet, yet comparable to Jay Gould's ***ATALANTA*** at 250 feet, and larger than William Astor's ***NOURMAHAL***, a mere 233 feet overall. Perhaps to further reassure himself of his new status, Pierpont bought George Washington's sword to add to his growing collection of artifacts.

By the year 1890 America had been divided into states and territories that ostensibly were part of the whole, but it still remained economically divided by the ethnic differences in East and West. Western and Eastern financiers generally did not trust one another, often with good reason. The East, said the West, was crowded into cities full of immigrants, who took American jobs and salaries, and drove men to the West's cheap land, where a fortune, or at least a good living, could still be made from the fertile soil.

Farming, however, is a hard life, and dependent upon many things outside of the farmers' control. Nature did not always cooperate, and in fact, she often rampaged against the frailties of man. Adversity breeds organization, and farmers began to bond together in their hatred of the East. The big Eastern trusts became a prime target of these new rural bondings.

But Western banking houses needed to communicate with those on Wall Street, and farmers needed transportation to sell their products back East, in those very cities from whence they had fled. And farmers, with their families, were dependent upon the manufactured goods from the East. The westward growth of the railroads, with smooth connections between rival Eastern and Western lines, was mandated by the burgeoning population along the West Coast. In twenty years that population had more than doubled, growing from seven million to seventeen million, and it was still growing rapidly. Every place along the way where farmland was good, where engines needed to replenish water and coal, a town sprang up. The towns which had been necessary for stagecoach stops were no longer needed. Horses could go only ten miles at top speed before they were worn out, and another team had to take over the stagecoach. Steam engines went hundreds of miles before refueling. As stagecoach towns died, their occupants were forced to move, usually west. Men blamed the railroads, and their owners, the new railroad trusts, for their forced moves, their hardships. Yet many men knew that their very lives depended upon what they hated most, the railroads. There is no hatred like that of one who knows he is indebted, and has no control over his own life. Pierpont Morgan, the new rail baron, became a symbol of railroad domination, and thus became the target of public hatred, the scapegoat for everyman's problems.

Jay Gould of the Union Pacific shared Morgan's ambition to gain control of a transcontinental rail system. But Morgan had the money, and Gould needed Morgan's financial backing. Morgan accepted Gould's notes, but Gould rebelled at Morgan's domination. He reverted to the old rate-cutting on the Union Pacific, while Morgan was trying to organize western roads into price fixing associations, as he had done in the East. On 26 December, 1892, Gould's daughter Helen made her debut into New York Society. Gould had invited 3,000 people to attend the affair, but only a few hundred showed up. The Astors and the Vanderbilts were conspicuous by their absence. But Pierpont and Fanny had the courtesy to attend. Jay Gould died a few days later, and Morgan had the Union Pacific.

By default Morgan had won control of one of the biggest western railroads. He had transcontinental service now. The New York Central ran from New York to Chicago, and the Union Pacific picked up traffic there and carried it all the way to the West Coast. Along the railroad right of ways had gone the telegraph lines. East and West were linked by transportation and communication into one great country, for all time.

Jay Gould had been the last of the great railway raiders. Farmers and reformers who had hated Gould's trickery with a passion could now turn all of their animosity toward Morgan. But Morgan could claim patriotism, and he really believed it. Whatever else motivated Pierpont, and unquestionably the drive for moneyed power did, he sincerely believed that his control was in the country's interest, and certainly it appears to have been. Having conquered the northern transcontinental railroad route, Pierpont now turned to the south. No less than thirty five railroads competed in a chaos of tracks and rate wars across the southern part of the United States. Morgan moved to reorganize the key road, the Richmond and West Point Terminal Line, but not without receiving controlling stock. With the line in such poor financial condition, its owners had to accept Morgan's terms. Patiently, he watched the other thirty four roads plunge toward bankruptcy. Morgan's fee for creating the new Southern Railway System out of this mishmash of small railroads was $850,000, while the voting stock majority was placed in the hands of his own men. As usual, the whole transaction had to be rushed and secret, finished before Congress and minority stockholders knew what was going on. In 1890 the Sherman Antitrust Act had been created to prevent just such monopolies. In particular the Sherman act was directed at eliminating Morgan's railroad trust and Rockefeller's Standard Oil trust. Actually the Sherman Act did no such thing. It merely quieted the rumbling Western dissidents, and left the Eastern magnates in power.

The men behind the fierce railway rate wars had gone too far in forcing employees into starvation wages. In 1892 the Carnegie steelworkers at Homestead, Pennsylvania struck, and two years later the class war blazed anew in a strike at George Pullman's luxury railroad car company.

Carnegie, rather than give up his forced twelve hour work day and lower piece rate, locked out the union men, and sailed off to Europe, leaving his partner, Henry Clay Frick, to handle the dangerous situation. Frick reacted as all big employers did; he hired 300 Pinkerton strikebreakers, who arrived in armored scows. Gunfire came from both sides. Three Pinkerton men and five of the strikers died before the strikebreakers broke ranks and ran. The Governor of Pennsylvania sent in the militia, 8,000 strong, to restore order. Frick had been shot and stabbed, and almost died. Carnegie's reputation as a coward never left him, while Frick was seen as the capitalists' hero.

George Pullman fared no better. When he tried to cut wages to the bone, Eugene Debs's American Railway Union backed the Pullman strikers and 150,000 Railway Union men refused to handle Pullman cars on any railroad. Two thirds of the country's railway system was shut down. President Grover Cleveland called in federal troops, and invoked the Sherman Antitrust Law... against Debs and the Railway Union! Coxey's Army of unemployed marched on Washington, increasing the hostility against the big money men of the East, of whom Morgan was still the symbol. The country was in the middle of a four year depression, the worst yet seen.

As his financial empire grew, Morgan diversified. As he rescued railroads, so he rescued governments. When the Argentine government defaulted on bond payments, Morgan guaranteed the sale of $75 million in government bonds to bail out the South American country.

The Panic of 1893 was a repeat of other periodic financial crises, for all the same reasons. Before the year was out 550 banks had failed, 6 mortgage companies had gone under, along with over 15,000 companies and businesses of varying sizes. Thirteen trust companies went into bankruptcy. The nouveau riche speculators, who had amassed their holdings on credit, went down with the poor. Morgan loaned money to those with flawless reputations. The others he let struggle, and most of them did not make it through the depression. Just after the worst of the panic, Morgan's partner, Anthony J. Drexel, died, leaving an estate of $30 million. Morgan was free now, no longer restrained by Drexel's conservatism. Within two years he dropped Drexel's name from the firm. Others were leaving him, some taken by death, some retiring after years of overwork. Morgan replaced them with young blood, those who had the youth and vigor that he was now losing. He was at the height of his power now, yet he was accessible, with a genuine warmth that hid his depression and headaches. His business reputation was impeccable. Morgan's word was absolutely good in any boardroom in the world. His judgement of men was just as good as his word.

Morgan still found solace in his church. Reverend W. S. Rainsford, rector of St. George's Episcopal Church, and Morgan's confessor, often found Pierpont in church at night, alone with an organist to play hymns while he sang them in his booming voice. There were those on Wall Street who said that Pierpont could not live much longer, because he had "fits." He still suffered from his nervous collapses, his melancholia. His disfigurement had worsened with age. But his piercing dark eyes stopped short any who would stare at his flaming, engorged nose. His social position had been ascertained not so much by his great wealth, as by his dynamic virility and showmanship, which remains unparalleled to this day. Pierpont's son, Jack, growing up in his shadow, remained reclusive and shy. Pierpont hid his own self doubts behind a facade of legendary grandeur which successfully concealed the real man.

Morgan clashed again with his old adversary, Edward H. Harriman, first over the bankrupt Erie Railroad, which Morgan had been called in to save. Backed by the prestigious investment firm of Kuhn, Loeb and Co., which was representing the Rothschilds and the Astors, Harriman objected, on the grounds that Morgan's plan was financially unsound. The Supreme Court found for Morgan, but the Erie defaulted, not just once but twice on Morgan's newly issued bonds. The creditors, siding with Harriman, demanded another plan.

The Union Pacific now went into the hands of the receivers, and Morgan was on the committee headed by Senator Brice which was formed to rescue it. Congress, surprisingly, blocked Morgan's attempts to reorganize the railroad and pay off its government debts. A disgusted Morgan divorced himself from the line, a great mistake. Suddenly and mysteriously, with Morgan out and Harriman on the committee. Congress changed its collective mind and approved the reorganization and loan settlements. Harriman's plan all along had been to acquire the Illinois Central, to link it to his Union Pacific. Harriman had become an opponent worthy of Morgan's talents.

But Harriman's victory came as much from Morgan's loss of interest as from the Western rail baron's talents. Morgan now spent three months out of every year on vacation, either in Europe or aboard ***CORSAIR II.*** He enjoyed an active social life, not always with Fanny. His friends included the famous, and the infamous, the titled and the merely very wealthy. His ostentatious lifestyle naturally attracted attention, especially from those too poor to afford even life's necessities. Morgan had always been a Republican, except when he voted for Democrat Grover Cleveland in the election of 1884. Morgan's father-in-law, Charles Tracy, had been a prominent New York attorney with political connections. His law firm. Bangs, Stetson, Tracy and McVeagh, had represented the Morgan interests for some time. When Tracy died, Francis Lynde Stetson became head of the firm, and Morgan's chief legal adviser. Stetson used his influence with Cleveland to win favors for Morgan, a move which served to bolster the believe of the western farmers that big money men of the east were running the government for their own self-aggrandizement. This conviction was reinforced when the Cleveland administration repealed the Sherman Compromise Silver Act of 1893.

Excessive silver mining had caused the price of silver to drop to nearly half its face value. The U.S. treasury was forced to redeem silver certificates with its gold reserves, which quickly fell below the legal limit of $100 million. European investors became nervous and cashed in their U.S. Treasury bonds. The Secretary of the Treasury implored Morgan to pick up the second issue of government bonds, a matter of $50 million, in a desperate attempt to stave off the country's economic collapse. Morgan called on James Stillman, his rival at the National City Bank, for help. Stillman found Morgan near a breakdown, complaining that $50 million was too much to expect from him. Stillman cabled his European contacts and quickly raised $20 million. Morgan provided the remainder. It seemed that Morgan was more solvent than the United States Treasury, an image which did nothing to increase his popularity with the man in the street, or on the farm.

In two months, however, the situation had worsened. There was an even greater run on gold, by those who either hoarded it at home out of panic, or shipped it abroad at great profit to themselves. In one month alone the U.S. Treasury was forced to hand out $45 million in bullion. At that rate the Treasury would collapse in a matter of weeks. It was then considered unthinkable to leave the gold standard, although many years later the United States as well as other countries would be forced to do so.

The November election spelled victory for the eastern financiers. Although the Democratic vote of the South and West, led by William Jennings Bryan, had risen, nevertheless Republicans claimed a clean sweep of both the Presidency and Congress. Only four Democratic senators were reelected, and they were pledged, along with two known sympathizers, to push for an income tax on the rich. American workers were fed up with toiling twelve, and more, hours a day, six and sometimes seven days a week, to build the tremendous fortunes of a few men on Wall Street.

Hard on the heels of the failure of the second government gold bond issue, came news that European investors were selling their American securities in return for gold. There were two choices. Either leave the gold standard, in favor of the silver lobby from the West, and thereby destroy American credit abroad, or turn again to the bankers, meaning Morgan. Once more the Secretary of the Treasury, John G. Carlisle, went to Morgan, who had already been apprised of the seriousness of the situation by his London office.

Morgan and his associates agreed, and asked for 3 3/4 percent on the needed $100 million, far less than the interest rate demanded by European investors. Rumors of a new bond issue spread rapidly, and helped to stop the Treasury's outflow, while the Western and Southern interests were infuriated. They saw more profiteering by the Eastern financiers, and the fact that Cleveland himself did not favor Morgan's offer encouraged them. Under this pressure Secretary Carlisle refused Morgan's offer, and decided to try once again a public offer of Treasury bonds.

Believing that the new government move was nothing but folly, Morgan and his associate, August Belmont, went directly to Washington and saw President Cleveland. The meeting came to nothing. Cleveland decided to risk all on another public bond offer. Morgan cabled his London office, saying strongly that he would fight to save the U.S. currency, but he feared what might happen to the United States if he could not.

The House of Representatives seemed to agree with Morgan, and two days after his futile meeting with Cleveland, the House voted against allowing the administration to issue more gold bonds. Morgan, along with Stetson and Bacon, boarded his private car, bound for Washington again. Secretary of War Lamont met the train, with a message from Cleveland. The President was adamant. He would not negotiate a private bond sale to Morgan interests, and he would not even see Morgan. Pierpont informed Cleveland that he would stay in Washington until Cleveland changed his mind. Some historians say that Morgan did indeed consider giving up and returning to New York. At any rate, he took a room for the night at the Arlington Hotel, and played solitaire alone in his room, after receiving several visitors who braved a raging blizzard to offer him their support.

Morgan thought back to his gold speculation during the Civil War. There was a law on the books, he remembered, which had been passed in Lincoln's administration, and it allowed the Secretary of the Treasury to buy gold without Congressional approval when it was needed. If the law had not been repealed, and Morgan thought it had not, then Cleveland did not need the approval of Congress to deal with Morgan.

Cleveland capitulated. He agreed to see Morgan the next morning, February 8th. The President was with the Attorney General, Richard Olney, and Secretary Carlisle. Morgan's associate, Robert Bacon, was also with Cleveland when Morgan entered the office. Cleveland announced that he would still prefer to offer gold bonds to the public again, provided that an interim loan could be obtained to keep up the gold reserves until the bond sales receipts came in. Morgan mentioned the Lincoln law of 1862 he had been thinking about the night before. Cleveland had never heard of it. Morgan reminded him that the Civil War had been financed by private contracts made with the government. Why should such a thing not be done now? The alternative was probably complete destruction of United States currency.

Morgan then surprisingly told Cleveland that he and his associates could find all the gold the government needed. In effect this meant that Morgan was ready to control the entire international gold market, in the interest of the United States, and of course, his syndicate.

Cleveland mulled over Morgan's claims and offer. He had his doubts at first, then came to see Morgan as a "man of large business comprehension and of remarkable knowledge and prescience... of clear-sighted, far-seeing patriotism." Morgan offered $100 million in gold, raising his interest rate to 4 percent. Cleveland needed only 3.5 million ounces, valued at $65 million. Morgan dropped the interest to 3 per cent, provided that the bonds were redeemable in gold. The two men drew up and signed a contract, never expecting Congress to approve it.

News of the contract became known immediately in New York's financial community. From the specie rooms of liners ready to sale for Europe, $18 million in gold was removed, to stay in the United States. Morgan cabled his European associates, ordering them to send their gold to America, while he let the bankers know that he would pay more for their gold than they could get overseas. Morgan's plans worked well. The Treasury reserve was once again up to a safe level of

$100 million.

But Morgan had little thanks from the public, who noticed only that his group had cleared about $7 million profit from their "patriotism." Morgan's own share was probably no more than $300,000. Morgan always refused to give any figures for his profit, even when under oath at a Senate inquiry into the transaction. It hardly mattered. The Treasury had been shorn up, the deep depression was over, economic recovery was rapid. Morgan had risked his reputation and disastrous personal loss to save his country He could see it no other way.

John Q. Public saw it differently, of course. The Supreme Court had struck down any chance of an income tax law. There were different laws for the rich and the poor. Working men continued to scratch for a living, although jobs were beginning to open up again, and bread lines and soup kitchens gradually shut down as men went back to work, albeit at the same twelve hour days and six or seven day weeks. Cleveland's own party turned against him, saying that he had become too much of a Republican.

Morgan now clashed with Cleveland in another matter. Threat of war loomed over Europe, and Morgan naturally sided with the British. Cleveland did not. In fact, Cleveland's foreign policy was now directed against the British, hated for their increasingly large investments in American businesses. While Morgan wanted to, and was, increasing foreign investments in America, Cleveland was trying to put a stop to it. Americans naturally rallied round the flag, and Cleveland. *"America for Americans"* was the cry. No more foreigners moving in to take American jobs. Never mind that "Americans" and their ancestors, except for those hapless, exploited native American "Indians," had come from elsewhere, most from the British Isles, or the European Continent.

Just before Christmas in 1895, there was another run on gold. Morgan went to Washington again, to offer $200 million in gold coin to the U.S. Treasury. He named the members of his syndicate, prudently leaving out any with Jewish or European taint, as well as his British sources. Cleveland and Morgan moored their yachts side by side in a secluded cove, and met once again. But Cleveland knew that he could make political points for himself by turning away the unpopular Wall Street barons, and he turned a deaf ear to Morgan's blandishments.

Cleveland tried other national banks, including the Bank of France, for emergency loans. Congress grew furious over Morgan's new intervention, and Cleveland continued to balk. He refused to see Morgan again, or to negotiate with him in any way. Joseph Pulitzer's *New York World* continued to rail against the Morgan syndicate, inflaming the American populace even more. Pulitzer made a public pledge to buy $1 million in gold bonds at the highest market price. The offer brought in telegrams from all over the country, with pledges totaling $235 million. A Pulitzer editorial exhorted Cleveland to "smash the ring" of Wall Street barons who controlled the American economy. A contemporary cartoon showed Morgan in a pirate costume, demanding $12 million ransom from Uncle Sam. The politically prudent Cleveland continued to ignore Morgan's offers.

Secretary Carlisle announced the fourth public issue of gold bonds in the amount of $100 million. Morgan declared his support for the public issue and made one of the highest offers through his own firm, which was now called simply J. Pierpont Morgan and Company. Morgan claimed $33 million worth of bonds, with another $5 million going to him by default. It was enough to solve the latest gold crisis. The government had learned that it was difficult to get along without Morgan.

Again a Senate investigation failed to find any government conspiracy with Morgan. Senator Marcus Alonso Hanna, the Cleveland, Ohio, iron-ore magnate, schoolmate and lifelong friend of

John D. Rockefeller, was Morgan's next political contact. Hanna had won infamy from his alleged statement that *"a man in public office owes the public nothing"* Now Hanna was promoting McKinley for Republican candidate in the next presidential election. Morgan invited Hanna and McKinley to dinner aboard ***CORSAIR II.***

The Republicans needed a middle-of-the road politician to placate both sides and win the election. McKinley remained silent on the currency issue throughout his campaign. The Democratic candidate, William Jennings Bryan, was the candidate of small-business owners who could not compete with the big trusts. Morgan was one symbol of the trusts. But Morgan knew that if the United States did not maintain its gold standard, then European financiers would not buy American securities. It was that simple. McKinley won the election with Morgan's tremendous backing. The long depression ended, and Morgan continued to reorganize America's railroads, with financial backing from London, and Berlin. He dominated the Erie, he controlled the Reading; he controlled the Northern Pacific and the Great Northern; he had a large interest in the Atchison, Topeka and Santa Fé. Morgan controlled the Hocking Valley, the Chesapeake and Ohio, the Baltimore and Ohio, the Central of Georgia, and he was the financial backing of Vanderbilt's vast rail system, including the big New York Central.

But Morgan was not content with an American financial empire. Junius Morgan had used British capital to finance the development of the western United States. Pierpont rescued the British Empire during the Boer War, by funding one fifth of the war costs through American loans underwritten by his banking firm. Through his German affiliate, the Deutsche Bank, Pierpont shored up the Mexican economy by funding that country's national debt.

Pierpont balked, however, when ***CORSAIR II*** was requisitioned by the U. S. Navy during the Spanish American War. Her name changed to ***USS GLOUCESTER***, Morgan's little yacht acquitted herself well, surviving the war to serve just as well in World War I. Pierpont soon replaced ***CORSAIR II*** with ***CORSAIR III.*** And with his railroad empire thriving, Morgan began to collect art treasures, an expensive hobby that eventually alarmed the old British families whose treasures were enlarging Morgan's collection.

Morgan turned his organizing talents to other industries. He consolidated the steel industry, the banks, trust and insurance companies. He organized the giant combine General Electric. And he worked the men who ran these companies for him as hard as he worked himself, often to the destruction of their health, their family lives, and in the end their own lives. When McKinley came back to the White House for a second term in the election of 1900, his vice president, Theodore Roosevelt, courted Morgan. Coal miners, working in foul conditions for starvation wages, a situation forced upon the mine owners by the low price of coal paid by steel and railroad owners, had rebelled and struck. Senator Hanna called in Pierpont Morgan to settle the strike. Morgan ordered the mine owners to accept the miners' compromise terms. Such, then, was Pierpont Morgan's power at the turn of the century, and it continued to grow.

After reorganizing America's railroads and steel industry, Pierpont turned his gaze eastward. America's merchant fleet was in a mess similar to that of the railroads when Morgan stepped in, due to price wars and too much competition. Morgan set out to reorganize North Atlantic shipping lines in the same way he had consolidated railroads, then to operate them at a profit to him, and for the good of the United States.

The British, whose lines were among those raided by Morgan, protested in Parliament and the media. But Morgan naturally had his defenders on both sides of the Atlantic. He had quickly acquired two old British lines, the Leyland and the White Star, but he had bought them partly in stock and bonds, but partly in $22.5 million in gold. Morgan had also paid inflated prices for the shares in each company, and in fact, the chairman of the Leyland Line had told his shareholders that Morgan's offer was so "extravagant that no management had the right to refuse it." While Morgan had plans for efficiency that had never before been seen on the Western Ocean, for a liner sailing nearly every day of the week in each direction rather than three rival lines sailing on the same day with no service for the remainder of the week, and he wanted transatlantic voyages to be as simple as transcontinental train trips, Morgan was still a patriot. He wanted these ships to fly the Stars and Stripes. In the end it did not work out that way, for by law only vessels built in the United States could fly its flag.

It is beyond the scope of this book to recount the massive financial labyrinth which was Morgan's International Mercantile Marine Company. Suffice it here to say that it was a highly complex structure which encompassed the two big German lines, Hapag and the Lloyd, with which I.M.M. had a profit-sharing agreement; the Holland-America Line, of which I.M.M. owned a large block of stock; the Red Star Line, White Star Line, Leyland Line, Dominion Line, American Line and the American Transport Line. Additionally Lord Pirrie of Harland & Wolff was on the board of directors of the I.M.M., and an agreement with Harland & Wolff assured that all ships and repair work done in Great Britain would be undertaken by Harland & Wolff. Some I.M.M. vessels would be built in the United States, however, because the lines flew the American flag. The Belfast shipyard would be paid on a cost plus 5% on new building, plus 10% on new machinery installed in old ships, and plus 15% on repairs. In return Harland & Wolff agreed not to build for any other shipping line outside of the I.M.M. combine and its Continental associates as long as the latter's orders kept the yard fully employed. The voting control of the new trust was assumed by a five member board consisting of Morgan, P. A. B. Widener, a director of the Pennsylvania Railroad (whose son George would perish in ***TITANIC***) and Charles Steele, a junior partner in J. P. Morgan Co. and a member of the board of directors of the Erie Railroad, as well as General Electric, the Hocking Valley Railway Company, the Southern Railway Company, and United States Steel. White Star's Managing Director J. Bruce Ismay and Harland & Wolff's Lord Pirrie completed the quintet. I.M.M.'s president was Clement Acton Griscom, a Philadelphian who had amassed most of his fortune in shipping. Among Griscom interests was the International Navigation Company, which had in 1873 bought the Belgian Red Star Line. In 1884 the INC had taken over the Keystone Line, which operated a Philadelphia-Queenstown-Liverpool service under American registry. Keystone was backed by the Pennsylvania Railroad. In 1886 Griscom had purchased the Inman Line, and in 1893 he combined Keystone and Inman into the American Line, which took over Red Star's Philadelphia service. Griscom also had interests in New York and New Jersey companies, including Standard Oil. We may remember Bill Müller's assessment of the hard-driving Griscom from Chapter 7. I.M.M.'s vice president was no less than Harland & Wolff's chief, Lord Pirrie. Although Morgan knew very little about shipping or ships, he surrounded himself with men who did.

The mention of "New Jersey" companies was significant. In 1889 a New Jersey attorney named James B. Dill had promoted an amendment of that state's corporation laws which would allow one corporation within its jurisdiction to own the stock of another. In 1896 New Jersey law was further amended to allow any corporation to own shares in another, whether the company was chartered in New Jersey or another state. This was the reason why so many companies were reorganizing in the state of New Jersey.

When President McKinley was shot by Polish anarchist Leon Czolgosz on 6 September, 1901, in

Buffalo, New York, Morgan was devastated. McKinley had, by his non-intervention policy, become a Morgan ally, albeit a reluctant one. Vice President Theodore Roosevelt had gone immediately to Buffalo to attend to any matters the President might want, but doctors pronounced McKinley's wounds not fatal, not even dangerous. Roosevelt left Buffalo cheerfully, but one week later, on Friday the 13th, the Vice President received word that McKinley's condition had worsened. Before Roosevelt could get to Buffalo McKinley was dead. When Roosevelt was sworn in as President he responded with: *"I shall take the oath of office in obedience to your request, sir, and in doing so, it shall be my aim to continue absolutely unbroken the policies of President McKinley for the peace, prosperity, and honor of our beloved country."* Theodore Roosevelt, the leader of the "Rough Riders" of San Juan Hill fame, the descendant of 17th century Dutch immigrants, was the twenty sixth president of the United States and at the age of forty three the youngest man yet to occupy the White House.

Morgan had just come from a battle with the new Amalgamated Association of Iron, Steel and Tin Workers union, a labor problem he inherited with Carnegie's United States Steel Corporation. The union had been trying to establish a union closed shop. Instead of using Carnegie and Frick's armed tactics, Morgan starved the union workers by using scab labor. The police suspected that a "secret anarchist organization" was dedicated to killing important capitalists, with the result that Morgan had a police bodyguard for some time, and he lived as much as he could aboard his yacht for safety.

Morgan dashed off to San Francisco aboard a special train to attend the Triennial Convention of the Episcopal Church. All other trains were sent to sidings while the Morgan special passed, allowing Morgan to make a transcontinental speed record. When he returned to New York Morgan continued his progress in acquiring two large British steamship lines.

Vanderbilt, the wily old Commodore, had once allegedly remarked, *"The public be damned."* Senator Hanna had said, *"A man in public office owes the public nothing."* And Pierpont had once said, *"I owe the public nothing."* This, believed the public, epitomized the feelings, or lack thereof, of the bankers behind the big trusts and the politicians they controlled. Roosevelt, who had vowed to uphold McKinley's hands-off policies, was an idealist who understood perfectly well how the big trusts caused laws to be made in their favor, and how they evaded current laws which were inconvenient for them. The big money men were naturally not going to relinquish control to satisfy Roosevelt's idealism, yet they recognized that he operated on a rational system of principles which would not allow him to cross over to their side. So they began a propaganda campaign which questioned his competence, his integrity and his sanity.

The time had come when almost every boardroom in America was part of a vast interlocking directorate and at the center of that huge spiderweb sat Pierpont Morgan and John D. Rockefeller. If they themselves were not on every board of directors their affiliates and/or relatives were. And while in some cases the first generation was gone, for example Commodore Vanderbilt and Jay Gould, the names were perpetuated in succeeding generations which continued to dominate the boardrooms of America. Although in many cases there was personal animosity between these men, their financial positions demanded that they be more than business acquaintances. Their extreme wealth naturally threw them together socially as well, for who else could keep up with their entertainment expenditures? And they had another thing in common… their dislike and distrust of the trustbuster, Rough Rider Colonel Teddy Roosevelt.

William Roscoe Thayer, a friend of Roosevelt's for forty years as well as his biographer, wrote in 1919 that Roosevelt was so "natural, so unguarded, in his speech and ways, that he laid himself open to calumny." Certainly Roosevelt was a man larger than life, and full of life, full of enthusiasm, which he expressed without reserve. He was accused of being egotistical, always wanting to be the central figure wherever he went. One of his sons had remarked, *"Father never likes to go to a wedding or a funeral, because he can't be the bride at the wedding or the corpse at the funeral."* But Roosevelt was well aware of his flaws, if they were that, and laughed at them. As Thayer also wrote, *"The truth is, that he could no more help being the central figure than a lion could in any gathering of lesser creatures."* This, then, was the man who took it upon himself to "bust the trusts," the man who called the bankers "plutocrats and monopolists," and "malefactors of great wealth," and "the wealthy criminal class." Such rhetoric served to bring the bankers closer together to fight the common enemy. The public saw Roosevelt as the man of the square deal, the friend of the underdog, and the man who could fight the trusts. It was said that no other president until that time had kept Congress so busy. Among other laws pushed through Congress by Theodore Roosevelt were the Elkins Anti-Rebate Law, which applied to the railroads" price-fixing; the creation of the Department of Commerce, also aimed at the railroad barons; the creation of the Pure Food and Meat Inspection laws; the law creating the Bureau of Immigration; the Employers' Liability and Safety Appliance Laws, which limited working hours of employees; the law making the U.S. Government liable for injuries to its employees; the law forbidding child labor in the District of Columbia; the Hepburn Bill, which amended and put teeth into the Interstate Commerce Act. And Roosevelt fought to save the environment from big companies who would strip land for their own profit. He was also responsible for the prohibition of campaign contributions from corporations, which was intended to put a leash on the big money men who bought Congressmen. It was inevitable that Roosevelt would clash with Morgan.

Roosevelt, along with his Attorney General Philander Knox, decided to start with Morgan's Northern Securities Company. On 19 February, 1902, Knox announced that the U.S. Government would file suit asking for the company's dissolution. Morgan was livid. And so was Wall Street. Stocks spiraled downward. Pierpont raced to Washington to meet with Senator Hanna. Together Morgan and Hanna met with Roosevelt and Knox. Why had he not been warned? Morgan asked. If he had done anything wrong, Morgan told the President, you may send your man to meet with my man and fix it. *"We don't want to fix it up,"* responded Knox. *"We want to stop it."* Morgan asked if Roosevelt intended going after the Steel Trust as well. Roosevelt said they would not, unless it was proven that the law had been broken. Morgan for once was defeated, at least temporarily. No longer did he have control over the White House. Morgan was King of the Trusts, therefore he was the man Roosevelt had to beat.

Pierpont continued to organize his new shipping monopoly, the I.M.M., while he continued to expand his collection of art objects. Morgan and his family retired to the privacy of the Jekyll Island Club, an exclusive resort off the Georgia coast where he and other millionaires could relax, yet discuss business with their peers in guaranteed privacy. When he returned to Washington Pierpont was subpoenaed to testify in the suit against his Northern Securities railroad trust. Morgan believed that the railroad trusts should regulate themselves without government intervention. In the end, after three years of litigation, neither really won. Morgan continued in control of his railroads, while the Supreme Court found in favor of the government by one vote. Roosevelt's victory was symbolic only.

Morgan's younger henchmen were overworked and exhausted while the older Morgan tried to pace himself. He sailed for England in a White Star liner, having ***CORSAIR III*** brought over besides to impress his European associates. An editorial cartoon of the day showed a crowned Morgan seated on a dollar throne with the Kaiser polishing his boots while King Edward VII held up a silver salver for a tip.

The British were alarmed. Not only was Morgan buying up all their shipping lines, now he aimed at the London subway. Alarm increased when Morgan headed a syndicate of his own bank, the Barings and the Rothschilds, to take up half a British government loan for £32 million.

Queen Victoria was gone, and her son prepared for his coronation as Edward VII. Morgan had often met Edward when he was Prince of Wales, usually in Germany at spas frequented by them both. Possibly Morgan advised Edward financially as he did Edward's relative King Leopold of Belgium. There were those who believed that Morgan had loaned money to Edward, for it was known that the latter had lived beyond his means, entertaining lavishly and keeping expensive mistresses. But there was one thing at which Edward had excelled as King-in-waiting… diplomacy. He would be sure that Morgan was his friend before Morgan went on to visit the Kaiser, not only for patriotic reasons. There was intense personal rivalry between Edward and his nephew Wilhelm, an enmity that grew unchecked after Queen Victoria's death. But first Morgan joined ***CORSAIR III*** for a relaxing voyage to Italy, where he met with that country's king, another monarch for whom he was financial adviser. Morgan returned to London, where he was invited to attend Edward's coronation. Then, suddenly, on the eve of his coronation, Edward was stricken with appendicitis and lay near death. When Edward recovered, Morgan continued on in ***CORSAIR III,*** to Kiel, to the Kaiser's royal welcome. The Kaiser wanted to examine Morgan's shipping plans. Morgan declared to the press, *"I have met the Kaiser, and I like him."*

On went the Morgan entourage, overland to Paris, and to London via the boat train, where Pierpont, the king of international finance, finally attended the coronation of the new King of England. Throughout his travels in Europe Morgan had continued to add to his art collection.

Suddenly Morgan was called home to America. Even his great adversary, Roosevelt, needed him to solve a new financial crisis created by a lengthy strike of anthracite miners. Morgan won again. Roosevelt, for the good of the country, had to negotiate with Pierpont, the symbol of the hated trusts.

Morgan first met with the leader of the miners' union, John Mitchell. Among other grievances, Mitchell pointed out the lack of safety precautions in the mines. In 1901 alone 441 miners had died. Mitchell, backed by 140,000 miners, asked the owners, led by George F. Baer, for fair wages, a shorter working day, union recognition and fair weighing of the coal they mined. Mitchell negotiated quietly, reasonably, while his men starved without violence, and Baer was obstinate in defending the rights of the owners to do whatever they wanted. Roosevelt summoned Baer and his associates to Washington to meet with Mitchell. Morgan, in the meantime, brought coal from England, and sold some of it at a special cheaper rate to the poor. Even Roosevelt lost his temper while Baer behaved like an insolent bully, and Mitchell remained composed and gentlemanly. Morgan later praised Mitchell while saying that Baer and his associates had abused Mitchell and the President alike. Morgan in this instance as well as others exhibited a little known side to his personality. Even in labor disputes he could see the other side when necessary and judge men as what they were, not who they were.

Roosevelt issued an order for 10,000 regular Army men to support the 10,000 militiamen already at the mines to prevent violence. These men would now work the mines and allow any citizens to take coal from them as their right for the preservation of life in the cold winter weather.

Only Morgan could bring the coal operators, led by Baer, into line. A conference was arranged aboard ***CORSAIR III***, where Elihu Root, who was a general counsel to the J. P. Morgan Company in its Northern Securities lawsuit, while serving at the same time as Secretary of War in Roosevelt's cabinet, proposed a plan to settle the strike through a special commission to be appointed by Roosevelt.

Morgan got Baer and Mitchell to sign an agreement accepting binding arbitration by the President's commission. Just how Morgan pulled it off remained secret.

Roosevelt was re-elected President in 1904, but his campaign was financed mostly by the big money men he had previously eschewed, $150,000 coming from Morgan, $125,000 from Standard Oil. But if the contributions were supposed to be bribes, they failed. Roosevelt went after the Standard with a vengeance, but he did ease off on Morgan, apparently having recognized Morgan's contributions to the national economy. But Morgan continued to move inside his own little world. Despite his cross-country railroad junkets, during which he never strayed from his private car, Pierpont saw little of the United States except his stately homes in New England and New York, and of course his yacht ***CORSAIR III***. Thus Morgan never knew what effect his reorganizations had on millions of poor people, the workers who kept his empire running smoothly. Roosevelt, on the other hand, did keep in touch with the vast working class and understood their problems. And he knew how disenchanted they had become with the big money men and their trusts. The mere mention of the names Rockefeller or Morgan invoked hatred from these people who slaved for a bare living, who had begun to realize that the United States was governed not from Washington, but from Wall Street. Still, Roosevelt understood how badly he, and the country, needed Morgan.

Morgan's I.M.M. did not do well. He had paid too much for what he got. The American public did not buy I.M.M. stock, and the British government paid enormous sums in subsidies to the Cunard Line to build their more-than-competitive new ***LUSITANIA*** and ***MAURETANIA***, both of which promptly took the Blue Riband and passed it back and forth between them. With public feeling running high against the trusts, of which Morgan remained their symbol, Morgan could not get subsidies from Congress for his lines.

Roosevelt continued his reforms in conservation, health, pure foods, and government control of monopolies, while he insisted that he would not run again in 1908, it being customary to limit presidents to two consecutive terms in office. Roosevelt therefore needed a successor of his own ilk, someone to carry on the reforms he had begun. He settled on William Howard Taft, the Ohioan who was his Secretary of War.

But Roosevelt needed Morgan again, to finance the building of the Panama Canal.

In 1850 the United States and Great Britain had signed the Clayton-Bulwer Treaty, in which the two countries agreed to "maintain free and uninterrupted passage across the Isthmus of Panama," and, further, that neither country should obtain or maintain to itself any "control over the said ship canal, or assume or exercise any dominion… over any part of Central America." During the Spanish-American War the battleship ***USS OREGON*** had been forced to voyage around Cape Horn to get to Cuba from San Francisco. This had impressed upon Americans the need for a canal to cut through the Isthmus so that in time of war either the Atlantic or Pacific fleet could quickly reach the other ocean. Additionally, of course, the merchant fleet would greatly cut the time taken to go from one coast to another, thus increasing its ability to compete with railroads. About 1880 French engineers headed by Count De Lesseps had begun construction of the canal, but after about six years had abandoned the work due to the enormous loss of life caused by what eventually became known as "yellow fever," or malaria. Roosevelt had long understood the necessity for the canal, but he was wary of its being used by enemy vessels as well, or to its being completely taken by an enemy in war time. It was obvious that the canal, if built, must be under government control, and that government should be the United States, with possibly one ally,

England. Secretary of State John Hay had negotiated a treaty with England to this effect, but it was defeated by Senatorial amendments which angered the British so much that they refused to accept it. Hay was so chagrined by the senators' interference that he tried to resign. In February of 1900 Roosevelt, who was then Governor of New York, wrote to Hay suggesting that the United States alone should own the Panama Canal. When Roosevelt finally had the chance as president he was determined to finish the proposed Canal

The French had bought the rights to dig the canal through the Isthmus of Panama from the Columbian government, which owned the State of Panama. At first the Columbian leaders were happy to transfer the French rights to the Americans, and they sent their agent, Dr. Herran, to Washington to negotiate a contract. Herran and Hay composed a treaty which both deemed satisfactory. But by this time the Columbian leaders had other thoughts, realizing that if the United States wanted the rights from the French company so badly, then it ought to be worth more money to themselves. The Columbian government therefore refused to ratify the treaty and warned the French Canal Company that Columbia would charge an additional $10 million for the privilege of transferring the French rights to America. The French balked. In one of the early contracts with the French company, the Columbians had stipulated that if the Canal was not finished by a certain date in 1904 the entire concession would revert to the Columbian government. It was now September, 1903, and Roosevelt needed Morgan.

The French company, however, became alarmed at the possibility of losing the money that the United States had promised to pay for the digging rights. The French decided that the best way to force the Columbian government into line was to foment a revolution in Panama. This was not too difficult because the Panamanians had long been mistreated by Columbia and had in fact made more than fifty attempts at revolt. M. Jean Philippe Bunau-Varilla, a zealous officer of the French company, came from Paris to confer with Roosevelt and Hay. He tried to draw Roosevelt into his conspiracy, but Roosevelt told him that he could do no more than order U. S. Navy vessels, which were already near the Panamanian coast, to prevent any attack from outside. Consequently Bunau-Varilla announced publicly that the revolution would begin at noon on November 3rd. It went off as announced, and resulted in the killing of one "foreigner" and one dog. Columbia had tried to send troops to put down the rebellion, but the U.S. warships would not allow them to land. With suspicious speed, on the following day the United States formally recognized the Republic of Panama. Roosevelt immediately signed an agreement with the new republic by which the United States would lease a zone across the Isthmus for building, owning and operating the Canal. Columbian government leaders tried to persuade Roosevelt to reverse the agreement, for they had lost the $50 million which now went to the Republic of Panama. Roosevelt remained firm. The new treaty stood. There was no evidence that Hay, Congress or anybody else had been consulted. Years later when Roosevelt was chided for being a "wicked conspirator" he replied laughingly, *"What was the use? The other fellows in Paris and New York had taken all the risk and were doing all the work."* One of the "*other fellows*" was Morgan, without whom Roosevelt could not have pulled off the deal.

Roosevelt and Morgan had set up dummy corporations, through which the French Company's rights had been purchased. In November of 1903 Morgan agreed to act as financial adviser to the new Republic of Panama. He immediately advanced $100,000 for expenses to keep the new country running. Morgan then went to France to orchestrate the transfer of $3.5 million in gold bullion to cover the payment to the Republic of Panama. In all the United States paid $50 million to acquire the Canal Zone, more than it had paid for Alaska, the Louisiana Territory and the Philippines together. Later, however, Roosevelt admitted that he had taken the Isthmus and begun building the canal without first consulting Congress. It was a case of necessity, forced by the contract limitation between the original French company and Columbia. Nevertheless, the deed was started, and the strategic importance of a canal across the Isthmus of Panama was recognized by Congress and the American public as well. During Roosevelt's administrations Morgan money was increasingly used to pave the way to diplomacy abroad. Morgan financed railroads in Panama, and government loans to several Central and South American countries.

In March of 1907 Wall Street was again in panic, and blamed it on Roosevelt and his "anti-business" crusade. But Roosevelt defended his policies, saying that they were in fact in the best interests of the financiers, if they but knew it. Their only hope of survival was to accept his regulation of the worst of them in order to save them all. Actually the panics of that year were due to the same causes as any other year… overspeculation, stock watering, which in turn caused the loss of foreign investments. In the fall it got worse. Morgan had again been attending the Triennial Convention of the Episcopal Church, this time in Richmond, Virginia. He was called back to New York, but refused this time to help. He watched banks fail; he was seventy years old and tired. But in the end he brought his money and his influence to bear on the other bankers, on Rockefeller, Harriman, Stillman and Frick, and on the U.S. government, all of whom put up cash to stop the run on the financial institutions. Morgan had again saved the day and Roosevelt had to admit it. He stopped an anti-trust suit against Morgan's International Harvester Company.

Morgan and Roosevelt looked to a round the world transportation network, as Edward H. Harriman had begun with his Union Pacific Railroad, his Pacific merchant fleet, and now Harriman was persuading the Chinese government to link one of their ice free Pacific ports with Russia's Trans-Siberian Railroad. Roosevelt conferred more and more often with Morgan.

William Howard Taft was elected handily in 1908, and took office in March, 1909. He was not a carbon copy of Roosevelt by any means. In fact, the public believed that Taft did not whole-heartedly pursue Roosevelt's goals, one of which was trust-busting. Roosevelt still had a large following, mostly younger men, "Radicals" of the Republican Party, or "Insurgents" as they were sometimes called, in opposition to the "Regulars" led by Taft.

Taft continued, however, to rely upon Morgan for his dollar diplomacy. By 1910 Taft had appointed Robert Bacon as Secretary of State. Bacon was a retired Morgan partner who was also one of Roosevelt's old classmates.

The race was on in 1911 for the presidential candidates of 1912. The Insurgents had now become the "Progressives," and they actively backed Roosevelt as their candidate. It was his duty as a patriot, they told Roosevelt, to run again for the presidency. Privately, to his eventual biographer Thayer, at a pre-convention meeting Roosevelt said, *"I can name forty six Senators who secured their seats and hold them by the favor of a Wall Street magnate and his associates, in all parts of the country."* The next day, 26 February, 1912, less than two months before ***TITANIC***'s loss, Roosevelt announced that he was a candidate for the Republican nomination. The Republican Convention would open on 18 June, 1912, in Chicago.

Pierpont mellowed as he aged. Many of his early friends, associates and enemies had died, and Morgan began to think of putting his affairs in order. He was in Paris when Edward VII died in 1910. Pierpont raced to London to attend the funeral and the private luncheon for the royal family afterward. He gave more and more responsibility to his son Jack.

Morgan returned to the States, and learned that the Supreme Court had declared Rockefeller's Standard Oil trust guilty of "an unreasonable restraint of trade." Congress turned its interest to an investigation of Morgan's steel trust, which, surprisingly, had found that twelve-hour work days and six day work weeks were inefficient in the long run. Taft was riding the wave of public opinion and the public believed that trusts were "un-American." Taft next went after two more of Morgan's combines, the International Harvester and American Telephone and Telegraph. The latter was forced to divorce itself from Western Union. Eventually, unfortunately after Pierpont was gone, these suits would come to nothing. But they did their damage to Morgan personally. His periodic bouts of depression worsened. A Congressional committee called him to Washington to answer questions about his campaign donations to Roosevelt in 1904, to Taft in 1908.

When ***TITANIC*** sank Pierpont was in Europe, leaving Jack in charge at home. Morgan lost friends and business associates in Benjamin Guggenheim, George Widener and John Jacob Astor IV. But worse, Morgan was accused personally of causing the disaster. And then came the Pujo hearings.

It is, of course, unknown just who originated and orchestrated the coverup of the ***TITANIC*** disaster. Was it Pierpont in Europe, or Jack in New York? No doubt they were both involved,· but probably Pierpont ordered it. False wireless messages were sent all day on Monday, 15 April, to the effect that ***TITANIC*** was still afloat with passengers all safe, that she was being towed to Halifax and special trains had already been chartered and were on their way to pick up survivors and bring them to New York. Certainly ***TITANIC*** was reinsured by a Lloyd's underwriter just after 5:30PM on Monday in London, which was 12:30 in the afternoon in New York, many hours after she had sunk. News of ***TITANIC***'s loss was not released by newspapers, or admitted by the White Star Line, until after the New York stock exchange closed on Monday. There can be no doubt that this was done deliberately to protect the price of I.M.M. shares. Morgan can hardly be blamed for doing all he could to protect shareholders. On April 18th an article in the *Philadelphia Inquirer* quoted Thomas J. Stead (no relation to W. T. Stead who died in ***TITANIC***), a local official of the Cunard Line, as saying that a friend of his had come into his office on Tuesday morning seeking information about the disaster. *"Didn't your people know about this yesterday?"* the man asked Stead. When Stead replied that he had not known about it, his friend said, *"I knew at 10 o'clock yesterday morning that* ***TITANIC*** *had sunk."* When Stead pressed him for details his friend finally admitted that the information had come in strictest confidence from Jack Morgan.

In spite of the upcoming inquisition of the Pujo investigation into Morgan's trusts, it would be extremely naive to even suggest that Morgan's power to sway senators and the press was gone. Newspapers were and are greatly dependent upon advertising revenue, thus big companies who threaten to withdraw that advertising revenue may intimidate editors and owners into keeping matters detrimental to the companies out of the papers. Not only did senators who had received large campaign donations from Morgan interests remain loyal to Morgan, but they had influence on other senators as well, and many remembered the debts owed to Morgan for the many times he bailed out the U.S. government. Although Senator Smith may have begun his *TITANIC* investigation in good faith, it is obvious that sometime during the first few days, after testimony had begun, the word had been passed around that certain subjects were *verboten*. By the time the British investigation opened it was certainly known that these subjects must at all costs be kept hidden from the public. So many companies, so many governments, had so much to conceal that they all cooperated, each for its own reasons, and every one of them owed Morgan. He had only to call in their debts. It should be clearly understood, however, that the coverup had nothing to do with the cause of ***TITANIC***'s demise, and certainly Pierpont Morgan had no guilt in it.

While legend has it that Pierpont was so devastated by ***TITANIC***'s loss that it brought him to an early death, the truth is that he simply was getting old, he had never really been well in spite of what seemed robust strength, and he was increasingly frustrated by the investigations into his financial empire. One of the major reasons for Morgan's rise to power had been his integrity. His word was absolutely good, anywhere, any time. He dealt fairly always. To have his every move investigated, flaunted before a public which was incapable of understanding his dealings, was too much. Not all bankers were villains, but the few who were turned the public against the one they perceived as the strongest and richest of them all, Pierpont Morgan. Even after the Pujo Committee Investigation Morgan wanted President Wilson to know that he and his resources were still available any time his country needed them.

Pierpont traveled to Egypt, and back to Rome, always besieged by reporters and art dealers. He was tired, melancholy, and found it difficult to eat. He seemed to have lost the will to live. Just after midnight, on 31 March, 1913, in his usual suite at the Grand Hotel, he pointed upward and said, *"I've got to go up the hill."* He seemed to fall asleep, and never woke up. He had lived almost exactly 11 months after ***TITANIC***'s loss. There was never another like him.

Chapter Thirteen

Other Shipwrecks

Like the ***TITANIC***, the wreck of the British registered Lamport and Holt liner ***VESTRIS*** was investigated both in the United States and Britain because she plied between the United States and South American ports, she operated under an American certificate for passenger vessels, and she carried a number of American citizens, many of whom were lost. Also like the ***TITANIC*** investigation the British crewmen often were reluctant to testify before an American investigation committee and they publicly questioned the competence of the Americans who conducted the inquiry. The British Board of Trade inquiry into the loss of ***VESTRIS*** lasted forty days, even longer than the ***TITANIC*** investigation. There were other similarities. The master of ***VESTRIS***, Captain William J. Carey, in true British tradition, went down with his ship as had Captain Smith of ***TITANIC***. Allegedly Captain Carey's last words were, *"My God! My God! I am not to blame for this!"* And no doubt he was not, nor was Captain Smith of *TITANIC* to blame for events which led to her loss. While the naive traveling public believes that shipmasters are free agents, in absolute authority aboard their respective vessels, reality is an entirely different matter. It was and is commonly known among seamen that while many shipping companies drew up imposing and seemingly ironclad safety rules and regulations, which were solemnly handed to their masters to allegedly follow to the letter, any master who did adhere strictly to every safety regulation would be relieved of command before his next voyage. In the airline industry we used to say that "we would never turn a wheel if we adhered strictly to safety regulations," and in fact "slowdowns" at contract time were nothing more than strict compliance with the safety edicts imposed by government regulations, which by the way had been demanded mostly by labor unions, not owners and rarely by governments. It is exactly the same thing at sea. But, as Karl Baarslag wrote in his *SOS to the Rescue* (Grosset & Dunlap, New York, 1935) *"... in any disaster the captain, generally an experienced, capable, and sorely tried man, invariably becomes the scapegoat."* Certainly we have seen how Captain Smith of ***TITANIC*** is still a scapegoat even after over eight decades have passed, and while Captain Carey of ***VESTRIS*** is hardly as well known today, he was just as vilified as Smith in his time. The master, alone on the bridge of his sinking ship, knows perfectly well that if he saves his own life he has to face the inquiry and a hostile public. He must either lie to protect the ship's owners against the results of their own avarice, or he may tell the truth and give up all hope of pursuing his career and the only means he knows of making a decent living. His third choice, which most took to avoid being the inquiry's scapegoat, was literally suicide. For surviving families it was better to see him as the heroic figure who went down with his ship. At least, his widow might get his pension, such as it was.

William McFee, a British marine engineer and writer mentioned in earlier chapters, had been an employee of Lamport and Holt, thus wrote at length and with inside knowledge of the ***VESTRIS*** and her officers. While McFee wrote at least one short story based upon the subject, he wrote an excellent, informative chapter titled *"The Captain of the **VESTRIS**"* in his *"Sailor's Wisdom"* Jonathan Cape, London, Toronto, 1935).

Captain Carey, master of ***VESTRIS***, was a Liverpool Irishman, a breed of man who, according to McFee, took one of two forms. Either he was a man of large physical stature and enormous physical strength who had "a disciplined, but inexorable thirst," who went into the stokeholds or fo'c'sle and stayed there for his entire career at sea, never rising above the rank of bo'sun or donkeyman, or he was a steady and ambitious youth who set his sights on command of a passenger liner belonging to one of the many prestigious lines which operated out of Liverpool at that time, those lines including the Cunard, White Star, the Blue Funnel, Bibby's, Donaldson, and Lamport and Holt, the line which specialized in the South Atlantic trade and based some of its crews in New York. Either way the Liverpool Irishman was a good man to have behind you in a fight, or an emergency, said McFee, who happened to be a Liverpool Irishman. William Carey belonged to the latter category. In either case, however, the sea was the usual destiny of a Liverpool man when that was the home port of some of the greatest ships that plied the seven seas. Like ***TITANIC***'s officers Carey went to sea in the 1880s, when steamships still carried sails. In due course he acquired all of his certificates, was accepted by the Lamport and Holt, which named its ships after poets and artists. Carey was a fine officer, much esteemed by his company, and in due course he was appointed to command. Carey had served his time in North Atlantic waters before he came into the warmer South Atlantic where there were no icebergs, no shrouds and rigging encased in ice for the entire voyage. He served his time in freighters before he achieved command of a passenger ship. During the Great War Carey continued his fine record as master of ***TITIAN***, a Lamport and Holt liner commandeered as a troop transport. When ***TITIAN*** was torpedoed Captain Carey's conduct was exemplary. He saw to it that everybody was safely into the boats before he finally left his command, and lived to tell of it. Coming up behind Carey were his two sons, one master of ***RAPHAEL***, the other second mate in ***LEIGHTON***. Mrs. Carey was a much-envied woman. Not every wife, even in Liverpool, could say she had a husband and son commanding in the same line while another son was already a watch officer on his way to command. Captain Carey was sixty two years old and had been appointed to command in the company's new ***VOLTAIRE*** when he returned from this voyage in ***VESTRIS***.

A name familiar to all ***TITANIC*** enthusiasts, Mr. Butler Aspinall, K. C., who appeared on behalf of the Board of Trade in 1912, as Wreck Commissioner in 1928 presided over the ***VESTRIS*** inquiry. Like the ***TITANIC*** inquiry, evidence presented at the ***VESTRIS*** inquiry was said by the Board of Trade to be, "*... unsatisfactory, contradictory, inconsistent, and piecemeal. Much of it is unreliable, some of it untruthful.*" All of this made the sinking of the ***VESTRIS*** every bit as mysterious as that of ***TITANIC***. The only reason ***VESTRIS*** is not now the subject of organizations to perpetuate her memory and solve her "mysteries" is the fact that nobody named Astor, Guggenheim, Thayer, etc., died in ***VESTRIS***.

The Board of Trade inquiry disclosed the fact that ***VESTRIS*** had been loaded beyond her loadline, a fact which was contributory to her loss. In fact, according to the B.O.T., five definite cases of such overloading had been apprehended in Lamport and Holt vessels, and the Board believed there were probably more. The company's excuse was that vessels were loaded as cargo was delivered for shipment, often within 24 hours of departure time. If Lamport and Holt did not accept the cargo, some other line would. It was assumed by the company that masters would anchor off the Statue of Liberty, and pump out tanks to bring the ship to allowable draft. But this took time, and time was money to a shipowner. Schedules were to be kept at all cost. The master brave enough to take his ship out on time with all cargo intact, with no time lost in pumping ballast tanks, whether stability was affected or not, was the one who would keep his job. If he balked, there were plenty more to take his place, and in fact one such man was always on board... the Chief Officer, a "master-in-training." Lamport and Holt officials admitted on the stand that they never ascertained whether or not their masters did indeed pump out tanks, or whether overloading might adversely affect the vessel's stability. When the ship left her pier, she became entirely the master's responsibility. Nothing had changed at sea since the loss of ***WARATAH,*** or the loss of ***TITANIC,*** or ***VOLTURNO,*** the names were endless. Promotions for officers came slowly, in every line. Berths were few. Passenger lines paid better than tramps. Blacklists were far-reaching and powerful. Dangerous cargoes and fittings, overloading, unseaworthiness, speed no matter what the conditions, too little lifeboat space, the wise master played along, kept quiet. Captain Smith and Captain Carey were not exceptions. They were the rule, and they played by the rules, knowing those rules that were unwritten as well as those put down in black and white.

Lamport and Holt had other regulations for masters, with which the Board of Trade found fault, as well they should have. *Always* think twice, and more, before calling for help. Be *absolutely certain* you cannot get her to shore, to safety in port. *Be absolutely certain* before you risk having the company pay out a salvage fee, is what the regulation meant. Because the risk is yours, and it means your job. This is what really sank ***VESTRIS***... and ***TITANIC,*** and ***REPUBLIC,*** and many other fine ships.

The 10,494 ton ***VESTRIS*** departed Hoboken, New Jersey, on Saturday afternoon, 19 November, 1928, bound for Barbados and South America. She carried 128 passengers, with a crew of 198, including officers. ***VESTRIS*** was owned by the Liverpool, Brazil, and River Plate Steam Navigation Company, commonly known as the Lamport and Holt Line. Launched by Harland & Wolff the same year ***TITANIC*** was lost, ***VESTRIS*** had served well during the Great War, carrying troops and supplies. Early in the War ***VESTRIS*** had a narrow escape from the German raider ***KARLSRUHE,*** which had sunk her sister ***VANDYCK.*** After the War, in 1921, ***VESTRIS*** went into the New York-South American trade. This was to be her last voyage.

The British inquiry eventually established the fact that ***VESTRIS*** had departed Hoboken in an unsafe condition. Although she had been "substantially upright," some evidence was given that she had a slight list to port. On her first night out the wind increased. By 0200 on Sunday Captain Carey reported a fresh northeaster. ***VESTRIS*** now had a list to starboard of from 3 to 5 degrees, measured by her clinometer. By 0800 stokers complained that their feet were wet. There was water in her bunkers and cross-alleyway. Water was coming in the ash-ejector, but repairs seemed to have stopped this leak by noon. The starboard half-door leaked, but was recaulked and apparently gave no more trouble, at least for a while. Most passengers were violently seasick, few came to breakfast.

By Sunday noon ***VESTRIS*** was about 240 miles south of Sandy Hook. The wind had risen to gale force. ***VESTRIS*** steered wildly, rolling from upright to 5 degrees to starboard. At 1145, according to a surviving quartermaster, when the helm was put hard aport her head still went over to port. Wind and sea were off her port quarter, while Captain Carey let her lie in the trough, under starboard helm, keeping her head somewhat to the wind with the starboard engine turning over slowly. ***VESTRIS*** now listed 6 degrees. From this time until she foundered 24 hours later she never recovered steering ability.

The starboard half-door began leaking again on Sunday afternoon. It was recaulked but apparently the caulking was forced out almost immediately by the inrushing sea. Wind increased, with the starboard list now 8 degrees, her starboard rail going under on the roll. By 1600 water was sloshing into the cross-alleyway too fast to run off. Passengers were finally uneasy, but officers and stewards reassured them. At about 1900 the center of the tropical disturbance passed close to ***VESTRIS.*** The wind backed north-northwest and increased to minimum hurricane strength, 75 miles per hour. The seas rose proportionately. About half an hour later two heavy waves struck the ship in quick succession on her port bow. ***VESTRIS*** staggered, rolled sharply to starboard and recovered very slowly. This was actually her death blow, but nobody, not even Carey, realized it.

The few passengers in the dining saloon were thrown from their chairs, while china went crashing against the bulkhead as everything was swept off the tables toward the starboard side of the saloon. Two lifeboats were lifted from their chocks, three crated automobiles crashed through the bulkhead into the forecastle, bunker coal shifted and some spars battered the door to the wireless cabin. Third Operator Charles Verchere was swept from his chair, the earphones torn from his head. He was on his second trip at sea.

VESTRIS carried three wireless operators, the chief having a name familiar to all ***TITANIC*** enthusiasts... Michael J. *O'Loughlin.* He and the second operator, James MacDonald, were trying to eat their dinner in the saloon. ***VESTRIS*** now rolled through an arc of 5 to 15 degrees, with a permanent list of 10 degrees which brought the sill of the starboard half-door permanently under water. While water hissed and spurted under this door sill, two other mysteriously untraceable leaks puzzled Captain Carey and Chief Engineer Adams. (McFee later speculated, as did other Merchant Navy engineers, that the coaling ports had not been properly secured.) By midnight Adams advised Carey that the bunkers were full of water, the bulkheads were leaking, but he thought he was holding it with the pumps. Carey ordered Nos. 2, 4, and 5 tanks pumped out, hoping to bring her to an even keel again, but instead the effort increased her list ominously. Captain Carey had not been provided with his ship's stability curves or he would have known better than to pump these tanks. By 0400 ***VESTRIS*** was rolling her mooring deck under. And still Carey refused to send a distress call, remembering his company's admonishment to be "absolutely certain" that help was needed. Nor did Carey make any attempt to turn ***VESTRIS*** and head for land to the west.

For 12 hours ***VESTRIS*** had barely moved, her engine power devoted to pumping while she wallowed helplessly in the trough. When Carey inspected the engine room shortly after 0400 on Monday, he asked Chief Adams how things were going. *"Things look pretty bad,"* Adams replied, and pointed out where water was coming into the engine room through the bulkhead and from the overhead. Rising water gurgled over the floor plates, forcing the Chief to shut down all starboard boilers. Carey returned to the bridge and admitted to Chief Officer Johnson that, *"It looks serious."* Still Carey sent no SOS.

According to Baarslag, a former marine wireless operator who interviewed MacDonald, one of the two surviving wireless operators from ***VESTRIS***, Carey gambled with his ship, the lives of his passengers and his own life, for one reason... salvage. We have already defined salvage in earlier chapters. Lamport and Holt's admonishment in its *"General Instructions to Masters,"* stated: *"In the event of a serious disaster happening to one of the vessels of this line while at sea, the master must in the first instance calmly consider the actual amount of peril there may be to the lives of those under his charge, and then judge if he will be justified infighting his own way unaided to the nearest port. His being able to succeed in this will always be considered a matter of high recommendation to him as master."* Nothing in writing to say just what his not being able to succeed in this endeavor might bring, but Carey knew as all masters before and since him knew. The Board of Trade concluded that this instruction was *"highly undesirable."* They suggested that it be cancelled. And so Captain Carey, encouraged by improving weather, decided to wait a while.

McFee's evaluation of the ***VESTRIS*** disaster matched that of Baarslag. Every sailor knew what every passenger never learned, that the economics of salvage overruled the master, and the passengers' safety, on the high seas.

Sixty stewards and firemen were organized into a bailing party, but their efforts in the "battle of the buckets" were futile and they gave up after trying for several hours during which the sea gained three feet. Efforts were made to jettison some of the heavy cargo, but this, too, was given up when one crated automobile got hung up on the rail.

At 0700 even passengers became convinced that ***VESTRIS*** could not survive. Women and children were assembled in the smoking room. The list had increased to 20 degrees, the whole starboard side of the upper deck was under water, ***VESTRIS*** was very nearly on her beam ends. No breakfast was served, and still Carey did not call for help.

Wireless operator MacDonald, however, having followed the sea for 13 years, in good weather and bad, was not yet alarmed. He had, after all, been through typhoons in the China Seas. He copied the press so that passengers would have their morning news, and otherwise carried on his usual routine. About 0500 O'Loughlin had communicated with a sister ship, that same ***VOLTAIRE*** that Carey was slated to command, northbound but 500 miles south of ***VESTRIS***. Not the master, not an officer, had given the wireless operators the slightest hint that ***VESTRIS*** was in deep trouble.

But Captain Carey had not been able to get a celestial observation since departing Hoboken, and so he ordered Third Officer Welland to have O'Loughlin get a bearing from a shore station, which was taken on Tuckerton Radio. Carey, still reluctant to formally request aid, asked O'Loughlin to send out a stand-by message to all ships in the vicinity. O'Loughlin sent a CQ, asking all ships to keep a good radio watch on ***VESTRIS***. O'Loughlin now realized that the situation was serious and awakened MacDonald, who called Verchere. ***VESTRIS*** now had a list of nearly 30 degrees.

Ray Myers, chief at the Bethany Beach Naval Radio Compass Station, was practicing plotting exercises. Myers took a series of bearings on ***VESTRIS***, just for practice, but he noticed that she had been making little or no progress when he calculated her course and speed. Before he went off duty Myers gave instructions to the night operators to guard her carefully. When Myers came back on duty early on Monday morning he noticed that ***VESTRIS*** had almost stopped. He took another bearing on her at about 0730 when she was working another ship. Finally, an hour later, Myers called ***VESTRIS*** and asked if anything was wrong. The answer came back in a question, where was the nearest Coast Guard cutter located? Myers replied *"Cape May."* He asked the ***VESTRIS*** operator if they needed a cutter. *"No, not now, old man,"* was the reply.

Myers, fortunately, took it upon himself to telephone the Coast Guard base, suggesting that a cutter be dispatched, and he explained that ***VESTRIS*** had not moved for hours. At 0900 a cutter headed for the position Myers had given, 37°20'N, 70°30'W. While the cutter was enroute Carey finally sent his distress call, with a slightly different position, and the cutter altered course to the new position, which was found to be erroneous.

When they had sent the CQ none of the wireless operators had been alarmed. No ships who answered altered course. They were merely asked to keep a sharp radio watch on ***VESTRIS***.

Tuckerton Radio acknowledged the first SOS immediately and relayed the call on his powerful transmitter. Fifty six ships logged the SOS. O'Loughlin and MacDonald were working the apparatus, one at the key, the other phoning messages to the bridge. When MacDonald later went on deck to see what was going on, he found the port side boats were being readied for lowering. MacDonald spotted Captain Carey at No. 6 boat and told the master that a German ship with a direction finder, ***SS BERLIN***, was on her way. Carey asked if they were okay in the wireless room. MacDonald told him they were, and not to worry about them. With great difficulty he made his way across the slanting deck, back to the wireless cabin. By 1000 ***VESTRIS*** was on her beam ends, only two boilers could be fired, and those who remained below to fire them, slipping in black, greasy water up to their knees, hoped that the ship would not roll completely over without a bit of warning. Some of the firemen deserted and went topside. Carey pleaded with them to return to work. A few went back and stayed below before leaving the fireroom about an hour later for the last time. From then on all firing was done by the engineers, just as it had been done in ***TITANIC***. With rank goes obligation as well as privilege. At 1100 Chief Adams advised Carey that the pumps were working well. As long as he could keep up steam Adams thought he could keep the ship afloat. Carey told Adams he expected two U. S. Navy destroyers alongside by 1700. The engineers worked, two men bracing a third, passing coal in sacks over their heads until about 1330, an hour and a half after the bunker bulkhead gave way, showering them with coal and water. Still they stayed. There had been no order to abandon ship. Like ***TITANIC***'s engineers, they fought a losing battle to the very end to provide power for the pumps and radio, to buy a little time to save the passengers. And like ***TITANIC***'s engineers they knew that at any moment their ship could roll over and they would be trapped below. Only five of the engineers in ***VESTRIS*** survived.

By 1330 Chief Adams had to make the painful decision… they were fighting a battle that could not be won. Steam pressure was going down while water was rising higher and higher. Adams ordered his main stop valves closed and safety valves opened to prevent boilers from exploding when the water hit them. Fourth Assistant Engineer George Johnstone Prestwich completed the job. The day before Prestwich had worked in water up to his neck for two hours, cutting through the ash ejector pipe so the chief could him it into an auxiliary pump. At 1345 Adams ordered his men to abandon the engine room. ***VESTRIS*** had 30 minutes to live. An interesting message from the owners to Captain Carey was received at 1040. Carey had never informed Lamport and Holt that he was in trouble. A shore station intercepting the SOS had telephoned his agents and apprised them of the situation. The owners accordingly wirelessed, *"Wire us immediately your trouble."* Via Tuckerton Radio Carey answered: *"**VESTRIS** is hove-to since yesterday noon, last night developed 32 degree list to starboard, impossible to proceed anywhere. Sea moderately rough."* The wireless operator had added, *"We are getting worse; decks all under water, and ship lying on beam ends."*

The last message Captain Carey received from his employers was significant in its content. Although several ships had responded, some giving an earlier estimated time of arrival alongside ***VESTRIS***, Lamport and Holt advised, *"**USS DAVIS** proceeding to your assistance."* The inference was clear. Wait for ***USS DAVIS***, a United States Navy destroyer, a government vessel… no salvage fees. And this order in spite of the wireless operator's information that ***VESTRIS*** was already on her beam ends.

By 1315 O'Loughlin was ready when an electrician informed him that the boilers were being shut down, the wireless power from the dynamo would cease. O'Loughlin had anticipated this and switched to his emergency battery. At 1329 O'Loughlin sent, *"Going to abandon ship in a few minutes, getting lifeboats ready now."* Then, *"So long, Tuckerton, SK."* With the ship sinking out from under him the very calm, very professional O'Loughlin sent *SK*, meaning finis... all transmissions from ***VESTRIS*** would cease. As it turned out, it was O'Loughlin's final transmission, not only from ***VESTRIS***, but forever. Like his namesake Dr. O'Loughlin of ***TITANIC***, the chief wireless operator of ***VESTRIS*** did not survive.

Surprisingly, 5 out of the 6 starboard boats were safely launched, but Captain Carey had been reluctant to send passengers to the ship's low side, thus starboard boats were filled mostly with crew members. Carey was criticized posthumously for allowing his passengers' fears to sway his judgement. When ***VESTRIS*** finally rolled over and went under she took two of her port boats with her, filled with women and children. Survivors reported that ***VESTRIS*** went down with very little suction. The seas were still high, rain squalls and hail pelted those in the boats. Unlike ***TITANIC***'s survivors, those who lived through the loss of the ***VESTRIS*** were in the warmer waters of the Gulf Stream, which saved them. The first rescue ship, the French tanker ***MYRIAM***, picked up Boat No.

7 at 0500. At 1930 ***SS AMERICAN SHIPPER*** arrived at the position given in the shore bearings and found nothing. Her master, Captain Schuyler Cummings, continued south toward the position given by ***VESTRIS***, arriving there at 2230. All he found was another searching vessel. From 2300 to 0220 of 13 November Cummings searched the area where ***VESTRIS*** was supposed to have gone down, and found nothing. At 0340 a lifeboat flare was sighted and ***SHIPPER*** subsequently rescued 124 people in 5 boats, while ***MYRIAM*** found boat No. 11, saving a total of 53. ***BERLIN*** saved 23, the American battleship ***USS WYOMING*** saved 9 swimmers, bringing the total of those saved to 209, while 153 were lost. It was later learned that the American freighter ***MONTOSO*** had been less than 45 miles away, but she had no wireless. MacDonald and Verchere survived. The British Marconi Company paid O'Loughlin's mother the usual £100 for loss of life at sea, and in addition £4 per month for two years. The men who had worked with O'Loughlin in ***VESTRIS***, and those who heard him transmitting to the end praised his calm professional heroism. His name was added to the list of those wireless operators lost at sea on the Memorial at the Battery m New York City. Few persons today know who Michael J. O'Loughlin was, while many know of ***TITANIC***'s Jack Phillips. The former was no less a hero than the latter.

And Republic

The 15,378 ton White Star liner ***REPUBLIC*** departed New York on Friday, 22 January, 1909, bound for Gibraltar and the Mediterranean. She ran into thick fog as soon as she passed out of the Narrows, which was normal for that time of year. ***REPUBLIC*** carried one wireless operator, Jack Binns, who was employed by the British Marconi Company. Binns worked until well after midnight completing all of the usual "Bon Voyage" and "Good-bye" messages. He turned in, knowing that he would have to be up early in the morning.

Binns later said that he slept well until about 0540, when the increased frequency of ***REPUBLC***'s foghorn blasts awakened him. Then, suddenly the ship trembled and her engines were stopped. Binns' first thought was of collision, and immediately there was a terrific crash. Binns leaped out of his bunk and ran into the adjoining wireless room to find that the port bulkhead had been torn away and the overhead was sagging menacingly. But Binns had been lucky. The other vessel's sharp, straight stem had gone into the wireless cabin, just a few feet from where he was sleeping. Binns naturally looked out immediately and saw what he thought was a rock, giving him the impression that ***REPUBLIC*** had run aground.

Binns at once began checking out the wireless apparatus. It was still operable, the antenna was intact. The old ten-inch spark coil with its earthed gap sprang to life as Binns threw the power switch and touched the key. Then, the power failed and lights went out as swiftly rising water reached the generators.

Below, the engineers quickly drew fires under the boilers, and Fourth Engineer J.G. Legg turned on the injector valves, reducing boiler pressure. Binns switched to his storage batteries, which would give him a range of no more than 50 or 60 miles. With the wireless cabin laid completely open, Binns was completely exposed to the bitter cold of the North Atlantic winter. He put on all the clothes he could find and tried to look outside. He still had no idea what had happened. His telephone to the bridge had been destroyed in the collision so he could not get any information from that source. On his own responsibility he sent out Marconi's CQD call.

Jack Irwin, operator at Marconi's Siasconsett, Massachusetts, station, call letters SC, had dozed off because the ether had been so quiet. Irwin awakened with a start when Binns' CQD blasted through his earphones. Irwin recognized ***REPUBLIC***'s call sign, MKC. Binns did not know ***REPUBLIC***'s position or extent of her damage, but he asked Irwin to clear the air for this information as soon as he could get it.

Binns had no sooner sent this than a steward arrived with a message from Captain Sealby, asking if Binns and the wireless apparatus were all right. Binns decided to report personally to the master, and followed the steward to the bridge, picking his way through wreckage, noticing that passengers were already assembling near the bridge, where Sealby used a megaphone to address them. Binns reported to Sealby that he had already been in communication with Siasconsett. Binns returned to his wireless cabin and had just contacted Irwin again when Chief Officer Crossland came to him with the message, *"**REPUBLIC** rammed by unknown steamship, 26 miles southwest of Nantucket. Badly in need of assistance."*

We may note that at no time was an SOS call suggested, even though SOS had been the internationally recognized wireless distress call since July of the previous year. Binns preceded Sealby's message with Marconi's CQD, and never did Binns use any other call. Irwin at Siasconsett repeated Binns' CQD and added, *"Do utmost to reach her!"* From this time until about noon when ***REPUBLIC*** was in direct contact with White Star's ***BALTIC***, Binns conserved his battery power and let Irwin handle traffic. Irwin was then working both ***BALTIC*** and the French liner ***LA TOURAINE***, both ships being Marconi-equipped. By this time Irwin had a U. S. revenue cutter dispatched from Wood's Hole as well. Irwin informed Binns that help was on its way, Binns in turn informed Captain Sealby, who used his megaphone to tell passengers. They immediately sent up a great cheer. Binns would later report that passengers remained calm, although at first there was some problem with "Italian and Portuguese" steerage passengers, until they were "calmed by stewards of their own race." Like passengers aboard ***TITANIC*** *would* do three years later, and like nocturnally shipwrecked passengers of all time, ***REPUBLIC***'s passengers hurried to the boat deck clad in nightclothes and whatever they could grab quickly. Many were barefoot in the extreme cold. Men gave their coats to women who wore none. Stewards raided cabins for all the warm clothes they could find and distributed them indiscriminately to the most scantily clad passengers. Stewards also brought hot coffee, snacks and the more welcome whisky. Passengers began to joke about their apparel, while the bravest of them ventured below to retrieve their valuables.

REPUBLIC of course lay dead in the water, drifting with the current. In the fog they had managed to establish contact with the ramming vessel, which had properly remained nearby. Captain Sealby thus learned that ***REPUBLIC*** had been struck by the Italian Lloyd emigrant steamer ***FLORIDA***, which had lost 30 feet of her bow, but she was afloat and likely to remain so, with her engines still intact. ***FLORIDA***'s collision bulkhead was holding and the gaping hole was patched with an immense stretch of canvas. Sealby thus made the decision to transfer ***REPUBLIC***'s people to ***FLORIDA***, although the Italian vessel was crowded with 830 immigrants, many of them recent survivors of the catastrophic Messina earthquake. Having just come from this horrifying experience these passengers at first panicked, but Captain Angelo Ruspini quickly brought them under control. Ruspini was later described by Binns as being "young and very cool."

Captain Sealby now made a controversial, yet normal for the time, address to his passengers. He informed them that they would be transferred to ***FLORIDA***, which had been less damaged than ***REPUBLIC***. But Sealby's words were, *"I expect you will be cool and not excited. Take your time in getting into the lifeboats. Remember!.... women and children first, then the First Cabin and then the others. The crew will be the last to leave this vessel."*

Sealby's declaration that First Cabin men would leave before any other men nearly started a riot, as should have been expected. It was indicative of the times, however, and the class distinction that prevailed. Captain Smith of ***TITANIC*** would follow the same routine, but without the ensuing publicity sparked by Sealby's declaration. With every transatlantic liner's bread and butter being immigrant traffic, and that included the most elite and fanciest of the floating palaces, it was not politic to flaunt this kind of class privilege before the steerage passengers. Yet it was always inferred by the simple fact that First Class accommodations were closest to the boat deck. It was not easy for Third Class to find their way topside in any liner, and normal barriers being up enroute precluded any exploration of emergency escape routes from the lower decks.

The transfer of 460 passengers began soon after Sealby's announcement, and was completed without mishap within two hours. Two of ***REPUBLIC***'s passengers, however, had been killed when ***FLORIDA***'s sharp stern entered their cabins, killing them as they slept in their berths. Another passenger died later from his injuries. Two of ***FLORIDA***'s crewmen died in their forecastle.

FLORIDA's accommodations naturally did not match those of ***REPUBLIC***, and now the emigrant ship's supplies were overburdened. Officers and men divided what little they had to offer. The Italian immigrants learned that ***REPUBLIC***'s passengers were mostly Americans. Remembering all too well how the American fleet had cared for the Messina earthquake's victims, ***FLORIDA***'s passengers did all they could to help ***REPUBLIC***'s survivors. But the situation worsened when ***REPUBLIC***'s crew was ferried to ***FLORIDA***. Rumors started by "two cowardly men" who insisted that ***FLORIDA*** was doomed and had not long to live were squelched by a young woman who went about reassuring her fellow passengers with the news that ***REPUBLIC*** was in constant communication now with the approaching ***BALTIC***.

Captain Sealby and a crew of 45 volunteers, including Binns, remained aboard ***REPUBLIC***. ***BALTIC***, inbound from Liverpool and near Montauk when her operator caught the CQD, was only 64 miles away. But in the thick fog ***BALTIC*** covered 200 miles in the next 12 hours searching for ***REPUBLIC***. Binns later said, *"By noon of Saturday the **BALTIC** was within ten miles of us; I could tell by the strength of her signals."* The fog grew denser and ***BALTIC*** reduced speed to avoid crashing into ***REPUBLIC***.

Twenty five years later Binns still remembered the intense cold. At about 1400 a steward brought him food and hot coffee, which Binns consumed while he transmitted. He was now in constant touch with ***BALTIC*** and ***LA TOURAINE. The*** latter's wireless operator asked how Binns felt. Binns replied with his famous, *"I'm on the job, ship sinking, but will stick to the end."* Every wireless operator afloat would admire Binns for that, and wish to emulate his heroic coolness if the chance arose. There can be no doubt but what Binns' behavior influenced Jack Phillips three years later in ***TITANIC***. Finally, an officer brought Binns some woolen overshoes and a steward brought him blankets, which Binns wrapped around his legs.

In the early winter darkness those aboard ***REPUBLIC*** lost sight of ***FLORIDA***. Sealby was not convinced that his people aboard the badly damaged Italian liner were all that safe. Meanwhile, ***BALTIC*** and ***REPUBLIC*** played their deadly game of hide and seek. Each fired rockets and exploded detonating bombs, and ***BALTIC*** inquired by wireless whether those aboard ***REPUBLIC*** could hear her foghorn. Still they could not hear each other. While one ship's officers fired a signal bomb, aboard the other her wireless operator advised officers so they could listen. It was to no avail. All afternoon this went on, but neither ship heard the other. By 1800 each vessel had only one signal bomb left. ***REPUBLIC*** agreed to detonate her last bomb. Chronometers were synchronized by wireless and at a given moment the bomb went off. Binns listened anxiously, but in a few seconds he was disappointed again. Nobody in ***BALTIC*** had heard it.

Now it was ***BALTIC***'s turn. Carefully the times were checked, and a quartermaster stood by ***BALTIC***'s chronometer to signal the exact moment. It was a desperate gamble now, for they all knew that ***REPUBLIC*** could not live out the night. The quartermaster raised his arm, the bomb was detonated, the signal was given by wireless, and Binns strained his ears to listen. He thought he heard a faint "boom," and so did the Third Officer standing next to him. A bearing was taken on the direction reported by Binns and the Third Officer, and Sealby had the information flashed to ***BALTIC***'s master, Captain Ranson. Within fifteen minutes they heard ***BALTIC***'s foghorn. Binns rushed to his key and informed Tattersall, ***BALTIC***'s operator, that they heard her. Ten minutes later Binns heard the cheer that went up, not from the 45 desperate men scattered throughout ***REPUBLIC,*** but from ***BALTIC***'s crew and passengers, who lined her rail, straining their eyes to be first to pick up ***REPUBLIC***'s dark outline. It had taken ***BALTIC*** 13 hours to find ***REPUBLIC.***

Sealby and Ranson conferred and agreed that ***BALTIC*** must find ***FLORIDA*** and take off all her passengers as well as those from ***REPUBLIC.*** Then, suddenly the fog lifted and was replaced by a hard, driving rain. Although Sealby and his skeleton crew abandoned ***REPUBLIC,*** the master and one boat's crew circled her all during the wet, cold night. Binns went aboard ***BALTIC,*** found Tattersall and introduced himself, then snatched a few hours' much needed sleep.

At 2330 on Saturday the transfer of 1,650 passengers from ***FLORIDA*** to ***BALTIC*** began. The double transfer remains unique in maritime history. Boats from all three ships were used. A strong wind, which had sprung up since the original transfer from ***REPUBLIC*** to ***FLORIDA,*** stirred up a long, rolling swell which, along with a cold, drenching rain made those in the boats miserable. Many of them were still ill-clad. The immigrants aboard ***FLORIDA*** became furious when they learned that ***REPUBLIC***'s First Class men would be transferred before any of them, including their women. Somebody had started a rumor that ***FLORIDA*** had not long to live and her passengers would be left to die with her. A male passenger aboard ***BALTIC*** later commented that the women behaved better than many of the men. The transfer was completed just before 0700 on Sunday.

Captain Sealby reboarded his command and sent word to Captain Ranson that he still might save ***REPUBLIC.*** Binns and a skeleton crew returned to her, and Binns found that ***REPUBLIC***'s wireless set was still working. ***BALTIC*** proceeded to New York with her triple load of passengers as ***FLORIDA*** limped off in the same direction. ***REPUBLIC*** was going down at the rate of about one foot per hour. The U. S. revenue cutter ***GRESHAM*** took her in tow while the Anchor liner ***FURNESSIA*** made fast to her stern to serve as a rudder. Two hours later the derelict-destroyer ***SENECA*** arrived. She put a tow line aboard ***REPUBLIC*** in tandem with ***GRESHAM. FURNESSIA*** cast off and was on her way. The little government vessels strained mightily, but the big liner was now so weighted down with water that they made little progress. To make matters worse, they were bucking the current. As water began coming into the wireless cabin Binns wondered if he should go to the bridge to find out if they were going to abandon ship, or wait for orders. His batteries were almost gone. Then the Third Officer came to tell him that Sealby had given the order to "abandon ship." Binns obeyed quickly He sent a final message, *"Current going, wireless now closed."* He had been at his key for 36 hours, excepting for the brief respite when he boarded ***BALTIC.***

In spite of his officers' pleading, Sealby would not leave his command. He asked for one volunteer to stay with him. Of course they all volunteered, so Sealby chose Second Officer Williams, the senior unmarried man among them. Binns and the others rowed to the ***GRESHAM.*** Sealby and Williams could still communicate by Morse lamp. Sealby requested that the steel-wire towing hawsers be replaced by rope lines that could be cut quickly. He would burn a blue light as a signal to cut the lines when he felt ***REPUBLIC*** going under. Several other ships stood by, playing their searchlights on the sinking liner.

One of those other ships was the U. S.-flagged Standard Oil whaleback tanker ***CITY OF EVERETT***, Captain Thomas Fenlon commanding. Fenlon gave a statement to reporters when he arrived at Point Breeze on 26 January.

*If Captain Sealby of the liner **REPUBLIC** had accepted the aid I offered him immediately after the collision with the **FLORIDA**, on Saturday last, that ship would be safe in port now, and the cargo and the effects of the passengers would have been saved, beyond the shadow of a doubt."*

The ***EVERETT*** *had* been one of the first vessels to catch Binns' CQD. Her United Wireless operator had immediately informed Fenlon, who had turned ***CITY OF EVERETT*** at once toward the position given in the CQD message. According to Fenlon, she had arrived alongside ***REPUBLIC*** only minutes after ***BALTIC*** did, and he was the first to speak directly with Captain Sealby, probably by megaphone.

"The ship under my command contains some of the most powerful apparatus for wrecking purposes afloat," continued Fenlon. *"Our pumps have a capacity of 40,000 barrels, or 2,000,000 gallons, an hour. The barge we were towing would have held all the baggage of the passengers of the **REPUBLIC** and a large part of the cargo besides. The **CITY OF EVERETT** was built for ocean towing, and is equipped with tremendously powerful machinery and towing cables seven inches in diameter. With such magnificent facilities right at hand. Captain Sealby declined our assistance, saying that a couple of Government boats were coming to his relief. These little Government boats could have towed a rowboat as well as they could have towed that big liner. We offered our assistance, mind you, at 8:30 that evening. We could have worked all night. All it would have cost the White Star Line would have been about $20,000. As it was, property of all kinds to the value of some $2 million was lost.*

"The first intimation that we had of anything wrong was a wireless message from the Nantucket Lightship," continued Fenlon. *"We have a De Forest instrument on the **CITY OF EVERETT**, and there was another on the barge we had in tow. We put about at once and cruised toward the scene of the wreck. Messages of 'still afloat' kept coming in, and finally we received word that the passengers had been transferred to the **FLORIDA**. At 8:30 o'clock we ran alongside the **REPUBLIC**, and I offered the use of my outfit to Captain Sealby. He answered that he needed no assistance whatever, but asked us to go to the **FLORIDA**, as all his passengers were aboard that boat. At 9:30 we ran alongside the **FLORIDA**.*

*"Men and women cried to us from the liner and offered us large sums of money if we would only take them off. When my First Officer, Mister Tucker, went on board the **FLORIDA** her First Officer handed him a blackjack and told him to use it on the passengers if necessary to keep them from trying to jump from the deck of the **FLORIDA** to the **CITY OF EVERETT**.*

*"On Sunday morning at nine o'clock we once more ran alongside the **REPUBLIC**, and once more I asked Captain Sealby to allow me to help him. Once again he refused my offer, saying that his ship was all right. He said that he had engaged assistance from New York by wireless. I felt desperate at the way things were going, but my hands were tied. The capacity of my barge was 6,000 tons.*

*"On board the **CITY OF EVERETT** were nine heavy deep-sea towing hawsers and two spare ones. The **CITY OF EVERETT** is a whaleback, built for towing oil barges across the ocean, and our pumps are the most powerful it is possible to build. The fact that **REPUBLIC** kept afloat by her own effort until Sunday night is proof positive, to my mind, that with very little help of the proper kind she would have weathered it out and would be lying safe in New York Harbor today,"* concluded Fenlon.

Fenlon's statement speaks for itself. As we saw in Lamport and Holt's final wireless message to the hapless Captain Carey, the inference, the standing order was always clear... *wait for the government vessels, if none of your own line are near.* When Fenlon said that ***CITY OF EVERETT*** carried a "De Forest instrument," he no doubt was going by the manufacturer's name stamped, or etched, on the equipment. It had been built by de Forest, under de Forest patents, but by 1909 the company had become United Wireless, as told in Chapter 8.

One or two questions must arise... why did ***BALTIC*** not attempt a tow of her sister liner ***REPUBLIC?*** The answer to that is probably twofold. Captain Sealby did put his passengers' safety first, and once he had them safely aboard ***BALTIC*** she must be on her way, to keep her imperative schedule. And why did Sealby refuse aid from ***CITY OF EVERETT?*** The answer is one word, the same word that Baarslag used in reference to ***VESTRIS***... salvage.

But let us return to Captain Sealby and Mister Williams on the bridge of the sinking ***REPUBLIC***, which was going down fast. Sealby ordered Williams to set off the blue lights, then he fired his revolver five times, in case the blue lights had not been seen. Sealby and Williams dropped down the ladder on to the saloon deck, each carrying a blue light. Only ***REPUBLIC***'s taffrail was above water now, and ***REPUBLIC*** was listing 30 degrees. The two officers had to hold on to the rail and crawl along the wet, slippery deck. *"Explosions of the air driven out by water and the rending of frames amidships told us that the stern was already under water. I managed to get to the foremast and climbed the rigging as far as the running light about 100 feet up,"* Sealby told reporters when he landed in New York. *"Below me half the ship was visible and she tipped up like a rocking chair about to go over backward. My blue light would not burn because it was wet, so I fired the last shot from my revolver. Then everything dropped and I was in the water with the foremast slipping down beside me like an elevator plunger. There was a boiling, seething mass of water about me and a great roaring noise. I went under, but bobbed up again immediately as the air under my great-coat buoyed me up."*

This indicates that Sealby did not wear a life vest. He managed to catch hold of a spar and then a hatch cover, while wreckage swirled all around him. He spread out on the hatch cover, keeping only his head and shoulders above water. He could see the searchlights of the revenue cutters sweeping the black water, looking for him and Williams. Desperately Sealby put one round in the revolver's chamber and pulled the trigger. Surprisingly, it fired and the sharp report was heard by officers on the bridges of the searching ships. Both Sealby, and Williams who was found nearby, were rescued, but they were *"about finished,"* said Sealby later. ***REPUBLIC*** had lived for 39 hours after her mortal wound.

Binns meanwhile had been taken aboard ***SENECA***, where he promptly fell asleep. He slept around the clock and did not see ***REPUBLIC*** go down. When they landed in New York Sealby and Binns were greeted as heroes. Binns especially was feted and cheered. He was welcomed even more enthusiastically in England. The shy Binns actually hid from reporters, however, when he could. Everywhere he went women chased him, usually hugging and kissing him enthusiastically, which embarrassed him no end. After ***REPUBLIC***'s loss Binns served for two years in ***ADRIATIC***, most of the time under Captain E. J. Smith. Binns knew most of ***TITANIC***'s officers very well. In fact, he had almost sailed in ***TITANIC***, having left Marconi and taken employment in New York. He had debated whether to wait for the new ***TITANIC***, or to take the earlier ***MINNEWASKA***. He was in a hurry to get to his newspaper job in New York, and thus decided upon ***MINNEWASKA***. Binns remained in newspaper work until the War began, then he joined the Royal Canadian Flying Corps and became an instructor. After the War he returned to New York and his career in journalism, until he eventually went into the radio business.

With Captain Sealby's new hero status. White Star could not immediately dismiss him.

However, when Sealby was interviewed by reporters on the subject of ***TITANIC***'s loss, it is interesting to note that Sealby was, in 1912, a maritime law student at the University of Michigan. The master who loses his ship, but survives to talk about it, rarely continues his career at sea.

Epilogue

The truth about the ***TITANIC*** disaster is simple. She was a ship, and like any other ship, she was bound to obey the laws of physics. Her demise, like any other disaster, was caused not by one incident, but by a combination of incidents escalating into one final catastrophe. If any early link in the fatal chain had been broken, ***TITANIC*** would not have been lost. After a certain number of flawed links, she was doomed, yet many ships had sunk without a loss of life. ***TITANIC***'s people could have been saved, all of them, but for the final defective links in the death chain. She was completed and entered into White Star service at the wrong time of year for the spectacular maiden voyage that Ismay wanted. When the coal bunker fire was discovered it would have been prudent, but not economically sound to return to Belfast to repair the bulkhead. In fact, of course, it was common practice to continue a voyage when coal ignited by spontaneous combustion. Two chances gone; two fatal links woven into the final chain. She could have taken a longer route, could have slowed down, both of which were not economically sound—two more fatal links. After she struck ice, her wireless operator could have communicated freely and courteously with the ***FRANKFURT***. One more link. And finally, her master could have seen to it that regulation distress rockets were fired, bringing every ship within a radius of thirty miles, possibly more, to her aid. That Captain Smith did not do this indicates that Ismay called the shots there, too. While many shipmasters have waited too long to call for help, it is doubtful that Smith would have put his passengers last in that respect. Ship *owners,* however, generally see dollars, pounds, marks, francs, whatever, first. ***TITANIC*** researchers can fantasize and romanticize all they want to, but it won't get them anywhere near the truth about the loss of the ***TITANIC***. The bottom line was money; pure, and simple.

No monetary value has ever been put on human life. While it has been said that the sea is a profession, which is defined as meaning it is something done because you want to do it, and not for money, and most sailors would not shirk rescue of human life (some have, however) it was and is money that talks. Salvage. Ismay knew full well that any ship arriving while ***TITANIC*** remained afloat could claim salvage, and would, on the value of the vessel and the cargo. The very fact that he took such a chance surely indicated that he did not expect ***TITANIC*** to founder, at least not for many hours. The rapidity of her sinking was unprecedented under the circumstances, and the unknown factor was the weakened bulkhead. A gamble with very high stakes, indeed.

Thus we have the facts, and now the ***ifs***. If ***TITANIC***'s maiden voyage had been in the summer, like ***OLYMPIC***'s was, there would have been no ice to worry about. ***If*** 1912 mariners had known to factor wind and current into plotting their courses. ***If*** they had known that field ice drifts with surface current; ***if*** they had known that surface current is deflected by strong winds, then they would not have been south of their estimated position and they would not have turned south so soon. ***If TITANIC*** had not been so huge, with such a deep draft, she could have crossed the Grand Banks without fear of running aground, as early liners did. She could have stayed North of the ice altogether. ***If*** the DAPG tanker ***DEUTSCHLAND*** had not run short of coal, and she would not have if masters had not been encouraged to take minimum fuel, then ***TITANIC*** would not have come so far south so far east that she failed to miss the ice fields which had been drifting south instead of east-northeast as the charts said they should. ***If*** the coal fire had been in a different bunker; ***if TITANIC***'s rockets had been red or green as prescribed by the International Rules of the Road; ***if CALIFORNIAN***'s wireless operator had drunk enough coffee to stay awake all night; ***if***

Jack Phillips had not disliked Germans—and ***if*** the German operator in the ***FRANKFURT*** had not disliked Englishmen; ***if*** *that* mutual dislike had not been encouraged by propaganda preparing both country's citizens for war; ***if MOUNT TEMPLE***'s master had had a bit more gumption… the ***ifs*** seem ***endless***. But all the ***ifs*** bring us back to the same cause for ***TITANIC***'s loss—*force majeure.* Act of God. For after all, does not Man claim to have been created in His image?

ABOVE: TITANIC passing Lower Manhattan. (Artwork by James A. Flood.)

Acknowledgments

Gathering the material to write this book would have been impossible without the help of the following people. In order to be fair, they are listed in alphabetical order. Because this research has spanned such a long period of time, I hope not to forget anyone. My humblest apologies if I do.

In Canada: Ken Carter, H.C. Murdoch.

In England: Captain Jeremy Caro, David Bristow, Lydia Bristow (neither of whom are related to me), Leslie Harrison, Alan Hayward, Martin Lewis, Alan McGiffin, Joy and Leo Morley, Stuart Partridge, Edwin Steele, F.D. Swift, Brian Ticehurst, Stephen Tucker, John Turner.

In Finland: Juha Feltonen.

In Germany: Arnold Kludas, Elfriede Sieta.

In New Zealand: William A. Blogg, E.G. Butland, Maureen Landreth and her father, the late James O. McGiffin, and Ada Murdoch's nephew L.R. Webbley, with his son Derek.

In Northern Ireland; the late John Brown, Max Maccabe, Donal McCloskey, James R. Walker.

In Norway: Pete Elverhøi.

In Scotland: Scott Murdoch and the late Jimmy Murdoch.

In Sweden: Claes-Goran Wetterholm.

In Switzerland: Günter Båbler.

In the Netherlands: Cornelis J. Hettema, Rob Kamps.

In the United States: Jeffrey Anderson, Leland Anderson, Richard Brown, Joseph A. Carvalho, Margaret Cheney, Second Officer Larry Fosgate, William Kerka, Melony Lockwood, John Luchau, Philip B. Mahony, Raphael Dante Mancinelli, Robert Phillips, Ray Redwood, Bette Reiter, John Whitman, and John Bryant Williams.

Thank you also to Marti at Gables Booksellers, who patiently found many obscure books for my research. Special thanks to all the kindly editors worldwide who published my letters searching for relatives of ***TITANIC***'s people.

A special thank you to fellow Mensans Jeffrey Anderson, Second Officer Larry Fosgate, John Luchau, Philip B. Mahony, Stephen Tucker, and John Bryant Williams, all of whom provided their technical and professional expertise, and to Martin Lewis who patiently escorted me through museums, bookstores, and the lovely English countryside, and who did tedious newspaper research in my behalf. Without them this book could not have been written.

I apologize to my readers for repetition in my text, which I have used for emphasis of certain important points.

Bibliography

Adler, Dorothy R.; *British Investment in American Railways*, 1834-1898, University Press of Virginia, Charlottesville, VA, 1970.

Allen, Frederick Lewis; *The Great Pierpont Morgan*, Dorset Press, New York, 1948.

Angas, W. Mack, Comdr. USN; *Rivalry on the Atlantic*, Lee Furman, Inc., New York, 1939.

Baarslag, Karl; *Famous Sea Rescues*, Grosset & Dunlap, New York, 1935 formerly titled *SOS to the Rescue.*

Bebie, Jules, Ph.D.; *Explosives, Military Pyrotechnics and Chemical Warfare Agents*, The Macmillan Company, New York, 1943.

Beesley, Lawrence; *The Loss of the SS TITANIC*, Houghton Mifflin Co., Boston, New York, 1912.

Behrman, Cynthia Fansler; *Victorian Myths of the Sea*, Ohio University Press, Athens, OH, 1977.

Bennet, H. L.; *A Glimpse of Wall Street and Its Markets*, Greenwood Press, New York, 1968, reprint of 1904 edition, Jacob Berry & Co.

Bes, J.; *Chartering and Shipping Terms*, Barer & Howard, Ltd. London, 1951.

Bisset, Sir James, with Stephensen, P. R. *Tramps and Ladies*, Criterion Books, New York, 1959.

Blunt, Wilfred Scawen; *My Diaries, Parts One and Two*, Alfred A. Knopf, New York, 1921.

Bonsor, N. R. P.; *North Atlantic Seaway, Volumes 1, 2, and 3*; David & Charles, London, and Brookside Publications, Jersey, Channel Islands.

Born, Karl Erich; *International Banking in the 19th and 20th Centuries*; originally published as Geld und Banken im 19. und 20. Jarhundert, Alfred Kröner Verlag, Stuttgart, 1977. English translation by Volker R. Berghahn, Berg Publishers, Limited, Warwickshire, 1983.

Bowditch, Nathaniel, *American Practical Navigator*, United States Hydrographic Office, Washington, DC, 1914.

Chadwick, F. E., U.S.N.; Gould, John H.; Kelley, J. D. J., U.S.N.; Rideing, William H.; Ridgely, Hunt, U.S.N.; Seaton, A.E.; *Ocean Steamships*; Charles Scribner's Sons, 1891.

Cheney, Margaret; *Tesla, Man Out of Time*, Dorset Press, New York, 1981.

Chernow, Ron; *The House of Morgan*, Atlantic Monthly Press, New York, 1990.

Croly, Herbert D.; *Marcus Alonzo Hanna*, Chelsea House, New York, 1983.

Cugle, Charles H.; *Cugle's Practical Navigation*, E. P. Dutton Co., Inc., New York 1942.

Cullen, Tom; *Crippen, The Mild Murderer*, Penguin Books, London, 1988.

Davison, Ian Hay; *A View of the Room*, Lloyd's, St. Martin's Press, New York, 1987.

De Forest, Lee; *Father of Radio*, Wilcox and Follett, Chicago, 1949

De Mierre, H. C. *Clipper Ships to Ocean Greyhounds*, Harold Starke, Limited, London, 1971.

Etherington-Smith, Meredith and Pilcher, Jeremy; *The "It" Girls*, Harcourt Brace Jovanovich, San Diego, New York, London, 1986.

Evans, R. J., *The Victorian Age, 1815-1914*; Edward Arnold & Co. 1950.

Gabler, Edwin; *The American Telegrapher, A Social History 1860-1900*, Rutgers University Press, New Brunswick and London, 1988.

Gibb. D. E. W.; *Lloyd's of London*, MacMillan & Co., Ltd., London, 1957.

Griffiths, Denis; *The Power of the Great Liners*, Patrick Stephens, Ltd., Teovil, Somerset, 1990.

Gröner, Erich; *German Warships 1815-1945, Vol. 1, Major Surface Vessels*, English edition Naval Institute Press, Annapolis, Maryland, 1990.

Harrison, Leslie; *A TITANIC Myth, The CALIFORNIAN Incident*, (second edition revised) S.P.A. Ltd. Hanley Swan, Worcs., 1992.

Hayes, Sir Bertram; *Hull Down*, The MacMillan Co., New York, 1925.

Hodgson, Godfrey; *Lloyd's of London*, Penguin Books, Ltd., 1984.

H.O. Pub. No. 151; *Distances Between Parts*, U. S. Government Printing Office, Washington, 1965.

Hurd, Archibald, and Castle, Henry; *German Sea Power*; John Murray, London, 1913.

Jolly, W. P. ; *Marconi*, Stein and Day, New York, 1972.

Jolly, W. P.; *Sir Oliver Lodge*, Fairleigh Dickinson University Press, 1974.

Knight, Austin M., Rear-Admiral, USN; *Modern Seamanship*, D. van Nostrand Company, New York, 1917.

Kurylo, Friedrich, and Susskind, Charles; *Ferdinand Braun*, The MIT Press, Cambridge, MA, 1981.

LaFore, Laurence; *The Long Fuse*; J. B. Lippincott, Co., Philadelphia and New York, 1965.

Lambert, Angela; *Unquiet Souls*; Harper & Rowe, New York, 1984.

Lewis, Tom; *Empire of the Air*, Harper Perennial, New York, 1993.

Lord, Capt. William R.; *Reminiscences of a Sailor*, Mackenzie and Storrie, Leith, 1894.

MacLeish, William H.; *The Gulf Stream*, Houghton Mifflin Company, Boston, 1989.

Massie, Robert K.; *Dreanought*, Random House, New York, 1991.

Mayes, Thorn L.; *Wireless Communication in the United States*, The New England Wireless and Steam Museum, Inc., East Greenwich, R.I., 1989.

McDowell, Carl E., and Gibbs, Helen M.; *Ocean Transportation*, McGraw Hill, New York, 1954.

McFee, William; *Sailor's Wisdom*, Jonathan Cape, London, Toronto, 1935.

McFee, William, *Watch Below*, Random House, New York, 1940.

Mixter, George W.; *Primer of Navigation*, revised for the 4th edition by Capt. Donald McClench, USNR, Ret., D. van Nostrand, Princeton, NJ, 1960.

Mott, N. F., and Jones, H.; *The Theory of the Properties of Metals and Alloys*; Dover Publications, New York, 1958. (An unabridged republication of the work first published in 1936 by Clarendon Press, Oxford, New England.)

Nicolls, A. E., Extra Master; *Nicholl's Seamanship and (Viva Voce) Guide*, 9th edition revised by F. W. Maxwell, Extra Master, James Brown and Sons, Glasgow, 1918.

Nitske, W. Robert, and Wilson, Charles Morrow; *Rudolf Diesel*, University of Oklahoma Press, Norman, OK, 1965.

Plimpton, George; *Fireworks*, Doubleday, New York, 1984.

Plummer, Carlyle J., Lieut. Commdr. USCGR; *Shiphandling in Narrow Channels*; Cornell Maritime Press, 1945.

Pugsley, Capt. R. M.; *The Navigator or Mariner's Guide*, New Jersey Paint Works, Jersey City, NJ, 1902.

Quinby, E. J. Comdr. USN (Ret.); *IDA Was a Tramp*, Exposition Press, Hicksville, New York, 1975.

Raymond, E. T.; *Mr. Lloyd George*, George H. Doran Co., New York, 1922.

Redwood, Ray; QTC, *A Seagoing Radio Officer's Scrapbook*, Sequoia Press, Austin, TX, 1989.

Reisenberg, Felix, Master Mariner, Lt. Comdr. USNR, Ret.; *Standard Seamanship for the Merchant Service*, D. van Nostrand Co., Inc., New York, 1922.

Richards, Phil, and Banigan, John J.; *How to Abandon Ship*; Cornell Maritime Press, Centreville, MD., 1942.

Rostron, Sir Arthur H.; *Home from the Sea*, Cassell & Co., Ltd., London, 1931.

Sinclair, Andrew; Corsair; *The Life of J. Pierpont Morgan*, Little Brown and Company, Boston and Toronto, 1981.

St. Aubyn, Giles; *Edward VII, Prince and King*, Atheneum, New York, 1979.

Stevers, Martin D., and Pendlebury, Captain Jonas; *Sea Lanes*, Minton, Balch & Co., New York, 1935.

Talbot, Frederick A.; *Steamship Conquest of the World*, J. B. Lipincott Company, Philadelphia, William Heinemann, London, 1913.

Torbell, Ida; *The History of the Standard Oil Company, Volumes I and II*, McClure, Phillips, and Co., New York, 1904.

Thayer, William Roscoe; *Theodore Roosevelt, An Intimate Biography*, Houghton Mifflin Company, Boston and New York, 1919.

The Shipbuilder; *Ocean Liners of the Past, White Star Liners OLYMPIC and TITANIC*, reprint, Patrick Stephens, Cambridge, 1970.

Tuchman, Barbara W.; *The Proud Tower*; The McMillan Co., New York, 1962.

Turpin, Edward A., and MacEwen, William A. Master Mariners; *Merchant Marine Officers' Handbook*; Cornell Maritime Press, Inc., Cambridge, Maryland, 1965.

Vale, Vivian; *The American Peril*, Manchester University Press, 1984.

Vosseller, Perry, Master Mariner, *Navigation*, Rudder Publishing, New York, 1935.

von Bülow, Prince Berhard; *Imperial Germany*; reprint by Greenwood Press, Inc., Westport, CT., 1979 from Original, Copyright Reimar Hobbing, 1914.

Watson, Thomas H.; *Naval Architecture, A Manual on Laying-off Iron, Steel, and Composite Vessels*, Longmann, Green, & Co., London, 1917.

Williams, Frances Leigh; *Matthew Fontain Maury, Scientist of the Sea*, Rutgers Univ. Press, New Brunswick, NJ, 1963.

Wood, Major Eric Fisher; *The Note-Book of an Intelligence Officer*, The Century Co., New Yor, 1917.

Woollard, Lloyd; (revised by) *Mackrow's Naval Architect's and Shipbuilder's Pocket Book*, 15th edition, The Technical Press, Ltd., London, 1954.

Wulle, Armin; *Der Stettiner Vulcan*, Koehlers Verlagsgesellschaft mbH, Herford, 1989.

Yergin, Daniel, *The Prize*, Touchstone, Simon & Schuster, New York, 1991.

Plus: Newspaper sources: *New York Times*, *Philadelphia Inquirer*, *Washington Post*, *Wall Street Journal*, *San Francisco Chronicle*, *Chicago Tribune*, *Toronto Star*, etc. etc., for appropriate dates.

Plus: Publications and books too numerous to mention individually, all of which are in my personal library.

Appendix

In preparing this book, we have included illustrations and artwork within the text that best serves the point the author is stressing. However, there were several reference items that were repeatedly mentioned throughout the book. For our readers' benefit, we are including any examples or illustrations that were not included within the body of our chapters within our appendix.

SHIPS' BELL TABLE, American Merchant Marine. The bell is struck every half hour to indicate the time.

1	bell	12:30AM	(0030)
2	bells	1:00	(0100)
3	"	1:30	(0130)
4	"	2:00	(0200)
5	"	2:30	(0230)
6	"	3:00	(0300)
7	"	3:30	(0330)
8	"	4:00	(0400)
Ends Middle Watch, Begins Morning Watch			
1	bell	4:30	(0430)
2	bells	5:00	(0500)
3	"	5:30	(0530)
4	"	6:00	(0600)
5	"	6:30	(0630)
6	"	7:00	(0700)
7	"	7:30	(0730)
8	"	8:00	(0800)
Ends Morning Watch, Begins Forenoon Watch			
1	bell	8:30	(0830)
2	bells	9:00	(0900)
3	"	9:30	(0930)
4	"	10:00	(1000)
5	"	10:30	(1030)
6	"	11:00	(1100)
7	"	11:30	(1130)
8	"	12:00	(1200)
Ends Forenoon Watch, Begins Afternoon Watch			
1	bell	12:30	(1230)
2	bells	1:00	(1300)
3	"	1:30	(1330)
4	"	2:00	(1400)
5	"	2:30	(1430)
6	"	3:00	(1500)
7	"	3:30	(1530)
8	"	4:00	(1600)
Ends Afternoon Watch, Begins First Dog Watch			
1	bell	4:30	(1630)
2	bells	5:00	(1700)
3	"	5:30	(1730)
4	"	6:00	(1800)
End First Dog Watch, Begins Second Dog Watch			
5	"	6:30	(1830)
6	"	7:00	(1900)
7	"	7:30	(1930)
8	"	8:00	(2000)
Ends Second Dog Watch, Begins First Watch			
1	bell	8:30	(2030)
2	bells	9:00	(2100)
3	"	9:30	(2130)
4	"	10:00	(2200)
5	"	10:30	(2230)
6	"	11:00	(2300)
7	"	11:30	(2330)
8	"	12:00	(2400)
Ends First Watch, Begins Middle Watch			

The British custom was to strike 1, 2, 3 in the two hours of the second day watch. In the French service there were no Dog Watches, but there were two six-hour watches

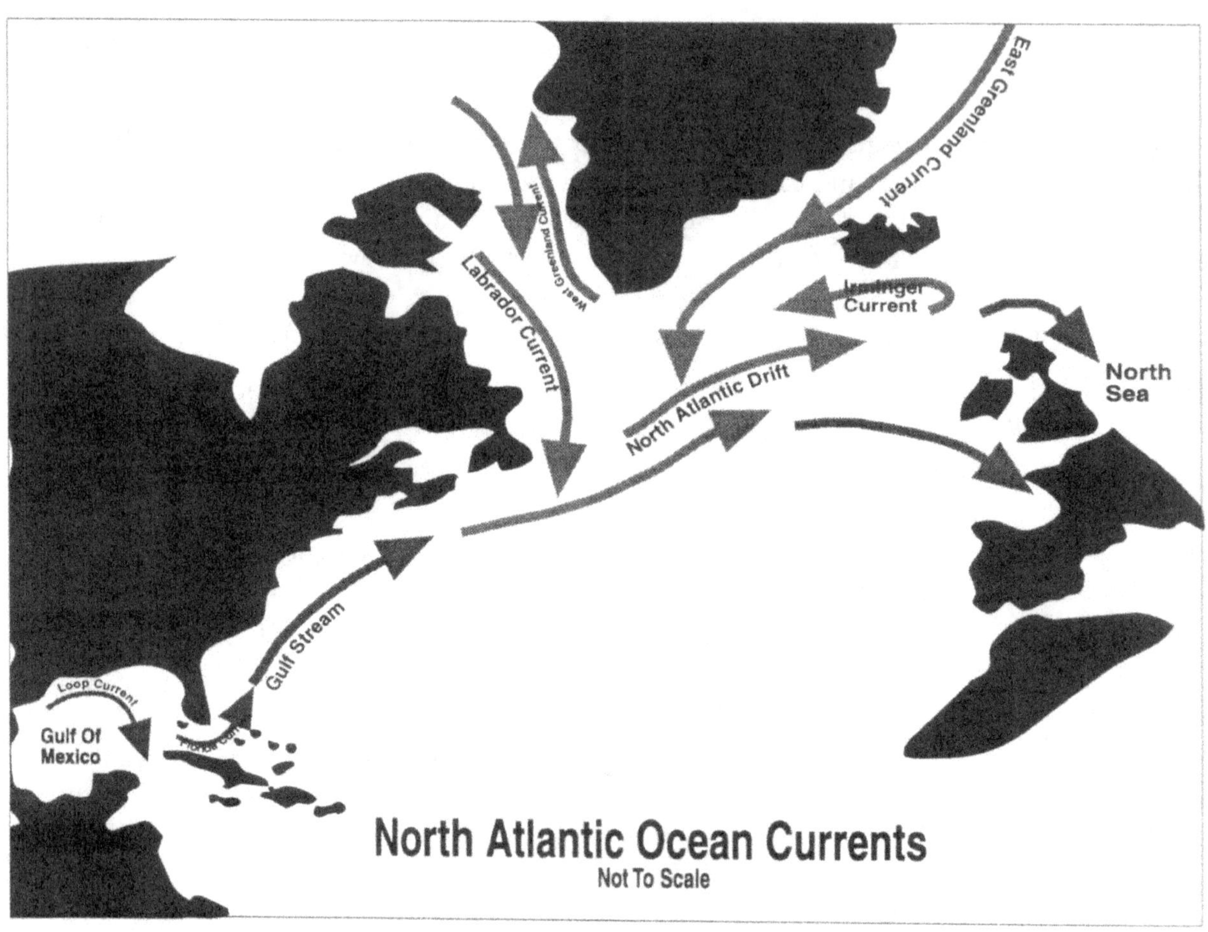

THE BRIDGE OF THE *TITANIC*

A close-up of ***TITANIC*** cutaway model showing starbord wheelhouse door, bridge wing and cab, with engine telegraphs forward of the wheelhouse. Photo copyright 1995, by Model Builder, Author, and ***TITANIC*** enthusiast Pete Elverhei.

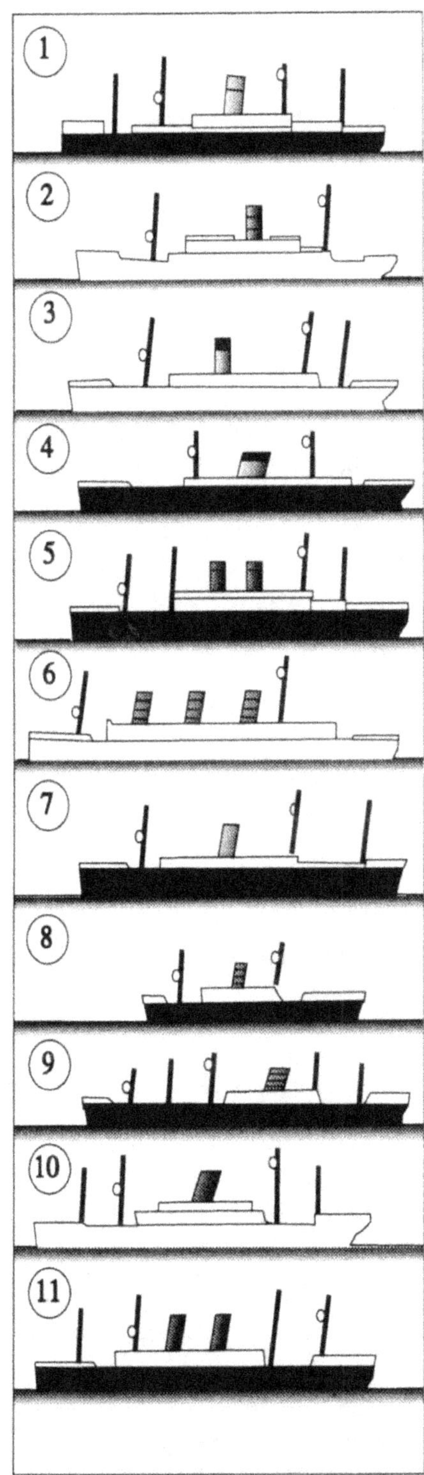

Answer To Ship Mastlight Test

International Morse Code Symbols

Meaning	Symbol	Meaning	Symbol	Meaning	Symbol
A	·—	H	····	Q	——·—
Ä	·—·—	I	··	R	·—·
Á	·——·—	J	·———	S	···
B	—···	K	—·—	T	—
C	—·—·	L	·—··	U	··—
CH	————	M	——	Ü	··——
D	—··	N	—·	V	···—
E	·	Ñ	——·——	W	·——
É	··—··	O	———	X	—··—
F	··—·	Ö	———·	Y	—·——
G	——·	P	·——·	Z	——··

NUMERALS

Meaning	Symbol
1	·————
2	··———
3	···——
4	····—
5	·····
6	—····
7	——···
8	———··
9	————·
0	—————

PUNCTUATION

Meaning	Sign	Symbol
Period (full stop) (.) and decimal point	AAA	·—·—·—
Bar indicating fraction (/)	XE	—··—·

Morse Code is a system of dots and dashes which represent letters. The only difference between American Morse and International Morse or a modification of it called Continental Code, was the provision of Morse symbols to represent linquistic symbols not found in English. For example, ä would be dotdashdotdash, ü would be dotdotdashdash, ñ would be dashdashdotdashdash, etc.,

Dot = 1 unit
Dash = 3 units
interval between letters = 3 units
interval between word or group = 5 units

American Morse Code Symbols

Alphabet

A	·—	N	—·
B	—···	O	———
C	—·—·	P	·——·
D	—··	Q	——·—
E	·	R	·—·
F	··—·	S	···
G	——·	T	—
H	····	U	··—
I	··	V	···—
J	·———	W	·——
K	—·—	X	—··—
L	·—··	Y	—·——
M	——	Z	——··

Numerals

1	·————	6	—····
2	··———	7	——···
3	···——	8	———··
4	····—	9	————·
5	·····	0	—————

Index

A

B

C

D

E

F

G

H

I

M

N

O

P

Q

R

S

T

Y

Z

Experience the Art of JAMES A. FLOOD

Jim's paintings can be viewed throughout the world in galleries, museums, ships, private collections, books, and magazines.

Visit JamesAFlood.com for more of his amazing art.

JAMESAFLOOD.COM

About D. E. Bristow

Ohio native Diana E. Bristow was a retired Eastern Airlines flight attendant who was a member of the British TITANIC society, TITANIC International, Steamship Historical Society, the Antique Wireless Association, Pyrotechnics Guild International, the National Maritime Historical Society, and Mensa.

About Ryan H. Katzenbach

Ryan Katzenbach began working as a freelance journalist at the age of 15 for his local Ohio hometown newspaper while attending both high school and art school. Upon moving to California a few years later, he found himself in the entertainment business as a producer. Since then, he's produced, written and directed multiple TV shows for REELZ Channel, including the docudrama adaptation of this book, "TITANIC: Sinking The Myths" which is still airing on REELZ today. Ryan resides in Los Angeles, California.

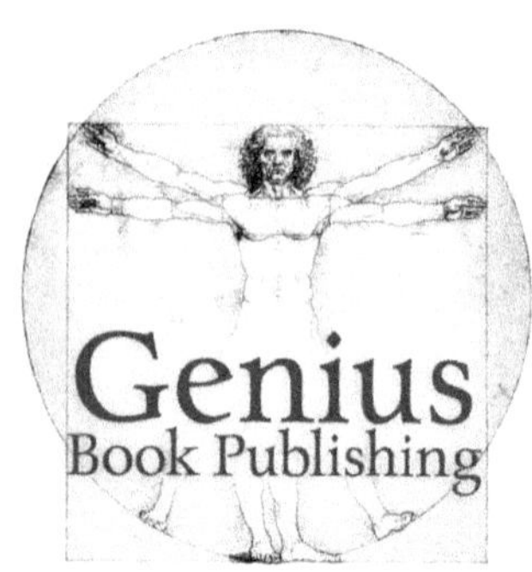

Genius Book Publishing Milwaukee Wisconsin USA

www.ingramcontent.com/pod-product-compliance
Lightning Source LLC
Chambersburg PA
CBHW080943120626
46546CB00010B/2822

* 9 7 8 1 9 5 8 7 2 7 2 6 3 *